STUDIES IN BAPTIST HISTORY AND THOUGHT

Interfaces: Baptists and Others

International Baptist Studies

STUDIES IN BAPTIST HISTORY AND THOUGHT

Series Editors

Anthony R. Cross	Bath, England
Curtis W. Freeman	Duke University, North Carolina, USA
Stephen R. Holmes	King's College, London, England
Elizabeth Newman	Baptist Theological Seminary at Richmond, Virginia, USA
Philip E. Thompson	North American Baptist Seminary, Sioux Falls, South Dakota, USA

Series Consultants

D.W. Bebbington	University of Stirling, Stirling, Scotland
Paul S. Fiddes	Regent's Park College, Oxford, England
Stanley J. Grenz	Carey Theological College and Regent College, Vancouver, British Columbia, Canada
Stanley E. Porter	McMaster Divinity College, Hamilton, Ontario, Canada

> A full listing of titles in this series appears at the end of this book

STUDIES IN BAPTIST HISTORY AND THOUGHT

Interfaces: Baptists and Others

International Baptist Studies

Edited by
David Bebbington and Martin Sutherland

Copyright © David Bebbington and Martin Sutherland, and contributors 2013

First published 2013 by Paternoster

Paternoster is an imprint of Authentic Media
52 Presley Way, Crownhill, Milton Keynes, Bucks, MK8 0ES, UK

www.authenticmedia.co.uk
Authentic Media is a division of Koorong UK, a company limited by guarantee

09 08 07 06 05 04 03   8 7 6 5 4 3 2 1

The right of David Bebbington and Martin Sutherland to be identified as the
Editors of this Work
has been asserted by them in accordance with the Copyright, Designs
and Patents Act 1988.

All rights reserved. No part of this publication may be reproduced, stored in a retrieval system, or transmitted, in any form or by any means, electronic, mechanical, photocopying, recording or otherwise, without the prior permission of the publisher or a license permitting restricted copying. In the UK such licenses are issued by the Copyright Licensing Agency, 90 Tottenham Court Road, London W1P 9HE.

British Library Cataloguing in Publication Data A catalogue record for this book is available from the British Library

ISBN 978-1-84227-674-7

Printed and bound in Great Britain
for Paternoster
by Lightning Source, Milton Keynes

Series Preface

Baptists form one of the largest Christian communities in the world, and while they hold the historic faith in common with other mainstream Christian traditions, they nevertheless have important insights which they can offer to the worldwide church. Studies in Baptist History and Thought will be one means towards this end. It is an international series of academic studies which includes original monographs, revised dissertations, collections of essays and conference papers, and aims to cover any aspect of Baptist history and thought. While not all the authors are themselves Baptists, they nevertheless share an interest in relating Baptist history and thought to the other branches of the Christian church and to the wider life of the world.

The series includes studies in various aspects of Baptist history from the seventeenth century down to the present day, including biographical works, and Baptist thought is understood as covering the subject-matter of theology (including interdisciplinary studies embracing biblical studies, philosophy, sociology, practical theology, liturgy and women's studies). The diverse streams of Baptist life throughout the world are all within the scope of these volumes.

The series editors and consultants believe that the academic disciplines of history and theology are of vital importance to the spiritual vitality of the churches of the Baptist faith and order. The series sets out to discuss, examine and explore the many dimensions of their tradition and so to contribute to their on-going intellectual vigour.

A brief word of explanation is due for the series identifier on the front cover. The fountains, taken from heraldry, represent the Baptist distinctive of believer's baptism and, at the same time, the source of the water of life. There are three of them because they symbolize the Trinitarian basis of Baptist life and faith. Those who are redeemed by the Lamb, the book of Revelation reminds us, will be led to 'fountains of living waters' (Rev. 7.17).

In Memory of Silas Mead (1834-1909), Baptist Pioneer in the Southern Hemsiphere

Contents

Contributors xiii

Introduction
David Bebbington and Martin Sutherland xv

Part One: Early Baptists 1

Chapter 1
Brian C. Brewer
Free Church Sacramentalism: A Surprising Connection
between Baptists and Anabaptists 3

Chapter 2
Ruth Gouldbourne
Episcope without Episcopacy: Baptist Attitudes to the
Bishops in Seventeenth-Century England 29

Part Two: Nineteenth-Century Baptists in Britain and America 47

Chapter 3
Derek Murray
The Scotch Baptists and the Birth of the Churches of Christ 49

Chapter 4
Timothy Whelan
An Evangelical Anglican Interaction with Baptist
Missionary Society Strategy: William Wilberforce and
John Ryland, 1807 – 1824 56

Chapter 5
Daniel Dunivan
General Baptists, Cumberland Presbyterians and
Denominational Identity in Frontier Indiana in the
Early Nineteenth Century   86

Chapter 6
Terry G. Carter
Baptist Reactions to Catholics in the United States,
1830 – 1860   103

Part Three: Baptists in the Twentieth Century   117

Chapter 7
Michael J. Collis
Baptists and Church Unity in Wales in the
Twentieth Century   119

Chapter 8
Callum N. Jones
Western Canadian Baptists and Ecumenical Initiatives
in the Early Twentieth Century   136

Chapter 9
Brian R. Talbot
Baptists and Other Christian Churches in the First
Half of the Twentieth Century   156

Chapter 10
Geoffrey R. Treloar
Baptists and the World, 1900-1940: A "Great Reversal"?   177

Part Four: Baptists in Australia   199

Chapter 11
Ken R. Manley
Australian Baptists and the State: Partner or Peril?   201

Chapter 12
John S. Walker
Christians First and Baptists Second? South Australian
Baptists and Other Denominations, 1836-1936   216

Chapter 13
Ian Breward
From Baptist Leader to Presbyterian Leader:
The Rev. Donovan Mitchell (1890-1954)   242

Chapter 14
Graham Paulson
Baptists and Indigenous Australians   251

Part Five: Baptists in New Zealand   263

Chapter 15
Laurie Guy
Three Countries, Two Conversions, One Man:
J. J. Doke: Baptists, Humanity and Justice   265

Chapter 16
John H. Tucker
Prophets at the Gate? New Zealand Baptists and
Social Justice in the 1990s   277

Chapter 17
Steve Taylor
Baptist Worship and Contemporary Culture:
A New Zealand Case Study   292

Part Six: Baptists in Asia and Africa 309

Chapter 18
Rosalind M. Gooden
The First Australasian Baptist Missionary: Ellen Arnold
and the Bengalis, 1882 – 1931 311

Chapter 19
David A. Groves
Baptists and the Reformed in Mission: Indonesian
Papua in the Late Twentieth Century 323

Chapter 20
Samuel Ngun Ling
Baptists and Buddhists in Burma, 1813-2009 334

Chapter 21
Matthews A. Ojo
Baptists and New Christian Movements in West Africa 362

Index 391

Contributors

David Bebbington, Professor of History at the University of Stirling, Scotland.

Ian Breward, Senior Fellow, School of Historical and Philosophical Studies, University of Melbourne, Australia.

Brian C. Brewer, Assistant Professor of Christian Theology, George W. Truett Theological Seminary, Baylor University, Waco, Texas, USA.

Terry G. Carter, W.O. Vaught Professor of Christian History and Ministry, Ouachita Baptist University, Arkadelphia, Arkansas, USA.

Michael J. Collis, retired Baptist minister, formerly pastor, Sarn Baptist Church, near Newtown, Powys, Wales.

Daniel Dunivan, Dean of the Chapman School of Religious Studies and Chapman Seminary, Oakland City University, Oakland City, Indiana, USA.

Rosalind M. Gooden, retired Director of Training for Global Interaction (formerly Australian Baptist Missionary Society), Adelaide, South Australia.

Ruth Gouldbourne, Minister, Bloomsbury Central Baptist Church, London; Associate Research Fellow, Spurgeon's College, London.

David A. Groves, former Baptist missionary and development officer and currently member, Missiological Advisory Committee and History Project, Global InterAction, Australia.

Laurie Guy, Lecturer in Church History, Carey Baptist College, Auckland, New Zealand.

Callum N. Jones, Senior Pastor, First Baptist Church, Penticton, British Columbia, Canada.

Samuel Ngun Ling, President of Myanmar Institute of Theology, Insein Township, Yangon, Myanmar.

Ken R. Manley, Distinguished Professor of Church History, Whitley College, University of Melbourne, Australia.

Derek Murray, Chair of the Scottish Baptist History Project; retired Baptist minister, Inverurie, Scotland.

Matthews A. Ojo, Professor of Religious Studies, Obafemi Awolowo University, Ile-Ife, Nigeria.

Graham Paulson, first Australian Indigenous Baptist minister, served among Indigenous peoples for over forty years; former President of the Baptist Union of Queensland.

Martin Sutherland, Vice-Principal, Laidlaw College, Auckland, New Zealand.

Brian R. Talbot, Fellow, Centre for Baptist Studies, Regent's Park College, Oxford; Extraordinary Associate Professor of the NWU Faculty of Theology, South Africa, and minister, Broughty Ferry Baptist Church, Dundee, Scotland.

Steve Taylor, Director of Missiology, Uniting College of Leadership and Theology; Senior Lecturer, Flinders University, Adelaide, Australia.

Geoffrey R. Treloar, Co-ordinator of Coursework Development, The Australian College of Theology; Visiting Fellow in the School of History and Philosophy, University of New South Wales, Australia.

John H. Tucker, Director Ministry Training, Carey Baptist College, Auckland, New Zealand.

John S. Walker, Service Fellowship International/Global Interaction worker, Cambodia.

Timothy Whelan, Professor of English, Georgia Southern University, Statesboro, Georgia, USA.

Introduction

David Bebbington and Martin Sutherland

'Although Baptists have for so long held a position separate from that of other communions', ran a statement by the council of the Baptist Union of Great Britain and Ireland in 1948, 'they have always claimed to be part of the one holy catholic Church of our Lord Jesus Christ'.[1] Baptists have formed a separate body of Christians and yet they have been part of the broader Christian church. The resulting links have often been fruitful, but the resulting tensions have sometimes been acute. Baptists, furthermore, have had a similar ambivalent relationship with other human collectivities – with their society, culture or state; with other peoples and communities of faith. They have been in the world and yet (sometimes) not of it. At the points of contact between Baptists and others there have been varied and evolving relationships in thought and practice. This volume collects a series of papers on the theme of how Baptists have dealt with other Christians and other bodies. It covers the whole period of their existence from the early seventeenth until the early twenty-first century. It also touches on many parts of the world. How, the papers ask, have Baptists engaged with the 'other'?

The issue certainly arose for the early Baptists. There was an affinity, and perhaps a stronger bond, between the first Baptists and the Anabaptists of the continent. One of the papers in this volume, chapter 2 by Brian Brewer, explores how there was a surprising degree of common ground in a high view of the sacraments. Chapter 3 by Ruth Gouldbourne shows, however, that the relationship with contemporaries could be aversion. Her article examines the reaction of early Baptists against the episcopal theory and practice of the Church of England that coloured their attitude to translocal oversight of their churches. So from the beginnings of the Baptist movement a strong degree of kinship with other Christians coexisted with a sharp sense of difference from some of them.

In subsequent generations the variations in relationships with other branches of the Christian church persisted. The diversity of relationship was particularly apparent with Presbyterians, a body with whom Baptists shared many beliefs and practices. Thus, as chapter 6 by Daniel Dunivan argues, the Cumberland Presbyterians, an American denomination that adopted Arminian doctrines in the nineteenth century, exerted an influence over the emergence of the General

---

[1] 'A Statement approved by the Council of the Baptist Union of Great Britain and Ireland, March 1948', in H. Leon McBeth (ed.), *A Sourcebook for Baptist Heritage* (Nashville, TN: Broadman Press, 1990), p. 369.

Baptists in Indiana. But Presbyterians could also attract Baptists because of their Reformed heritage. Chapter 14 by Ian Breward shows how one distinguished Australian Baptist was drawn to Presbyterianism in the twentieth century. A missionary organisation of the related Dutch Reformed community was able to co-operate with Baptists in Indonesian Papua in the late twentieth century, but chapter 20, by David Groves, explains how the experiment collapsed, chiefly because of suspicions by third parties. Bodies from the Presbyterian/Reformed confessional family therefore wielded influence, acted as a haven and functioned as a partner for Baptists.

Other groups could actually be fostered within Baptist communities. The Churches of Christ, originally simply a reform movement in Baptist life, operated in this way. Derek Murray demonstrates in chapter 4 that one branch of the Baptist denomination, the Scotch Baptists, was particularly susceptible to the appeal of the reformers. In the years around the opening of the twenty-first century, as Matthews Ojo explains in chapter 22, charismatic renewal became a major force among the Baptists of Nigeria and Ghana, transforming the ethos of the churches it affected. The relationship with others could therefore be very close indeed, even while creating serious strains. For much of their history, however, Baptists had an opponent from which they felt totally remote, the Roman Catholic Church. Anti-Catholicism was a potent force within Baptist life, as Terry Carter illustrates in chapter 7, a study of mid-nineteenth-century America. Other Christian churches could be seen as entirely alien organisations.

Ecumenical bonds could nevertheless be forged with the likeminded. In early contacts the bonds were often informal, as between William Wilberforce, an Evangelical Anglican, and John Ryland, a prominent English Baptist of the early nineteenth century, the topic of Timothy Whelan's essay that forms chapter 5. During the twentieth century the organised ecumenical movement emerged, creating dilemmas for Baptists about how far to go in compromising with fellow-believers for the sake of institutional unity. The standard preference, as Brian Talbot suggests in his worldwide survey in chapter 10, was for co-operation with Evangelicals but little further. A similar stance is evident among the Baptists of Western Canada, as Callum Jones contends in chapter 9, and among those of South Australia, as John Walker reveals in chapter 13. For a while some of the most enthusiastic Baptist advocates of church union were in Wales, as Michael Collis shows in chapter 8, but even there zeal for the cause waned as the century wore on. Their deepest corporate convictions about baptism usually acted as a brake on the ecumenical endeavours of Baptists.

The dealings of Baptists with others went far beyond their stance towards other Christians. At many times they addressed the issues of society at large. That was true, as Geoff Treloar argues in chapter 11, even in the early twentieth century when it is usually supposed that Baptists, like fellow Evangelicals, retreated from social questions. A case study, an account of the career of J.J. Doke in Australia and South Africa by Laurie Guy in chapter 16, illustrates that Baptists could be outspoken on questions of racial injustice. Another, however,

Introduction

chapter 17 by John Tucker on New Zealand Baptists in the 1990s, recounts how they could retire from the field of public issues at a time when other Christian bodies were forthright in raising questions about the direction of national policy. There was a reclusive tendency in Baptist life as well as a prophetic strain.

Two studies, one of Australia and the other of New Zealand, depict additional aspects of the ways in which Baptists engaged with their setting. In chapter 12 Ken Manley traces the changing relationship between Baptists and the state over nearly two centuries. After early uncertainties Australian Baptists settled into the conviction that they must refuse state aid; but as the twentieth century advanced found that position untenable. Chapter 18 is an analysis by Steve Taylor of an effort by a twenty-first century New Zealand Baptist congregation to adapt its worship to the cultural climate of the times. In the first case the other remained dangerous; in the second the other was accommodated.

The other could appear in yet further guises. In Burma, as Samuel Ngun Ling suggests in chapter 21, Buddhism, taken up as a component of national identity, was a powerful rival religion and so compelled Baptists to deal with it circumspectly. The Bengalis of India, according to Rosalind Gooden's chapter 19, received the gospel through the first Australasian Baptist missionary and formed a national denomination that she championed. On the other hand, as chapter 15 by Graham Paulson makes clear, the Indigenous Australians, robbed of their land and their dignity by white settlers, were long reluctant to heed a message brought by those who despised them. The missionary movement, whether at home or abroad, necessarily brought Baptists into contact with others but with varying outcomes.

The papers collected here were delivered at a conference at Whitley College, Melbourne, Australia, from Wednesday 15 to Saturday 18 July 2009. It was the fifth triennial meeting of the International Conference on Baptist Studies and also the biennial meeting of the Australian Baptist Research Forum. The theme of the conference, 'Interfaces: Baptists and Others', accounts for the thread running through the papers in this book; the place helps explain the emphasis in this volume on the experience of Australia and New Zealand. It would be hard to draw a single conclusion from this broad assembly of papers, but together they illustrate the principle that Baptists, though usually separate from other Christians and other human groups, were also irrevocably part of the wider communities of the church and the world.

PART ONE

Early Baptists

CHAPTER 1

Free Church Sacramentalism: A Surprising Connnection between Baptists and Anabaptists

Brian C. Brewer

Whether the Anabaptist movement originating from the Grebel circle in sixteenth-century Switzerland and carrying over to seventeenth-century Dutch Collegiant Mennonites had some connection to the Baptist movement in Holland and England has long been debated. However, whilst the most strident voices on the two sides have either completely denied any sort of direct connection or made British Baptists direct heirs of Anabaptism, most historians have actually and more accurately studied the degree to which one associated with the other. It is undeniable that the English Separatist group led by John Smyth and Thomas Helwys had some sort of relationship with the Waterlanders in Amsterdam between 1607 and 1609. Additionally, it is well documented that Smyth and the majority of his Separatist congregation decided to remain in Holland after 1609 and attempted to join the Anabaptists because Smyth had come to the conclusion that Anabaptism was a correct and historical church. Thus historians have attempted to deduce what aspects of Baptist theology and practice have been shaped by the early Baptists' connection with Anabaptism and what parts are merely typologically or coincidentally related.

The purpose of this paper is not to review the old debates or to survey the connections which have already been established or attempted. Instead, this work will suggest a surprising link between the two movements that has heretofore not been formally developed: that both Baptists and Anabaptists share a sacramental tradition within their Free Church[1] ecclesiology. This

---

[1] This essay will use the terminology 'Free Church' to refer to those Christian traditions which show either historical rooting in or at least an affinity with the Radical or left wing of the Reformation. This usage is in congruence with Curtis Freeman's definition of the tradition which he characterises with the following five traits: '1. freedom of the church (non-hierarchical order/congregational polity); 2. freedom of worship (non-prescribed liturgy/spiritual worship); 3. freedom of confession (non-binding confession/gathered community); 4. freedom of conscience (non-coercive authority/soul liberty); and 5. freedom of religion (non-established religion/separation of church and state)'. See Freeman, '"To Feed Upon by Faith": Nourishment from the Lord's Table',

notion, at first glance, would seem absurd. In fact, most historical theologians would categorize both traditions as 'non-sacramental'. Anabaptist scholar Walter Klaassen observes that 'Anabaptism testifies uniformly that sacredness or holiness does not attach to special words, objects, places, persons or days . . . . There are no sacred things.' In the Lord's Supper, for instance, Klaassen argues for Anbaptism: '"The bread is nothing but bread". . . . Therefore ordinary bread ought to be used and it should be treated like ordinary bread.'[2] What is particularly noticeable in Klaassen's comments is his avoidance of the term 'sacrament' even in his rejection of the concept. Other Anabaptist scholars have long held that the movement should be described as both 'anticlerical' and as 'antisacramental'.[3]

For accuracy's sake, it is important to concede that antisacramentalism was indeed a prominent feature for a number of Anabaptism's theologians, past and present. Conrad Grebel, the leader of the early Anabaptist splinter from Zwinglianism, and Hans Denck tended to use the simple word 'ceremonies' to describe the Lord's Supper and baptism, for fear of implying that the rites were *ex opere operato* effecting salvation. Instead, Grebel argued for discontinuing priestly customs such as vestments, special water, special bread and cup. Jakob Kautz even noted in his *Seven Articles* that 'No word, no sign, no promise and no sacrament can make a man completely certain.' Melchior Hofmann charged Luther with making an idol out of the sacraments, and he called Catholic priests 'sacramental sorcerers and conjurers'. And in his trial in 1570, one Anabaptist contended that the word 'sacrament' was apocryphal, and the term should cease being used by Christians altogether.[4] Instead, many Anabaptists propagated the use of the term 'ordinance' in lieu of 'sacrament'. Such an alternative term tended to mitigate conveying any sort of divine action in the rites, while underscoring the significance of sign and symbol.

Likewise, Baptists are typically portrayed as continuing this non-sacramental tradition. In his commentaries on Baptist beliefs, Herschel H. Hobbs repeatedly stated that the rites of baptism and communion 'are not sacramental but symbolic in nature'.[5] This idea was substantiated by numerous other scholars such as Baptist historian Robert A. Baker, who opined: 'Even the English use

---

in Anthony R. Cross and Philip E. Thompson (eds), *Baptist Sacramentalism* (Carlisle: Paternoster, 2003), p. 194.

[2] Walter Klaassen, *Anabaptism: Neither Catholic Nor Protestant* (Waterloo: Conrad Press, 1973), pp. 11-12.

[3] For instance, see John Rempel 'Worship: A Multitude of Practices looking for a Theology', in D. Schrag & J. Juhnke (eds), *Anabaptist Visions for a New Millennium* (Kitchener: Pandora, 2000).

[4] Gerhard J. Neumann, 'The Anabaptist Position on Baptism and the Lord's Supper', *Mennonite Quarterly Review* 35 (April 1961), p. 147.

[5] See Herschel H. Hobbs, *Fundamentals of Our Faith* (Nashville: Broadman Press, 1960), p. 114; and Hobbs, *What Baptists Believe* (Nashville: Broadman Press, 1964), p. 82.

of the word *sacrament* has unsavory connotations. It sounds strange on Baptist lips.'[6]

Thus, it would at first appear that if there is a connection between the Anabaptist and Baptist movements regarding the sacraments, it would be in their non-sacramental sympathies. However, an increasing number of Baptists, primarily in Europe but also in North America and elsewhere, have called for this interpretation of Baptist theological history to be revisited, to the astonishment of other Baptists and onlookers alike. For example, J.I. Packer, when invited to write the foreword to a book on Baptist sacramentalism, registered his surprise: 'I had thought that . . . Baptist thought about the church and its life was mainly along Anabaptist lines, with careful distancing from the Reformed emphasis on God's sovereignty in grace, and on local congregations as microcosmic outposts of the worldwide visible church, and on sacraments as means of grace.'[7] What Packer observes has long been held as the popular view regarding Anabaptists, Baptists, and most Christians within the Free Church tradition. However, much of the Baptists' discomfort in using this terminology, or about other historians using the term on the Baptists' behalf, has been culturally conditioned by relatively recent historiography and not by a deep understanding of early Baptists and Anabaptists. A broad reading of Anabaptists and early Baptists, while showing that they upheld views that differed from various other Christian interpretations of sacramentalism, manifests nonetheless that many in both traditions held that baptism and the Lord's Supper are 'a means of conveying what [they] signify',[8] and thus that they attributed more significance to the rites than mere symbolism.

Early Anabaptist Sacramentalism

Balthasar Hubmaier (ca. 1480-1528)

To establish the purposeful use of the term 'sacrament' among Anabaptists, one can look no further than Balthasar Hubmaier (c.1480-1528), Anabaptism's greatest first-generation theologian. Like numerous Anabaptists, Hubmaier's sacramentalism has been misrepresented by researchers. For instance, Eddie Mabry argued:

> . . . Hubmaier also rejected the medieval term 'sacrament' itself. Historically the term 'sacrament' had meant the visible sign of an invisible grace, which communicated that of which it was the sign. Hubmaier rejected the notion that the

---

[6] Robert A. Baker, 'Baptist Sacramentalism', in H.C. Brown, Jr. and Charles P. Johnson (eds), *Chapel Messages* (Grand Rapids: Baker Book House, 1966), p. 24.

[7] J.I. Packer, 'Foreword', to Cross and Thompson (eds), *Baptist Sacramentalism*, p. xiii.

[8] Stanley K. Fowler uses this language to argue for Baptist sacramentalism in his excellent study, *More Than A Symbol: The British Baptist Recovery of Baptismal Sacramentalism* (Carlisle: Paternoster, 2002), p. 156.

sacraments conveyed grace. As they did not convey grace, but were only done in obedience to the commands of Christ, Hubmaier called them, not sacraments, but 'ordinances'.[9]

Yet Mabry's interpretation probably portrays less Hubmaier's theology and more Mabry's own modern Free Church sacramentarianism,[10] for one may note Hubmaier's intentional use of the term 'sacrament' if his writings are read more than cursorily. Following the trend of the Protestant Reformation, Hubmaier posited only two sacraments as biblically legitimate and rejected the Roman Catholic interpretation that their effectiveness occurred *ex opere operato*. Instead, as a converted Humanist, like Luther, Hubmaier studied philology and observed that the original and simple meaning of the word 'sacrament' is 'promise' or 'pledge'. Martin Luther had previously interpreted 'sacrament' to convey God's promise to humanity, when accepted in faith.[11] Hubmaier instead exchanged the idea of divine promise with a human one. And he exchanged the Catholic notion that grace was communicated through the elements of bread, wine and water with the public profession and commitment of the participant(s). He wrote in his *Form zu Taufen* (*A Form for Water Baptism*):

> That we have called the water of baptism, like the bread and wine of the altar, a 'sacrament'; and held it to be such, although not the water, bread, or wine, but in the fact that the baptismal commitment or the pledge of love is really and truly 'sacrament' in the Latin; i.e., a commitment by oath and a pledge given by the hand which the one baptized makes to Christ, our invincible Prince and Head, that he is willing to fight bravely unto the death in Christian faith under his flag and banner.[12]

Hubmaier's baptism is then sacramental in that the new Christian responds to God's saving grace by promising to follow Christ. Likewise, Hubmaier understood the Lord's Supper as the covenantal and ethical response in Christian community of each believer who demonstrated his or her willingness to love, serve and sacrifice for the others. Ultimately, Hubmaier developed

---

[9] Eddie Mabry, *Balthasar Hubmaier's Doctrine of the Church* (Lanham: University Press of America, 1994), p. 166.
[10] 'Sacramentarianism' refers to the movement which regarded the consecrated bread and wine of the eucharist metaphorically only and not as the physical body and blood of Christ Jesus.
[11] See Martin Luther, 'The Babylonian Captivity of the Church', in Abdel Ross Wentz (ed.), *Luther's Works* 36, *Word and Sacrament,* II (Philadelphia: Muhlenberg Press, 1959), p. 38.
[12] G. Westin and T. Bergsten (eds), *Balthasar Hubmaier Schriften* (Gütersloh: Gerd Mohn, 1962) [hereafter *Schriften*], 352; H. Wayne Pipkin and John H. Yoder (eds), *Balthasar Hubmaier: Theologian of Anabaptism,* Classics of the Radical Reformation, vol. 5 (Scottdale, PA: Herald Press, 1989) [hereafter *Hubmaier*], p. 391.

liturgies for both rites in which the baptisand and the congregation might orally participate in such pledges.

At the same time, however, Hubmaier's Anabaptist sacramentalism did not mitigate 'sacramentality',[13] but merely transposed it from the symbols of bread, wine and water to their accompanying human actions of promise and oath. Thus, sacraments are understood as actions of the converted Christian and the gathered church. Yet Hubmaier did not relegate the accompanying signs as *exclusively* symbolic. In his *Von Der brüderlichen Strafe* (*On Fraternal Admonition*), Hubmaier maintained:

> So all of those who cry: 'Well, what about water baptism? Why all the fuss about the Lord's Supper? They are after all just outward signs! They're nothing but water, bread and wine! Why fight about that?' They have not in their whole life learned enough why the signs were instituted by Christ, what they seek to achieve or toward what they should finally be directed, namely to gather a church, to commit oneself publicly to live according to the Word of Christ in faith and brotherly love, and because of sin to subject oneself to fraternal admonition and the Christian ban, and to do all of this with a sacramental oath before the Christian church and all her members, assembled partly in body and completely in spirit, testifying publicly, in the power of God.[14]

Hubmaier understood the sacramental oaths and their accompanying symbols as both powerful for and integral to maintaining a believers' church. The signs of water, bread and cup attest to the Christian community's genuineness of faith and intention to serve, and the pledges made by participating Christians were properly guarded by church discipline. Hubmaier understood, then, the sacraments as human promises to God and fellow believers that one will abide in faith and live within the discipline of the Christian community. Thus, Balthasar Hubmaier, Anabaptism's first significant theologian, provided the Free Church tradition with a model for sacramental theology.

Bernhard Rothmann (1495-1535) and Pilgram Marpeck (ca. 1495-1556)

This general notion of Anabaptist sacramentalism continued in the subsequent generations of the movement. Bernhard Rothmann, an evangelical reformer in Münster, is known in Christian history for inspiring the Anabaptist Münster kingdom. However, his positive theological intentions have only recently been

---

[13] James F. White points out that the term 'sacramentality' is a relatively modern term which can appropriately, if anachronistically, be applied to sixteenth-century figures. He writes: 'By *sacramentality* we mean the concept that the outward and visible can convey the inward and spiritual. Physical matters and actions can become transparent vehicles of divine activity and presence. In short, sacraments can be God's love made visible.' Here cited from White, *The Sacraments in Protestant Practice and Faith* (Nashville: Abingdon, 1999), p. 13.

[14] Westin and Bergsten (eds), *Schriften*, 346; Pipkin and Yoder (eds), *Hubmaier*, p. 384.

restored, and his influence on the Münster Rebellion was probably tragically twisted by the political order.[15] Regardless, Rothmann serves as another example of the continuation of Anabaptist sacramentalism. Like Hubmaier, Rothmann accepted the term 'sacrament' as technically appropriate for the church ordinances. And also like Hubmaier, he understood the word's initial meaning to convey a pledge or covenant, as had been rendered from the original Latin root.[16] Rothmanm perceived baptism's sacramentality as grounded in its purpose of incorporating the individual into the saving community of Christ.[17]

Rothmann became an important link to the better respected and more significant South German Anabaptist leader, Pilgram Marpeck. Marpeck also argued for a sacramental construal of the ordinances. In an important section of his writings entitled, 'What the Word Sacrament Really Means and Is', Marpeck wrote:

> Sacrament is a Latin word derived from *sacer, sacra, sacrum,* and it means holy. . . . Sacrament refers to anything done in connection with an oath or a similar obligation, and refers to an event that is special and holy or a work that has that kind of connotation; similarly, the knight commits himself to serve his lord by the raising of a finger in battle where, on his honor and with his oath, he commits himself not to yield in combat. *Now, the raising of his finger is not the battle, nor a fight, nor endurance, nor is it victory; the action is a covenant, made in the firm hope that, according to the command and the desire of his Lord, he will diligently attack the enemy of his Lord, even risking his life until death.*[18]

Marpeck also used the analogy of one who receives an unexpected gift. In response, the receiver of the gift would want to act in such a way that shows her appreciation and love for the one who first expressed that love to her. Marpeck concludes: 'Thus, sacrament is not to be understood as a single essential thing, but only as the act that is carried out. If the act is carried out with an oath or a similar commitment, then it can be called a sacrament.'[19]

Baptism and the Lord's Supper are sacraments for Marpeck only when they are carried out with the earnest heart of the participants. If one obeys the commands of Christ in this action, it carries the 'same kind of force and binding

---

[15] See Jack W. Porter, 'Bernhard Rothmann 1495-1535, Royal Orator of the Münster Anabaptist Kingdom' (Ph.D. dissertation, University of Wisconsin, 1964).

[16] Rollin S. Armour, *Anabaptist Baptism: A Representative Study* (Scottdale: Herald Press, 1966), p. 185, n. 132.

[17] Hans-Jürgen Goertz, *The Anabaptists* (London: Routledge, 1996), p. 81.

[18] Pilgram Marpeck, *The Writings of Pilgram Marpeck* [hereafter, *Writings*]. trans. and ed. William Klassen and Walter Klaassen (Scottdale: Herald Press, 1978) [editor's italics], p. 169.

[19] Marpeck, *Writings*, p. 170.

quality as the oath'.[20] And the spirit of participating in the sacrament is even more important than the elements themselves. Observes Timothy Reardon:

> For Marpeck, sacrament is more than simply following a command or the bare rituals of baptism and the Lord's Supper. Sacrament is instead an incarnational act where the church lives as Christ on earth: first, in the action of baptism, and subsequently, in the life of baptism. Sacrament itself is a meeting of the divine and creation, the pinnacle of which is accomplished in the incarnation of Christ.[21]

Baptism and the Lord's Supper, then, for Marpeck, were far more than signs. They served as witnesses to what God had already done and was currently doing. In baptism, the Holy Spirit witnesses to the baptisand and to the gathered church one's participation in the new life of Christ. 'Witness' (*Zeugnis*) is to be understood kinetically, not passively. Thus, the sacraments become the incarnational reality for the church when the congregation actively participates in them. One's conscious personal confession and wholehearted commitment are required for the witness to be effective. Children who cannot fully believe and make such commitments, therefore, are not appropriate candidates for sacramental participation.[22]

The sacraments then serve as 'embodied action' for Marpeck. In baptism, one pledges to follow Christ and participate in Christ's suffering. Interestingly, too, Marpeck notes that the waters of baptism actually convey 'the secrets of the cross', and demarcate the personal sacrifice of the new Christian, whereby the candidate is actually 'crucified with Christ'.[23] The participating congregation embodies this life of sacrifice and common suffering. Thus, the sacrament of baptism for Marpeck served as the entrance into the church and as 'a work that Christ entrusted to the congregation', each participating member becoming a co-witness to the event.[24] Said Marpeck: 'Since we all are already washed in sin, baptism (which means the outer action of immersion or pouring) is a co-witness (*mitzeüge*) of the inner reality (*wesen*) which is the covenant of a good conscience with God.'[25]

Just as Christ was argued to be spiritually present in the commitment sealed through water baptism, Marpeck held that the incarnate Christ, who now is physically on the right hand of God the Father, can still be spiritually received in the Supper: 'The soul is fed and given drink in communion . . . through faith in the words and proclamation of Christ's death, that he offered his flesh and

---

[20] Marpeck, *Writings*, p. 170.
[21] Timothy W. Reardon, 'Pilgram Marpeck's Sacramental Theology: Based on His Confession of 1532', *Mennonite Quarterly Review* 83 (April 2009), pp. 294-95.
[22] Reardon, 'Pilgram Marpeck's Sacramental Theology', pp. 311-13.
[23] Pilgram Marpeck, 'Pilgram Marpeck's Confession of 1532', in *Writings*, p. 154.
[24] Goertz, *The Anabaptists*, p. 81.
[25] Marpeck, *Writings*, pp. 129-30.

shed his blood. It is this food and drink alone which the soul tastes in its already-mentioned hunger and thirst.'[26]

Through much of his writings, Marpeck had entered into a lengthy debate with the famous spiritualist of his day, Casper Schwenckfeld. In his polemical works against spiritualism, Marpeck struck a careful sacramental balance between Catholic *ex opere operato* sacramentalism and Schwenckfeld's spiritualism, with what Marpeck perceived as an overemphasis on the inner life to the diminution of the outward symbols. Marpeck observed that the spiritualists submitted themselves to and argued based upon the authority of scripture. Yet Marpeck noted that the Bible itself serves as a witness external to the human heart. He then built his own definition of sacrament as co-witness (*mitzeugnus*), arguing that baptism and the Supper serve parallel functions to the preacher who proclaims the Word. They are all agents of proclamation:

> Thus you can see how both baptism and the Lord's Supper are called sacraments, namely, because both of them take place with a commitment and sanctification, which is actually what a sacrament is. For merely to plunge somebody into water or to baptize them [sic.] is no sacrament. You must baptize in such a manner that the one who is baptized dies to his sins in a sincere way and in the power of a living faith in Christ. From henceforth, he commits himself to a new life, and only then is baptism a true sacrament, that is, when the content and action of baptism happens with the commitment to a holy covenant. It is the same way with the Lord's Supper.[27]

Thus, the elements are not effective for Marpeck without their reception in faith. At the same time, the actual physical signs must be enacted by the congregation in order for their co-witnessing power to be appropriated spiritually. In this unique way, Pilgram Marpeck evinced an Anabaptist sacramentalism.[28]

Sacramentalism among the Dutch Anabaptists

Having established the use and Anabaptist variation of 'sacrament' among the members of the first generation of the movement, it is now essential to demonstrate the continuation of Anabaptist sacramentalism among the Dutch Anabaptists, those whom the first English Baptists would ultimately encounter.

---

[26] Marpeck's words are here cited in John D. Rempel, *The Lord's Supper in Anabaptism: A Study in the Christology of Balthasar Hubmaier, Pilgram Marpeck, and Dirk Philips* (Scottdale: Herald Press, 1993), p. 112.

[27] Marpeck, *Writings*, pp. 171-72.

[28] It is important to point out, however, that Marpeck later wrote that he maintained the technical definition of sacrament but lamented that its use should be discontinued given the Catholic interpretation's hegemony of the term and its consequent openness to misunderstanding by others. See Marpeck, *Writings*, pp. 262-63.

Free Church Sacramentalism 11

This task, however, would appear problematic. While it is often said to have nearly dominated the Reformation movement in the Netherlands in the mid-sixteenth century,[29] Dutch Anabaptism often characterised sacramentarian tendencies regarding the ordinances as symbolic only.[30] Yet, Dutch Anabaptism might well have become the seedbed of heretical and extremist reformers and fringe movements were it not for the brothers Obbe and Dirk Philips and also Menno Simons.

Dirk Philips (1504-1568)

While Obbe was the original organiser of the peaceful, moderate Dutch Anabaptist wing, Dirk became 'one of its major spokesmen, theologians, and church leaders'.[31] Some modern Anabaptist scholars have posited that Dirk preferred the term 'ordinance' to 'sacrament',[32] construing his thought to be more in keeping with Free Church tendencies today. However, such a preference cannot actually be detected in Dirk's writings. Instead, one can observe in both Dirk Philips and in his Dutch Anabaptist contemporary, Menno Simons, a robust sacramental theology. William E. Keeney rightly notes that

> They both used the term 'sacraments' (*Sacramenten*). They also referred to them as ordinances of God, signs and ceremonies. Again, they made some attempt to free themselves from Roman Catholic terminology, yet they were not as rigid as some others who would break completely with traditional usage unless it was scriptural.[33]

Even more precisely, Dirk understood the terms 'sacrament' and 'ordinance' as related but not necessarily as synonymous. For Dirk Philips, 'sacrament' is rooted in Christ, who is the only means to salvation.[34] The Lord's Supper and

---

[29] For instance, J.G. de Hoop Scheffer argued that 'with few exceptions the history of Anabaptism constitutes the history of the Reformation in our country [the Netherlands] from 1530 to 1566'. While somewhat diminishing this claim, Cornelius Krahn later affirmed that de Hoop Scheffer's remark 'contains enough truth to be repeated even in our [modern] day'. See Cornelius Krahn, *Dutch Anabaptism: Origin, Spread, Life, and Thought* (Scottdale: Herald Press, 1981), p. 188.
[30] Krahn, *Dutch Anabaptism*, p. 118.
[31] Cornelius J. Dyck, *An Introduction to Mennonite History*, 3rd edn (Scottdale: Herald Press, 1993), p. 101.
[32] See Cornelius Dyck's biographical notes in Cornelius J. Dyck, William E. Keeney, and Alvin J. Beachy (trans. and eds), *The Writings of Dirk Philips, 1504-1568* (Scottdale: Herald Press, 1992) [hereafter, Philips, *Writings*], p. 40.
[33] William Echard Keeney, *The Development of Dutch Anabaptist Thought and Practice from 1539-1564* (Nieuwkoop: B. de Graaf, 1968), p. 74.
[34] Note that Dirk argues: 'Nevertheless, Christ is and remains the true and only sign of grace, and all external signs direct us from themselves to him, admonish us from themselves to him, admonish us and remind us of him, witnessing about him, witness to

baptism serve as the two 'sacramental signs' which point to and testify about the true sacrament. Dirk emphasized:

> Thus Christ fulfills in us what the sacraments signify. Therefore, whenever we utilize or receive the external signs of baptism and the Lord's Supper, we look not primarily upon the external sign but upon Jesus Christ himself, 'from whose fullness we have all received, grace upon grace'.[35]

To Dirk Philips, then, the sacraments represented externally what God granted internally.[36]

In writing about 'The Congregation of God', Dirk noted that Christ gathered the church and instituted some six general 'ordinances' by which the church might be known: the proper ordination of 'true ministers', the two sacraments (namely baptism and the Lord's Supper), the ordinance of footwashing, 'evangelical separation' (which includes church discipline and the ban), the *mandatum novum* to love one another (which Dirk called 'brotherly love'), and the divine mandate to keep all the commandments of Christ.[37] These six ordinances mark the true church of Christ Jesus. Though baptism and the Lord's Supper are included as one type among the other five 'ordinances' in Philips' list, John Rempel observes that 'their designation as "sacraments, sacramentalism" underscores their special character as concentrated moments in the divine-human encounter by which believers "are made partakers of all that belongs to Christ"'.[38]

For Dirk, a 'sacrament' must include faith, confession, mystery, a good conscience, and God's leadership and continual activity in the believer leading to 'full salvation'.[39] Both the Lord's Supper and baptism demand these acts of faith and divine movement. While the other five ordinances respond to or

---

him, Exod. 25:22; Rom. 3:25; Heb. 5: [5], and in the use of these signs nothing is accomplished for our salvation except that which Christ himself works in us, which we receive and accept through faith, John 1: [12]. For Christ is the one who baptizes us inwardly with the Holy Spirit and with fire, Matt. 3:11, who accepts us into his fellowship as members of his body, [I Cor. 12:12], who sprinkles our conscience with his blood, cleansing and washing away all sin, Heb. 9:14. Christ makes us partakers with him in the Supper, feeds us with true heavenly bread, Exod. 16:5; Wisd. of Sol. 16:20, gives us his flesh to eat and his blood to drink, John 6:32[-33]. It is by his grace and work in us that we through faith in the spirit, and the power of his Word, have eternal life from his body and blood which was sacrificed for us on the cross, John 19:34.' See Philips, *Writings*, p. 103.

[35] Philips, *Writings*, p. 103.
[36] Philips, *Writings*, p. 116.
[37] Philips, *Writings*, pp. 363-72.
[38] John D. Rempel, *The Lord's Supper in Anabaptism: A Study in the Christology of Balthasar Hubmaier, Pilgrim Marpeck and Dirk Philips* (Scottdale: Herald Press, 1993), p. 173.
[39] Philips, *Writings*, p. 101.

represent the relationship of the believer to the Christian fellowship, 'the principal mode of a sacrament is vertical communion',[40] one's union with Christ. And though Philips at times referred to baptism and the Supper as sacramental signs (*sacramentlije teecken*) which represent the saving sacrament of Christ Jesus, Philips also carefully distinguished his position from mere spiritualism. The signs of water, bread and cup cannot be completely divorced from the Spirit. Because Christ commands the use of the sacraments, they become effective when both the Spirit and genuine belief are at hand. Dirk underscored the potential power of the sacraments, most strongly emphasised when he wrote about the Supper, which not only represented the spiritual experience which had already occurred but actually strengthened and intensified the Christian in the experience. Thus, William Keeney writes of the Dutch Anabaptist sacramentalism of Dirk Philips and Menno Simons:

> though they treated the sacraments as signs or symbols, it is incorrect to say that to them they were 'only' or 'merely' signs and symbols. The sacraments were closely correlated with the spiritual reality or true being which must support or sustain the outward or external expression. Menno and Dirk's tendency to look upon the commands of Christ as positive law and their reaction against any form of sacramentarianism may obscure the fact that their view was dynamic and not static or formal. Nevertheless, their view of the sacraments had a certain mystical quality. . . .[41]

Menno Simons (1496-1561)

Menno Simons' organizational and spiritual leadership of the Dutch Anabaptists was so influential that they ultimately adopted a form of his name for their movement. Not surprisingly, Menno's sacramentalism complemented the thought of his friend and colleague, Dirk Philips. Like Philips, Menno outlined six signs by which the church of Christ might be known, namely, 'unadulterated doctrine', the sacraments of baptism and the Supper, the Christian life (obedience to scripture), love of neighbour, faithfulness to Christ even during persecution, and the cross of Jesus Christ.[42] Thus, while somewhat different from his Dutch colleague's characteristics, the sacraments still constitute the second place among the signs and also a special designation. Notes J.C. Wenger: 'Although Menno rejected the sacramental theory of the Roman Catholic Church, he did not hesitate to use the term "sacrament" in reference to the Lord's Supper [and baptism]. In this he was followed by many other Anabaptist authors.'[43]

---

[40] Rempel, *The Lord's Supper in Anabaptism*, p. 173.
[41] Keeney, *The Development of Dutch Anabaptist Thought and Practice from 1539-1564*, p. 76.
[42] J.C. Wenger (ed.), *The Complete Writings of Menno Simons* (Scottdale: Herald Press, 1956) [hereafter, Simons, *Complete Writings*], pp. 739-42.
[43] See editor's footnote in Simons, *Complete Writings*, p. 143, n. 22.

While showing similarities to Philips' sacramentalism, Menno's theology also bore likeness to those of Balthasar Hubmaier and to Pilgram Marpeck. At times Menno argued that God's action preceded the rites and thus the sacraments became the human response to the grace of God, much as in Hubmaier's writings. The sacraments then serve as pledges on behalf of the person or congregation to follow in God's ways. For instance, in the case of baptism,[44] Menno wrote:

> Oh, no, outward baptism avails nothing so long as we are not inwardly renewed, regenerated, and baptized with the heavenly fire and the Holy Ghost of God. But when we are the recipients of this baptism from above, then we are constrained through the Spirit and Word of God by a good conscience which we obtain thereby, because we believe sincerely in the merits of the death of the Lord and in the power and fruits of His resurrection, and because we are inwardly cleansed by faith. In the spiritual strength which we have received, we henceforth bind ourselves by the outward sign of the covenant in water which is enjoined on all believers in Christ . . . that we will no longer live according to evil . . . but walk according to the witness of a good conscience before Him.[45]

In this way, baptism serves as a sacramental pledge to God to be Christ's disciple. However, as Hans-Jürgen Goertz has noted, this confession and pledge

> not only affirmed the salvific action of God in man, but also occupied a special place within it. Only through confession, that is to say water-baptism, did God's action become redemptive reality, as if God felt himself bound by man's acceptance of his gift of grace. In this sense, Menno regarded baptism as more than a mere symbol of obedience, occasionally speaking of its effects and of the 'forgiveness of our sins in baptism'. By this he meant that, through the act of confession, what man confessed was actually effected.[46]

Along these lines, Menno's teaching resembled Marpeck's account of the sacramental structure of witness and co-witness.[47] Menno himself wrote that 'the believing receive remission of sins not through baptism, but in baptism',[48] whereby they are transformed through Christ. The power of the sacrament, then, lies not in the water itself but in the God who chooses to use the water, or the bread and wine, for those who have faith.

---

[44] For more development of Menno's eucharistic thought regarding the real presence of Christ, see Sjouke Voostra, *Menno Simons: His Image and Message* (North Newton: Bethel College, 1997), esp. pp. 62-81.
[45] Simons, *Complete Writings*, p. 125.
[46] Goertz, *The Anabaptists*, p. 84.
[47] Goertz, *The Anabaptists*, p. 84.
[48] See John Horsch, *Menno Simons: His Life, Labors, and Teachings* (Scottdale: Mennonite Publishing House, 1916), p. 261.

Regardless, one might easily observe the heritage of Anabaptist sacramentalism, perhaps initiated by Balthasar Hubmaier and Pilgram Marpeck and appropriated by Dirk Philips and Menno Simons, which became clearly influential among the Dutch Mennonites in the succeeding generations. In the decades following Dirk Philips' and Menno Simons' organizational work and thought, Anabaptist sacramentalism competed with theologies of memorialism and even spiritualism, the latter of which often sought to do away with physical ceremonies altogether. However, a sense of Free Church sacramentalism seemed to survive among the early seventeenth-century Waterlander Mennonites in Amsterdam. In fact, the Waterland Confession (1580), though written years before the Dutch Mennonite-Baptist interaction, reflects the abiding Free Church sacramentalism of the Waterlander congregation led by John de Ries and Lubbert Gerrits. Its theological assessment of the sacraments is informative. Regarding baptism, for instance, the confession states:

> The whole action of external, visible baptism places before our eyes, testifies and signifies that Jesus Christ baptizes internally (a) in a laver of regeneration (b) and renewing of the Holy Spirit, the penitent and believing man: washing away, through the virtue and merits of his poured out blood, all the spots and sins of the soul (c) and through the virtue and operation of the Holy Spirit, which is a true, heavenly (d), spiritual and living water, [washing away] the internal wickedness of the soul (e) and renders it heavenly (f), spiritual (g) and living (h) in true righteousness and goodness. Moreover baptism directs us to Christ and his holy office by which in glory he performs that which he places before our eyes, and testifies concerning its consummation in the heart of believers and admonishes us that we should not cleave to external things, but by holy prayers ascend into heaven and ask from Christ the good indicated through it [baptism]: a good which the Lord Jesus graciously concedes and increases in the hearts of those who by true faith become partakers of the sacraments.[49]

Clearly articulated here is an understanding of the sacraments as both carrying a symbolic function and conveying Christ's benefits, contingent upon the sacraments being received in faith. Thus, a form of believers' sacramentalism from the previous century's Anabaptism remained among the Dutch Mennonite congregation the following century. This influence became marked when the Separatist congregation led by John Smyth and Thomas Helwys encountered the Waterlander congregation in 1607 or 1608. Jason Lee affirms that 'while John Smyth was never in direct contact with . . . Menno Simons, or Dirk Philips, their influence lived on in the Mennonites with whom Smyth did interact'.[50]

---

[49] *The Waterlander Confession*, here cited in William L. Lumpkin (ed.), *Baptist Confessions of Faith* (Philadelphia: Judson Press, 1959), pp. 60-61.

[50] Jason K. Lee, *The Theology of John Smyth: Puritan, Separatist, Baptist, Mennonite* (Macon: Mercer, 2003), p. 33.

Dutch Mennonite Influence on the First Baptists

While Anabaptists ultimately made their way to England in the sixteenth century, the best known point of contact between Anabaptist Mennonites and those English Separatists who would ultimately become Baptists was that interaction between the Mennonite Waterlander church and John Smyth's congregation, which encountered the former while in exile in Amsterdam in the early years of the seventeenth century. William Estep, who contributed enormously to understanding the complexity of the Mennonite-Baptist relationship, wrote:

> The first English Baptist church, of which there is documentary evidence, emerged out of English Separatism only after direct contact with the Waterlander Mennonites in Holland. Possibly as early as December, 1608, John Smyth and his congregation unchurched themselves and reconstituted a church on the basis of believer's baptism in the place of a church covenant.[51]

However, according to one Mennonite scholar, the connection between the two groups went further: 'To the Smyth congregation, which accepted adult baptism as a result of contact with Dutch Mennonites, the General Baptists owe their origin.'[52] Discussion regarding the overarching amount of influence the Mennonites had on Smyth and those who would become English Baptists goes well beyond the scope of this work. However, both Baptist and Mennonite scholars perceive an affinity between the Dutch Mennonite understanding of baptism and the formation of early Baptist theology.

As his congregation's interactions with the Mennonites developed, Smyth wrote *The Short Confession of Faith in XX Articles*, probably in 1609. One of the principal duties of the church, Smyth said, was 'administering the sacraments' of baptism and the Lord's Supper (Art. 13). He referred to baptism as an 'external sign' of a spiritual reality, but he did not develop the nature of the timing of that reality in his confession. Whether baptism was an external sign of what had already occurred or it represented externally what was occurring spiritually in the heart of the baptisand during the rite was not specifically addressed. Thus, Stanley Fowler writes: 'This imprecision regarding what exactly happens in baptism is characteristic of much Baptist literature of the 17th century, because the writers were in most cases concerned primarily about the question of pedobaptism, secondarily about the mode of baptism, and only to a limited degree about the sacramental issue.'[53]

---

[51] William R. Estep, Jr. (ed.), *Anabaptist Beginnings (1523-1533): A Sourcebook* (Nieuwkoop: B. de Graaf, 1976), p. 5.

[52] Originally cited in *The Mennonite Encyclopedia*, vol. 2, 218; here cited in Dyck, *An Introduction to Mennonite History*, p. 118.

[53] Fowler, *More Than a Symbol*, p. 12.

Regardless, after months of fellowship with the Anabaptists, Smyth recognised so many commonalities between his church and its Waterlander counterparts that he and the majority of his congregation applied for membership in the Mennonite congregation. Upon receiving a formal application for church membership from Smyth on behalf of his followers, Hans de Ries, the leader of the Mennonite community, produced 'A Short Confession', which outlined some thirty-eight articles of the Waterlanders' beliefs. Smyth and his congregation willingly accepted and signed the document.[54]

What is telling about this confession for the purpose of this essay is Ries' description of the 'two sacraments appointed by Christ' (Art. 28), in which he called them 'outward visible handlings and tokens' which marked both divine work and human obedience. The confession concludes regarding baptism: 'Therefore, the baptism of water leadeth us to Christ, to his holy office in glory and majesty; and admonisheth us not to hang only upon the outward, but with holy prayer to mount upward, and to beg of Christ the good thing signified.'[55] While the wording here seems to mimic some of Dirk Philips' ideas regarding inner baptism and outward expression, the full meaning is nebulous. Regardless, the language intimates that outward baptism is a form of prayerful request for God's action in the life of the baptisand and 'is in some way instrumental in the personal enjoyment of the benefits of Christ'.[56] At the very least, Ries's confession signed by the Smyth congregation seems to imply a sacramental quality of God's mysterious action in the outward rite and establishes a connection between Dutch Anabaptist sacramentalism and the first Baptist congregation.

The Continuance of Baptist Sacramentalism

However, it must be conceded that Thomas Helwys and a small remnant of the former English Separatist congregation returned to England in rejection of Smyth's application for union with the Waterlanders. Therefore, one must establish not only the continuance of the Anabaptist conviction of believer's baptism among the new English Baptists (which seems apparent), but also the survival of the former's sacramental appropriation of the outward rites. In other words, the argument hinges not on whether the outward form but on whether the inner theological expression remained among early Baptists. Wrote William Estep: 'It would appear that the association with, and thinking of, John Smyth as well as Mennonite thought had left an undeniable and indelible imprint [on Helwys and the early Baptists]'.[57] This imprint conceivably included not simply

---

[54] Lee, *The Theology of John Smyth*, p. 87.
[55] See Lumpkin (ed.), *Baptist Confession of Faith*, p. 98.
[56] Fowler, *More than a Symbol*, p. 13.
[57] Estep, *Anabaptist Beginnings*, p. 7.

the Anabaptist convictions regarding church and state, religious freedom, and believer's baptism, but also integrated a lingering Free Church sacramentalism, which underwent reshaping and revising but nevertheless abided from Hubmaier and Marpeck ultimately to Smyth and other early Baptists.

Early Baptist Confessions

A number of the early Baptist confessions of faith demonstrate sacramental themes resembling those found in the Anabaptist tradition. While Baptist historians and theologians have commonly concluded that 'Smyth's descendants in faith, in their anxiety to purify Christianity and to purge it of heathen and magical notions, have often despised the material elements of bread and wine in the Lord's Supper, and have spoken as though they did not believe that the grace of God is given in the sacraments',[58] some early seventeenth-century Baptist confessions and leaders prove otherwise. For instance, the General Baptist *Orthodox Creed* (1678) noted: 'Those two sacraments (baptism and the Lord's Supper) are ordinances of positive, sovereign, and Holy institution, appointed by the Lord Jesus Christ, the only Lawgiver'.[59] Under each rite it again refers to them as sacraments. However, careful historians have shown that the words 'sacrament' and 'ordinance' were used by Baptists interchangeably in the seventeenth century, 'often both in the same sentence'.[60] Therefore, a closer examination into their usage is necessary. *The Orthodox Creed*, though, appears to convey a sense of the Free Church sacramentalism already characteristic of the Anabaptists. In its description of the purpose and effects of the Supper, for instance, it notes:

> The supper of the Lord Jesus was instituted by Him . . . to be observed in His church to the end of the world for the perpetual remembrance and showing forth the sacrifice of Himself in His death; and for the confirmation of the faithful believers in all the benefits of His death and resurrection and spiritual nourishment and growth in Him; sealing unto them their continuance in the covenant of grace and to be a band and pledge of communion with Him, and an obligation of obedience of Christ, both passively and actively, as also of our communion and union each with other, in the participation of this Holy sacrament.[61]

---

[58] Robert C. Walton, *The Gathered Community* (London: Carey Press, 1946), p. 157.

[59] *The Orthodox Creed*, here cited in Timothy and Denise George (eds), *Baptist Confessions, Covenants and Catechisms* (Nashville: Broadman and Holman Publishers, 1996), p. 112.

[60] Paul Fiddes, 'The Baptism of Believers', in Thomas F. Best (ed.), *Baptism Today: Understanding, Practice Ecumenical Implications* (Collegeville: Liturgical Press, 2008), p. 76.

[61] *The Orthodox Creed*, p. 116.

The notion of the Supper being a confirmation of faith in Christ's spiritual work and being a seal in the divine covenant portrays both a human and divine participation in the rite itself. Additionally, the idea of the sacrament being a 'band', 'pledge', and a communal 'obligation of obedience' is representative of Anabaptist sacramentalism. However, the creed went further. Beyond being a sacramental promise, the elements convey something of spiritual substance. As Israel 'had the manna to nourish them in the wilderness to Canaan; so have we the sacraments, to nourish us in the church, and in our wilderness-condition, till we come to heaven'.[62] Thus, the sacraments for these collective General Baptists appeared to be a means by which God grants strength to the faithful.

While many scholars have conceded some connection between the Anabaptists and General Baptists, some have maintained that the relationship does not carry over to the Particular Baptists, whose origins came somewhat later and whose birth derived from reformed Separatist, Puritan or at least Calvinistic stock. However, during the schism of the main church in this tradition regarding baptism, Richard Blunt sailed to Holland in 1641 to confer with and probably receive immersion baptism from the Waterlander Mennonites.[63] For a significant number of early Particular Baptists, then, this gesture of sacramental succession was essential.

It is not surprising, then, to find Free Church sacramentalism also among the Particular Baptists. Thus, the *Second London Confession* (1677) of the Particular Baptist tradition, written two years before the publication of the General Baptists' *Orthodox Creed*, also emphasised the sacraments as a 'bond and pledge',[64] portraying a congruent understanding of 'sacrament' to those of Balthasar Hubmaier and other Anabaptists the century prior. However, its language, particularly regarding communion, went further. While eschewing the Catholic doctrine of transubstantiation and the Lutheran doctrine of holy union of Christ's physical presence with the elements, the confession revealed another form of sacramentalism:

> Worthy receivers, outwardly partaking of the visible Elements in this Ordinance, do then also inwardly by faith, really and indeed, yet not carnally, and corporally, but spiritually receive, and feed upon Christ crucified & all the benefits of his death: the Body and Blood of *Christ*, being then not corporally, or carnally, but spiritually present to the faith of Believers, in that Ordinance, as the Elements themselves are to their outward senses.[65]

---

[62] *The Orthodox Creed*, p. 107.

[63] H. Leon McBeth, *The Baptist Heritage: Four Centuries of Baptist Witness* (Nashville: Broadman Press, 1987), p. 43.

[64] *Second London Confession*, here cited in Lumpkin (ed.), *Baptist Confessions of Faith*, p. 291.

[65] *Second London Confession*, p. 293.

This argument for the special spiritual presence of Christ in the eucharist, perhaps influenced from Calvin's theology, at the very least portrays a position different from mere memorialism and demonstrates a continued understanding of the sacraments as more than symbols among seventeenth-century Baptists.

Perhaps even more striking, however, is *The Baptist Catechism*, written as a sort of theological commentary to complement the *Second London Confession*.[66] It was ultimately nicknamed 'Keach's Catechism' because it was co-authored by William Collins and Benjamin Keach. Question and Answer number 93 is especially instructive regarding an early Baptist sacramentalism:

> Q. (93) What are the outward means whereby Christ communicateth to us the benefits of redemption?
>
> A. The outward and ordinary means whereby Christ communicateth to us the benefits of redemption are his ordinances, especially the word, baptism, the Lord's Supper, and prayer; all which means are made effectual to the elect for salvation (Matt. xxviii. 19, 20; Acts ii. 42, 46, 47).[67]

While the first phrase of the answer might be interpreted only to say that the ordinances, along with scripture and prayer, are the ordinary symbolic means of expressing Christ's redemption, though the Word and prayer could hardly be interpreted symbolically, the latter phrase brings further explanation: baptism and the Lord's Supper join the Word and prayer as the ways in which a Christian comes to salvation in Christ Jesus. Stanley Fowler notes of this passage: 'Furthermore, it was indicated here that it is Christ himself who communicates the benefits of his saving work through the ordinances, which is to say that baptism [and the Supper are] means of grace as well as [acts] of personal confession.'[68]

Early Baptist Leaders

Yet, not only do some of the early confessions but also certain formative Baptist leaders demonstrate the continuation of Free Church sacramentalism. While the writings of numerous seventeenth-century Baptists could be highlighted as representative of this movement, this essay will briefly focus on the thought of two Particular Baptist ministers, Robert Garner and Henry Lawrence, as well as the sacramental formulations of the General Baptist leader, Thomas Grantham.

---

[66] Fowler, *More than a Symbol*, p. 18.
[67] 'Keach's Catechism', here cited in Tom J. Nettles (ed.), *Baptist Catechisms: 'To Make Thee Wise Unto Salvation'* (Tom J. Nettles, 1983), pp. 91-92.
[68] Fowler, *More than a Symbol*, p. 19.

ROBERT GARNER (D. 1649)

In his useful little book printed in 1645, *A Treatise of Baptisme,* Particular Baptist pastor Robert Garner wrote an apologetic work against infant baptism and for the exclusive practice of believer's baptism. Garner's work, though relatively brief, is significant theologically, for he outlined four privileges of believer's baptism. In the first place, Garner noted that

> Believers (in submitting to this Ordinance) have the name of the Father and of the Sonne, and of the holy Spirit called upon them therein. . . . For through the Lord Jesus, believers have a glorious interest in the Father, and in the holy Spirit. And this is expressed elsewhere, by being baptized into Christ. Rom. 6.3, Gal. 3.27. Now to be baptized into Christ, or into the Name of Christ, or in the Name of Christ, have one and the same sense and signification in Scripture. . . . Now his name holds forth unto believers, especially two things: Authority, and Grace: as such 'know' to whom the Lord giveth understanding. And to have his Name called upon them in baptisme, implyeth two things. First, the Lord declareth or promiseth to them that he Calleth or Putteth his Name, that is, his Authority and his Grace, upon them in baptism: for these words, Baptizing them in the Name of the Father, and of the Sonne, and of the Holy Spirit, carry the force of a promise in them: for in that the Lord hath commanded his servants to baptize believers in his Name, to Put or Call his Name upon them in baptisme he saith Amen to it, he confirmeth the word of his servants, he performeth what he promiseth to them.[69]

Likewise, Garner argued that the believer 'profits to put or call' God's Name, thereby promising herself that God will be her Father and Maker and she God's child, servant and member of God's people.[70] What is remarkable about these two points is the acknowledgement from an early Baptist that baptism serves, as both Luther and the Anabaptists had argued, as a promise. Yet Garner combined both divine and human participation in such a promise. And it seems that while the act of water baptism serves as symbolic of this promise, Garner apparently still maintained that some kind of divine blessing occurs in the rite, to the spiritual benefit of the participant.

This idea of divine promise and work for the benefit and blessing of the new Christian is more than an intimation or an item cursorily mentioned in Garner's work. In fact, the second 'privilege' of believer's baptism for Garner is that baptisands are incorporated into the church, which grants them the spiritual communion with Christ and other believers that is requisite for the faith. Said Garner: 'for to be added to the Church of the Lord, or the body of the Lord, is to be added to the Lord himself, in a mysticall externall union'.[71]

Thirdly, the Christian receives the privilege, 'through the faith of the operation of God', to enter into fellowship with Christ through his death and

---

[69] Robert Garner, *A Treatise of Baptisme* (London: n.p., 1645), pp. 10-11.
[70] Garner, *A Treatise of Baptisme*, p. 11.
[71] Garner, *A Treatise of Baptisme*, p. 15.

resurrection. Through baptism, Garner argued, 'the strength of the body of sinne is more subdued, and they are more enabled to walk in newnesse of life'. The idea of one's union with Christ in death and resurrection is far more than symbolic in Garner's writing. Instead, the Christian experiences a sort of mystical union with Christ through the act of water baptism. Stanley Fowler notes that, from at least 1640, Particular Baptists connected baptism to the death, burial and resurrection of Christ.[72] Yet, Robert Garner held that through baptism God gives 'in unto their hearts (in what proportion he pleaseth) the power of the death and resurrection of Jesus Christ, acting faith in them to receive the same, whereby they are in some measure enabled to perform that which their baptisme doth engage them unto.'[73]

Finally, the fourth privilege granted in baptism to the believer, in Garner's mind, was that God's assurance of forgiveness is conveyed, which 'doth more richly seal up or confirm to him the free and full remission of all his sinnes, through the blood of Christ'.[74] Here, Garner was careful to note that baptism does not remit the sins of the baptisand but does mysteriously communicate, through God's confirmation and witness, the assurance of that forgiveness. 'For when a Believer is baptized in the Name of Christ, and the Spirit of God acts faith in him in his baptisme, then is his heart more sweetly assured, that though this Name all his sins are remitted, and he is at peace with God.'

Thus, Garner exhibits a baptismal theology which incorporates a kind of sacramentalism in which promises are made by both the participant and God, and the baptisand experiences God's confirmation and sealing assurance, whereby the new Christian is mysteriously united with Christ and his church and is divinely strengthened in faith during the rite. The glory of the Lord is 'put forth' onto Christians in baptism, 'crucifying the power of sin in them, and raysing up their heart and minde as it were into heaven to sit with Christ, to walke with him in a holy and heavenly conversation, and to live a new life.'[75] The 'newness of life' then is not only a Christian duty but it also becomes a Christian privilege, bestowed by God, through the waters of baptism.

HENRY LAWRENCE (1600-1664)

Garner's Particular Baptist contemporary, Henry Lawrence, echoed the notion of one's mystical union with Christ through the sacraments. In his systematic work entitled, *Of Baptism,* published in 1659, Lawrence argued that the mystical union that the Christian experiences in Christ is the 'ground of all that is good and happy in us' and that it 'is the first and great thing that is made ours by Baptisme'.[76] Through this union, Christ becomes the 'middle person, the

---

[72] Fowler, *More than a Symbol*, p. 21.
[73] Cited in Fowler, *More than a Symbol*, p.22; cf, Garner, *A Treatise of Baptisme*, p. 19.
[74] Here cited in Fowler, *More than a Symbol*, p. 24.
[75] Fowler, *More than a Symbol*, p. 20.
[76] Henry Lawrence, *Of Baptism* (Amsterdam?, n.p., 1646), p. 2.

bond'[77] between God and the believer. Through the waters of baptism, the Christian is assured of and sealed in this divine-human connection.

Yet, as Fowler notes, this sealing for Lawrence is not merely a token of that which had already been established spiritually. While baptism and the Supper both presuppose the faith of the participants, these sacraments also affect some spiritual work in the hearts of the recipients. Said Lawrence: 'God by his sealing lets us know, what a vallew he puts upon us, how he separates us from refuse and base things, therefore we should not defile ourselves.'[78] Yet, in the course of one's salvation, Lawrence maintained, unbelievers find themselves 'pricked at the heart' and in a lost condition, cry out to the Lord for help, and find their hope in the divine ordinance of baptism. Lawrence underscored the association between baptism and forgiveness. Thus baptism serves as a sign and seal of salvation.[79] However, Lawrence was careful to note that the outward washing is not merely a 'carnall ceremony' but corresponds also to an inward conveyance of confidence and assurance that the baptisand is reconciled to God.[80] Wrote Lawrence:

> This is that which is the effect of Baptisme, and which Baptisme seals up to you; for what Baptisme findes it seals, although it doeth also exhibit more of the same kind; Baptisme and so all the ordinances of Christ, those we call Sacraments, seale up what is already, else how could it be a seale, but doth also conveigh more of the same.[81]

Thus, Lawrence emphasised the sealing work of God in the sacraments both as a securing of what has already been established in faith and as a strengthening of the same. Moreover, Lawrence argued that both the Lord's Supper and baptism cannot confer grace without the presence of the Holy Spirit, just as the Word is a 'dead letter' without the same Spirit.[82] He asked: 'Now if there be not virtue in the flesh of Christ, but by the personall union, how shall bodily actions about bodily elements confer grace, but by the mediation of the Spirit.'[83] The Supper and baptism are akin to the Word of God in that they emanate from the same Christ in whom 'all his benefits is offered and confirmed to us in the word and Sacraments, the same union, the same communion in the death & resurrection of Christ,' and both the Word of God and God's sacraments are 'ineffectual without faith'.[84] Lawrence furthered this comparison between the

---

[77] Lawrence, *Of Baptism*, p. 2.
[78] Lawrence, *Of Baptism*, p. 17. See also Fowler, *More than a Symbol*, p. 25.
[79] Lawrence, *Of Baptism*, p. 21.
[80] Lawrence, *Of Baptism*, p. 22.
[81] Lawrence, *Of Baptism*, pp. 22-23.
[82] Lawrence, *Of Baptism*, p. 103.
[83] Lawrence, *Of Baptism*, p. 103.
[84] Lawrence, *Of Baptism*, p. 104.

Word and the sacraments by articulating that one is audible and the other the visible Word:

> The word signifies according to such expressions as men have given a value unto, to signify thinges by, but the Sacraments represents by such similitudes and proportions as the signes have with the things signified; therefore we read the word and heare the word, but we see and feel the Sacraments. . . . Those signes and visible elements affect the sences outward and inward, the sences conveigh the object to the understanding, there the Holy Ghost takes them, and brings us into the present enjoyment of things, as if we saw Christ with our eyes, toucht him with our hands, felt him by our tast, and injoyed him with our whole man: all this in a rationall and discoursive way, raysing an analogy & proportion beweene the signe and the thing signified. . . . [While] the word especially teacheth, the Sacraments especially seale and confirme: the word indeed signifies and applyes spiritual things, but the Sacraments more efficatiously represent & apply.[85]

While the Word is essential to salvation for Lawrence, the sacraments are helpful for the security of and confidence in the salvation effected in the heart of the believer.[86] In this sense, the elements of bread, wine and water are sacramental for Henry Lawrence.

THOMAS GRANTHAM (1634-1692)

However, not only did Particular Baptists manifest a Free Church sacramentalism, but there is also significant evidence that many seventeenth-century General Baptists appropriated a similar understanding, evidenced already in this chapter by the *Orthodox Creed* (1678). Thomas Grantham serves as an outstanding example of a prominent seventeenth-century General Baptist leader whose writings affirmed a style of Baptist sacramentalism.

In a work entitled *A Sigh for Peace: or The Cause of Division Discovered* (1671), Grantham wrote of the ordinance of baptism:

> Baptism in the ordinary way of God's communicating the grace of the Gospel is antecedent to the reception thereof, & is propounded as a means where in not only the Remission of our sins shall be granted to us, but as a condition whereupon we shall receive the gift of the Holy Ghost. . . . [It] was fore-ordained to signifie and sacramentally to confer the grace of the pardon of sin, and the inward washing of the Conscience by Faith in the Bloud of Jesus Christ.[87]

Clearly Grantham was arguing for something other than mere symbolism in the sacrament of baptism. Yet, like the Anabaptists and other Baptists reviewed in this chapter, Grantham fully saw the faith of the participant in the sacrament

---

[85] Lawrence, *Of Baptism*, pp. 109-11.
[86] See Lawrence, *Of Baptism*, pp. 111-12.
[87] Thomas Grantham, *A Sigh for Peace: or The Cause of Division Discovered* (London: n.p, 1671), pp. 87-88; here cited in Fowler, p. 28.

playing a vital role in its efficacy, distinguishing a Protestant if not Free Church sacramentalism.[88] Nevertheless, through the waters of baptism, Grantham seemed to maintain, God communicates his grace and confers the Holy Spirit upon the baptisand.

Grantham bolstered the importance and spiritual power of baptism in his magisterial work, *Christianismus Primitivus* (1678), in which he closely associated baptism with the remission of sins. After outlining how Christ demonstrated the priority of baptism by participating in it himself and commissioning his disciples to perform it upon others, Grantham wrote:

> And thus was our Lord himself the chief founder of the Gospel in the Heavenly Doctrine of *Faith, Repentance, ann* [sic.] *Baptism for the remission of Sins. . . .* This Baptism is joyned with this Gospel of repentance, that as repentance being now necessary to the admission of Sinners into the Church of Christ, even so Baptism being joyned thereto by the will of God, is necessary to the same end.[89]

Thus, while the previous citation seemed to show Grantham as understanding baptism as the 'ordinary means' of receiving God's grace, in this latter comment, the General Baptist leader argued that baptism joins repentance as the keys to enter the church. Furthermore, faith, repentance and baptism combined appear requisite for the remission of sins. On this point Stan Fowler comments that: 'This would surely make baptism not merely a sign, but an effective sign.'[90]

Yet, Grantham also extended this sacramental language to the ordinance of communion, what he commonly called 'The Table of the Lord'. He argued for a trifold divinely instituted purpose of the Lord's Supper, namely, to obviate the need for future offerings for human iniquity, to represent and remind believers of Christ's death, and to demonstrate that Christ shed his blood visibly before human witnesses.[91] Additionally, the Table is intended to teach

---

[88] On the analysis of this passage of Grantham's, Stan Fowler writes: 'To say that baptism effects a purification of the conscience is to say that it seals or assures the baptizand of forgiveness, and to say that it is effective "by faith" is to deny that it functions *ex opere operato* or that it is applicable to those who are not yet capable of faith. Furthermore, to say that it is the "ordinary" means of conferring these benefits is to deny that it is an absolutely necessary means of salvific union with Christ, as if the grace of God were tied to the sacrament. All the qualifications simply tell us what his sacramental language does *not* mean, but they in no way refute the idea that his thought is sacramental in concept as well as terminology', *More than a Symbol*, p. 28.

[89] Thomas Grantham, *Christianismus Primitivus* (London: Francis Smith, 1678), Book 2, Part 2, Chapter 1, Section 5.

[90] Fowler, *More than a Symbol*, p. 28.

[91] Originally from Grantham's *Christianismus Primitivus;* here cited from Grantham, 'The Primitive Christian Religion', in Curtis W. Freeman, James Wm. McClendon, Jr.

Christian humility, brotherly love and spiritual unity in response to Christ's humility and love for humanity. Grantham took seriously the notion that the Lord's Supper was a spiritual communion:

> Can anything be more effectually spoken to unite the members of Christ or will any man say these things are not spoken of this ordinance? . . . Yea here Christ gathers his people together at his own Table as one family. And it is that Table to which all saints are to approach with such preparation as may render them fit for communion in that mystical body, the Church, which is also called Christ because of that unity they have in him and one another in him.[92]

Such a statement is remarkably consistent with those of previous Free Church sacramentalists, such as Pilgram Marpeck, who interpreted one's incorporation into Christ to be the very same as the incorporation into Christ's church. Additionally, Grantham's phraseology resembled the mystical union language of the Dutch Anabaptism of Dirk Philips and Menno Simons, through which a believer finds herself bound to Christ and the church sacramentally by means of the Table.

Finally, Grantham viewed the goal of communion as 'to assure the saints as by a pledge or token that the new testament is ratified and confirmed by the death of the testator, so that whether we regard the certainty or sufficiency of the gospel, both declared in this ordinance as much as any other'.[93] This notion of the sacrament as a promise echoes the sacramental theology of Hubmaier, Marpeck and Menno. The promise found in the Supper established for Grantham 'God's blessing and Spirit going along with them all such as love Christ and wait for his appearing'.[94] Thus, consistently with his view of baptism, Thomas Grantham perceived the Supper as not merely a token but as an effective sign which powerfully and especially communicates God's blessing. It is here, Grantham wrote, that Christians 'feed upon [Christ] as meat and drink indeed'.[95]

Conclusion

Baptist historians have only recently uncovered a number of other seventeenth-century Baptist leaders and documents that also articulated a form of Free Church sacramentalism which harkened back to their Anabaptist

---

and C. Rosalee Velloso da Silva (eds), *Baptist Roots: A Reader in the Theology of a Christian People* (Valley Forge: Judson Press, 1999), pp. 91-92.

[92] Grantham, 'The Primitive Christian Religion', p. 95.
[93] Grantham, 'The Primitive Christian Religion', p. 95.
[94] Grantham, 'The Primitive Christian Religion', p. 97.
[95] Grantham, 'The Primitive Christian Religion', p. 96.

predecessors.[96] If John Smyth was influenced by the baptismal practice of Collegiant Mennonites in Amsterdam, it seems probable that he was additionally shaped by their theological rationale for the practice. That Baptists throughout the remainder of the century and into the eighteenth century repeated these themes it stands to reason that such a Free Church sacramentalism was a natural and conscious extension of its Anabaptist forerunners, and not a continually repeated coincidental occurrence. While the potential of Reformed (Puritan) theology and other Magisterial Protestant forces probably also played a role in influencing especially the Particular Baptist branch regarding the sacraments, Anabaptism's abiding afflation on the movement still remains unavoidable.

Still, the use of sacramental language and, especially, the appropriation of sacramental cogitation among Baptists, and, by extrapolation, among their predecessors, looms as uncharacteristic to their latter-day counterparts. But as Curtis Freeman observes:

> In the seventeenth century, Baptists used a variety of almost interchangeable terms to describe the Lord's Supper [and baptism], frequently invoking the language of sacrament. But the range of words narrowed during the years of rapid growth for Baptists in America as a result of eighteenth and nineteenth-century revivals. Growing gradually less comfortable with sacramental language that attempted to say something about God's activity in the Supper [or the water], they began to speak of it more as an 'act of obedience'.[97]

Thus, baptism and the Lord's Supper are today commonly called only 'ordinances' and are relegated through rationalism to the category of symbol, memorialism and real absence for most Baptists. Yet, to the astonishment of those not well-read in Baptist theology, the twentieth and early twenty-first centuries have seen a modest but significant return to both the language and the understanding of a Free Church sacramentalism, especially among British Baptists whose denominational fruit has fallen closest to the historical Baptist trunk.[98] While the traditional definition of sacrament as 'an outward and visible sign of an inward and spiritual grace' can be interpreted as congruent with long

---

[96] For instance, see Fowler's development of the *Propositions and Conclusions concerning True Christian Religion* which elaborated John Smyth's 1610 confession and also Fowler's discussion of such seventeenth century figures as Benjamin Keach and William Mitchill, and eighteenth century Baptist sacramentalists such as John Gill, Abraham Booth, and Andrew Fuller, among others in his *More Than a Symbol*, pp. 13-57. See also Anthony R. Cross, 'Dispelling the Myth of English Baptist Baptismal Sacramentalism', *Baptist Quarterly* 38.8 (2000), pp. 367-91.

[97] Curtis W. Freeman, '"To Feed Upon by Faith": Nourishment from the Lord's Table', in Cross and Thompson (eds), *Baptist Sacramentalism*, p. 200.

[98] For examples, see the works of H. Wheeler Robinson, G.R. Beasley-Murray, Paul Fiddes, Anthony Cross and E.A. Payne, among others.

established Baptist views, its usage has been all but eliminated by a modern Free Church misunderstanding that forces the term 'sacrament' to be tantamount to Catholic *ex opere operato* interpretations, appearing to Protestant minds to undercut the necessity of faith and to Baptists to mitigate the necessity of the personal response of the participant(s). Yet this rejection of sacramental language and action is not representative of the Baptist tradition as a whole. And Baptists who wish to deepen their understanding of their ecclesial practices would find a rich Free Church sacramental heritage in both their seventeenth-century Baptist progenitors and their Anabaptist antecedents.

CHAPTER 2

Episcope without Episcopacy: Baptist Attitudes to Bishops in Seventeenth-Century England

Ruth Gouldbourne

About seven months ago, I was sent a photograph. It shows the consecration of a bishop in Georgia, the independent state in the Caucasus. It is a scandalous photo, for two reasons: the bishop being consecrated is a) female and b) Baptist. Her name is Rusadan Gotsiridze, and she is that wondrous thing, a Baptist bishop. For those who have been nurtured in the Anglo-American tradition of Baptist identity, such a phase has a clear oxymoronic quality. For many continental Europeans, too, the phrase has a strange sound. But that is not true everywhere. In Georgia (in the Caucasus), there are bishops, and an archbishop. In Latvia, there is a bishop, and in Moldova too. And in other parts of the world, we also come across the phrase. Valdis Teraudkalns has written an important piece on the contemporary situation, 'Episcopacy in the Baptist Tradition', in which he compares and contrasts the English and Latvian situations.[1]

Nevertheless it remains the case that for the Baptist tradition I come from, Baptists and bishops do not go together – indeed, one of the defining features of being Baptist is that we do not have bishops. I cannot count the number of times I have told a mixed Baptist and Anglican class that we cannot simply equate regional ministers of the Baptist Union of Great Britain with episcopal bishops, and that is one of the things that must be grasped about who we are. And yet it is clearly not true. There are places – and there are times – when Baptist have bishops. But for many Baptists, for a significant part of the tradition, the language of episcopacy, of a structure that is in parallel or continuity with the ordering of the wider church in time and space, is one we have rejected.

The argument of this paper is that a significant reason why on the whole we have refused both the language and the structure of episcopacy has at least as much to do with the context in which the early Baptists were exploring their

---

[1] Valdis Teraudkalns, 'Episcopacy in the Baptist Tradition', in Philip E. Thompson and Anthony R. Cross (eds), *Recycling the Past or Researching History: Studies in Baptist Historiography and Myths* (Milton Keynes: Paternoster, 2005), pp. 279-93.

identity as it has to do with theology *per se*. The first Baptists, both General and Particular, were operating in the context of seventeenth-century England. In the case of the Generals, even while they were in the Netherlands, their identity and the arguments they were having and were reacting to were those of England and English theological reality. And so, if we are going to make sense of the visceral rejection of episcopacy – and the ongoing struggles to find both a language and structure to deal with the questions of oversight that continued to need addressing - then it is not only to the emerging Baptist theology of what the church is that we need to look but to the historical context and to the theology which was driving it.

The Episcopacy that Early Baptists Repudiated

That the rejection of episcopacy as early Baptists experienced it was bitter and defiant is clear when we start to read what was written. Helwys' *The Mistery of Iniquity* (1612) is always a good place to start in order to understand early Baptists. He pulls no punches in attacking what he sees as the evil and idolatrous structure of the episcopacy. Having attacked the papacy as the first of the beasts of revelation, he then sets about identifying the second:

> Which way now (in finding out the second beast) shall we be able to look beside that great hierarchy of archbishops and lord bishops. Are not you they that pretend (in meekness and humility) the words and power of the Lamb who says learn of me that I am meek and lowly etc, but exercise the power of the beast and speak like the dragon.[2]

He continues with his attack in various forms, and it culminates in:

> Lastly to make it appear plainly enough that this hierarchy of apbs and lord bps is the image of the beast, let all behold the names of blasphemy which it bears and they are these
> Apb, primate, metropolitans, Lords spiritual, reverend father, lords' grace. What names of blasphemy are here. They are the titles and name of our Lord and our Christ. But is it not sufficient to despoil and rob Christ of all his power. But you will also take from him the titles of honour due to his name?[3]

Helwys was by no means the only one to attack the episcopal structure as he experienced it. The author of *Religion's Peace: Or a Plea for Liberty of Conscience* (1614), possibly Leonard Busher, wrote:

---

[2] Thomas Helwys, *The Mistery of Iniquity, 1612*, ed. Richard Groves (Macon, GA: Mercer University Press, 1998), pp.15-16.
[3] Helwys, *Mistery*, pp. 20-21.

> But as the church of Rome, people of all sorts are by persecution forced there into by the bishops and ministers thereof, so it is in the church of England also. Which showeth that the bishops and ministers of Rome and England are one spirit. In gathering people to their faith and church, which is the spirit of Satan, who knoweth well that his kingdom, the false church, would greatly decay, if persecution were laid down.[4]

Even Thomas Grantham, to whom we will return, for he has a great deal to say about oversight, was less than happy with the pattern as he saw it practised in the Church of England of his day. Writing in 1678, he declared:

> But this I will say, That it's hard for a Bishop to be very rich and very good, otherwise our Saviour could have chosen such.[5]

Whatever we can glean that the early Baptists wanted to say about ecclesiastical oversight, we can be pretty sure that they did not like the forms of episcopacy that they saw around them.

It is worth, in the light of such strong reactions, taking a moment to understand something of the episcopacy they were rejecting. With the Elizabethan settlement of 1559, the Reformation in England was established by law, and the church was organised on episcopal lines, with the monarch as the head or, in deference to the concerns about a woman ruler, when Elizabeth eventually came to the throne, the governor of the church. There was a clear distinction made then, and worked out in more detail in the reigns of Elizabeth's successors, between the temporal jurisdiction of the monarch and the spiritual jurisdiction of the rulers of the church, the archbishops and bishops.

The church in England under the Elizabethan settlement understood itself as the *continuation*, reformed and restored it is true, but the *continuation* of the ancient church, which had been distorted by Rome. It mattered that this was not a new beginning, but a re-formation of the original. Central to this self-perception was the conviction that that continuity was carried not only in buildings, practices and creeds, but also, and primarily, in the episcopate. The continuing of the episcopate and that through a proper succession was crucial to the sense of and claims for catholicity. The question they faced was whether this new form of organisation was to be trusted as church, especially after the break from Rome under Henry VIII. Its authenticity was guaranteed by the episcopal succession. Thus, John Jewel, in his *Apology of the Church of England* written in 1562, said:

---

[4] E.B. Underhill (ed.), *Tracts on Liberty of Conscience* (London: Hanserd Knollys Society, 1846), p. 19.

[5] Thomas Grantham, *Christianismus Primitivus* (London: Francis Smith, 1678), Book 2, Chapter 9, Section VI, p. 125.

> We believe that there is one Church of God, and that the same is not shut up (as in time past among the Jews) into some one corner of the kingdom, but that it is catholic and universal and dispersed throughout the whole world; so that there is now no nation which can truly complain that they be shut forth and may not be one of the church and people of God; and that this church is the kingdom, the body and the spouse of Christ; and that Christ alone is the prince of this kingdom; that Christ alone is the head of this body; and that Christ alone is the bridegroom of this spouse.
> Furthermore that there be diverse degrees of ministers in the church; whereof some be deacons, some priests, some bishops; to whom is committed the office to instruct the people and the whole charge and setting forth of religion.[6]

Thus, bishops were crucial to the catholicity of the church – a vital factor in preserving the church through the chaos of the Reformation and the challenges offered by the old church about the validity both of sacrament and of authority.

At the heart of maintaining this catholicity was the doctrine of succession. It mattered first in the consecration of bishops, and there was great controversy over the consecration of Elizabeth's first archbishop, Matthew Parker, who actually became the narrow channel through whom all succession from the old church into the Church of England passed. Whether he was properly consecrated or not remained, indeed remains, an open question. It mattered, too, in the continuity of the priesthood. The bishops were responsible for the ordination of those who were the sacramental ministers. The power of ordination resided in them alone, in order, precisely to protect this succession.

There was another aspect too, that of divine right. Matthew Sutcliffe, Dean of Exeter, argued in 1591:

> That order which Jesus Christ prescribed, the Apostles diligently observed and maintained. For they did not only keep an Apostolical dignity themselves and shewed their authority in their actions, but on the Ministers they appointed, they set notable marks of difference.[7]

The order of the church was God's structure and made valid by God's action, creating a divine right of episcopacy. This was a position that, in England at least, was deeply united with the recognition of the monarch as the head of the

---

[6] John Ayre (ed.), *The Works of John Jewel* (London: Parker Society, 1848), Vol. 3, p. 59.

[7] Matthew Sutcliffe, A Treatise of Ecclesiastical Disicipline, cited by Norman Sykes, Old Priest and New Prebyter: Episcopacy and Presbyterianism since the Reformation with especial relation to the Churches of England and Scotland (Cambridge: Cambridge University Press, 1956), p. 63.

church, and, even more, with the sense of the nature of the church as the religious facet of the civil community.[8]

Following the break with Rome, there had to be some way of validating both church and monarchy. Previously, the validation of both had been dependent on the Roman supremacy. It came to rest in the divine right of the crown, and what Henry had started, Elizabeth developed. The theory of divine right argued that the monarch was not monarch through the appointment by Rome, but was such by direct divine appointment. In England this included the role as head of the church, though the distinction between temporal and spiritual office was always maintained. And so the divinely appointed monarch delegated the interpretation of his or her will over the church to the spiritual officers, the episcopate. The understanding of episcopacy, therefore, in the Church of England was not simply a theological statement about the nature of the church. Or rather, it was a theological statement, but it started from the assumptions inherent in a theology of establishment. Church and state were understood as one body. They existed under the divinely appointed headship of the monarch. Just as the monarch had temporal ministers to conduct the temporal affairs of the nation, so there were spiritual ministers to conduct the spiritual affairs, the bishops.

These two aspects – catholicity and establishment – were the two particular historical realities that shaped the episcopacy in the Church of England as the seventeenth century opened. The great articulator of Anglican identity at that juncture was Richard Hooker. He wrote *The Laws of Ecclesiastical Polity*, some parts of which were so contentious that he chose not to publish them. However, after his death, the final books were published. Part of his definition of a bishop is this:

> A bishop is a minister of God unto whom with permanent continuance is given not only the power of administering the word and sacraments, which power other presbyters have, but also a further power to ordain ecclesiastical persons and a power in chiefty over presbyters as well as laymen, a power to be by way of jurisdiction to a pastor even to pastors themselves.[9]

Hooker's definition insists on three things. Firstly, that a bishop is ordained, and therefore is part of the continuing succession. Secondly, he insists that the bishop has the power of ordination. He is the conduit of the succession. And then thirdly, and as a result of these two, a bishop has a ruling role over those whom he ordains, and thus by extension over the whole of the flock.

---

[8] For a further discussion of this theology, see Sykes, *Old Priest and New Presbyter*, especially chapter 1, 'The Godly Prince and the Godly Bishop'. See also Paul Avis, *Church, State and Establishment* (London: SPCK, 2001).

[9] Richard Hooker, *The Laws of Ecclesiastical Polity*, Book VII, 2/3, in P.G. Stanwood (ed.), *The Works of Richard Hooker* (Cambridge, MA:Harvard University Press, 1981), Vol. 3, p. 152.

In the context of the establishment this role was part of and sustained by political force, and so we begin to reach some of the objections that the Baptist writers were offering to what they experienced as episcopacy. The right to ordain, the theology of succession and its location in the episcopate were exercised in part through the forcible suppression of those who preached without licence, which was the bishop's to give. So, for example, John Bunyan was imprisoned so memorably in Bedford for preaching without a licence, while John Sims was arrested in 1646 for his evangelistic preaching in the West of England.

For those committed to this policy, it was about protecting the truth of the gospel: limiting its proclamation to those who were duly trained, approved and accepted, and so protecting the church from the danger of heresy. From the earliest days, the view was articulated by, for example Cyprian, that the bishop was held to be responsible for the doctrinal purity of the church.[10] The right of jurisdiction, including but not limited to the maintaining of doctrinal purity, was exercised, as Hooker made clear, over both pastors and laity. In a context where the church was so closely identified with the power structures of the community, this meant that in effect the bishops had the power to impose fines, to confine to prison and even to require the state to carry out execution. The dissenters of all sorts experienced these powers. This was the oppression that shaped their world; hence the energy in the attacks on the power of bishops.

Thus, at first reading, many of the attacks that we hear from the early Baptists on episcopacy as an ecclesiastical structure were shaped by the particular context – the Elizabethan settlement, the role of the monarch and the theologies of divine right – which had a specific place in the English situation. What they were rejecting, we might conclude, is not so much episcopacy as the experience of oppression, the absence of liberty of conscience and the lack of freedom to organise as they desired. And this is true. As we will see, they were not in fact rejecting the idea of oversight as a theological concept and indeed an ecclesiastical necessity.

The Anglican Theology of Episcopacy

Even with that said, the theology of oversight that they developed was not just episcopacy with the nasty bits taken out. It was, in several significant ways, profoundly different from the theology that developed within the seventeenth-century Anglican Church. In order to see more clearly not only the ways in which these early Baptists thought about oversight, but also the distinctiveness of their position, we need to examine first the deeper theology that was being expressed in Anglican practice, then the reasons for Baptist rejection of this.

---

[10] Cyprian, *Treatise 5*, chs 9-10, in *A Library of Fathers of the Holy Catholic Church*, Vol. 3 (Oxford: John Henry Parker, 1839), p. 138.

Then we will go into more detail of how Baptists did think about oversight, and the different ways in which it was practised.

As we have seen, Anglican theology of episcopacy had within in it convictions about the relationship of the church in England to the wider church: the concept of catholicity, and the relationship between the nation in its spiritual aspect and in its political aspect, establishment.

Deep in the notion of catholicity as it was grasped by the Anglican theologians was the conviction that the church drew its life from its historical roots, and so its life and legitimacy came from its foundation by Christ and the calling of the first apostles. It is this principle that gives power to the notion of succession: the continuity of the life, passed from faithful hand to faithful hand links the community of the faithful across time and across geography. This is quite explicit, for example, in Hooker's writing:

> The first bishops in the church of Christ were his blessed apostles; for the office whereunto Matthias was chosen the sacred history doth term episcope, and episcopal office; which being spoken expressly of one agreeth no less unto them all than unto him.[11]

And later in the same section:

> The apostles there were the first which had such authority and all others who have it after them in orderly sort are their lawful successors....For to succeed them is after them to have that episcopal kind of power which was first given to them.[12]

The identity and being of the church emerge from its continuity with the past. Cut off from its past, it ceases to be the church. The church is in relationship to the risen Christ – the validator of the church – through the mediation of the historic process, embodied in the successive episcopate. Without the episcopate, therefore, there is no church – not primarily because there is need of an episcopate to organise or rule the church, but because it is in the episcopate that the Christ of the past is linked to the church of the present. The connection between Christ and the church as presently experienced is mediated through the episcopate, and if that succession is broken, the connection to Christ, and so to the roots of the church's being is marred.

The notion of establishment is deeply, though not inherently, connected to the theology of episcopacy. It is quite possible for a church that is the spiritual aspect of the state and established church not to be episcopal. The Presbyterian church in Scotland at the time we are talking about demonstrates this. However, the particular circumstances of the Reformation in England, and the especial

---

[11] Hooker, *Laws of Ecclesiastical Polity*, Book VII, 4/1, in Stanwood, *Works of Hooker*, Vol. 3, p. 155.
[12] Hooker, *Laws of Ecclesiastical Polity*, Book VII, 4/3, in Stanwood, *Works of Hooker*, Vol. 3, p. 158.

link between the monarch and the reformed church gave that identity an appearance of inevitability. Although the link is not in fact a necessary one, through the historical processes which shaped seventeenth-century England, the link was unquestioned. When he succeeded Elizabeth 1, James VI and I articulated this link in his motto 'no bishop, no king'. He had grown up and come to power in a Presbyterian context. His experience of that polity was that it provided a force of resistance to his reign. He was much more contented with the pattern he found when he went to England, and so he set about strengthening the episcopate as a way of strengthening his own power. 'No bishop, no king' for James was less a statement about the church and more about his understanding of kingship. Both issues were, for James and for the bishops, theological statements. He found among the bishops those who were equally convinced that the episcopal church government was the most compatible with a church headed by a monarch. The characteristically Anglican loyalty to the idea of the identity of church and state as one body has its roots here and was worked out in the unquestioning assumption that the bishops were part of the nature of the church as the spiritual life of the nation.

The rejection of episcopacy that we encounter among the early Baptists is not only the rejection of the power and corruption that they often name in their attacks. It is also a rejection of the theologies underlying the practice. They are rejecting not only the oppression that they experience. They are also rejecting the theology that Christ is present to the church through the historic succession, and they are rejecting the conviction that the religious and civic aspects of the nation are inextricably linked.

It is in this that we find the most profound effect of their context on the Baptists' understanding of oversight; in rejecting what they believed to be an unjustified and unbiblical theology, they set themselves on the way to find the patterns of oversight that were to become characteristic. For most of the seventeenth century it is piecemeal or developing; there is clear evidence of various strands of thought being worked at and worked out, not least in differences between Particular Baptist and General Baptist patterns. But there are some continuing themes or better some common features that emerge, and from which we can draw some conclusions about the theology of oversight or *episcope* that the Baptists were developing – *episcope* without episcopacy.

Baptist Messengers

To help understand this, it will be useful to sketch in something of what we know about what happened. For this section of my discussion, I am deeply reliant on J.F.V. Nicholson's paper in the *Baptist Quarterly* in January 1958.[13]

---

[13] J.F.V. Nicholson, 'The Office of Messenger amongst British Baptists in the Seventeenth and Eighteenth Centuries', *Baptist Quarterly* 17.5 (January 1958), pp. 206-25.

In that article, Nicholson examines the different references that there are to messengers, the most common term that Baptists adopted as the century went on to refer to those who exercised a ministry beyond the immediate and local and who therefore in some way were fulfilling a ministry of *episcope*.

The first thing to say about messengers is, that as far as we can tell, the General Baptists and the Particular Baptists, although they both developed this category, treated it in very different ways. Thus, to take the simpler one first, the Particular Baptists regarded messengers basically as those who were appointed for particular occasions to represent one congregation to another in cases of mutual contact, or to go with the minister, leading elder or whichever term was used, to represent the congregation at an association or even national gathering. The *London Confession* of 1644 is signed by 'elders and messengers', representatives of the congregations who took part in the meeting to draw it up. This pattern continues in the reports we have of association meetings, for the 'delegates' are referred to as messengers.

Messengers were also those who, commissioned by their local church, had the role of preaching where there was currently no baptised congregation, planting a local church, and, to some extent at least, ordering and leading it. Indeed, this role of evangelism appears, for most of the century, to be the main function among the Particular Baptists of those whom they called messengers. This role might very well be long-term and, in that sense, permanent. However, it is quite clear that the role of messenger practised this way was a subset of preaching or ruling elder, not in the sense that somebody would be both, though that did happen, but that there was no separate order of messengers apart from the regular recognition of those who served the churches in preaching and leading. Oversight therefore was not over those who were already leading churches, it was over local churches in their formative days, before there were fully recognised leaders.

For the General Baptists, the picture was more complex. Both of these roles were involved – evangelism and representation. But there was also a more juridical role, of governing and of oversight of 'the churches', often in a collegiate model. The messengers, at least towards the end of the century, were recognised as a separate order, and there was some sense of wider representation. Thus, although it is clear that among the Particular Baptists, messengers were ordained within and by the local church to which they belonged (with possibly some representation from the association, but not necessarily), among the General Baptists, at least some of the messengers were ordained by other messengers, and on one occasion at least we read of the national assembly ordaining and settling messengers.[14]

Thus, Thomas Grantham described his own ordination as a messenger in this way:

---

[14] Nicholson, 'The Office', p. 213.

I was elected by the consent of many congregations and ordained to the office of a messenger by those who were in the same office before me. The place where I was ordained was in my own mansion or dwelling house, the place where thechurch usually met.[15]

In such practices, we see the outworking of the sort of theology that Grantham is outlining in *Christianismus Primitivus*, when he states:

> The Rubbish of men's Devices being removed [he has been attacking the episcopacy as presently practised], we shall apply our selves to the Word of God, where we find only these four sorts of Ordained Officers or Ministers given to the Christian Churches, *viz. Messengers*, (or Apostles), *Bishops* (or Elders), and Deacons....For this Office [of itinerant evangelist, which is one of the roles that he assigns to a messenger] is as firmly settled in the Church, as any other, and therefore the Abrogation of this is in effect to abolish them all....And that Commission, *to teach all Nations*, must have a Ministry authorized by it...yet no Officers as such in the Church, save that of Messengers or Apostles, are obliged to do that Work, but to look to their particular Charge.[16]

He starts from the assertion that Christ has commanded that the gospel is to be preached, and from that proceeds to the conviction that such a command presupposes and even creates an office for its fulfilling. This he identifies with messengers. This work of evangelism is their primary function. Then, however, Grantham moves on to describe more of their work, giving several summaries of the activity that he is describing:

> Now this Work consists of divers Parts; they are to be as Eyes to the Church, to *oversee* or *provide*. They are to feed or nourish the Flock with the sincere Milk of the Word. They are to rule with diligence, and to keep good order in the Church of God, &c.[17]

In putting forward this definition, Grantham is going beyond the first role, as travelling evangelists and organisers of new churches, into what was clearly a more juridical role: they are to rule and keep good order.

This work is further discussed in 1659 by Will Jeffery, also a messenger, who described the kind of intervention that he and others were called on to make:

---

[15] Nicholson, 'The Office', p. 211.
[16] Grantham, *Christianismus Primitivus*, Book 2, Chapter 9, Section III, p. 119.
[17] Grantham, *Christianismus Primitivus*, Book 2, chapter 9, Section V, p. 122.

it is good and safe for a particular church in times of high concernment to call for, or desire help from sister churches, and so messengers, who are to take care of all churches in an especial manner, are to go in such cases.[18]

But alongside this authoritative role there was another strong theological conviction playing out. The *Orthodox Creed* of 1679 described the role of the messenger thus:

> The visible church of Christ, being completely gathered and organized, according to the mind of Christ, consists of officers and members; and the officers, appointed by Christ, to be chosen by his church, for the peculiar administration of ordinances, and execution of the power and duty Christ hath enjoined them to the end of the world, are these three, viz. Bishops or Messengers; and Elders, or Pastors; and Deacons, or Overseers of the poor; ... and those bishops so ordained, have the government of those churches that had suffrage in their election, and no other ordinarily; as also to preach the word, or gospel, to the world or unbelievers.[19]

Grantham refers to rule before preaching and planting, though, noticeably, limiting, or defining that rule, in terms of the link to the local churches. Juridical capacity is here founded on and contained within an overriding theology of the authority of the local congregations. Grantham also explores this from another angle. In Treatise 5, book 4, of *Christianismus Primitivus*, he answers various objections to his theology of oversight. To the objection,

> *But do you not give to these Ministers or Messengers a superintendency over Bishops or Elders? And may not this in time lead to the setting up Arch-Bishops, or some Anti-christian Usurpation?*

he answers,

> There is no better way to prevent such Usurpation than by preserving the Ministry by us contended for, because it preserves all particular Churches Right to send forth such Ministers as there is occasion for them so to do, and no one Church is herein priviledged above another....We give them no more superintendency than *Timothy* or *Titus* had, whose care was for the Churches indifferently, so that there preheminence was only a degree of Honour, (not of Power)...[20]

The messenger, however wide the ministry spreads, remains within and held by the local church.

---

[18] Will Jeffrey, *The Whole Faith of Man* (1659), p. 109, cited in Nicholson, 'The Office', p. 208.
[19] William L. Lumpkin, *Baptist Confessions of Faith* (Valley Forge: Judson Press, 1989), pp. 319-20, article 31.
[20] Grantham, *Christianismus Primitivus,* Book 4, Treatise 5, p. 164.

Intriguingly, of course, we see the language of 'bishop' used here, in the objection that Grantham imagines being raised, the danger of setting the messenger over bishops or elders. Here, 'bishop' as a term is being used in the way we often find it among these early Baptists, to refer to the leader of a local church, what in Anglican terms of the period would be a vicar, and what today we would usually call minister. He – and others as we shall see when we we consider the Second London Confession - were not afraid of the term. But they insisted on giving it their own definition, and of separating it both from succession and from state authority.[21]

There is a strong sense in all these writings that, even as Baptists are exploring the need of and scriptural warrant for authoritative ministry beyond the local church, still the local gathered congregation remains the locus of authority. Grantham continues:

> It is meet every Christian (and so every Minister) be a Member of some particular Church, and this Church is the most proper Judg to execute Justice (as far as it concerns the Church) against such Offenders.[22]

He takes this location in the local church even farther when he contrasts the election of such overseers with the consecration of the episcopate that he is rejecting: '…'tis certain none are ordained to any Office in the Baptized Churches till elected by the Consent of the Church'.[23] And he makes a theological and political point of it, as he continues:

this right of the people hath been invaded in many ways.

1. By great Personages and Magistrates.

2. When the Bishops grew to great pomp and the Clergy began to be enriched by Benefices, Elections were, and to this day are, made according to the Interests of the Rich and Strong, whilst the People are not only deprived of, but become ignorant that any right remains in them to chuse their own Ministers or Pastors. Now this Priviledge is restored and maintained in the Baptized Churches, where none are elected *Messengers*, *Bishops*, or *Deacons* without the free Choice of the Brotherhood where such Elections are made.[24]

---

[21] See for example, Grantham, *Christianismus Primitivus,* Book 4, Treatise 5, p. 165: 'It is true, the Ancients call these seven Messengers Bishops, or Chief Ministers, But them we know by Bishops, they mean ordinarily such as had the care of many particular Societies or Churches.'

[22] Grantham, *Christianismus Primitivus,* Book 4, Treatise 5, p. 165.

[23] Grantham, *Christianismus Primitivus*, Book 2, Chapter 9, Section 8, p. 129.

[24] Grantham, *Christianismus Primitivus*, Book 2, Chapter 9, Section 8, p. 130.

The choosing, election, owning, discipling and presumably ending if necessary of such a ministry is firmly and explicitly rooted in the local church.

This practice of ordination is an important one in understanding one of the distinctives of the polity of the Baptists as it developed. There was a great deal of consciousness about just what they were doing in the ways that they ordained messengers in particular. We have already seen how, for the existing Anglican episcopate, the valid consecration of Parker, and through him the bishops of the newly ordered Anglican church, was of supreme significance in maintaining catholicity and therefore validity. The Baptists addressed this, if not always head on, at least always as an issue to be considered. By what right, if any, were their ministers to be known as valid ministers of the gospel and in particular, what was the authority of their messengers?

We have seen already that, at least towards the end of the century, there was a move among General Baptists to involve, if not completely rely on, the existing body of messengers in the ordination of new messengers. But there was, alongside this, an explicit rejection of a pattern of succession. In 1656, the General Agreement of the General Assembly stated: 'messengers may not without the common consent of ye churchs chuse messengers'.[25] And in 1659, Jeffery argued, in *The Whole Faith of Man*: 'so the churches are to choose messengers still for the gathering of the church, and establishing of the same, so that they are to go forth to preach the gospel'.[26] It is one of the topics that concerns Grantham greatly, and so he deals with it at length:

> And thus the Divine Institution of this Sacred Office is clearly found, both in the Original, and after Ordinations in the Apostolical Churches [he is maintaining that there is an office which is the one he is calling Messenger]. And therefore, by what Right or Power True Churches may be (and are) gathered this day, by the same these Officers may be revived also, even there, where a Succession of Churches and Officers have failed. Christ Jesus by his Holy Spirit being always powerfully present with his own Doctrine, to put those into a capacity to manage the Affairs of the Gospel, who receive the Truth thereof in the Love of it: ...What can make any Office to be of Divine Institution, if to be made so by the Holy Ghost will not do it?[27]

He rejects succession, yet he is clear that the ordination by their churches of those appointed to this office is valid and effective. That is the key: it is by the churches, because it is in the churches that the Spirit is present. And the ordination is effective because it is the Spirit that makes it so.

---

[25] W.T. Whitley (ed.), *Minutes of the General Assembly of the General Baptist Churches in England* (2 vols; London: Kingsgate Press, [1909-10]), I, p. 6, cited by Nicholson, 'The Office', p. 207.

[26] Jeffery, *Whole Faith of Man*, p. 96, cited by Nicholson, 'The Office', p. 208.

[27] Grantham, *Christianismus Primitivus,* Book 2, Chapter 9, Section IV, pp. 120-21.

Anglicans also deal with the question of ordination to the ministry *per se*. The context in which they work insists that only those who are ordained by those who have been ordained within the episcopal succession are validly ordained. This is rejected by the Baptists. Not only do they insist that the messengers are chosen by the churches as a whole, but they also refuse to limit the power of ordination to the messengers.

In book 4, the questions and answers at the end of *Christianismus Primitivus*, Grantham cites the objection, *But do you not give the sole Power of Ordination to your Messengers, or Apostles?* He answers it:

> In no wise: for though we say they only are in a regular capacity to ordain Elders in Congregations newly planted, which have no Officers: yet where the Churches have an Eldership, there they are in a capacity to ordain their own Officers; yea, they many ordain and send forth Messengers...[28]

We find this too in the Second London Confession of 1677:

> A particular Church gathered and compleatly Organized, according to the mind of Christ, consists of Officers and Members; And the Officers appointed by *Christ* to be chosen and set apart by the Church (so called and gathered) for the peculiar Administration of Ordinances and Execution of Power or Duty, which he intrusts them with, or calls them to, to be continued to the end of the World, are Bishops or Elders and Deacons.

And in the next article, the way is laid out:

> by the common suffrage of the Church it self; and Solemnly set apart by Fasting and Prayer, with imposition of hands of the Eldership of the Church, if there be any before Constituted therein.[29]

The capacity to ordain is not inherent in the office of messenger, but is part of, indeed, comes as the final part of, church planting. Therefore, the time when others from outside the local congregation are called to ordain is when a local congregation is in process of being formed. Otherwise, ordination is a function of the local church.

In reaction to an episcopate which they experience as oppressive, unscriptural and corrupting, the Baptists, especially the General Baptists, begin to explore a practice of oversight that is shaped by different convictions. In exploring such a ministry, the convictions that make them who they are, what we are accustomed to term Baptist distinctives, begin themselves to be explored and explicated. They are not yet fully worked out, but we can see them developing as the implications are explored.

---

[28] Grantham, *Christianismus Primitivus*, Book 4, Treatise 5, p. 165.
[29] Lumpkin, *Baptist Confessions*, p. 287, ch. 26.8 and 9.

That they were not afraid to use the word 'bishop' is also clear. It was not only Grantham, but also the drafters of the 1644 Confession, that took the term, and redefined it along what they were convinced were lines more in keeping with the biblical usage. In this redefinition, and in their practice, we can see several theological convictions being worked out.

Distinctive Features of Baptist Oversight

Firstly, there is the conviction that the church matters. One of the distinguishing features of Baptist identity is that the church is important. In their concern to identify and explore the various offices of the Christian congregation according to their reading of scripture, these early Baptists took seriously the ordering of the people of God for the service of God. To be the church was no small thing for these people. It is what it meant to be followers of Jesus, and ordering that common life was not a matter of convenience, nor of political expediency. It was a theological and spiritual matter, and one that they took very seriously. In our exploration of their theology and practice of oversight, there are two aspects of this commitment to the seriousness of church that we need to consider.

The first aspect that we see is that both parts of Baptist life, Particular and General, took the oversight and the interconnectedness of the churches seriously. For all that they did not develop the strongly connexional ministry of the General Baptists with a separate office of messenger, the Particular Baptists nevertheless did appoint messengers as a way of keeping churches in touch with each other. The common life of the community mattered. There was a sense of catholicity. Unlike the episcopate that they experienced in the Church of England, they did not *locate* it in or identify it with the overseer, but they did make it happen *through* the overseers. For the General Baptists this was even more marked. The ones they charged with oversight had a distinctive role in keeping the churches together. We have seen how this was worked out for Anglicans through the doctrine of episcopacy, particularly successionism. There was a conviction about the nature of the church, and its dependence on its historic identity, the mediation of the presence of Christ through the continuing unbroken line. In the rejection of successionism, there was an equally distinctive theology of the nature of the church at work. We see it outlined in Grantham's conviction about the authority of ordination quoted already: 'What can make any Office to be of Divine Institution, if to be made so by the Holy Ghost will not do it?'[30]

The second aspect is that there was the conviction that the church is the church because of the divine presence in and with it. That presence in the contemporary church is the same as the presence with the disciples; the encounter between the first disciples and the risen Christ, the head of the

---

[30] Grantham, *Christianismus Primitivus*, Book 2, Chapter 9, Section IV, p. 120.

church, is not different in kind, not closer, than the encounter between the contemporary church and the risen Christ. We can see this worked out in various ways in Baptist thinking and practice, but this is one of the clearest. The church, to be church, does not depend on a transmission from the past of the presence of the head of the church. Rather, it depends on the actual presence among the believers of the risen Christ. This conviction – that where two or three are gathered, Christ is present – is deep in Baptist identity, and it shapes the way in which oversight is worked out. Although the messengers were frequently referred to as successors of the apostles, this was not in the way that the previous Roman pattern, nor the current Anglican pattern, had insisted, by the passing on of grace and authority through an unbroken line. Rather it is that, just as Christ called and commissioned the first apostles to plant and care for the churches, so Christ now calls and commissions these to do the same. It is a succession through the call, activity and presence of Christ, by the Spirit.

This conviction about the nature of oversight and its authority is an aspect of the Baptist conviction about the nature of the church: the current people of God in relationship to God through the presence of Christ in the midst. It reflects a radical dependence on the presence of the Spirit, and a conviction that James W. McClendon describes thus: 'the church now *is* the primitive church; *we* are Jesus' followers; the commands are addressed directly to *us*'.[31]

This is the conviction that allows Baptists to develop the strong commitment to the local church as the full church that marks their identity and that shapes their practice of oversight. We see this perhaps more clearly among the Particular Baptists. In the 1644 confession, they state:

> That Christ hath here on earth a spirituall Kingdome, which is the Church, which he hath purchased and redeemed to himself, as a peculiar inheritance: which Church, as it is visible to us, is a company of visible Saints, called & separated from the world, by the word and Spirit of God, to the visible profession of the faith…To this Church he hath made his promises and given the signes of his Covenant, presence, love, blessing, and protection: here are the fountains and springs of his heavenly grace continually flowing forth;…That being thus joyned, every Church has power given them…to choose to themselves meet persons into the office of Pastors, Teachers, Elders, Deacons…and that none other have power to impose them, either these or any other….And as Christ for the keeping of this Church in holy and orderly Communion placeth some speciall men over the Church who by their office are to governe, oversee, visit, watch; so likewise for the better keeping thereof in all places by the members he hath given authoritie, and laid dutie upon all, to watch over one another….And although the particular Congregations be distinct and severall Bodies, every one a compact and knit Citie in it selfe; yet are they all to walk by one and the same Rule, and by all meanes

---

[31] James W. McClendon, Jr, *Systematic Theology: Ethics* (Nashville: Abingdon Press, 1986), p. 33.

convenient to have the counsell and help one of another in all needfull affaires of the Church...[32]

What is at the heart of this conviction about the church is the sense that the church exists here and now as the place where Christ is present and active, and the relationships with him that make church are actualised not by a historic process, but by the activity of the Spirit.

If the first facet of identity is these two strands about the importance of church, the second facet of Baptist identity worked out in their theology of oversight is also present in both General and Particular thinking. It is a conviction that overrides every other conviction about the function of these overseers, and it is that evangelism and church planting form the heart of the messengers' ministry. The impetus to preach the gospel to those who have not yet heard is present at the heart of Baptist theology and practice from these earliest days.

This had a very particular theological reality in the context in which they were operating. The Anglican episcopal theology also identified bishops as those who, in the succession of the apostles, have a duty of evangelism. But there is less urgency about this when a Christendom model of church and state is the dominant one. To whom is the gospel to be preached if all are already baptised, and thus included in the church?

With this emphasis on evangelism, we see not only a significant Baptist practice of preaching, but also the working out of the conviction that church and state are not the same thing; being born in one does not automatically make a person a member of the other, and nor should it. The call to preach and plant churches is part of the Baptist conviction that the church is a free, voluntary and called community, not a legislated and government-ordained one. Thus, in the very clear and overriding call to evangelism as the role of an overseer, we see not only (to be anachronistic) Baptist Evangelicalism, we see also the rejection of the state church, and so the insistence that the bishops are not an arm of the state power.

Thus, inherent in the theology and practice of messenger as evangelist is the conviction not only that the gospel must be preached, but also that such preaching, together with the responding to it that is sought, is a matter of conscience, and more specifically, a free conscience. This link is explored by the writer of *Religion's Peace*, writing in 1614:

Certain reasons against persecution

First because Christ hath not commanded any king bishop or minister to persecute the people for difference of judgement in matters of religion.

---

[32] Lumpkin, *Baptist Confessions,* pp. 165,165-66,166, 168, 168-69, articles 33, 34, 36, 44, 47.

Secondly – because Christ hath commanded his bishops and ministers to persuade prince and people to hear and believe the gospel, by his word and Spirit, and, as ambassadors for him, to beseech both prince and people to be reconciled to God, and not as tyrants, to force and constrain them by persecution.[33]

Throughout this book, the writer outlines what he thinks bishops ought to be. Evangelist comes top of the list. But that has to be in the context of freedom, and as those who allow freedom of conscience. The rejection of the episcopacy as an arm of state power and therefore persecution is not, for these early Baptists, simply about being allowed to order their church the way they chose without facing hardship. It was part and parcel of their conviction that the church was composed of the chosen people of God and exists without constraint, and that people have, in God's providence, the right to reject the invitation to share in it. This is not just about being free themselves. It is a deeply felt theological conviction about the nature of religious freedom and the nature of conversation and faith as that which cannot be constrained.

While the picture with which we started might well surprise the early English Baptists, this would (apart from the fact that it is a woman being consecrated) be as much about the context as about the theology. In their experience, episcopacy was practised in and was representative of a state church which denied them the right to worship and organise according to conscience. It was an institution which they regarded as corrupt and corrupting. This was true not only for those who were bishops, but for the church as a whole. But that was not because they rejected a theology of oversight, but because they were concerned to explore, and indeed, were just beginning to find a way to articulate and live out, a different theology of the nature of the church, and of the calling of the church in the civic community. Within that exploration, they remained convinced of the need for oversight, a need that in other times and places, Baptists have forgotten and have as a result, suffered loss. Their reflections on oversight – what it was for and how it should work – were necessarily incomplete, contextually shaped and experimental. But they did not reject *episcope* as a theological reality among the people of God. The Anglican theology with which they were faced not only drove them to reject episcopacy as they experienced it. It also gave them the context and the impetus to work out what Baptist-shaped *episcope* might look like and in so doing to work out more of what it means to live with a Baptist vision of church and discipleship.

---

[33] Underhill (ed.), *Tracts,* p.27.

PART TWO

Nineteenth-Century Baptists in Britain and America

CHAPTER 3

The Scotch Baptists and the Birth of the Churches of Christ

Derek Murray

This is an enquiry into one of the streams of Christian thought and life which have contributed to the denomination known in the USA. as the Disciples of Christ, the Independent Churches of Christ and the A Cappella Churches of Christ, and in the United Kingdom as the Church of Christ, which is now a component of the United Reformed Church, and as the Old Paths Churches of Christ. These related branches of the church descend from the teaching and evangelistic activities of Alexander Campbell, Barton Stone and Walter Scott in America during the early part of the nineteenth century. Some historians, particularly in the more conservative Churches of Christ, have become interested in the Scottish roots of this movement, which sought to embody the restoration of Primitive Christianity.[1]

John Glas (1695-1773) was deposed as minister of the parish of Tealing near Dundee for obstinate Independency and for opposition to certain articles of the Westminster Confession and for refusing to keep quiet! He gathered followers in several Scottish towns, and mainly through the efforts of his son-in-law Robert Sandeman, churches were formed in England, Wales and New England. Peculiar doctrines of this Calvinist body included an intellectualist view of saving faith, a sceptical view of the possibility of assurance of faith, and an attempt to emulate the Christian customs of the primitive church before it became contaminated by philosophy and Roman power. Therefore an unpaid plural eldership, the use of the lot, the weekly observance of the Lord's Supper, the holy kiss, the avoidance of personal insurance and soon of the worshipping company of other Christians, and a strong emphasis on unanimity in all church matters became mandatory on all Sandemanian societies.[2]

---

[1] For example, Lynn A. McMillon, *Restoration Roots* (Dallas, TX: Gospel Teachers Publications, 1983).

[2] For the most recent account of the Glasites/Sandemanians, see J. H. Smith, *The Perfect Rule of the Christian Religion* (Albany, NY: State University of New York Press, 2008). See also G.N. Cantor, *Michael Faraday, Sandemanian and Scientist* (Basingstoke: Macmillan, 1991).

In 1765 Robert Carmichael and Archibald McLean, briefly in the Glasgow Glasite church, came to believer Baptist conclusions and the first Scotch Baptist Church, in Edinburgh, was formed. Apart from the practice of the baptism of believers, the main difference between Scotch Baptists and Glasites was that they were more open to fellowship with other Christian and indeed became strong supporters of the Baptist Missionary Society. Scotch Baptists, by the end of the eighteenth century, were to be found in many Scottish towns, and in England in Beverley, Nottingham, Liverpool and London. They divided in 1810 and again in 1834 over the same issue, the necessity for elders to be in place before a church could be set in order to eat the Lord's Supper, and they were increasingly focused on internal order and somewhat obscure points of doctrine. Although they were theoretically independent bodies, there was a strong sense of 'sisterhood' with the church in Edinburgh under McLean and later the church in London under William Jones taking a certain precedence.

Alexander Campbell and the Beginnings of the Churches of Christ

Campbellism began in the early nineteenth century as a movement seeking to avoid denominational issues and to rediscover primitive Christianity. It had a strong eschatological emphasis (its journal being the *Millennial Harbinger*), and it appealed to the newly independent and in many places unevangelised United States. By 1816 there were churches with an order similar to that of the Scotch Baptist in New York, Philadelphia, and Danbury, Connecticut, where Sandeman died, earnestly Calvinistic and restorationist, but not evangelistic, and some Church of Christ leaders such as Isaac Errett and Walter Scott came from that background.

The Campbells, father Thomas and son Alexander, came from Ulster, and the Scottish AntiBurgher Secession Church. Thomas, born in 1763, studied under Archibald Bruce of Whitburn, strictest of the Seceders, and served a congregation in Ahorey, in Ulster, near which was an Independent church where Thomas worshipped on Sunday evenings, and where the influence of the Haldanes, leading Scottish Evangelicals outside Presbyterianism, was strong. Thomas immigrated to America in 1807. Alexander attempted to follow but was shipwrecked and had to return to Glasgow where he studied at the university and came into contact with Greville Ewing, Haldane's friend who remained faithful to paedobaptism at the split in 1808.[3] There Alexander became familiar with the works of Glas and Sandeman and always admitted a debt to them, although he diverged in many ways in later life. He inclined towards a Sandemanian view of faith as simple belief, and like Sandeman sought for primitive simplicity. He strongly disapproved of the Sandemanian narrowness and intolerant spirit, and indeed of their Calvinism. In 1809

---

[3] When James and Robert Haldane accepted believer's baptism in 1808 there was a breach in their movement.

Alexander arrived in America, sought fellowship with Baptists by 1813, but by 1829 the 'Reformers', as Campbell's followers were named, had largely been removed from Baptist fellowship and were on the way to becoming the Churches of Christ. Thomas Campbell's *Declaration and Address* of 1809 sets out the principles of the movement, and stresses the unity of the Church of Christ, the supreme authority of scripture, the futility of human creeds, the essential brotherhood of all Christians, and the restoration of the church as pictured in the New Testament.

William Jones and the Introduction of Campbellite Ideas into Great Britain

William Jones, author and publisher originally from North Wales and then Liverpool, was an elder in the Scotch Baptist church in Windmill Street, Finsbury Square, London,[4] when in the summer of 1833 a young American portrait painter, Peyton C. Wyeth, came to a service searching for a church like his own in Pennsylvania. He was admitted to membership in Windmill Street a few weeks later. Jones was delighted to find that there were churches in America which also sought the simplicity of the New Testament church and were anti-emotional and anti-revival. Jones corresponded with Campbell, and published a new journal in 1835, *The Millennial Harbinger and Voluntary Church Advocate*, which reprinted Campbell's articles and which circulated widely amongst Scotch Baptist churches for the sixteen months of its existence. But division appeared. Jones and Campbell disagreed about the work of the Holy Spirit in conversion and on the vexed question of whether the Lord's Supper could be eaten in the absence of an elder. Campbell asserted in correspondence with Jones that the Scotch Baptists were bound by legalistic cords and by what he termed Hyper-Calvinism, and Jones indignantly refuted these comments. Jones, holding strict McLeanite views, then withdrew his support from Campbell, but the damage to Scotch Baptist unity, always fragile, had been done.

The most effective advocate of Campbellite ideas in England was James Wallis, a member of the Scotch Baptist church in Nottingham, a relatively large congregation under the leadership of the Bayley family of shoemakers. In the 1830s the Scotch Baptists were bitterly divided over the question of eating the Lord's Supper without elders. Wallis read a treatise by Henry Grew, *A Tribute to the Memory of the Apostles*, which argued, as did Campbell, that it was more important to celebrate the feast than that elders should preside. In the ensuing controversy Wallis and his followers broke away in 1836 to form a church of

---

[4] http://www.oxforddnb.com/view/article/15109, accessed 11 November 2011—Derek B. Murray, 'Jones, William (1762–1846)', *Oxford Dictionary of National Biography* (Oxford: Oxford University Press, 2004)

New Testament Disciples.[5] Wallis travelled in his trade as a tailor, and also published journals which circulated among Scotch Baptist churches in England and Scotland.

There was and still is a small group of Welsh churches following the teachings of McLean and known as Scotch Baptists to this day. They too were influenced by Jones and then by Campbell and in the early 1840s a number of churches broke away from the Scotch sisterhood. In Criccieth the majority of the fellowship embraced Campbellite views and retained the chapel. It was in this chapel that David Lloyd George was nurtured. Some six other churches were disrupted.[6]

Campbellism in Scotland

Already in 1830 a Haldanite/Scotch Baptist church in Auchtermuchty, Fife, founded in 1809 and led by the brothers George and John Dron had discovered Campbell and John visited him in America in 1834. Campbell visited Auchtermuchty in 1847 on a tour of Britain, and the church must have been Campbellite from the 1830s. The history of the Churches of Christ in Kirkcaldy, a larger town a few miles south of Auchtermuchty, is complex. The original Scotch Baptist church was formed, first as a branch of the Edinburgh church in the late 1780s. By 1819 a new meeting house in Rose Street was opened and it was there until demolition in 1967, when a redundant Church of Scotland building in Hayfield was acquired and there the Old Path church remains, still declining to use musical instruments. One of the first elders appointed in 1809 was Ninian Lockhart, a linen manufacturer, many of whose descendants became leaders in Baptist Union churches. Campbell visited the church in 1847, after a separate Church of Christ had been formed in 1842. In 1852 a more liberal group seceded to found the extant Baptist Union Church in Whyte's Causeway, and the Rose Street Church finally moved from isolation as a Scotch Baptist church in 1883 when it acceded to the Association of the Churches of Christ, moving out of the Association to become an independent Church of Christ in 1947.[7]

Other Scotch Baptist churches may have gone over wholly to the Campbellites in the 1830s and 1840s. A church of twelve members in Auchterarder, previously served from Crieff in Perthshire, went over in 1848. A correspondent of the Campbellite magazine gave a report of the transfer of allegiance: 'Perth January 5th 1848: I have also the pleasure to inform you that a

---

[5] David M. Thompson, *Let Sects and Parties Fall* (Birmingham: Berean Press 1980), p. 20.

[6] A.C. Watters, *History of the British Churches of Christ* (Birmingham: Berean Press, 1948), pp. 30-31.

[7] R.W. Hughes, *Churches of Christ in the County of Fife, Scotland* (Kirkcaldy: Hayfield Publications, 1998), pp. 9-23.

Church of Baptist believers in Auchterarder formerly in connection with the Baptists have renounced all human bonds of Union and are determined to be united with the brethren of the Restoration.'[8] Here we see a typical pattern. A group of believers moves from the Baptist fold into isolation and then moves to the Campbellites. In Ayrshire churches in Kilmarnock, Newmilns and Saltcoats ceased as Baptist churches around 1850 and subsequently appeared as Churches of Christ. In other towns there were divisions, and in Edinburgh Thomas Milner moved from a Calvinist Scotch Baptist stance to an Arminian position and then to the Churches of Christ in 1852, another two-stage conversion. His church at Roxburgh Terrrace in Edinburgh is listed in the standard history of the Baptists in Scotland as existing from around 1850-1860,[9] and a church in Drumclair, apparently always Church of Christ, is listed from 1860-1870, with its first pastor as Charles Abercrombie, a Church of Christ evangelist active in the area, indications that denominational lines were not always tightly drawn at this time.[10]

The short-lived Baptist church in Dunbar ceased in 1847. John Muir, who became an eminent environmentalist, emigrated about this time to the United States with his father who had become a supporter of the Churches of Christ, and we may speculate that this may indicate the transfer of allegiance in Dunbar.[11]

Australia and Canada

Scotch Baptists emigrated in the early part of the nineteenth century, especially to South Australia, and the transition from Scotch Baptist to Church of Christ seems to have been concentrated on Adelaide. David McLaren, a prominent Scotch Baptist elder in Glasgow, was sent for business reasons to Adelaide, and pioneered Baptist life in the colony from 1838 until his return to Britain in 1841. He left a predominantly Scotch Church, with its besetting sin of divisiveness. Some of its members had arrived from Newmilns and Kilmarnock in 1839, and they came from newly divided Scotch Baptist communities. The subject of the necessity of baptism for the remission of sins, which was becoming a recognisable Campbellite doctrine, was discussed and the group divided evenly. For many, Calvinism ceased to be important, and when Thomas

---

[8] Robert Anderson to editor, 5 January 1848, *British Millennial Harbinger*, 3rd series 1 (February 1848), p. 93.

[9] For Milner, see B.R. Talbot, *The Search for a Common Identity* (Milton Keynes: Paternoster, 2003), pp. 260-75.

[10] George Yuille (ed.), *History of the Baptists in Scotland* (Glasgow: Baptist Union of Scotland Publications Committee, 1926), pp. 280, 279.

[11] http://www.oxforddnb.com/view/article/40906 accessed 11 November 2011—Dennis R. Dean, 'Muir, John (1838-1914)', *Oxford Dictionary of National Biography* (Oxford: Oxford University Press, 2004).

Magarey from Ireland and then New Zealand arrived in 1845 he became the catalyst for the formation of a Church of Christ, leaving the Scotch Baptists weak and increasingly marginal to the story of Australian Baptists. In the 1880s Magarey himself moved to the Brethren.[12]

In Canada the story was somewhat different, as although there were Scotch Baptists among the pioneers in Ontario and the Maritimes, the greatest impetus for the Churches of Christ came from Baptists of the Haldane tradition or, though from Scotland, of the English type. In Prince Edward Island some silk weavers, Scotch Baptists from Paisley, arrived in the early nineteenth century and were the nucleus of later Churches of Christ. 'These old Scotch Baptists were sturdy stock and the roots of their religion ran deep.'[13] In Nova Scotia Scotch Baptists arrived in 1815 as precursors of the Campbellites. They were very rigid and legalistic in their church relations, but some gradually broadened into the Church of Christ stream.

Many Scots emigrated to Ontario, and among them were Highland pastors following their flocks or seeking, like Donald McArthur, religious freedom. These people were Particular Baptists and some of their descendants formed the Old-School Baptists of Ontario, with several settlements continuing to worship in Gaelic. Dugald Sinclair, whose career has been carefully examined by Donald Meek, was set apart by the Scotch Itinerant Society in 1810 and served at Lochgilphead from 1815.[14] In 1831, whether finding that his usefulness in Scotland was diminishing or that he was being strongly invited by emigrés from Knapdale, he moved to Lobo Township Middlesex County, where he was among friends. Sinclair, though technically supporting the English pattern of one-pastor Baptist churches, nevertheless became the leader of a group of neighbouring churches, known until 1850 as Sinclair Baptists. In that year he appears to have identified his churches as Churches of Christ. A local historian of the Lochgilphead church asserted that Sinclair imbibed peculiar views on prophecy, the man of sin and successive forms of the great tribulation. He believed that Europe was to be involved in a universal war with Britain at its centre. America was to be excepted and it was there that the Church of Christ was to be preserved till his return.[15] Campbell, with his magazine the *Millennial Harbinger*, also looked forward to a great calamity and to the preservation of the faith in America. Mormons and other new sects in this period held similar apocalyptic views. Whatever the exact story, Sinclair became the leader of the

---

[12] K.R. Manley, *From Wooloomooloo to 'Eternity': A History of Australian Baptists* (2 vols; Milton Keynes: Paternoster, 2006), I, pp. 47-52.

[13] Reuben Butchart, *The Disciples of Christ in Canada since 1830* (Toronto: Canadian Headquarters Publications, Churches of Christ (Disciples), 1949), p. 102.

[14] D.E. Meek, 'The Preacher, the Press-gang and the Landlord: The Impressment and Vindication of the Rev. Donald McArthur', *Records of the Scottish Church History Society* 25. 2 (1994), pp. 256-87.

[15] Yuille (ed.), *Baptists in Scotland*, p. 117.

Church of Christ in Upper Canada until his death in 1870, and is an example of a Baptist from Scotland rather than a Scotch Baptist who contributed much to the Campbellite movement.[16]

Conclusion

Scotch Baptists and Campbellites both owed much to Glas and Sandeman, although it became unfashionable to claim such an inheritance. An intellectualist idea of faith, a distrust of emotional religion and revivalism, an aversion to professional clergy, the practice of weekly communion, and a certain exclusiveness were held in common. The search for Primitive Christianity was their watchword. But the Campbellites upbraided the Scotch Baptists for their Calvinism, their rigidity and legalism and their lack of evangelistic zeal. The distinguishing mark of the Campbellites, their belief in baptism for the remission of sins, was not so different from what McLean had held,[17] but the emphasis given to this tenet became a dividing line between Baptists of all sorts and the Churches of Christ.

---

[16] For a full account see D.E. Meek, 'Dugald Sinclair: The Life and Work of a Highland Itinerant Missionary', *Scottish Studies* 30 (1991), pp. 59-91.

[17] A. M'Lean, 'The Commission given by Jesus Christ to His Disciples Illustrated' [1786], in *Miscellaneous Works*, Vol. 1 (Elgin: Peter MacDonald, 1847), p. 121.

CHAPTER 4

An Evangelical Anglican Interaction with Baptist Missionary Society Strategy: William Wilberforce and John Ryland, 1807-1824

Timothy Whelan

William Wilberforce (1759-1833), after a disagreement with some of his Anglican friends, wrote in his diary, 'they think I cannot be loyal to the Established Church because I love Dissenters'.[1] Some thought Wilberforce 'half Methodist' as it was, and his collaboration with Dissenters 'akin to treason'.[2] Wilberforce's pronounced Evangelical faith and ecumenical spirit did little to stay such opinions. For nearly forty years he was the most visible, vocal, and vital parliamentarian link between Dissenters and the established church, working closely on numerous issues important to both parties, beginning with the first debates on the abolition of the slave trade in 1787 and ending with his death on 29 July 1833, just three days after the third and final reading of the bill to abolish slavery throughout the British Empire. Though the twin evils of the slave trade and slavery itself formed the alpha and omega of Wilberforce's political agenda, his passion for Christian missions was the chief driving force behind that agenda after 1792, an agenda marked on both accounts by a remarkable cooperation between the Clapham Saint and his Dissenting friends, especially the Baptists. Biographers of Wilberforce have had little, if anything, to say about his relations with Baptists; however, Wilberforce's correspondence, especially with John Ryland of Bristol, demonstrates a consistent and substantial relationship, revealing his sincere admiration for Baptist missions and his willingness, as an M.P., to protect the interests of the missionaries in the face of oppressive governmental regulations in India and Jamaica.

Much of the correspondence between Wilberforce and various Baptist figures is no longer extant, but some forty letters, written between 1792 and 1827, have survived. None of these letters, however, appeared in *The Life of William Wilberforce* (1838) or *The Correspondence of William Wilberforce*

---

[1] Quoted in John Pollock, *Wilberforce* (London: Constable, 1977), p. 153.
[2] Reginald Coupland, *Wilberforce* (London: Collins, 2nd edn, 1945), p. 311.

(1840) (both edited by his sons, Robert and Samuel Wilberforce), or any biography of Wilberforce thereafter.[3] One letter from Wilberforce to Thomas Langdon, dated 23 February 1792, was published in Langdon's *Memoir* (1837); two other letters, both to John Ryland in 1807, can be found in F. A. Cox's *History of the Baptist Missionary Society, 1792 to 1842*.[4] All the rest remain in manuscript. One letter from Ryland to Wilberforce, dated 26 March 1821, resides in the Wilberforce Papers at Duke University. The Wilberforce Collection at the Bodleian Library, Oxford, contains eleven letters to Wilberforce, written by such Baptist figures as Robert Hall, Andrew Fuller, Olinthus Gregory, Joshua Marshman and Mrs Adoniram Judson, and one letter by Wilberforce to John Fawcett. Two more letters can be found at the Angus Library at Regent's Park College, Oxford: one from Fuller to Wilberforce, dated 5 December 1801, and the other, dated 15 November 1825, from Wilberforce to W.B. Gurney, a prominent Baptist layman from the congregation at Maze Pond, Southwark. More significantly, in a bound volume at Bristol Baptist College are twenty-one letters from Wilberforce to John Ryland, Jr (1753-1825), pastor of the two congregations (Baptist and Independent) at Broadmead in Bristol, president of Bristol Baptist Academy, and a leading member of the Baptist Missionary Society committee, 1793-1825. The volume also contains one letter by Ryland to Wilberforce, and one by Wilberforce to Ryland's son, J.E. Ryland. At some point after the death of Wilberforce, these letters came into the possession of the younger Ryland. In 1850 he presented the volume as a gift to the prominent Baptist railway magnate and M.P., Samuel Morton Peto. Eventually, the volume found its way to the library at Bristol Baptist College, where it resides today.[5]

Wilberforce and the Baptists

Prior to his correspondence with Ryland, however, Wilberforce had had substantial contact with Baptists concerning several issues, the most prominent being the abolition of the slave trade and the repeal of the Test and Corporation Acts. Between 1788 and 1792, several leading Baptist ministers and laymen

---

[3] Robert and Samuel Wilberforce (eds), *The Life of William Wilberforce*, (5 vols; London: J. Murray, 1838); idem, *The Correspondence of William Wilberforce* (2 vols; London: Murray, 1840).

[4] See *A Brief Memoir of the Rev. Thomas Langdon, Baptist Minister at Leeds* (London: Simpkin and Marshall, 1837), p. 151; F.A. Cox, *A History of the Baptist Missionary Society, 1792 to 1842* (2 vols; London: T. Ward, and G. and J. Dyer, 1842), II, pp. 19-21.

[5] Shelfmark MS. G97a. Photocopies of the 23 letters can also be found at the Bodleian Library, Oxford, MSS. Wilberforce, Don. e. 164-165. Baptist historian Daniel Potts refers to two of these letters in *British Baptist Missionaries in India, 1793–1837* (Cambridge: Cambridge University Press, 1967), pp. 17, 180.

served on local auxiliaries of Granville Sharp's London Society for Effecting the Abolition of the Slave Trade, contributing monies to the London committee and assisting Wilberforce, the committee's primary voice in parliament, in gathering petitions from within their congregations and local communities to be presented to parliament prior to votes on the bills to prohibit the slave trade. Among the Baptist ministers were Robert Robinson (Cambridge), Caleb Evans and Robert Hall (Bristol), Joseph Horsey (Portsmouth), James Dore (Maze Pond, Southwark), and Abraham Booth (Little Prescot Street, London), as well as several prominent London Baptist laymen, including Joseph Gurney, John Barton, William Fox and Joseph Gutteridge.[6] Baptists were also actively involved in the boycott of sugar and other West Indian products that began in the summer of 1791 with the publication of *An Address to the People of Great Britain, on the Propriety of Abstaining from West India Sugar and Rum* by William Fox (a London Dissenting bookseller and political writer, not to be confused with the Baptist layman William Fox mentioned above), one of the most widely distributed pamphlets of the eighteenth century, with most of its twenty-six editions printed and sold by Martha Gurney (1733-1816), Baptist bookseller, printer, and member of James Dore's congregation at Maze Pond.[7]

Not only were Baptists assisting Wilberforce in his parliamentary efforts to end the slave trade, they were also involved in the campaign to repeal the Test Acts in the late 1780s, a campaign Wilberforce, though reluctantly, was nevertheless drawn into as well. Wilberforce's Dissenting constituents in Yorkshire were fairly certain the Evangelical M.P. would vote in favor of the repeal. His failure to do so led to a series of letters between Wilberforce and the Committee of Protestant Dissenting Ministers for the West Riding of Yorkshire, led by William Wood and Thomas Langdon, two ministers (Unitarian and Baptist) from Leeds. Other Baptist ministers who served on the committee (and some sub-committees) included John Fawcett, William Crabtree, William Price and two Baptist laymen, John Ashworth and William Hudson. Wilberforce's defence for not supporting the repeal failed to satisfy the members of the committee, and a series of letters, both private and printed,

---

[6] See Fair Minute Books, Committee of the Society for Effecting the Abolition of the Slave Trade, British Library, ADD. MS. 21255, ff. 57r, 58r, 73r, 86v, 112v, 135v; also ADD. MS. 21256, ff. 26v, 41r-v, 42v, 46r, 49r.

[7] See Timothy Whelan, 'Martha Gurney and William Fox: Baptist Printer and Radical Reformer, 1791-1794', in J.H.Y. Briggs (ed.), *Pulpit and People: Studies in 18th Century Baptist Life and Thought* (Studies in Baptist History and Thought, 28; Milton Keynes: Paternoster, 2009), pp. 165-201; Timothy Whelan, 'Martha Gurney and the Anti-Slave Trade Movement, 1788-94', in Elizabeth J. Clapp and Julie Roy Jeffrey (eds), *Women, Dissent and Anti-Slavery in Britain and America, 1790-1865* (Oxford: Oxford University Press, 2011), pp. 44-65; for the complete text of Fox's pamphlet, see John Barrell and Timothy Whelan (eds), *The Political Writings of William Fox: Abolitionist, Tory, and Friend to the French Revolution* (Nottingham: Trent Editions, 2011), pp. 1-10.

passed between them and Wilberforce.[8] Much to their consternation, Wilberforce believed that a full toleration of the Dissenters would only further weaken a clergy already contaminated by various forms of deism, latitudinarianism, scepticism, and Socinianism. Because many of the established clergy no longer believed the Thirty-Nine Articles of the Church of England 'and would easily part with them', as Wilberforce wrote to Wood on 8 September 1789, 'Dissenters must have civil grievances continued upon them, to prevent them from joining the supposed disaffected part of the establishment, in attempting to abolish or to alter the Articles and the Liturgy, and to weaken their efforts if they should use any for this purpose'.[9] In the spring of 1790, when another repeal vote came before the House, Wilberforce voted against the motion for repeal, acknowledging, however, that though the defeat of the motion for repeal gave him 'satisfaction' it was 'by no means unalloyed'.[10]

Wilberforce may have protested that he truly 'love[d] Dissenters', the majority of whom were sympathetic to his efforts to abolish the slave trade, but, as his actions concerning the repeal of the Test Acts revealed, Wilberforce was first and foremost an Anglican. Wilberforce's sons would argue that their father always considered membership in the established church superior to the meeting house. Even attendance at a Methodist meeting was 'no compensation for the general evils of dissent', Wilberforce once said, adding, 'dissenters could do nothing if it were not for the established church'.[11] The Quaker banker John Harford of Blaise Castle, near Bristol, agreed that his friend from Hull was always 'an attached member of the Church of England', but unlike the characterisation created by Wilberforce's sons, Harford contended that Wilberforce was 'superior ... to an exclusive or sectarian spirit'.[12] Ryland seems to have appreciated this side of Wilberforce better than Andrew Fuller, yet both men, arguably the two most prominent leaders of the Baptist Missionary Society (BMS) in its early years, would have agreed without hesitation that in his support of Christian missions, distribution of Bibles and religious tracts, establishment of Sunday schools, and promotion of itinerant preaching and general public morality, as well as his membership in nearly seventy nondenominational societies devoted to the spread of religion and morality, the Evangelical Anglican William Wilberforce demonstrated a remarkable ecumenical spirit. By 1797, the proliferation of the war with France in Europe, coupled with growing political turmoil and the fear of the spread of

---

[8] These letters can be found in the Test Act Papers, a little known volume of autographs and printed materials collected by Wood, now belonging to the John Rylands University Library of Manchester, shelfmark D1/18.
[9] Test Act Papers, f. 38.
[10] Wilberforce and Wilberforce (eds), *Life of William Wilberforce*, I, p. 260.
[11] Wilberforce and Wilberforce (eds), *Life of William Wilberforce*, I, p. 249.
[12] John S. Harford, *Recollections of William Wilberforce, Esq.* (London: Longman, 1864), p. 263.

French 'infidelity' at home, had caused most Baptists to forget Wilberforce's lack of support during the campaign to repeal the Test Acts. In fact, by that time Wilberforce's popularity among Baptists had increased considerably as a result of his influential book, *A Practical View of the Prevailing Religious System of Professed Christians in the Higher and Middle Classes* (1797), as well as his advocacy of Christian missions in Africa, India and the West Indies during the parliamentary debate on the renewal of the charter of the East India Company in the spring of 1793.[13]

Wilberforce sought to include provisions in the new charter that would grant the legal admission of missionaries and Christian teachers into India. Though his Evangelical friend, Charles Grant, was a notable exception, the majority of the East India Company's directors believed that any attempt to Christianise India would be 'dangerous to the peace and good order of the British possessions in India'; consequently, the motion failed in the House of Commons that May.[14] From that point on, as Charles Hole contends in his history of the Church Missionary Society, the cause of missions became 'a part of [Wilberforce's] programme', second only to the abolition of the slave trade.[15] Less than a week after the House vote, Wilberforce met with William Carey and John Thomas in London just prior to their departure for India as the first BMS missionaries. He recommended that they go out in a foreign ship, since the Company would probably be suspicious of their mission. Andrew Fuller wrote to John Saffery at Salisbury on 30 May 1793, informing him that he had just read in a London paper that Wilberforce was 'endeavouring to get an Episcopal Mission, under the Sanction of parliament, but his scheme is frustrated; and therefore they will probably be the more friendly to us'.[16] Fuller may have read too much into Wilberforce's actions at this time concerning an ecclesiastical establishment in India, but he would continue to maintain suspicions as to the intentions of Wilberforce and his Clapham friends toward

---

[13] Fuller reviewed *A Practical View* in the *Protestant Dissenter's Magazine* 4 (1797), pp. 196-98, hoping it would 'meet with more than common attention', although he was somewhat critical of Wilberforce's diffuse style. Ann Judson, wife of the American Baptist missionary, Adoniram Judson, while on furlough in London in 1822, expressed to Mrs Wilberforce her appreciation of her husband's book, a perusal of which 'was the means, not only of my removing my doubts & restoring my mind to its former state of tranquility, but gave those high & elevated ideas which that work is so admirably calculated to produce.' See Ann Judson to Mrs William Wilberforce, 23 July 1822, MSS. Wilberforce, d.13, ff. 301-302, Bodleian Library, Oxford.

[14] Cyril Henry Philips and Patrick J.N. Tuck, *The East India Company 1784-1834* (Manchester: Manchester University Press, 1940), p. 159.

[15] Charles Hole, The Early History of the Church Missionary Society for Africa and the East (London: Church Missionary Society, 1896), p. 22.

[16] Fuller to Saffery, 30 May 1793, BMS Letters, Angus Library, Regent's Park College, Oxford. A typescript of the Fuller letters can also be found at the Angus Library; see Fuller Letters, 4/5/1 (1780-1808) and 4/5/2 (1808-1815).

the work of the BMS. Like Ryland, Sutcliff, and the other members of the BMS committee, Fuller knew only too well the important role Wilberforce could play in securing the future success of the society. Fuller and his Baptist friends would also discover that Wilberforce could play a similar role at home, especially in protecting the rights of Dissenters to evangelise through the means of itinerant village preaching.

In 1800 the Bishop of Rochester, in an address to the clergy of his diocese, accused Dissenting preachers of conducting village evangelism for the purpose of disseminating radical political ideas among the poor rather than propagating the gospel.[17] The Baptists had been itinerating for much of the 1790s in Cornwall and the West Country, even forming a national society to promote such activities in 1797.[18] They had evangelised without incident, yet now they were being classed as radical Jacobins and disloyal citizens by a leading bishop. Fuller understood the implications of the bill, informing William Carey on 12 May 1800 that he was 'using all the interest I can with H[enry]. Thornton and Wilberforce ag^t it: but God knows what is coming upon us ... For ought I know your friends here may be soon in a prison.'[19] Wilberforce recommended that, for the moment at least, Fuller and his Baptist preachers keep quiet. A few weeks later Fuller related the substance of Wilberforce's advice to John Sutcliff, Baptist minister at Olney and, like Ryland and Saffery, a key member of the BMS committee. Fuller acknowledged the importance of Wilberforce's assistance but he also recognised the complications that came from depending too much upon an Anglican, no matter how Evangelical and sympathetic he was to the cause of missions. 'He [Wilberforce] thinks the Church is in *more danger* from such a measure', Fuller complained to Sutcliff,

> than the Dissenters, they of *doing* wrong, we only of *suffering* wrong. As a friend to the Church therefore he is deeply concerned to oppose it; earnestly requests me to use all my influence to keep dissenters still; but desires his name not to be mentioned [or] as little as possible. I wrote to several quarters merely in this way – that a member of Parliament who was deeply concerned to prevent the measure advised so and so.[20]

Fuller and the Baptists did keep 'still', but by December 1801, Fuller was ready to make a public defence of village preaching, especially after the recent appearance of two virulent pamphlets, both written by Anglicans and aimed

---

[17] See Samuel Horsley, The Charge of Samuel Lord Bishop of Rochester, to the Clergy of his Diocese, delivered at the Second General Visitation in the year 1800 (London: Nichols and Sons, 1801).

[18] The Baptist Society for the Encouragement of Itinerant Preaching; the name was later changed to the Baptist Itinerant Home Missionary Society, and finally to the Baptist Home Missionary Society (BHMS).

[19] Fuller to Carey, 12 April 1800, BMS Letters, Angus Library, Oxford.

[20] Fuller to Sutcliff, 5 May 1800, BMS Letters, Angus Library, Oxford.

primarily at the Methodists and Baptists.[21] 'I am aware', he wrote to Wilberforce on 5 December, 'that we have heady and foolish individuals amongst us, and so has the church; but to the best of my knowledge of both Dissenters and Methodists, the body of them are far from being what they are represented by these men.'[22]

Fuller believed the Bishop of Rochester had completely misread the motives of the Baptists, to whom village preaching was simply another form of missionary activity, and had never been used for political purposes. 'We make no parade, nor ever think of preaching agst the church, or depreciating the clergy,' Fuller writes, warning Wilberforce that if the Baptists should choose 'to retaliate, we could bring five charges to their one.'[23] Fuller was probably aware that Robert Hall's blistering response to the Bishop of Rochester's sermon had been circulating in manuscript in London since the summer, but Hall chose not to publish it, apparently following Wilberforce's advice.[24] Fuller and Wilberforce would correspond again concerning this issue in 1811, during the battle over the Sidmouth Bill, a similar attempt to curtail evangelism by Dissenters among the poor and uneducated, especially in the country villages. With the help of Wilberforce and other Evangelicals in parliament, the Sidmouth Bill was defeated and the ten-year effort by the established church to stop Dissenters from engaging in village preaching finally came to an end.[25]

---

[21] The pamphlets were A Candid Inquiry into the Democratic Schemes of the Dissenters, during these Troublesome Times (Bradford, 1801), by William Atkinson, and Hints to Heads of Families (London, 1801), by T.E. Owen.

[22] Fuller to Wilberforce, 5 December 1801, acc. 27, Angus Library, Oxford.

[23] Fuller to Wilberforce, 5 December 1801, acc. 27, Angus Library, Oxford.

[24] Eliza Flower, visiting the family of Joseph Gurney in Southwark, wrote to her husband, Benjamin Flower, editor of the *Cambridge Intelligencer*, the week of 16 July 1801, that 'Hall has been lately in Town he came up on Monday afternoon, & returned on Friday, he passed most of the time with Phillips of Clapham. Hall is about they say to reply to the Bishop of Rochester's attack on itinerant preaching, & had part of the copy with him which Phillips has read. I have heard nothing of the sort at Cambridge.' James Philips was the Independent minister at Clapham, 1807-24, and a close friend of Hall. Hall would revise his pamphlet in defence of village preaching again in 1810, but after the defeat of the Sidmouth Bill the next year, chose not to publish it. Gregory published the manuscript in his *Works of Robert Hall* in 1832. Hall's main purpose was to assure the public that 'as nothing is more remote from the views of those who are most active in promoting village preaching than an intention to promote political discontent, so nothing is more removed from the practice of the preachers'. See Olinthus Gregory (ed.), *Works of Robert Hall* (6 vols; London: Henry G. Bohn, 1853), III, p. 337; for Eliza Flower to Benjamin Flower [postmark 16 July 1801], see Timothy Whelan, *Politics, Religion, and Romance: The Letters of Benjamin Flower and Eliza Gould Flower, 1794-1808* (Aberystwyth: National Library of Wales Press, 2008), p. 239.

[25] See Fuller to Wilberforce, 21 August 1811, MSS. Wilberforce, d.17, f. 174, Bodleian Library, Oxford.

Wilberforce, Ryland, Jamaica and India

If Baptists and Methodists could freely evangelise in England, the same was not true in India or the British colonies in the West Indies. The granting of legal toleration to missionaries throughout the British Empire would unite Wilberforce and the Baptists more than any other issue after 1800, and would be the chief focus of the letters that passed between Wilberforce and John Ryland. Their correspondence began in August 1807 after news reached Ryland of a crackdown in Jamaica on village preaching among black Baptist preachers, especially Moses Baker, Ryland's correspondent.[26] The oppressive measures began on Christmas day, 1802, when the planters pushed through a new ordinance in Jamaica outlawing the teaching of negroes or people of colour by Dissenters.[27] The ordinance was disallowed in June 1804, but the planters continued to find ways to stifle the activities of the Dissenters and the black preachers. In June 1807 a new ordinance was passed by the Common Council, this one designed 'to prevent meetings from being held before sunrise, or after sunset – thus aiming', as John Clarke, BMS missionary and one of the society's earliest historians, contended, 'at the prevention of religious services, excepting on the Sabbath day'.[28]

Ryland wrote to Wilberforce in the summer of 1807, enquiring if he was aware of the religious persecution occurring in Jamaica. Wilberforce responded on 27 August from Brighton, describing the June ordinance as 'a shocking Violation of all Religious Liberty'. However, he could provide no advice until he returned to London 'to talk the Matter over ... with 2 or 3 intelligent friends'.[29] One was his brother-in-law, James Stephen (1758-1832), lawyer,

---

[26] Moses Baker (1755-1822), a free black, came to Jamaica from New York in 1783 and worked in Kingston as a barber. Converted under the ministry of George Liele (1750?-1828), he began preaching in a house in Kingston and formed the first Baptist church there. He would later found the second Baptist church in Jamaica at Crooked Spring, on the estate of I.L. Winn, a Quaker. About 1805 Baker became a correspondent of Rippon and Ryland, pleading for the cause of the slaves. For more on Baker, see Christopher Brent Ballew, *The Impact of African-American Antecedents on the Baptist Foreign Missionary Movement, 1782-1825* (Lewiston, NY: Edwin Mellon Press, 2004); *Baptist Annual Register* (4 vols; London, 1790-1802), III, pp. 212-14; John Clarke, *Memorials of the Baptist Missionaries in Jamaica* (London: Yates and Alexander, 1869), pp. 18-30.

[27] Only 'duly qualified, authorized and permitted clergymen', such as Roman Catholics and Episcopalians, could teach or preach to the blacks. According to John Clarke, the new law effectively shut up the Baptist and Scottish churches, and lessened the operations of the Methodists for two years, even imprisoning some of their ministers. See Clarke, *Memorials*, p. 30.

[28] Clarke, *Memorials*, p. 44.

[29] Ryland's letter to Wilberforce, unfortunately, has not survived. Wilberforce's letter of 27 August 1807 (the first letter in the bound volume at Bristol Baptist College), as well as another letter to Ryland, dated 19 November 1807 (autograph no longer extant), appeared in Cox, *History*, II, pp. 19-21.

abolitionist, and member of the Clapham Sect. The previous year Stephen had been largely responsible for drafting the bill to abolish the slave trade, which was formally enacted on 25 March 1807, just a few months before Wilberforce's letter to Ryland. Wilberforce returned to London and met with Stephen, who believed the new ordinance to be 'illegal' and something 'to be resisted in a legal course'. By the time Wilberforce relayed Stephen's opinions to Ryland on 19 November, the Consolidated Slave Law had been passed, prohibiting slaves from attending *any* Dissenting place of worship, including those of the Methodists.[30] Wilberforce was convinced the new law was not only 'illegal' but would 'not be allowed in any court or country which is governed by law ...'. Unfortunately, 'in such a community' as Jamaica, Wilberforce admits, 'it is difficult to say what may not be done with impunity'.[31] Ryland had also expressed concern that Methodist ministers ordained by Thomas Coke, who began establishing Methodist missions in Jamaica in the 1780s, might be exempted from the new restrictions. Wilberforce could not confirm that suspicion, but he was fairly certain (and he was correct in this regard) that the primary issue was less Methodist vs. Baptist and more white vs. black. He warned Ryland

> that preachers in a white skin would be likely to be treated better and respected more than black ones. This is all I can now say. When the meeting of parliament shall bring me within reach of West Indians again, I will try in private to soften the prejudices of some leading men connected with that country; but I fear that the prejudices of the resident colonists, and their irreligious habits, are such as to render all attempts to soften them unavailing. May the Almighty open a door which no man can shut![32]

That last sentence struck a vibrant chord with Ryland, who had been hearing similar sentiments from Moses Baker for some time. Ryland was provoked enough to write the following note at the foot of Wilberforce's letter: 'I cannot but think it is of great importance for us to send out some one speedily. *I have waited with great anxiety several years for some one to send.*'[33] Ryland's anxiety would not be abated until John Rowe sailed for Jamaica as the first BMS missionary to the West Indies on 31 December 1813.[34]

Jamaica, however, was not the only front under attack. Between 1807 and 1813, BMS missionaries in India would face their own brand of persecution by

---

[30] Clarke, *Memorials*, pp. 44-46.

[31] Cox, *History*, II, p. 20.

[32] Cox, *History*, II, p. 21.

[33] Ibid.

[34] The Jamaica law would eventually be overturned by the British government on 26 April 1809. See Clarke, *Memorials*, p. 48.

the East India Company.[35] Once again, Wilberforce would play a prominent role in negotiating between the two entities. The issue came to a head, just as it had in 1793, during the debate over the renewal of the Company's charter, a process that began in 1812. Early that year several proposals circulated around London calling for an ecclesiastical establishment in India. Wilberforce, the devoted Anglican, was obviously not opposed to the plan, but, at the same time, advocated toleration for all missionaries, especially the Baptist mission at Serampore led by William Carey, whom Wilberforce greatly admired. Wilberforce believed, however, that the best way to gain a legal toleration for the missionaries would be for the established church to initiate the new proposals for a change in the charter, thereby eliminating any backlash from those in the church whose opinion of the Baptist missionaries was unfavorable and who would have resented and even resisted any attempt to change the charter to allow for a greater toleration for the missionaries. Ryland, Fuller and other members of the BMS Committee were naturally suspicious and began to make their opinions known about the Anglican proposal, much to Wilberforce's dismay. On 12 February he wrote in his diary, 'I am sadly disappointed in finding even religious people so cold about the East India Instruction, partly produced, I think, by the sectaries having had a notion that the Church of England is to be established. Alas! alas! let us have some substance before we differ about form.'[36] He wanted the Church of England to assume its proper station and in order to do that, he believed, it would be necessary for the time being to 'keep back the Dissenters and Methodists, until the Church fairly come forward, from fear that if the sectaries begin the Church will not follow'.[37]

The Church Missionary Society (CMS) met on 24 April, passing resolutions 'framed by Wilberforce & his friends', according to Fuller, that 'were so worded that if their requests [for an ecclesiastical establishment in India] were granted ours would be included in them'. Fuller was writing at the time to Joshua Marshman at Serampore,[38] but he must have sent news of the meeting to Ryland as well, for Ryland quickly sent a letter to Wilberforce about the matter. That letter is now lost, but in his follow-up letter dated 2 June 1812 (Wilberforce had failed to respond to his first letter), Ryland apologised for his bluntness.

'Now I recollect that I had (perhaps incautiously) observed', he writes,

---

[35] See Brian Stanley, *The History of the Baptist Missionary Society 1792-1992* (Edinburgh: T & T Clark, 1992), p. 54; Hole, *Early History*, pp. 227-233; E.D. Potts, *British Baptist Missionaries in India, 1793–1837* (Cambridge: Cambridge University Press, 1967), pp. 177-200.
[36] Wilberforce and Wilberforce (eds), *Life of William Wilberforce*, IV, p. 10.
[37] Quoted in Hole, *Early History*, p. 211.
[38] Fuller to Marshman, 15 May 1812, BMS Letters, Angus Library, Oxford.

that it w.^{d} not be expected that Dissent.^{s} w.^{d} write in a petition for such an Establishm.^{t} and there[fore] if all parties were to be invited to concur in an applicat.^{n} in favour of the propagation of X.^{y} in Ind.^{a} that object sh.^{d} not be introduced into the *general* petition.

The observation was perfectly legitimate, but to the politically conscious Ryland, offending Wilberforce was the last thing he wanted to do. Yet knowing the political and spiritual inclination of the majority of the clergy of the Church of England, Ryland could not help but plead with Wilberforce that if bishops were indeed appointed for India,

they may *neither* be good men of the High Ch. stamp, who w.^{d} not all[ow] full Liberty of conscience to other Denomin.^{s} nor yet (which w.^{d} be still worse) more worthy formalists, unacquainted with vital, evang.^{l} X.^{y} who w.^{d} oppose those of their own persuasion who were most zeal.^{s} for the Gosp.^{l} of X.^{t}

These 2 Classes I recollect I term'd, to avoid Circumlocut.^{n} High Church.^{n} & Dry Church.^{n}; if by those phrases I gave you any offence, I sincerely beg your pardon; tho I did not at the time suspect the express.^{s} w.^{d} be misunderstood or that moderate Chris.^{ns} w.^{d} be unwilling to allow, that some of their Breth^n deserve the form^r Appellation, or that there are those that might justly be designated by the latter.

In his postscript, Ryland reiterated that he had no desire to oppose the establishment of a bishopric in Calcutta; he simply wished that it be proposed as 'a separate measure, and not introduced in a *gen.^{l}* application wherein Dissenters were expected to join'.[39]

Wilberforce responded on 3 June, reassuring Ryland that he was not offended by his remarks and promising him that 'there is room enough in ye East Indies for all Denominations of Xtians, & it will certainly be my earnest Endeavour to secure free Scope for ye Exertions of all.' 'Certainly he must be a strange man', he added in his postscript, 'who could expect conscientious Dissenters to join in applying for a Church Estab.^{t} in India.'[40] Wilberforce got the message, and on 14 and 15 July, accompanied by Lord Teignmouth and James Stephen, he met twice in the home of William Burls, a member of John Rippon's congregation at Carter Lane and the BMS's primary financial trustee in London. 'They were some hours together,' Fuller wrote to James Hinton of Oxford, another member of the BMS Committee. 'They seem hardly to know

---

[39] Ryland to Wilberforce, 2 June 1812, Bristol Baptist College Library. About this time, Ryland reiterated some of these same points in a speech at a meeting at the Guildhall in Bristol. See J.E. Ryland (ed.), *Pastoral Memorials* (2 vols; London: J. Holdsworth, 1828), II, pp. 27-29.

[40] Wilberforce to Ryland, 3 June 1812, Bristol Baptist College Library.

what is the best mode of proceeding, but think something should be immediately done by *each denomination separately…*'.[41]

At the same time as Wilberforce and the Dissenters were attempting to change the charter, news came from India that a fire had destroyed much of the Serampore Mission printing office, with damages totalling nearly £12,000. Wilberforce quickly sent a contribution to Ryland, with the promise of another £5 if the subscription drive proved insufficient, demonstrating not only his generosity but also his ecumenical spirit at a time when sectarian tensions were running high.[42] Wilberforce and the Dissenters, however, would eventually put their differences aside and join together in a remarkable demonstration of unity around the proposed changes in the new charter. Friends of the BMS in London, led by Joseph Gutteridge, deacon at the Baptist church in Little Prescot Street, drew up a petition on 6 April 1813; Fuller and his Kettering congregation sent theirs on 8 April. These were two of the more than 800 petitions, signed by more than 500,000 individuals (55,000 appeared on petitions attached specifically to the BMS) that deluged the House of Commons.[43]

Wilberforce was the parliamentary leader throughout the petitioning drive and the subsequent debates, presenting the petition for the BMS on 19 May in a speech that earned the praise of the *Baptist Magazine*. 'We feel much obliged to Mr. Wilberforce', the *Magazine* noted, 'for his conduct on this occasion. The advocate of humanity is the friend of christianity; and we cannot but hope that the victory of the former over the cause of slavery, will be the presage of the triumph of the latter over that of infidelity.'[44] Wilberforce spoke again on behalf of the missionaries on 22 June 1813, a speech the Baptist essayist John Foster believed would be 'regarded as one of the most distinguished efforts ever made in the assembly'. Wilberforce mentioned many of the BMS missionaries by name, 'and there is no part of this most powerful Speech', Foster argued, 'animated by a more generous fire than that in which he pronounces at great length the panegyric of these "fanatics and anabaptists", as a lofty and assuming speaker denominated them.'[45] Wilberforce believed Carey

---

[41] Fuller to Hinton, 16 July 1812, cited in J.H. Hinton, *A Biographical Portraiture of the late Rev. James Hinton, M.A.* (Oxford: Bartlett and Hinton, 1824), p. 312 (emphasis mine).

[42] Wilberforce to Ryland, 2 November 1812, Bristol Baptist College Library.

[43] See Wilberforce and Wilberforce (eds), *Life of William Wilberforce*, IV, p. 123; G.E. Smith, 'Patterns of Missionary Education: The Baptist India Mission 1794-1824', *Baptist Quarterly* 20.5 (Winter, 1964), p. 300.

[44] *Baptist Magazine* 5 (1813), pp. 260-61.

[45] John Foster, 'Wilberforce on Christian Missions', from the *Eclectic Review*, May 1814; reprinted in J.E. Ryland (ed.), *Critical Essays contributed to the* Eclectic Review, *by John Foster* (2 vols; London: Bohn, 1856), II, pp. 237-51 (quotations from pp. 248, 250). General Gascoigne, MP for Liverpool, referred to Carey and the other BMS missionaries as 'anabaptists' on the floor of the House; he was rebuked by Wilberforce

and his colleagues were 'entitled to our highest respect and admiration' not only for their missionary zeal and their remarkable work in learning and translating the scriptures into Bengali, Sanscrit, Mandarin, and other native languages, but also for their selflessness in turning over the profits of the Serampore press to the mission. Wilberforce not only praised 'these great and good men', as he termed them, but also the BMS 'for having selected and sent forth agents so admirably fitted for their important functions', a legacy, he admonished his fellow M.P.s, that 'entitles the Society to our confidence in future'.[46] This overwhelming display of public opinion in favour of the BMS missionaries, as well as Wilberforce's brilliant and persuasive speeches, convinced Lord Castlereagh to add another provision to the charter legalising missionary activity. Wilberforce's sons would later write that their father was 'the link [at that time] between the most dissimilar allies. Bishops and Baptists found in him a common term.'[47]

Wilberforce, Ryland and Prudent Missionary Policy

After the victory over the East India Company, Wilberforce turned his attention to the West Indies, helping Ryland get approval from the colonial government for John Rowe to begin his mission work in Jamaica.[48] Wilberforce wrote to Ryland that he had procured a recommendation from a member of the House of Lords who had agreed to present Rowe to the Duke of Manchester. The peer, however, did not want his name to become public; Ryland did his part by carefully marking out the peer's name each time it appeared in Wilberforce's

---

and eventually 'retraced his steps, as to express his hearty concurrence' in supporting the mission at Serampore. See *Baptist Magazine* 5 (1813), p. 260.

[46] William Wilberforce, Substance of the Speeches of William Wilberforce, Esq. on the clause in the East-India Bill for promoting the Religious Instruction and Moral Improvement of the Natives of the British Dominions in India, on the 22d of June, and the 1st and 12th of July, 1813 (London: Printed for John Hatchard, J. Butterworth, and Cadell and Davies, 1813), pp. 62, 65.

[47] Wilberforce and Wilberforce (eds), *Life of William Wilberforce*, IV, p. 113.

[48] John Rowe (1788-1816), originally from Somerset, was baptised at Yeovil in 1807 and entered Bristol Academy in 1810. Rowe and his wife sailed on 31 December 1813 and arrived in Jamaica on 23 February 1814; his ministry, however, was short-lived, as he succumbed to a fever on 27 June 1816. Moses Baker would later say of Rowe, 'Though at a place where the most minute parts of his conduct were liable to the severest scrutiny, he conducted himself with such prudence and meekness as, at length, to gain the confidence and respect of the most prejudiced.' See Broadmead Church Book, 1779-1817, f. 345 (Bristol Record Office, Bristol); *Periodical Accounts Relative to the Baptist Missionary Society* (6 vols; Clipston: J.W. Morris; London: Burdett and Morris, 1800-1817), VI, pp. 72-73; Clarke, *Memorials*, pp. 18-30; Leslie Brooke, *Baptists in Yeovil: History of the Yeovil Baptist Church* (Bath: Ralph Allen, 2002), pp. 13-14.

letter. Wilberforce was 'fearful', he wrote to Ryland on 10 January 1814, two weeks after Rowe sailed for Jamaica,

> lest I may be using an undue Liberty ... in letting you see the Note I have this day receivd from him; but I send it for your perusal, trusting to your promising me (& if you promise I know you will perform) not to mention [his] name. Tho I have no objection to your telling our common friends, that Mr Rowe would be recommended to the Duke of Manch.^{r} by one of ye principal members of Government, in reliance on his prudence, sobriety &c as well as the other requisite qualifications.

'Mr Rowe should be warnd', Wilberforce added in his postscript, 'that ye Credit of men in high Stations as well as that of his friend is involvd in his Good Conduct.'[49]

Rowe's 'prudence', 'sobriety', and 'Good Conduct' were important to Wilberforce, for it represented an ideal he had long harboured about missionary activity. In 1796 Robert Haldane (1764-1842), a future Baptist and supporter of the BMS but at that time a member of the Church of Scotland, requested permission of the East India Company to conduct missionary activity in India. Wilberforce inadvertently played a key role in the Company's decision to reject the application. After meeting with Haldane and his co-workers, Wilberforce wrote in his diary that they were 'all perfect democrats, believing that a new order of things is dawning, &c'. He told Haldane that they 'had by their imprudence seriously injured their cause with Mr. Dundas'. Despite their 'imprudence', Wilberforce was impressed by their zeal for missions and tried to convince Dundas that Haldane and his friends could do little harm in 'the back settlements' of India. Unfortunately, Wilberforce's characterisation of their political radicalism was sufficient for Dundas and the other directors of the East India Company to reject their application.[50] Wilberforce learned his lesson: politics and missions did not mix, and if such 'imprudence' on the part of a missionary candidate would prove unacceptable to the directors of the East India Company, it would be just as abhorrent to the colonial authorities and planters in the West Indies.

Fuller, Ryland and the BMS committee would follow Wilberforce's lead in this regard. Though many Baptist ministers and ardent supporters of the BMS had been outspoken proponents of political reform in the early 1790s, including Robert Hall in Bristol and Cambridge and Samuel Pearce in Birmingham, by 1797 some of these same ministers were stifling political expression among BMS missionaries and demanding a level of submission to authority both in England and abroad that they had once considered servile and even

---

[49] Wilberforce to Ryland, 10 January 1814, Bristol Baptist College Library.
[50] Hole, *Early History*, p. 156.

unchristian.[51] The examples of Jacob Grigg and John Rodway in Sierra Leone and John Fountain in India in 1796-1797 demonstrated the need for adhering to the Wilberforce doctrine.[52] Fuller admonished Fountain about his political views even before he left for India, writing to him on 25 March 1796, 'Whatever you think about the downfal of Despotism I beseech you say little or nothing upon it. Birds of the air Carry news: and every thing said by a person who is going on such an errand as yours will be noticed and reported.' 'All political concerns', Fuller continued,

> are only *affairs of this life*; with w^h. he that will please *Him* who hath chosen him to be a soldier, must not *entangle himself*. Eye the providence of *God*; and mark the operation of *his* hands: but beware of your passions being immoderately interested in the concerns w^h. *men* have in the business. He that will be Christ's disciple must *deny himself* even of many of his natural rights: Not only Liberty and friends, & property but even life itself require to be set at nought when they stand in competition with him, or the dissemination of his cause.[53]

The next year Fuller would share much the same thoughts with Carey. 'When I think of these things [the growing power of Napoleon in France] I am more and more convinced that political changes are matters from w^h. it becomes good men in general to stand aloof ... the political world is a tumultuous ocean; let those who launch deeply into it take heed lest they be drowned in it.'[54] The lesson seemed to stick with the BMS thereafter. In 'An Address from the Committee of the Baptist Missionary Society to the Missionaries' (7 May 1799), the committee warned Carey and his associates to beware

> both from a principle of conscience, and from sound policy, and regard to your own interest and that of the mission, to keep at the utmost distance from intermeddling with any political concerns ... Study to be quiet, and mind your own business ... Set a pattern yourselves of ready obedience to human authority, in all things that are lawful in the sight of God.[55]

---

[51] Hall argued in *Christianity Consistent with a Love of Freedom* that the Christian minister is not forbidden to engage actively in 'regenerating the civil constitutions of nations'. To Hall, the changes Dissenters like himself wanted in 1791 – a repeal of the Test Acts, an end to unequal representation in parliament, the end of ministerial corruption and the 'encroachments of an hierarchy equally servile and oppressive' upon parliament – were all 'parts of God's plan of government'. See *Christianity Consistent with a Love of Freedom* (London: J. Johnson, 1791), pp. 32, 34.
[52] See Basil Amey, 'Baptist Missionary Society Radicals', *Baptist Quarterly* 26.6 (Spring, 1976), pp. 363-76.
[53] Fuller to Fountain, 25 March 1796, BMS Letters, Angus Library, Oxford.
[54] Fuller to Carey, 18 January 1797, BMS Letters, Angus Library, Oxford.
[55] Periodical Accounts, I, pp. 515-516.

Concerning the issue of mixing politics and evangelism, Fuller, Ryland, Carey and Wilberforce all spoke the same language: missionaries were to exhibit prudent behaviour at all times and maintain a proper submission to authority.

Ryland and Wilberforce were also of one mind in maintaining an ecumenical spirit concerning missions and evangelism. In the spring of 1814 Ryland sent Wilberforce a letter from Stephen West, aging Congregational minister at Stockbridge, Massachusetts, about a revival occurring in America.[56] Wilberforce responded to Ryland on 5 April 1814, declaring, 'The thought of this Xtian fellowship & Love over all considerations & feelings of political Hostility, is quite healing.' To Wilberforce, the war with America (which began in 1812) was a 'Subject of unfeign'd & deep concern, I mean more so than Wars in common, from ye Consideration of its being carried on with the Descendants of ye best of our own forefathers – men united to us by ye bond of common principles of Religion Morals, civil & political as well as relig^s Liberty &c &c.' Wilberforce was also acting once again as Ryland's special agent in London on behalf of new BMS missionaries in need of assistance from high-ranking officials. This time Wilberforce was procuring help for Thomas Trowt, a recent student at Bristol Academy who was attempting to go to Java as a BMS missionary. Though the provisions in the new charter of the East India Company had done much to facilitate the work of missions in India, they did not eliminate the requirement of government approval of missionaries. Thus, the aid of well-connected men like Wilberforce would continue to be a necessity for the BMS. 'I fear there has been some mistake in applying to Lord Bathurst', Wilberforce writes, 'However both Mr Ivimey[57] thro Mr Grant, & I are attending to ye Object (of securing Mr Trouts permission I mean to go to Java)[58] I trust we shall succeed.'[59]

---

[56] The letter appeared in *Periodical Accounts*, V, p. 210, and another one by West in the *Baptist Magazine* 8 (1816), p. 83.

[57] Joseph Ivimey (1773-1834), Baptist minister at Eagle Street, London, 1805-1834.

[58] Thomas Trowt (1784-1816) joined the Baptist church in How's Lane, Plymouth (at that time pastored by John Dyer), in 1811. After serving as a layman in Kingsbridge and Plymouth, Trowt answered the call to the mission field, entering Bristol Baptist College in August 1813. He was set apart by the Pithay congregation in Bristol as a BMS missionary in April 1814, arriving in Java on 16 September 1814. Before he left Bristol, he married John Dyer's sister-in-law, Eliza. As the *Periodical Accounts* notes, John Ryland, who spoke at Trowt's dedication service, observed that 'since Mr. Trowt came to Bristol . . . at the expense of the Baptist Missionary Society, he has discovered much ardent piety, and remarkable diligence in the acquisition of learning.' Trowt's service in Java, however, was short-lived; he died from dysentery in October 1816. See *Periodical Accounts*, V, pp. 295-96; Cox, *History*, I, pp. 253, 310-11; W. H. Carey (ed.), *Oriental Christian Biography, Containing Biographical Sketches of Distinguished Christians who have Lived and Died in the East* (3 vols; Calcutta: J. Thomas, Baptist Mission House, 1852), II, pp. 368-72.

[59] Wilberforce to Ryland, 5 April 1814, Bristol Baptist College Library.

In December 1814 Wilberforce wrote again to Ryland, this time turning the tables and asking Ryland's help in the formation of a Bristol auxiliary of the London Society for Promoting Christianity among the Jews. Wilberforce was scheduled to accompany two of the vice-presidents[60] of the society to the meeting in Bristol, but circumstances precluded his attending the meeting. He hoped Ryland could attend in his place and give 'a fair hearing to the advocates of the Society & an impartial Attention to its Claims'. Once again, Wilberforce's approach to this society, much like his work with the BMS, CMS, the Religious Tract Society and the British and Foreign Bible Society, demonstrated a belief that such societies could and, indeed, *should* be of an ecumenical nature. The society for the conversion of Jews, Wilberforce writes, 'is an Undertaking at least on which we are far from approaching towards that point at which the paths of Conscientious Churchmen & Dissenters begin to separate & therefore we may all labour for ye Common purpose without Jealousies on either Side'.[61] Wilberforce would have found a sympathetic ear with Ryland, but not with the Evangelical clergy in Bristol, who refused to support the Society due to its 'undenominational constitution'.[62]

By May 1815 Ryland's correspondence with Wilberforce took on even greater importance, for now Ryland was the titular head of the BMS. Sutcliff had died in the autumn of 1814 and Fuller in late April 1815. Eventually the BMS committee, largely composed of London Baptists, would select John Dyer as the society's first full-time secretary, moving the society's headquarters from Kettering to London in 1818. In the meantime, Ryland, along with Christopher Anderson of Edinburgh and James Hinton of Oxford, shouldered much of the burden of the BMS leadership before its transfer to the London committee. On 22 May 1815 Wilberforce returned a crumpled Rowe letter to Ryland accompanied by the M.P.'s deepest regret over the death of Andrew Fuller. 'All this time', he writes, 'I have been thinking of *our* departed friend – for *ours* not *yours*, I must term him – at least it will go ill with me or with any one who does not belong to that blessed Society to which he belong'd – There is a part of his work The Gospel its own Witness[63] which is enough to warm the coldest Heart.' Fuller would have been pleased that Wilberforce had lost none of his concern for the fragile nature of the work in Jamaica and the continuing attempts by the plantation owners and the colonial government to persecute those who were working among the black population. 'How dreadful to see such Hostility to ye Cause of Christ in a Country calling itself Christian', Wilberforce writes. 'I wish it were in my power to suggest any useful Hint for

---

[60] Charles Simeon, Evangelical vicar from Cambridge, and Lewis Way, Esq.
[61] Wilberforce to Ryland, 8 December 1814, Bristol Baptist College Library.
[62] Hole, *Early History*, p. 591.
[63] Andrew Fuller, *The Gospel its own Witness* (London, 1799).

Jamaica, but what can any one say, except that which the Scriptures furnish Be wise as Serpents & Harmless as Doves'.[64]

In the same letter, Wilberforce also admonished Ryland to 'contend for *prudence* in all y^r publications & proceedings', a reference to some reports that had appeared in the *Periodical Accounts* of the BMS that Wilberforce thought might be offensive to those whose support of missionary activities was less than warm. 'When we may as Christians encounter Opposition & even Persecution, then as Xtians let us meet them,' he writes. 'But let us not call for the Opposition & Persecution by our own Imprudence.' To be 'wise' and 'harmless' meant not only remaining silent about certain evils which the colonial governments and plantation owners were not yet ready to eradicate but also avoiding any inflammatory language in the publications of the missionary society. What could be gained by the missionary raising his voice against slavery in Jamaica or the discriminatory policies of the East India Company except inevitable prosecution and expulsion? To Wilberforce, Ryland and the BMS, the fear of *losing* the freedom to evangelise among the slaves of Jamaica or the natives of India as a result of 'imprudent' political activity on the part of the missionaries outweighed any potential *gain* in freedom for the slaves or the missionaries that such political activity might produce.

Wilberforce returned another Rowe letter to Ryland on 6 December 1815, glad to see that 'Mr Rowe appears to be of the right Spirit', which to Wilberforce meant that Rowe was avoiding politics, something the Dissenting ministers in London were not doing.[65] Wilberforce was upset about a recent meeting at Dr Williams's Library where a large group of Dissenters resolved to petition the British government about the recent persecutions of the Protestants in the south of France. At a second meeting on 28 November the ministers passed a resolution full of emotionally charged language, depicting Protestants being 'ravaged' and 'driven into exile', with 'their children dragged from the arms of their parents in order to be rebaptized according to the Roman Catholic ritual, and whole families brutally massacred'.[66] Such language was too provocative for Wilberforce. Though he was sympathetic to the plight of the French Protestants, the resolution violated Wilberforce's dictum that preachers should not engage in politically sensitive issues. 'I respect & love the warmth of their Xtian Sympathy,' he tells Ryland,

---

[64] Wilberforce to Ryland, 22 May 1815, Bristol Baptist College.
[65] Wilberforce to Ryland, 6 December 1815, Bristol Baptist College Library. As Stanley notes (*History*, p. 71), Rowe 'had fulfilled to the letter the BMS Committee's parting instructions to avoid interference in political matters and "endeavour by a respectful demeanor to recommend yourself and the gospel to the white inhabitants of the Island."'
[66] A deputation committee, which included the Baptist minister and educator William Newman, was appointed to meet with the Earl of Liverpool, who expressed much regret over the horrible scenes occurring in France. See *Baptist Magazine* 7 (1815), p. 528; 8 (1816), pp. 37-39; quotation from p. 38.

but I own I fear they will greatly injure the Cause not only of the Protestants of the South of France, but also of Protestantism itself, & of the new System of Instruction. O let them consider well the course they are pursuing.

Wilberforce reminds Ryland that 'our Saviour has himself instructed us to confine the Wisdom of the Serpent with the Harmlessness of ye Dove',[67] a dictum that the BMS missionaries in Jamaica, despite the pleas of Ryland and Wilberforce, would eventually violate in favour of a new principle of a militant Christianity that attempted to mediate between the poor and those in power, critiquing and correcting government practices and societal ills, most particularly the continuing proliferation of slavery in the Caribbean and America.

Wilberforce returned to the subject of the Baptist mission in Jamaica in his next letter to Ryland, suggesting that a plan might be devised that would make it easier to get missionaries into the islands and avoid their having to apply solely to the government. 'An Idea has struck me,' he writes on 29 June 1816,

> that considering the prejudices of the W. Indians &c &c – it might be an adviseable measure, if it could be effected, to prevail on them to come into an agreement that a Committee of Missions should be constituted of some of ye most respectable Proprietors – and also a committee consisting of 2 or 3 of the most respectable Ministers of each Denomination that sends Missionaries, & that the Selection of Missionaries for ye West Indies should be left to these Bodies ... who, being thus recommended & certified for, should then have their Certificate countersigned by the W[est]. I[ndian]. Committee –

Wilberforce was concerned that if societies such as the BMS sent too many missionaries to Jamaica, the planters would feel threatened and might try to end the mission operation altogether. The planters were already fearful of the growing number of blacks on the islands, a situation, Wilberforce concludes, that could easily make parliament

> disposed to be more influential than it ought by the fears of ye Planters & to consent to shut ye door against you altogether, unless a plan could be devisd which should secure the Planters on ye one hand from incompetent fanatics & on ye other should secure the Religious Denominations at Home from being discredited by the real or allegd Misconduct of Missionaries, tow^d whose going over they had had no Concern.[68]

As this letter reveals, Wilberforce's chief concern about the work of missions remained unchanged from his encounter in 1796 with an 'imprudent' Robert Haldane. This same concern would also dominate Wilberforce's efforts to bring

---

[67] Wilberforce to Ryland, 6 December 1815, Bristol Baptist College Library; Wilberforce actually wrote 'Servant', not 'Serpent'.

[68] Wilberforce to Ryland, 29 June 1816, Bristol Baptist College Library.

Protestantism to the fragile state of Haiti under the new government of Christophe, King Henry I.

The former French colony, at that time known as St Dominigue, had been dominated by Roman Catholicism but was now amenable to Protestant influence. Christophe, a former slave himself, chose Wilberforce specifically as his agent within the Anglican church and the British government, sending him £6000 to pay for the expenses of locating and transporting seven schoolmasters, a tutor for Christophe's son, and seven professors for his new Royal College.[69] Wilberforce was thrilled with the opportunity of helping to shape the first black government of freed slaves in the Western hemisphere, and he readily shared the news with Ryland. Anxious to spread the influence of the BMS beyond Jamaica, Ryland asked Wilberforce if he would be inclined to send a Baptist to teach in the school. Wilberforce responded on 1 January 1818, informing Ryland that he had recommended a classical scholar, 'a truly good Man, a Clergyman of the Church of England', to teach at the Royal College Christophe planned to establish. 'But I dare not recommend any Ministers of your Denomination', Wilberforce adds, 'to go to Hayti; at least, until circumstances sho'd be materially different – I durst not indeed answer for the consequences even to themselves; but, I own, I sho'd deprecate the measure with a view even to the interests of the Haytians.' 'In their present circumstances', Wilberforce explains, 'any religious controversy among their new Teachers, might be extremely injurious; and wo'd at least be very unadvisable.'[70] Like his response to the renewal of the East India Charter and the creation of the bishopric in India, Wilberforce could not hide his obvious allegiance to the Anglican church.

Ryland was not completely persuaded by Wilberforce's reasoning, confident that he could find a Baptist teacher who would avoid any doctrinal controversies with the Anglican teachers in the new college. To make matters worse, Ryland soon heard that some Methodists might be sent to teach in the college, and he pressed Wilberforce once again about appointing a Baptist

---

[69] Wilberforce would later tell his sons, 'In this Haytian instance, we are sowing the seeds of civilization and knowledge in a new society, which (may it please God) you may live to see exhibiting the new spectacle of a community of black men, of which the mass will be as well instructed as any nation upon earth.' See Wilberforce and Wilberforce (eds), *Life of William Wilberforce*, IV, p. 359; also Eric Metaxas, *Amazing Grace: William Wilberforce and the Heroic Campaign to end Slavery* (New York: Harper, 2007), pp. 249-50.

[70] Wilberforce to Ryland, 1 January 1818, Bristol Baptist College Library. Writing to William Steadman at Bradford, 28 January 1818, Ryland comments that some in the BMS were thinking it better to give up Haiti and concentrate on Jamaica. He remarks about the letter from Wilberforce, noting to Steadman that Wilberforce is of the opinion that 'a diversity of sentiment would be puzzling to the Haytians'. See 'Calendar of Letters, 1742-1831, Collected by Isaac Mann', *Baptist Quarterly* 7.1 (Winter, 1934), p. 42.

teacher. Wilberforce remained steadfast in his refusal to accept Ryland's proposal, fearful that his own efforts at securing Anglican teachers were sufficient to anger the Catholic bishop in Haiti. 'If this idea sho'd seize him,' he tells Ryland on 7 February, 'it is highly probable he wo'd use his utmost efforts to counteract my design, and what wo'd be so likely to infuse this idea into him as any noise about Religion in Hayti.' As to Methodist teachers, he admits he was 'not altogether without some uncomfortable feeling at sending them without permission', but he was fairly confident that there should be no disagreement between them and the Anglican clergyman already there. Wilberforce hoped Ryland would understand his concerns. 'It wo'd be gross imprudence,' he argues (using one of his favourite terms in regards to mission work), 'to incur the risk of calling forth a Bull from Rome ... in order to unmask to his Haytian Children the real Designs of their Sovereign and his heritical [sic] Advisers, and to keep them from straying into new pastures.' Given the 'bitter hostility' the white colonial governments in the West Indies demonstrated toward the new Haitian government, Wilberforce was convinced that Ryland 'wo'd feel as nervous as I do lest any mischief sho'd happen from even the imprudence of zealous friends'.[71] Wilberforce's inordinate concern for social stability, in this case, allowed him to restrict the presence of the BMS in Haiti in an effort to avoid any possible religious and social conflict that might ensue from the clash of different sects and opinions. Similarly, he was also willing to allow the continuation of slavery in the West Indies (an evil he obviously detested) in exchange for a degree of social order and stability necessary, he believed, to ensure a continued toleration by the planters of a missionary presence among the slaves.

Wilberforce, Ryland and Politics

The next year, during a vacation at Malvern Hills in Worcestershire, Wilberforce learned that Ryland himself had become embroiled in local politics. During the last week of September and the first week of October 1819, meetings were held in London and in numerous towns and villages for the purpose of raising petitions on behalf of several people killed by the militia during a political demonstration in St Peter's Fields, Manchester, on 16 August 1819 (an event that became known as the Peterloo Massacre). Many viewed the actions of the militia as a clear violation of the rights of the people to assemble and address political issues. Others viewed the demonstrators as 'a ragged crew' misled by the demagoguery of radical political leaders.[72] In Bristol, some fifty citizens signed a requisition calling for a public meeting in the Assembly

---

[71] Wilberforce to Ryland, 7 February 1818 (but not sent until 19 February), Bristol Baptist College Library.

[72] *Bristol Mercury* 11 October 1819, p. 1. The 'ragged crew' was language used by the ministerial London paper, *The Courier*, as quoted in the *Mercury*.

Rooms to discuss the Massacre. The Mayor of Bristol, however, refused to comply with the requisition and would not allow use of the Guildhall Assembly Room for the meeting. The citizens defied the mayor and met on 4 October at Brandon Hill, passing resolutions supporting the protestors and calling for changes in the current government. The mayor, clearly angered by the group's defiant attitude and anti-ministerial resolutions, held his own meeting on 9 October at the Council House in which resolutions were passed denouncing the Manchester protestors as 'wicked and designing men, [attempting] to excite a Spirit of Disaffection amongst the lower Orders of the People that no Loyal Subject [could] contemplate without feelings of the utmost alarm'.[73]

After the meeting, the Mayor asked Ryland to circulate among the members at Broadmead a petition supporting the government and its actions against the Manchester protestors. Ryland, fearful that the petition might divide his congregation and place him at political odds with many in his congregation, wrote to Wilberforce about the matter, attaching some accounts of the incident taken from the Bristol newspapers. Wilberforce responded on 16 October. Though once viewed as 'radical' by many conservatives during his initial campaign to end the slave trade in the 1780s and early 1790s, Wilberforce had consistently identified with conservative politics in England throughout most of his parliamentary career, especially after 1795. What was paramount to Wilberforce was social order and political stability, even if it meant suppressing certain freedoms, such as the rights of the persecuted Protestants in France in 1815 or the massacred protesters in Manchester in 1819.[74] As he had demonstrated in his letters about the work of missions in India, Jamaica and Haiti, Wilberforce was capable of tolerating for a time a clear social evil in exchange for the privilege of propagating Christianity. In this instance, the conservative Wilberforce agreed with the Bristol mayor about the unsavoury, even dangerous, nature of the protestors in Manchester, though he also agreed with Ryland that the mayor's request was inappropriate. 'I really feel much for you on the very unpleasant & even distressing Circumstances in which you are plac'd,' Wilberforce writes, and he advised Ryland to 'take no part in calling forth ye political opinions of [your] congregation'. He recommended 'a general declaration of attachment to the Constitution & Loyalty to the Crown' be signed by all citizens, especially at this time, when attempts are being made, he added, 'to extinguish all religious principles & with them all patriotic feelings from ye Mass of ye people. I was greatly shockd by a passage in one of Carlisle's periodical publications the very name of which the Republican, plainly indicates its intent.' Wilberforce asked Ryland for more time to digest

---

[73] *Bristol Mercury* 11 October 1819, p. 1.
[74] Wilberforce would also express concern about Robert Hall's engagement in radical politics during a protest by members of the Spencean Society and the Hampden Club in Leicester in January 1817. See Hall to Wilberforce, 27 February 1817, MSS. Wilberforce, d.17, ff. 269-270, Bodleian.

all the newspaper accounts of the incident in Manchester in order to arrive at the truth, but he was confident the authorities had acted appropriately.[75]

During 1820 and 1821, the *Works of Andrew Fuller* appeared in eight volumes; Ryland had already published his memoir of Fuller in 1818. As the volumes began to appear, Wilberforce contacted Ryland about purchasing a set. Ryland responded on 26 March 1821, with information on the cost of each volume and places where Wilberforce could place his order. Ryland, however, used the occasion to engage Wilberforce once again in a political discussion, this time on the nagging issue of Catholic Emancipation. Ryland says he 'never busied [himself] much in political concerns', a disingenuous statement, at best, given his participation in the extremely anti-Catholic *Protestant Magazine* in the early 1780s, his brilliant letter to the London *Evening Post* in November 1781 demonstrating his support for the American War, his involvement with the Northampton committee of Dissenting ministers for the repeal of the Test and Corporation Acts in 1790, his support of Wilberforce in his campaign to abolish the slave trade, and his near twenty-year record of actively preserving the interests of the BMS and its missionaries in India, Java, Sierra Leone and Jamaica, as well as Baptist itinerant preachers in Great Britain. Wilberforce had straddled the fence for years on the Catholic Question,[76] and Ryland was struggling as well to arrive at a decision. 'On the *one hand*,' Ryland writes,

> I have been afraid of seeming to distrust my own sword, and to ask for the aid of the civil magistrate to defend the cause of Christ.
>
> On the *other hand*, while I am willing that the worst enemies of the truth should be approved only by the word of God, and be left to try all that they can do by means of argument ag.^{t} it, I have tho't the case of the Catholics differ'd from that of other erroneous persons. A man may indeed be a Catholic, and disbelieve the power of the Pope to dispense wth the obligation of an oath: tho I should fear that out of 12 men, who now think themselves sincere in denying that power, 8 or 9 w.^{d} be likely to change their opinion in case of a *Crisis*, when they might essentially serve their Church, by adopting it. But another point weighs more with me, viz. A man cannot be a Roman Catholic, and yet be heartily disposed to allow Liberty of Conscience to others. If then a man had his hands tied behind him, and I was sure that if they were untied, he w.^{d} immediately tie mine behind me, I should hesitate about cutting the string. Hence the scale has hitherto preponderated in my mind ag.^{t} the measure.

As convincing as this logic seemed to be to Ryland, he was nevertheless not convinced. 'The more I think of it,' he continued,

---

[75] Wilberforce to Ryland, 16 October 1819, Bristol Baptist College Library.

[76] For more on Wilberforce and the Catholic Question, see Wilberforce and Wilberforce (eds), *Life of William Wilberforce*, III, pp. 362-363; vol. 4, pp. 94-98, 323-324; Metaxas, *Amazing Grace*, pp. 264-265.

the more I dread distrusting the sufficiency of scripture and argument to defend our cause; and I have almost felt inclined to risque all consequences. Surely if Protestants of all denominations do their Duty, we cannot have much room to fear the prevalence of popery in England.[77]

The Catholic Question was not the only political issue prompting Ryland's letter. A new attack on Dissenters was looming on the horizon in the form of Henry Brougham's Education Bill. In 1820 Brougham, an abolitionist and close friend of Wilberforce, introduced his Education Bill, in which he sought the assistance of the church and state in the formation and equipping of schools.[78] Eventually his goal of a system of national education would come to fruition, but his initial effort in 1820 failed, much to Ryland's relief.[79] Ryland complained to Wilberforce that the bill was 'not so much intended for the increase of education to the poor, as it [was] to prevent Dissenters and Methodists, from instructing the Children of Absenters, and thereby causing many of them to become conscientious Dissenters'. He admitted there might be some instances of 'intemperate or imprudent' Sunday School teachers among the Dissenters, but every one he had known had been 'purely and earnestly concern'd to do good, by alluring the most neglected children, who used totally to profane the Lord's day, to come and be instructed in the common faith'. More than 500, he tells Wilberforce, were being instructed in Broadmead's Sunday Schools at that time.[80]

Wilberforce responded on 29 March, ordering the entire set of Fuller's *Works*, as well as Ryland's memoir of Fuller. He thanked Ryland for the missionary reports he had sent him and assured him that 'Mr Brougham [has] laid aside his intention of prosecuting his [Education] bill this year; & this

---

[77] Ryland to Wilberforce, 26 March 1821, Wilberforce Papers, Duke University.

[78] According to one historian, Brougham's educational efforts were stymied by Anglicans and Dissenters – the former believing they had a right to control education and Dissenters believing their children (and any child whose parents so wished) were free to be educated by Dissenters. See Frances Hawes, *Henry Brougham* (London: Jonathan Cape, 1957), p. 111.

[79] One of the key provisions of the bill was that the master was to be a 'member of the established church', although not an 'officiating minister'. The church catechism was to be taught one half day each week, but 'no child [was] to be punished, rebuked, admonished, or otherwise molested, for being absent with leave of its parents, guardians, or persons having care of it, at the times when the Church catechism is taught.' Students were to attend the parish church once on Sunday unless they attended elsewhere with their parents, but once again, they were not to be 'punished, rebuked, admonished, or otherwise molested' for attending a Dissenting chapel. See *An Abstract of Mr. Brougham's Education Bills* (London: Longman, 1821), pp. 11, 16.

[80] In his postscript, Ryland attached a portion of the journal of Stephen Sutton, a BMS missionary working at that time in Midnapore, India, and a brief account of a Baptist slave in Jamaica who, after many years of extreme hardship, finally purchased his freedom for £250.

seems so probable,' Wilberforce adds, 'that I believe it.'[81] As to the Roman Catholic question, Wilberforce says he did not have time to address it fully, 'but I cannot acquiesce,' he tells Ryland, 'in your manner of putting it, – that the Hands of the R. C. are not tied behind them. On the contrary I believe that their power is great, & the influence of their Priests more operative now than it would be if they were allowed themselves to come into Parliament, instead of Electing Representatives who are called Protestants.'[82]

The next spring would find Wilberforce at Marden Park, Godstone, where he received a packet from Ryland that included a political pamphlet by an unnamed friend of Ryland. Wilberforce did not think 'much of [Ryland's] political Economist', he writes on 7 March 1822, but he was glad Ryland was continuing 'to receive good accounts' from the missionaries in India, for 'there is no part of the World,' he writes, 'to which I look with greater pleasure & more elevated hopes'. In fact, his interest was so great that when he returned to London he attended the annual meeting of the BMS at Great Queen Street Chapel, London, on 20 June, accompanied by his friends Joseph Butterworth (1770-1826), a former Baptist turned Methodist, printer of law books, and former M.P. for Dover; Jabez Bunting (1779-1858), leader of the Methodist Missionary Society; and the Baptist layman Benjamin Shaw, London financier, insurance broker, and M.P. for Westbury, who chaired the meeting and served as treasurer of the BMS from 1821 to 1826. At the meeting, Wilberforce briefly spoke and then made a motion, seconded by F.A. Cox of Hackney, that the BMS should form 'a Corresponding Committee, to act, in various parts of the empire, in connexion with the General Committee'.[83] 'Wilberforce spoke charmingly', William Newman, principal of Stepney College, noted in his diary after the meeting, 'his silvery tones, his musical voice, his evangelical spirit highly interesting. But there are strong marks of debility; he seems to be shattered.'[84]

Final Correspondence

Wilberforce would remain an M.P. for another four years, but his health was not good and the level of his public work slowed considerably as he devoted much of his time now to his family. His letters to Ryland from 1820 and 1821

---

[81] In a brief letter to Ryland dated 23 April 1821 (Bristol Baptist College Library), Wilberforce repeats once again that he was 'all but absolutely sure' Brougham's Education Bill would not come up this session; however, he would rather Ryland 'not quote me as your authority as yet'.
[82] Wilberforce to Ryland, 29 March 1821, Bristol Baptist College Library.
[83] Annual Report of the Committee of the Baptist Missionary Society (London: J. Haddon, 1822).
[84] R.E. Cooper, 'The Diary of William Newman - II', *Baptist Quarterly* 18.5 (Winter, 1960), p. 278.

do not reveal anything of great significance. In one from 1820 Wilberforce seeks a copy of one of the 'Reports of the Society under the Serampore Missionaries for setting up Schools in Hindoostan – I dont recollect the exact name of the Society,' he admits, 'but I have mentioned the Reports themselves (*two*, out of *three*, which I think are all that are published, I have read with great pleasure)[85] to some friends of mine, people of considerable rank & influence ....'[86] In April 1821 he writes twice: in one letter he confesses his inability to procure a job for a friend of Ryland, declaring that it had always been his rule 'not to ask any favor of Government', not even when his close friend, William Pitt, was Prime Minister.[87] The second letter was about the death of the Evangelical clergyman and biblical commentator, Thomas Scott (1747-1821), a close friend of both Wilberforce and Ryland and a leading figure in the CMS from its founding in 1799.[88]

The final two letters in this collection, however, deserve a closer look. Sometime in October or early November 1823, Ryland wrote to Wilberforce about some concerns he had about a new law, probably in Jamaica or India, and apparently one that was likely to have a negative effect upon the work of the Baptist mission. Ryland's paramount concern, as it had been since the beginning of their correspondence in 1807, was always the welfare of Baptist missions and evangelism, at home and abroad, and Wilberforce was still

---

[85] An Abstract of the Second Report of the Institution for the Support and encouragement of Native Schools, begun at Serampore, November, 1816, appeared in the Periodical Accounts of the BMS, VII, pp. 44-49, prepared by Joshua Marshman. The Third Report would appear in 1821. The education of native children had long been a concern of the Serampore mission, its teachers instructing primarily in the vernacular languages. Carey had opened his first school at Mudnabatty in 1794. In 1802 the mission published its Plan for the Education of the Children of Converted Natives, patterned at that time after traditional models of English Nonconformist education. Marshman was instrumental in founding the Benevolent Institution in Calcutta in 1810, and by 1813 sixteen schools were operating in India under its auspices, all of them patterned now after a Lancastrian model. Between July 1816 and October 1817, as G. E. Smith notes, BMS missionaries opened 103 schools, instructing more than 6,700 students. Joshua Marshman chronicled the mission's achievements and its educational practices in Hints Relative to Native Schools, Together with the Outline of an Institution for Their Extension and Management (Serampore, 1816, 1817). By 1819, BMS missionaries in the East were operating 126 schools with a student population of more than 9000. See Cox, History, I, pp. 231-33, 315; Smith, 'Patterns of Missionary Education', p. 300; M.A. Laird, 'The Serampore Missionaries as Educationists 1794-1824', Baptist Quarterly 22.5 (Winter, 1968), pp. 320-25; Keith Farrer, William Carey: Missionary and Botanist (Kew, Victoria, Australia: Carey Baptist Grammar School, 2005), pp. 41-46.

[86] Wilberforce to Ryland, 29 December 1820, Bristol Baptist College Library.

[87] Wilberforce to Ryland, 10 April 1821, Bristol Baptist College Library.

[88] In the collections of Bristol Baptist College resides an important though little known set of letters that passed between John Ryland and Thomas Scott, as well as two of his sons.

Ryland's first point of call when in need of political assistance. Wilberforce responded on 24 November 1823 from Elmdon House in Coventry. He promised Ryland that when he returned to London to take his seat in parliament he would try 'to have the Law altered in such a way as to render it no longer open to the objection you state'. 'At all Events,' he promised, 'when Parliament shall reassemble if I am then alive and well, I trust I shall be able to ascertain the actual state of the Law, and the probability of an acceptable settlement.'[89]

The final letter, though undated, is from late 1823 or early 1824, about a year before Ryland's death.[90] It provides a fitting close to the correspondence that passed between the two men, for it speaks eloquently to their ecumenical spirit and undying support for the work of missions around the world. Ryland had written to Wilberforce (his letter is now lost) expressing sentiments of Christian fellowship that struck a vibrant chord in Wilberforce. 'I must indulge the strong disposition I feel to thank you for y^r last friendly Letter,' Wilberforce writes,

> & to express the cordial Gratification with which I welcome & I trust I can truly say, I return, y^r Catholic Xtian Sentiments, & feelings – I cannot tell you how much I delight in them – They seem to unite us more closely than if our opinions were on all points ye same and so they are on all points of any Importance – for I cannot think that those ab^t which Churchmen & Dissenters differ, are *in themselves* of any *essential* Value.[91]

In this regard, Wilberforce hit upon the one point more than any other that distinguished Ryland from Fuller and probably made Ryland Wilberforce's favourite Baptist, for throughout the years of their correspondence, Ryland and many of his Baptist colleagues, especially those working closely with the BMS, demonstrated an ecumenism that had significant repercussions for the growth of the BMS. Wilberforce, as much as any other non-Baptist friend of the BMS, understood this, and his final statement to Ryland, 'I rejoice to hear of y^r Success in India – O that God may prosper still more abundantly ye Labours of y^r Ministers', mirrors a declaration in an earlier letter to Ryland in which Wilberforce boasted that the Serampore mission was 'one of the chief glories of

---

[89] Wilberforce to Ryland, 24 November 1823, Bristol Baptist College Library.
[90] Wilberforce to J.E. Ryland, 20 August 1824, Bristol Baptist College Library. Attached to this letter is a note by Wilberforce to Jonathan Edwards Ryland, Ryland's son and soon to be educator at Mill Hill and Horton Academy as well as a fairly significant writer and editor. In the note, dated 10 August 1824, Wilberforce thanks the younger Ryland for his gift of a print of his father, which his 'Esteem for the Original,' Wilberforce declares, 'will render valuable to him'.
[91] Wilberforce to Ryland, undated [*c.* 1824], Bristol Baptist College Library.

our Country.'[92] Both statements must have provided great satisfaction to Ryland.

The BMS, certainly in Wilberforce's eyes, had indeed achieved a degree of 'respectability' that could not be denied, yet ironically that very 'respectability' was something Andrew Fuller had feared, even resented. Fuller reminded William Ward in March 1813, during the battle over the renewal of the East India charter, that

> When your translations began to make a stir, tho' we had no 'respectability' in us, yet it seemed as if some thing of the kind would be bred amongst us. Hence the eager struggles of [Anglicans] on your side the water & of the Church party in the Bib. Soc^y, to w^h. Mr [Joseph] Hughes condescended to lend himself, on ours. Here was a feather, and surely you plebeians, you low-minded anabaptists will not pretend to wear it. Give it us 'respectable men,' it will just fit our hats. Be you our journeymen s^d B[uchanan]. & B[rown]. to you – Let us have the translations and you confine yourselves to your Missions ... But as we had made shift to do without 'respectability' at the beginning, both you and we were for going on in the same Track.[93]

Fuller was suspicious of Joseph Gutteridge's desire to bring 'the management of [the BMS] to London' after he and Sutcliff and Ryland were dead, so that 'it might be managed,' Fuller tells Ward, 'by "respectable men" without disgracing or committing themselves'. As Fuller's health declined in 1812, several Baptist laymen in London became concerned that too much power resided in the hands of Fuller. Gutteridge was the leader among them. In 1811 he had written to Fuller, requesting permission to have a likeness of Carey engraved as a means of promoting the BMS. In May 1812 he wrote again, this time anonymously (but Fuller tells Ward that he recognized 'the handwriting of the same "respectable" gentleman who sent for Mr Carey's likeness'), expressing great respect for Fuller, Ryland and Sutcliff, 'and ascribing much,' Fuller writes, 'to our prudent and well directed measures; and adding that during our life no one could wish it to be in other hands; but that as we certainly did not wish the work to end with us, proposing that Corresponding committees sh^d be formed in our life time, one in London, one in Bristol, & one

---

[92] Wilberforce to Ryland, 28 September 1819, Bristol Baptist College Library. After Ryland's death, Wilberforce paid a visit to Harford, during which the conversation turned to India and the Baptist mission. Wilberforce 'poured forth an eloquent eulogium,' Harford writes, upon William Carey, marvelling how he had risen from his 'lowly origin as a shoemaker' to such a 'dignified position in the learned world' at the College of Fort William. After reminding Harford that the first BMS collection 'netted only £13 for Carey', Wilberforce declared that from 'such small beginnings emerged a society which has since produced very striking and beneficial results to the cause of Christianity'. See Harford, *Recollections*, pp. 90, 178.

[93] Fuller to Ward, 5 March 1813, BMS Letters, Angus Library, Oxford.

in Edinburgh; and that the management on our decease sh^d go into these channels.'[94]

Fuller was wary of the idea of three committees, convinced that ultimately control of the BMS would reside in London, led by a group of wealthy businessmen, a situation that could lead to a fragmentation in the BMS, Fuller warned, primarily, over a desire for 'respectability'. Ryland was fearful as well, but he was pragmatic enough to understand that the inevitable power residing in London could not be withstood indefinitely by a group of provincial preachers, telling John Saffery shortly after Fuller's death that the BMS 'must have a man near London, who can easily slip up to meet persons of conseq.^{ce}'.[95] After 1818, London, not Kettering, would indeed be the home of the BMS, and by the time of Wilberforce's final letter to Ryland, Gutteridge was the leading layman on the BMS's Central Committee, the society's treasurer was Benjamin Shaw, and annual meetings were graced by the presence of Shaw, Wilberforce, Joseph Butterworth, and Jabez Bunting. For ten years after the death of Sutcliff and Fuller, Ryland was the chief link between the original idea of the BMS – a society largely controlled by a select group of local church pastors – and the post-Fuller idea of an organisation operating in conjunction with local Baptist churches but answering primarily to a central committee in London largely controlled by wealthy laymen.[96]

Ryland was not able to stop the move to London or the development of a centralised organisation during the tenure of John Dyer as BMS secretary. His correspondence with Wilberforce, despite the loss of most of Ryland's letters, nevertheless reveals a desire on Ryland's part to continue, as best he could, Fuller's role as the guardian of the society, recruiting new missionaries (like John Rowe and Thomas Trowt), opening new mission fields (like Jamaica and possibly Haiti), promoting and protecting the interests of the BMS (whether in India or the West Indies), and seeking whenever necessary the assistance of William Wilberforce, who, as the leading Evangelical MP and friend of missions, was uniquely qualified to accomplish those ends which Ryland and the BMS could not do on their own. Though Ryland understood the threat posed to the BMS by an inordinate attraction to 'respectability', he also recognised that Wilberforce provided a degree of 'respectability' that could be used as a positive good. Ryland's friendship with Wilberforce would indeed

---

[94] Ibid.

[95] Ryland to Saffery, 28 September 1816, Reeves Collection R/8, Angus Library, Regent's Park College, Oxford. Ryland would write during this time that he 'trembled for the ark of the mission, when it should be transported to London, and fall into the hands of mere counting-house men'. See J.C. Marshman, *The Life and Times of Carey, Marshman, and Ward* (2 vols; London: Longman, Brown, Green, Longman, and Roberts, 1859), II, p. 190.

[96] For more on the Gutteridge-Fuller controversy and the BMS's move to London, see Stanley, *History*, pp. 30-35.

leave a lasting mark on the history of the BMS. Had Ryland lived to see the passage of the Abolition Bill in 1833, his continued correspondence with Wilberforce would unquestionably have been filled with vivid accounts from Jamaica about the rise of the abolitionist movement there led by William Knibb and his Baptist co-workers. Though his ultimate loyalty was always to the Church of England, Wilberforce's final wish stated to Ryland, 'that God may prosper still more abundantly ye Labours of y^r Ministers',[97] was a genuine expression of his gratitude and admiration for a mission whose labours and accomplishments, he would have been the first to admit, between 1792 and 1833, were second to none.

---

[97] Wilberforce to Ryland, undated [c. 1824], Bristol Baptist College Library.

CHAPTER 5

General Baptists, Cumberland Presbyterians and Denominational Identity in Frontier Indiana in the Early Nineteenth Century

Daniel Dunivan

Historical narratives are important not only because they tell what happened, but also because they speak about who we are and guide us in becoming who we will be. In the practice of Baptist historiography such an insight has long been understood at least implicitly. Successionist historians from past generations utilised a particular way of narrating the past to position Baptists as the embodiment of the true church which never ceased to be authentic biblical Christianity and thus had never been and did not need to be reformed.[1]

This type of historiography unashamedly flowed from an understanding of what constituted being Christian, and more specifically from a detailed understanding of Baptist theological/ecclesial identity.[2] The definitions of what it meant to be Baptist were primary while a rigorously developed historical

---

[1] For prominent examples of successionist historiography, see Thomas Crosby, *A History of the English Baptists from the Reformation to the Beginning of the Reign of King George I* (4 vols; London: Thomas Crosby, 1738-1740); G.H. Orchard, *A Concise History of the Baptists from the Days of Christ their Founder to the 18th Century, with Notes, Illustrative of their Sufferings, from Papal and Episcopal Hierarchies*, ed. J.R. Graves (St Louis, MO: St Louis Baptist Publishing Co., 1859); Adam Taylor, *The History of the English General Baptists* . . . (2 vols; London: T. Bore, 1818); and J.M. Carroll, *'The Trail of Blood': Or, Following the Christians Down through the Centuries from the Days of Christ to the Present Time* (Lexington, KY: American Baptist Publishing Co., 1931). For a sample of Graves' theological argumentation in favor of successionism and its ecclesiologial offspring, Old Landmarkism, see *Old Landmarkism: What is It?* (Memphis, TN: Baptist Book House; Graves, Mahaffy and Co., 1880).

[2] The term 'Baptist theological/ecclesial identity' will be used throughout this article to refer to what Baptists usually call 'Baptist identity'. The extra identifying terms are an attempt to clarify the nature of such an 'identity'. At issue has always been what doctrinal and often specifically ecclesiological distinctives make an individual or a church 'Baptist'.

narrative was secondary and often simply served to prove the theological identity already assumed.³

This historiography also conveniently allowed these same historians to define exactly what being a Baptist meant; it was to hold the principles that Baptists had always held.⁴ Baptists from any period in history were considered to be basically the same, and Baptists in the present were cast rather monolithically as they all emanated from the same set of biblical/Baptist principles. When individuals departed from the canonical measures of identity as a given historian/theologian defined them, they were removed from the annals of Baptist history, and their stories were perceived as separate from the stories of the true Baptist tradition. At the same time, individuals or groups who were never, or only for the shortest of periods, called Baptist could be incorporated as central examples of being Baptist or proto-baptist if they represented some desirable virtue.⁵ Successionist history married the definition of Baptist theological identity to historical narrativity.

---

³ It is common to delineate two separate types of successionism: one of a succession of Baptist principles (ideological) and another of a succession of Baptist churches (institutional). For an example of this taxonomy, see Leon McBeth, *The Baptist Heritage: Four Centuries of Baptist Witness* (Nashville, TN: Broadman Press, 1987), pp. 56-60. Actual disagreements about how each category declines and which historians/theologians fit into those categories is a common issue. In fact, a survey of book-length Baptist histories would yield several different taxonomies.

⁴ It was this understanding that allowed J.R. Graves to push for Baptists to pay more attention to their history. In the 'Introductory Essay' to Orchard's work, he says, 'Excepting the study of the Bible, the life and teaching of Christ, the teachings and Acts of his Apostles, what study can or should be more delightful or more intensely interesting to the Christian than the study of the history of the churches which succeeded those planted in the days of the Apostles, and which have existed, preserving a pure faith and a pure practice through centuries of the fiercest persecutions and martyrdoms, unto this time?' Graves, *Old Landmarkism*, p. iv. In a more recent and sophisticated work, Tom Nettles has argued for a particular view of Baptist identity that is directly tied to historic Baptist confessions while at the same time arguing them as more or less timeless because truth is coherent. He explains this by saying that 'truth exists and can be communicated clearly from one mind to another, from one generation to another, and from one culture to another'. As a result all parts of the Baptist past have the same marks of identity. *The Baptists: Key People Involved in Forming a Baptist Identity: Vol. 1: Beginnings in Britain* (Fearn, Ross-shire, Scotland: Christian Focus Publications, 2005), p. 35.

⁵ It is common for successionists to trace the Baptist lineage through groups such as the Donatists or Waldenses and reformers prior to the Reformation such as Jan Hus. In more recent historiography, individuals such as Roger Williams who was only for the shortest time a Baptist have received an inordinate amount of attention. It is insightful to compare Williams to Alexander Campbell. Campbell was a Baptist from 1812 to1830; however, he is rarely mentioned as a part of the Baptist family. In the only work dealing with this oversight, Austin Bennett Amonette has said: 'Few readers of Baptist history

As a result of this overt theologising of the practice of history the accounts became significantly skewed as critiques of successionism have shown.[6] One of the greatest problems with such an approach is that it almost completely shuts out the ability of non-Baptists to make contributions to Baptist life, particularly to what it means to be Baptist. In other words, as non-Baptists were marginalised from the narratives of the Baptist past as told by successionist historians, they were also cut off from any contribution to Baptist theological identity. In this essay, an example of such a narrative will be set forth in the story of the frontier American group of General Baptists. After surveying the possible impact of the Cumberland Presbyterians upon the General Baptists, the questions of historiographical practice and its importance for ongoing questions of theological identity will be re-engaged.

An Overview of General Baptist Beginnings

In the 1820s in frontier Indiana, a new group of Baptists was born out of controversy emanating from the revivals that had swept much of the region in the first two decades of the nineteenth century. The movement began when a young Baptist preacher named Benoni Stinson migrated across the Ohio River from Kentucky into southern Indiana in the spring of 1822. Stinson quickly became pastor of a United Baptist church named New Hope in present day Evansville, and began holding camp meetings. In these revivals, Stinson emphasised the doctrine of general atonement; however, the majority of the

---

query the Baptist identity of either Smyth or Williams, but few Baptists have been willing to accept Campbell as a real Baptist: among historians, for instance, Torbet and McBeth maligned Campbell, while Leonard virtually ignored him. Why is this? Perhaps Baptists perceive that Smyth and Williams contributed something positive to Baptist life whereas Campbell was simply a destructive presence. Perhaps the time has arrived for Baptists to forgive Campbell for whatever damage he may have caused and to acknowledge him as a real Baptist who made Baptist life more robust.' 'Alexander Campbell and Baptist Identity: Contributions and Challenges', in Ian Randall, Toivo Pilli and Anthony Cross (eds), *Baptist Identities: International Studies from the Seventeenth to the Twentieth Centuries* (Milton Keynes: Paternoster, 2006), pp. 136-37.

[6] Discrediting successionist historiography is often traced to William Whitsitt, who famously resigned his position at the Southern Baptist Theological Seminary in Louisville, KY, in 1898 as a result of a controversy over his view that Baptists had not recovered immersion until 1641. For important relatively recent contributions in discrediting successionism see W. Morgan Patterson, *Baptist Successionism: A Critical View* (Valley Forge, PA: Judson Press, 1969); James Edward McGoldrick, *Baptist Successionism: A Critical Question in Baptist History* (Metuchen, NJ: Scarecrow Press; Philadelphia, PA: ATLA, 1994).

Baptists in the area were Calvinistic and intolerant of both Stinson's preaching and practices.[7]

Stinson soon became frustrated[8] and attempted to make room for himself through the constitution of a new church. He accomplished this move by starting a mission church from New Hope, and placing members in it of like mind with himself. Then upon their constitution as a church, they called Stinson as their pastor.[9] The name of this new church was Liberty.

Stinson seems to have been trying to avoid the control of the local Baptist associations, the Wabash District and Salem Associations. It is unclear whether he initially intended to remain outside all other associations because he would attempt to secure relationships with others in later years, including the Freewill Baptists.[10] However, when the churches of those associations charged that Stinson was out of order and spoke of him as a heretic who preached works-righteousness as a result of his statements in favor of general atonement, any participation with another association became impossible.[11] Therefore, in 1824, Stinson's church, along with four others that he had helped constitute through his revival efforts, formed the Liberty Association of General Baptists. The statements of faith for the new association remained substantially the same as the statements of the Wabash District and Salem Associations save one point: Liberty held to general atonement. The new statement read, 'Jesus Christ, by the grace of God, tasted death for every man; yet none can partake of his Divine benefits only [i.e. 'except'] by repentance towards God, and faith in the Lord

---

[7] William Reavis, 'The Life of Elder Benoni Stinson, together with a short history of the General Baptist denomination, as organized by him; to which is added short biographical sketches of the life and times of several other prominent Baptist Elders and Laymen', *General Baptist Herald* 2 August 1877, p. 5.

[8] This was primarily as a result of his personal interactions with the incumbent Baptist associations in the area—the Wabash District and Salem Associations. Particularly, Stinson was upset by a meeting he attended in Patoka, Indiana, where a hot dispute over the support of missions was boiling. He was also upset by his inability to get a statement placed in the newly constituted Salem Association's Articles of Faith which would allow for tolerance of the preaching of general atonement.

[9] Reavis, 'Sketches', p. 5.

[10] For an overview of the failed attempt at this merger see Douglas Low, 'Strangled at Birth with Newsprint: The Failed Merger of General Baptists with the Freewill Baptists, 1868', *American Baptist Quarterly* 25.2 (2006), pp. 175-95.

[11] They questioned whether he had properly 'lettered off' from New Hope. They also accused Stinson and the churches the followed him of being too liberal in their acceptance of social aberrants. Reavis, 'Sketches' 16 August1877, p. 5; 23 August 1877, p. 5; 13 September 1877, p. 5; 20 September 1877, p. 5.

Jesus Christ.'[12] In the years that followed, the group came to be distinguished by Arminian soteriology[13] and the practice of open communion.[14]

Since Stinson's death in 1869, multiple histories of his life and the formative period of the movement have been written.[15] In all these stories, the picture is primarily painted as an internal Baptist controversy revolving around the theology of general atonement and/or controversies about proper church order.[16] Non-Baptists are present in the story, but only in order to portray Stinson as liberal in his associations with them. The story never includes possible influence upon Stinson or the General Baptists from these 'others'.

No doubt the most immediate context of the early General Baptists was within Baptist life; however, they modified the accepted theology, liturgy, and polity of the Baptists out of which they arose and did so in unique ways. These developments of more or less traditional frontier Baptist life were not likely created *ex nihilo*. This essay will provide evidence that interactions with the Cumberland Presbyterians played some role in these innovations.

The Cumberland Presbyterians supply a set of interesting comparisons and similarities to the General Baptists that seem to go beyond pure coincidence. First, the formative years of the General Baptists were also the formative years for the Cumberland Presbyterians in the same area of Indiana. As early as 1817,

---

[12] The first clause in this statement, closely tied to the King James Version's translation of Hebrews 2:9, became and remains the watchword for the entire movement. *Minutes of the Liberty Association of General Baptists*, 1824.

[13] At first the General Baptists continued to hold to the final perseverance of the saints. The fifth article of faith in 1824 read 'the saints will finally persevere, through Grace, to Glory'. However, in 1844 the Liberty Association changed this article by quoting Mark 13:13, 'we believe that he that shall endure to the end, the same shall be saved', as a compromise between those who accepted and those who rejected the possibility of apostasy. Later statements make the possibility of apostasy much more adamantly.

[14] Daniel Dunivan, 'Closed, Close, and Open', *General Baptist Messenger* February 2006, p. 13.

[15] Reavis, 'The Life of Elder Benoni Stinson, together with a short history of the General Baptist denomination, as organized by him; to which is added short biographical sketches of the life and times of several other prominent Baptist Elders and Laymen', *General Baptist Herald* 2 August 1877 to 3 November 1878, was published in the denominational newspaper in weekly vignettes just a few years after the death of Stinson and at the outset of the formation of the national body for the movement, the General Association of General Baptists. The other histories include A.D. Williams, *Benoni Stinson and the General Baptists* (Owensville, IN: General Baptist Press, 1892); D.B. Montgomery, *General Baptist History* (Evansville, IN: Courier Company, 1882); T.A. Laslie, *Laslie's History of the General Baptists*, ed. L.O. Roberts (Poplar Bluff, MO: General Baptist Publishing House, 1938); Ollie Latch, *History of the General Baptists* (Poplar Bluff, MO: The General Baptist Press, 1954); Craig Shull, *The God of Our Fathers* (Poplar Bluff, MO: Stinson Press, 1983); Randy Mills, *Christ Tasted Death for Every Man* (Poplar Bluff, MO: Stinson Press, 2000).

[16] Mills, *Christ Tasted Death*, pp. 49-51.

Cumberland Presbyterian ministers began preaching in houses and holding camp meetings in the southern counties of the state,[17] and on 18 April 1826, the Indiana Presbytery of the Cumberland Presbyterian Church was organised,[18] just two years after the formation of the Liberty Association. Secondly, during the earliest years of the Cumberland Presbyterian ministry in Indiana, the ministers rode on circuits preaching and building up churches in a variety of communities. Stinson was close to the two primary circuit riders in Indiana at the time, Alexander Downey and Hiram Hunter.[19] Thirdly, the primary mode of expansion for both groups was the camp meeting. Stinson began holding them as soon as he started preaching and success in them was a primary concern for Stinson,[20] and the camp meeting lay at the heart of the formation of the original Cumberland Presbyterians in Kentucky.[21]

In order to examine possible influences of Cumberland Presbyterians on the early General Baptists, interactions and similarities in the areas of liturgy and polity will be surveyed. Through this exploration, Cumberland Presbyterians will be shown to be more than spectators of the development of the General Baptists, as the earlier histories of Stinson and the General Baptists have portrayed. In fact, they have left a lasting mark upon important elements of the General Baptist identity.

---

[17] W.J. Darby and J.E. Jenkins, Cumberland Presbyterianism in Southern Indiana: Being a History of the Indiana Presbytery and an Account of the Proceedings of Its Fiftieth Anniversary Held at Princeton, Indiana, April 13-18, 1876. Together with Various Addresses and Communications, and a Sermon on the Doctrines of the Church (Indianapolis: Printing and Publishing House, 1876), p. 18.

[18] Darby and Jenkins, Cumberland Presbyterianism in Southern Indiana, p. 20.

[19] The case of Downey will be explored below under the discussion of open communion. Concerning Hunter, Reavis, 'Sketches' 7 March 1878, p. 5, states: '. . . among the great pulpit orators of the West, he has few equals and no superior. He and Elder Stinson often preached together, and were much attached to one another. Elder Stinson entertained for him the kindest feelings until the day of his death.' No other close relationship like this is presented with any other individual Baptist or otherwise in Reavis' work.

[20] I have argued elsewhere that the primary impetus for Stinson's Arminian theology was its serviceability in calling sinners to repentance at the camp meetings. Daniel Dunivan, 'American Frontier Revival Piety and the Development of the General Baptists' (unpublished paper given at the Midwestern meeting of the American Academy of Religion, Chicago, IL, 5 April 2005).

[21] The beginning of the Cumberland Presbyterian Church is a tangled story of the overlay of anti-revivalist rhetoric and disagreements over ordination. For an extended discussion of the origin and history of the Cumberland Presbyterian Church, see Ben Barrus, Milton L. Baughn, and Thomas H. Campbell, *A People Called Cumberland Presbyterians* (Memphis, TN: Frontier Press, 1972).

Liturgy: The Open Communion Question and the Camp Meetings

When Stinson found himself outside of the Baptist associations in the area, he was also forbidden to preach in the meeting houses of other Baptists or to hold camp meetings with them.[22] Lacking the support of others of the same faith and order, he turned to non-Baptists of similar soteriology and revival piety and began holding protracted meetings with them. In one such meeting in 1824, Stinson co-operated with the Cumberland Presbyterian circuit rider, Alexander Downey.[23] During the week, Stinson and Downey traded off the jobs of preaching and exhorting, but on Sunday when it came time for the Lord's Supper, Stinson was unable to share the table with Downey because it was considered out of order. General Baptists up to this time held to close communion, as did the other Baptists in Southern Indiana; however, in the course of his encounter with Downey, Stinson began to question the viability of this practice. Looking back on the event he said:

> I did not say it in so many words, but our former practice said, we have been well pleased with you all the week, but now you will please take a back seat until after this solemn duty and binding service is over, then we will be glad to have you assist us in our services . . . I must confess to you brethren, that I felt mean, and there and then I told my brethren that I intended to invite all of God's people to the Lord's table.[24]

Following this encounter, Stinson started pushing for the practice of open or free communion in the General Baptist churches.[25]

All of the histories of Stinson's life and the early years of the movement, except that of his close friend William Reavis,[26] convey either this story or some part of it in their explanation of the move towards open communion. However, the prevailing tendency is to present Stinson as an open

---

[22] Reavis, 'Sketches 15 November 1877, p. 1.

[23] Alexander Downey (1799-1848) was one of the first Cumberland Presbyterian circuit riders in Southern Indiana and one of the charter members of the Indiana Presbytery of the Cumberland Presbyterian Church. He later pastored the Shiloh Cumberland Presbyterian Church in Shiloh, Indiana, for several years. He was also a teacher in the Cumberland Presbyterian training institute in Southern Indiana called the Delaney Academy which Stinson supported through an advertisement in the *General Baptist Herald* in 1845. For more on Downey see Darby and Jenkins, *Cumberland Presbyterianism in Southern Indiana*, p. 55.

[24] Montgomery, *General Baptist History*, p. 215.

[25] Some of the incoming churches to the General Baptist movement were also open communionists, a fact that made this move easier. See Williams, *Benoni Stinson and the General Baptists*, p. 69.

[26] Reavis states that Stinson's liberality on the issue of atonement led logically to his liberality on the issue of communion participation. Reavis, 'Sketches' 13 December 1877, p. 5.

communionist incognito and the encounter with Downey as the impetus to making Stinson a spokesman for open communion.[27] This is part of a larger tendency to portray Stinson as having held to all of the doctrines of the later General Baptists from the very beginning, a framework that has been effectively challenged in other areas by recent studies.[28]

It seems more likely that Stinson became disillusioned with the close communion position because of his relationships with non-Baptists in the revivals, not prior to them. In fact, the arguments made for open communion by Stinson and others who supported liberality on this issue substantiate this conclusion. Stinson's associate Reavis summarises the argument:

> These pedobaptist Christians are as certainly children of God as we are. They, like us, preach the doctrine of free grace and free salvation to all men, upon the terms of the gospel; they have good characters, and live holy lives; then, if we can worship with them in so many ways and forms, and fellowship them as Christians, why not commune with them?[29]

This same line of argument is taken up by Stinson himself in at least two extant sources of his own writing. In a sermon on open communion, Stinson stated, 'we agree about preaching, praying and singing together. Why not in communing together?'[30]

Again in an article published in the *General Baptist Herald* in 1845, Stinson addresses this topic and says:

> "But," says another, "by communing with those that are in error, we encourage them in that which we believe to be wrong." Not at all. We never can convince a man of his error, by taking him by the throat; but let the man know that you have some regard to his feelings; and then you many convince him of his error. So we may see many brethren in other denominations that we think to be in error: yet by their fruit it appears that God loves them, and owns them for his children. And can we not commune with, and bear with him whom God receives and loves?[31]

In each of these defences of open communion, the central reason for the practice is the affirmation of the non-Baptists in the same way that Stinson wanted to affirm Downey at the camp meeting in 1824. This leads one to believe that the 1824 episode and others like it acted as catalysts in the General Baptist move to open communion.

---

[27] For instance, Latch, *History of the General Baptists*, p. 131. Latch characterises close communion and perseverance of the saints as issues Stinson 'had to go along with for the time being'. He also states that the Downey incident 'fortified' Stinson's 'determination' rather than changing his mind on the issue.

[28] Mills, *Christ Tasted Death*, pp. 52-62.

[29] Reavis, 'Sketches' 13December 1877, p. 5.

[30] Williams, Benoni Stinson and the General Baptists, p. 66.

[31] Benoni Stinson, 'Free Communion', *General Baptist Herald* 1.4 (15 May 1845), p. 2.

The Cumberland Presbyterian influence on the issue of the Lord's Supper, however, goes even further than the move to open communion. Another element in the Downey story points towards a particularly Presbyterian influence on the General Baptist practice at the time, namely that the Lord's Supper was held at the end of a camp meeting. It is has been shown that the popularisation of the camp meeting on the American frontier arose from the Scottish-Presbyterian sacramental seasons, defined by several days of preaching on repentance and public confession followed by the observance of communion. Furthermore, the marriage of the camp meeting and the Lord's Supper seems to have been a uniquely Presbyterian influence.[32] However, among other groups, like the Baptists and the Methodists who took up and broadened the practice of the camp meeting, the element of the Lord's Supper as the climax of the revival was quickly dropped. In fact, by around 1805, the eucharistic aspect of the camp meeting seems to have been almost entirely lost among Baptists.[33]

The fact that Stinson and his church were holding a camp meeting climaxed by an observance of the Lord's Supper in 1824 is, therefore, unusual, and the fact that a Cumberland Presbyterian was helping him conduct the revival is telling. In 1800, the camp meetings were popularised by the Presbyterian minister, James McGready, and while he never joined the Cumberland Presbyterian Church, McGready was one of the foundational figures on the pro-revivalist side in the controversy which brought about the division leading to the establishment of that denomination. It seems highly probable, then, that Stinson was borrowing the practice from his Cumberland Presbyterian friends.

Whether is was through simple interaction or by direct borrowing, the co-operation between the two groups in this early period influenced General Baptist practices on the Lord's Supper. Into the present, one of the strongest components of General Baptist self-understanding stems from the acceptance of all Christians at the table, and this theological position has been used even in recent years to argue for continued involvement in groups like the Baptist World Alliance and the National Association of Evangelicals.[34]

---

[32] Leigh Eric Schmidt, Holy Fairs: Scottish Communions and American Revivals in the Early Modern Period (Princeton, NJ: Princeton University Press, 1989).
[33] William L. De Arteaga, *Forgotten Power: The Significance of the Lord's Supper in Revival* (Grand Rapids, MI: Zondervan, 2002), pp. 128-29.
[34] The author of this article was the chairperson of an ad hoc committee that assessed involvement in these organisations and Stinson's statements on open communion were included in the oral report to the General Association of General Baptists on 28 July 2009. General Baptist historian and statesmen, Ollie Latch, seems to have also used a similar argument during the period when General Baptists first joined the BWA.

Polity: Presbyterian-ish Presbyteries among the General Baptists

Because of the controversy surrounding the open communion question, the number of sources on the subject is fairly plenteous; however, in examining the issues of polity, evidence is much less forthcoming. In fact, the evidence is deficient with respect to Cumberland Presbyterian influence in particular and the history of the development of General Baptist polity in any of its facets. What is known is that General Baptists have differed markedly from other Baptists on the process of ordination since relatively early in their history.

Normative practice among most Baptists was and has generally remained that the ordination of ministers is done within the bounds of the local church and/or under the power of the local church, echoing the generally agreed upon Baptist principle of local church autonomy.[35] In Baptist life, pragmatism and common sense have demanded that most churches also be connected with other local churches and thus invite them to be involved in the ordination process.

On the American frontier among the Baptists out of whom the General Baptists arose, a council of other leaders of sister churches could be called for a variety of purposes, including ordaining, installing or dismissing pastors.[36] To do so, a church desiring the services of the council sent letters to surrounding churches listing the time, place and object of consideration. These sister churches were then to send their pastor and one or two laymen.[37] The council was only to deal with the issue presented to them, and then it was to be dissolved; thus, there were no standing councils. Sometimes these councils could be referred to as presbyteries,[38] but they were never standing and never given exclusive rights over the ordained. Instead, they acted in an advisory capacity to the local congregation, wherein laid the sole authority to ordain.

---

[35] For instance, in The Church Member's Manual of Ecclesiastical Principles, Doctrine, and Discipline: Presenting a Systematic View of the Structure, Polity, Doctrines, and Practices of Christian Churches, as Taught in the Scriptures, William Crowell says, 'It is evident that the right to consecrate, is involved in the right to elect; and this, as we have seen, the Lord Jesus Christ has vested in each church. All questions, therefore, respecting the validity of any ordination, must be settled by reference to this cardinal principle: the choice or election of a man to ministry, is a greater act than that of consecration or induction into office; consequently the church which is competent to do the greater, must possess in itself all inherent power essential to the valid performance of the less. The church,—not the ministry,—is the body of Christ, the organ of his will on the earth.' (Boston, MA: Gould, Kendall, and Lincoln, 1847), p. 166.

[36] Crowell, *Church Member's Manual*, pp. 263-64. He also lists 'aid in organizing churches', 'to assist in adjusting difficulties between churches', and 'to depose or silence unworthy ministers'.

[37] Crowell, Church Member's Manual, p. 265.

[38] Crowell does so on two occasions when referring to the theology of ordination, but never in referring to the practice. Stinson's own ordination certificate states that the church called for a 'presbytery', but then only two 'presbyters' are involved—one of whom is the pastor of the church which called for the 'presbytery'.

The General Baptists seem to have had this type of polity at least at first; however, by the 1860s a different polity for the ordination of ministers was in place. General Baptist historian, A.D. Williams, in 1892 described the General Baptist polity on ordination as 'peculiar'.[39] The peculiarity of the General Baptists was in the way they used the presbytery. The General Baptist presbytery was like the councils found in traditional Baptist polity, in that they respected the autonomy of the local congregation to select their own ministers, but they went beyond the limits place on the ordaining councils in two ways.

First, the General Baptist presbytery mixed the traditional ordaining council with another common institution among Baptists of the time, the ministers' meeting. In the polity manual by William Crowell published in 1847, ministers' meetings were described as being 'formed by the ministers within certain limits uniting, and agreeing to meet statedly once in two or three months, for mutual improvement, and the communication of intelligence from their respective churches'.[40] Thus, these meetings, unlike councils, were standing and for the ordained only.

General Baptist presbyteries took the power of ordination from the councils and placed it in the hands of the ministers' meeting, a standing body constituted by the ordained. Additionally, General Baptists began to include deacons as equally ordained members of these bodies.[41] As early as the 1834 meeting of the Liberty Association, churches were instructed to send their requests for licensing[42] and ordination to the quarterly meeting of ministers.[43]

Secondly, General Baptist presbyteries wield a larger authority than the traditional councils. As stated above, the councils were advisory to the ultimate power of the local church. It was normally the local church that ultimately held the power to ordain and discipline its ministers, but it was not so with the General Baptists. Of course, the local General Baptist church was independent of the presbytery, in so far as the presbytery could not dictate whom a church could call as their pastor, but the presbytery did hold absolute jurisdiction over

---

[39] Williams, Benoni Stinson and the General Baptists, p. 128.
[40] Crowell, p. 267. He goes on to explain exactly what this meant: 'Essays, doctrinal and practical, interpretations of difficult passages of Scripture, and plans of sermons, are exhibited, for mutual remark and friendly criticism. Questions of discipline are introduced and discussed, and mutual advice and encouragement imparted. In many places it is usual to have one or more sermons preached during the meeting, which sometimes occupies nearly two days.'
[41] Deacons were charged with the physical ministry of the congregation (visitation of the sick, benevolence, etc.), and the ministers were charged with the spiritual needs (preaching, conducting revival meetings, etc.). As co-members of the presbytery, deacons came to have a function in the local church much like the Presbyterian ruling elders. It is unclear exactly when this move took place.
[42] A licentiate refers to someone desiring to become an ordained minister but not yet proven or educated.
[43] Minutes of the Liberty Association of General Baptists, 1834.

the ordination of any of its members. This meant that a General Baptist minister could lose his credentials and thus the authorisation to preach and officiate at the ordinances as a result of the dissatisfaction of the presbytery and regardless of the sentiments of his church.[44] Conversely, he could not lose his ordination as a result of the actions of one church, for it took the actions of the presbytery. Williams describes this approach to ordination polity by saying:

> ... the principle of the Presbytery is that of the old English doctrine that one shall be governed by his peers. The minister is not responsible to the laity, but to his brother ministers - both as to securing official position, and to being degraded from it. The logic of the principle requires the whole body to act in any given case, one individual having no more right to act for the body than one member of the church to act for the church.[45]

Williams here and in other places uses the model of the upper and lower houses in the parliament of Great Britain to point out that there should be two levels of authority in the denomination—each wielding power in its own sphere—one for the churches and one for the ordained.

In making this move, the General Baptist presbytery took elements found in the broader Baptist polity, mixed them, and then vested them with independent power. Interestingly, the presbytery's jurisdiction over the ordained is remarkably similar to that of the presbyteries of the Presbyterians. Obviously the power of Presbyterian presbyteries extends into the workings of the local congregations in ways that the power of presbyteries among General Baptists do not. However, the power of the presbytery to ordain and discipline its own members is more analogous to the practice of Presbyterianism than to traditional Baptist polity, because the presbytery holds power which is not under the authority of the local church but in the hands of the other ordained members.

The histories of the General Baptist movement provide no indication of when the institution of this kind of presbytery began. The history of the rise of the power of the presbytery must almost exclusively be reconstructed through the minutes of the associations. What is known is that by the middle 1830s General Baptists had turned over the work of the council to the ministers' meeting, and before the 1860s the system was fully functional.[46]

---

[44] The use of the masculine to refer to General Baptist ministers is intentional here. There is no evidence that the earliest General Baptist churches contain ordained women; however, this practice is accepted by several contemporary presbyteries in the denomination including the Presbytery of Liberty Association.

[45] Williams, *Benoni Stinson and the General Baptists*, p. 127.

[46] Reavis describes the process of his own ordination as well as that of others, and the presbytery was working as an independent body by that point. Reavis, 'Sketches' 11 April 1877. Also the first extant minutes of the Liberty Presbytery are for the 1860s.

The answer to the question of why General Baptists chose a polity of this type is also not entirely clear. In fact the histories are again mysteriously quiet. Stinson and Liberty were experimenting in several different areas, both theologically and in practice, and as an independent group without the structures and tradition of other Baptist associations they must have seen this as the most effective way to deal with the ordination process. It should be noted that since Stinson and the General Baptists had been labelled as disorderly as early as 1822, the possibility exists that stronger connectional structures were already being introduced as a type of insurance of good practice among General Baptist ministers.

It is also possible that Stinson simply wanted to be able to control the direction of the association by moulding the leadership of the constituent churches. An example of the type of minister Stinson wanted to exclude could have been found in the anti-missions advocate and father of the 'two-seed' doctrine, Daniel Parker.[47] In 1822 when Stinson attended his first local association meeting in southern Indiana, Parker and his church brought another church up on heresy charges for financially supporting the Baptist Board of Foreign Missions, and it was ultimately the work of Parker that caused Stinson to step away from the Baptists of the other associations in southern Indiana.[48] Furthermore, Parker was infamous for starting trouble. He had done so in Tennessee before he moved to Illinois and became embroiled in the anti-missions controversy in the Wabash District Association.[49]

If the General Baptists had become sceptical about the ability of traditional Baptist polity to deal with agitators like Daniel Parker, they might have been seeking ways to secure stronger oversight. By placing ordination and discipline over the ordained in the hands of the ministers and deacons, the General Baptists were in effect taking away the power of the laity to support malcontents who might hijack the work of the movement. This assumes that Stinson was confident in his own abilities to sway other ministers. Presbyterian

---

[47] The 'two-seed' doctrine was Parker's claim that the elect were of the seed of the woman (Eve) and the non-elect were of the seed of the serpent based on his reading of Genesis 3. Daniel Parker, *Views on the Two-Seeds* (Vandalia, IL: Robert Blackwell, 1826). For a discussion of Parker's life, see Jeffrey Wayne Taylor, 'Daniel Parker (1781-1844): Frontier Baptist Warrior for the Old Way', *Baptist History and Heritage* 32 (April 1997), pp. 54-64.

[48] Mills, *Christ Tasted Death*, pp. 28-33.

[49] The figure of Daniel Parker drew no small amount of criticism at the hands of the General Baptists. For instance, in the 15 May 1845 volume of the *General Baptist Herald*, Stinson takes direct aim at Parker's hyper-Calvinist theology, and yet the readers are told in the section of the paper dedicated to news that Parker had died within the previous week in his home in Texas. Parker had left a lasting impression upon Stinson and the General Baptists long after he left the area of southern Illinois and southern Indiana.

polity in this way could provide the control that traditional Baptist polity could not.

Whether it was to centralise control over ordination in general or to eliminate a problem over a specific ordination, the reality is that General Baptist ordination became Presbyterian-like. If the General Baptists had become sceptical about the ability of traditional Baptist polity to deal with specific issues, the relative peace in the formation and period of growth of the Indiana Presbytery of the Cumberland Presbyterians might have presented an attractive alternative. The data is only suggestive, but if General Baptist historians were reluctant to include the influence of the Cumberland Presbyterians because of their status as 'others' their silence on this issue would be understandable.

Implications for General Baptists

In comparing the encounters and similarities between the General Baptists and the Cumberland Presbyterians in the areas of liturgy and polity, the evidence seems to suggest that the Cumberland Presbyterians played a role in the development of the General Baptists. Another area that could be explored, but which space will not permit here, is that both groups were involved in camp meeting revivalism and their theologies were impacted in similar ways by the experience of those revivals.[50] Moreover, such a mutual experiential theology seems to have made way for the relationships between Stinson and his Cumberland Presbyterian friends. Both had simultaneously evolved or softened Calvinism to fit the experiences they were having in the revivals, and this revival piety set both groups in opposition to the traditional lines of associations in their own denominational bodies. In other words, because the General Baptists identified with the theology, revivalism and alienation of the Cumberland Presbyterians from other Presbyterians, they were willing to listen and learn from them.

In spite of the relative silence in General Baptist histories, it seems that several key components of General Baptist theological/ecclesial identity were developed at least in part out of their partnerships with the Cumberland Presbyterians. One might ask the question why this story was not told. The answer lies in the historiographical skewing of successionism. The earliest General Baptist historians followed the paradigm of successionist historiography including long accounts of the New Testament roots of Baptists

---

[50] Both came out of Calvinistic traditions and cited their revival experiences as the ethos behind their rejection of predestination, or as the Cumberland Presbyterians called it 'fatalism'. For a history of the expurgating and ultimate rejection of Westminster Calvinism by Cumberland Presbyterians, see Joe Ben Irby, *Cumberland Presbyterianism and Arminianism Compared/Contrasted on Selected Doctrines* (Chelsea, MI: Cumberland Presbyterian Resource Center, 1998), pp. 5-17.

(especially General Baptists)[51] and even interspersing successionist theological points into the story of Stinson.[52] It seems that such an approach did not allow the early historians to explore the influence of the non-Baptist Cumberland Presbyterians, but instead seems to have silenced them either intentionally or inadvertently based on their preconceived notions of what could have taken place. This is a terrible loss for General Baptists who have been robbed of the opportunity for better understanding of their own past as well as guidance for their ongoing life.

Marginalisation of the 'Other' in Baptist Historiography and Theological Identity

Even though the last several decades have seen the demise of successionist approaches to telling Baptist stories, the questions of theological identity engendered in such approaches have not been so easily removed. Even the most rudimentary of searches on Baptist identity will show that the questions are alive and well among contemporary Baptist theologians and historians. The war over what it means to be a Baptist did not end with the demise of successionist historiography. The question of origins may have been relatively settled, but the power for determining present identity and thus guiding the future of Baptist life is still up for grabs.[53] The intersection of history and theological identity continues to be an important battleground. The dangers of successionist exclusion may have waned but other types of theologically-driven exclusion remain a threat to those marginalised from the sites of power in such debates. As a result self-aware historical methodologies for narrating the intersection of Baptist identity and history should be explored.

---

[51] For instance, Reavis' sketches were presented along with histories of the pre-Reformation 'Baptists' and Montgomery goes over a third of the way through his work before reaching the story of Stinson.

[52] For instance, D.B. Montgomery includes extended arguments about the connection between American frontier General Baptists and the General Baptists in England in order to secure succession. Montgomery, *General Baptist History*, pp. 181-82. The important work of A.D. Williams, *Benoni Stinson and the General Baptists*, is an exception to this pattern in that successionism is not found in the argumentation of his account; however, while Williams received some material from other sources besides those of Montgomery and Reavis, they provide nearly all of his information about the developments described above. After Williams, the works of other General Baptist historians until those by Shull and Mills returned to successionism along the same lines as Montgomery.

[53] Tom Nettles has correctly observed, 'Renewed zeal for the issue of Baptist identity emerged in the last two decades of the twentieth century and has, in fact, replaced the question of origin as the chief interest of Baptist historical studies.' *The Baptists: Key People*, p. 12.

A methodology of this type would require that the historical writings themselves become the objects of historical concern. There is scope for examining the ways in which the writings about the Baptist past have conveyed, created and marginalised conceptions of the identities present among specific Baptists. In so doing, this methodology becomes historiography as a second-order operation. As David O'Brien has said, 'Historiography can be seen as a category of intellectual history which relates historical works to the periods in which they were written and attempts to uncover their basic assumptions, revealing more immediately the limitations of the historical discipline, suggesting new questions to be asked, new avenues to be explored, new techniques, new metaphors, new models to be utilized.'[54] In the case of Baptist history, the new questions, avenues, techniques, metaphors and models will all be dually focused on the historical narratives and the ways they impact Baptist theological identity.

While not advocating all the implications or complexities of deconstruction as Jacques Derrida has defined it,[55] the general process of the subversive reading of texts becomes a centrepiece of this historiographical process. The primary emphasis is placed on the classical deconstructive value of decentring. First, the written narratives of the Baptist past, both remote and recent, have supported the definitions of theological identity that have functioned as centres for Baptist thought. This should be acknowledged and become an object of study itself. Then, counter-proposals can be presented in the form of the voices of marginalised positions. Non-Baptists are one group of 'others' that need to be explored in this regard, but there are also 'others' within Baptist enclaves that need to be given opportunity to speak equally for what it means to be Baptist (many of which are represented in the other narratives in this volume): for example, smaller Baptist groups, non-Westerners, non-whites, laypersons and women.

Some good work has begun in each of these areas, but to them must be added critical re-evaluation of how they might revise the discussions of what it means to be Baptist. These counter-proposals will themselves show what other centres of theological identity can and should be explored: not that a new concrete identity should replace the former, but there should be 'freeplay',[56] as

---

[54] David O'Brien, 'American Catholic Historiography: A Post-Conciliar Evaluation', *Church History* 37.1 (1968), p. 80.
[55] Jacques Derrida, *Of Grammatology*, trans. G.C. Spivak (Baltimore, MD: John Hopkins University Press, 1976).
[56] For a discussion of freeplay in Derrida's thought, see the review of two of his works by James S. Hans, 'Derrida and Freeplay', *MLN* 94.4 (May 1979), pp. 809-26.

Derrida has described it, of the multiple centres around which theological identity can be discussed.[57]

In the case of the General Baptists outlined in this essay, the discovery of this link came through the critical questioning of the historical narrative told by General Baptists themselves with special attention to 'others' who might have been marginalised from the story in ways that fitted the historical contexts of the middle to late nineteenth century. Also, illuminated in this quest were the ways this context and marginalisation allowed the shaping of General Baptist identity to fit historiography and theology about broader Baptist identity. In turn this led back to a reformulation or revisioning of both the narrative and the historical theological identity exposed by that narrative. Such a narrative and the identity inherent therein both reinforce and call into question components of the self-understanding of General Baptists from the past and the present. It is this action that is most significant for allowing these historical narratives to continue to pose the question of who a specific group like the General Baptists will be today. It opens the story to new interpretation and new application.

Such a re-envisioned historical methodology is not ceaselessly required, nor universally applicable in Baptist historiography, but with regard to hearing the voices of the marginalised it can open one's historical ears. And unless Baptist historians attend to the ways that tellings of the Baptist past create identity or narrow identity issues for others, then their historical methods will be no less invasive and destructive of their stories than those of the successionists.

---

[57] Cross-disciplinary and cross-cultural historiographical practice of this type can already be seen in the International Conference on Baptist Studies of which the essays in this volume are a product.

CHAPTER 6

Baptist Reactions to Catholics in the United States, 1830-60

Terry G. Carter

In 1938 Ray Allen Billington published a monograph entitled *The Protestant Crusade: 1800-1860* tracing the history of an increasing anti-Catholicism which characterised the United States (US) during the nineteenth century. American Protestant prejudice against Catholics touched virtually every denomination. It should be noted that during the nineteenth century one would be hard pressed to find any positive Protestant attitudes toward the Roman Catholic Church (RCC) and the papacy. Billington argued the bias was transplanted from Europe and then intensified in the colonies:

> The isolation of the people, the introspection to which they resorted in their wilderness homes, the distance which separated the colonies from the mother country and from Europe, all fostered bigotry which they had brought from the old world…In this sense the colonies represented a form of intellectual inbreeding where the worst as well as the best of the original characteristics of the people were unduly magnified.[1]

Early American Christianity strongly identified with Protestantism. In 1790 only about 30,000 Catholics resided in the US, most in Maryland. By 1840 that number had grown to 84,000 and by 1854 to 400,000.[2] Catholic growth caused Protestant negative reaction and fear. Men like Samuel Morse even accused the RCC of being a political entity rather than a spiritual one. Morse believed Catholics were scheming to take the United States as a new seat for the pope.[3]

Protestant prejudice against the RCC took various forms. Anti-Catholic statements appeared in school books as well as pamphlets, periodicals and other books. Billington argued that by the 1850s the average American had been

---

[1] Ray Allen Billington, *The Protestant Crusade: 1800-1860* (New York: Macmillan, 1938), p. 4.
[2] Colin Brummitt Goodykoontz, *Home Missions on the American Frontier* (Caldwell, Idaho: Caxton Printers, 1939), p. 222.
[3] John R. Bodo, *The Protestant Clergy and Public Issues, 1812-1848* (Princeton, NJ: Princeton University Press, 1954), pp. 70-71.

'trained from birth to hate Catholicism'. By '1838 an observer complained that books on the subject had become so numerous that it was impossible to read them all, and bookstores were established in the larger cities to deal solely in anti-Catholic works'.[4] Periodicals representing several Protestant groups such as the *Presbyterian Boston Recorder* (1816), the *Baptist Watchman* (1819) and the *New York Observer* dedicated magazine space to attack the RCC.

As early as 13 February 1832 Protestants in New York organised the crusade forming the New York Protestant Association. Over 500 attended the second meeting in March 1832.[5] In May 1836 the Protestant Reformation Society commenced. The stated purpose was to 'combine their energies for the illumination of the public mind on the subjects which were controverted by Protestant churches and the followers of the Court of Rome'.[6] In the next fifteen years several broadly Protestant organisations followed.

Political efforts grew out of a fear of growing Catholic numbers. As standing political parties used the immigrant vote to buttress their influence, nativists (native-born or non-immigrant), mostly in the larger cities, reacted. In 1841 the American Protestant Union formed in New York, seeing itself as a 'national defense society' with a goal to protect American and religious institutions.[7] This trend continued with the establishment of the American Republican Party in New York in 1843 that supported a twenty-one year naturalisation period for foreigners which no doubt targeted new Catholics. Finally, in the 1850s the American or Know Nothing Party developed.[8] According to William Ganna Brownlow, the party 'was against political Romanism – against all who acknowledge any allegiance to a foreign Prince, Potentate or Power: or who acknowledge an authority on earth, higher or more binding than the Constitutions of our states and General Government'.[9]

Unfortunately the anti-Catholic prejudice moved beyond rhetoric, organisation and politics to violence. As early as 1834, prompted by stories of supposed immorality in convent life, Protestants burned a convent in Charlestown, Massachusetts.[10] This event was the first of a series between 1830 and 1860 which included riots in Philadelphia and Louisville, Kentucky.[11]

---

[4] Billington, *Protestant Crusade*, pp. 345-46.
[5] 'Notice', *Protestant* 25 February 1832, p. 63; 3 March 1832, p. 89.
[6] Billington, *Protestant Crusade*, pp. 96-98.
[7] Billington, *Protestant Crusade*, p. 168.
[8] Bodo, *Protestant Clergy*, pp. 169-70.
[9] William Ganna Brownlow, *Americanism Contrasted with Foreignism, Romanism and Bogus Democracy, in Light of Reason, Scripture, in which Certain Demagogues in Tennessee and Elsewhere are Shown in their True Colors* (Nashville: n. p., 1856), pp. 88-89.
[10] Louisa Whitney, *The Burning of the Ursuline Convent* (Boston, n.p., 1877), pp. 1-158.
[11] Thomas T. McAvoy, *A History of Catholic Church in the United States* (Notre Dame: University of Notre Dame Press, 1969), pp. 143-44,170.

One interesting phenomenon of the anti-Catholic movement was the mission response of Protestants. As German and Irish Catholics moved into the west and Jesuit activity grew, American Protestants reacted with a call to missions.[12] Believing the RCC was 'sending men and money into this country, for the purpose of establishing here, the Kingdom of the beast', Protestants desired to counteract that plan.[13] This call to missions extended even beyond the home missions. Fearing Catholics across the world, Protestants urged mission endeavours to convert countries like France.[14] Even the American Bible Society exhibited anti-Catholic impulses in its distribution of scriptures worldwide. Nineteenth-century Protestants from most denominations in America harboured negative feelings toward Roman Catholics. These prejudices surfaced in writings, politics, organisations, missions and, unfortunately, even violence. The bias against the RCC in the US grew more intense as the numbers of Catholics increased. Only a perceived greater issue like the fight over slavery could draw attention from the crusade against the RCC in America.

But how did one of the largest denominations in America, which had played a leading role in the constitutional guarantees of religious liberty in the US, react to a growing RCC? Billington offered scant detailed information on the Baptist reactions in particular. So we ask the question. What was the general Baptist reaction to Catholics during this time? Using similar categories noted in the introduction, we will trace the Baptist reaction to the perceived Roman Catholic threat in nineteenth-century America.

Baptist Anti-Catholic Literature

The written word became by far the most popular weapon in anti-Catholic attacks in the US between 1830 and 1860. Baptists claimed to be liberally tolerant concerning other religious groups, yet Baptist anti-Catholic monographs, pamphlets and periodicals concerning the Catholic question surfaced in great quantities. Baptist publication societies entered the battle as well. In order to grasp the scope of the literary crusade, we will borrow some of James Leo Garrett's categories listed in an article concerning Baptists postures toward Roman Catholics and add a few new ones.[15]

One category of Baptist literature directed against Catholicism might be called historical refutation. Nineteenth-century American Baptists interpreted

---

[12] Goodykoontz, *Home Missions*, p. 31.
[13] Charles I. Foster, *An Errand of Mercy: The Evangelical United Front, 1790-1837* (Chapel Hill: North Carolina University Press, 1960), p. 206.
[14] Whitney R. Cross, *The Burned-Over District: The Social and Intellectual History of Enthusiastic Religion in Western New York, 1800-1850* (Ithaca, NY: Cornell University Press, 1950), p. 231.
[15] James Leo Garrett, 'Polemic, Conversion, and/or Dialogue: Baptist Postures toward the Church at Rome', *Review and Expositor* 60 (Summer, 1963).

the history of the Christian church with a definite anti-Catholic slant. Like most Protestant groups, Baptist historiography used Christian history to refute the RCC and favour Protestant forms. John Dowling served as a prominent Baptist pastor in Philadelphia and New York. A noted speaker and prolific writer, Dowling refuted Catholicism through his *History of Romanism* (1848). In the preface Dowling openly admitted his bias. He believed history revealed the dangerous story of the existence of 'Romanism', its most famous and infamous popes, its tyranny, inquisition, massacres, tortures, burnings and the efforts of the reformers 'to rescue the world from its thralldom'. Dowling intended the work as a reference book for Protestant defence against Jesuitical apologists.[16] He spelled out the purpose of the book clearly:

> To that God, who has declared in the sure word of prophecy, that 'Babylon the Great' must fall, the author humbly commits this book. If the work shall be the means of extending light throughout our yet happy America, upon the history and character of that hierarchal despotism which is straining every nerve to reduce the people of this land to its tyrannical sway, and of arresting the efforts of Rome to spread over the western continent, the darkness, the superstition and the mental and spiritual thralldom of the middle ages, he will feel that he is richly rewarded.[17]

Dowling used derogatory phrases like 'man of sin' in reference to the pope and highlighted supposed Catholic atrocities carried out through the ages. He spent time refuting RCC doctrine as false and contradictory to scripture. Dowling concluded, 'The result of our examination is the solemn conviction – strengthened the more attentively we study the subject – that the "Romish", so far from being the true church is the bitterest foe of all true Churches of Christ'.[18]

Garrett describes another Baptist polemical method as 'rebuttalism or argumentation' directed toward disproving Catholic doctrine and practice.[19] This approach utilised a Baptist view of biblical teaching to support arguments against Catholic doctrine. One particularly hot issue surfaced concerning perceived Roman Catholic opposition to the Bible. William Plumer in *Rome Against the Bible* (1854), published by the American Baptist Publication Society, rebutted the Roman Catholic doctrine of the Bible. Plumer attacked Catholics viciously when he compared 'papists' with the Pharisees of the New Testament. He claimed Roman Catholic priests and Pharisees obstructed light, denied private judgment, rejected Jesus, established their own righteousness, trusted in themselves, exemplified a cruel and persecuting spirit and still won

---

[16] John Dowling, *The History of Romanism: From the Earliest Corruptions of Christianity to the Present Time* (New York: Edward Walker, 1848), p. iii.
[17] Dowling, *History of Romanism*, p. 5.
[18] Dowling, *History of Romanism*, pp. 69-77, 645-46.
[19] Garrett, 'Baptist Postures', p. 320.

the confidence of thousands. Plumer attacked the RCC for holding that scripture is not the only rule of faith, a doctrine which stood in opposition to Baptist thought. He even accused the Catholic church of going further than the Pharisees in subordinating scripture.[20]

Periodical articles rebutting Roman Catholic views appeared weekly. For instance, Baptists attacked the practice of infant baptism. Stephen Ray wrote 'Devil's Ladder to the Papal Throne' in 1851 as part of a running debate on the baptismal regeneration question. Other paedobaptist groups were included in the attack. However, Ray saw infant baptism as one step on the ladder to papal control.[21] An earlier series of articles in the *Baptist* agreed, saying one cannot stop at paedobaptism but must go on to 'popery'.[22] Baptists rebutted Catholic views on sacraments, church organisation, images, the papacy, infallibility, transubstantiation, relics and any other Catholic idea believed to be false.

Perhaps the basest form of literary attack was what Garrett called exposurism.[23] Baptists sought to expose supposed Catholic atrocities. They used near slanderous propaganda to warn others concerning Catholics. Richard Fuller, a pastor in South Carolina, chaired a temperance society committee in 1839 which drafted a memorial to be sent to the legislature. The memorial's purpose was to encourage the restriction of the sale of liquor and it included an anti-Catholic reference:

> When the legislators of a Christian community will regard an enactment to license the retail of ardent spirits with the same abhorrence which they feel toward the statute formerly passed by the Roman Chancery, making assassination and murder, and prostitution and every crime, subjects of license and taxation and regulating the price at which each might be committed.[24]

In a written debate with Bishop John England, Fuller defended the memorial's statement claiming a tax book existed containing the pope's tariff for indulgences. Fuller even called Pope John XXII a blood-sucker who must have chuckled as he concocted a scheme for replenishing church coffers.[25]

---

[20] William S. Plumer, *Rome against the Bible, and the Bible against Rome; or Pharisaism, Jewish and Papal* (Philadelphia: American Baptist Publication Society, 1854), pp. 3-50. See also *Minutes of the Genesee Baptist Association, 1854*, p. 9. A resolution passed indicating the American Baptist Publication Society tried 'to supply poor ministers with small libraries, to counteract the tendencies of an immoral press, to meet the influence of Romanism in our country'.

[21] Stephen Ray, 'The Devil's Ladder to the Papal Throne', *Western Recorder* 4 June 1851, p. 93.

[22] 'Baptism VII', *Baptist* March 1836, p. 234.

[23] Garrett, 'Baptist Postures', p. 324.

[24] Richard Fuller and John England, *Letters Concerning the Roman Chancery* (Baltimore: Fielding Lucas, Jr, 1840), p. 9.

[25] Fuller and England, *Letters*, pp. 14, 16, 21, 54-55, 147-48.

Another example of this form of attack can be seen in Thomas Ford Caldicott's *Hannah Corcoran* (1853). Caldicott, a Baptist pastor in Charlestown, Massachusetts, helped lead Hannah out of Catholicism and into his Baptist church. The book chronicled a supposed abduction and persecution of Hannah by her mother and a Catholic priest. Caldicott tried to expose the Roman Catholic spirit of persecution as immutable. He even quoted a Catholic periodical called *The Shepherd of the Valley*. 'If Catholics ever gain, – what they surely will do, though a distant day, – an immense numerical majority, religious freedom in this country is at an end.' Caldicott used the story to make pointed jabs at the RCC concluding that Catholicism and liberty of conscience cannot co-exist.[26]

Protestants established some periodicals for the sole purpose of anti-Catholic propaganda. Baptists, not only gave column space in their own papers to the issue, but supported multi-denominational anti-Catholic periodicals and even helped produce them.[27] C.C.P. Crosby, a Baptist, purchased the *Reformation Advocate* in 1833 changing its name to the *Protestant*. The magazine proposed to prove that anyone who felt 'popery' had changed was deceived. Crosby called 'popery' a most harmful force that destroys holy truth.[28] Some Baptist periodicals expressed anti-Catholic purposes. *The True Light and Baptist Monthly Visitor* (1837) explained, 'When we hear and see the extensive progress that Papists are making in our country – when they have almost crossed our threshold – it is high time that we should awake to the interests of the Christian church.'[29] Baptists engaged heavily in the use of the written word to attack Roman Catholic beliefs, history and activity.

Baptists and Anti-Catholic Organisations

Many Baptists expressed reservations concerning Protestant anti-Catholic organisations. The *New York Baptist Register* in an 1842 article considered organisational involvement 'questionable' since Baptists did not admit to being Protestant.[30] However, an editorial in the same periodical earlier commented on a Protestant meeting designed to resist the papacy. The editor admitted apprehension to opposing the RCC through organisations while agreeing to the

---

[26] Thomas Ford Caldicott, *Hannah Corcoran: An Authentic Narrative of her Conversion from Romanism, her Abduction from Charlestown, and the Treatment she Received during her Absence* (Boston: Gould and Lincoln, 1853), pp. iii-v, 21-23. Caldicott stated that an added purpose was to help Catholics break from the chains of spiritual bondage and show them that Protestants only felt kindness toward them.
[27] 'The Protestant Platform', *New York Baptist Register* 8 April 1842, p. 32.
[28] 'Introduction', *Protestant* September 1833, pp. 1-3.
[29] 'Proposals for Publishing a Religious Paper in the Town of Jonesborough, to be Entitled—The True Light and Baptist Monthly Visitor', *Baptist* 1 February 1837, p. 18.
[30] 'The Protestant Platform', *New York Baptist Register* 8 April 1842, p. 32.

need for a more visible unity among Evangelicals. He suggested an alternative plan of converting, preaching and praying.[31]

However, Baptists generally supported anti-Catholic organisations. In January of 1831 the editors of the *Protestant* organised the first society to combat Catholicism. It lapsed for a while but was revived in 1832. The adopted constitution purposed 'to promote the principles of the Reformation by public discussion which shall illustrate the history and character of Popery'.[32] Nearly 300, including Baptists, attended the first meeting of the New York Protestant Association. Baptist meeting houses provided space for some of the debates. On 28 May 1832 nearly 500 gathered at the First Baptist Church on Pearl Street in Brooklyn.[33]

On 8 November 1842 several ministers in Philadelphia issued an invitation to Protestants to form an association. The invitation praised the Reformation of the sixteenth century and called respondents to protect their freedoms against an apostasy 'which for many centuries had blinded and oppressed a large portion of mankind'. Baptist pastors A.D. Gillette and George B. Ide signed the invitation.[34] Baptist churches responded, sending messengers to the meeting, including the Baptist ministers Burrow, Aldrich and Dodge. Ide served on a committee consisting of one representative from each denomination to prepare the association constitution. The new organisation, the American Protestant Association, hoped to aid the education of congregations on 'popery', highlight the distribution and study of scripture, circulate books on the errors of 'popery' and awaken attention to the dangers of Romanism in the United States.[35]

M.J. Gonsalves, an ex-Roman Catholic turned Baptist, served the American Protestant Society established in 1844 as a missionary and colporteur in Madeira, Trinidad and the United States. He visited many Baptist associations explaining the society's purpose and collecting funds.[36] Baptist papers like the *Christian Watchman, New York Recorder* and *Baptist Banner* reported on the society's functions.[37] Numerous Baptist associations passed resolutions of support for the society. Following a report by Herman Norton, the

---

[31] 'Editorial', *New York Baptist Register* 10 April 1840, p. 35.
[32] Billington, *Protestant Crusade*, p. 58.
[33] 'New York Protestant Association', *Protestant* 26 May 1832, p. 161; 'New York Protestant Association', *Protestant* 2 June 1832, p. 169.
[34] *Address of the Board of Managers of the American Protestant Association; with the Constitution and Organization of the Association* (Philadelphia: no pub., 1843), p. 5.
[35] *Address of the Board of American Protestant Association*, p. 7.
[36] M.J. Gonsalves, *Testimony of a Convert from the Church of Rome* (Boston: no pub., 1859).
[37] 'American Protestant Society', *Christian Watchman* 24 May 1849, p. 83; 'Special Notices', *New York Recorder* 10 May 1848, p. 23; 'American Protestant Society', *New York Recorder* 17 May 1848, p. 28; 'Letter from the Corresponding Secretary to the Executive Committee of the American Protestant Society', *Baptist Banner* 8 October 1846, p. 157.

corresponding secretary of the society, the Hudson River Baptist Association in 1847 resolved 'that the American Protestant Society, whose Corresponding Secretary, Rev. Herman Norton, had addressed this association, is worthy the confidence of the churches of this body, and is hereby commended to their Christian cooperation'. Similar resolutions appeared in the minutes of the Pennsylvania Baptist Convention (1845) and the Georgia Baptist Convention (1846), showing the northern and southern reach of the society.[38]

In 1844 a league of Presbyterian, Baptist and Methodist ministers formed in Louisville, Kentucky, for the purpose of conducting lectures against the doctrines of Rome. Two Baptists, F.A. Willard and T.S. Malcom, aided in its formation. The league conducted a series of lectures in various churches, including Baptist, on subjects such as purgatory and the apocrypha and published a semi-monthly paper called the *True Catholic*.[39]

In 1849 Protestants organised the American and Foreign Christian Union. A *Western Recorder* article applauded its specific work. 'Popery is justly regarded as a greater obstacle to the spread of truth than Mohammedanism or Paganism. When the former is removed the latter will soon follow.'[40] Other papers like the *Christian Watchman, New York Baptist Register,* and the *Christian Times* gave the union similar positive press.[41] The New Jersey Baptist Association, New Haven Baptist Association of Connecticut, the Philadelphia Baptist Association, the Connecticut Baptist Convention, the Indiana Baptist Convention and the New York Baptist Convention approved resolutions of support.[42] Baptists also supported the union monetarily. Baptist pecuniary gifts

---

[38] *Minutes of the Hudson River Baptist Association of New York, 1847*, pp. 22, 24; 'Resolution of the Hudson River Baptist Association', *American Protestant* August 1847, p. 93; *Minutes of the Pennsylvania Baptist Convention for Missionary Purposes, 1845*, p. 8; 'Baptist Convention at Griffin, Ga.', *American Protestant* July 1848, p. 57.

[39] Sister Agnes McGann, *Nativism in Kentucky to 1860* (Washington, D.C.: The Catholic University of America Press, 1944), p. 6; 'Another Hero of the League', *Catholic Advocate* 16 March 1844, p. 55; William Brownlow Posey, *Religious Strife on the Southern Frontier* (Baton Rouge: Louisiana State University Press, 1965), p. 107.

[40] 'American and Foreign Christian Union', *Western Recorder* 26 November 1851, p. 228.

[41] 'American and Foreign Christian Union', *Christian Watchman* 6 June 1850, p. 90; 'New York Anniversaries', *New York Baptist Register* 19 May 1853, p. 66; 'Religious Liberty', *Christian Times* 9 February 1854.

[42] 'The New Jersey Baptist Association', *American and Foreign Christian Union* October 1850, p. 458; *Minutes of the New Jersey Baptist Association of New Jersey, 1850*, p. 11; 'Extract from the Minutes of the New Haven Baptist Association, held in Southington, Conn.', *American and Foreign Christian Union* January 1852, p. 26; *Minutes of the Philadelphia Baptist Association of Pennsylvania, 1851*, p. 20; *Minutes of the Connecticut Baptist Convention, 1852*, p. 20; *Minutes of the Indiana State Baptist Convention, 1851*, p. 9; *Minutes of the New York Baptist Convention, 1857*, pp. 6-7.

came to the union from at least twenty-four states extending as far north as Maine, as far south as Georgia and as far west as Iowa and Mississippi.[43]

New York Baptists even established a Baptist Protestant Society. The First Baptist Church in Brooklyn, New York, became concerned over the prevalence of 'Romanism' in America and the increased propagation efforts by Roman Catholics. As a result, the China Mission Society of the First Baptist Church recommended the formation of a Protestant society. The Baptist Protestant Society formed as an auxiliary of the American Protestant Society:

> Resolved, that the Society heretofore known as the China Mission Society of the First Baptist Church in Brooklyn, drop its distinctive name, and become, at such time as the Society determines, auxiliary to the American Protestant Society of the city of New York. June 27, 1847.[44]

Thus Baptists in the northeastern and western US readily involved themselves in the anti-Catholic Protestant organisations of the period. Even some Southern Baptists like those in Georgia expressed support.

Baptists and Political Organisations

While Baptist attitudes toward the RCC appeared almost exclusively negative, a political solution to the problem did not prove amenable to all Baptists. The *Western Recorder* ran several articles opposing political activity for Baptist ministers. It attacked ministers who used the pulpits to urge partisan voting. The magazine even boldly suggested ministers who did so should resign. 'The Lord does not have ministers to use any carnal weapons in his behalf for the purpose of maintaining his honor on earth.'[45]

Nevertheless, some Baptists actively engaged in an expressly nativistic and anti-Catholic political activity. Several Baptist papers urged members to utilise the right of voting to accomplish their goals. Baptists also aligned themselves with the new nativist movement targeted at political action. In June 1843 local native American associations in New York came together to form the American Republican Party. The party originally formed to stand against Bishop Hughes 'who would turn the Bible out of our schools, and overthrow the foundation of our free institutions'. The *New York Baptist Register* explained that when corrupt politicians sacrificed true public interests to secure the aid of Roman

---

[43] 'Receipts', *American and Foreign Christian Union,* November 1850 – December 1856. Many Baptists became life members based on donations of $30.00. Most were pastors of Baptist churches.
[44] 'Another Sign of the Times', *American Protestant* November 1847, pp. 172-73.
[45] 'Politicians', *Western Recorder* 8 February 1857; 'Clerical Politicians in the North', *Western Recorder* 29 March 1854.

bishops, the spirit of the great mass of native Americans would raise up a standard against them.[46]

William Buck, editor of the *Baptist Banner*, printed the platform of the American Republican Party which called for a twenty-one-year naturalisation law, natives only in office, every man's right to worship as he pleased, limitations on immigration to avoid the introduction of political and religious disputes from other countries and the presentation of a pure and uncorrupted elective franchise.[47] Although the platform never blatantly claimed to be anti-Catholic, in practice foreign Catholic immigrants became the key target.

The most powerful expression of nativist political action with anti-Catholic attitudes surfaced in the form of the American or Know Nothing Party in 1854. Many Baptists supported the new party. J.R. Graves, known for his leadership in the Landmark movement among Baptists, surfaced as an adamant supporter of the Know Nothing Party. Graves wrote an article in the *Tennessee Baptist* (1854) predicting the new party would sweep the next elections. Describing the political scene, Graves called other political parties corrupt, Congress a shameful scene of drunkenness and the increasing foreign element fearful. He accused candidates of pandering for Catholic votes. Graves desired the protection of Protestant interests:

> Thousands and hundreds of thousands of American citizens and Christians who love their country better than party, and who nobly prefer to struggle and sacrifice even blood if it shall need it, to perpetuate this glorious legacy of our hero fathers, and martyrs of the Revolution, rather than to wrangle and prostitute their principles for the spoils of party, are banding together determined to Know Nothing but the safety and best good of their country, and of their whole country.[48]

While Graves endorsed the party through his paper, other Baptists endorsed it by participation. Daniel Clarke Eddy, a Baptist pastor in Lowell, Massachusetts, ran for and was elected to the Massachusetts State Legislature under the Know Nothing banner. He characterised ministers as ex-officio politicians with a duty to speak on the political obligation of man.[49] In his sermon, 'The Times and the Men for the Times', preached in 1854, Eddy listed the elements that threatened the US. 'Romanism' deserved inclusion because she wielded more power than the president and his cabinet. Rome would not shoot citizens, Eddy argued, but would suppress schools, control the ballot box, overthrow the press and silence the pulpit. Eddy suggested a requirement of

---

[46] 'The Native American Party', *New York Baptist Register* 19 April 1844, p. 42.
[47] 'Change of Character', *Baptist Banner* 14 November 1844.
[48] 'Know Nothings', *Tennessee Baptist* 26 August 1854.
[49] D.C. Eddy, *The Commonwealth: Political Rights of Ministers: A Sermon Preached on Fast Day, April 6, 1854* (Boson: Dayton and Wentworth, 1854), pp. 4, 19, 21.

fifteen to twenty-five years before a foreigner could vote, with reading and writing also being qualifications.[50]

Other Baptists engaged in party politics under the Know Nothing banner. Colonel James G. Hardy ran for Lieutenant Governor in Kentucky as the American candidate. The *Covington Journal* noted that he had been a member of a Baptist church for many years. Another Baptist, E.B. Bartlett, served as the president of the national council of the American Party.[51]

It should also be noted that some Baptists opposed the Know Nothing Party. In November of 1854 the *Religious Herald* printed an article accusing the American Party of holding principles of intolerance. The article called the Know Nothing Party the wrong method of dealing with Catholics.[52] J.L.M. Curry used harsh terms in referring to the party:

> That truism is only prefatory to my expressions of abhorrence for the recent anti-republican development of opinion, as exhibited in the 'Know Nothing' organization. In my humble opinion, nullification, succession, U.S. Bank, Mexican War, and such like existing questions were harmless to the government in comparison with this stupendous and far-spreading leprosy.[53]

Curry accused the party of espionage which would ruin the government if not stopped. He regarded principles of the party as ridiculous, believing the need to exclude foreigners was a minor issue compared to proscribing faith and taking away freedom of speech. Curry certainly entertained no pro-Catholic ideas but he rejected anything 'that militates against the individuality of character and the right of private judgment'. No doubt Curry's Baptist views on freedom of conscience and religious liberty guided his stance.[54]

Baptists and Anti-Catholic Violence

Unfortunately between 1830 and 1860, the US endured several instances of anti-Catholic violence. But fortunately, little evidence exists to connect Baptists directly to the violence. Baptist papers and associational minutes condemned the violent phase of nineteenth-century anti-Catholicism. After the burning of the convent in Charlestown, Massachusetts, in 1834 the *Christian Gazette* expressed Baptist disgust over the incident in an article entitled 'Disgraceful

---

[50] Eddy, *The Commonwealth*, pp. 34, 40-45.
[51] 'Col. James G. Hardy—A Sketch of His History', *Covington Journal* 16 June 1855; 'E.B. Bartlett, Esq.', *Covington Journal* 16 June 1855.
[52] 'Observations in Baltimore, No. 2', *Virginia Religious Herald* 9 November 1854, p. 174.
[53] J.L.M. Curry to C.C. Clay, 30 June 1854, Clement Claiborne Clay Papers and Letters, Duke University, Durham, NC.
[54] Curry to Clay, 30 June 1854.

Outrage, Nunnery Burnt'.[55] The *Christian Watchman* of Boston echoed that same distaste for violence and admitted a disbelief concerning a sufficient number of 'unprincipled beings in human form, who would so surrender themselves to the baser passions, as to perpetrate such acts of lawless violence'.[56] The Philadelphia riots in 1844 received similar treatment from Baptist periodicals. The *New York Baptist Register* claimed the riots cast deep disgrace on the American population.[57] The violence connected with the Know Nothing Party in the 1850s produced equal outrage from Baptists. Robert Middleditch addressed the New Jersey Baptist Convention in 1854 condemning the violence that erupted in Newark. He called the people who committed such violence 'professed' Protestants but unconverted. 'Bloody Monday' election riots which occurred 5 August 1855 in Louisville, Kentucky, caused deep mortification for Baptists. The *Western Recorder* called it a disgrace to the city and believed the gospel could do more than civil enactments to stop such events.[58]

Although Baptists generally abhorred the anti-Catholic violence, they followed suit with other Protestants in shifting the blame for such acts to the Catholics. For instance, a *Christian Watchman* article claimed Jesuit involvement contributed to the burning of the convent in Charlestown. Jesuit deception, lack of public inspection of the convent and even Bishop Fenwick were cited as causes for the violence.[59]

Baptist Missions and Anti-Catholic Impulses

At the opening of the nineteenth century Baptists in the US received a mission impulse from William Carey through a group of Congregational missionaries turned Baptist. No doubt Carey's view of the Great Commission served as the key motivation for American Baptist missions in the beginning. However, as the Catholic issue heated up between 1830 and 1860, anti-Catholic motivations entered missions rhetoric. In 1835 J. Going moved at the annual meeting of the Baptist Home Mission Society for a mission solution to the Catholic problem:

> ...and that in all our efforts to prevent the baleful influence of Romanism, our only weapons should be those of moral influence, and the chief thing to be attempted is, by prayer and the preaching of the gospel and kind offices to seek,

---

[55] 'Disgraceful Outrage, Nunnery Burnt', *Christian Gazette* 22 August 1834, p. 382.
[56] 'Burning of the Convent at Charlestown', *Christian Watchman* 15 August 1834, p. 131.
[57] 'Philadelphia Riots', *New York Baptist Register* 7 June 1844, p. 70.
[58] 'Election Riots and Mob Law in Louisville', *Western Recorder* 15 August 1855.
[59] 'Destruction of the Charlestown Convent', *Christian Gazette* 31 October 1834, pp. 118-20. This article cites the Baptist periodical *Christian Watchman*.

with the blessing of God, the conversion of the souls of Catholics to Jesus Christ.[60]

Baptists saw Roman Catholics as non-believers and in need of evangelisation.

Growing numbers of Roman Catholics in the US added fuel to the mission call. Baptists believed the eyes of all Europe looked to the US with great interest. 'Popery' had shown a great 'inward heaving of ambition' towards America to compensate for her losses in the old country. Baptists accused Rome of sending emissaries to the US to survey the new world with the goal of possessing it.[61] The Baptist Home Mission Society said thousands came annually and are 'located at places selected with systematic regard' to gain influence in the United States. The 'papal' immigrants were believed to be disciplined to the will of their spiritual guides and practised habits incongruent with American life.[62] A *Western Recorder* article estimated 1,600 priests and 1,700 Catholic churches in America in 1855, with immigration cited as the cause for such numbers.[63]

The Western Baptist Convention saw Catholicism as a major reason for home mission efforts. They accused the RCC of warring with God's saints and opposing religion and scripture:

> …until it can be shown that Heathenism, is more to be abhorred and dreaded than Catholicism; and until it can be shown, that on some other portion of the globe the cause of human rights depends more essentially, than upon this republic, your committee will not yield the position they have taken, in favor of Home missions.[64]

Similar statements came in from Texas, California, Oregon and Canada.

The Catholic problem also motivated foreign missions. The *American Baptist* magazine printed several articles concerning the religious condition of France and the need for more Protestant mission effort. A Professor Chase noted that the priests were numerous and owned the religious favour of the

---

[60] *Third Report of the Executive Committee of the American Baptist Home Mission Society* (New York: American Baptist Home Mission Society, 1835), p. 12.

[61] *Minutes of the Connecticut Baptist Convention, 1847*, p. 15.

[62] 'Reasons for Vigilance and Activity', *Fifteenth Report of the Executive Committee of the American Baptist Home Mission Society* (New York: American Baptist Home Mission Society, 1847), p. 17; 'Popish Efforts—Protestant Supineness', *Twelfth Report of the Executive Committee of the American Baptist Home Mission Society* (New York: American Baptist Home Mission Society, 1844), pp. 61-62.

[63] 'The Intolerant Spirit of Romanism', *Western Recorder* 1 August 1855.

[64] 'Proceedings of the Second Anniversary of the General Convention of Western Baptists at Cincinnati commencing Nov. 4, 1835; including the First Annual Meeting of the Western Baptist Educational Society held Nov. 5, 1835', *Baptist Advocate* December 1835, pp. 272-73.

people. They christened infants and pagan children. He gladly reported that many Roman Catholics would listen to Protestant preachers.[65] Baptists also expressed concern for Catholic Ireland largely because of the growing number of Irish Catholics in the United States. The Home Mission Society reported the religious condition of Ireland in terms of money. Irish Catholic clergy were said to receive seven million dollars a year from the people for services which included confession and purgatory prayers. This burden on the people was seen as reason to bring them to conversion.[66] Southern Baptists targeted Italy later in 1870 for similar reasons.

Conclusion

Although many Baptists of nineteenth-century America claimed not to be Protestant, most aligned themselves with Protestants when a common enemy was perceived. Baptists participated actively in the main avenues of expressing anti-Catholic prejudice during the nineteenth century. They engaged in prejudicial writing often vicious in character. Baptists supported and participated in anti-Catholic organisational efforts. In fact, New York Baptists formed a society for that purpose. Some were involved politically although other Baptists discouraged such activity. Baptists, however, for the most part condemned violence directed at Catholics, perhaps because of the long-standing Baptist belief in religious liberty.

By far the most common method selected by Baptists in confronting Roman Catholicism was missions. Baptists home and foreign mission efforts treated Catholics as unbelievers. Mission anti-Catholic rhetoric often bordered on slander. Baptists perceived missions and evangelism as the best biblical response to a Catholic threat worldwide. Generally American Baptists supported the Protestant establishment and saw the RCC as a dangerous threat to true Christianity and the American way of life.

---

[65] 'Professor Chase's Letter to Reply to Certain Inquiries Respecting the Religious State of France', *American Baptist* September 1833, pp. 325-26.
[66] 'Financial Statements of the Church of Rome in Ireland', *Sixteenth Report of the Executive Committee of the American Baptist Home Mission Society* (New York: American Baptist Home Mission Society, 1848), p. 77.

PART THREE

Baptists in the Twentieth Century

CHAPTER 7

Baptists and Church Unity in Wales in the Twentieth Century

Michael J. Collis

The twentieth century was a significant period for change politically and ecclesiastically in Wales. In late Victorian Britain Wales was thought of by many as little more than a geographical area and not as a distinct nation within the United Kingdom. There was an infamous entry in the *Encyclopaedia Britannica* which read 'for Wales, see England'.[1] However, there was at the time the beginning of national self-consciousness. Tom Ellis, who was elected the Liberal M.P. for Merioneth in 1886, was a staunch advocate of home rule for Ireland and his election manifesto was the first to include self-government for Wales.[2] In 1914 E.T. John, the Liberal M.P. for East Denbighshire, introduced into the House of Commons a private member's bill for Welsh Home Rule. It proceeded no further than its formal first reading. However, there was little enthusiasm for Welsh Home Rule apart from E.T. John's wife, Beriah Gwynfe Evans, and a few churchmen of nationalist outlook such as the Anglican layman, J. Arthur Price,[3] and the Baptist minister, the Rev. Gwilym Oswald Griffith.[4] It was not until 1997 that devolved government was set up in Wales following elections to the National Assembly of Wales.

At the beginning of the twentieth century the Christian faith in Wales seemed in an impregnable position, but by the dawn of the twenty-first century Wales had become a secular post-Christian society. The Evan Roberts Revival

---

[1] Kenneth O. Morgan, *Rebirth of a Nation: Wales 1980-1980* (Oxford: Oxford University Press & University of Wales Press, 1982), p. 3.
[2] 'Ellis, T(homas) E(dward) (1859-99)', John Davies *et al.* (eds), *The Welsh Academy Encyclopaedia of Wales* (Cardiff: University of Wales Press, 2008), p. 252.
[3] Morgan, *Rebirth of a Nation*, p. 119. For John Arthur Price (1861-1942), see *The Dictionary of Welsh Biography, 1941-1970* (London: The Honourable Society of Cymmrodorion, 2002), p. 211; and for the Rev. Gwilym Oswald Griffith (1882-1972), see *The Baptist Union Directory*, 1973-74 (London: Baptist Union of Great Britain and Ireland, 1973), p. 289.
[4] Gwilym O. Griffith, *The New Wales: Some Aspects of National Idealism with a Plea for Welsh Home Rule*. Introduction by E.T. John, Esq., M.P. (Liverpool: Hugh Evans & Sons, 1913).

swept through Wales in 1904-05 and the Baptist Union of Wales *Handbook* for 1905 noted that there were 24,651 *baptisms* in 1904. However, it is widely recognised that it was the 1914-18 War that marked a change in the fortunes of the Christian Church in Wales, initiating a period of persistent decline.[5]

In 1901 most Baptist churches in Wales were in membership with either the Baptist Union of Great Britain and Ireland (BUGBI, often known in Wales as the 'English Union') or the Baptist Union of Wales and Monmouthshire (BUW), while some churches were in membership with both Unions.[6] Both Unions subsequently simplified their names: the English Union dropping the words 'and Ireland' in 1988 and the Welsh Union the words 'and Monmouthshire' in 1959. The churches in the English Union were English-speaking while the majority of churches in the Welsh Union were Welsh-speaking. Statistically the Baptist denomination lost some ground in the decade 1910-1920, but, with the exception of the Breconshire and East Glamorgan Associations, some of the lost ground was regained during the middle twenties, and the total membership showed some small gains between 1920 and 1930.[7] In the following decades the membership declined as shown in Table 1 for the period 1901-1971. Table 2 shows the decline in the numbers of pastors serving Baptist churches in Wales between 1991 and 2001.[8]

Table 1: Statistics for Baptist Churches in Wales and Monmouthshire 1901-1971[6]

Year	Churches	Branches	Church members	Sunday School scholars	Pastors in charge	Baptisms
1901	835	922	105,566	119,373	543	
1911	921	1024	126,863	140,493	596	
1914	940	1047	124,795	140,810	527	
1921	939	1048	123,798	134,696	550	
1931	953	96	124,891	126,333	524	3,986
1941	958	98	115,833	97,945	538	2,679
1951	960	62	105,214	73,416	420	1,989
1961	948	47	91,802	51,950*	433	1,601
1971	925	53	69,515	32,701**	373	644

*42,666 children under 14 plus 9,284 young people 14-20

---

[5] See, for example, D. Densil Morgan, The Span of the Cross: Christian Religion and Society in Wales, 1914-2000 (Cardiff: University of Wales Press, 1999).
[6] BUW is a union of associations and not churches, and so Baptist churches are in membership with the Union by virtue of their membership of an association.
[7] T.M. Bassett, The Welsh Baptists (Swansea: Ilston House, 1977), p. 392.
[8] Figures for the years 1901-71 are taken from the Baptist Handbook (London: Baptist Union of Great Britain and Ireland).

** 25,373 children under 14 plus 7,328 young people 14-20

Table 2
Numbers of Pastors serving Baptist Churches in Wales in 1991 and 2001
(excluding independent Baptist Churches and Baptist churches in membership with the Associating Evangelical Churches of Wales)[9]

	1991	2001
The Baptist Union of Wales	134	116
North Wales English Baptist Union of The Baptist Union of Great Britain	12	11
South Wales Area of The Baptist Union of Great Britain	87	72
Baptist Churches in the Fellowship of Independent Evangelical Churches	4	10
Total number of pastors	237	209

Ecumenical Movement until 1914

By the end of the nineteenth century there was a desire among some for the visible unity of the church in fulfilment of Christ's prayer that his people might be one (John 17:22). The 1888 Lambeth Conference of Anglican bishops issued a call for church unity. The four essential points were: (i) the acceptance of the Bible as the rule and ultimate standard of faith; (ii) the acceptance of the Apostles' Creed as a baptismal creed and the Nicene creed as an a sufficient declaration of the Christian faith; (iii) the acceptance of the two sacraments, baptism and the Lord's Supper; and (iv) the acceptance of the historic episcopate, with its administrative methods 'adapted to the needs of the nations and people whom God calls to the unity of his Church'. This declaration was important because in Wales it modified Anglican attitudes to the question of unity with other churches.[10] Other denominations formed international bodies, the World Alliance of Reformed and Presbyterian Churches (1875), the Methodist Ecumenical Conference (1881), the World Congregational Conference (1891), and the Baptist World Alliance (1905). However, R. Tudur

---

[9] Numbers are taken from the *Baptist Union Directory*, 1992 & 2002 (Didcot: Baptist Union of Great Britain) and *Llawlyfr/ Handbook*, 1992 and 2002 (Abertawe/Swansea: Undeb Bedyddwyr Cymru /Baptist Union of Wales). Information for FIEC churches was supplied by Rod Baddams, administrator, The Fellowship of Independent Evangelical Churches.

[10] R. Tudur Jones, *Faith and the Crisis of a Nation: Wales, 1890-1914*, ed. Robert Pope (Cardiff: University of Wales Press, 2004), p. 49.

Jones has pointed out that 'if new bodies had any influence at all, they tended to intensify denominational pride'.[11]

At the local level co-operation between the various Nonconformist denominations was often good and John Jones, the historian of the Radnorshire Baptists, contrasted the situation in 1895 with that in 1840s: 'There was not much talk then as there is now of the Baptists and Congregationalists amalgamating.'[12] In 1901 there was a joint assembly of the Baptist Union of Great Britain and Ireland and the Congregational Union of England and Wales. Even though the only difference between Baptists and Congregationalists was on the subject of baptism, many Congregationalists preferred to look to the Presbyterians for unity.[13]

One of the chief promoters of fuller co-operation between the denominations was Owen Owen (1850-1920), the headmaster of Oswestry High School and chief examiner for the Mid Wales Board between 1897 and 1915. In 1889 he corresponded with no fewer than 200 denominational leaders and persuaded them that it would be a good idea to discuss church unity. Some twenty-six of them met at Tabernacle, the Welsh Independent chapel at Shrewsbury, on 22 and 23 April 1890 to discuss possibilities and it was decided to recommend to their denominations the formation of a Union of Welsh Nonconformists in order to ensure more effective co-operation 'with regard to social, moral and spiritual questions'. A general conference was held in Swansea in October 1891 and although subsequent meetings were held it made little contribution to the permanent co-operation between the denominations.[14]

The specifically Welsh Nonconformist Union lost some of its appeal because of interest in the corresponding movement in the whole of England and Wales. After its Manchester congress in 1892, the National Free Church Council was established, and immediately began to set up local councils throughout England and Wales, each containing representatives from local Evangelical churches. The National Council was not comprised of official representatives from the denominations, but rather committed and interested individuals. There were those who wanted the movement to be more tightly organised and as a result the National Council of Evangelical Free Churches was formed with the Carmarthen-born Wesleyan Methodist Hugh Price Hughes as its first president. There was considerable enthusiasm for the National Council in Wales and by 1908 167 local councils had been established.

By 1908 about a dozen denominations in Wales belonged to the National Council. The most prominent exceptions were the Baptists, for whom

---

[11] Jones, *Faith and the Crisis of a Nation*, p. 54.
[12] John Jones, *The History of Baptists in Radnorshire* (London: Elliot Stock, 1895), p. 61.
[13] J.H.Y. Briggs, *The English Baptists of the Nineteenth Century* (A History of English Baptists, 3; Didcot: Baptist Historical Society, 1994), pp. 239-41.
[14] Jones, *Faith and the Crisis of a Nation*, pp. 55-56.

communion was the stumbling block. In the Cardiff meetings, 12-14 March 1901, for instance, the 'Alliance' (as it was called in the Welsh-language press) arranged for communion to be administered at one of its meetings. This naturally offended the Welsh Baptists because it violated their conviction that only those baptised on profession of their faith should attend communion. The Welsh Baptists tried many times to explain their position. The Anglesey Assembly, for instance, passed a strong motion in June 1899 stating 'that it would be a great error for us to join the Alliance of Free Churches', because it would be contrary to their principles and would 'endanger our honesty and consistency'. The Baptist Union also corresponded with officials of the National Council in London, and in Rhymney in 1899 the Union declared its willingness to co-operate on condition that no branch of the Alliance was permitted to celebrate communion. However, the officials in London were unyielding. The Baptist Union could not approve the answer it received from them and subsequently it had no choice but to withdraw from the Alliance.[15]

Unquestionably, the issue of admission to communion was a significant barrier to co-operation of the Free Churches in Wales and sometimes even between Baptist churches in the principality. However, some Baptist churches in Wales were adopting open communion. As early as 1861 the Denbigh, Flint and Merioneth Association saw the formation of a Welsh Baptist Union as a bulwark against the open communion tendencies of the English-speaking churches.[16] In his presidential address in 1897 to the Radnorshire and Montgomeryshire Baptist Association, the oldest association in Wales founded in 1790, Thomas Edmunds, of Newtown, said, 'It is a grievous fact that our associated churches are not as united as they used to be in the past. The practise [sic] of open communion has crept in like a thief in the night, has robbed those few churches, it has attacked their fidelity to the truth and their loyalty to the great principles for which are forefathers were so cruelly treated.'[17] By a large majority in June 1899 the delegates passed a motion requiring all member churches to observe close communion. Those churches which had allowed non-Baptists (that is, those not baptised as believers) to sit at the Lord's Table were permitted to allow them to remain as communicants but these churches were not permitted to allow any further admissions to the Table of those who had not been baptised. The Baptist church at Sarn, Montgomeryshire, was practising open communion and so it withdrew from the Welsh association and joined the Shropshire Baptist Association.[18] However, its sister church at Cwm, which

---

[15] Jones, *Faith and the Crisis of a Nation*, pp. 56-57.

[16] Bassett, *The Welsh Baptists*, p. 338.

[17] Thomas Edmunds, 'Our Privileges and Duties: A Circular Letter to the Churches of the Radnorshire and Montgomeryshire Baptist Association For the Year 1897 and A Report of the Annual Meeting held at Presteign, June 2nd and 3rd 1897'.

[18] Minutes of the Sarn Baptist Church Members' Meetings held on 14 & 28 June and 20 September 1899.

shared the same pastor, continued to observe close communion and remained in membership with the Welsh Association.[19] William Edwards, principal of the South Wales Baptist College, provided a strong defence of practice of close communion in a book written for the Welsh and English Baptist Sunday School Unions of Wales.[20] As the English associations in South Wales tended towards open communion, in 1907 ten churches formed the Glamorgan English Strict Baptist Association and by 1916 there were sixteen churches in membership. T.W. Chance, tutor and later principal of the South Wales Baptist College, was a personal member of the association.[21] However, in 1912 three churches left this association, which appears to have closed the following year when the churches rejoined the existing Baptist associations, which contained both open and close communion churches. One of the churches which belonged to the short-lived Glamorgan Strict Baptist Association was Llandaff Road, Cardiff, whose minister, Robert Lloyd, had served as president of the Baptist Union of Wales in 1884.[22] Gradually Baptist churches in Wales adopted open communion and by the year 2000 Nantgwyn Baptist Church, Radnorshire, was the only church in the Radnorshire and Montgomeryshire Association still observing close communion.

The need for army chaplains during World War I meant that Baptist ministers, whatever their views on admission to the Lord's Supper, co-operated with ministers of other denominations. The Territorial Force was created in 1908, its own Chaplains' Department was formed and a Baptist chaplain was attached to the 3rd Welsh Field Ambulance on the outbreak of war.[23] Despite being formally recognised by the army, neither Baptists nor the Congregationalists had any commissioned or acting chaplains when war broke out. However, by the end of August 1914 temporary or acting commissions were granted to ministers of these denominations.[24] E.L. Watson, an Australian Baptist serving in London, was the first Baptist chaplain [25] and he was followed

---

[19] Open communion at Sarn appears to have been introduced during the ministry of Dr Arthur George Jones (1895-98). He served previously as minister of (open communion) churches of the Free Will Baptist Conference of Nova Scotia at Halifax (1889-91) and Beaver River and Sandford (1892-93).

[20] William Edwards, *A Handbook of the Lord's Supper Designed Mainly for Young People* (Bristol: W. Crofton Hemmons, 1904), pp. 121-66.

[21] Bassett, *The Welsh Baptists*, p. 337, and information in *Llawlyfr/ Handbook*, 1909-1914, (Abertawe/Swansea: Undeb Bedyddwyr Cymru /The Baptist Union of Wales).

[22] His memoir (*The Baptist Handbook for 1925*, p. 314) does not mention that his church, Llandaff Road, Cardiff, was in membership with the Glamorgan English Strict Baptist Association, from 1908 to 1912.

[23] Michael Snape, *The Royal Army Chaplains' Department: Clergy Under Fire* (Studies in Modern British Religious History, 18; Woodbridge: Boydell, 2008), pp. 182-83.

[24] Snape, *Royal Army Chaplains' Department*, p. 199.

[25] Edward Lodge Watson was pastor of West End, Hammersmith, and had served as a denominational evangelist in Victoria, Australia, 1909-11.

shortly by W.C. Charteris from Scotland, T.N. Tatersall from England and Thomas Jones from Wales.[26] Densil Morgan concluded from lists published in the denominational handbooks that 14 Welsh Anglican clergymen, 8 Calvinistic Methodists, 10 Baptists and 14 Congregational ministers served in a full-time capacity with the Welsh regiments.[27] In fact 12 ministers from Baptist churches in Wales became army chaplains. In addition Thomas Tudor Rhys, a student from Regent's Park College, and A.E.O. Jones, W.E. Jones, and A.M. Rees, students from the North Wales Baptist College, served as chaplains. A.E. O. Jones later transferred to the Presbyterian Church of Wales, while Thomas Tudor Rhys and Abraham Morgan Rees subsequently served as Baptist pastors in Wales.[28] W.E. Jones initially enlisted in the ranks and he was wounded. At the request of the Welsh Baptist Union he was accepted as a chaplain and was ordained in Caersalem Caernarfon with that in mind. He was later killed in France.[29] In all, nine army chaplains returned to Wales to serve Baptist churches in the principality. The Great War had a considerable impact on all those who served as chaplains as well as other men in the army. W.C. Charteris preached the gospel during a revivalist-type rally attended by eight to nine hundred Welsh troops who had walked through gale force winds and torrential rain in order to attend. The rally was likened to an 'Evan Roberts' revival meeting with soldiers praying and weeping in repentance before God. Unusually at such a revival meeting the Lord's Supper was celebrated.[30] The willingness of Charteris to conduct the Lord's Supper under such circumstances is remarkable, since he had been pastor of the Scotch Baptist Church at Westray, Orkney, from 1905 to1909. It was said of a Scotch Baptist Church that the discipline of such a church was 'uncompromising, strict and severe. Most carefully was the work and worship of the church scrutinized lest any unscriptural practice creep in.'[31] However, for many Free Churchmen participating in the Lord's Supper in a trench, or within the sound of a battle, was frequently a very moving experience.[32] Charteris moved to Ayr Baptist Church in 1909 and in a sermon there in 1916 while on leave from the front he called for the recognition of the need for theological reconstruction and adaptation in view of the changed attitude created by the upheaval of the war. The men that will return to the church will be changed for 'they have been in

---

[26] Neil E. Allison, 'Shakespeare's Man at the Front: The Great War Ministry of the Revd William Cramb Charteris, OBE, MC', *Royal Army Chaplains' Department Journal* 44 (2005), pp.40-45.
[27] Morgan, *The Span of the Cross*, p. 285, n. 37.
[28] I am grateful to the Rev. Ieuan Elfryn Jones for information about A.E.O. Jones.
[29] Bassett, *The Welsh Baptists*, pp. 388, 390.
[30] Allison, 'Shakespeare's Man at the Front', p. 41.
[31] George Yuille (ed.), *History of the Baptists in Scotland* (Glasgow: The Baptist Union of Scotland, 2nd edn, c. 1927), p. 107.
[32] Morgan, *The Span of the Cross*, pp. 50-51.

the mouth of hell, and have lived in presence of life and death. There they have met and touched God. ... Should they refuse to subscribe the shibboleths that have served a past generation, don't conclude that they have not the truth. The truth is eternal, but demands new expression to meet the ever changing needs of experience.'[33] Baptist chaplains who had administered the Lord's Supper to soldiers on the field of battle and Baptist soldiers who had shared communion with those of other denominations were unlikely in the future to support the observance of close communion in their home churches. Henry James, who had been minister of the Dr Pritchard Memorial Church, Llangollen, before his army service, insisted when he was called to Windsor Baptist Church in 1921 that it should become an open membership church. However, it is not known whether his views were influenced by his experience as an army chaplain or by the fact that his fiancée was an Anglican.[34] Henry Mander, who served as an army chaplain before coming to Mount Pleasant Baptist Church, Swansea, ended his ministry at the open membership church of Heath Street, Hampstead.[35] Another former army chaplain who served in Wales was F.J. Miles, who had been a senior chaplain with the Australian forces.[36] He was pastor of the English Baptist Church at Commercial Street, Newport, Monmouthshire, from 1923 to 1930.

Ecumenical Movement between the World Wars

Dr J.H. Shakespeare, the able secretary of BUGBI from 1898 to1924, pressed on Free Churchmen the need for more effective union between the denominations. It was his conviction that this could not be attained through the existing National Free Church Council and he urged the need for a body composed of official representatives of the churches. In 1916 he proposed to the National Free Church Council the creation of such a body and after a series of preliminary conferences it was constituted as the Federal Council of Evangelical Free Churches. Many Free Churchmen were distrustful of Shakespeare's plans because in *The Churches at the Crossroads*, which was published in 1918, he argued not only that union with the Church of England

---

[33] Allison, 'Shakespeare's Man at the Front', p. 43.

[34] Brian Neal and Ruth Smith, *A Royal Heritage: History of the Baptist Church, Victoria Street, Windsor, 1838-1982* (n.p., n.d.), pp. 17-19. After his pastorate at Windsor, 1921-26, Henry James ministered at Lower Circular Road, Calcutta, 1926-31. He returned to Wales and had a distinguished academic career, being awarded the D.D. degree of the University of London and served as lecturer, Extra-Mural Department, University College, Swansea, 1945-69.

[35] Frank Buffard, *Heath Street Baptist Church Hampstead, 1861-1961* (Hampstead: Heath Street Baptist Church, 1963), pp. 8, 34.

[36] K.R. Manley, *From Woolloomooloo to 'Eternity': A History of Australian Baptists* (2 vols; Milton Keynes: Paternoster, 2006), II, pp. 419-20.

was imperative for the future health of English Christianity but that the new church must be an episcopal one. This distrust was somewhat softened by the conciliatory tone of an *Appeal to All Christian People*, which was issued by the bishops of the Anglican church at the end of their Lambeth Conference in 1920. The *Appeal* was similar to the Lambeth Quadrilateral of 1888, and affirmed that the four articles were the only proper basis for unity. There were, however, differences, both in content and tone, between the statements of 1888 and 1920. The fourth article was modified, so that the explicit reference to the historic episcopate in the earlier document was replaced by a reference to 'a ministry acknowledged in every part of the Church as possessing not only the inward call of the Spirit, but also the commission of Christ and the authority of the whole body'.[37] Both Baptists and Congregationalists gave serious consideration to the Lambeth *Appeal* but, in the words of the Baptist historian, Ian Randall, 'although the Lambeth *Appeal* ultimately ran out of steam, it did open up the thinking of some Baptists to the ecumenical dimension'.[38]

Inter-church discussions held at Murren, Switzerland, in 1924 included the Baptists Charles Brown, T.R. Glover and Thomas Phillips.[39] Phillips was a native of Rhydwilym, and it is said that he spoke no English when he was admitted to Llangollen Academy in 1866, yet the whole of his pastoral ministry was spent in England. He returned to Wales in 1928 to become principal of Cardiff Baptist College and he saw his task as being to raise a new generation of *preachers* for the denomination.[40] He appears to have made no further contributions to ecumenical discussions.

In England in the twentieth century the influence of the ecumenical movement can be seen in the growth of the numbers of union churches, which practise baptism of both infants and believers. By 1937 there were sixty-five such churches, but none in Wales or Scotland.[41] The first union church in Wales was formed in 1947 at Colwyn Bay when the Congregational church united with Tabernacle Baptist Church.

---

[37] G.K.A. Bell, *Documents on Christian Unity, 1920-24* (London: Oxford University Press, 1924), p. 5.

[38] See R. Tudur Jones, *Congregationalism in England, 1662-1962* (London: Independent Press, 1962), pp. 363-64; Ian Randall, *The English Baptists of the Twentieth Century* (A History of English Baptists, 4; Didcot: Baptist Historical Society, 2005), pp. 114-19; Peter Shepherd, *The Making of a Modern Denomination: John Howard Shakespeare and the English Baptists, 1898-1924* (Carlisle: Paternoster, 2001), pp. 93-135.

[39] Randall, *The English Baptists of the Twentieth* Century, p. 119

[40] D. Hugh Matthews, *From Abergavenny to Cardiff: History of the South Wales Baptist College (1806-2006)* (Abertawe: Gwasg Ilston, 2007), p. 27.

[41] A.R. Cross, *Baptism and the Baptists: Theology and Practice in Twentieth-Century Britain* (Carlisle: Paternoster, 2000), pp. 91-96.

Ecumenical Movement since 1948

A fresh impetus to ecumenical endeavour in Wales was afforded by the First Assembly of the World Council of Churches in Amsterdam in 1948:

> The World Council of Churches came into existence because we acknowledged a responsibility towards each other's churches in our Lord Jesus Christ. There is only one Lord and one body. Therefore we cannot be at peace with our present divisions. Before God we are responsible for one another.[42]

The Amsterdam Assembly was one of the main impulses for the formation of the Council of Churches for Wales, which met for the first time in May 1956. During the years that followed much effort was devoted to the search for Christian unity among the churches and denominations of Wales. In 1963 a suggested scheme for church unity was published under the title *Tuag at Uno* (*Towards Union*). Following criticism of the proposals and comments on the scheme, the Committee of the Four Denominations, Baptist, Methodist, Union of Welsh Independents and Presbyterians, issued a revised scheme for 'The United Church of Wales' ('Eglwys Unedig Cymru') in 1964. There were 14 Baptist members of the Four Denominations Committee which prepared the scheme, including W. Davies, General Superintendent of the South Wales Area of the Baptist Union of Great Britain and Ireland, J. Ithel Jones, principal of the South Wales Baptist College, and M.J. Williams, secretary of the Welsh Baptist Union.[43] Discussions on the scheme were complicated by the offer of Sir David Jones, a Cardiganshire millionaire, to share a million pounds between the four denominations on condition of their becoming one. Both Baptist bodies withdrew from the talks in 1966 due to the compromise they would have to endorse over believer's baptism. Among the Welsh Independents there emerged a sense that criticisms that had been made of *Tuag at Uno* from the Congregational point of view had largely been ignored. The ecclesiastical pattern was deemed to be unbiblical, resorting to centralised bureaucracy and Presbyterianism. There emerged among Welsh Independents a sense that organic unity was not the only way to pursue Christian unity.[44]

---

[42] The First Assembly of the World Council of Churches: *The Official Report* (Geneva, 1949), p. 57. A translation into Welsh for Welsh-language publication is the basis of the present text. This is a re-translation into English by Noel A. Davies *A History of Ecumenism in Wales, 1956-1990* (Cardiff: University of Wales Press, 2008), p. 217, n. 2.

[43] Four Denominations Committee, Pwyllgor Y Pedwar Enwad, A Scheme of Union: The United Church of Wale; Cynllun Uno: Eglwys Unedig Cymru (Llanfair: Caereinon, 1965).

[44] R. Tudur Jones, *Congregationalism in Wales*, ed. Robert Pope (Cardiff: University of Wales Press, 2004), p. 264.

During the 1960s there were worldwide and British factors which influenced the ecumenical scene in Wales.[45] An ecumenical Faith and Order Conference was held in Nottingham in 1964 and the 550 delegates from 15 denominations invited the members of the British Council of Churches to work for unity by Easter Day 1980. The Council of Churches for Wales endorsed the move with a document entitled *Yr Alwad i Gyfamodi* ('The Call to Covenant'), published in 1965. Further reports published in 1968 and 1971 called on the denominations to enter into covenant for union by 1974. Although the covenant came into being in 1975, R. Tudur Jones concluded that 'support for it was at best half hearted'. The Commission of Covenanting Churches was made up of the Presbyterian Church of Wales, the United Reformed Church, the Methodist Church of Great Britain and the Church of Wales. Eleven or twelve English-speaking congregations of South Wales Area of the Baptist Union of Great Britain and Ireland joined the covenant.[46] However, some of the Baptist churches like Ararat, Whitchurch, which initially supported the covenant ceased to do so, while others like Lammas Street, Carmarthen, and Kensington, Brecon, subsequently joined the covenant.[47]

On 7 May 1985 representatives of thirty-two churches and denominations in Britain and Ireland met at Lambeth Palace to launch an Inter-Church Process 'on the nature and purpose of the church in the light of its mission in and for the world'. The Roman Catholic Church in England and Wales was a full member of the process from the beginning. In due course new ecumenical bodies were formed, Churches Together in England (CTE), the Council of Churches for Britain and Ireland (CCBI), and Cytûn: Churches Together in Wales. The Roman Catholic Church was a full member of these bodies too. Roman Catholic involvement was a serious obstacle for many Baptists. At the 1989 assembly of the Baptist Union of Great Britain (BUGB), approval was given for the Baptist Union to join the new ecumenical bodies. The positive vote caused much heart-searching among those who opposed participation in CTE and CCBI and by November 1989 thirteen churches had left the Union.[48] The *Baptist Times* listed the names of sixty-five churches, including six in Wales, which had asked the Union to note that they dissociated themselves from the Union's decision to be full members of the new ecumenical bodies.[49] In 1992

---

[45] Davies, *A History of Ecumenism in Wales*, pp. 11-20.

[46] Jones, *Congregationalism in Wales*, p. 266. The text of the covenant is given in *Churches Together in Pilgrimage* (London: British Council of Churches, 1989), p. 74, and has been reprinted in David M. Thompson, J.H.Y. Briggs and John Munsey Turner (eds), *Protestant Nonconformist Texts: Vol. 4: The Twentieth Century* (Aldershot: Ashgate, 2007), p. 385.

[47] I am grateful for information supplied by the Rev. John Garland, chairman of the Covenanted Baptist Churches in Wales.

[48] Randall, *The English Baptists of the Twentieth Century*, pp. 444-49.

[49] *Baptist Times* 23 November 1989, p. 13.

the *Spirit of '88 Directory* was published listing those churches and organisations that opted out of Churches Together and the Inter-Church Process. Amongst the churches listed was Moriah Baptist Church, Risca, which remained in membership with the Baptist Union of Wales.[50] However, during the 1990s over twenty former Baptist Union churches joined the Fellowship of Independent Evangelical Churches (FIEC),[51] which requires both its churches and their ministers to subscribe to its doctrinal basis, which sets out the 'truths of historic, biblical Christianity'.[52] The formation of the *Churches Together* movement in 1991 brought pressure on the FIEC to join other churches in united services, prayer meetings, marches and other evangelistic activities. At its assembly in 1996 the FIEC issued its 'Statement on Ecumenism', which effectively limits co-operation to churches and leaders which believe and hold 'those essential gospel truths which are embodied in our FIEC Doctrinal Basis or a Similar Statement of Faith'.[53]

The churches in Wales belonging to the BUGB decided not to become a member of Cytûn. There was a difficult debate within the Baptist Union of Wales and it was agreed to affiliate to Cytûn for a trial period of three years. However, at the end of the three-year period, following a referendum of all the churches (in 1993), it was agreed to remain in membership with Cytûn, although the Union's contract with Cytûn will be reviewed in 2012.[54]

The 1964 Nottingham Faith and Order Conference encouraged the formation of 'Area of Local Ecumenical Partnership' (more recently known as 'Local Ecumenical Projects (LEP) or Partnerships)'. They are defined as follows:

> A LEP may be said to exist where there is at the level of the local church a formal, written agreement affecting the ministry, congregational life and/or buildings of more than one denomination, and the recognition of that agreement by the appropriate denominational authorities.[55]

The development of Local Ecumenical Projects was much slower in Wales than in England and by 1991 there was only one LEP in membership with the Baptist Union of Wales at Ebbw Vale (Waunlwyd, Caersalem), where the pastor was Mary Davies, a minister of the United Reformed Church.[56] In other

---

[50] *Spirit of '88 Directory* (Gerrards Cross: Spirit of '88, 1992).
[51] Randall, *The English Baptists of the Twentieth Century*, p. 495 note 107.
[52] *FIEC Directory*, 2005 (Croydon: Fellowship of Independent Evangelical Churches), pp. 194-97.
[53] 'Statement on Ecumenism', April 1996, in *FIEC Directory*, 2005, p. 209.
[54] I am grateful to the Rev. Peter M. Thomas, general secretary of the Baptist Union of Wales, for this information.
[55] *Guidelines for Local Ecumenical Projects* (London: Consultative Committee for Local Ecumenical Projects in England, 1975), pp. 6-7.
[56] Mary Davies served in the Congregational and later United Reformed Church ministry 1980-98 but then became an accredited minister of The Baptist Union of Wales.

areas, such as Llanuwchllyn, Merioneth and Banycyfelin/Carmarthen, an interdenominational pastorate was formed between the Union of Welsh Independents and the Presbyterian Church of Wales, with one minister serving both denominations. More recently, these have been termed 'community ministries (*gweinidogaethau bro*)'.[57] By 1991 there were community ministers serving at Baptist churches at Llansilin, Denbighshire, and Tymbi, Llanelli, Carmarthenshire. The Interdenominational Advisory Committee, representing the Four Denominations, produced *Guidelines on Community Ministry* in 2000.[58] In other places, such as Llangollen, a united Welsh-speaking church was formed. This meant that at Llangollen, where there had been a Baptist academy from 1869 until 1892, there was no longer either an English or Welsh Baptist church.[59]

Discussions on the proposed United Church for Wales were resumed in 1995 with the Welsh Baptist Union being a full participant in the discussions and the BUGB sending observers. Politically, the nation was moving in a new direction towards devolved government and it was felt that an attempt at ecclesiastical union would concentrate the minds of Christians on the specific spiritual tasks facing the nation. The Baptist Union of Wales sent out the discussion document entitled *The United Church of Wales: The Way Forward* to the associations and the churches for their consideration. The annual assemblies of the Welsh and English wings of the Baptist Union of Wales in 2001 discussed *The Way Forward* document and the replies from the associations and churches. It was clear that many found it unacceptable that the scheme involved the acceptance of the validity of infant baptism. There was concern that the document *The Way Forward* failed to safeguard that believer's baptism would be adequately taught in the united church. The document was also felt to undermine the independence of the local church and links with the Baptist institutions around the world such as the European Baptist Federation and the Baptist World Alliance. Although both the Welsh and English assemblies expressed a willingness to continue in discussion with the other denominations, it was felt that a more acceptable approach might be to form a federation of Welsh denominations. Each denomination would then decide those areas of its work which it could hand over to a central body.[60]

---

[57] Davies, *A History of Ecumenism in Wales*, p. 39.
[58] Canllawiau ar gyfer Gweinidogaeth Bro, *Guidelines on Community Ministry* (Y Pwyllgor Ymgynghorol Cydenwadol ar y Weinidogaeth, The Interdenominational Advisory Committee on Ministry, 2000).
[59] The Welsh Baptist Chapel (Y Capel) closed in 1982 and united with three other Welsh congregations to form a church meeting in the premises of Seion Welsh Methodist Wesleyan Chapel: *Discovering Chapels in Llangollen* (Capel: Chapels Heritage Society, 2008). The Dr Pritchard Memorial English Baptist Church closed in 1968.
[60] *The Way Forward: The Baptist Response*, 2001; The Baptist Union of Wales: The English Assembly, The Annual Report, 2001-2003, p. 51.

In 1993 an inter-denominational committee comprising representatives of the Baptist Union of Wales, the Church of Wales, the Methodist Church, the Presbyterian Church of Wales and the Union of Welsh Independents was set up to produce a new hymn-book. It was published in 2001 as *Caneuon Ffydd* ('Songs of Faith') and it has enriched the singing of many Welsh-language congregations.[61]

The ecumenical movement was not without its critics and in Wales, unlike in England, there was a tendency for Evangelicalism and ecumenism to be seen as mutually exclusive. For the Evangelical the crying need was for the *individual* to be redeemed, whereas the ecumenist emphasised the renewal of the *church*, believing that the concept of the 'denomination' had served its purpose. Evangelicals suspected the ecumenical movement of compromising the gospel in a worldly desire to form a 'super-church' and strong criticism of the movement was voiced by Dr Martin Lloyd Jones and the Evangelical Movement of Wales.[62]

Unity among Baptist churches in both England and Wales was threatened by an address given at the 1971 annual assembly of the Baptist Union of Great Britain and Ireland by Michael Taylor, principal of the Northern Baptist College, with the title 'The Incarnate Presence: How much of a man was Jesus Christ?'. Taylor said that he must stop short of saying categorically, 'Jesus is God.' For Taylor, God was present in Christ 'as God is in every man', but in Jesus Christ 'God acted in a unique and decisive way for our salvation'.[63] His views led to a number of Baptist ministers resigning from the accredited list of ministers and a number of churches, including Wrexham, Bradley Road, leaving the Baptist Union and the local Baptist association. Some ministers and churches also left the Baptist Union of Wales.[64] For ministers, resignation from the accredited list often meant the loss of pension rights, and when Swansea, Penlan, left the West Wales (English) Baptist Association it lost its BUGBI initial pastorate grant which had enabled it to support its minister. Probably the most significant loss to the Baptist denomination in Wales was the withdrawal of Alfred Place Baptist Church, Aberystwyth, whose minister, H. Geoffrey Thomas, had trained at the conservative Westminster Theological Seminary in

---

[61] Jones, *Congregationalism in Wales*, p. 290.
[62] Morgan, *The Span of the Cross*, pp. 215-17.
[63] For an account of the 'Michael Taylor Affair' see Randall, *The English Baptists of the Twentieth Century*, pp. 366-82.
[64] The list given in Noel Gibbard, *The First Fifty Years: The History of the Evangelical Movement in Wales 1948-98* (Bryntirion, Bridgend: Bryntirion Press, 2002), p. 96, is neither complete or correct. A total of 8 accredited ministers and probationers resigned from the lists of ministers of BUGBI and BUW. Two churches left BUGBI, namely, Newport, Alma Street, and Swansea, Townhill. Three non-Union churches left their local Baptist associations, namely, Bethel, Cefn-Hengoed, Hengoed, Mount Pleasant, Maesycwmer, and Penlan, Swansea. Two churches left BUW, namely, Aberystwyth, Alfred Place, and St Mellons, Cardiff.

Philadelphia.[65] The church declared that it was making this stand because of the doctrinal shift it perceived in the denomination, in particular the denial of Christ's deity by Michael Taylor and the unwillingness of the Baptist Union to remove his name from the list of recognised ministers. The church declared its adherence to the Evangelical creed on the person of Christ and expressed a desire to be in communion with every other church of like faith.[66] The church joined the Associating Evangelical Churches of Wales when the organisation was formed in 1988.[67]

Anthony Cross has compiled a list of British Baptists who have played a significant role in the ecumenical movement and lists three ministers who served in Wales.[68] Of these Neville Clark and Hazel Sherman were ministers in membership with or serving BUGB churches. Clark, who was tutor at Cardiff Baptist College 1975-85 and principal 1985-91, was a member of the Joint Liturgical Group from its inception in 1963, while Dr Hazel Sherman, who was minister of Kensington, Brecon, 1995-2006, was a member of the CTE Working Group, which produced *Called to be One* (1996). Gethin Abraham-Williams, who is a Welsh speaker, served 1990-98 as General Secretary to the Covenanted Churches in Wales, which was renamed Enfys (Welsh for 'rainbow') in 1990. He was then General Secretary of Cytûn from 1998 until his retirement in 2008. Another minister who should be mentioned for his ecumenical involvement was J.S. Williams, who was president of the BUW Welsh Assembly 1985-86. He was one of the Baptist ministers involved in writing the report *Tuag at Uno* and a member of the Faith and Order Committee of the Council of Churches for Wales.[69]

Concluding Reflections

The story of the ecumenical movement in Wales is one of high hopes followed by subsequent disappointment. There now appears to be little enthusiasm for a United Church in Wales or a federation of the denominations. However, the most significant contribution of the ecumenical movement must be a new translation of the Bible into contemporary Welsh sponsored by a joint committee representative of all churches in Wales. *Y Beibl Cymraeg Newydd* ('The New Welsh Bible') was published in 1988. A Welsh-English diglot of the New Testament using the text of *Y Beibl Cymraeg Newydd* and the English version found in *The Good News Bible: Today's English Version* was published

---

[65] *The Baptist Handbook* (London: Baptist Union of Great Britain and Ireland), 1972, p. 341.
[66] Gibbard, *The First Fifty Years*, p. 96.
[67] Gibbard, *The First Fifty Years*, p. 97.
[68] Anthony R. Cross, 'Service to the Ecumenical Movement: The Contribution of British Baptists', *Baptist Quarterly*, 38: 3 (July 1999), pp. 107-22.
[69] Davies, *A History of Ecumenism in Wales*, p.19.

by the British and Foreign Bible Society in 1975. A revision of the New Welsh Bible was published in 2004 and in 2006 this revised translation was used in a Welsh-English New Testament, which was again published by the Bible Society, the English version this time being *The Holy Bible: English Standard Version*.

The work of Cytûn will be reviewed in 2012. The Roman Catholic and Anglican churches are no longer actively involved in the work and the three Nonconformist denominations (Presbyterian, Congregationalist and Baptist) have found a new impetus in sharing ideas and joint ecumenical projects. The cost of sustaining an ecumenical body has also been questioned and so it is likely that the present structure will come to an end in 2012. The future of ecumenical endeavour in Wales is not likely to lie in schemes to unite denominations but in cooperation at the local level between the denominations to form Local Ecumenical Projects.

The Baptist Unions in Wales have drawn closer together and in 2008 the North Wales English Baptist Union affiliated with the Baptist Union of Wales while retaining its membership of BUGB. Since June 2009 the BUGB South Wales Baptist Association has joined the BUW English Assembly and BMS World Mission to hold 'The Baptist Assembly in Wales' at Carmarthen.

The missionary task that the churches face in Wales is immense. In a recent essay Paul Chambers noted that Christianity in Wales is facing the most rapid rate of decline within the United Kingdom. The decline is most rapid in Nonconformist congregations. He considered how far Nonconformity is equipped to meet the challenges it now faces. His findings are not encouraging. Ageing and shrinking congregations, shortage of ministers, the gradual loss of a shared memory of religious values in society and a general inability to adapt mean that 'with the best will in the world it is only possible to say that the prognosis is not good'. His final sentence offers a bleak summary: 'The challenge for the churches is clear, but how far can they renew themselves to meet these changes with ever-decreasing resources and a growing climate of public indifference to institutionalised religion remains highly problematic.'[70]

A recent encouraging development has been the formation in 2005 of Waleswide (Cymrugyfan), an Evangelical organisation which seeks to plant and strengthen churches in Wales. Amongst the leaders of Waleswide are Marc Owen, Church Life Secretary, the Baptist Union of Wales, Dave Norbury, General Secretary of the Evangelical Movement of Wales, and Elfed Golding, National Director of the Evangelical Alliance Wales and an accredited FIEC minister.[71] Nick Bradshaw, the regional minister for the BUGB South Wales Baptist Association is a member of the council of reference of Waleswide. The Baptist Union of Wales is currently seeking to plant a Welsh-language church

---

[70] Paul Chambers 'Out of Taste, Out of Time: The Future of Nonconformist Religion in Wales in the Twenty-First Century', *Contemporary Wales* 21 (2008), pp. 86-100.

[71] http://www.waleswide.org; http://www.cymrugyfan.org

in Swansea, a venture actively encouraged by Waleswide. Since 2007 Penybryn, the Welsh Baptist church at Wrecsam (Wrexham), has been cared for by a community minister (Gweinidogaeth Bro), Rhun Murphy, but in October 2011 he will be joined by a Baptist ministerial student (minister-in-training) who will be studying at the Northern Baptist Learning Community.[72] There is now a slow and encouraging growth in the number of ministers serving BUW churches and this gives hope for the future.

The hope and prayers of many in the principality can be expressed in the Caleb Prayer for Wales:

O Uchel Frenin Nef,
Trugarha wrth ein Gwlad.
Bywha dy Eglwys;
Danfon yr Ysbryd Glan
Er mwyn y plant.
Deled dy deyrnas I'n Cenedl.
Yn enw nerthol Iesu. Amen.

O High King of heaven,
Have mercy on our Land.
Revive Your Church;
Send the Holy Spirit
For the sake of the children.
May Your kingdom come to our nation.
In Jesus' Mighty Name. Amen.[73]

---

[72] Formerly known as Northern Baptist College
[73] The prayer originated at the Ffald-y-Brenin Christian Retreat Centre, Pembrokeshire.

CHAPTER 8

Western Canadian Baptists and Ecumenical Initiatives in the Early Twentieth Century

Callum N. Jones

Following Canadian Confederation, on 1 July 1867, churches in the new Dominion were presented with, in the words of John Webster Grant, 'the challenge of laying a Christian foundation for a new and expanding nation'. This required 'not merely greater resources than the existing fragments could command but a broader vision than their sectarian bases could support'.[1] As a result, Canadian churches embraced organic ecumenical union ahead of all other western nations.[2] In the latter years of the nineteenth century they explored denominational union within each tradition,[3] and then, at the dawn of the twentieth century, formulated inter-denominational union. Of all these unions the most dramatic, begun in 1904 between the Methodists, Congregationalists, and Presbyterians, was the formation of the United Church of Canada on 10 June 1925.[4] Canadian Baptists, however, stumbled; while other denominations formed national organisations, they failed in 1909 to constitute a Baptist Union of Canada.[5]

This essay explores how the Baptist Union of Western Canada (BUWC) negotiated its way through the ecumenical initiatives among Protestant churches up to 1925 and the emergence of the United Church of Canada.[6]

---

[1] John W. Grant, *The Canadian Experience of Church Union* (Richmond, VA: John Knox Press, 1967), pp. 17, 18.
[2] Anon., 'The United Church of Canada', *Presbyterian Record* May 1904, p. 217; cf. Ernest Thomas, 'Church Union in Canada', *American Journal of Theology* 23:3 (July, 1919), p. 257; Grant, *Canadian Experience of Church Union*, p. 2.
[3] For a summary of nineteenth-century union movements see John W. Grant, *The Church in the Canadian Era* (Vancouver: Regent College Press, 1998), pp. 37-43.
[4] One third of the Presbyterians eventually refused to join.
[5] Lutherans also failed to create a national body by the turn of the century.
[6] The two main articles exploring Canadian Baptist ecumenical relations are I. Judson Levy, 'Canadian Baptist Ecumenical Relationships', *Foundations* 23:1 (January-March, 1980), pp. 84-96, and Jarold K. Zeman, 'Baptists in Canada and Cooperative Christianity', *Foundations* 15 (July-September, 1972), pp. 211-40. Both, however, give little attention to Baptists in Western Canada. The published BUWC histories are C.C.

Though confronted with the same challenges as other denominations, it was their allegiance to Baptist distinctives which, as we shall see, kept Western Baptists out of formalised ecumenical union.

Ecumenical Impulses

Scholars have identified several impulses towards Canadian church union in the early twentieth century. Beside broader national and political motivations,[7] these include the appearance of biblical criticism, increased negativity towards sectarianism from such advocates of traditionalism as the Oxford Movement, widespread social optimism, joint action against the liquor trade, concerted efforts to maintain the sanctity of the Lord's Day, co-operation under the banner of the Laymen's Missionary Movement and the advance of Roman Catholicism.[8] We shall focus upon three, the social gospel, immigration and limited denominational resources, to illustrate how Baptists in Western Canada identified with these concerns.

Early in the twentieth century Canadian church leaders believed social reformation was best achieved through conversion of the individual. Presbyterians, for example, pointed to the decrease in social evils resulting from the Welsh Revival and called for prayer for a similar revival in Canada.[9]

McLaurin, *Pioneering in Western Canada: A Story of the Baptists* (Calgary: C. C. McLaurin, 1939); Margaret E. Thompson, *The Baptist Story* (Calgary: Baptist Union of Western Canada, 1975); Joseph E. Harris, *The Baptist Union of Western Canada: A Centennial History, 1873-1973* (Saint John, NB: Canadian Baptist Federation, 1976); Walter E. Ellis, 'A Place to Stand: Contemporary History of the Baptist Union of Western Canada', *American Baptist Quarterly* 6:1 (March, 1987), pp. 31-51. The denomination has changed its name three times. It was the Baptist Convention of Western Canada (BCWC) between 1907 and 1909, the BUWC between 1909 and 2007 and the Canadian Baptists of Western Canada (CBWC) thereafter. For national Canadian Baptist histories see E.R. Fitch, *The Baptists of Canada* (Toronto: Standard Publishing Company, 1911), and Harry A. Renfree, *Heritage and Horizon: The Baptist Story in Canada* (Mississauga: Canadian Baptist Federation, 1988).

[7] Frank A. Peake, 'Movements towards Christian Unity in the Post-Confederation Period', *Journal of the Canadian Church Historical Society* 9:4 (December, 1967), pp. 84-108, questions whether national and political motivations were substantive. However, Henry O'Hara, chairman of the Congregational Union of Ontario and Quebec, specifically attributed nineteenth-century church union to prior political initiatives. See the *Canadian Congregational Year Book* (1904-5), p. 71.

[8] See for example Grant, *Church in Canadian Era*, p. 107; S.D. Clark, *Church and Sect in Canada* ([Toronto]: University of Toronto Press, 1948), p. 431; Samuel H. Reimer, 'Lay Cooperation in Canada: Catholic and Mainline and Conservative Protestant Attitudes Toward Interdenominational Cooperation', *Journal of Ecumenical Studies* 41:2 (Spring, 2004), p. 227.

[9] *Acts and Proceedings of the Thirty-First General Assembly of the Presbyterian Church of Canada* (1905), pp. 246-47.

Congregationalists charged that the sacrifice of Jesus was the basis for a renewal of religion capable of revitalising everyday life: 'The Cross is not only a revelation of the atoning grace of God, it is the revelation of a law of life'.[10] In 1914 the Methodist committee on evangelism affirmed that '[t]he heart of the message of the Church must still be, as it has ever been, the call for surrender to Jesus'.[11] And by 1922 reports from the Methodist Board of Evangelism and Social Service applauded the success of 'intensive personal evangelism' through Circuit Evangelistic Campaigns.[12]

New emphases, however, emerged. As early as 1902 Methodists were reminded of 'the unfortunate lack of harmony at present prevailing between the equity of the Gospel proclaimed by Jesus Christ and the inequitable conditions which mark our present social relationships'.[13] In 1906 a Committee on Sociological Questions ventured, 'We hold that the work of the Church is to set up the Kingdom of God among men, which we understand to be a social order founded upon the principles of the Gospel – the Golden Rule, and the Sermon on the Mount – and made possible through the regeneration of men's lives.'[14] By 1910 Methodists were informed: 'Those who insist on individual regeneration and those who call for social reforms are coming together'.[15] Presbyterians, meanwhile, amalgamated the Committee on Evangelism and the Board of Moral and Social Reform into the Board of Social Service and Evangelism in 1911.[16] This produced a 'Statement of the Attitude of Christianity to Christian Social Questions' which recommended '[t]hat the General Assembly ... urge the ministers of the Church to recognize and fulfil the obligations resting upon them as ministers of Jesus Christ with respect to the social applications of His Gospel'.[17] A few years earlier, J.B. Silcox, denominational chairman, informed fellow-Congregationalists that '[t]he revival of religion ... will be concerned for the salvation of the individual soul, and will be equally concerned for the salvation of society. ... The program of

---

[10] *Canadian Congregational Year Book* (1906-7), p. 73.

[11] *Journal of Proceedings of the Ninth General Conference of the Methodist Church* (1914), p. 325.

[12] *Journal of Proceedings of the Eleventh General Conference of the Methodist Church* (1922), p. 233.

[13] *Journal of Proceedings of the Sixth General Conference of the Methodist Church* (1902), p. 175.

[14] *Journal of Proceedings of the Seventh General Conference of the Methodist Church* (1906), p. 274.

[15] *Journal of Proceedings of the Eighth General Conference of the Methodist Church* (1910), p. 415.

[16] This was soon merged with the Home Mission Board. However, this did not detract from the social emphasis. See H.H. Walsh, *The Christian Church in Canada* (Toronto: Ryerson Press, 1956), p. 333.

[17] *Acts and Proceedings of the Thirty-Seventh General Assembly of the Presbyterian Church of Canada* (1911), p. 276.

Jesus includes the Christianizing of society as well as the Christianizing of the individual.'[18] This shared understanding contributed to the desire for greater unity; the Anglican Committee of Christian Union, for example, recommended 'more effective co-operation in Christian, Social and Moral Reform work'.[19]

Western Baptists also emphasised evangelism and individual conversion. J. Willard Litch, pastor of First Baptist, Vancouver, delivered a sermon in 1904 entitled 'Do the Work of an Evangelist'. He declared, 'There must first be new life received from above. The "spark of good" is implanted not by birth but by the new birth. ... Growth begins with the sprouting seed planted when the Holy Spirit turns the yearning eyes to the Atonement of Christ on the Cross.'[20] Litch went on to become a noted evangelist within the BUWC; accounts of his work among local churches frequent the BUWC's periodicals.

Similarly, in 1905, F.W. Auvache, pastor of New Westminster Baptist Church, extolled 'the fundamental doctrine of the vicarious sacrifice offered on Calvary' at the British Columbia Baptist Convention in Vancouver.[21] In a 1918 letter Britton Ross, BUWC evangelist for Manitoba, testified to the encouragement conversion brings: 'What stronger demonstration could we ask, as proof of the mighty power of the blood of Christ to cleanse from all sin, than these transformed lives, and here also we must realize the value and power of evangelistic preaching'.[22] Local churches not only valued the work of the denomination's evangelists – Saskatoon Baptist Church, for example, requested an evangelist for a planned campaign in April 1918[23] – they were encouraged by H.H. Bingham, pastor of First Baptist, Calgary, one of the denomination's flagship churches, to emphasise evangelism.[24] And in 1923-24 several BUWC churches in Vancouver participated in healing meetings held by the evangelist Charles Price. One, Jackson Avenue Baptist Mission, reported, 'Great blessing has been received as a result of the Price evangelistic meetings where we were

---

[18] *Congregational Year Book* (1906-7), p. 84.

[19] *The General Synod of the Church of England in the Dominion of Canada: Journal of Proceedings of the Fifth Session* (1908), p. 229.

[20] J. Willard Litch, '"Do the Work of an Evangelist"', *The Northwest Baptist* (*TNWB*) 20 December 1904, p. 2.

[21] As reported by Robert Lennie, 'Baptist Convention of British Columbia', *TNWB* 20 August 1905, p. 4. Auvache would later side with the Regular Baptists of British Columbia, the fundamentalist group which split from the BUWC in 1927.

[22] Britton Ross, 'The Monthly Letter', *The Western Baptist* (*TWB*) January 1918, p. 5.

[23] Church minutes, 30 January 1918, Saskatoon Baptist Church Minute Book September 28, 1916 to January 3, 1934, First Baptist Church Saskatoon files, CBWC Archives, Calgary. As of 2011 CBWC church archives were undergoing cataloguing. Saskatoon's minute book was uncatalogued when viewed. Archival access was graciously given by denominational staff.

[24] H.H. Bingham, 'Evangelism in the Local Church', *TWB* 15 December 1919, pp. 4-5, 15.

privileged to assist in the altar work. We were impressed with the many who sought the salvation of the Lord entirely apart from physical healing.'[25]

Alongside this evangelistic outlook, Western Baptists embraced the social gospel agenda. Prominent leaders had trained under the leading Baptist social gospeller Walter Rauschenbusch, among them Dores R. Sharpe who pastored in Edmonton, Calgary and Moose Jaw before becoming superintendent for missions in Saskatchewan in 1917,[26] and during the first twenty-five years of the century they openly addressed this agenda.[27] In June 1908 Avery A. Shaw, pastor of First Baptist, Winnipeg, and former Rauschenbusch student, outlined the social gospel to Manitoba Baptists gathered in Brandon.[28] In November, he presented an expanded three-part adaptation to the assembly of the Baptist Convention of Western Canada (BCWC) in Vancouver.[29] In the second he declared:

> The primary function of the church is, we all agree, the regeneration of human character. It has been charged against socialism that at its best it seeks the salvation of the individual through the regeneration of society; while the church seeks salvation of society through the regeneration of the individual. But we must recognize clearly that the church has before it this larger aim. Its function does not cease with the regeneration of the individual. In fact, is it not true that the church can best reach her goal through a combination of these two ideals? The church can never content itself with seeing the new life implanted in men, and then saying to them, 'Go out now and live out this life in society;' it has the added duty of organizing and directing that new life for social betterment.[30]

In 1908 the denomination created the Board of Moral and Social Reform and sought collaboration with equivalent Methodist and Presbyterian committees. Within a year this board recommended that all pastors closely study questions of labour relations; churches pursue involvement in temperance, Lord's Day observance and anti-gambling organisations; and the denominational paper list

---

[25] 'Report of the work of the Mission for the Month of May' ([1924]), Jackson Avenue Baptist Mission files, CBWC Archives. This is an uncatalogued handwritten report.

[26] See John Brian Scott, '"Responding to the Social Crisis": The Baptist Union of Western Canada and Social Christianity, 1908-1922' (PhD thesis, University of Ottawa, 1989), pp. 83-86, 116-49, for further details about these personalities.

[27] This is not to say they ceased to be Evangelical. At one of his final services at Moose Jaw, for example, Sharpe was instrumental in leading twenty-five boys and girls to Christ, with many seeking baptism. See Anon., 'Church News', *TWB* January 1918, p. 6.

[28] Avery A. Shaw, 'The Church of To-Day and To-Morrow', *The Western Outlook (TWO)* 1 October 1908, pp. 5-7. *TWO* preceded *TWB* as the denomination's paper.

[29] *BCWC Year Book* (1908), pp. 117-38.

[30] *BCWC Year Book* (1908), p. 124. Years later, D.R. Sharpe addressed similar themes with Saskatchewan Baptists. See *BUWC Year Book* (1921), pp. 80-93.

publications related to moral and social issues.[31] As this board noted in 1910, 'The Christian Churches are beginning to realize that they not only need the Gospel of the Man of Calvary that the Kingdom may be advanced in the individual heart, but the teaching of the Man of Nazareth that the Kingdom of Heaven may be seen among men'.[32] The social gospel was also promoted by D.B. Harkness, BUWC general secretary and editor of the *Western Outlook*,[33] and in the education programme of the denomination's school, Brandon College.[34] By 1920, according to George A. Rawlyk, the social gospel was 'the point of view of the majority in the Western Baptist Union'.[35]

The paramount issue fuelling this desire for social reconstruction was immigration. The federal minister of the interior from 1897 to 1905, Clifford Sifton, believed the nation's future prosperity depended in part upon development in the West. Under Sifton, immigration policy focused less upon racial origin than occupational skill. As a result, immigrants often established settlements along ethnic lines, failing to integrate with the larger population and its British values. Even Sifton's successor, Frank Oliver, a staunch supporter of Anglo-Saxon values, failed to prevent business leaders from recruiting non-British aliens for, for example, railroad construction.[36] Between 1901 and 1911, therefore, more than a million people ventured into Western Canada, including many from Eastern Europe.

Churches' reactions were mixed. E.D. McLaren, Presbyterian home mission secretary, described non-Anglo-Saxon immigrants as 'a mass of crude material',[37] while the Anglican synod considered many arriving in Eastern

---

[31] P.C. Parker, 'Report Of General Board On Moral And Social Reform', *TWO* 1 January 1909, p. 6.
[32] *BUWC Year Book* (1910), p. 63.
[33] D.B. Harkness, 'The Message Must be Social', *TWO* 1 October 1909, p. 4.
[34] In his inaugural address, D.C. Macintosh, professor of biblical and systematic theology, spoke of Christianity as the religion of the future in part because it fostered 'social betterment'. See D.C. Macintosh, 'The Religion of the Future', *TWO* 1 November 1908, p. 4. Shailer Mathews, a prominent Baptist social gospel advocate from Chicago Divinity School, visited Brandon in 1909. See Anon., 'Personals', *TWO* 1 June 1909, p. 2. On the role of the social gospel at Brandon see John Brian Scott, 'Brandon College and Social Christianity', in Jarold K. Zeman (ed.), *Costly Vision: The Baptist Pilgrimage in Canada* (Burlington: Welch, 1988), pp. 139-63.
[35] George A. Rawlyk, 'The Champions of the Oppressed? Canadian Baptists and Social, Political and Economic Realities', in Robert E. Vander Vennen (ed.), *Church and Canadian Culture* (Lanham, MD: University Press of America, 1991), p. 108.
[36] Gerald Friesen, *The Canadian Prairies: A History* (Toronto/Buffalo/London: University of Toronto Press, 1987), pp. 245-47. Friesen further notes that Robert Borden's Conservative government, sensitive to business needs, granted free entry to thousands of 'navvies' between 1910 and the outbreak of World War I.
[37] E.D. McLaren, 'The Perils Of Immigration', *Presbyterian Record* January 1906, p. 11.

Canada to be of a 'most refractory and difficult character'.[38] At the same time the missionary responsibility did not escape the churches. The Methodist General Board of Missions reported, 'The importance of our Western work can scarcely be exaggerated. Instead of our having to go to the ends of the earth with the Gospel, the ends of the earth, it would seem, are coming to us, as if to hear the Gospel at our doors'.[39] Congregationalists, Methodists and Presbyterians co-operated, appointing immigration officers at Eastern Canadian ports to direct newcomers and exemplifying, in the view of one Congregational immigration superintendent, the proposed value of church union.[40]

The missionary imperative, however, equated 'Christianisation' with 'Canadianisation'. If the social order required moral correction through the preaching and ministry of the churches, the social vices displayed by non-Anglo-Saxons intensified the churches' proclamation of superior British ideals as the basis for citizenship. Again, E.D. McLaren asked: 'In view of the large foreign element in our population are we not compelled to ask ourselves how we are going to maintain in this new land, which we proudly call "the greater Britain beyond the seas," those principles and usages and ideals that have made Great Britain so strong and prosperous and influential'?[41] As it was put to Methodists, regarding oriental settlement along the Pacific Coast, '[T]he tendency of our mission work...is to change the pagan into a Christian and the alien into a citizen'.[42] After the war, when the federal government, under pressure from Eastern European settlers, relaxed immigration requirements, the main denominations – Anglican, Baptist, Congregationalist, Methodist and Presbyterian – claiming that the weight of responsibility for integrating immigrants fell upon them, made representation to Ottawa reiterating the urgency of increased British immigration.[43]

Throughout, Western Baptists shared these concerns.[44] An early report from the Baptist Convention of Manitoba and the Northwest to Baptists in Ontario and Quebec noted:

---

[38] *The General Synod of the Church of England in the Dominion of Canada: Journal of Proceedings of the Sixth Session* (1911), p. 17.
[39] *Journal of Proceedings of the Methodist Church* (1906), p. 369.
[40] *Canadian Congregational Year Book* (1907-8), p. 88.
[41] McLaren, 'Perils', p. 12.
[42] *Journal of Proceedings of the Methodist Church* (1906), p. 364.
[43] *The General Synod of the Church of England in the Dominion of Canada: Journal of Proceedings of the Tenth Session* (1924), pp. 287-92.
[44] The most comprehensive study of Baptist response is Robert R. Smale, 'For Whose Kingdom? Canadian Baptists and the Evangelization of Immigrants and Refugees, 1880 to 1945' (DEd thesis, University of Toronto, 2001). Baptist work among, for example, Scandinavian, German, Ukrainian, Russian, Japanese and Chinese settlers was often conducted by pastors from these ethnic groups.

Now the people who are coming represent a great variety as to nationality, language, customs, and other social conditions. The various needs and responsibilities that they bring with them, the educational, social and political problems that develop after their coming, combined with the immediate importance and magnitude of the present opportunities in this new and growing country, make it absolutely necessary that our noblest efforts be given to the immediate dissemination and establishment of the principles of the Christian religion. This then is the day of supreme opportunity for the Christian people of this Dominion, and no effort should be withheld that may aid God's work at this crucial stage in its growth.[45]

Similarly, in 1916, Mrs G.H.V. Bulyea, president of the BUWC's Board of Women's Work, lamented the church's missionary indifference towards immigrants. She warned of demographic shifts in favour of immigrants as a result of the death of Canadian troops from British stock in the Great War and spoke of the need to Christianise and Canadianise settlers.[46] And in 1925 M.L. Orchard, general secretary of the Baptist Union, emphasised the denomination's commitment to this process:

To be truly Canadian must include being truly Christian. If we would Canadianize these people we must surely Christianize them. The New Birth is a prime essential to the New Canadian. Baptist churches, just because they claim to be New Testament churches and because they emphasize a spiritual religion, are under a peculiar obligation to present the need of and the way of the New Birth to every New Canadian.[47]

Finally, inadequate resources, spread among different denominations, spurred the call for union. An anonymous prize-winning essay in the *Presbyterian Record* in 1904 declared: 'Consider the waste of men and money in the present system; the overlapping, with all the consequent rivalry and irritation, the vast work at home and abroad which might be done...and it must be seen that unbelief in organic unity is a sentiment not to be wisely entertained.'[48] These

---

[45] *BCOQ Year Book* (1903), p. 42.
[46] Mrs G.H.V. Bulyea, 'Non-English Work', *TWB* July 1916, pp. 14-15.
[47] M.L. Orchard, *The Time for The Sickle* (Winnipeg, MB: The Baptist Union of Western Canada, 1925), p. 53. By 1930 Jackson Avenue Baptist Mission would report: 'Nationality does not interest us so much as at the beginning. We have learned that the gospel of Jesus Christ reaches the heart of the alien in exactly the same way as the Canadian.' 'Report of the Jackson Avenue Baptist Mission, Vancouver, B.C., for the year ending December 31, 1930', Jackson Avenue Baptist Mission files, CBWC Archives.
[48] Anon., 'United Church of Canada', p. 217.

views were echoed by Methodists and Congregationalists.⁴⁹ As Grant states, denominational rivalry in a town or village 'seem[ed] wasteful and frivolous'.⁵⁰

Western Baptists were similarly stretched. In a letter decrying organic union, G.J. Coulter White, missionary along the Crowsnest Pass, lamented the waste expended on Baptist Union administration to the detriment of effective field ministry.⁵¹ Social Service Committee member and managing editor of the *Western Outlook*, J.N. Maclean, also lamented the organisational and financial challenges hindering Baptist mission. 'We are not reaching the opportunity', he wrote.⁵² Meanwhile, another letter, from W.J. McCormick, pastor at Minnedosa, Manitoba, stated:

> ...in many of the newly-settled districts the people themselves are taking the initiative in shutting out denominational competition. Their claim is that they can give good, hearty support to one strong central church, which will conserve within itself all the spiritual strength and enthusiasm of the community... But they absolutely refuse to be burdened down with the support of four or more weak, struggling churches, whose ministry is bound to be inefficient because of lack of proper support.⁵³

In Western Canada in the early twentieth century inter-denominational union appeared as a practical and necessary solution to these challenges. Western Baptists felt the pressure of these impulses, but, significantly, did not consider them sufficient to embrace ecumenical union. How did they respond?

Western Baptist Responses to the Ecumenical Climate

In 1906 Methodists, Presbyterians and Congregationalists formally invited Baptists and Anglicans into union negotiations.⁵⁴ Though Western Baptists

---

⁴⁹ *Journal of Proceedings of the Methodist Church* (1902), p. 172; *Canadian Congregational Year Book* (1918-19), pp. 27-28. A joint Presbyterian, Methodist and Congregational committee noted, in 1911, that though overlap may not be as extensive as presumed, 'there are yet more cases of the unnecessary multiplication of religious effort than are creditable either to the Christian spirit or to the good judgment of the Churches concerned'. See *Acts and Proceedings of the Presbyterian Church of Canada* (1911), p. 5.

⁵⁰ Grant, *Church in Canadian Era*, p. 107.

⁵¹ G.J. Coulter White, 'Christian Union' *TNWB* 5 April 1905, p. 3. The Crowsnest Pass links southern Alberta and British Columbia over the Rockies.

⁵² J.N. Maclean, 'Christian Co-Operation', *TWO* 1 July 1915, p. 3.

⁵³ W.J. McCormick, 'Can We Co-operate', *TWO* 15 December 1911, p. 8.

⁵⁴ See *The Acts and Proceedings of the Thirty-Second General Assembly of the Presbyterian Church in Canada* (1906), p. 42, and *Journal of Proceedings of the Methodist Church* (1906), p. 292.

never officially responded,[55] Maritime and Baptist Convention of Ontario and Quebec (BCOQ) Baptists replied in 1906 and 1907.[56] Both replies were courteous, but explained that Baptist principles prevented participation: 'It is because of these principles which represent to them the Divine will that the Baptists find it necessary to maintain a separate organized existence'.[57] In the West, C.C. McLaurin, Alberta superintendent for missions, considered such responses worthy explications of the Baptist position, though he deeply regretted that they never caught the attention of local church members.[58] As a result, though the BCOQ response informed Baptists in ecumenical debates in the 1960s and 1970s,[59] we shall not consider either here.

Nevertheless, matching the tone of these responses, Western Baptists were equally irenic. Maclean stated in 1914, '[I]n the deep soul of the Christian world there is a note of gladness that a movement so sublimely in line with the whole tenor of the Christ life is possible'.[60] Similar sentiments were echoed at BUWC assemblies.[61] Baptists also welcomed representatives from other denominations to their assemblies,[62] and graced local ecumenical services.[63]

Only a minority of Western Baptists advocated organic union. Against the background of Baptist-Disciples of Christ negotiations,[64] Professor D.C. Macintosh of Brandon proclaimed 'spiritual religion', the regenerative experience, as the key Baptist principle. From this, other Baptist principles,

---

[55] Western Baptists, at this time, had not forged a single Western Convention from the Prairies to the Pacific coast. In any case, Prairie Baptists, formed and financed as a mission extension of the Ontario and Quebec Convention, still deferred to that Convention.

[56] *United Baptist Convention of the Maritime Provinces Year Book* (1906), pp. 128-29; *BCOQ Year Book* (1907), pp. 223-25. Anglicans declined participation because of insistence upon the historic episcopate. See *General Synod Journal of Proceedings* (1908), pp. 224-29.

[57] *BCOQ Year Book* (1907), p. 225.

[58] *BUWC Year Book* (1921), p. 29

[59] See Russell F. Aldwinckle, *A Baptist Response to the Principles of Union between the Anglican Church of Canada and the United Church of Canada* (Brantford, ON: Baptist Federation of Canada, 1970); Philip Collins, *The Church of Tomorrow: The Believers' Church – A Study Guide for the Text: The Believers' Church in Canada* (Baptist Federation of Canada, 1980), pp. 93-95.

[60] J.N. Maclean, 'Church Union', *TWO* 1 July 1914, p. 3.

[61] See *BUWC Year Book* (1911), p. 106; *BUWC Year Book* (1921), p. 140.

[62] For example, Methodist and Presbyterian representatives brought greetings to the Baptist Convention of Saskatchewan in 1916. See Anon., 'Church Union Is Discussed At Baptist Meeting', *Morning Leader* 2 June 1916, p. 10.

[63] Baptists shared a Good Friday service at Vancouver's Wesleyan Church alongside Congregationalists, Methodists, Presbyterians and Salvation Army officers in 1923, for example. See Anon., 'Wesley Church (Vancouver)', *Western Methodist Recorder* April 1923, p. 11.

[64] See discussion below.

including believer's baptism, followed. Accordingly, in his letter to the *Western Outlook*, Macintosh suggested Baptists enter wider union dialogue on the basis of a common 'evangelicalism'.[65] And in 1921, as BUWC general secretary F.W. Patterson observed, several struggling Baptist congregations demanded 'whether there is sufficient reason to justify separate existence'.[66] The majority in the West, however, opposed union, affirming believer's baptism and opposing all forms of authority over the individual or congregation.[67]

Non-Baptists considered believer's baptism the defining Baptist principle.[68] It was also, according to N. Keith Clifford, the chief obstacle to union with Baptists.[69] Unsurprisingly, the practice of paedobaptism provoked Baptist opposition to formal union. Harkness wrote, 'The one practise which more than anything else separates and keep [sic] separated, Baptists and Methodists, is that of infant baptism.'[70]

Western Baptists frequently extolled believer's baptism and critiqued paedobaptism in the denomination's newspapers. James Black, pastor at Didsbury, Alberta, submitted a letter in 1904 describing believer's baptism by immersion (and the Lord's Supper) as 'pictorial of the most essential verities of the Christian faith'. Baptism was only effective in the 'understanding heart and

---

[65] D.C. Macintosh, 'The Baptist Perspective', *TWO* 1 March 1909, p. 5. Macintosh defined 'evangelicalism' as 'faith in the Grace of God as manifested in Jesus Christ'. His suggestion was not without merit. Congregationalists also appealed to a common evangelical bond which transcended denominational distinctives. See *Congregational Year Book* (1904-5), p. 73.

[66] F.W. Patterson, 'Denominational Propaganda', *TWB* 15 April 1921, p. 2.

[67] See Philip Griffin-Allwood, 'The Canadianization of Baptists: From Denominations to Denomination, 1760-1912' (PhD thesis, Southern Baptist Theological Seminary, 1986), p. 256. Congregationalists believed their contribution to future union included their heritage as Separatists. See *Congregational Year Book* (1904-5), p. 85. Since Baptists could also claim this heritage, it is perhaps unsurprising that believer's baptism became one of their main reasons to oppose union. Citing an article from the *Baptist Argus*, Baptists had already accused Congregationalists of rejecting congregationalism if they entered organic union. See Anon., 'Baptists and Congregationalists', *TNWB* 1 June 1906, p. 6.

[68] Harkness observed: 'The only thing which the pedo-Baptist and a great majority of Baptists themselves conceive as distinctive in our tenets is the mode of baptism'. D.B. Harkness, 'What is the Baptist Message?' *TWO* 1 October 1909, p. 4. Similarly, in correspondence with the *Western Outlook*, J.N. Maclean, pastor of Tabernacle Baptist Church, Winnipeg, reported how, at a recent Laymen's Missionary Movement gathering, believer's baptism had been described as the Baptist 'shibboleth' by a Methodist professor. See J.N. Maclean, 'A Methodist Professor on the Baptist Position', *TWO* 15 April 1909, p. 6.

[69] N. Keith Clifford, *The Resistance To Church Union In Canada 1904-1939* (Vancouver: University of British Columbia Press, 1985), p. 27. Clifford primarily explores Presbyterian opposition to union.

[70] D.B. Harkness, 'The Passing of Denominations', *TWO* 1 November 1909, p. 3.

mind', and therefore it automatically precluded infants.[71] Early in 1914, F.W. Walker Pugh, pastor of Tabernacle Baptist Church, Winnipeg, preached against infant baptism, outlining four points: 'the church consists only of converted people'; 'the absolute supremacy of Jesus in the church' and thus the rejection of any other form of power; the sole authority of the New Testament; and the right to private judgment.[72] And with the United Church of Canada merger just three years away, D.G. Macdonald, pastor at Ladner, British Columbia, declared, 'Infant baptism in any form has no support in reason or Scripture, and it opens the door of the church for the influx of the unregenerated world'.[73] Moreover, Western Baptists claimed the support of contemporary scholarship. General secretary Orchard wrote, 'As to the New Testament form of baptism, there is really no controversy. *All* scholars agree that the word means "immerse".'[74]

Baptists also rejected union because of their principles of individual and congregational autonomy. In a paper to have been given at the BUWC's Vancouver assembly in 1912, W.J. McCormick, from Minnedosa, detected in the proposed basis of union 'all those elements of ecclesiasticism which has [sic] ever tended toward the suppression of soul liberty and the hampering of spiritual initiation'.[75] And in a letter to the *Western Outlook*, William Hay, pastor of Nassau Street Baptist Church, Winnipeg, stated, 'Not one of our churches is organically united to another. If our congregational polity prevents organic union amongst ourselves, how can we possibly enter into such union with others?'[76]

Beyond allegiance to specific principles, Western Baptists defended denominationalism, the notion that separate existence better advanced Christ's cause than the lofty but compromising ideals of organic union, against a growing impatience with distinct denominations. In 1908 William T. Gunn, chairman of the Congregational Union of Canada, observed, 'The old red-hot denominational loyalty has grown cool. Men are groping towards one another in their church life with the feeling that in some as yet not clearly discerned way the things that unite are greater than those that divide.'[77] That same year O.B. Stockford, church clerk at Okotoks Baptist Church, Alberta, noted, 'Ten

---

[71] James Black, 'Why did Christ institute baptism? An open letter to Christians of all denominations', *TNWB* 5 August 1904, p. 3.

[72] F.W. Walker Pugh, 'Why do not Baptists Christen Babies?' *TWO* 1 March 1914, pp. 6-7.

[73] D.G. Macdonald, 'The Church and her Ordinances', *TWB* May 1922, p. 3.

[74] M.L. Orchard, 'The Battle of the Baptist Principle, Part 1', *TWB* October 1924, p. 2, emphasis added.

[75] W.J. McCormick, 'Co-operation of Baptists with Other Denominations in Missionary Enterprises', *TWO* 1 June 1912, p. 12.

[76] William Hay, 'Organic Union or Federation?' *TWO* 15 April 1914, p. 10.

[77] *Congregational Year Book* (1907-8), p.63. See also G.A. Johnston Ross, 'Church Union', *Presbyterian Record* May 1904, p. 227.

years ago denominationalism was upheld in the vast majority of the pulpits of the church: to-day it can hardly find an advocate'.[78] Western Baptists therefore faced the charge that separate existence constituted a denial of Christian unity, as McLaurin, Alberta superintendent for missions, reported in 1921: '[T]he people in general...are constantly accusing us of narrowness and even bigotry'.[79]

Baptists responded, first, by proudly claiming the scriptural basis of their principles. An anonymous contributor to the *Western Outlook* announced, '[O]ur Baptist doctrine and polity are founded on the New Testament. If this New Testament is not the common law of the church, then our separate existence as a denomination is impertinence and schism.'[80] In 1917 Saskatoon Baptist Church affirmed, 'This Church shall subscribe to the principles upon which Baptist Churches generally are founded, and shall adopt as its rule of Faith and Practice, Christ's Law as laid down in the New Testament.'[81] Others argued that Jesus' prayer in John 17 intended not organic, but spiritual, union.[82] J.N. Maclean and A.M. McDonald, co-editors of the *Western Outlook*, placed scripture at the forefront of ecumenical dialogue: 'Admit our assumption that the "Scripture, when rightly interpreted, is an infallible guide for faith and practice," and our conclusions must follow.'[83] And, in assembly, Saskatchewan Baptists stated that even if they could enter organic union, 'the principles of the Baptist faith must and could not be allowed to disappear'.[84] Unsurprisingly, in combative words reprinted from *Baptist World*, we read, 'We have no sympathy at all with the notion advocated by some flabby-faithed Baptists that our people have no future, that we have served our purpose in the world, that we had best now merge with other denominations for the spread of New Testament principles.'[85]

Secondly, Western Baptists distinguished between organic union and co-operation. Though they had enjoyed inter-denominational interaction for many years, including participation in the Laymen's Missionary Movement[86] and the

---

[78] O.B. Stockford, 'Union of Baptists and Disciples: Article 1', *TWO* 15 June 1908, p. 6. One pastor, F. A. McNulty, left the denomination in 1918, taking half the congregation of Heath Baptist Church, Calgary, with him, because he opposed 'all denominationalism'. 'History of Heath Baptist Church 1907-1957', handwritten brief ([1957]), Heath Baptist Church files, Box C0000228536, CBWC Archives.

[79] *BUWC Year Book* (1921), p. 29.

[80] Anon, 'The Baptist Outlook', *TWO* 1 June 1911, p. 5.

[81] Church minutes, May 2 1917, Saskatoon Baptist Church Minute Book.

[82] McCormick, 'Co-operation', p. 11.

[83] J.N. Maclean and A.M. McDonald, 'Baptists and Christian Union', *TWO* 1 January 1914, p. 3.

[84] Anon., 'Church Union Is Discussed', p. 10.

[85] Anon., 'Baptists and the Future', *TWO* 1 May 1914, p. 4.

[86] In 1909 W.T. Stackhouse resigned from his position as Western Baptist secretary of missions to become general secretary of the Layman's Missionary Movement for the

Inter-Church Forward Movement,[87] when presented with the growing fortunes of organic union they proposed a federation concept. Hay, from Winnipeg, offered this template: '[A] federation would have its representative council, but no church and no denomination need lose its identity or its distinctive name, or polity or ideals. Each would be as truly autonomous as any Dominion of the British Empire.'[88] Similarly, Harkness championed federation in order to minimise wasted energy and resources.[89] The BUWC even federated with Presbyterians in two towns in Alberta in 1916, though this experiment failed.[90] And by 1921 the British Columbia Convention had a notice of motion commending 'the formation of an Interdenominational Council or Parliament of Churches in which the great national problems could be deliberated upon from the Christian point of view'.[91] Since it preserved denominational distinctives, federation was ecumenically preferable for the Baptist Union.

Thirdly, Western Baptists believed proposals for union were more mechanical than spiritual. A resolution passed by the Alberta Baptist Association in 1904 declared:

> [W]e express our desire to see brought about a closer union between all true Christians in harmony with the prayer of our Lord Jesus Christ expressed in John 17 – and the principle of love and forbearance enumerated elsewhere in the New Testament, but that we believe a merely organic union..., a uniformity established apart from the above principles would be purchased at too high a cost.[92]

In 1914 a letter from G.F.C. Kierstead, pastor of Central Baptist Church, Regina, stated, 'For the true test of Catholicity is not in adherence to prescribed dogma, no matter how historic or venerable, but loyalty to the abiding facts of New Testament Christianity and participation in the experience that constitutes

---

Baptists of Canada. See W.T. Stackhouse, Letter dated 12 January 1909, *TWO* 15 January 1909, pp. 6-7.

[87] See, for example, D.R. Sharpe, 'The Inter-Church Forward Movement', *TWB* 15 October 1919, p. 4.

[88] Hay, 'Organic Union or Federation?' p. 10.

[89] D.B. Harkness, 'Christian Unity', *TWO* 1 September 1910, p. 3.

[90] In Viking the pastor of the combined congregation was Baptist; in Blairmore, Presbyterian. By 1918 the Alberta Baptist Convention reported unsatisfactory 'spiritual' results in both congregations. By 1919 the church at Blairmore had called a Methodist minister who received over two-thirds of his salary from the Methodist Church. See *BUWC Year Book* (1916), p. 99; *BUWC Year Book* (1918), pp. 33, 107-108; *BUWC Year Book* (1919), p. 94.

[91] *BUWC Year Book* (1921), p. 140. This motion, due to be voted on at the BC Convention in 1922, was deferred to 1923 but never received further attention, probably because of emerging modernist accusations against Brandon College. See *BUWC Year Book* (1922), p. 144.

[92] A.W. Ward, 'The Alberta Baptist Association', *TNWB* 20 October 1904, p. 6.

the abiding worth of that Christianity.'[93] He concluded, 'We have no desire for a formal mechanical union which at heart is not spiritually demonstrated'.[94] As Hans Mol notes, '[Baptists] took the wind out of the union sails by denying the close link between organic union and Christian unity; and there the matter came to rest'.[95]

Denominationalism was not only necessary but vital if the church in Canada was to move in a biblically viable direction. Alexander 'Pioneer' McDonald, the first Baptist to establish a mission in the West, had urged Ontario Baptists to 'assist in planting firmly in the developing country, the old and apostolic standard of "One Lord, One Faith, One Baptism"'.[96] He arrived in Winnipeg in 1873 declaring, reputedly, that he had come 'to make Baptists'.[97] By 1900, in a report to the BCOQ, Western Baptists were to seize 'every opportunity to leaven society with their elevating and saving principles'.[98] Even S.D. Chown, Methodist general superintendent, noted in 1921 that '[t]he Baptist Church' had declined union involvement 'on the conviction that she was needed in the world as a separate Church, and had a particular mission to perform in the world'.[99] For Western Baptists, therefore, organic union was impossible, regardless of social or economic challenges, or theological argument. They believed they had a distinct message to offer, the purity of which could only be advanced by remaining separate.

Contingencies on the Eve of Formation of the United Church of Canada

Nevertheless, by the early 1920s, faced with the prospect of a new, large and well-resourced United Church of Canada, Western Baptists adopted several contingencies. In 1923 A.J. Bowbrick, pastor of Stettler Baptist Church, Alberta, anticipated that Baptist churches would provide the obvious alternative for dissident Methodists, Presbyterians and Congregationalists. He urged Baptists to welcome such people.[100] At the same time, he feared some Baptists might gravitate to United Church congregations, attracted by less sacrificial discipleship and because 'bigness and popularity are more important

---

[93] G.F.C. Kierstead, 'Baptist Principles and Their Programme', *TWO* 1 October 1914, p. 5.
[94] Kierstead, 'Baptist Principles', p. 6.
[95] Hans Mol, *Faith and Fragility: Religion and Identity in Canada* (Burlington: Trinity Press, 1985), p. 237.
[96] Cited in McLaurin, *Pioneering*, p. 47.
[97] See Mrs J.R. McDonald, *Baptist Missions in Western Canada, 1873-1948* (Edmonton, AB: Baptist Union of Western Canada, 1948), p. 27.
[98] *BCOQ Year Book* (1900), p. 346.
[99] Anon., 'Banquet and Address at Metropolitan', *Western Methodist Recorder* December 1921, p. 1.
[100] A.J. Bowbrick, 'How will Church Union affect the Baptist Churches?' *TWB* September 1923, p. 9.

considerations than fidelity and usefulness'.[101] Already, he alleged, some Baptist pastors had accepted charge of union churches offering larger congregations and salaries.[102]

Baptists also intensified confessional instruction. In 1922 Norman McNaughton, pastor of Olivet Baptist Church, New Westminster, restated 'Some Baptist Principles' to fellow Baptists in British Columbia.[103] Two years later, BUWC general secretary, Orchard, defended what he considered the primary Baptist principle, soul freedom, which he defined as 'the voluntary, intelligent and unconditional response of the individual to the appeal of God in Jesus Christ'.[104] And, just eight days before the United Church of Canada was constituted, the Baptist Women's Missionary Society of Manitoba '[r]esolved that we believe the time has come when we…should declare more clearly and more frequently our New Testament principles'.[105]

Whether such contingencies were effective is difficult to determine; the dark clouds of the fundamentalist/modernist debate filled the horizon. What may be said is that after Bowbrick's article there was no direct mention of the United Church's imminent formation in Baptist Union publications, assembly minutes or reports.[106] Instead, articles and addresses expounded the history and evolution of the Baptist genius. On the eve of union Western Baptists elevated the substance of their position rather than argue against union.

---

[101] Bowbrick, 'Church Union affect Baptist Churches?' p. 9. Evidence of migration is hard to substantiate since, if such transfers did occur, records are meagre. For example, in July 1925, B.R. Davies, a founding member of Stirling Baptist Church, Estevan, Saskatchewan, in 1908, resigned. Stirling Baptist had indicated in 1923 it would not issue letters of transfer to other denominations. If Davies had transferred to another Baptist church a letter of transfer would have been issued and recorded in the minutes. Instead, Davies requested his name be removed and no letter was issued. No more is known. One is left wondering why a founding member would leave just days after the United Church was formed. See Church minutes, 2 May 1923 and 8 July, 1925, Stirling Baptist Church Minute Book 1 (June 1908-December 1925), Stirling Baptist Church files, Box C0000228602, CBWC Archives. Interestingly, elderly members at St Paul's United Church, Estevan, do not remember a B.R. Davies, and unfortunately, since St Paul's membership records are not held at the church, confirmation is unavailable (private e-mail correspondence with St Paul's church office, 12 September 2011).

[102] Bowbrick, 'Church Union affect Baptist Churches?' p. 9.

[103] Norman McNaughton, 'Some Baptist Principles', *TWB* October 1922, pp. 3-5.

[104] M.L. Orchard, 'The Battle of the Baptist Principle, Part 2', *TWB* November 1924, p. 2. For Part 1 see n. 74; M.L. Orchard, 'The Battle of the Baptist Principle, Part 3', *TWB* December 1924, p. 2.

[105] Anon., 'The Manitoba Convention', *TWB* 18:6 (July 1925), p. 14.

[106] Western Baptists would no doubt have read the anti-union stance of T.T. Shields in the weeks before the United Church was formed. See, for example, T.T. Shields, 'Will the Methodist Whale be able to Digest the Presbyterian Jonah – Is Church "Union" likely to be Permanent?' *Gospel Witness* 21 May 1925, pp. 1-11.

Baptists and the Disciples of Christ

While rejection of organic union with paedobaptist denominations is unsurprising, this is not the whole story. In the first decade of the twentieth century Western Baptists considered mutual co-operation and organic union with one denomination of similar faith and practice: the Disciples of Christ.[107]

Following a joint meeting between the two denominations in April 1907, the Baptist Convention of Manitoba and the Northwest unanimously adopted the following recommendations: for mutual and shared pastorates where possible, for a raised profile of co-operation in both denominations' convention programmes and press, and for the exchange of delegates at each denomination's assemblies.[108] As in other ecumenical debates, limited resources became the impetus for union. W.T. Stackhouse, Baptist superintendent on home missions, reported, '[I]n this country with its many smaller towns and sparsely populated districts, it would be to say the least, a woeful waste of energy and money, to establish in these places at the present time, two churches whose faith and practise are identical'.[109] Stackhouse then advocated organic union:

> ...as a body we should not only continue to foster, by every wise and candid measure, the happy relations now existing, but should do all in our power to hasten the ultimate organic union of these two great bodies, that as the followers of our Lord Jesus Christ we may unitedly perpetuate those New Testament principles for which we have always stood, and do now unswervingly stand.[110]

Following this, seven Prairie congregations united.[111]

The only detailed exploration of the Baptist/Disciples relationship is found in a series of letters to the *Western Outlook* in 1908, evaluating the context, importance and process of union.[112] The author, O.B. Stockford, church clerk at Okotoks Baptist Church, one of the united congregations, states, 'If we can give a practical demonstration of the benefits to be derived from true union, then we will have served a great purpose.'[113] However, this series halted abruptly.

---

[107] Typically, Disciples were anti-denominational, preferring the terms 'Christian' or 'Disciples of Christ'. Use of the term 'denomination' at this juncture is more for convenience than description.
[108] *BCWC Year Book* (1907), p. 47.
[109] *BCWC Year Book* (1907), p. 18.
[110] *BCWC Year Book* (1907), p. 18.
[111] Vermillion, Ponoka, Okotoks, Nanton, Yellow Grass, Innisfree, and Portage La Prairie. See McLaurin, *Pioneering*, p. 153.
[112] See Stockford, 'Union: Article 1', p. 6; O.B. Stockford, 'Union of Baptists and Disciples: Article 2', *TWO* 1 August 1908, p. 6; 'Union of Baptists and Disciples: Article 3', *TWO* 1 September 1908, pp. 8-9; 'Union of Baptists and Disciples: Article 4', *TWO* 15 September 1908, pp. 7-8.
[113] Stockford, 'Union: Article 1', p. 6.

Stockford planned five letters. The fifth, intended to address matters of divergence between Baptists and Disciples, never appeared. In another letter from 1908, James McDermid, pastor at Edrans, Manitoba, challenged 'a peculiar silence' within the BCWC. Observing no negative appraisal of the 'amalgamation movement' in the denomination's media, he objected to 'airy unions' and the infiltration into Baptist congregations of Disciple doctrines of baptismal regeneration, open communion and falling from grace.[114]

According to McLaurin, after 'a few short years' the initiatives collapsed.[115] What is intriguing is why. If McDermid correctly perceived an underlying favourableness towards union, then apparent sudden termination suggests reasons of considerable significance and immediacy. However, we are met with silence in official BCWC minutes and reports, and surprisingly, in the two main analyses of Canadian Baptist ecumenical relations.[116] The only hints of collapse appear in the *BCOQ Year Book* for 1908 and local church reports. The *Year Book* identifies four points of tension: the relation of baptism to regeneration and the remission of sins, the role of the Spirit in conversion, the eternal security of the Christian and, more pragmatically, the new denomination's name should union proceed.[117] These are matched by local church reports. In a letter to the *Western Outlook*, Ponoka Baptists spoke not only of Disciples' duplicity and attempts to secure the Baptist church building for themselves, but also of '[r]apid progress in the direction of eradicating Baptist views and practices' and the imposition of '[e]very distinctive feature of Disciple practise'.[118]

While simultaneous breakdown in union discussions in the United States may shed some light,[119] there are reasons peculiar to the Canadian scene. First, as noted, it was the BCOQ, a wealthier Baptist convention less hindered by limited resources, which raised theological and practical concerns. Secondly, the focus for the Baptist Convention of Western Canada at this time was upon constitutional transition to the Baptist Union of Western Canada and another proposed Baptist Union of Canada. Thirdly, all attempts at localised union were restricted to the Prairie provinces.[120] Significantly, Baptists in British Columbia, enjoying a rise in giving in 1906 – thus negating any need of

---

[114] James McDermid, 'Is That So?' *TWO* 1:14 (1 August 1908), p. 6.
[115] McLaurin, *Pioneering*, p. 153. The union in Portage La Prairie lasted only from January to June 1909. See Winfred E. Garrison and Alfred T. DeGroot, *The Disciples of Christ: A History* (St. Louis, MI: The Bethany Press, rev. edn, 1958), p. 457.
[116] Levy, 'Canadian Baptist Ecumenical Relationships'; Zeman, 'Baptists in Canada'. The histories in n. 6 are also largely silent.
[117] *BCOQ Year Book* (1908), p. 221.
[118] G. Edwards, 'The Ponoka Situation', *TWO* 15 February 1909, p. 6.
[119] See Bill J. Leonard, *Baptist Ways: A History* (Valley Forge, PA: Judson Press, 2003), p. 408.
[120] See n. 111 above.

amalgamation to consolidate resources – and inspired to make 1907 'the greatest year in our history',[121] appeared uninterested. Lastly, the repeated focus on Baptist principles in official reports, assembly minutes and the *Western Outlook*, demonstrates that greater space was given to exonerating and advocating Baptist principles in the face of all ecumenical overtures than to how such principles might assist dialogue and union with the Disciples of Christ.

The significance of this potential union with Disciples lies in the broader ecumenical context. John Webster Grant has claimed that Baptist capacity to respond to the invitations to union by the Methodists, Presbyterians and Congregationalists was 'hampered by the lack of a national consultative body'.[122] Such a lack did not prevent Western Baptists debating a union with Disciples. In other words, failure to create a Baptist Union of Canada may not have been as debilitating a reason for rejecting wider ecumenical union as presumed. Instead, another, more significant reason for not entering formal union with the Methodists, Presbyterians and Congregationalists, can be advanced: namely the importance of faith and practice. That Western Baptists and Disciples, who shared several common convictions, failed to unite indicates how essential allegiance to their convictions was for Baptists. If they were not prepared to compromise with Disciples to obtain union, why would they ever consider doing so with other denominations? It is no surprise that the question of baptism – a point of departure with Disciples – was a chief point of contention in the wider ecumenical debates. Nevertheless, let us not forget, for a brief moment, the possibility of formal, organic union with the Disciples of Christ, which might have forever altered the face of Baptist life in Canada, existed and was endorsed among Prairie Baptists.

Conclusion

Like their neighbours in other denominations, Western Baptists were caught up in the moods and aspirations of Canadian society in the early twentieth century. They faced similar struggles and questions over allocation and distribution of resources; they addressed the social implications of immigration with the same belief in 'Canadianisation'; and they confronted social challenges with the social gospel. However, adherence to their principles meant separate denominational existence and rejection of organic union. Separatism did not mean Western Baptists were unwilling to co-operate with other denominations where these distinctives were not questioned or sacrificed, but co-operation could not be the same as organic union. Equally, separatism did not mean unsympathetic and uncharitable attitudes. But fundamentally, Western Baptists believed their principles to be New Testament principles, granting them a

---

[121] *BCOQ Year Book* (1906), p. 178.
[122] Grant, *Church in Canadian Era*, p. 109.

natural superiority and keeping them out of ecumenical union. In fact, Western Canadian Baptists in the first quarter of the twentieth century anticipated the day when other denominations would recognise the scriptural basis of their position and concede to Baptist wisdom.

CHAPTER 9

Baptists and other Christian Churches in the First Half of the Twentieth Century

Brian R. Talbot

This study of one aspect of the collective life of some Baptist bodies in the first half of the twentieth century will of necessity be a very brief overview of their relationships with other Christian churches. Baptists have been committed to world mission as part of their core identity, at least since the 1790s. The first part of this study will note the different Baptist groups that participated in the 1910 World Missionary Conference, a highly significant event in the history of the Protestant missionary movement. Edinburgh 1910 laid the foundations of interdenominational understanding for the ecumenical movement of the twentieth century and is, therefore, an appropriate place to begin a study of the relationship of Baptists with other churches in the first five decades of the twentieth century. The second theme under consideration will be the relationship of Baptists with other churches in their own countries, followed by their approach to international ecumenical initiatives, in particular the founding of the World Council of Churches.

Baptists and World Mission

The key event that had a major impact on ecumenical relations between Protestant churches in the early twentieth century was the World Missionary Conference held during 1910 in Edinburgh. It has been with hindsight that historians have recognised its pivotal importance.[1] John Mott, the chairman of that event, described it as 'the most notable gathering in the interest of the worldwide expansion of Christianity ever held, not only in missionary annals,

---

[1] S.P. Mews, 'Kikuyu and Edinburgh: The Interaction of Attitudes to Two Conferences', in G.J. Cuming & D. Baker (eds), *Councils and Assemblies* (Cambridge: Cambridge University Press, 1971), p. 346. K.S. Latourette, 'Ecumenical Bearings of the Missionary Movement and the International Missionary Council', in R. Rouse & S.C. Neill (eds), *A History of the Ecumenical Movement, 1517-1948* (London: SPCK, 2nd edn, 1967), pp. 356-57. A.R. Vidler, *The Church in an Age of Revolution: 1789 to the Present Day* (Harmondsworth: Penguin, 1961), p. 257.

but in all Christian annals'.[2] However, as C.E. Wilson, the foreign secretary of the Baptist Missionary Society, openly acknowledged in the *Baptist Times and Freeman*, the English Baptist periodical, this conference would be a Protestant, primarily Evangelical conference 'because the great Romanist and Greek Churches will not be represented'.[3] A number of scholars have suggested that this gathering of Protestant church leaders was more limited in its scope than is sometimes assumed.[4] This missionary conference was restricted to delegates from missionary societies operating among non-Christian peoples. This policy was carefully upheld to ensure that a greater variety of ecclesiastical and theological convictions would be represented than at any previous gathering of this kind.[5] The Baptist Union of Scotland (BUS) wholeheartedly welcomed this event taking place in Edinburgh.[6] Two Scottish Baptists were included in the twenty-two strong (male) Baptist Missionary Society (BMS) delegation,[7] though four female British Baptists attended as representatives of the Baptist Zenana Mission and some other British Baptists were present in some other capacity.[8] Half of the British delegates were Anglican and a quarter Presbyterian, with the other quarter consisting of Baptists, Congregationalists and Methodists in roughly equal numbers.[9] Baptists from North America were well represented at this event. The largest contingent that included nine women in its forty-three representatives came from the American Baptist Foreign Missions Society (ABFMS). The Northern Baptist Convention had been

---

[2] Cited without a reference in C.H. Hopkins, *John R. Mott, 1865-1955* (Grand Rapids: Eerdmans, 1979), p. 342.

[3] C.H. Wilson in *Baptist Times and Freeman* 3 June 1910, p. 362.

[4] For example, B. Stanley, 'Edinburgh 1910 and the Oikoumene', in A.R. Cross (ed.), *Ecumenism and History: Studies in Honour of John H. Y. Briggs* (Carlisle: Paternoster, 2002), pp. 89-105. H.H. Rowdon, 'Edinburgh 1910, Evangelicals and the Ecumenical Movement', *Vox Evangelica* 5 (1967), pp. 53-54.

[5] Latourette, 'Missionary Movement', pp. 357-62. B. Stanley, *The World Missionary Conference, Edinburgh 1910* (Grand Rapids: Eerdmans, 2009), p. 320.

[6] BUS Council, 10 May 1910, Baptist Union of Scotland Minute Book, 1906-1915, *Scottish Baptist Magazine* (*SBM*), 36.6 (June 1910), pp. 86-87.

[7] Details given in B.R. Talbot, 'Fellowship in the Gospel: Scottish Baptists and their Relationships with Other Christian Churches, 1900-1945', *Evangelical Quarterly*, 78.4 (October 2006), p. 342.

[8] For example, Sir G.W. Macalpine, president of the Baptist Union of Great Britain and Ireland, and Timothy Richard, a BMS missionary in China, were special delegates of the British Executive Committee. *World Missionary Conference, 1910: The History and Records of the Conference* (12 vols; Edinburgh: Oliphant, Anderson & Ferrier, 1910), IX, pp. 39-41.

[9] Ashley Carus-Wilson, 'A World Parliament on Missions. The Meaning and Methods of the Edinburgh Conference of 1910', *Quiver* 45 (1910), p. 632—www.theologicalstudiesorguk.blogspot.com/2007/02/contemporary-account-of-edinburgh-1910.html accessed 29 May 2009

enthusiastic about working with other Protestant churches since its own inception in 1907. Prior to that date these American Baptists had participated in the Foreign Missions Conference of North America in 1893.[10] The Foreign Mission Board of the Southern Baptists had eight delegates, two of whom were women. Three other American Baptist agencies were present in Edinburgh. The Foreign Mission Board of the National Baptist Convention, the Foreign Mission Board of the General Conference Free Baptists and the Missionary Society of the Seventh Day Baptists had two, three and one representative respectively. There were two societies present from the ranks of Canadian Baptists, the United Baptist Foreign Mission Board with two delegates and three from the Baptist Foreign Mission Board in Canada.[11] Baptists in the rest of the world had only one delegate, W.T. Whitley, on behalf of the Victoria Baptist Foreign Mission from Australia. Overall, out of the 1,215 official delegates, 509 were British, 491 came from North America, 169 from continental Europe, 27 from the white colonies of South Africa and Australasia and only 19 from the non-Western world, of whom eighteen came from Asia. Only one black African attended, Mark Hayford from Ghana, and his name was not on the list of official delegates.[12] No-one was present from the Pacific islands and the Caribbean. Latin America was also unrepresented, as Protestant missionary representation from those countries would have led to the withdrawal of Anglo-Catholic Anglicans who considered those countries to be Roman Catholic and therefore without a need of any Christian missionaries. A similar view was taken by these High Churchmen of Protestant missions in Orthodox territories. Protests from various independent Evangelical mission agencies went unheeded.[13] The pragmatic rather than doctrinal basis of invitations to prospective delegates has been viewed as a major error by some Baptists and other conservative Evangelicals,[14] but no-one, including the various Baptist bodies from around the world, in the early twenty-first century, could be comfortable in hindsight with the balance of ethnic representation in evidence at the 1910 World Missionary Conference.

Edinburgh 1910 had been viewed at the time as 'The Third Ecumenical Missionary Conference', following previous Protestant international missionary

---

[10] R.G. Torbet, 'American Baptist Churches in the U.S.A.', in J.L. Garrett (ed.), *Baptist Relations with Other Christians* (Valley Forge: Judson Press, 1974), p. 54.

[11] World Missionary Conference 1910: The History and Records of the Conference, IX, pp. 52-53.

[12] Contra J.J. Hanciles, *Beyond Christendom* (Maryknoll: Orbis Books, 2008), p. 123, who stated that 'not a single African was present'.

[13] Stanley, World Missionary Conference, pp. 12-13. Talbot, Fellowship in the Gospel, p. 342

[14] D.J. Hesselgrave, 'Will we Correct the Edinburgh Error? Future Mission in Historical Perspective', *Southwestern Journal of Theology*, 49.2 (Spring 2007), pp. 121-49.

gatherings held in London in 1888 and New York in 1900.[15] The term 'ecumenical' in the title of these events implied a global geographical reach rather than a comprehensive or inclusive conference at which all the major sectors of Christendom were represented.[16] At these events in London and New York their purpose had been to impress and inspire the Christian public. However, an alternative model of a 'consultative conference' of authorised delegates had been in evidence at the fourth Indian Decennial Missionary Conference, held in Madras in 1902, and the Shanghai Missionary Conference in 1907, and this approach was adopted for Edinburgh 1910.[17] Following these meetings in Scotland, a 'Continuation Committee' had been formed to continue the work commenced at Edinburgh. A quarterly journal, the *International Review of Missions*, was launched under the editorship of J.H. Oldham, with the first issue appearing in January 1912.[18] John Mott, chairman of the Continuation Committee, undertook a tour of the Far East between October 1912 and May 1913. He held no fewer than eighteen regional and three national conferences in Ceylon, India, Burma Malaya, China, Korea and Japan.[19] These initiatives gave birth to a series of national and regional missionary councils or congresses. In China, for example, the China Continuation Committee took seriously the model of Edinburgh 1910 for its National Christian Conference in Shanghai in 1922, with half of all delegates Chinese and a large proportion of those present representing Chinese churches. This event was followed by the formation of the National Christian Council in China. It became a member of the newly-formed International Missionary Council. As early as 1917 a comity agreement had been drawn up setting out principles for Protestant mission agencies proposing to work in an area in which another Protestant society was already established. Most mission agencies had signed up by 1919, including the BMS. H.R. Williamson, who served with that body in China from 1908 to 1938, stated that its missionaries did their utmost to promote the spirit of comity and co-operation between the different denominational missions and churches in the vicinity of their own work and played a full part in the work of the National Christian Council.[20] American (Northern) and Southern Baptists from the USA had jointly established the Shanghai Baptist College in 1908 and were full partners in Ginling College in Nanking, founded in 1911. They were

---

[15] W.R. Hogg, Ecumenical Foundations: A History of the International Missionary Council (New York: Harper Brothers, 1952), pp.102-103.

[16] Stanley, World Missionary Conference, pp. 18-19, 23.

[17] W.H.T. Gairdner, *Edinburgh 1910* (Edinburgh: Oliphant, Anderson & Ferrier, 1910), p. 13; Stanley, *World Missionary Conference,* pp. 26-28.

[18] *Report of Commission VI,* pp. 53-54; K. Clements, *Faith on the Frontier: A Life of J. H. Oldham* (Edinburgh: T. & T. Clark, 1999), pp. 105-108.

[19] Latourette, 'Ecumenical Bearings of the Missionary Movement', p. 364.

[20] H.R. Williamson, *British Baptists in China* (London: Carey Kingsgate Press, 1957), p. 216.

also committed to a Union Educational Commission that represented five American missions (Southern Methodist, Northern and Southern Presbyterian, together with Northern and Southern Baptist). It became the East China Educational Union for the entire lower Yangtze Valley, co-ordinating a programme of higher education. The East China Missionary Conference of 1912 had approved a Baptist share with two Presbyterian missions in a Union Institutional Evangelistic Centre in Hangchow. Baptists had also agreed to work with the China Inland Mission in evangelistic and educational work in the Kinhwa region.[21] Furthermore, the American Baptists had attended comity meetings, for example in Shanghai in 1913, and agreed to co-operate in future union projects in education and medical missions, but had declined to enter into any organic union with other denominations in China.[22] Most of the Lutheran agencies and American Southern Baptists had also declined to participate in supporting the National Christian Council in that country. Within a few years a number of other conservative Evangelical bodies, for example the Christian and Missionary Alliance and the China Inland Mission, together with some national Chinese Christian groups, withdrew due to what they perceived as the increasingly modernist or liberal tendencies of the National Christian Council in China. A rival League of Evangelical Churches was formed under mainly Chinese leadership.[23] The future tensions in relationships between theologically liberal and conservative Christians that would become a major problem by the second half of the twentieth century, were already in evidence amongst the various mission bodies working in China, but not uniquely in that country.[24]

The International Missionary Council (IMC) was constituted in October 1921 with sixty-one representatives present from fourteen different countries,[25] though overwhelmingly from the West with only seven delegates from the younger churches in the two-thirds world.[26] However, it was only a small natural step forward in uniting mission agencies because it built on the successful work of regional mission bodies amongst the Christian churches. For example, the Committee of (Twelve) German Evangelical Missions had been founded as early as 1885 and the Continental Missionary Conference of Europe

---

[21] R.G. Torbet, Venture of Faith: The Story of the American Baptist Foreign Mission Society and the Women's American Baptist Foreign Mission Society, 1814-1954 (Philadelphia: Judson Press, 1955), pp. 291, 310-11.

[22] Torbet, *Venture of Faith*, p. 295.

[23] Latourette, 'Ecumenical Bearings of the Missionary Movement', pp. 378-82.

[24] Adrian Hastings, in *The Church in Africa 1450-1950* (Oxford: Clarendon Press, 1994), pp. 550-52, perceptively noted that the majority of Protestant missionaries were more conservative in their theology than their respective denominations prior to Edinburgh 1910. This conference had retained the famous Student Christian Movement motto 'the evangelisation of the world in this generation', but it was quickly dropped thereafter.

[25] Hogg, Ecumenical Foundations, p. 202.

[26] Latourette, 'Ecumenical Bearings of the Missionary Movement', p. 366.

in 1886. This later body had brought together representatives of missionary societies in Germany, Denmark, Finland, France, the Netherlands, Norway, Sweden and Switzerland in Bremen, Germany, every four years from 1886 to its last meeting in 1935.[27] The largest of the member bodies of the IMC was the Foreign Missions Conference of North America, founded in January 1893 by twenty-three organisations in Canada and the United States. Edinburgh 1910 undoubtedly contributed to the founding of the Conference of Missionary Societies of Great Britain and Ireland in 1912.[28] Other national missionary councils were formed after the IMC. These included in Europe: the Northern Missionary Council in 1923, with representatives from Sweden, Norway and Finland and further afield, the United Missionary Council of Australia constituted in 1920, together with its sister body in New Zealand in 1926, both agencies formed after visits by John Mott to these countries.[29] Although Edinburgh 1910 had not created the conditions for the formation of national missionary councils, it had encouraged the spirit of co-operation between different denominational mission agencies in a number of countries and enabled the formation of the IMC to take place with a much wider representation of participating countries.

One example of the impact of Edinburgh 1910 on a specific country can be seen in its influence on the host country. In Scotland 'The Missionary Congress of Scottish Churches' that took place in Glasgow in October 1922 was inspired by the 1910 World Missionary Conference. Baptist minister John MacBeath, the conference secretary,[30] was convinced that this 'occasion would be a landmark in the history of the Scottish Churches and their missions overseas'. There were seventy-five Scottish Baptists registered as official delegates, a significant number of representatives from a small denomination. MacBeath was convinced that a people with vision who prayed hard for God to be at work in the world would see that 'the churches shall be full of increase and all lands shall see the glory of the Lord'.[31] One of the follow-up events to this gathering was a major mission week in Aberdeen in which all the Protestant churches participated. 'The campaign from Monday, October 30, to Sunday November 12, succeeded in arousing interest in Aberdeen as no religious effort has done for the past decade... All the churches...co-operated in the enterprise, thus affording a superb demonstration of the unity that lies deeper than their

---

[27] 'Zahn, Franz Michael, 1833 to 1900, Bremen Mission, Germany', *Dictionary of African Biography* (New Haven, CT: Overseas Ministries Study Centre, 2002), no p. [www.dacb.org/stories/non%20africans/legacy_zahn.html accessed 20 June 2009]. See also Latourette, 'Ecumenical Bearings of the Missionary Movement', p. 373.
[28] Stanley, World Missionary Conference, pp. 318-20.
[29] Latourette, 'Ecumenical Bearings of the Missionary Movement', pp. 373-77.
[30] *SBM*, 48.11 (November 1922), p. 125.
[31] *SBM*, 48.8 (August 1922), p. 92. MacBeath echoed similar sentiments in a final article before the conference in the same periodical, 48.10 (October 1922), pp. 115-16.

differences.'[32] MacBeath, in his summary of the two year missionary campaign in Scotland, sought to underline the uniqueness of its successes:

> It was the first effort in which all the Reformed Churches united together. There were no precarious negotiations concerning union - there was rather the impulse of a great task that could best be done together. The Campaign has created a new spirit of fraternity throughout the churches which will do much to facilitate common service in the future.[33]

This event underlined the benefits of co-operation, first of all in mission and then in other forms of united action.

Baptists and Other Churches in their Own Countries

Baptists, like other branches of the Christian family in the first half of the twentieth century, recognised that closer ties with other churches would be beneficial for work at home as well as overseas. American Baptists in the Northern Baptist Convention had joined the Home Mission Council in their country in 1908 and that same year were charter members of the Federal Council of Churches of Christ in America. In 1950 this denomination participated in the formation of the National Council of Churches of Christ. However, working closely with other churches is not the same as merging with them. That took place only when core principles were held in common. As a result a merger with the Free Will Baptists in 1911 was acceptable, but a potential union with paedobaptist denominations in 1919 and the Disciples of Christ between 1930 and 1947 were rejected.[34] The Southern Baptist Convention (SBC), by contrast, was more cautious about ecumenical relationships.[35] In 1914 it produced its most conciliatory statement on inter-church relations in America entitled 'Pronouncement on Christian Union and Denominational Efficiency'. However, the American War Department's decision to continue allowing Roman Catholics freedom to promote their principles amongst men in the armed forces in 1917, a concession that had previously been available to the various Protestant churches, whereas Protestant bodies were subsequently forced to channel their efforts through interdenominational agencies like the YMCA, led to growing protests from Southern Baptists. James B. Gambrell, who gave the first presidential address to the SBC in its history, in 1919, reversed his earlier favourable thoughts on inter-church co-operation and thundered against the government plan that

---

[32] *SBM*, 48.12 (December 1922), p. 147.
[33] J. MacBeath, 'The Close of the Missionary Campaign', *SBM*, 49.6 (June 1923), pp. 75-76.
[34] Torbet, 'American Baptist Churches in the USA', p. 54.
[35] J.C. Fletcher, *The Southern Baptist Convention* (Nashville: Broadman Press, 1994), p. 121.

'allowed three expressions of religion in the camps: "Judaism, Catholicism and YMCA-ism".[36] A minor concern in 1917 had grown into full-scale resentment of this policy in 1919. As a result, the SBC decided in 1919 to reject participation in further ecumenical initiatives, a policy that continued to express the convictions of a majority of its constituency for at least the next fifty years.[37] The two major African-American denominations, the National Baptist Convention of America and the National Baptist Convention, U.S.A., Inc., were both full participants in the National Council of the Churches of Christ in the USA in the twentieth century.[38] Of the smaller Baptist bodies in the USA, only the Seventh Day Baptist General Conference has been a constituent member of the National Council of the Churches of Christ.[39] The overwhelming majority of American Baptists were happy in this period to work with other Christians on a wide range of issues, but were equally opposed to attempts at organic union or merger between Baptist and paedobaptist bodies.

Inter-church relations in Canada in the first half of the twentieth century were dominated by the foundation of the United Church of Canada in 1925,[40] a merger of the large Methodist Church, the smaller Congregational Churches and around half of the Presbyterian Church. The Baptist Convention of Ontario and Quebec (BCOQ) articulated a clear and unequivocal rejection of the invitation to join this new body in 1907, declaring that Baptists had a necessity to 'maintain a separate organised existence' and also had a distinctive baptistic witness to proclaim to the world, although they commended these paedobaptist denominations on their plans for union.[41] A year earlier the United Baptist

---

[36] W.W. Barnes, *The Southern Baptist Convention, 1845*-1953 (Nashville: Broadman Press, 1954), pp. 270-84. See also J.B. Gambrell, *Baptists and Their Business* (Nashville: Sunday School Board, Southern Baptist Convention, 1919), pp. 95ff, cited by R.O. Ryland, 'Southern Baptist Convention', in Garrett (ed.), *Baptist Relations with Other Christians*, p. 76.

[37] Ryland, 'Southern Baptist Convention', pp. 73-77. A good analysis of why Southern Baptists held this conviction is given in S.J. Grenz, 'Baptist and Evangelical: One Northern Baptist's Perspective', in D.S. Dockery (ed.), *Southern Baptists and American Evangelicals* (Nashville: Broadman & Holman, 1993), pp. 64-67.

[38] E.A. Freeman, 'Negro Conventions (U.S.A.)', in Garrett (ed.), *Baptist Relations with Other Christians*, pp. 88-92.

[39] G L. Borchert, 'Other Conferences and Associations (USA)' in Garrett (ed.), *Baptist Relations with Other Christians*, pp. 93-104.

[40] The movement towards church union both within denominations and then across their boundaries since the confederation of Canada in1867 is explained succinctly in P.D. Airhart, 'Ordering a New Nation and Reordering Protestantism, 1867-1914', and R.A. Wright, 'The Canadian Protestant Tradition, 1914-1945', in G.A. Rawlyk (ed.), *The Canadian Protestant Experience, 1760-1990* (Montreal & Kingston: McGill-Queen's University Press, 1990), pp. 98-101, 149-154.

[41] Canadian Baptist 12 September 1907; Baptist Convention of Ontario and Quebec Year Book (1907), pp. 223-25; E.L. Morrow, Church Union in Canada (Toronto:

Convention of the Maritime Provinces (UBCMP) had replied to this invitation with a similar response.[42] The wide range of beliefs and cultural backgrounds of the small Baptist bodies in a vast country hindered attempts to form any kind of workable organisation amongst Canadian Baptists until 1944 when the Baptist Federation of Canada (BFC) was constituted, embracing the three regional conventions, the BCOQ, the UBCMP and the Baptist Union of Western Canada. Although an organic union with other Christian bodies was ruled out, Canadian Baptists willingly agreed to participate in the production of a new hymnbook with the United Church of Canada in the 1930s. Further collaboration with the United Church resulted in the publishing of the Canadian Baptist-edited Sunday School materials as well. However, a minority of Baptist churches declined to use these publications.[43] Baptists on the Atlantic coast, unlike their denominational colleagues in the rest of Canada, played a more central role in the life of their region and were happy to work with other churches in most initiatives that stopped short of formal mergers.[44] During the early 1940s, for example, the UBCMP showed its confidence in the co-operative principle in Christian education through the Maritime Religious Education Council. Its social service board recorded its links with the Christian Social Council of Canada. Also, a strong inter-church Committee on Protestant-Roman Catholic Relations was formed in 1943 to watch for movements infringing on religious liberty and to promote Protestantism. In addition, the new general secretary of this Baptist convention was appointed to attend the organisational meeting of a proposed national Christian agency, the Canadian

---

Thomas Allen, 1923), pp. 34-39. See also H.A. Renfree, Heritage and Horizon: The Baptist Story in Canada (Mississauga, Ontario: Canadian Baptist Federation, 1988), pp. 205-206.

[42] *UBCMP Year Book* (1906), pp. 128-29. For more details on Canadian Baptist responses to ecumenical initiatives in their own country see chapter 9, C. Jones, 'Western Canadian Baptists and Ecumenical Initiatives in the Early Twentieth Century'. I am grateful to Callum Jones for information on the approaches of the different Canadian Baptist bodies in this period.

[43] Renfree, *Heritage and Horizon*, p. 241. J.K. Zemen, 'The Changing Baptist Identity in Canada since World War II: Prolegomena to a Study', in P.R. Dekar & M.J.S. Ford (eds), *Celebrating the Canadian Baptist Heritage* (Hamilton, Ontario: McMaster University Divinity College, n.d.), p. 3.

[44] 'Convention Minutes', *Yearbook of the UBCMP*, 1921, p. 15, cited by Renfree, *Heritage and Horizon*, p. 236. The Regular (Calvinistic) Baptists in the Maritime Provinces had united with their Free Will Baptist colleagues in New Brunswick and Nova Scotia, five years earlier than a similar merger of Northern and Free Will Baptists in the USA, in 1906, and for similar reasons. For details of these mergers see G.E. Levy, *Baptists of the Maritime Provinces, 1753-1946* (Saint John, New Brunswick: Barnes Hopkins, 1946), pp. 267- 82.

Council of Churches, that was operational by 1946.⁴⁵ It is not surprising that the branch of the Canadian Baptist family most secure in its own identity, the UBCMP, was the one that had the closest ties with other Canadian churches.

Baptists in East Asia, like their colleagues in Latin America, were a small minority that sought to promote their distinctive witness in countries where other Christian traditions had established a presence a good number of years earlier. Congregations planted by various Baptist mission agencies in China, for example, tended to reflect the ecumenical sympathies or otherwise of their 'parent' body. As a result, those causes associated with the BMS joined with others planted by missionaries from Presbyterian, Congregational, United Church of Canada, Reformed Lutheran, United Brethren (USA) and Swedish Missionary Society backgrounds, together with some independent Chinese churches, to form the Church of Christ in China. This denomination by 1950 had a membership of 177,000 out of a registered total of 950,000 Protestant Christians in that country. However, congregations associated with Baptists from North and South America and Sweden made the decision not to seek formal affiliation with this national institution.⁴⁶ Burmese Baptists were enthusiastic about partnership with other churches in their country and joined the Burma Christian Council at its formation in 1950.⁴⁷ Japanese Baptist Churches began through the work of Northern and Southern Baptists in the second half of the nineteenth century. Prior to the 1930s, under the influence of American missionaries, these causes had held back from significant ecumenical involvement until Dr William Axling (ABFMS), together with some Japanese colleagues, encouraged congregations associated with his mission agency to retain an affiliation with the United Church of Christ in Japan. After Axling left Japan some of these Baptist churches left the United Church to form the Japan Baptist Union, though others remained and lost their Baptist identity. By contrast, congregations related to the Southern Baptists remained aloof from ecumenical engagement until forced to do so between 1941 and 1946, when, together with most denominations, they were compelled to join the United Church of Christ (Kyodan). In 1946, when free to do so, these churches withdrew and formed the Japan Baptist Convention (JBC), though they were willing to work with other Christian churches through the National Christian

---

⁴⁵ *Yearbook of the UBCMP*, 1939, pp. 18, 153-54; 1944, pp. 44, 179-80; 1946, p. 211, cited by Renfree, *Heritage and Horizon*, p. 243.

⁴⁶ H.R. Williamson, *British Baptists in China* (London: Carey Kingsgate Press, [1957]), pp. 216-19. P.S. Hsu, 'East Asia', in Garrett (ed.), *Baptist Relations with Other Christians*, pp. 155-57, while broadly agreeing with Williamson's position, disagreed over the position of churches associated with the American (Northern) Baptists. Hsu maintained that some of these churches did affiliate with the Church of Christ in China, though none associated with Southern Baptists had taken this step.

⁴⁷ I am grateful to Samuel Ngun Ling of the Myanmar Institute of Theology for providing this information.

Council of Japan.[48] East Asian Baptists were inclined to engage in ecumenical initiatives, mindful as they were of being a small religious minority in these countries.[49] However, guidance from the mission agencies whose workers had planted these churches provided, in some cases, advice that pointed in a contrary direction. As a result, some East Asian Baptists were significantly less open to working with Christians from other churches in formal inter-church bodies.

Australian Baptists in general have worked happily with all other Protestant denominations in their own country, although their involvement in ecumenical initiatives in the first half of the twentieth century had been limited due to a fear of increasing the power of the Roman Catholic Church, which represented around 30% of the population.[50] On 1 January 1901, by an act of the British parliament, Australia was made a nation. Federation between the different Australian colonies led to a Presbyterian General Assembly of Australia that same year and Methodist union was achieved as early as 1902, but Baptists, although stimulated both by political union in the nation and denominational union amongst other churches, could not agree on a federal structure in their own ranks. There were even moves at that time to establish a United Evangelical Protestant Church, but this initiative did not succeed.[51] However, in the different regions of Australia there had been a variety of approaches to inter-church relations. The New South Wales Baptist Union, the largest and the dominant power in national Baptist life, was firmly opposed to ecumenical engagement, whilst South Australia and Victoria were far more open.[52] It had taken until 1925 for the different state Baptist Unions to agree on a constitution

---

[48] Hsu, 'East Asia', pp. 157-58. There was, though, some pressure from the SBC as its money and missionaries would not have been sent back to Japan to work with JBC congregations after World War II had these churches remained in the United Church of Christ. I am grateful to Dr Eiko Kanamaru of the Seinan Gakuin University, Fukuoka, Japan, for providing this information.

[49] Torbet, *Venture of Faith*, p. 349.

[50] D.M. Himbury, 'Australasia', in Garrett (ed.), *Baptist Relations with Other Christians*, pp. 178-79. A more detailed study of the relationship of Australian Baptists with other Christian churches was given by David Parker in 'Baptists and Other Christians in Australia', a paper given in July 2009 at the ICOBS V, Melbourne, Australia.

[51] K.R. Manley, *From Woolloomooloo to 'Eternity': A History of Australian Baptists* (2 vols; Milton Keynes: Paternoster, 2006), I, p. 182. See also F. Engel, *Australian Christians in Conflict and Unity* (Melbourne: Joint Board of Christian Education, 1984).

[52] Manley, *From Woolloomooloo to 'Eternity'*, II, p. 580. See also K.R. Manley, 'The Shaping of Baptist Identity in Australia', in Ian M. Randall, Toivo Pilli and Anthony R. Cross (eds), *Baptists Identities* (Milton Keynes: Paternoster, 2006), pp. 291-94, for more details of different Australian Baptist identities in this era.

for the newly formed Baptist Union of Australia.[53] As a result, a much longer timescale would be required for the formation of an agreed position concerning relationships with other Australian denominations.[54] New Zealand Baptists, by contrast, had always had cordial relationships with the other churches, even in the settlements which had a distinctly ecclesiastical origin such as Christchurch and Dunedin. A possible merger with the Congregationalists in Timaru led to discussions between the two denominations, but by 1912 the Baptists had decided to maintain a separate witness, both locally and, by implication, as a denomination. Relations were also good with the other Free Churches, and this experience had led to a New Zealand equivalent of the Free Church Councils in Britain being established in various parts of the country.[55] It was, therefore no surprise that when the New Zealand Council of Churches came into being in April 1941 that the Baptist Union was a founder member of that body.[56] Although New Zealand Baptists had been committed consistently to ecumenical engagement, they were equally opposed to any involvement in the moves towards reunion which had been a feature of the life of the other major denominations in that country in the twentieth century.[57] In addition, like Australian Baptists, the majority in their ranks were deeply hesitant about ecumenical engagement with the Roman Catholic Church. It is likely that the slight differences between Baptists in the two countries on this subject can be accounted for by a more powerful and influential Roman Catholic Church in Australia, together with the geographical and communication challenges Australian Baptists faced in seeking to work together in the first half of the twentieth century.

Baptists in continental Europe presented a varied series of responses to the subject of inter-church relations. In Northern Europe, Sweden, Denmark, Finland and Norway, together with Germany, Switzerland and the Netherlands, were historically Protestant, holding the Lutheran or Reformed understanding of the Christian faith, although sizeable numbers of Roman Catholics were

---

[53] *Australian Baptist,* 10.31 (1 August 1922), p .1; 14.30 (27 July 1926), p .1; 14.33 (17 August 1926), pp. 1-2; 14.35 (31 August 1926), pp. 1-2; 14.36 (7 September 1926), pp. 1-3, 8;

[54] Parker, 'Baptists and other Christians in Australia', p. 13, after acknowledging some support for ecumenical initiatives noted that 'most Australian Baptists have been indifferent, opposed, or in some cases, vociferously hostile' to such ventures.

[55] J.B. Chambers, *'A Peculiar People': Congregationalism in New Zealand* (Levin: Congregational Union of New Zealand, 1984), pp. 282-86.

[56] 'Baptists and the Ecumenical Movement', *New Zealand Baptist* (June 1972), pp. 8-9, cited by L. Guy (ed.), *Baptists in Twentieth Century New Zealand* (Auckland: New Zealand Baptist Research and Historical Society, 2005), pp. 56-57. See also M. Sutherland, 'The Basis of Union: New Zealand Baptists forge a Denomination in the 1940s', *Journal of Religious History* 27.1 (February 2003), pp. 72-73, gives an unusual example of ecumenical co-operation in which Baptists played a leading part.

[57] Himbury, 'Australasia', pp. 182-84.

found in Germany and Switzerland. The state churches, with which the vast majority of the population were nominally associated, had severely persecuted smaller denominations, for example, the Baptists, in the nineteenth century. Although this oppression had ceased, it had been replaced merely by a civil toleration until the second half of the twentieth century. Baptists in these countries had close ties with the other smaller Free Churches, for example Methodists and Congregationalists, and were associated with the Evangelical Alliance.[58] Conditions for witness in the former Union of Soviet Socialist Republics in this period were extremely difficult. In 1944 the Baptists and Evangelical Christians united to form the All Union Council of Evangelical Christians-Baptists (AUCECB) and a majority of Pentecostals also joined this body the following year.[59] In Eastern Europe, prior to World War II, Baptists had also suffered greatly at the hands of the larger denominations - for example, from Roman Catholicism in Poland, the Orthodox Church in Romania and Reformed and Lutheran churches in Hungary. Baptists were considered to be sectarians and ecumenical engagement with state churches became possible only much later in the century. The small Baptist community in Poland has been an enthusiastic participant in the Ecumenical Council with the majority of other churches in that country.[60] However, it has always been determined to maintain a distinctive witness in Poland since that country gained its independence in 1918. After World War II, for example, Polish Baptists refused to enter the United Evangelical Church, a body that contained the various Free Church denominations, because they feared the influence of Pentecostals.[61] Some of the most intense persecution experienced by Baptists in this era took place in Romania at the hands of the government and at the instigation of the Orthodox Church. This problem was at its most severe in the 1930s, when, in spite of all their claims to be in favour of promoting religious tolerance, Archbishop Colan was the minister of cults and the patriarch of the Orthodox Church was the Prime Minister.[62] This oppression culminated in the notorious 1938 decree enforcing the closure of all the approximately 1,600 Baptist churches in Romania, a policy enforced for over five months.[63] Baptist protests at this infringement of basic religious and civil liberties had some

---

[58] R. Thaut, 'Northern Europe', in Garrett (ed.), *Baptist Relations with Other Christians*, pp. 21-24.
[59] A. Bichkov and I. Ivanov, 'The Union of Soviet Socialist Republics', in Garrett (ed.), *Baptist Relations with Other Christians*, pp. 30-33.
[60] D. Lotz, 'Eastern Europe', in Garrett (ed.), *Baptist Relations with Other Christians*, pp. 35-36.
[61] A.W. Wardin (ed.), *Baptists Around the World* (Nashville: Broadman & Holman, 1995), pp. 206-208.
[62] *SBM*, March 1938, p. 4.
[63] Decizie [Law] No.26, 208, cited by B. Green, *Tomorrow's Man: A Biography of James Henry Rushbrooke* (Didcot: Baptist Historical Society, 1997), p. 152. The BWA letter of protest at this law is printed in the *SBM*, October 1938, p. 16.

impact on the Romanian government, especially when presented in person in Romania by J.H. Rushbrooke, a leading English Baptist and a passionate advocate of human rights.[64] Relations with Lutherans and Reformed Christians in this era were minimal but good.[65] Baptists in Hungary, like the other Free Churches, were persecuted not only by Roman Catholics, but also by the other two 'accepted' denominations, the Lutheran and Reformed churches. However, Hungarian Baptists were committed to working with other churches and were members of the Free Church Council of Churches and the Hungarian Evangelical Alliance.[66] In a context where religious liberty was often significantly restricted, Baptists, along with other Free Churches, struggled to maintain an effective witness for their faith. Inter-church relations with other oppressed denominations were cordial, but having any kind of ecumenical engagement with state churches needed to wait until after World War II.

British Baptists in England and Wales, in the Baptist Union of Great Britain (BUGBI), in the last decade of the nineteenth century, had played a leading part in the establishment of local Free Church Councils and in the formation of the National Council of the Evangelical Free Churches (NCEFC) in 1896. Dr Richard Glover (Bristol), C.F. Aked (Liverpool), Alexander McLaren (Manchester) and J.C. Carlile (Folkestone) were amongst the prominent Baptist members of this body.[67] Welsh Christians had shown great enthusiasm for the new bodies and by 1908 167 local Free Church Councils had been established in Wales. However, Welsh Baptists, in the largely Welsh-speaking Baptist Union of Wales (BUW), had felt unable to join the councils because these bodies by celebrating the Lord's Supper at some of their meetings had violated their Baptist conviction that only those baptised on profession of faith could participate in this ordinance. Interdenominational communion services, therefore, on these terms was impermissible.[68] Some British Christians, including J.H. Shakespeare, secretary of BUGBI from 1898 to 1924, had been dissatisfied with the NCEFC's perceived lack of vision for a closer federation of Free Churches[69] and formed a Federal Council of the Evangelical Free Churches in 1919 as a step towards a United Free Church of England. These two bodies were later united at a meeting held in Baptist Church House,

---

[64] *SBM*, November 1935, p. 2; May 1938, p. 7, are examples.
[65] Lotz, 'Eastern Europe', pp. 39-40.
[66] Lotz, 'Eastern Europe', pp. 57-58; Wardin, *Baptists Around the World,* pp. 262-63.
[67] A.R. Cross, 'Service to the Ecumenical Movement: The Contribution of British Baptists', *Baptist Quarterly,* 38.3 (July1999) pp. 108-109.
[68] M.J. Collis, 'Baptists and Church Unity in Wales in the Twentieth Century', chapter 8.
[69] P. Shepherd, The Making of a Modern Denomination: John Howard Shakespeare and the English Baptists, 1898-1924 (Carlisle: Paternoster, 2001), pp. 94-95.

London, in September 1940.[70] The vast majority of Baptists in BUGBI did not share Shakespeare's vision for a United Free Church, but ironically his 1912 proposal for a United Board to supervise a redistribution of Free Church resources and to undertake a wide social and evangelistic ministry[71] was later accepted with reference to one particular form of Christian ministry, namely army and navy chaplaincy. The British government had declined to accept chaplains from a number of Free Church denominations, including Baptists, for service with regiments in World War I. In response to this problem the United Navy and Army Board was constituted in March 1915 with Shakespeare and R.J. Wells, secretary of the Congregational Union of England and Wales, as its joint secretaries.[72] Shakespeare was delighted with its success. In 1916 he declared: 'we have seen the working in miniature and for a specific purpose of a partially United Free Church of England. It has worked well.'[73] Shakespeare had sought reunion of all the Free Churches with the Church of England, but this vision had died after an Anglican conference in July 1923, in which it was suggested that Free Church ministries might be 'irregular or defective' without episcopal ordination.[74] However, many British Baptists had accepted the need for closer ties between the churches and when the two Free Church bodies merged in 1940, the Federal Council was the model for the amalgamated body.[75] This crucial decision paved the way for the next steps in inter-church relations in the 1940s. A further milestone in British ecumenism took place in the council chamber of Baptist Church House, London, when the British Council of Churches (BCC) was formed in September 1942. A number of Baptists from the BUGBI played key roles from the very beginning of the BCC. These included M.E. Aubrey, BCC vice-president, 1948-50; Hugh

---

[70] E.K.H. Jordan, *Free Church Unity: History of the Free Church Council Movement, 1896-1941* (London: Lutterworth Press, 1956), pp. 127-35. See also Cross, 'Services to the Ecumenical Movement', pp. 108-109; E.A. Payne, 'Great Britain', in Garrett (ed.), *Baptist Relations with Other Christians*, p. 15.

[71] Jordan, Free Church Unity, p. 127.

[72] For more details of the work of this organisation, see N.E. Allison, *The Official History of the United Board: Volume One: The Clash of Empires, 1914-1939* (Great Bookham: United Navy, Army and Air Force Board, 2008).

[73] J.H. Shakespeare, 'Forward', in F.C. Spurr, *Some Chaplains in Khaki* (London: Kingsgate Press, 1916), p. 8. See also Shepherd, *Making of a Modern Denomination*, pp. 96-100. Idealist chaplains in the RAF during World War II did call for the creation of a United Free Church after the war, although it was recognised that there were serious obstacles to overcome before Baptists could be incorporated into such a body, due to their understanding of baptism. See W.E. Mantle, 'The Theological Significance of the P.M.U.B. Church of the Royal Air Force and its Contribution to the Reunion of the Churches' (M.A. dissertation, University of Bristol, 1965), pp. 76-77.

[74] G.K.A. Bell, *Documents on Christian Unity, 1920-1924* (London: Oxford University Press, 1924), pp. 156-63, cited by Shepherd, *Making of a Modern Denomination*, p.126.

[75] Shepherd, Making of a Modern Denomination, p. 129.

Martin, chair of the BCC administrative committee (1943-1956); J.H. Rushbrooke, acting chair of international affairs (1945), together with Clifford Cleal, secretary of the BCC Social Responsibility Department from 1948 to 1953.[76] Baptists in Scotland were more cautious than the BUGBI over ecumenical engagement, but did not hesitate to join the Scottish Council of Churches (SCC) on its formation in 1924.[77] The success of the SCC was the reason why Scottish Baptists were to reject a Continuing United Free Church proposal for the establishment of a Free Church Council in Scotland.[78] British Baptists in the BUGBI had been committed to developing ever closer ties with other churches in the first half of the twentieth century, but stopped short of any thoughts of a merger with other denominations. Scottish Baptists had taken a similar approach. Welsh Baptists in the BUW, by contrast, had struggled over ecumenical engagement due to their strict communion principles.

Baptists and Other Churches on an International Level

After the traumatic events of World War I, progress in inter-church relations was inevitably slow. A small gathering of ninety delegates from fifteen countries assembled at Geneva in 1920 and began the process of rebuilding and strengthening relationships damaged during the previous decade. Momentum increased following the Universal Christian Conference on Life and Work at Stockholm (1925) and the first World Conference on Faith and Order at Lausanne (1927), which bore fruit in the increased representation at the second World Conference on Faith and Order at Edinburgh in August 1937, when 344 delegates from 123 denominations were present.[79] This latter conference had been preceded by two smaller meetings in London and Oxford in July 1937 at which the proposal for a world council of churches had been propounded. At the Oxford conference Anglican Archbishop William Temple had proclaimed 'the need for a body which would provide "a voice for non-Roman Christendom", and the desirability of basing the whole ecumenical movement more directly on the Churches themselves'. His proposal was adopted with only two dissentient voices. After a vigorous debate the Edinburgh 1937 delegates approved the Oxford resolution with only one expression of dissent.[80] A special

---

[76] Cross, 'Service to the Ecumenical Movement, pp. 107-11.
[77] D.B. Forrester, 'Ecumenical Movement', in N.M. de S. Cameron (ed.), *Dictionary of Scottish Church History & Theology* (Edinburgh: T. & T. Clark, 1993), pp. 273-74.
[78] BUS Council, 25 May 1943, Baptist Union of Scotland Minute Book, 1942-1945, p. 245.
[79] A helpful summary of this process of events is given in W.R. Estep, *Baptists and Christian Unity* (Nashville: Broadman Press, 1966), pp.26-40.
[80] William Temple cited by W.A. Visser'T Hooft, 'The Genesis of the World Council of Churches', in Rouse and Neill (eds), *History of the Ecumenical Movement, 1517-1948*, p. 703.

advisory conference met in Utrecht in May 1938 to draw up the basis for the proposed World Council of Churches. The agreed statement, which was confirmed at the first assembly of the World Council of Churches in Amsterdam in August 1948, read: 'The World Council of Churches is a fellowship of Churches which accepts our Lord Jesus Christ as God and Saviour.' Utrecht delegates had not imagined the length of the delay that resulted, due to World War II, before the vision for the WCC became a reality.[81] The work of the International Missionary Council (IMC), although distinct from this process, was not in competition with it. In fact through its engagement with churches in parts of the world virtually unrepresented at Edinburgh 1910 it enabled interaction between and fellowship with Christian bodies from a greater proportion of countries in the world. Its 1928 Jerusalem conference attracted nearly a quarter of its delegates from the 'younger churches' in lands traditionally viewed as 'mission fields'. A major breakthrough came at its 1938 gathering at Madras Christian College, Tambaram, India, where 471 representatives from sixty-nine countries were present, with the majority of those present coming from the 'younger churches'. This truly representative conference of Christian churches was also the first IMC event held in Asia.[82] The groundwork had been laid for Amsterdam 1948, at which 351 official delegates of 147 churches in forty-four countries had gathered, together with many other invited guests to launch this new body. Of the major Christian denominations, only the Roman Catholic Church, the Russian Orthodox Church, the Southern Baptist Convention and the Missouri Synod of Lutherans were not officially represented. In assessing the significance of Amsterdam 1948 it is clear that it was in many respects only a significant milestone on an ecclesiastical journey, but one in which the churches themselves had accepted responsibility for this process and that the ecumenical movement had gained a firm foundation in the continuous life of the churches.[83] However, churches in Asia, Africa and Latin America were still under-represented,[84] but this new venture had gained significant momentum and represented the ecumenical mobilisation of the vast majority of Christian churches.

How did the various branches of the Baptist family interpret the formation of the World Council of Churches (WCC) and its vision for future inter-church co-operation? The majority of American Baptists had seen the formation of the

---

[81] Visser'T Hooft, 'The Genesis of the World Council of Churches', in Rouse and Neill (eds), *History of the Ecumenical Movement*, p. 705.
[82] Estep, Baptists and Christian Unity, pp. 40-44.
[83] Visser'T Hooft, 'The Genesis of the World Council of Churches', pp. 719-724. See also Estep, *Baptists and Christian Unity*, pp. 49-54.
[84] W.A. Visser'T Hooft, 'The General Ecumenical Developments since 1948', in H E. Fey (ed.), *The Ecumenical Advance: A History of The Ecumenical Movement: Volume 2: 1948-1968* (Philadelphia: Westminster Press, 1970), p. 4.

WCC as a natural development for churches already in membership with the National Churches of Christ in the USA. They did not see it in any way as compromising the unique witness of their Baptist constituency.[85] However, a minority of their members holding firmly to a more conservative theological position than many in their ranks, left the Northern Baptist Convention in 1933 to form the General Association of Regular Baptists. Others with a similar theological framework who remained in the Convention opposed these ecumenical developments. In 1939 a motion was passed at the Convention declaring that the Northern Baptists could continue their relationship with the ecumenical organisations only if 'their unique and historic Baptist principles' were recognised. The decision to affiliate with the WCC, taken in 1947, led to a further secession of members known as the Conservative Baptist Association. The majority of members had won the day, at the price of the withdrawal of a significant proportion of their constituency.[86] The National Baptist Convention of America joined the WCC at its inception,[87] as did the Seventh Day Baptist General Conference.[88] The National Baptist Convention U.S.A., Inc., took a more cautious line, but joined the WCC outside the time frame of this study.[89] Southern Baptists, by contrast, had a minimal involvement in such initiatives. In 1937 the president of the SBC was authorised to attend the Edinburgh Conference on Faith and Order and George Truett from Dallas was appointed as the delegate for the Oxford Conference on Church, Community and State that same year. As Truett was unable to attend, Convention president John R. Sampey and his wife and two others represented the SBC at both these events. Three times in 1938, 1940 and 1948, the SBC affirmed its policy of isolation from the ecumenical movement. The 1948 rejection letter included the phrase 'with perhaps increased conviction' indicating the strength of feeling in that constituency.[90] On this subject Canadian Baptists were closer in sentiments to the Southern Baptists. Full consideration was given to joining the WCC in 1948, but only the Convention of Ontario and Quebec voted, in 1949, to affiliate to this world body. The Union of Western Canada did not approve the proposal and the Maritime Baptist Convention voted formally against it in 1951. As a result of these decisions, the Baptist Federation of Canada was prevented from joining the WCC.[91] The majority of Baptists in the Americas

---

[85] Torbet, 'American Baptist Churches in the U.S.A.', p. 62.
[86] Estep, Baptists and Christian Unity, pp. 135-41.
[87] Estep, Baptists and Christian Unity, p. 141.
[88] Borchert, 'Other Conferences and Associations (U.S.A.)', pp. 99-100.
[89] Estep, Baptists and Christian Unity, p. 141.
[90] 'Proceedings of the Southern Baptist Convention', 1948, p. 58, cited by Ryland, 'Southern Baptist Convention', pp 77-79. Helpful information on the Southern Baptist position is given in E.A. Payne, 'Baptists and the Ecumenical Movement', *Baptist Quarterly* 18.6 (April 1960), p. 263.
[91] Zeman, 'Canada', in Garrett (ed.), *Baptist Relations with Other Churches,* pp. 112-13.

had not joined the WCC in 1948. This decision was in line with the majority of Baptists in other countries.

Australian Baptists were open to joining the WCC,[92] but were determined to take time to work through their collective viewpoint through the various state Unions. They were represented in Amsterdam by Ernest Brown, a former English government minister.[93] Many Australian Baptist leaders believed that their denomination would join this body early in 1949, but the meetings of the state Unions later that year revealed very mixed opinions about the way ahead. The leaders of the Tasmanian Baptists appeared to be committed to joining the WCC, but had delayed taking a formal vote on this matter. However, the Western Australian Baptists voted against affiliation by what the *Australian Baptist* called 'a surprisingly large majority'. New South Wales Baptists at their assembly referred the subject to their council so that both sides of the argument could be thoroughly considered. At the triennial meeting of the Baptist Union of Australia in 1950 it was reported that Queensland, New South Wales and Western Australia had voted against affiliation; Victoria and South Australia were in favour, with Tasmania having postponed a vote. The Baptist Union decided not to seek affiliation with the WCC, but requested the right to continue to send observers to WCC meetings. However, at the 1953 Baptist Union assembly even the attendance of observers at WCC meetings was questioned.[94] Australian Baptists were enthusiastic about working with other Christians, but attitudes concerning the WCC became increasingly polarised, with the majority against any involvement with it. The majority of New Zealand Baptists, by contrast, chose to affiliate with the WCC in 1948 and the East Asian Christian Conference in 1957, though up to a quarter of its constituency was unconvinced of the wisdom of taking this course of action.[95] Like Baptists in the Americas, Australasian Baptists were divided over the extent of their involvement in the ecumenical movement.

The responses from Baptists in Europe were very similar to those of their sister bodies in other parts of the world on this subject. In 1948 Baptists in Holland and Great Britain had chosen to join six other Baptist bodies represented in Amsterdam. In addition to the three American conventions and Baptists in New Zealand already discussed, Baptists from the Burma Baptist Convention and the China Baptist Council had also chosen to affiliate with this

---

[92] *Australian Baptist*, 36.47 (23 November 1948), p. 4.

[93] Brown was appointed to the WCC Central Committee from 1948 to 1954 despite the withdrawal of Australian Baptists from the WCC. Cross, 'Service to the Ecumenical Movement', p. 113.

[94] Opposition to involvement in the WCC was equally clear in 1955. See the *Australian Baptist* 43.1 (12 January 1955), pp. 1, 8; 43.3 (26 January 1955), p. 15; together with Manley, *Woolloomooloo to 'Eternity'*, II, pp. 579-88; and Himbury, 'Australasia', pp. 180-81.

[95] Himbury, 'Australasia', pp. 182-83.

new venture. However, Chinese Christians were forced to withdraw from the WCC after the Communist takeover in China, no later than 1950.[96] The Dutch Baptists were to leave the WCC in 1963,[97] though Baptists in Denmark joined shortly after the formation of the WCC in 1948[98] and Baptists in Hungary a few years later in 1956.[99] Baptists in BUGBI were committed to the work of the WCC and a number of its members took an active part in its proceedings. These included, in 1948, Ernest Payne, who became a member of the Faith and Order Commission of WCC that year and who was then elected to the WCC Central Committee, becoming its vice-chair in 1954 and retiring as one of its presidents at Nairobi in 1975. Percy Evans, principal of Spurgeon's College, London, who was both a BUGBI delegate and a Faith and Order Commission member, like Ernest Payne in 1948, was also a participant in a follow-up WCC Commission on the Church at Cambridge in 1950.[100] M.E. Aubrey, secretary of BUGBI and C.T. LeQuesne, the BUGBI president in 1946-1947, were the other two delegates from this Baptist Union.[101] The Baptist Union of Wales was not represented at the formation of the WCC in Amsterdam in 1948.[102] Scottish Baptists, likewise, had no representation at Amsterdam, though they had decided to affiliate with the WCC by one vote that year. However, there was much opposition to this decision in the years that followed, leading to a withdrawal from membership in 1955.[103] Only a minority of European Baptist bodies joined the WCC. British Baptists in the BUGBI were amongst the most enthusiastic advocates on this continent for this inter-church body.

Baptists in the various unions and conventions covered in this brief study showed a willingness to work with Christians of other denominations throughout the first half of the twentieth century. Although the total number of Baptists present at the World Missionary Conference in Edinburgh in 1910 was limited, their commitment to world mission was not in doubt. They, together

---

[96] Payne, 'Baptists and the Ecumenical Movement', pp. 258-67.

[97] Thaut, 'Northern Europe', p. 25.

[98] B. Hylleberg, 'Denmark' in Wardin (ed.), *Baptists Around The World,* pp. 238-39. Danish Baptists had been prevented from joining the WCC in 1948 due to interference with their application to join this body by the Danish State Lutheran Church. See K. Jones, *The European Baptist Federation: A Case Study in European Baptist Interdependency, 1950-2006* (Milton Keynes: Paternoster, 2009), p. 73, n.60, for more details.

[99] Payne, 'Baptists and the Ecumenical Movement', p. 265.

[100] Cross, 'Service to the Ecumenical Movement', pp. 112-14.

[101] Ian M. Randall, *The English Baptists of the Twentieth Century* (Didcot: Baptist Historical Society, 2005), pp. 254-55.

[102] Nor did it join the WCC that year, contra Payne, 'Baptists and the Ecumenical Movement', p. 263. See Collis, 'Baptists and Church Unity in Wales', pp. [?], for more details of BUW engagement with the ecumenical movement in the twentieth century.

[103] Details are given in Talbot, 'Fellowship in the Gospel: Scottish Baptists and their relationships with other Christian Churches 1900-1945', pp. 352-53.

with other Christians, formed various inter-denominational mission bodies to facilitate good relations on the mission fields and to aid effectiveness in the task of world evangelisation. Co-operation overseas was largely mirrored by partnerships in the gospel at home. Baptists were often serving as a bridge between various mainline denominations and some of the more separatist Evangelical churches and mission agencies. However, within the different Baptist bodies there had been tensions over the extent to which ecumenical engagement was desirable or permissible. Establishing good relations with some state churches had proved to be problematic as they often refused to recognise Baptists as equal partners in the work of the gospel. There was, though, far less enthusiasm for the proposed WCC. A minority of Baptist bodies did affiliate, but the majority of this constituency was unconvinced of the wisdom of such a course of action. Overall, though, relationships within and across Christian denominations had taken major steps forward between 1900 and 1950. As a result, this pointed forward to further encouragements in inter-church relationships in the second half of the century.

CHAPTER 10

Baptists and the World, 1900-1940: A 'Great Reversal'?

Geoffrey R. Treloar

In 1911 the Englishman, John Clifford, reminded the Baptists of the world that they were people of the Bible.[1] He also asserted that they were in touch with, and had nothing to fear from, the new biblical criticism that had burst upon the scene in the closing decades of the nineteenth century. If Clifford was right about their knowledge and critical understanding of the scriptures, three things followed for Baptists. First, they could not but be aware of what the Bible taught about the world, and, more specifically, the relation of the Christian to it. They were well placed to understand this teaching in all its tantalising ambiguity.[2] Second, they were bound to follow the Bible's teaching about the world, to embody it in their lives and structures. This placed them in a delicate position. Baptists knew they were to set their minds on the things above and not the things below which were all around them; that they were to be 'in the world but not of the world'. It followed, third, that they could neither deny the world nor surrender to it. In this dilemma a dialectical relationship with the world was required. Baptists must have dealings with the world, but it must seem that they had no such dealings. The quandary is of course perennial, but the early twentieth century, the era of such major global events as two world wars, the Great Depression, the reign of anti-God ideologies and the beginnings of decolonisation, was a time of particular difficulty. What kind of interface with the world, we might then ask, was sustained by the Baptists of these decades?

The particular interpretative issue on which an investigation into the relation of early twentieth-century Baptists to their world might be expected to shed

---

[1] John Clifford, 'The Baptist World Alliance: Its Origin, Character, Meaning and Work,' *The Baptist World Alliance: Second Congress ... 1911: Record of Proceedings* (Philadelphia: Harper & Brother, 1911), pp. 53-72, esp. pp. 58-59.
[2] My understanding of 'world' in the Bible is informed by Colin Brown (ed.), *The New International Dictionary of New Testament Theology* (4 vols; Grand Rapids: Zondervan, 1986), I, pp. 517-26.

some light is 'the great reversal'.³ According to the standard historiographical view, Evangelicals, among whom the Baptists of the period included themselves, evinced a weakened commitment to social ministry. This was a significant departure from the historical norm. For Evangelicals, as we have been accustomed to saying now for some twenty years, are activists.⁴ From the first they have been doers of the word – as individuals, in their denominations and in transdenominational parachurch groups. This activism has always involved preaching the gospel. It has also involved works of service and philanthropy in the wider society. The humanitarian activity of Evangelicals has embraced an enormous range of activities, and some great successes have been won at the level of political and social structures, most notably the emancipation of the slaves in the British Empire.⁵ But it is said that in the early twentieth century, particularly in the 1920s and 30s, Evangelicals resiled from this commitment which was only recovered after 1945. In the book that marked the beginning of the new Evangelical historiography of the last quarter of the twentieth century, Robert Linder observed that 'the great majority of evangelicals appeared to forget their own heritage of social concern and ministry in this period', turning instead to private prayer and personal evangelism as the primary means of dealing with modern social problems.⁶ Twenty years later, in a more nuanced account which allows that some interwar Evangelicals never ceased to engage with the social questions of the day, David Bebbington identifies an unmistakable weakening of social commitment among British conservative Evangelicals, arising from their premillennial theology, preoccupation with personal holiness and alarmed reaction to modernism and rampant Catholicism within Christianity, and to socialism and Communism without.⁷ Bebbington's refinement exposes what is implicit in Linder's account, viz. the equation of the Evangelical right with the movement as a whole in the

---

³ The term was popularised by David Moberg, *The Great Reversal: Evangelism and Social Concern* (rev. edn; Philadelphia & New York: J.B. Lippincott, 1977).

⁴ David Bebbington, *Evangelicalism in Modern Britain: A History From the 1730s to the 1980s* (London: Unwin Hyman, 1989), ch. 1.

⁵ Evangelical activism is one of the major themes in the IVP 'History of Evangelicalism' series: Mark Noll, *The Rise of Evangelicalism: The Age of Edwards, Whitefield and the Wesleys* (Leicester: IVP, 2004); John Wolffe, *The Expansion of Evangelicalism: The Age of Wilberforce, More, Chalmers and Finney* (Leicester: IVP, 2006); and David Bebbington, *The Dominance of Evangelicalism: The Age of Spurgeon and Moody* (Leicester: IVP, 2005).

⁶ Robert D. Linder, 'The Resurgence of Evangelical Social Concern (1925-1975),' in David F. Wells & John D. Woodbridge (eds), *The Evangelicals: What They Believe, Who They Are, Where They Are Changing* (Grand Rapids: Baker Book House, 1975), pp. 209-30.

⁷ David Bebbington, 'The Decline and Resurgence of Evangelical Social Concern, 1918-1980,' in John Wolffe (ed.), *Evangelical Faith and Public Zeal: Evangelicals and Society in Britain, 1780-1980* (London: SPCK, 1995), pp. 175-97.

'great reversal' interpretation. But is it true that 'conservative Evangelicals', in general, withdrew from social engagement? And what of the Evangelical centre and left?

Given their individualism, Baptists provide an apt case study of the early twentieth century Evangelical social perspective. Here, if anywhere in a denomination, might be found the alleged absorption with the salvation and sanctification of the self at the expense of wider social concern. To be sure, Baptists are treated in some of the literature as a 'mainline denomination', an entity often set over against Evangelicals. As a denomination the Baptists also encompassed great variety of outlook and theology. But, on the whole, early twentieth-century Baptists thought of themselves as Evangelicals, so that the diversity within the denomination reflects the diversity of the larger movement of which they were part. They are therefore an appropriate group with which to test the 'great reversal' thesis. Do early twentieth-century Baptists, in fact, evince this preoccupation with individual salvation and fit the pattern of decline and resurgence of social concern?

Baptists and Others

The first step taken by Baptists collectively in the new century recognised the world as the *oikoumene*, the inhabited earth, the place where humanity lives and functions. This was a dimension of the world of which they were obliged to take heed. For by 1901 Baptists were spread all around the globe. At that time there were said to be about 8 million Baptists in some 40 countries on 6 continents.[8] This wide distribution was the result of the expansion of British settlement since the seventeenth century and missionary effort in both the old world and the new since the end of the eighteenth. In recognition of the fact that Baptist Christianity had become a global religion, at the suggestion of J.N. Prestridge of Louisville, Kentucky, and under the leadership of the British Baptist Union, Baptists convened their first world congress in London in 1905.[9] Its foremost achievement was the creation of the Baptist World Alliance. From that point the two organisations functioned alongside one another symbiotically, the Alliance 'to unite Baptists in different countries and to create and express a Baptist world consciousness', the Congress to 'inspire, to educate

---

[8] *Baptist World Alliance ... 1911*, p. 56. See also David W. Bebbington, *Baptists Through the Centuries: A History of a Global People* (Waco, Texas: Baylor University Press, 2010), esp. ch. 14.

[9] J.H. Shakespeare, 'Introduction,' in *The Baptist World Congress ... 1905: Record of Proceedings* (London: Baptist Union, 1905), pp. v-vi. On the origins, see also Horace O. Russell, 'Early Moves in the Direction of Greater Cooperation,' and J.H. Briggs, 'From 1905 to the End of the First World War,' in Richard V. Pierard (ed.), *Baptists Together in Christ, 1905-2005: A Hundred-Year History of the Baptist World Alliance* (Falls Church, Virginia: Baptist World Alliance, 2005), chs 1 & 2.

and to further Baptist work'.[10] In the first half of the twentieth century subsequent Baptist World Congresses met in 1911 at Philadelphia, in 1923 at Stockholm, in 1928 at Toronto, in 1934 at Berlin, in 1939 at Atlanta and in 1947 at Copenhagen. Because of the obvious diversity of the environments in which world Baptists lived, it was never the intention for the Congress to function like an ecumenical council, dominating and controlling the expression of faith. The intention, rather, was to maintain and propagate the principles of Baptist Christianity for application in individual and local circumstances. At the beginning of the twentieth century Baptists organised to send their collective voice out into the world.

In fact, they had been slow to do so. Other denominations had been functioning globally in this manner for a generation.[11] In creating the Baptist World Alliance, Baptists were catching up with and, as they liked to think in emphasising the absolutely voluntary nature of their association, surpassing the others. Given this clear acceptance that they did not have the world to themselves, it is not surprising that the Baptist World Congress was from the first a platform for the assertion of Baptist identity. Of course, the world conferences of the other denominations did the same, and Baptists lose nothing by comparison. A succession of presidents, secretaries, local hosts and keynote speakers returned again and again to the matter of who the Baptists are and what makes them different.[12] Almost without exception, they identified the lordship of Jesus Christ as the fundamental principle of the Baptists. From this cardinal teaching, five distinctives flowed. First, the conviction that 'the believing soul stands immediately in the presence of Christ and receives [salvation] from Him' without the interposition of any other entity or power sustained a radical individualism. The same salvific reality meant, second, that Baptists must be champions of religious liberty (for believers and unbelievers alike) and practitioners of democracy in their own polity. The Baptist churches were held up, third, as spiritual bodies, with membership open only to those who confess a personal faith in God and his Son. Baptist life was based, fourth, on the authority of the Bible. This was one reason why, although Baptists experienced as much broadening and diversification as the other denominations, the leaders insisted, fifth, that their churches were Evangelical

---

[10] J.H. Shakespeare, 'Introduction,' *Third Baptist World Congress ... 1923: Record of Proceedings* (London: Kingsgate Press, n.d.), p. vi.

[11] See, for example, Hilary Carey, *God's Empire: Religion and Colonialism in the British World, c. 1801-1908* (Cambridge: Cambridge University Press, 2011).

[12] Especially J.D. Freeman, 'The Place of Baptists in the Christian Church,' *Baptist World Congress ... 1905*, pp. 22-29; 'A Message of the Baptist World Alliance to the Baptist Brotherhood, to Other Christian Brethren, and to the World,' *Third Baptist World Congress ... 1923*, pp. 223-28; Z.T. Cody, 'The Vital Principles of the Baptist Faith,' *Fourth Baptist World Congress ... 1928: Record of Proceedings* (London: Kingsgate Press, n.d.), pp. 106-11, & esp. p. 107 for the quotation that follows.

fellowships, embodying the traditional beliefs of Evangelical Christianity.[13] What outsiders might have regarded as a sixth distinguishing mark, believer's baptism, was presented as no more than a sign of entry into the *communio sanctorum*. Early twentieth-century Baptists were assured of their place in the world as a distinctive Christian community.

Maintaining their view of themselves and their role in the world required continual differentiation from other denominations.[14] At one level Baptists readily acknowledged their connection with the church throughout the world. At the same time it was necessary as a condition of maintaining the cardinal principles of Baptist faith and life to uphold difference and remain separate from 'ecclesiastical Christianity'. In particular they rejected the claim of established churches that entry into a visible church gives or is a condition of salvation. They were equally opposed to sacramentalism and sacerdotalism, both seemingly in the ascendant in an age of Anglo-Catholic congresses. In taking this line Baptists fully recognised that they set themselves against the three historic churches of Christendom – the Roman Catholic, the Orthodox and the Anglican. They were also well aware that they were criticised for being exclusive, intolerant and illiberal. Their response was that other communions owed their religious liberty to Baptists as the foremost champions of soul-freedom. Nor had the need for the distinct historic contribution of Baptists abated. As the leading representatives of 'the doctrine of "a Free Church in a Free State" [which] shall have absolute supremacy, in every land, whether great or small, around the encircling globe', they needed to stand firm. To the extent that such a stand stemmed from their fidelity to apostolic teaching, Baptists assigned themselves, in addition to their other characteristics, a pre-eminence of authenticity among the world's denominations.

A challenge to this sense of apartness and unique importance came from the church world itself. The early years of the twentieth century were the foundation years of the ecumenical movement with its attempt to transcend historic differences between the churches and focus on practical unity through service. Although the myth that the Edinburgh Missionary Conference of 1910 marked the birth of the ecumenical movement has recently been exposed by

---

[13] E.g.: 'we stand in the great evangelical tradition': J.B. McLaurin, 'A Key-Note Address,' *Fifth Baptist World Congress ... 1934: Official Report* (London: Baptist World Alliance, 1934), p. 206.

[14] Apart from those of John Clifford and J.D. Freeman cited in nn. 1 & 12 above, the important speeches on this are the presidential addresses of E.Y. Mullins, 'Baptist Life in the World's Life,' *Fourth Baptist World Congress ... 1928*, pp. 55-63, and George W. Truett, 'The Baptist Message and Mission For the World Today,' *Sixth Baptist World Congress ... 1939: Official Report* (Atlanta: Baptist World Alliance, 1939), pp. 22-36, esp. p. 28 for the quotation that follows.

Brian Stanley,[15] it was nevertheless a catalyst of the forces for interdenominational co-operation among Protestants that had been building across the nineteenth century. John Clifford seems to have responded to this in 1911 when he observed that 'the forces making for ecclesiastical federation and unity are working with unprecedented strength'.[16] At such a time the Baptist response was to offer co-operation with efforts to achieve unity among followers of Christ provided that they were not merely 'visible, formal, and mechanical', but led rather to 'unity of life, of love, and of governing ideas and ideals'.[17] After the war and its crushing demonstration of Christian disunity and the power of nationalism over international ideologies, the impetus to unity was renewed by the Lambeth Appeal of 1920 and sustained throughout the interwar decades by the International Missionary Council and by the 'Faith and Order' and 'Life and Work' movements that led up to the formation of the World Council of Churches in 1948.[18] In this new ecclesiastical setting Baptists both recognised the practical advantages of unity and also felt the pressure to join. Yet the general reaction in the interwar years echoed the earlier statement of John Clifford. Baptists welcomed the possibility of co-operation with all true believers, a condition the terms of which they themselves would set.[19] There could not, of course, be any truck with sacerdotal churches. Nor could there be any compromise of the spirituality of the church, a requirement which seemed to preclude organic connection with Congregationalists and Presbyterians (to whom in other respects they were close) because of their practice of infant baptism. In any case, as a voluntarily united body and as the bearers of authentic Christianity, Baptists constituted the truly catholic church because they reflected the catholicity of Christ.[20] By 1939 a survey tabled by H. Wheeler Robinson confirmed that Baptists did not believe that any kind of organic unity could be achieved without impairing the truths for which they stood.[21] Co-operation with other churches in Christian service commended itself as both a means to greater effectiveness in the world and as preparation for some kind of federation in the future. In the meantime the reflexive effect had been to make Baptists think more seriously about internal unity, in itself a

---

[15] Brian Stanley, *The World Missionary Conference, Edinburgh 1910* (Grand Rapids: Eerdmans, 2009) ch. 1.
[16] *Baptist World Alliance ... 1911*, p. 62.
[17] *Baptist World Alliance ... 1911*, pp. 62-63.
[18] David M. Thompson, 'Ecumenism,' in Hugh McLeod (ed.), *The Cambridge History of Christianity. Volume 9. World Christianities c. 1914-c. 2000* (Cambridge: Cambridge: University Press, 2006) pp. 50-70.
[19] *Fifth Baptist World Congress ... 1934*, p. 205; *Sixth Baptist World Conference ... 1939*, pp. 28-29.
[20] E.g. John MacBeath, 'The Catholicity of Our Faith,' *Fourth Baptist World Congress ... 1928*, pp. 116-21. Cf. *Baptist World Alliance ... 1911*, pp. 56-57.
[21] 'The Baptist Contribution to Christian Unity,' *Sixth Baptist World Congress ... 1939*, pp. 115-25.

relatively new development for a denomination that emphasised the autonomy of local churches.[22] The most effective way for Baptists to be in the world was to remain separate from the other churches and to be better Baptists.

Baptist identity and relations with other churches were worked out in the spiritual world, the order of redemption. However, there was another world. This was the *kosmos*, the natural order of communities of states and peoples. It was the domain of society, politics, economics, culture and conflict. In all of its dimensions it could be a source of anguish, but it was also a place of opportunity. Against the background of the Nazi seizure of power, the dualism of the church's existence was pinpointed poignantly in 1934 by the German Baptist, Paul Schmidt:

> The Church stands in two orders, in one of which war and confusion must continue, and she must face the facts and perform the duties arising out of the double relation if she is to avoid fanaticism on the one hand and dull resignation on the other.[23]

In its interface with the world order, the work of the church was proclamation of redemption, on the one hand, and of the God-given rules for the nations and their collective life, on the other. It was a matter, as Schmidt said, of facing the facts and performing the duties.

In the spirit of confronting the facts, the Baptist interface with the early twentieth-century world order was grounded in a view of the meaning of the events of their day. Before World War I Baptists were bold, not to say brash, in their estimate of the world. In what must be a high point in Baptist self-confidence, John Clifford asserted that 'the "stream of tendency" amongst the progressive peoples' was with Baptist principles. By this he meant that the world was moving towards greater freedom, with Protestantism to the fore and the idea of social service dominant.[24] Philip Jones, chairman of the 1911 publications committee, agreed:

> It is the era of the people. Democracy is in the air. Despotism at all points is feeling its breath. It must feel its breath more and more, and it is our mission to make it feel more.[25]

Immediately after the war Baptists recognised that everything had changed and set out to take their part in reconstructing a devastated world.[26] By the time of

---

[22] On which, see for example Peter Shepherd, *The Making of a Modern Denomination: John Howard Shakespeare and the English Baptists, 1898-1924* (Carlisle: Paternoster, 2001).
[23] 'Discussions on Reports of Commissions. No. 1. Nationalism,' *Fifth Baptist World Congress ... 1934*, p. 64.
[24] *Baptist World Alliance ... 1911*, esp. pp. 65-9, quoted at p. 65.
[25] *Baptist World Alliance ... 1911*, p. vi.

the 1928 Congress, democracy was much more problematic and Baptists, now far from being in the vanguard of world history, were accused of advocating a destructive principle in modern life.[27] Following the onset of the Depression, the world was seen at the next Congress to be 'in commotion', socially and economically, as well as politically. The material conditions of life were being transformed in the age of the machine, and new patterns of living were characterised by a 'groping for novelty, the casting off of moral restraints, skepticism as to moral principles'.[28] With 'the many attacks of crime, greed and hatred in personal, national and international affairs' in mind, Canadian J.B. McLaurin asserted that 'the world cannot keep on in the path in which it is going without moral and social paralysis and disaster'.[29] By the summer of 1939 the failure to build a new world order was clear. Texan, George Truett, told the 1939 Congress that they had

> come together in one of the most ominous and epochal hours in the life of the world ... Vast changes are rapidly sweeping the world as swirling ocean currents sweep the seas. These changes are economic and financial, political and governmental, educational and social, moral and religious. The world is still in the dreadful aftermath of the most ghastly and widely desolating war in all the history of mankind. The instability of reconstruction continues to plague the nations, both large and small. Misunderstandings, both national and international, seem relentless in their persistence. Wars and rumours of wars even now are casting their dark shadows across the earth.[30]

The world of early twentieth-century Baptists was manifestly turbulent, and the spectre of war loomed large. Pre-1914 optimism gave way to increasing apprehension and resignation to further conflict.

Witness to the World

The primary duty recognised by early twentieth-century Baptists was to be 'a witnessing church'. During these decades they never lost sight of the world as the object of God's love, and thus the sphere to be penetrated by the gospel. Before 1914, in the heyday of Protestant missionary endeavour, Baptists were second to none in their commitment to the evangelisation of the world.[31] Foreign missions were easily the most important concern at both of the first two

---

[26] *Third Baptist World Congress ... 1923*, pp. v-vi.
[27] *Fourth Baptist World Congress ... 1928*, pp. 55-63, 58.
[28] Corwin S. Shank, 'A World in Commotion,' *Fifth Baptist World Congress ... 1934*, pp. 176-80.
[29] *Fifth Baptist World Congress ... 1934*, p. 200.
[30] *Sixth Baptist World Congress ... 1939*, p. 23.
[31] See the extensive consideration of 'the evangelization of the world' at the 1911 Congress.

Baptist World Congresses. The enterprise itself was uncontested. Alongside reviews of what was taking place on the field, the main concern was how to maximise missionary impact by use of the most effective methods and increasing home support. In the interwar years foreign missions were no longer dominant, but they remained a leading issue. The importance of missions for the construction of a new world order characterised by peace and co-operation was readily allowed.[32] The Congresses also continued taking reports from the field. Indeed, allowing the churches established by missionaries increasingly to speak for themselves in recognition of their aspiration for self-determination reflected one of the important changes of the post-war era in Christian missions.[33] While Western Baptists were prepared to embrace this new heterogeneity within the denomination, they did not countenance the pluralisation inherent in the view that missionaries should collaborate with men and women of other faiths in the struggle against materialism and secularism. Against the background of the Jerusalem world missionary conference in 1928 and the publication of the controversial *Re-thinking Christian Missions* in 1932, both of which supported the liberalisation of contact with non-Christian religions, Baptists at the World Congress level continued to insist on the uniqueness of Christianity.[34] Only through Christ could the salvation of the world in all its senses be accomplished.

While home mission never rose to the same level of interest as foreign work, it remained a constant on the Congress programme throughout the era. However, despite the primacy of the individual in Baptist thinking, it was frequently asserted that the gospel was not for the individual alone. It was for society as well. In 1905 the connection was made by Augustus Strong: 'It is a great Gospel that we have to preach – a Gospel of salvation both for the individual and for Society.'[35] Effective social ministry remained an aspiration throughout the pre-war era. Welshman, Thomas Phillips, with his experience in London (at Bloomsbury) clearly in mind, revealed that 'we pray for social regeneration as we pray for personal conversion'.[36] After the war the commitment to the wider society was undiminished. In 1928 another Londoner, Charles Brown, asserted: 'The Church must get completely away from the idea

---

[32] E.g. H.L. Taylor, 'The Layman and Foreign Missions,' *Fifth Baptist World Congress ... 1934*, pp. 142-46.

[33] On which, see Robert Wright, *A World Mission: Canadian Protestantism and the Quest for a New International Order, 1918-1939* (Montreal & Kingston: McGill-Queen's University Press, 1992), chs 4 & 5.

[34] E.g. C.E. Maddry, 'The Great Commission: The Unchanging Imperative for the Missionary Enterprise,' *Fifth Baptist World Congress ... 1934*, pp. 146-52; Charles Koller, 'Evangelism as the Primary Task of the Church,' and Earle V. Pierce, 'Look on the Fields,' *Sixth Baptist World Congress ... 1939*, pp. 62-65 & pp. 81-85.

[35] *Baptist World Congress ... 1905*, p. 61.

[36] *Baptist World Alliance ... 1911*, pp. 159-60.

that its efforts are to be confined to its own premises and to what are specifically termed religious exercises and efforts.'[37] But the relationship between gospel and social ministry was never straightforward. The danger, as Phillips recognised, was 'for the church to degenerate to be a merely secular society, an institute, or an academy'.[38] Anxiety about social Christianity meant that the primacy of conversionism was repeatedly asserted. But for most early twentieth-century Baptists it was not a question of 'either-or', as it could be with fundamentalists on the one side and advanced liberal modernists on the other. The typical Baptist position was that the efficacy of social Christianity depended upon the effectiveness of preaching the gospel. The proper relationship was presented vigorously in 1923 by George Truett:

> We are not primarily social agitators or reformers ... When men are born again it will be natural for them to bear fruits, praise God. We have much preaching of ethics and social service in these times. This is well only as it is a corollary and application of the Gospel of the crucified and risen Christ. Doctrine without duty is indeed a tree without fruits. But it is also true that a tree without doctrine is a tree without roots.[39]

Presumption of the overlap between the salvation of the individual and of society was why the American, Hermann Von Berge, speaking under the shadow of the Depression, could say in 1934 that the prayer for our daily bread 'becomes one for a job, for a decent wage, for a social order that makes for security and justice'.[40] Looking back on a devastated world after World War II the importance of the gospel for the well being of society was even clearer. The American, H.C. Phillips, observed:

> The key to a city's life, or, indeed, to the world's life is not to be found in its stones, or in its steel for that matter, or any material thing whatever. The key is spiritual, not material... When we reverse the process, put material considerations first, and to gain material ends betray spiritual values, the things are not added. They are subtracted, as this poverty-stricken world attests.[41]

At the level of rhetoric at least, Baptists remained wedded to the gospel as the basis of an effective society and accepted the responsibility to Christianise the social order.

One important area in which this duty was pursued, particularly after World War I, was the economic system. The post-war period was a time of varying

---

[37] *Fourth Baptist World Congress ... 1928*, p. 35.
[38] *Baptist World Alliance ... 1911*, pp. 156-57.
[39] *Third Baptist World Congress ... 1923*, p. 119.
[40] *Fifth Baptist World Congress ... 1934*, p. 121.
[41] *Seventh Baptist World Congress ... 1947: Official Report* (London: Baptist World Alliance, 1948), pp. 84-85.

economic fortunes. For some countries the years after the war brought recovery and prosperity down to the Depression, which caused a dramatic economic downturn and widespread social distress. For others, post-war recovery was partial at best; the Depression only brought further deterioration. As a result, industrial strife and tension were widespread. Against this background, economic and industrial relations – now seen as 'a world phenomenon, and its problems [as] world problems'[42] – were extensively considered by the Congress.[43] Taking a long perspective, Baptist leaders recognised a result of the new organisation created by the ongoing Industrial Revolution. They also accepted that the church had a responsibility for ensuring that the operation of industry was Christian as well as scientific. Indeed, in relation to industry the gospel was 'the meaning of Jesus' way for the world of work'.[44] At the same time they were careful not to overstep the mark. Many of the problems of industry were technical and required no specifically Christian evaluation. Yet the task of the church was to bring the economic system and industry within the ethical framework of Christianity, a task for which Baptists felt they were well fitted. At the end of a sophisticated analysis of the world economic order, U.M. McGuire of Chicago noted: 'our ideals of liberty, equality and democracy ... have given us a specially clear understanding of the way to realize these ideals in economic life'. It followed that 'as long as we stand for freedom and fraternity in worship for all mankind we shall not cease to strive for equal freedom and fraternity for all in the world's work'.[45]

The whole subject was put on a considered basis in a report on 'Economics and the Mind of Christ' presented to the 1934 Congress.[46] The report summarised the Christian ethical framework for considering socio-economic problems: 'the supreme worth of personality in the sight of God, the brotherhood of all men as children of the one Father, the obligation of service to one's fellows, the law of love and mutuality as the ruling motive of life, and the duty of faith in God and in humanity.' It then presented a fourfold programme of action: maintenance of an atmosphere of goodwill for discussion of the reshaping of economic systems; ministers to function as prophets to inform and direct the social conscience about evils and injustice; support by the people for legislation curbing rapacity and anti-social exploitative practices; and encouragement to Christian industrial leaders to experiment with methods and plans which embody the goodwill of Christianity and the findings of careful economic research. This was a programme that allowed for the

---

[42] *Fourth Baptist World Congress ... 1928*, p. 263.
[43] Beginning with J.C. Carlile, 'Christianity and Industrial Relations,' *Third Baptist World Congress ... 1923*, pp. 61-66.
[44] *Fourth Baptist World Congress ... 1928*, p. 262.
[45] *Fourth Baptist World Congress ... 1928*, p. 265.
[46] *Fifth Baptist World Congress ... 1934*, pp. 57-61. The quotations that follow occur on p. 58 and p. 61.

reconstruction of the economic order if existing arrangements could not be made to serve the wellbeing of the people instead of exploiting human labour and life. The report concluded: 'Social evangelism seeking to convert the strong to the principles of Jesus and his way of life must supplement the older individualistic evangelism. Christian capacity will then be available for economic reconstruction.' Far from abandoning the economic order, inter-war Baptists were more than ever committed to the Christianisation of the economic life of the world.

The other leading social duty of Baptists in this era concerned the people of the world. In the judgment of one Congress speaker, 'the outstanding fact of the twentieth century [is] the dominating strides of the white man who is veritable master of our colour struck world'.[47] Awareness that all was not as it should be in racial relations was present at the Baptist World Congress from the beginning. If the gap between Christian teaching and reality was recognised, it was certainly not closed in the first half of the twentieth century. For in 1947 it was pointed out that those who had fought against the racism of the Nazis themselves still practised racial segregation.[48] The accusation reflected the rising importance of the issue across the century's early decades. In 1928 F.C. Spurr percipiently pointed to a rising clash of civilisations as the coloured people of the world reacted against the injustices to which they had been subjected by whites.[49] For all of its shortcomings on the other hand, the church could take the credit for advances in the humanisation of relations between whites and indigenous peoples. Past achievement, Spurr insisted, should be both incentive and obligation to see the job through to completion. But in 1934 it was commented that 'racial animosities are sharper and more explosive than ever in the immediate past'.[50] The need for testimony to the Christian brotherhood possible in Christ was becoming urgent. The report of the commission on racialism in 1934 accepted the responsibility to discover what was wrong in the racial relationships of the world and to set Baptists against it. It acknowledged racial difference as a fact to be celebrated as part of the providential plan for the world. It found that biological difference was not really the issue; racial antagonisms were more ethical than biological, and therefore subject to reformation. It identified the extent of the problem, mentioning in particular the problems of anti-Semitism, caste in India and the rivalry of Jew and Arab in Palestine. If the problem of segregation in the American South was omitted from the list in 1934, it was forced on Baptist attention in 1939 at Atlanta when J. Raymond Henderson spoke briefly on

---

[47] *Sixth World Baptist Congress ... 1939*, p. 269.
[48] J. Pius Barbour, 'The Colour Bar in the Light of the New Testament,' *Seventh Baptist World Congress ... 1947*, pp. 62-64.
[49] F.C. Spurr, 'Racialism,' *Fourth Baptist World Congress ... 1928*, pp. 270-72.
[50] *Fifth Baptist World Congress ... 1934*, p. 209.

'Negro Baptist History'.[51] At the same Congress Gordon Hancock of Richmond, Virginia, asserted that the church had to decide for 'the Barabbas of racialism or the Jesus of fraternalism', warning that 'the integrity of the Church is threatened, and that unless Christianity works immediately across racial and national lines it will not work ultimately within these'.[52] Hancock had no detailed programme for the church to follow, noting only that 'once the Church has engendered the fighting spirit, ways and means will suggest and multiply themselves'. The whole burden of his speech indicates that Baptists were not living up to their creed on the racial issue. Equally his protest showed that they were becoming increasingly troubled by what F.C. Spurr in 1928 had called 'the most vital question of our time'.[53]

Political Structures

Inevitably, social concern brought Baptists into contact with political structures. Speakers at the Baptist World Congresses liked to remind their audiences that the state was 'the other' against which Baptists had always defined themselves. With the progress of democracy, early in the twentieth century the religious liberty of the individual was not the problem it once had been, at least not in the English-speaking world. But it was still an issue. The *cause célèbre* before World War I was education in England where, under the terms of an act of 1902, denominational (mainly Anglican) schools were supported out of public money. As the leader of the passive resistance campaign, John Clifford was the hero of the denomination.[54] But dealing with affronts to religious liberty was only one side of the relationship with the state. In Britain the government had begun to take greater responsibility for the welfare of the people. None other than John Clifford himself applauded this development as 'foretelling the arrival of a new era in the commercial, industrial, and social condition and activities of the whole world'.[55] Clearly taken in by a wily politician and his own wishfulness, Clifford was delighted, moreover, that the change was being led by David Lloyd George, 'a political leader of splendid genius and captivating simplicity, who has been trained from childhood in Baptist ideas, who is now an active member of a Baptist church, and ... is absorbed in applying the doctrines of the Anabaptist of the sixteenth century to the needs of the men of our own day'.[56] In the work of social reform co-operation with the state and participation in politics could be part of the Baptist way of life. Yet a

---

[51] *Sixth Baptist World Congress ... 1939*, pp. 266-8.
[52] Gordon B. Hancock, 'The Colour Challenge,' *Sixth Baptist World Congress ... 1939*, pp. 269-72.
[53] *Fourth Baptist World Congress ... 1928*, p. 270.
[54] See Augustus Strong's remarks at *Baptist World Congress ... 1905*, p. 62.
[55] *Baptist World Alliance ... 1911*, p. 67.
[56] *Baptist World Alliance ... 1911*, p. 67.

broadly similar expansion in the role of the state in America in the 1930s caused George Truett some uneasiness.[57] Looking back on the initiatives of the 'New Deal', he warned American Baptists against encroachments on their liberty as the government contemplated inclusion of church employees in federal security pensions, allocation of public funds for sectarian schools and opening diplomatic relations with the Vatican. It remained a part of the Baptist mission to protect the great doctrine of religious liberty and its inevitable corollary, the separation of church and state. Political engagement, with and against the state, was another duty of the Baptist Christian.

In dealing with the state Baptists were obliged after World War I to take account of larger political units than the nation in much the same way as they were having to deal with the larger ecclesiastical units called into being by ecumenism. With the peace of the world now a major concern, they were soon involved in internationalism, the new dynamic in the post-war era. Following the horrors of the war, J.H. Shakespeare announced in 1923 that international peace is a true work of the church. In the 1920s this work ran along two main lines. Baptists opposed militarism.[58] They also worked for peace, setting themselves against the tendencies which promote war – international jealousies, suspicions, rivalries and greed – and pressing for the reference of disputes to international tribunals.[59] In line with this thinking the Alliance resolved 'to pray for peace, to counter-act everything that is likely to provoke governments to act against each other', expressed the earnest desire that 'all the nations should be brought into cooperative efforts to secure peace through a representative tribunal or court for the settlement of international quarrels' and appealed 'to the Governments of the world to make the maintenance of peace their first aim, for the sake of each nation and people, and for the sake of happiness and well-being of mankind'.[60] Later in the decade, while continuing to insist that the primary Baptist contribution to world peace would be the preaching that brings the new heart, Baptists were greatly encouraged by the work of the League of Nations and the disarmament conferences. But by 1934 the hopefulness of the 1920s had dissipated. With war again exalted as a legitimate method in international relations, they spoke out against it as contrary to the will of Christ and condemned the bellicose spirit emerging around them.[61] At the eleventh hour in 1939 Baptists were still actively considering how to avoid war and

---

[57] *Sixth Baptist World Congress ... 1939*, pp. 30-1.
[58] Henry Alford Porter, 'Militarism,' and J.H. MacDonald, 'Militarism,' *Fourth Baptist World Congress ... 1928*, pp. 244-50 and pp. 266-69.
[59] *Third Baptist World Congress ... 1923*, p. 35.
[60] *Third Baptist World Congress ... 1923*, pp. xxx, 212-13.
[61] E.g. Bela Udvarnoki, 'The Authority of Christ in International Relations,' and A.W. Beaven, 'Christ the Giver of Peace,' *Fifth Baptist World Congress ... 1934*, pp. 114-17 and 183-89.

promote peace.⁶² Recognising the failure of the League of Nations to provide for the settling of disputes by legal procedure, they again called for the creation of an international jurisdiction supported by an international police force and court of justice. All Baptists were exhorted not only to support the evangelistic ministry of the church but also to support the peace movement and work to influence public opinion in favour of international jurisdiction. The issues of peace and war required Baptist intervention.

The new factor in the international order between the wars was a non-Christian internationalism in the form of Communism following the revolutions in Russia in 1917. At first the Alliance was diffident. At a time when Western Christians were generally fearful of Communism, the subject did not find its way on to the agenda of the Baptist World Congress in the 1920s. Perhaps this is not surprising. By 1923 the revolutionary period was over, the Red Scare in America had passed, and there seemed a real possibility that the Soviet experiment would implode under the impact of civil war and mass starvation. In any case, disestablishment of the Orthodox Church and religious freedom gave promise of religious revival in Russia.⁶³ During the 1930s, in the wake of the failures of capitalism following the Wall Street crash, attitudes of many Western Christians towards the Soviet Union softened.⁶⁴ The Soviet Union was seen more as a challenge and a rival than an unqualified threat. Baptist thinking seemed to go in the opposite direction. Up-and-coming English Baptist, Ernest Payne, led the protest against the Five Year Plan of Atheism begun in 1932 and the anti-God campaign emanating from Russia designed to convince the rising generation 'that the fight against religion is a fight for socialism, a fight for better conditions of living and greater happiness'.⁶⁵ Moreover, the freedom enjoyed after the revolution had been replaced by persecution of Baptists as a group unwilling to give full allegiance to the Communist Party. Payne advocated a twofold response: refutation of the criticism of religion 'as the opium of the people and its leaders as exploiters of their fellows'; and the presentation of 'a full orbed adventurous Gospel, a faith willing to look all facts in the face, a devotion to truth, beauty and goodness, a patient and self-sacrificing discipleship'.⁶⁶ L.L. Gwaltney of Birmingham, Alabama, continued in this vein in 1939 when he said that the answer to the Communists must include the assertion that the attempt to banish God from human life was futile

---

⁶² 'Commission No. 1: "War and Peace",' and S.W. Hughes, 'World Peace,' *Sixth Baptist World Congress ... 1939*, pp. 96-114 and 221-25.
⁶³ E.g. P.V. Ivanov-Klyshnikov, 'The Work and Task of Baptists in the USSR,' *Fourth Baptist World Congress ... 1928*, pp. 75-78.
⁶⁴ Wright, *A World Mission*, ch. 2.
⁶⁵ *Fifth Baptist World Congress ... 1934*, p. 161.
⁶⁶ *Fifth Baptist World Congress ... 1934*, p. 164.

and foolish.[67] In the 1930s Baptists felt the need to continue as advocates of the gospel as the only true basis for international brotherhood.

At the same time as their opposition to Communism intensified, Baptists were confronted by another force in the world that seemed to run directly against the aspirations of internationalism. Fed by Japanese, Italian and German expansionist aspirations, nationalism was the new concern of the 1930s. Speaking under the shadow of the swastika at Berlin in 1934, the Swede, N.J. Nordström, was careful to point out that the commission on nationalism had been appointed in 1931 without reference to the policies of any one government or set of circumstances.[68] National identity, furthermore, was a gift of God which involved legitimate values and obligations. Yet the commission report insisted that nationalism, understood as theory in national and international relations of the absolute and unlimited authority of the state such that 'the citizens lose their liberty, and separations, hatred and enmity between the nations are created', was out of step with Christian ethics. Confronted by such phenomena, the church had no right to be passive or indifferent. Accordingly, the report called on Baptists to counter selfish nationalism by exposing its dangers, teaching against nationalistic arrogance, labouring unceasingly for peace and reconciliation in the world, building the moral foundation for the League of Nations and preaching 'the fatherhood of God and the brotherhood of men as revealed in the gospel'. In the same session Paul Schmidt bravely declared that 'the Church ... rebukes decadent nationalism and the exaltation of the state above God'.[69] By the mid-1930s Baptists had had openly to come out against the false nationalism of the modern nation state.

In Atlanta in 1939 there was not the same need to be diffident in expressing views about governments and their policies. By then the true bearing of Nazi ideology was plain for all to see, especially since the suppression of the Confessing Church. By then, too, what Nazism had in common with Russian Communism was clearly understood. With both in mind the Welshman, M.E. Aubrey, general secretary of the British Baptist Union, opened his address on 'Christianity and the Totalitarian State' with the claim, 'totalitarianism has presented to the Christian Church as great a challenge as any it has had to face since the fall of the Roman Empire'.[70] He made clear the stand that had to be taken: 'the claim that the need and the authority of the State must override every other loyalty is one which Christian men can never admit.' To sustain this position a twofold programme was necessary. With modern democracies

---

[67] L.L. Gwaltney, 'What have we to say to the Communist?' *Sixth Baptist World Congress ... 1939*, pp. 217-20.

[68] 'Report of Commission No. 1. Nationalism,' *Fifth Baptist World Congress ... 1934*, pp. 30-38.

[69] 'Discussions on Reports of Commissions. No. 1. Nationalism,' *Fifth Baptist World Congress ... 1934*, pp. 63-65.

[70] *Sixth Baptist World Congress ... 1939*, pp. 198-202.

having grown out of the Baptist demand for freedom but presently lacking moral authority, the first responsibility was to make safe the religious foundations of true democracy. 'We must go back to Christian teaching on basic Christian principles, to a fresh insistence on the truths in which our freedom is rooted.' The second responsibility was to make democracy worth saving. This requirement recognised the success of Communism and Nazism in meeting human material and emotional need. Solving the problems of unemployment, urban overcrowding and extremes of poverty and wealth followed as important components of setting the democratic house in order. The Christian response to totalitarianism was a recommitment to social Christianity in a democratic setting, a task for which Baptists, Aubrey asserted, were especially suited. After four decades of the new century the need for fidelity to Baptist duty in the world had, if it had changed at all, intensified.

Persistent Social Engagement

Their response to the international situation between the wars confirmed that for Baptists the spiritual and the socio-cultural dimensions of the world could not be practically distinguished. Grounded in the order of redemption, Baptists were not indifferent to the natural world and had an agenda for it as well as for themselves. That is, they moved easily back and forth between the kingdom of God and the *kosmos* as they endeavoured to bring their own distinctive Christian standpoint to bear on the great public questions of the day. The work of evangelism and conversion at home and abroad was fundamental as ever, but Christianisation of the social order and international brotherhood in relation to race and relations between the nations, for humanity at large as well as themselves, were at the same time the hallmarks of early twentieth-century Baptist concern for the world. Of course, this essentially unitary conception of the world was not held by all Baptists. There were Baptist fundamentalists and premillennial dispensationalists who were politically and socially disengaged— the names of T.T. Shields, A.C. Dixon and W.B. Riley come readily to mind. There were also Baptists who did give up active social interest—the outstanding example is F.B. Meyer.[71] But among Baptists as a whole there was no great reversal, and the practical Manichaeism of some Evangelicals of the era was not generally the view of Evangelical Baptists. They, at least, show that there are grounds for reconsidering the 'great reversal' interpretation of early twentieth-century Evangelical activism.[72] Indeed, there is good reason to

---

[71] Ian M. Randall, *Spirituality and Social Change: The Contribution of F.B. Meyer (1847-1929)* (Carlisle: Paternoster, 2003).

[72] Other works suggesting the need for revision of the 'great reversal' thesis include Nancy Christie and Michael Gauvreau, *A Full Orb'd Christianity: The Protestant Churches and Social Welfare in Canada, 1900-1940* (Montreal & Kingston: McGill-Queen's University Press, 1996); Gary Scott Smith, *The Search For Social Salvation:*

believe that in response to the conditions created by the Depression and totalitarianism's offence to Baptist sensibilities, their social and political interest actually strengthened during the 1930s.

One reason for the persistence of Baptist concern with society was the influence of clear-sighted and able leaders. In the front rank were the stars of the contemporary Baptist movement—John Clifford, J.H. Shakespeare, E.Y. Mullins, J.H. Rushbrooke and G.W. Truett. Each in his own way advocated social Christianity as he upheld the true scope of Baptist ideas and ideals as a counter to the parochialism into which they might easily descend. Behind the field marshals gathered a phalanx of lesser known but equally convicted generals from many countries to draw out the social applications of Christianity. From the newer Baptist lands also came leaders who knew persecution and repression to urge support for their struggle.[73] Baptist women played a smaller part at the Baptist World Congress, but, if sometimes maintaining something of a 'separate spheres' mentality, in pursuing the Baptist ideal of freedom for the emancipation of women they too put forward the social meaning of Christianity.[74] Each at his or her own level kept the Christianisation of the world in its many dimensions before the denomination as its calling and responsibility.

These leaders in turn were fired by a high estimate of the part they had to play in the world as the realm of both human need and divine power. As the custodians of authentic Christianity, and with the world needing 'nothing ... so much as saving power' in all of its dimensions, other-worldliness was not really an option for Baptists. Throughout the early decades of the twentieth century, their leaders never deviated from the faith in the scope and efficacy of Baptist principles declared in 1905 by the Canadian J.D. Freeman:

> They have in them ... the power to sanctify the family and make the home a place of richer spiritual culture. They have in them the power to secure for the Church a more intelligent, comprehensive, and universal consecration of her members. They have in them the power to mitigate the antagonism of commercial life. Setting before capitalist and tradesman alike the higher standards that necessarily accompany the sense of personal responsibility to Christ, they will go far to break the tyranny of both combined capital and organized labour. They have in them the

---

Social Christianity and America, 1880-1925 (Lanham, MA.: Lexington Books, 2000); and Brian Stanley, 'Evangelicals and Political Ethics: An Historical Perspective,' *Evangelical Quarterly* 62.1 (1990), pp. 19-36.

[73] E.g. 'Baptist Work on the Continent,' *Baptist World Congress ... 1905*, pp. 178-96; F. Fullbrandt, 'The Religious Situation in Russia,' *Fifth Baptist World Congress ... 1934*, pp. 154-59.

[74] E.g. Helen Barrett Montgomery, 'The New Opportunity for Baptist Women,' *Third Baptist World Congress ... 1923*, pp. 99-102; Frau Doctor E. Palm, 'The Service of Women Among German Baptists,' *Fourth Baptist World Congress ... 1928*, pp. 129-32; W.J. Cox, 'The Woman's Part,' *Sixth Baptist World Congress ... 1939*, pp. 228-32.

promise of succor and deliverance for millions who now groan under the oppressions of the autocratic Governments of the world.[75]

This was why they continued to see their task as, in the words of John Clifford, 'to lead and shape the religious life of mankind'.[76] Early twentieth-century Baptists had no doubt about the world's need of them.

In taking this high view of the world historical importance of Baptists, their leaders and others were inspired by the tradition they had inherited. Raising statues to the likes of C.H. Spurgeon, visiting important sites and celebrating 'great anniversaries' such as the Bunyan tercentenary and the centenary of German Baptists became a regular feature of the Baptist World Congress programme. After passing in review a long line of Baptist heroes, George Truett put his finger on the power of tradition as a vital force in the life of the denomination:

> We must not, dare not, be indifferent to the heritage of mighty names and vital principles that have come down to us. We must vindicate out faith and heritage by our deeds.[77]

The tradition he exalted impinged on Baptist consciousness in four main ways. Many great names sustained the Baptist enthusiasm for the Bible. The memory of William Carey and Adoniram Judson was a reminder that Baptists were 'missionary enthusiasts'.[78] A 'long line of Baptist prophets, priests and kings' kept alive the Puritan heritage, understood as 'a temper of mind that places the smallest act and thought ... over against eternal backgrounds and this appraises their true value ... that owes everything to inner worth and truth ... and that believes in the beauty of holiness that is eternal, because linked with the purposes of God and Christ'.[79] If social engagement was implicit in the first three, it was unavoidable in the fourth. The discovery of religious liberty created an obligation to uphold all legitimate freedoms as 'the consistent, insistent, and persistent contention of ... Baptist people, always and everywhere'.[80] It was, again, George Truett who pointed out that historically the gospel in the world 'has laid the corner-stone of our highest civilization ... founded institutions of learning ... inspired our best literature ... emancipated the slave ... conserved childhood, dignified womanhood, and glorified the home. Among all peoples and in all lands it has accomplished social and moral transformations which to the human view-point have seemed impossible.'[81]

---

[75] *Baptist World Congress ... 1905*, p. 29.
[76] *Baptist World Alliance ... 1911*, p. 65.
[77] *Sixth Baptist World Congress ... 1939*, p. 31.
[78] *Third Baptist World Congress ... 1923*, p. 122.
[79] *Fifth Baptist World Congress ... 1934*, pp. 204-205.
[80] *Sixth Baptist World Congress ... 1939*, p. 28.
[81] *Third Baptist World Congress ... 1923*, p. 121.

Ongoing social and political engagement was required for faithfulness to a heritage which demonstrated the potential of Baptists to change the world.

Finally, early twentieth-century Baptists were guided and sustained in their thinking by a wide-ranging theology of the kingdom of heaven. As successive Baptist World Congress speakers insisted, Baptist social thought was grounded in the dominical teaching of Jesus. This was a dual protest - against the tendency in the modern world to dismiss this teaching as irrelevant, and against the liberal-modernist tendency to concentrate on the teaching of the human Jesus as the residuum left over by historical-critical research. In the age of the social gospel, two doctrines, in particular, guided the thinking of Protestant Christians who adhered to the divine authority of Jesus. For Anglicans it was the incarnation, and this way of thinking was not absent from Baptist deliberations. But for Baptists the idea of the kingdom of God was much more powerful. It has been common to regard this as a liberal-modernist preoccupation.[82] In Shailer Mathews of Chicago University this perspective had a representative among Baptists, while a liberal evangelical interpretation was furnished by Walter Rauschenbusch.[83] Whatever its sources, the idea caught on and pervaded Baptist attitudes to the world. Its social implications were enunciated powerfully in 1911 by the moderate evangelical E.Y. Mullins:

> We must incorporate the conquering power of Jesus in grappling with these great [social] questions. It means that the kingdom is coming, for the kingdom is the correlative of the Lordship of Christ. The Kingdom means the end of predatory business methods, that know and give no quarter, the end of the sweatshop, the end of the disease-breeding tenement house, the cessation of the cry of children in factories overworked, the end of graft, the end of divorce in the sense in which men are practicing it in our time, the return of the Sabbath in its sacredness, and means of observing it, the purification of business, the purification of politics, the equalizing of human conditions... It is for the Christian man and woman, it is for the Church of Christ, to make the world see and appreciate that his sovereignty is destined to make its way in and through them.[84]

After the war Baptist leaders continued to take a broad and inclusive view of the kingdom and its obligations. Twenty years after Mullins' pronouncement,

---

[82] Claude Welch, *Protestant Thought in the Nineteenth Century: Volume 2: 1870-1914* (New Haven: Yale University Press, 1985), pp. 17-25. Gösta Lundström, *The Kingdom of God in the Teaching of Jesus: A History of Interpretation from the Last Decades of the Nineteenth Century to the Present Day* (trans. Joan Bulman; Edinburgh: Oliver & Boyd, 1963).

[83] Shailer Mathews, 'Sufficiency of the Gospel. For the Salvation of Society,' and Walter Rauschenbusch, 'The Church and Social Crisis,' *Baptist World Alliance ... 1911*, pp. 81-88 and 373-76. On Rauschenbusch, see Matthew Bowman, 'Sin, Spirituality and Primitivism: The Theologies of the American Social Gospel, 1885-1917,' *Religion in American Culture* 17.1 (2007), pp. 95-126.

[84] *Baptist World Alliance ... 1911*, pp. 390-91.

the Swede, George Fridén, represented the sentiment of the inter-war years in speaking on the authority of Christ in social relations:

> As to the workshop, be it the field of the farmer, the factory of the mechanic, the office of the businessman, the class room of the teacher, the hospital of the nurse and physician, or the study of the preacher, Christ wants to correct a defective notion about the things we often name our property. There is no property which man really owns and which he has the right to use according to his own pleasure. Positions, talents, properties are reduced, no, elevated, to nothing less than a sacred trust from God, which we are to administer for the purpose of establishing God's Kingdom and establishing the well-being of our fellowmen.[85]

For early twentieth-century Baptists the world was the domain for making the rule of Christ real and effective. Their calling to bring in the kingdom required the Christianisation of society.

The evidence of the Baptist World Congresses is, of course, highly rhetorical. Appearing before the denomination, men and women naturally expressed the attitudes they considered appropriate to the time and occasion. While there is no need to impugn their sincerity, the setting did create a tendency to state what ought to be rather than what was or might be. It meant too that the views expressed are those of the leadership elite, those appointed to official positions and able to take the time out from everyday occupations to travel long distances to the Congress venues. A quick review of the national backgrounds of speakers reveals, further, that these views are largely (although not entirely) Western, reflecting the contemporary Western hegemony of the world. They also represent what was said rather than what was done, and there is no shortage of evidence of different outlooks on the ground among Baptists around the world.[86] If not always representative of what was realistic and plausible in national and local settings, the deliberations at the Baptist World Congress nevertheless embody the ideals it was felt the denomination ought to espouse. As an expression of fidelity to scriptural teaching and Baptist identity, these ideals sustained an interface with the world that incorporated a distinctive response to a wide range of the public issues and awkward challenges of the day. If unable actually to bring about structural and political change, early twentieth-century Baptists, at least, sustained a critique of their world and countenanced the possibility of the reconstruction of society to achieve a more equitable social and economic order. In facing the facts of their times they were

---

[85] *Fifth Baptist World Congress ... 1934*, p. 113.
[86] What was happening on the ground may be gleaned from such works as Paul Harvey, *Redeeming the South: Religious Cultures and Racial Identities among Southern Baptists, 1865-1925* (Chapel Hill: University of North Carolina, 1997); K.R. Manley, *From Woolloomooloo to 'Eternity': A History of Australian Baptists* (2 vols; Milton Keynes: Paternoster, 2006); & Ian M. Randall, *The English Baptists of the Twentieth Century* (Didcot: Baptist Historical Society, 2005).

certainly 'in the world', while in continuing to advocate Baptist principles whatever the consequences they were often not 'of the world'.

PART FOUR

Baptists in Australia

CHAPTER 11

Australian Baptists and the State: Partner or Peril?

Ken R. Manley

'The separation of church and state has been something of a sacred cow in Baptist circles but only rarely have the theory and the practice been consonant the one with the other.'[1] This remark by John Briggs introduces the dilemma to be considered in this paper. Australian Baptists have waxed eloquent in advocating separation of church and state as a denominational distinctive but have often disagreed about precisely what this means in the Australian context. Contemporary Baptists are in partnership in many ways with the various levels of government: federal, state and local. What perils this may have created for the Australian Baptist movement is our question.

The relationship between the church and the state has, of course, been a problematic issue for believers from New Testament times. Changes in the time of Constantine broadly set the pattern for the middle ages and the Reformation era. Following the radicals of the sixteenth century, Baptists articulated a theology that broke with the Constantinian pattern and advocated a separation of church and state. Baptists have long been vigorous promoters of this ideal, especially in the United States.

Ernest Payne, over fifty years ago, argued that there are seven matters of concern for Baptists in considering state and church: freedom of conscience; freedom of the church from state control; separation of church and state; rejection of the idea of a national church; refusal of state subsidies; the right and duty of counsel or 'to wage war against evil'; the right of resistance.[2] Of these issues, the only one ever rejected by some Australian Baptists was 'refusal of state subsidies'. In early years this provoked harsh criticism from English Baptists who thought their honour was compromised by these either ignorant or wilful Australian Baptists.

But what is the relationship between a colonial church and the 'mother church'? Pamela Welch has questioned the common view that colonial

---

[1] J. Briggs, 'Foreword', in K.G. Jones and I.M. Randall (eds), *Counter-Cultural Communities: Baptistic Life in Twentieth-Century Europe* (Milton Keynes: Paternoster, 2008), p. xiii.

[2] E.A. Payne, *Free Churchmen, Unrepentant and Repentant* (London: Carey Kingsgate Press, 1965), pp. 56-74.

churches are to be regarded primarily as transplants, as re-located versions of their churches of origin. Rather they should be regarded as variants – at times highly distinctive variants – of their parent churches. 'Each evolved in its colonial setting into something new, which both resembled and also differed, sometimes considerably, sometimes subtly, from the original model. ... Australian conditions could require churches to alter religious practices and in so doing effectively re-shape doctrines fundamental to their identity.'[3] Were there special situations in the Australian colonies which prompted Baptists to adapt this traditional Baptist belief in the separation of church and state? Did the acceptance of grants from the government constitute a denial of their Baptist identity?

What does 'separation of church and state' really involve? The insights of Paul Fiddes are helpful. He notes that whilst Baptists in Europe do articulate a doctrine of the 'separation of church and state' this has not been to advocate an *absolute division*, along the lines of the 'wall of separation' urged by Thomas Jefferson. That is, engagement of the church in some corporate way in government is not *in principle* ruled out. He suggests that 'it should be the Baptist approach to ask how, *in each situation*, the relation between church and state accords with the sovereign rule of God and the place of Christ as the only covenant-mediator in the church'. What is ruled out by the doctrine of separation includes the following:

> (a) any kind of establishment in which Christian believers or a certain kind of Christian are privileged above other members of society; (b) a territorial view of religion in which a country or section of it is designated by government as the exclusive preserve of one church; (c) any interference by civil government in church government, or in religious belief or practices.[4]

None of these guidelines seems to have been compromised by Australian Baptist partnership with the state. The challenge, then, is to ask whether in the contemporary Australian scene the relation between church and state 'accords with the sovereign rule of God'. How to answer that question is far from easy.

---

[3] P. Welch, 'Constructing Colonial Christianities: With Particular Reference to Anglicanism, ca 1850-1940', *Journal of Religious History* 32.2 (2008), p. 234.

[4] P. Fiddes, *Tracks and Traces: Baptist Identity in Church and Theology* (Milton Keynes: Paternoster, 2003), pp. 263-64. See also the discussion in P. Weller, *Time for a Change: Reconfiguring Religion, State and Society* (London: T. & T. Clark, 2005), pp. 42-65.

Tensions over State Aid in the Australian Colonies

The first Baptist service was held in Sydney on 24 April 1831, by which time the number of convicts was 21,825 - still over 40% of the population of the colony of New South Wales.[5] The situation in the colony was difficult for all churches, although most of the other British denominations were already present. There was no established church, although the Church of England leaders, perhaps understandably, often acted as though they were the establishment. Governor Bourke successfully argued for the system embodied in the Church Act of 1836, which provided, under strict guidelines, aid for the building of churches and the maintenance of ministers of religion. This system ended any pretension of Anglicans being an established church since funds were available for all denominations equally. Roman Catholics, Presbyterians and Methodists benefited from this act over the next few decades whilst the few representatives of the voluntary system such as Independents and Baptists struggled to survive. By the 1840s in the three colonies of New South Wales, Van Diemen's Land (Tasmania) and South Australia, official aid for clergy and church buildings was provided, although in South Australia it was abandoned in 1851, when that colony became the first part of the British Empire to adopt this policy of separation of church and state.

John McKaeg, the unstable and impetuous minister who conducted that first service in 1831, attracted some followers of various religious backgrounds and in 1832 was granted a site for a church building by the governor. McKaeg was the only known Baptist among the sixteen appointed to the committee to raise funds and supervise a building project. This unusual crew would not have known they were breaking any time-honoured Baptist principle. In any case, McKaeg failed personally and the committee had to report in 1835 that the task could not be completed.

Meanwhile, some Baptists had sought help from the Baptist Missionary Society, which encouraged John Saunders, a young minister who had considered becoming a missionary, to come to Sydney. He travelled as a chaplain aboard a ship transporting female convicts, where among other duties he read the Anglican liturgy for the ship's company. Arriving in December 1834, Saunders soon gathered a respectable congregation of Baptists and other Evangelicals who applied for and received the land that McKaeg's group had earlier been given. On 23 September 1836 the first Baptist chapel in Sydney was opened.

What astonished English Baptists was to learn that the church, under the provisions of the Church Act, had been granted £741.6.10, half the cost of erecting the chapel. Reports of the grant were read with horror. Both the *Patriot*

---

[5] For details of Australian Baptist history in the following section, see K.R. Manley, *From Woolloomooloo to 'Eternity': A History of Australian Baptists* (2 vols; Milton Keynes: Paternoster, 2006).

and the *Baptist Magazine* asserted that this action impinged on 'the honour of our denomination' and hoped that the 'friends at Sydney' would soon realise how 'unsound was the ground upon which they had been treading'.[6] The account noted with pleasure, however, that additions of galleries were funded by voluntary contributions of over £500. The only other grant of land in New South Wales received by Baptists was at Kiama, though no chapel was ever built on this site.[7]

Meanwhile, in Van Diemen's Land the first Baptist church in Australia was formed in Hobart in June 1835. Strenuous efforts by the few Baptists to receive a land grant were unsuccessful. Henry Dowling, the Strict and Particular Baptist pastor who had arrived in 1834, was appointed a chaplain to convicts. His Congregational peers opposed this as an instance of receiving state aid, although Dowling asserted that the crown had a duty to provide religious instruction to such unfortunates and ministers should be appointed, 'exclusive of sect'. Dowling was a forerunner of many others who would later serve in various chaplaincy roles.

No Baptists received aid in the colony of South Australia during the brief period when such grants were available and the colony was held up to be a prime example of 'the success of voluntaryism' by Kerr Johnston in Tasmania in 1853. The Baptists there made a submission to Parliament on the subject in 1861, insisting that state aid was 'at variance with the New Testament dispensation ... unjust in principle... assisting equally to support truth and error'.[8]

The colony where state aid was to provoke the most controversy among Baptists was Port Phillip, from 1851 the colony of Victoria. Services were first held in 1839 and in 1843 the Collins Street Church was formed with John Ham from Birmingham as the first pastor. A grant of land was received from Lieutenant Governor La Trobe in 1845 and a fine chapel, funded entirely from church giving, was opened later that year.

During the next twenty years state aid was to be the subject of intense sectarian rivalry and led to internal tensions among Victorian Baptists. There were several reasons for this. Colonial churches were continually influenced by developments back 'home' as Australians avidly discussed religious news from Britain. Certainly, several English Baptists had argued energetically for voluntaryism, as Joseph Angus had in his prize-winning essay *The Voluntary System* (1839). Similarly, the English Baptist Union in 1839 resolved that state

---

[6] *Baptist Magazine* 29 (1837), p. 23.

[7] The land was sold in the twentieth century by the Baptist Union and used to help establish new churches in the area: A.C. Prior, *Some Fell on Good Ground* (Sydney: Baptist Union of NSW, 1966), p. 81.

[8] L. Rowston, *Baptists in Van Diemen's Land* (Launceston: Baptist Union of Tasmania, 1985), pp. 54-55.

establishments of religion were 'a palpable departure from the laws of Christ'.[9] Australian Baptists relished the news in 1848 that the Hon. and Rev. Baptist Wriothesley Noel had left the established church and become a Baptist. They saw this as a vindication of their views on baptism, but were also aware of his influential writings against church establishment. Ministers and other leaders who came to the colony in the 1850s and 60s, then, should have been well versed in the principle of the separation of church and state. Indeed, some of them had been active campaigners against discrimination. But establishment was one thing; receiving state aid, if equally distributed to all religions, was thought by some Australians to be quite another thing.

Local developments also continued to affect how churches faced the question of state aid. The 1836 Church Act had established a system of aid for the main denominations but had largely left unresolved the question of aid for education. Governments accepted they needed to subsidise schooling, but the debate was over what kind of funding and what type of schools. Sectarian rivalries and a mounting tide of secularism ended with the creation of public education systems that, as in Victoria in 1872, were 'secular, free and compulsory'. Churches were to maintain long and heated discussions about the type of Christian education, in particular the place of Bible readings in public schools, well into the new century.[10]

Baptists were heavily involved in numerous public debates about all aspects of state aid in every colony. James Voller, who came to Bathurst Street in 1854, proved to be a vigorous public advocate for Baptist ideals and was soon involved in public debates in 1855, when it was announced by the government that it intended to increase the amount reserved so as to place the clergy 'in a position similar to that occupied by other persons receiving salaries from the Government'. At the first protest meeting on 16 July 1855, Voller assured the audience that once people 'had to pay for their own pastors' many of the present stipendiary clergy would be forced to leave. As the *Empire* reported, 'He said of Christianity ... let it go and work for its own living (loud cheers) or let it starve.'[11]

Meanwhile, in Victoria Baptists were growing dramatically after the arrival in 1857 of James Taylor, an energetic and visionary evangelist and publicist.[12] He soon settled at Collins Street and a virile evangelistic ministry unfolded. Taylor's older Birmingham colleague, Isaac New, came to Melbourne and

---

[9] Baptist Union Minutes 1 May 1839, as cited by J.H.Y. Briggs, *The English Baptists of the Nineteenth Century* (Didcot: Baptist Historical Society, 1994), p. 384.

[10] See J.W. Gregory, *Church and State* (North Melbourne: Cassell, 1973).

[11] N. Turner, Sinews of Sectarian Warfare? State Aid in New South Wales, 1836 to 1862 (Canberra: ANU University Press, 1972), p. 159.

[12] For what follows, see Manley, *From Woolloomooloo to 'Eternity'*, pp. 63-76; K.R. Manley, 'A Colonial Evangelical Ministry and a "Clerical Scandal": James Taylor in Melbourne (1857-1868)', *Baptist Quarterly* 39.2 (2001), pp. 56-79.

served at the Albert Street Church. In the circular letter of the association in 1863, New outlined the denomination's beliefs, noting that the Baptists suffered a 'temporary disadvantage' because of their rejection of state aid: 'But we cannot sacrifice our honour and consistency for the sake of a questionable benefit'. It was a 'humiliating spectacle' to see professing Evangelicals receiving aid from a colony which supported both truth and error such as Catholics, Unitarians, Jews and, perhaps, 'the idolatrous Chinese too'.[13]

Thus, anyone with even a passing acquaintance with the Baptists of the colony would surely know that they were opposed in principle to any form of partnership with the state that involved a grant to a local church. Yet it was precisely during the 1860s when Baptists back in England as well as in the colonies were so outspoken on this subject that some Baptists in Melbourne applied for a crown grant for a Baptist church. In 1858 the Particular Baptists received a grant of land in Lonsdale Street with John Turner as pastor. But they were not in the association and had only limited contact with other Baptists. The church at Emerald Hill, later known as South Melbourne, was formed in 1854 and in 1862 the church applied for and was granted temporary reservation of a site at Howe Crescent.

In 1866 an application was made for a grant of land at East Melbourne for 'the Baptist denomination'. There was no church at East Melbourne and the association pointed out to the Commissioner of Public Lands that the association was completely opposed to any such grants and that they were the *bone fide* representatives of the Baptist denomination. Who had made the application? Taylor and the Collins Street church were thought to be responsible and the controversy precipitated a major breakdown between Collins Street and the association. In fact, the application was made by several individuals, including deacons from Collins Street, Edward Gibbs and Thomas McFarlane.[14] Indeed, the same group had made an earlier successful application in 1865 for land at Hotham or North Melbourne and Collins Street had commenced a Sunday School on the site - it later became the West Melbourne Baptist Church.[15]

These things could not be kept secret as temporary reservations and the names of trustees were published in the *Government Gazette*. In the Collins Street church on 19 November 1866, Brother Haller gave a notice of motion insisting that land grants were 'opposed to the revealed mind of God and that to participate in them was a sin'. Haller's motion was rejected on 19 December and a notice of motion was given that the church should withdraw from the association. Collins Street was by far the largest church (about 600 members).

---

[13] I. New, 'Our Denomination', Circular Letter of the Baptist Association of Victoria, 1863. The association at its annual meeting had adopted a strong statement on this issue: see *Australian Evangelist*, 4 (1863), p. 200.

[14] *Victorian Government Gazette*, 20 September 1872, p. 1731.

[15] *Victorian Government Gazette*, 5 September, 1865, p. 2002.

Conversations ensued and when the church did resolve to leave the association its withdrawal was not accepted.

New and nine other pastors then published in 1867 a pamphlet of twelve pages, *An Address to the Baptists in Victoria*. This criticised Collins Street for the North Melbourne application and insisted this was not 'persecution' but a fight for a great principle. How could Baptists give any sanction to error: 'Why not complete the circle by making a grant to the Chinese for building a Joss House and thus offer a direct insult to Heaven by patronising idolatry?' They lamented, 'We feel as if a great calamity had befallen us.'[16]

Just at this difficult time Taylor, who was clearly under great pressure, fell into moral failure with the wife of one of the deacons who had applied for the land and this 'clerical scandal', as the secular press hailed it, brought great humiliation on the Collins Street church and all Baptists in the colony. The church withdrew its resignation and rediscovered the strength of union when difficulties have to be faced. The one-acre site at East Melbourne between Gipps Street and Simpson Street, a short walk today from another 'holy' site, the Melbourne Cricket Ground, was never developed and the grant was revoked. What the site would be worth today defies calculation, but a Baptist principle was not to be denied.

Taylor's successor at Collins Street from 1869 was the scholarly pastor, James Martin, who soon had the church united and in good heart and no more foolishness about applications for state grants was entertained. But across the river at South Melbourne, where in 1863 William Potter had become pastor, things were not going well.[17] He had studied at the Congregational College in Carlton and at the university and in 1859 was ordained as pastor of the Mount Clear Union Church (near Ballarat on the road to Buninyong). Whilst he was at Mount Clear he had successfully applied on behalf of the Union Church for a grant of land. Potter's ministry at Emerald Hill proved to be disastrous and after he had refused to leave the pastorate, despite the advice of the association that he should do so, a schism ensued and a rival church was set up. Worse was to come. In 1870 the State Aid Abolition Act allowed churches which held land grants to dispose of these if they so wished. The question of what to do with granted lands was a neat little conundrum for those voluntarist congregations which had inherited crown grants. Most decided simply to do nothing. As a later Congregational conference observed, the government could not resume the land and abandonment of such lands would not be restoration but the 'giving up of the land to persons called jumpers'. In any case, some argued, the land had

---

[16] I. New, *An Address to the Baptists in Victoria* (Melbourne, 1867), pages unnumbered.
[17] For Potter and this controversy, see K.R. Manley, 'William Potter (1836-1908) at South Melbourne Baptist Church (1863-1875): Questions of Principle, Propriety, Property and Prosperity', *Pacific Journal of Baptist Research* 3.2 (2007), pp. 3-24.

been the property of the colonists of which the government was only a trustee and by taking it they were only receiving what was really their own.[18]

Such subtleties did not bother Potter and his supporters. Despite many protestations, he managed to sell the church land and personally obtained most of the proceeds. The secular press again had a field day with this further 'scandal' in which a Baptist was involved. Not the least intriguing was Potter's assurance that

> each Baptist congregation is, at law, a Denomination – a separate and distinct religious organization ... there is no Synod, assembly, or association that can interfere in any way whatever, either with the internal arrangement or with the property of the individual churches ... Each congregation is complete within itself and is independent of all others...[19]

The *Age* lambasted Potter:

> Persons of the Potter stamp ... preach morality, but heaven help the world if the morals of its inhabitants were regulated by such men ... Mr Potter has effectually prevented the congregation getting rid of him. The land and the church buildings are his own, and his salary is paid in advance until the end of 1879. If this be not fraud on a congregation, on the policy of the Abolition of the State Aid Act, and on the Government, then the English language is destitute of a term to express dishonesty.[20]

(It is worth observing that one of the leader writers for the *Age* at this time was William Poole who was also the pastor at the rival church in South Melbourne.) Potter, not surprisingly, did not remain a Baptist but became a public figure of some prominence as one of the founders of the Victorian Education League and became a close friend of Baron Sir Ferdinand von Mueller, the government botanist for Victoria, and was appointed his literary executor.

One of Potter's devices in the midst of the controversy was to form in 1871 what he called the Baptist Union of Victoria (recalling that the combined body was then known as an association and only itself adopted the title 'Union' in 1892). On a visit to Adelaide for the 1871 annual meetings James Martin ridiculed this initiative:

> There were only three little men with very little congregations and not very large minds ... One only preached to the elect, and would not have intercourse with him. ... The one man in Melbourne who preached to the elect few, and held most

---

[18] Report of the Intercolonial Conference held in Pitt Street Church, Sydney, May 15th to 23rd, 1883, to celebrate the Jubilee of the Introduction of Congregationalism in Australia (Sydney, 1883), pp. 255-56.

[19] The Rev. W.M. Potter's Reply to the Statements made on the 27th September 1873 in the "Age"... (Emerald Hill, 1873), pp. vii-viii.

[20] *Age* 29 December 1873, p. 4.

firmly to the doctrine of election, had come to the conclusion that God could not save His own elect without State aid.[21]

A recently located leaflet about this Union indicated that the president was Potter and the two other ministers were John Turner, the Particular Baptist of Lonsdale Street, and James Bassett of Ebenezer Chapel, another Particular Baptist church on Victoria Parade. The treasurer was Edward Gibbs, the former Collins Street deacon who had been active in the East Melbourne application. This Union was founded upon 'the distinctive principle of the Baptist denomination, namely, that the New Testament authorises every Christian Church to elect its own officers, to manage all its own affairs, and to stand independent of and irresponsible to all authority...'. Among the rules of the Union was that 'the President shall annually apply to the treasurer of the Colony for the proportion of the Donation-in-aid due to the Churches of the Baptist Union of Victoria, and shall act generally as its head or recognized organ of communication with the Government'.[22] Such a divisive and extravagant assertion of Baptist independency illustrated how far the quest for financial support had led those who wanted to become partners with the state.

The colonial period, however, finally settled into an agreement among all Australian Baptists that they should reject all forms of state aid. Some were occasionally tempted, such as when in 1879 various denominations received land to erect colleges associated with the University of Melbourne, but Baptists, so the story goes, declined any such help.[23] Given the heated tensions over the previous decade it is hard to see how they could have done anything else.

However, a new position was first articulated at the turn of the century. When Baptist work commenced in Western Australia, Samuel Fairey of South Australia wrote a long letter to the *Southern Baptist* in 1897 opposing the suggestion that they should receive any state aid. W.T. Whitley, the principal of the Victorian College, replied to Fairey and for the first time someone actually defended the possibility. He made the distinction between state control and state aid - in the 'old land' state control was the condition of state aid. 'But out here there is a singular state of affairs, that State aid is offered freely and hampered by no conditions as to State control. I am unaware of any reason in Scripture why a free gift should be refused'. He noted inconsistencies in those ministers who objected to any aid but claimed exemption from jury duties and served churches that were exempt from rates.[24] Whitley had anticipated the

---

[21] *Truth and Progress* November 1871, p. 110.
[22] *The Baptist Union of Victoria* (two page leaflet), copy in Public Records Office of Victoria, 00242/POOD.
[23] F.J. Wilkin, *Baptists in Victoria: Our First Century* (Melbourne: Baptist Union of Victoria, 1939), p. 24.
[24] *Southern Baptist* 1 January 1898, p. 12.

course of the debate over the next century or so and his position was to be adopted in ways and to an extent that he could not have anticipated.

Partnership with the State in Twentieth-Century Australia

Baptists participated in the debates leading up to the nation's federation. They supported the recognition of God in the preamble to the constitution and the saying of prayers in the federal parliament. The Seventh Day Adventists led a vigorous opposition to these moves on the basis of the separation of church and state, but the Baptists, from whom they might have anticipated some support, generally ignored their campaign.[25] One solitary Baptist leader, William Higlett, invoked this traditional Baptist principle, arguing that 'a civil government has no right to intermeddle with religion'.[26]

Over the next decades the Baptist principle of the separation of church and state seems to have been invoked only when Roman Catholics sought aid for their denominational schools. Baptists commenced their own schools in Victoria and South Australia but initially no aid was sought nor expected. But in 1939 F.J. Wilkin, a greatly respected home mission leader and tutor at the college, questioned the policy of Victorians on state aid. He echoed Whitley's views that in Australia state aid did not imply control or interfere with conscience: 'We can sympathise with the contention of our pioneer ministers, but for many reasons we cannot endorse it ... by their action Baptists were placed at serious disadvantage as compared with other churches'.[27]

After the Second World War things slowly began to change. The arguments of Whitley and Wilkin came to be utilised: aid was not the same as control. The church and the state surely could be partners in key social tasks such as education and care for the elderly. 'Strathalan', the first Baptist home for the elderly in Australia, was opened in Melbourne on 24 February 1945. This was achieved solely by the generosity and work of many ordinary Baptists. So began what has become a distinctive feature of Baptist work in every state of Australia: social ministries of various types have grown into a multi-million dollar enterprise with much of the income coming from government resources.

The expansion of this ministry has done much for Baptist credibility in the wider community, but it has only become possible because of a partnership with the federal and state governments. Running the homes was soon clearly beyond the capabilities of a small denomination and the government recognised the service to the community provided by church and community groups. Athol Townley, an active Baptist in the Menzies government, was appointed Minister for Social Services and developed the Aged Persons Homes Act in 1954 which

---

[25] R. Ely, Unto God and Caesar: Religious Issues in the Emerging Commonwealth of Australia (Melbourne: Melbourne University Press, 1976), pp. 42-47.
[26] *Queensland Baptist* 1 September 1897, pp. 114-15.
[27] Wilkin, Baptists of Victoria, p. 24.

granted capital aid to such projects. Baptists in Victoria had agreed to receive such aid on the basis that it helped Baptists render a service for the government. In 2008 the cumulative budget revenue of Baptist community agencies around the nation was over $400 million with more than 7,400 staff and thousands of volunteers.[28] Local churches are also engaged in numerous forms of social ministry for which they receive government funding, at the local, state or federal level. Australian Baptists are now partners with the state in a large social care enterprise which inevitably attracts a high degree of government regulation and control.

The 1950s and 1960s also saw renewed debate about aid for schools and it became a hot political issue, with Catholics stressing the injustice of the system as it operated. In 1951 Victorian Baptists set up an inquiry into the whole issue of church-state relations. There were many areas in which Baptists received assistance: exemption from rates for churches and manses, building grants for the erection of kindergarten halls and subsidies for running day kindergartens. The report, finalised in 1954, listed other areas where Baptists and state were co-operating: Aboriginal missions, the site for the Canberra church and chaplaincy privileges. The report also acknowledged that funding for schools was likely to be an issue and set up certain guiding principles such as that any aid was to be distributed equally, that nothing should compromise the church's freedom or the freedom of others and that the church had the right to criticise the state. Any grants would have to be for a task that the government could not meet from its own resources.[29]

Alarms were raised when the Government wanted to help denominational schools in Canberra in 1956. Protestants objected as Roman Catholics would principally benefit, it was feared. The *Victorian Baptist Witness* asserted that the people who wanted private education should pay for it and 'the price of freedom is eternal vigilance'.[30] Then in 1962 the assembly received a motion that expressed in strongest terms Baptist 'unfaltering opposition to the grant of Government aid to private and church schools'. A.F. Wright, the chaplain at Carey Baptist Grammar School, successfully moved an amendment which opposed in principle any subsidy of sectarian divisions in society but asked the Union to set up another committee to establish guidelines about Christian education. This committee duly reported that church and state should co-operate 'when the functions of each are fulfilled and protected'.[31]

Prime Minister Menzies during the 1963 election campaign promised substantial grants to the states for the purpose of science education. These were

---

[28] Data provided by Baptist Care Australia, courtesy of Mrs June Heinrich.
[29] Duplicated report of the committee in 'State Aid to Church Schools' file in Baptist Union of Victoria archives.
[30] Victorian Baptist Witness 6 August 1956, p. 2.
[31] Baptist Union of Victoria assembly minutes, October 1963, quoted by Manley, *From Woolloomooloo to 'Eternity'*, II, p. 528.

to be available to both state schools and denominational schools. As Michael Hogan observes: 'It was the formal entry of the Commonwealth into direct funding for schools. It was also the breakthrough to a policy of government assistance for denominational schooling which had disappeared eighty years before.'[32] The state where this change created most tension for Baptists was Victoria, where they had three schools, Carey, Strathcona and Kilvington, which would benefit from new policies. Victorian Baptists agreed in July 1964 that Baptist schools could accept state aid for the provision of capital items for the teaching of science.[33] That policy has been extended so that today a considerable part of school revenue comes from government funding, as it does in all private schools.

The decision to allow Victorian Baptists to accept state aid was timely for the Baptist College which, under the leadership of Mervyn Himbury, established a university residential college as well as continuing as a theological college. The Menzies government had resolved to enlarge university education and provide funding to assist the erection of residential colleges. The Prime Minister opened Whitley College, named after its founding principal who had argued that aid could be accepted, on 25 February 1965. The first stage of the building had cost £270,000 of which £120,000 came from the federal government and another £60,000 from the state government.

The New South Wales Assembly established a commission to investigate church-state relations in 1966 and this reported in 1968. Probably the most comprehensive statement on this issue by Australian Baptists, the familiar insistence on freedom of worship and religious association was sounded. Acknowledging the controversial nature of key issues, the report did allow exemption from rates and sales tax provided there was no interference by the state in church affairs and added that the church should not seek such exemptions (a clause that was impractical and has been consistently ignored). Financial support for chaplains was justified whilst government aid for charitable and social institutions was appropriate since the state sought the aid of voluntary organisations to serve in this way. State aid for schools received a lengthy discussion but was permitted if it was 'not used for religious purposes but for predominantly secular subjects' and there was no interference with religious liberty. Aware of the practical difficulties of these restrictions, the report also noted that 'as Baptists we accept grants in aid for teachers in our Mission schools'. Debate in assembly focused on one other recommendation, 'The institutional church should not endeavour to formulate specific pronouncements about political or economic problems'. This was rejected and replaced by the assertion, 'The institutional church is entitled to make specific pronouncements on moral and religious issues even though political and

---

[32] M. Hogan, *The Sectarian Strand* (Ringwood: Penguin, 1987), p. 253.
[33] Victorian Baptist Witness 5 August 1964, p. 3.

economic issues be involved'. This was strongly supported and a Public Affairs Committee to guide the churches was formed.[34]

A similar debate was held in Queensland and in 1972, after regular motions against any form of state aid in the preceding years, it was finally agreed to embrace the inevitable and accept the legitimacy of state aid for schools and social ministries.[35]

A new initiative in schooling among Baptists was commenced in New South Wales in the 1970s with the formation of Christian community schools which would be closely linked with local churches and were motivated largely by anxiety about the 'unchristian' influences in state schools. These new schools would be inexpensive, co-operative ventures between Christian staff, parents and interested Christians whilst Christ and the Bible would be central to all that happened in the school. The expansion of these parent-controlled schools is part of a dramatic switch in recent years from government to non-government schools. Prime Minister Howard positively encouraged this development as parents sought for schools that maintained what he described as 'traditional values'.[36]

Clearly, Baptists are now in an expanding partnership with the state. This has enabled Baptists to undertake a wide range of ministries which otherwise they could not possibly maintain. That is a positive outcome. But has the relationship with the government created real perils for the identity and mission of the church?

The Perils of State Partnership

Marion Maddox in her controversial book *God under Howard* (2005) argued that federal government support for Christian schools and social welfare programmes run by churches has tended to mute churches' criticism of political policies. Critics from the churches were branded as 'extreme' and leaders were urged to stick to 'spiritual leadership'.[37] This highly privatised model of religion reveals that politicians see churches as having a functional role in education and social care, but it is increasingly hard for mainline churches to exercise an independent voice in the public square. Patterns have developed of 'piecemeal mutual distancing between church and government, as well as

---

[34] Baptist Union of NSW Yearbook 1968-69, pp. 50-60; Australian Baptist 16 October 1968, pp. 1, 2, 6.
[35] K. Smith, 'The Rise and Fall of Opposition to State Aid for Schools', Baptist Historical Society of Queensland Newsletter, December 1991 and March 1992.
[36] For discussion of Howard and his support for 'traditional values', especially in schools, see M. Maddox, *God under Howard: The Rise of the Religious Right in Australian Politics* (Crows Nest: Allen & Unwin, 2005), pp. 73; 185.
[37] Maddox, *God under Howard,* pp. 147-50.

substantial areas of co-operation ... Australian religion-state relations have been worked out ad hoc.'[38]

Professor Elaine Graham in a review of British political emphasis on voluntary and community groups – the so-called 'third sector' – in the delivery of welfare provision, social services and social regeneration notes that many policy makers are looking to Australia for models and precedents in the role of voluntary agencies. Faith communities represent one of the wellsprings of 'social capital' in the state.[39]

Some British religious leaders, however, have wondered if this partnership will divert the church from other priorities more integral to their life and witness. Roland Sewell of the Salvation Army, for example, listed four substantial challenges which could fatally compromise the freedom of the faith-based sector. First was *competitive tendering* where the success of the bid may depend more on the 'narrative skill of the writer' than the competence of the provider. Many in the voluntary sector are finding that their essential mission is distorted by the cycle of funding and employing extra staff to prepare bids. Secondly, Sewell spoke of the risk of *compliance* to narrow outcomes or meeting prescriptive requirements leading to micromanaging and endless reporting protocols. Thirdly, is *corporatisation*, that is, the need to develop large administrative infrastructures to manage funding with the potential to lose flexibility. Finally, the imperatives of *commercialism* can undermine innovative services with the risk that those on the margins will suffer.[40]

One useful discussion in the Australian context, published in 2002, does explore dilemmas for church welfare agencies when accepting government contracts and some Baptist agencies are utilising this as a resource with their staff. The crux of the issue is stated by Marilyn Webster:

> Love ... Compassion ... Justice ... Mercy ... The poor ... the lame ... The least in the community: these are the gospel values which underpin the mission of the church through its community service agencies.
>
> Accountability ... Effectiveness ... Efficiency ... Best value, The consumer ... The individual: these are the market values which underpin the mission of the market through community services.[41]

---

[38] M. Maddox, 'Religion, Secularism and the Promise of Public Theology', *International Journal of Public Theology* 1 (2007), p. 88.

[39] E. Graham, 'Rethinking the Common Good: Theology and the Future of Welfare', *Colloquium* 40.2 (2008), pp. 133-56.

[40] Graham, 'Rethinking', pp. 141-42.

[41] M. Webster, 'A View from the Church Agency Perspective', in A. Nichols and M. Postma (eds), *The Church and the Free Market: Dilemmas in Church Welfare Agencies accepting Contracts from Government* (Melbourne: Victorian Council of Churches and Australian Theological Forum, 2002), p. 77.

Other theologians specifically repudiate the co-option of the churches into the government's agenda. They challenge the neutrality of the public domain and argue that much of what the church is being asked to do is a distraction from the essential and primary task of the church. Luke Bretherton of King's College, London, has argued that the church should refuse the terms and conditions of co-operation.[42] The partnership is an unequal one and can actually create distance between the targeted client group and the religious organisation acting as a conduit for state resources. 'Professionalisation' may actually distance such religious groups from those they serve in their communities. So much energy is needed to maintain government-sponsored projects that the 'core business' of the church suffers. Tangible outcomes become more important than 'spiritual goals' such as praying with and pastoring people. Bretherton claims that churches must understand the present debates as an opportunity to re-engage the churches in their mission. He sees what Stanley Hauerwas calls a 'discriminating engagement' as the goal rather than either complete withdrawal or general involvement. The real gift of the church to the state can be as a dissident or contrast society.

From several angles, then, the danger for the church as it engages with the state is significant. For Australian Baptists these are sobering questions. Thankfully, the days when Baptists in this country questioned the legitimacy of social action as an integral part of Christian mission have long gone. That is not the issue under review. Again, 'separation of church and state' remains a valued part of the Baptist heritage. But the present challenge is, as Paul Fiddes has suggested, to discern just how the relation between church and state accords with the sovereign rule of God. It is clearly arguable that the wide ministry of contemporary Baptists serving so many people, a ministry made possible only by a form of partnership with the state, truly does express a broad vision of the kingdom of God at work in our society. The ministry of dedicated leaders who serve with compassion, skill and care in our schools and social agencies is to be honoured. But in a changing political and social context caution is needed and questions such as those we have identified do need to be asked. John Briggs thought separation of state and church was a 'sacred cow' for Baptists, but not always followed as a principle. Luke Bretherton proposes a more sobering image for Australian Baptists to consider: 'Partnership, as it is currently envisaged by the state, is more of a Trojan horse than a gift horse'.[43]

---

[42] L. Bretherton, 'A New Establishment? Theological Politics and the Emerging Shape of Church-State Relations', *Political Theology* 7.3 (2006), pp. 371-92.
[43] Bretherton, 'A New Establishment?', p. 92.

CHAPTER 12

Christians First and Baptists Second? South Australian Baptists and Other Denominations, 1836 to 1936

John S. Walker

From the time when South Australia was founded as a British colony in 1836 until the 1930s, South Australian Baptists were, on the whole, more receptive to pursuing close ties with other Protestant denominations that had an Evangelical basis than were Baptists from other parts of Australia.[1] As J.D. Bollen has argued in his influential monograph on Australian Baptists, South Australian Baptists, comfortable in a society they helped to shape, were the prime example among Australian Baptists of the rejection of sect-type religion in favour of a more accommodating denominational style.[2] Although the contrast between South Australian Baptists and those elsewhere in Australia, particularly Victoria, should not be overdrawn, Bollen's assessment has a strong basis in fact. South Australian Baptists were unique amongst Australian Baptists in that the overwhelming majority of their churches followed an open-membership policy. Furthermore, South Australian Baptists not only co-operated with other Evangelicals in a range of joint activities, but also, unlike most other Australian Baptists, participated strongly in church union initiatives after the First World War. Indeed, in October 1919 the annual meetings of the South Australian Baptist Union (SABU) overwhelmingly supported a resolution approving amalgamation with the Methodist, Congregational and Presbyterian denominations in the proposed United Church of Australia on the condition that believer's baptism be one of the forms of baptism in the new church.[3]

Despite high hopes, church union did not eventuate. Church union negotiations between the Methodists, Presbyterians and Congregationalists broke down and Baptists in South Australia not only faced opposition from

---

[1] This article draws widely on the author's doctoral thesis, J.S. Walker, 'The Baptists in South Australia, circa 1900 to 1939' (PhD thesis, Flinders University, Adelaide, 2006).
[2] J.D. Bollen, *Australian Baptists: A Religious Minority* (London: Baptist Historical Society, 1975), pp. 27-32.
[3] South Australian Baptist Union and Furreedpore Mission, *Baptist Handbook for 1920* (Adelaide: South Australian Baptist Union, 1919), p. 20.

Baptists in other parts of Australia, especially New South Wales over their eagerness for church union, but they found it difficult to discern how they could be both true to their own heritage and give expression to Jesus' prayer that his followers might be one. Ultimately, they drew back from pursuing organic union with other denominations and focused on strengthening their own denomination. Some historians and sociologists of religion have sought to explain the growth of ties between denominations by mainly referring to social considerations.[4] To Bryan Wilson, for instance, the growth of ecumenicalism (Wilson coined this word) has been a result of secularisation. According to this perspective, church union initiatives were a response to the decline of institutional religion. Churches sought to resist further decline by combining their strength.[5] On the other hand, church leaders and theologians who supported closer ties between denominations have tended to explain the appeal of church union in theological terms such as the exemplary influence of Jesus' prayer for unity expressed not long before his death.[6] This chapter proceeds on the basis that while social considerations are important, theological explanations are an important resource for the historian as well. As Robert Towler has argued, it will not do for participants' own accounts to be treated as mere delusion.[7]

'Fair Field and No Favour': Baptists and the South Australian Religious Settlement

When compared with the other British colonies in Australia, South Australia had distinctive beginnings. Established in 1836 as a colony for free settlers, it was the only Australian colony not to receive convicts from Britain and, unlike other Australian colonies, no denomination receive preferential treatment from

---

[4] For a discussion of the different approaches to explaining the growth of church union sentiment, see D.M. Thompson, 'Theological and Sociological Approaches to the Motivation of the Ecumenical Movement', in D. Baker (ed.), *Religious Motivation: Biographical and Sociological Problems for the Church Historian* (Studies in Church History, 15; London: Blackwell, 1978), pp. 467-79.

[5] Bryan Wilson, *Religion in Secular Society* (Harmondsworth: Penguin, 1966), p. 202. For similar perspectives, see Alan Gilbert, *The Making of Post-Christian Britain: A History of the Secularization of Modern Society* (London/New York: Longman, 1980), p. 126.

[6] See, for example, the comments by John Raws supporting church union on the basis of Jesus' prayer for unity: supplement to *Australian Baptist* (*AB*) 28 October 1919, p. 14. On the failure of some participants in the ecumenical movement to take account of sociological aspects, see Christopher Lewis, 'Unity: A Sociological Perspective', in Rupert Davies (ed.), *The Testing of the Churches, 1931–1982* (London: Epworth Press, 1982), pp. 145-48.

[7] Robert Towler, *Homo Religiosus: Sociological Problems in the Study of Religion* (London: Constable, 1974), p. 165.

the government.⁸ This religious settlement reflected Enlightenment and British Nonconformist ideals concerning religious toleration and equality and can be seen as a side outcome of the campaigns in England in the 1820s and 1830s to eliminate legal restrictions on Nonconformists and Roman Catholics and to disestablish the Church of England.⁹

Not surprisingly, South Australia became a magnet for Nonconformists from Britain, including many Baptists, and also attracted Lutherans seeking to escape the threat of persecution in Prussia. By 1901, of 358,508 South Australians, 6 per cent described themselves as Baptist, compared to 1 per cent in New South Wales and 2.5 per cent in Victoria. The other non-Anglican Protestant churches were also proportionally much stronger in South Australia than in the other colonies while both the Anglican and Roman Catholic churches were much weaker.¹¹ Overall, Douglas Pike's description of early South Australia as a 'paradise of Dissent' is an apt one.¹²

The first Baptists arrived in the infant colony in February 1837 and a Baptist church was formed in the following year. South Australia presented opportunities not only for individuals to create for themselves a new beginning, but also for enthusiasts of all types to help shape the new colony. One principle that all Baptists supported and which affected interdenominational relations was religious voluntaryism. Baptists, as voluntaryists, were not only opposed to the Church of England becoming 'established' in South Australia but fought

---

⁸ This and the following paragraph draw from Douglas Pike, *Paradise of Dissent: South Australia, 1829–1857* (Melbourne: Melbourne University Press, 2nd edn, 1967); Eric Richards, 'The Peopling of South Australia, 1836–1986', in Eric Richards (ed.), *The Flinders History of South Australia* (2 vols; Adelaide: Wakefield Press, 1986), I, pp. 115-42; David Hilliard and Arnold Hunt, 'Religion', in Richards (ed.), *The Flinders History*, I, pp. 194-234. On the relationships between church and state in colonial Australia, see J.S. Gregory, *Church and State* (Melbourne: Cassell, 1973); John Barrett, *That Better Country: The Religious Aspect of Life in Eastern Australia, 1835–1850* (Melbourne: Melbourne University Press, 1966).

⁹ For an overview of the campaigns in England for full religious liberty and equality, see D.W. Bebbington, *The Nonconformist Conscience: Chapel and Politics, 1870–1914* (London: Allen and Unwin, 1982), ch. 2. On Enlightenment views regarding religious toleration, see Roy Porter, *Enlightenment: Britain and the Creation of the Modern World* (London: Allen Lane, 2000), pp. 105-10; D.W. Bebbington, *Evangelicalism in Modern Britain: A History from the 1730s to the 1980s* (London: Unwin Hyman, 1989), p. 52.

¹⁰ Statistics compiled from Pike, *Paradise of Dissent*, p. 493; David Hilliard, 'Religion', in W. Vamplew *et al.* (eds.) *South Australian Historical Statistics* (Kensington, New South Wales: Fairfax, Syme and Weldon, 1984), Tables 7:1, 7:2, and 7:13.

¹¹ In the 1901 Australian census, 29 per cent of the South Australian population claimed affiliation with the Church of England compared with an average of 41.6 per cent in the other Australian states.

¹² Pike, *Paradise of Dissent*.

against government aid to religion when it was introduced in South Australia in the 1840s.[13] They believed that any kind of state involvement in church affairs was deleterious to the advancement of true religion. This belief led many South Australian Baptists to join a voluntaryist pressure group, the League for the Preservation of Religion.[14]

The fervour of South Australian Baptists for voluntaryism was also an expression of their fear of Roman Catholicism. While South Australian Baptists treated most other Protestant denominations which shared an Evangelical basis as sister denominations, they distanced themselves from Roman Catholicism. Roman Catholicism was the religious 'other', an other which had few redeeming qualities and which provided the contrast against which they defined themselves and thus achieved a measure of denominational salience.[15] To Baptists, Roman Catholicism was the antithesis of true Christianity, the enemy of enlightened progress and a promoter of disloyalty to the British crown. George Stonehouse, for example, the first minister of North Adelaide Baptist Church, was greatly alarmed by the 'sophistry of Jesuitism' and warned in 1848 that 'popery' was 'putting forth every energy' in the infant colony.[16] He regarded Roman Catholic and Anglican support for state aid to religion as the 'thin edge of the wedge' which would result in the introduction of a state church.[17]

Voluntaryism became the governing principle for church-state relations in South Australia following the victory of voluntaryist forces at the first South Australian election in 1851.[18] With this victory, South Australia became the first colony in the British Empire to abolish state aid to churches for purposes other than education. South Australian Baptists could rejoice in a 'land of freedom' where there was a 'fair field and no favour'.[19]

---

[13] See Pike, *Paradise of Dissent*, ch. 11.

[14] Ken R. Manley, *From Woolloomooloo to 'Eternity': A History of Australian Baptists* (2 vols; Milton Keynes: Paternoster, 2006), I, p. 53; Pike, *Paradise of Dissent*, pp. 273, 367.

[15] The concept of the 'other' has been widely used in the social sciences and humanities. See, for example, Edward W. Said, *Orientalism* (New York: Routledge and Kegan Paul, 1978). For the use of 'other' in anthropology, see Johannes Fabian, 'The Other Revisited: Critical Afterthoughts', *Anthropological Theory*, 6. 2 (June 2006), pp. 139-52.

[16] *Baptist Magazine*, 40 (1848), pp. 226-27.

[17] This fear also contributed to the decision of South Australian Baptists and other Evangelicals to campaign, ultimately successfully in 1875, for the cessation of state aid to denominational schools and the introduction of an education system that was compulsory, secular and free. On South Australian Baptist attitudes to Roman Catholic schools, see *Truth and Progress* (*TP*) March 1869, p. 41; July 1869, p. 128; October 1871, p. 94.

[18] See Pike, *Paradise of Dissent*, ch. 17.

[19] *TP* November 1871, p. 147.

South Australian Baptists in Co-operation and Competition with other Denominations, 1836 to 1876

Baptists in South Australia could freely act on their own religious preferences, but what would their attitudes be to their fellow Protestants? Some groups of Baptists transplanted sect-type religion to the new colony and were happy to be a separate people, isolated in doctrinal purity. H.E. Hughes, the author of the first comprehensive history of South Australian Baptists, refers to a 'baker's dozen' of Baptists who formed their own church in the 1840s because they believed that Baptist preachers in the colony were not 'sufficiently High Calvinistic' in doctrine. Hughes records of this group that 'the doctrine that those people loved was strong, but their cause never became strong in numbers, and after some years it ceased to exist'.[20]

A similar but less exclusivist spirit was apparent in a range of small churches which held to believer's baptism but did not go under the name of 'Baptist' because they believed it was unbiblical.[21] One loosely affiliated group of such churches was begun by a battle of Waterloo veteran, Thomas Playford, who found no church to his liking when he arrived in the young colony in 1844. These 'Christian' churches, as they were known, embraced a premillennial eschatology and attracted many who would otherwise have worshipped in Baptist congregations.[22] The emerging Churches of Christ movement also added to the proliferation of small groups that held to believer's baptism.[23] One of the first two Churches of Christ congregations in South Australia emerged out of a Scotch Baptist Church that met in Franklin Street, central Adelaide. Such was the confusion of voices that it was not until 1863 that sixteen hitherto largely isolated and struggling Baptist churches decided to join forces to form the South Australian Baptist Association (SABA).

An entirely different note from the sectarian note of some was sounded by several prominent Baptists who believed that divisions between Christians were hindering the advance of God's kingdom. George Fife Angas, businessman, reformer, child of both the Evangelical Revival and the Enlightenment, and one of the founders of South Australia, was one of these.[24] Firmly committed to notions of progress and moral reformation, Angas dreamed that South Australia

---

[20] H. Estcourt Hughes, *Our First Hundred Years: The Baptist Church of South Australia* (Adelaide: South Australian Baptist Union, 1937), p. 34.

[21] See Hughes, pp. 24-28, 76-78.

[22] Hughes, *Our First Hundred Years*, pp. 77-78.

[23] On the intermingling of worshippers of Baptist, 'Christian' and Churches of Christ persuasion in the 1840s see Trevor Lawrie, 'Scotch Baptists and the First SA Church of Christ', *Australian Christian* 4 November 1995, p. 20.

[24] Pike, *Paradise of Dissent*, p. 127. Angas' combination of Evangelical and Enlightenment principles can be seen in his failed attempt in the 1820s to establish a 'Society for Promoting Christianity and Civilisation through the Medium of Commercial, Scientific and Professional Agency'.

would attract large numbers of Nonconformists who would help make it 'the headquarters for the diffusion of Christianity in the Southern hemisphere'.[25] Angas left an indelible mark on South Australia. He successfully used some of the techniques he learned from the anti-slavery campaigns in Britain to persuade many Nonconformists to migrate to South Australia. Demonstrating his largeness of vision, Angas also sponsored the first wave of Prussian Lutheran immigrants to South Australia.

Angas believed that for his vision to become a reality, Evangelical Christians needed to co-operate more fully and even put aside parochial differences and worship together. The Angas family showed the way in 1842, when they erected a church building at Angaston, their family 'seat' in South Australia, for the purposes of inter-denominational Protestant worship. With the support of the Angases, those worshipping there formed a union chapel in 1849. Independent in polity and Evangelical in doctrine, it was not prescriptive as regards the type of baptism.[26]

Angas' outlook was reflective of what has been termed 'pan-Evangelicalism'.[27] Pan-Evangelicalism imbibed something of both the Evangelical Revival's willingness to put denominational distinctives to one side in the interests of the spread of the gospel and the Enlightenment's embrace of pragmatism.[28] It involved an attempt to emphasise commonalties among Evangelicals rather than differences, to foster co-operation between Evangelicals through interdenominational societies and in some cases to bring about direct co-operation between denominations.

George Stonehouse was another shining exemplar of pan-Evangelicalism in South Australia.[29] Stonehouse, who was brought to South Australia by Angas, trained for the ministry in Bedfordshire at Newport Pagnell College, an institution run jointly by Baptists and Congregationalists. One of its tutors, Samuel Greatheed, was a leading pan-Evangelical activist and author of a 1798 work *General Union Recommended to Real Christians*.[30] Stonehouse advocated open-communion and open-membership principles, and frequently discussed with a leading Congregational minister, James Jefferies, the possibility of organic union between Baptists and Congregationalists in South Australia. In the 1870s he supported moves for the amalgamation of the two

---

[25] Quoted in Douglas Pike, *Paradise of Dissent*, p. 138.

[26] Hughes, *Our First Hundred Years*, p. 38.

[27] On pan-Evangelicalism, see R.H. Martin, *Evangelicals United: Ecumenical Stirrings in Pre-Victorian Britain, 1795–1830* (Metchuen, NJ: Scarecrow Press, 1983).

[28] On the influence of Enlightenment-inspired pragmatism on Evangelicalism, see Bebbington, *Evangelicalism in Modern Britain*, pp. 65-66.

[29] On Stonehouse, see Hughes, *Our First Hundred Years*, pp. 30-33.

[30] See Martin, *Evangelicals United*, p.32. Both Baptist and Congregational churches were a part of this union as were 'union churches' which were composed of both Congregationalists and Baptists.

denominations.[31] An article by Stonehouse entitled 'Speaking the Truth in Love' in the initial edition of *Truth and Progress*, the first periodical published by South Australian Baptists, exemplified his firm but irenical Evangelicalism. He declared that South Australian Baptists adhered to the 'grand and distinguishing doctrines of the Christian system' such as the divinity of Christ, the atoning sacrifice of his death and 'whatever else is usually designated by the term *evangelical*'. At the same time he argued:

> Believing that a perfect identity of opinion on subjects not so plainly revealed as some may desire, is neither possible nor desirable, let us not act as though we considered it ESSENTIAL. If called to defend those views of Divine Truth which we have conscientiously received, let us do so in a manner worthy of Him whose disciples we profess to be, and in accordance with the mild and benignant spirit of that dispensation under which it is our privilege to live.[32]

Some Baptists who shared similar sentiments to Stonehouse were involved in the establishment of union chapels.[33] Others were content to belong to non-Baptist Evangelical churches, even when there was a local Baptist church they could join. This was particularly so with 'Baptists' in Congregational churches. Baptists and Congregationalists shared a Separatist heritage, often viewed themselves as close relatives and, except for their theology and practice of baptism, had similar approaches to theology and church life. It is impossible to ascertain how many people from a Baptist background belonged to Congregational churches, but in the early years many Baptists worshipped in the Freeman Street Congregational Chapel in central Adelaide. One former member estimated that over half of the congregation was in fact 'Baptist'.[34]

Another option, one chosen by many Baptists, was to establish or join existing Baptist churches in the localities in which they resided. They saw themselves as part of the Evangelical mainstream, but believed that they held truths such as believer's baptism which were vital to the progress of the kingdom of God and which were best propagated by forming new Baptist churches. David Badger, a Baptist minister who had been in the Congregational ministry until he changed his views on baptism, expressed the conviction of many Baptists when he declared at the laying of the foundation stone of the Baptist church building in suburban Norwood (where a Congregational church and Methodist church already existed) 'that notwithstanding the activity and

---

[31] On Stonehouse's career, see Hughes, *Our First Hundred Years*, pp. 31-33, 70; Manley, *From Woolloomooloo to 'Eternity'*, I, p. 53; J.S. Walker, 'The Baptists in South Australia, 1863–1914' (Bachelor of Theology honours thesis, Flinders University, Adelaide, 1990), p. 31.

[32] *TP* January 1868, p. 6.

[33] Hughes, *Our First Hundred Years*, p. 63.

[34] *Southern Baptist* (*SB*) 29 January 1907, p. 30.

success of other religious bodies in the colony, there is still ample scope for the united energies and zeal of the Baptists'.[35]

In establishing new churches, however, South Australian Baptists were anxious not to exclude from membership those Christians who believed in infant baptism. They believed that in the matter of baptism and membership, liberty of conscience should be extended to all.[36] Until the second half of the twentieth century only a handful Baptist churches had a closed membership basis and most of these churches changed to an open membership basis over time. The SABA did not require that churches adhere to an open- membership policy as a condition of membership, but it strongly encouraged member churches to follow this policy.

While South Australian Baptists sought to accommodate their fellow Evangelicals, there were limits to how far South Australian Baptists were prepared to go. This became apparent in the 1870s when Silas Mead, the dominant figure among South Australian Baptists in the second half of the nineteenth century and their leading proponent of open membership, twice unsuccessfully pushed for Baptists to amalgamate with the Congregationalists. In line with modern views of rational organisation and efficiency, he believed that the mission of the Christian church could be better carried out if churches combined their strength. He was also concerned that divisions between churches gave reason to non-Christians to continue in their unbelief. But Badger and other leaders successfully argued that amalgamation would inevitably mean unacceptable compromise. Mead gained little support.[37]

By the mid-1870s, the SABA had rejected union chapels as being 'abominations which make desolate'.[38] It also chose competition over co-operation when it rejected an approach from the Congregational Union of South Australia to establish a 'towns of influence' policy in the newly settled agricultural districts whereby neither denomination would seek to establish a church in a town in which the other denomination was already established. Badger's argument proved persuasive that while Baptists should cultivate 'loving hearts' there should be 'no amalgamation of truth and error'.[39] Accordingly, when vast tracts of South Australia were opened up for settled agriculture in the 1870s and 1880s and as Adelaide continued to expand, Baptists often competed with other denominations to be among the first to form churches in new localities. By the mid- 1880s, South Australian Baptists took pride in the rapid expansion of their denomination but, as they were

---

[35] *TP* May 1869, p. 88.
[36] On the adoption of open membership by South Australian Baptists, see Walker, 'The Baptists in South Australia, 1863–1914', pp. 23-27.
[37] *TP* November 1870, p. 129; September 1876, pp. 97-98.
[38] *TP* October 1876, p. 127.
[39] *TP* October 1874, p. 114.

increasingly to find, sustaining churches often proved harder than establishing them.[40]

Evangelical Co-operation to 1918

Although South Australian Baptists had rejected amalgamation with the Congregationalists, they still liked to refer to themselves as Christians first and Baptists second.[41] They not only continued with an open-membership policy but they heartily co-operated with other Evangelicals in a range of social action, educative, missionary and evangelistic organisations such as the Evangelical Alliance, China Inland Mission and the Woman's Christian Temperance Union (WCTU). South Australian Baptists were determined to play their part in the evangelisation of their state and to help shape it in their own image. Rosetta Birks was but one Baptist example of co-operative Evangelical activism. She was a leading figure in the Ladies' Social Purity League, the WCTU and the Young Women's Christian Association (YWCA), and was the inaugural treasurer of the Women's Suffrage League.[42] In her work for the YWCA she tirelessly sought to provide recreational and educational opportunities for young women, particularly those from a poor background. She saw these efforts as part of the fight against 'all that tends to lower and degrade the character of the young'.[43]

The SABA exhibited the same pan-Evangelical spirit displayed by many individual Baptists. In 1872 it joined with the Congregational and Presbyterian denominations to establish a ministerial training institution, Union College. Its subsequent history was to show not only the possibilities of Evangelical co-operation but also some of the strains that co-operation engendered.[44] Although Union College functioned harmoniously for many years, in 1884 the Congregational Union complained to the Union College board that a recent Baptist graduate had been chosen to pioneer the commencement of a Baptist work in Port Pirie, a town where Congregationalists already had a presence. Both the board and the SABA rejected the Congregational complaint, and the Congregationalists did not pursue the matter further.[45] However, when the

---

[40] See Walker, 'Baptists in South Australia, 1863–1914', pp. 103-109.
[41] *TP* November 1871, p. 106; May 1875, p. 49.
[42] Helen Jones, *In Her Own Name: A History of Women in South Australia from 1836* (Adelaide: Wakefield Press, rev. edn, 1986), pp. 101-103.
[43] *SB* 13 October 1903, p. 231.
[44] On the history of Union College, see Walter Phillips, 'Union College Adelaide, 1872–1886: A Brief Experiment in United Theological Education', in G.R. Treloar (ed.), *The Furtherance of Religious Beliefs: Essays on the History of Theological Education in Australia* (Macquarie Centre, Sydney: Centre for the Study of Australian Christianity on Behalf of the Evangelical History Association, 1997), pp. 59-71.
[45] *TP* 1 February 1885, p. 19. Phillips makes no reference to this conflict in his article on Union College.

Presbyterians pulled out two years later following a decision to train their students in Melbourne, the Congregationalists, perhaps still smarting over the Port Pirie situation, decided to end their involvement with the college. This was a matter of deep disappointment to the SABA as it meant that Union College was forced to close.

Another expression of co-operative Evangelicalism on the part of the South Australian Baptist Union (SABU), as the SABA was re-named in 1894, was its membership of the Council of Churches in South Australia, a body which was established through a Baptist initiative in 1895. J. Viner Smith, a Baptist businessman, was its first president, and H.J. (Harry) Holden, another Baptist businessman whose automobile manufacturing company would later make the Holden name famous throughout Australia, was its first secretary.[46] The Council of Churches was a body of non-Anglican Protestant denominations which sought to represent the collective interests of member denominations to the government and the general public.

The exclusion of the Roman Catholic and Anglican churches from the Council of Churches revealed its defensiveness towards denominations it believed did not belong to the Evangelical fold. Baptists were particularly concerned about what they regarded as the 'Rome-ward' drift of the Church of England in Britain and South Australia. To their horror, one of their own leading ministers, A.E. Green, of the Semaphore Baptist Church, suddenly resigned his pastorate in 1893 and became an Anglican.[47] Particularly galling to Baptists was the fact that Green immediately espoused 'ritualistic' views and charged Baptists with being schismatics who belonged to a merely human society which was in rebellion against Christ and his church.[48] Green was later ordained in the Church of England and became the 'extreme high church vicar' of All Saints, Sydenham, London.[49]

As the new century dawned, South Australian Baptists had other concerns as well. South Australia was in the grips of a recession and the SABU was finding it difficult to assist the many small churches which had been established in the previous thirty years of strong denominational expansion. While Baptists still hoped for future growth, they had to come to terms with being a religious minority which was not able to compete on an equal terms with larger denominations, particularly the Methodists. One response by the SABU was to reverse its previous stance regarding not co-operating with other denominations

---

[46] On the formation of the council, see *SB*, 28 July 1910, p. 484. South Australian Baptist Union General Committee Minutes (SABUGCM), 21 October 1895, 10 February 1896, 20 July 1896, Society Record Group (SRG) 465, 51/7, State Library of South Australia (SLSA).

[47] On the Green affair see *TP* 19 January 1893, p. 25; 2 March 1893, p. 71.

[48] *TP* 19 January 1893, pp. 20-21.

[49] The description of Green is Hugh McLeod's. Hugh McLeod, *Class and Religion in the Late Victorian City* (London: Croom Helm, 1974), p. 179.

as to where it established churches. The most notable attempt at co-ordination commenced in 1913 when the Congregational Union initiated an inter-denominational committee to prevent the overlapping of churches.[50] This committee comprised representatives of the Methodist, Presbyterian, Congregational and Baptist denominations and on many occasions successfully co-ordinated the planting of churches in suburban Adelaide.[51] It continued its work until 1923 when Presbyterian withdrawal led to its collapse.[52]

The Push for Church Union

Hope emerged in the 1890s that if Baptists could not combine with the Congregationalists, then they might be able to amalgamate with the Churches of Christ. After an initiative from Charles Goode, a Baptist businessman, exchanges of views and unofficial discussions about church union between Baptists and members of the Churches of Christ took place in 1890 and 1894. Although both denominations practised believer's baptism by immersion, there were differences over denominational name, over practices such as the frequency of the observance of the Lord's Supper and most seriously over the meaning of baptism.[53] Baptists believed that water baptism symbolised what had already taken place at conversion while most Churches of Christ leaders insisted that baptism was not merely a symbolic act but one in which forgiveness was bestowed.

Although nothing concrete resulted from of these exchanges, hopes were raised in 1909 when through the enterprise of A.N. Marshall, a Baptist minister who had been chairman of the organising committee of the recently held Chapman and Alexander evangelistic campaign in South Australia, a combined gathering of Baptists and members of the Churches of Christ was held at the SABU annual meetings. Speakers highlighted the beliefs that members of the two denominations held in common, and pointed to the damaging results of denominational competition.[54] It is likely that the combined meeting contributed to the establishment in 1911 of a joint Churches of Christ and

---

[50] Little, if anything, came of a decision by the SABU and the Churches of Christ Conference in 1913 to establish a committee to prevent overlapping and pursue joint 'aggressive' work. SABUGCM, 10 February 1913, 9 November 1913, 14 December 1914, SRG 465/51/7/5, SLSA.

[51] For an example of its work, see SABUGCM, 14 July 1920, SRG 465/51/7/6, SLSA.

[52] SABUGCM, 12 March 1923, SRG 465/51/7/6, SLSA.

[53] For discussions between Baptists and members of the Churches of Christ over baptism and other issues, see *TP* April 1890, p. 61; June 1890, p. 105; July 1890, p. 121; 1 April 1894, p. 101; 1 March 1894, pp. 69-71; 15 March 1894, pp. 83-85; 1 April 1894, pp. 100-102. For a discussion of Churches of Christ teaching on baptism, see E. Roberts-Thomson, *Baptists and Disciples of Christ* (London: Carey Kingsgate Press, 1951), pp. 116-21.

[54] *SB* 12 October 1909, pp. 243-44.

Baptist church in Port Pirie, a port city north of Adelaide.[55] Following Churches of Christ principles, the church had a closed membership. Harmonious relations within this church continued until 1917, when a disagreement over the transfer into the united church of some who had been members in a Baptist church but who had never been baptised as believers led to the withdrawal of members from a Churches of Christ background.[56] Both denominations went their separate ways in Port Pirie and the experiment was not tried elsewhere. Baptists considered the Churches of Christ to be too sectarian, while the Churches of Christ concentrated on denominational expansion, sometimes at Baptist expense.[57]

In the first decade and a half of the twentieth century there was a surge of interest in church union among the Protestant denominations in Australia.[58] Although South Australian Baptists were attracted by the possibility of church union, until the First World War they held back from any strong move in that direction. The attitude of John Paynter to church union was probably typical of the outlook of many Baptists. He argued that the only sufficient reason for keeping a separate denominational existence was a consciousness of a distinct mission. He believed that Baptists had such a mission: spreading the observance of believer's baptism.[59] Paynter did not rule out the possibility of Baptist participation in a united church in the future if believer's baptism could be practised within that church. Nonetheless, he believed that the best policy for the present was to build up the Baptist denomination.

There were some who still harboured hopes that there would be progress towards church union.[60] John Raws, Mead's co-pastor then successor at Flinders Street Baptist Church, approvingly reported, for instance, that the impact of the World Missionary Conference in Edinburgh in 1910 had been felt in terms of a 'uniting spirit' that had 'spread and become more intense and devout'.[61] But a breakthrough was needed if union with other denominations was to be seriously considered by South Australian Baptists. The First World War precipitated just that. As was the pattern with Baptists in other states, South Australian Baptists co-operated with the Australian government and other denominations to provide chaplains under the designation of 'Other Protestant Denominations' (OPDs). Chaplains and YMCA workers with the

---

[55] *SB* 14 December 1911, p. 840; 21 December 1911, p. 857. South Australian Baptist Union Council Minutes (SABUCM), 10 July 1911, SRG 465/51/8/1, SLSA; 5 July 1917, SRG 465/51/8/1, SLSA; Hughes, *Our First Hundred Years*, pp. 118-20.
[56] SABUCM, 5 July 1917, SRG 465/51/8/1, SLSA.
[57] *AB* 1 June 1920, p. 2.
[58] C. Uidam, 'Why the Church Union Movement Failed in Australia, 1901–1925', *Journal of Religious History* 13. 4 (December 1985), pp. 393-410.
[59] *SB* 3 December 1902, p. 271.
[60] See John Raws' reflections, Supplement to *AB* 18 October 1919, p. 13.
[61] Supplement to *AB* 18 October 1919, p. 13.

troops reported that many soldiers expressed impatience with existing divisions between the churches. A conference of Australian military chaplains and other religious workers held in London in August 1919 claimed, for instance, that existing divisions among the churches were a source of great weakness and 'a reproach in the eyes of the soldiers'.[62] Donald McNicol, who had served as a military chaplain in France, thought the same. He urged South Australian Baptists to 'stop talking about the Union of the churches and do something. We are too much divided to possess moral influence over individuals and nations.'[63]

The case for church union amongst South Australian Baptists also received a boost from developments in Britain. As in Australia, the war had been a spur to address the question of church union with more urgency. J.H. Shakespeare, general secretary of the Baptist Union of Great Britain and Ireland, was influential in the cause of church union.[64] He envisaged a federation of Free Churches in England that would serve as a counterweight to the Church of England and which would minister more effectively to the war generation.[65] Shakespeare was not content to rest at this point. In *The Churches at the Cross Roads: A Study in Church Unity*, published in 1918, he startled many Baptists by advocating union with the Church of England.[66] Disillusioned with the individualistic excesses he observed in churches of independent order, Shakespeare was even prepared to accept episcopacy and the re-ordination of Baptist ministers.[67] Shakespeare's thinking received wide exposure in the British and Australian religious press and helped to bring the issue of church union to the fore. However, although Shakespeare's call for Free Church federation was favourably reported in the *Australian Baptist*, his plea for a

---

[62] *AB* 9 September 1919, p. 1.
[63] *AB* 24 September 1918, p. 3. See also *AB* 8 October 1918, p. 1.
[64] On Shakespeare's attitudes to interdenominational co-operation and church union, see Peter Shepherd, *The Making of a Modern Denomination: John Howard Shakespeare and the English Baptists, 1898–1924* (Carlisle: Paternoster, 2001), ch. 4; E.A. Payne, *The Free Church Tradition in the Life of England* (London: Hodder and Stoughton, 1965), pp. 158-61; Roger Hayden, 'Still at the Crossroads? Revd. J.H. Shakespeare and Ecumenism', in K.W. Clements (ed.), *Baptists in the Twentieth Century* (London: Baptist Historical Society, 1983), pp. 31-54.
[65] His call led to the establishment of the Federal Council of Evangelical Free Churches in 1919. This body, unlike the National Free Church Council, consisted of officially appointed denominational representatives who could speak on behalf of their respective denominations. See Payne, *Free Church Tradition*, p. 149.
[66] J.H. Shakespeare, *The Churches at the Crossroads: A Study in Church Unity* (London: Williams and Norgate, 1918).
[67] The Church of England did not recognise Free Church ordinations as 'lawful' as they were not performed by a properly consecrated bishop.

union of churches which embraced the Church of England was roundly condemned in the same paper.[68]

The mood in favour of church union had two initial outcomes for South Australian Baptists. Firstly, arising from a suggestion of the Port Pirie ministers' fraternal, a conference of delegates from the main Protestant and Anglican denominations was held in Adelaide in January 1919 to discuss union.[69] This and two conferences that followed it in 1921 based their deliberations around the two reports of conferences in England between a committee appointed by the archbishops of Canterbury and York and a commission comprising Free Church leaders. Nothing practical resulted from the Adelaide conferences but perhaps surprisingly to some, the three Baptist delegates gave assent to a proposal in the clause on episcopacy and church order which provided for the 'acceptance of the fact of episcopacy and not any theory as to its character' with all communions bringing their distinctive contributions to the methods of church organisation into any future united church.[70] While this was a major concession, it was not as large a step away from independency as it would have been ten years earlier, given that South Australian Baptists had already introduced a semi-connexional system of ministerial settlement.

A second ecumenical initiative seemed at first to provide a genuine opportunity for South Australian Baptists to combine with three denominations. In 1917, previously stalled church union negotiations between Presbyterians, Methodists and Congregationalists recommenced. In response, the 1918 SABU annual meetings appointed a committee to confer with committees from each of the three denominations about the proposed basis of union that had been put forward in Melbourne in September 1918. When the committee reported back a year later to the SABU annual meetings the atmosphere was 'tense with expectation, owing to the feeling of the immense issues... at stake'.[71] John Raws proposed that the delegates give general approval to the proposed basis of union of the Presbyterian, Methodist and Congregational churches, but with three amendments. These were:

> (1) Church membership shall be for those who profess faith in Jesus Christ and obedience to Him; (2) Baptism shall not be essential to church membership; (3) The subjects of baptism to be left open. The fact that some hold the proper

---

[68] *AB* 2 July 1918, pp. 6-7; 11 March 1919, p. 6.
[69] David Hilliard, *Godliness and Good Order: A History of the Anglican Church in South Australia*, (Adelaide: Wakefield Press, 1986), p. 94.
[70] *Report and Proceedings of a Meeting of Representatives of Christian Churches in South Australia* (Adelaide: no pub., 1919), p. 18.
[71] *AB* 21 October 1919, p. 4.

subjects of baptism are believers, and some infants presented in Christian faith, shall not be regarded as a barrier to Church Union.[72]

The polity for the proposed basis of union was mainly Presbyterian, except that settlement of ministers was to be by 'call'.[73]

Raws pointed to the practical benefits of union such as more efficient training of ministers, the elimination of overlapping and more effective evangelisation of the land.[74] McNicol introduced another reason for church union: the need for a united front against the 'sinister and aggressive policy of the Roman Catholic Church'.[75] His stance reflected a rise during the First World War of a vocal anti-Catholicism among Protestants. Many Protestants regarded Catholics as being disloyal to the British throne because of the 'Fenian' uprising in Ireland and because some Australian Catholic bishops had urged Catholics to vote against government attempts in two plebiscites to introduce conscription for overseas military service.[76]

It is significant that both McNicol and Raws spoke in favour of the proposals as, apart from being respected ministers, they represented two theological tendencies among South Australian Baptists. McNicol held fast to the type of conservative but co-operative Evangelicalism that Baptists had been long familiar with, while Raws embraced liberal strains in theology. In McNicol's case it seems as though his Evangelicalism combined with concerns about reaching the war generation for Christ were enough to galvanise him to support amalgamation with other Evangelical denominations. Raws shared McNicol's concerns about the negative impact of denominational divisions on the attitude of returning soldiers to Christianity, but as with many other South Australian Baptists who had been influenced by liberal theology, he was impatient with what he regarded as outmoded theological and ecclesiastical forms. Raws and others like him believed that the Bible gave no one system of theology, regarded systems of theology as being all too fallible and emphasised 'life' over 'dogma'.[77] On the whole, South Australian Baptists in the first forty years of the twentieth century were more influenced by liberal trends in theology than other Australian Baptists.[78] The theological fluidity that was characteristic of liberalism added to church union endeavours in that for union to be achieved, concessions and compromises needed to be made.

Apart from theological liberalism, two other tendencies substantially contributed to South Australian Baptists becoming more willing to embrace

---

[72] *AB* 23 September 1919, p. 8; 21 October 1919, p. 4.
[73] Engel, *Australian Christians in Conflict and Unity*, p. 175.
[74] *AB* 21 October 1919, p. 5.
[75] *AB* 21 October 1919, p. 5.
[76] See Walker, 'The Baptists in South Australia, circa 1900 to 1939', pp. 290-94.
[77] For an example of Raws' views, see *SB* 28 April 1898, p. 98.
[78] See Walker, 'Baptists in South Australia, circa 1900 to 1939', pp. 48-115.

church union. Firstly, the influence of Romanticism and Idealism which both stressed the organic connections between things, led many Baptists to adopt more holistic and less individualistic views of human society and community. This was seen in the social theology of many South Australian Baptists as they came to believe that social problems needed to be addressed not only through individual effort but through state intervention.[79] The impact of this type of thinking was seen in church polity too.[80] South Australian Baptists became increasingly disenchanted with the supposed virtues of the independence of local congregations and in 1903 introduced a council to oversee the accreditation of ministers and help in ministerial settlement. The SABU's powers were further enlarged in 1916 when the semi-connexional Ministerial Settlement Scheme was introduced. Given these changes and tendencies of thought, it was not a large step for Baptists not only to consider the advantages of forms of church government employed by other denominations, but also to be attracted by the benefits that a large combined church could bring.

Secondly, declining enthusiasm for baptism amongst South Australian Baptists had clear implications for church union endeavours. Baptists had argued that they were justified in sustaining their denomination because they had the important mission of spreading the observance of believer's baptism. But anecdotal and statistical evidence suggests that South Australian Baptists were placing less emphasis on believer's baptism than they had been prior to the 1880s. In 1911, Parkside Baptist Church, a medium-size suburban church, for example, complained that 'the ordinance of baptism, though recognised, is not followed as generally as we could wish'.[81] Statistical evidence makes clear that although many Baptist churches placed a strong emphasis on the importance of baptism, a substantial minority did not. In 1911, a survey of aspects of South Australian Baptist church life revealed that of the 39 churches which answered a question about whether baptism was a prominent feature in their church's life, 13 answered in the negative.[82]

A helpful statistical guide to the importance of baptism to Baptists is the number of baptisms as a percentage of additions to membership through profession of faith. Given the Baptist emphasis on baptism as an act carried out after conversion, one would expect to find the number of baptisms to be close to the number of additions to membership by profession of faith.[83] In fact, the number of baptisms as a percentage of additions to membership by profession

---

[79] See Walker, 'Baptists in South Australia, circa 1900 to 1939', pp. 201-20.
[80] See Walker, 'The Baptists in South Australia, circa 1900 to 1939', pp. 336-60.
[81] *Baptist Handbook for 1912*, p. 72.
[82] *Baptist Handbook for 1912*, pp. 59-76.
[83] Comparing the number of baptisms to the number of additions to church membership through profession of faith provides a better indication of the value that Baptists placed on baptism than does the number of baptisms alone, as the number of baptisms in any one year was heavily affected by the total number of conversions.

of faith declined from 97.6 per cent in the 1870s to 59.9 per cent in 1920–1924.[84]

Undoubtedly the open membership policy of South Australian Baptists contributed to this decline. South Australian Baptist leaders did not like to admit this, and they could point to the fact that the practice of open membership did not necessarily lead to infrequent observance of baptism. Nevertheless, church leaders were often reticent about placing much emphasis on believer's baptism lest they offend worshippers in Baptist churches who had different views on baptism, particularly in small rural towns or in suburbs where non-Baptists worshipped with Baptists because there were no other Evangelical churches nearby.[85] In 1911, for instance, the Canowie Belt Baptist Church in the north of South Australia reported that the 'subject of baptism [is] not very prominent, [because] the feelings of some non-Baptist families are regarded.'[86] The open-membership tradition – which was itself partly an expression of an Evangelical pragmatism that was redolent of Enlightenment values – was also behind the reported attitude of many at Magill Baptist Church that 'Believer's baptism is not given undue prominence, there being an impression that it is more important to make "Christians" than Baptists.'[87]

It is likely that spiritualising tendencies in Nonconformist theology that had always been present but were accentuated by Idealism, coupled with perceptions about the growing threats posed by Roman Catholicism and Anglo-Catholicism, resulted not only in a rejection of what Baptists called sacramentalism but also in a reduced emphasis on baptism.[88] These tendencies led to the exaltation of the inner, the spiritual and the spontaneous at the expense of the outward, the material and the formal. One unnamed South Australian Baptist minister declared, for instance, that South Australian Baptists did not emphasise the importance of baptism as much as formerly because 'as we are now recognising that it is possible to attach too much importance to the letter of the command'.[89]

Given the general tendencies of thought, declining interest in baptism, and the support of influential leaders of diverse theological perspective such as Raws and McNicol for church union, it is not surprising that the 1919 SABU

---

[84] These percentages were calculated from the annual statistics of the SABA and SABU as found in *Truth and Progress*, 1870–1894; *Southern Baptist*, 1895–1908; *SABU Handbook*, 1908–1925.

[85] *Baptist Handbook for 1912*, p. 68.

[86] *Baptist Handbook for 1912*, p. 63.

[87] *Baptist Handbook for 1912*, p. 69.

[88] On the impact of Idealism on Baptist and Congregational sacramental theology, see J.W. Grant, *Free Churchmanship in England, 1870–1940: With Special Reference to Congregationalism* (London: Independent Press, 1955), pp. 74, 76-77, 121, 272-79. See also, *AB* 9 April 1935, p. 2.

[89] *AB* 9 April 1935, p. 2. Although this statement was made after 1935, it illustrates the nature of what was a long-term trend.

annual meetings gave general approval to the amended basis of union with only two delegates dissenting. The one condition was that more detailed negotiations would have to occur between the denominations before a final vote for union was taken by the SABU. It was also decided that letters be sent to the Baptist Unions in other states asking them 'to consider and commend the matter in their several Assemblies'.[90]

The South Australian negotiating committee of the three denominations seeking union heartily endorsed the Baptist amendments and recommended them for favourable consideration by the central negotiating committee in Melbourne.[91] In response, the central committee decided to defer further action on the proposal as it wanted to negotiate on a national basis and not with state bodies individually.[92]

In effect, the South Australian proposal regarding church union was doomed as opposition from Baptists in other states emerged almost immediately, particularly from New South Wales. Many New South Wales Baptists leaders had long been critical of the open-membership stance of South Australian Baptists and had also expressed grave concerns about their liberal theological leanings.[93] Now, it seemed to New South Wales Baptists and some other Australian Baptists that their southern colleagues were 'going to desert' their 'colours'.[94] In response, the Baptist Union of New South Wales (BUNSW) used one of the evening sessions of the 1919 annual meetings to have two speakers give addresses opposing church union. The speakers, William Lamb and Stephen Sharp, two well known conservative Evangelical ministers, strongly rejected the idea of church union. Sharp argued that Baptists should remain an independent denomination until the whole Christian church accepted the Baptist understanding and practice of baptism.[95] Unlike conservative Evangelicals in South Australia, he linked the desire for church union to what he described as the modern view of scripture, a view which he claimed no longer regarded scripture as 'final and authoritative'.[96]

In response to the South Australian initiative, the BUNSW was clear that it regarded church union with paedobaptist denominations as compromising Baptist principles. It declared:

> That no basis of Union can be acceptable which compromises the acknowledged teaching of the New Testament in respect of the Church and Christian ordinances,

---

[90] *AB* 21 October 1919, p. 5.
[91] *AB* 21 October 1919, p. 5; 20 April 1920, p. 8.
[92] *AB* 20 April 1920, p. 8.
[93] See Walker, 'Baptists in South Australia, circa 1900 to 1939', pp. 95-99; Manley, *From Woolloomooloo to 'Eternity'*, I, pp. 187-88, 221-23.
[94] *AB* 30 September 1919, p. 8.
[95] Supplement to *AB* 7 October 1919, p. 13.
[96] Supplement to *AB* 7 October 1919, p. 14.

or which would in any wise fetter the perfect liberty to teach and administer the ordinances according to the conscientious convictions of the individual.[97]

The BUNSW also objected to the statement in the proposed amended basis of union that baptism was 'with' water rather than 'in' water. They believed that this was an unacceptable concession because although this statement allowed full immersion, it did not require it.

Baptists in other states did not react as strongly against the SABU resolution as in New South Wales, but they failed to endorse the South Australian initiative.[98] In any event, church union discussions between Methodists, Congregationalists and Presbyterians came to an end in 1925 when differences could not be surmounted.[99]

Despite the disappointment over failed church union negotiations, South Australian Baptists continued to pursue new opportunities for co-operation with other denominations. In 1921 a co-operative theological training scheme based at Parkin College, the Congregational theological college, was set up by Congregationalists, Baptists and Presbyterians. It was hoped that this co-operative training scheme would aid the cause of church union.[100] Other co-operative ventures were the establishment of Morialta Protestant Children's Home in 1924 and the founding of a boys' school, King's College, in the same year.[101] Concern over the drift to the Church of England of young Baptists and Congregationalists from well-to-do families was a major reason for the establishment of the college.[102]

---

[97] *AB* 20 April 1920, p. 6.

[98] *AB* 28 October 1919, p. 4; 20 April 1920, p. 4; 4 May 1920, p. 2; 18 May 1920, pp. 7-8; 15 June 1920, p. 1; 22 June 1920, p. 1; 29 June 1920, pp. 1-2. The Australian Baptist Congress in August 1922, a meeting of Baptists from across Australia which had no legislative power, resolved that Baptists were ready to co-operate with other denominations and would be willing 'to confer with a view to organic Church union with other bodies of evangelical Christian Churches upon the basis of Christian essentials'. *AB* 29 August 1922, p. 3. Of course for the majority of Australian Baptists, 'Christian essentials' included believer's baptism by full immersion. The resolution was acceptable to a wide cross section of Baptists because it could be interpreted in a variety of ways.

[99] Uidam, 'Why the Church Union Movement Failed in Australia', pp. 393-410.

[100] *AB* 15 March 1921, p. 2; John Cameron, *In Stow's Footsteps: A Chronological History of the Congregational Churches in South Australia, 1837–1977* (Adelaide: South Australia Congregational History Project, 1987), p. 89.

[101] For the establishment of Morialta Protestant Children's Home and King's College, see Walker, 'The Baptists in South Australia, circa 1900 to 1939', pp. 237-38, 320-22.

[102] *SB* 16 June 1898, p. 133; 1 October 1902, p. 218; 2 November 1911, p. 728; *AB* 24 March 1914, p. 1. On the drift of young people from well-to-do Nonconformist families in England to Anglicanism see Jeffrey Cox, *The English Churches in a Secular Society: Lambeth, 1870–1930* (Oxford: Oxford University Press, 1982), pp. 229-30, 244, 252.

Questioning Church Union

In the 1920s, some South Australian Baptists began to point to the costs of church union negotiations. Robert McCullough, for instance, claimed that the talk of church union had led many Baptists to be indifferent about the extension of their own denomination.[103] He had a point. When the Congregationalists enlarged their church building in 1922 at Henley Beach, a beachside suburb, a 'considerable number' of 'Baptists' who were members of this church chose to remain in membership with the Congregationalists rather than establishing a Baptist church or travelling to Grange Baptist Church less than two miles away.[104] Such was the importance of the 'Baptist' element to Henley Beach Congregational Church that a baptistry that provided for full immersion of candidates was installed during building additions.

South Australian Baptists were also much exercised about declining church member numbers and falls in church attendance. In 1924, one Baptist leader complained, for instance, that the 'habit of church going has fallen from the position of a duty to a compliment'.[105] For half a century Baptists had been used to steady membership growth, but total membership fell from a peak of 6,015 in 1914 to 5,231 in 1924.[106] Baptists were not alone in experiencing these problems as the impact of secularising influences was widely felt across the denominations. Indeed, Paul Barreira has concluded from statistical and other evidence that among Protestants in South Australia between the two world wars there was declining religious enthusiasm and a 'constantly contracting base for Protestant culture'.[107]

Another problem was the leakage of South Australian pastors from the Baptist ministry. In 1923 and 1924 six ministers left for other denominations.[108] The loss of these ministers was a substantial blow at a time when there was a shortage of ministers.[109] It is likely that the climate associated with church union initiatives made it easier for ministers to transfer between denominations than if high denominational fences existed.

In response to the problems facing them, South Australian Baptists took several steps to strengthen their position. First, they turned their attention towards the creation of a federal Baptist union in the hope that a federal body could help them address some of their most pressing problems such as

---

[103] *AB* 20 November 1923, p. 2.

[104] *AB* 5 December 1922, p. 3; *BR* 15 August 1923, p. 4.

[105] *Baptist Record* (*BR*), 15 January 1924, p. 14.

[106] These statistics have been taken from David Hilliard, 'Religion', pp. 144-48.

[107] Barreira, 'Protestant Piety and Religious Culture in South Australia', c. 1914–c. 1981' (PhD thesis, Flinders University, Adelaide, 2003), p. 129, ch. 7.

[108] Four became Presbyterians, one a Congregationalist and another an Anglican. SABUCM, 11 December 1922; 12 February 1923; 1 June 1923, SRG 465/51/8/2, SLSA; *AB* 12 June 1923, p. 10; 15 January 1924, p. 2; 22 January 1924, p. 10.

[109] *BR* 15 September 1924, p. 4.

ministerial supply.[110] South Australian Baptist leaders played a crucial role in preparing a draft constitution for the proposed federal Baptist union.[111] This draft was approved with only minor alterations at the next Australian Baptist Congress, held in Adelaide in 1925.[112] The Baptist Union of Australia was inaugurated in Sydney on 25 August 1926.

Secondly, the SABU sought to renew denominational consciousness and engage in more aggressive church extension efforts. Baptists did not abandon their desire for church union, but they also chose to place renewed emphasis on the importance of believer's baptism. An important step towards these things was the establishment in 1923 of the SABU's own paper, the *Baptist Record*. In the first edition of the *Baptist Record*, Norman Beurle, a co-editor, set the tone for the paper and made plain the attitude of denominational leaders. In an article entitled, 'The Need of an Awakened Baptist Consciousness', he claimed that South Australian Baptists, in standing for the 'two great traditions' of open membership and church union, had suffered from a reflex action on their thought. There had been, he claimed, a softening down of the sharp outlines of distinctive Baptist teaching:

> We have become so moderately Baptist that we have almost lost our raison d'être. Let us be frank and face the facts. We have let the Church of Christ folk run away from us in the matter of progress, largely because they meant something definite and were ready to say so, while we were too broad for definiteness and too unctuous for plain speaking. We make no plea for sectarian bigotry and intolerance that is foreign to the spirit of Christ. But we are not more loyal to Christ when we are disloyal to the claims of the Church that represents what ever we possess of religious principle. Our great need to-day is not so much more men nor more money, it is that we wake up as Baptists.[113]

A.C. Hill, who became general secretary of the SABU in 1924, thought similarly to Beurle. Although keen for church union, he declared that 'we have our own work to do as Baptists'.[114] The vision of Hill and Beurle for the immediate future of the denomination was the one that prevailed. Alongside the continued pursuit of closer ties with other denominations, the SABU put more energy and resources into church extension.[115] Between 1924 and 1926 it assisted in the establishment of six new causes in suburban Adelaide. Prior to their founding, there had been only one new Baptist church formed in South Australia since the end of the First World War.

---

[110] *BR* 16 August 1926, p. 5.
[111] *AB* 2 September 1924, p. 3.
[112] *AB* 25 August 1925, p. 13; Hughes, *Our First Hundred Years*, p. 259.
[113] *BR* 16 July 1923, p. 13.
[114] *AB* 10 October 1922, p. 2.
[115] For a comprehensive discussion of Baptist church extension efforts, see Walker, 'The Baptists in South Australia, circa 1900 to 1939', ch. 11.

Hopes Renewed and Frustrated

Although co-operative efforts such as King's College and the ministerial training consortium proved reasonably successful, there seemed little prospect of Baptists achieving union with any other denomination. Then in 1928, the Congregational Union forwarded a resolution to the SABU asking that 'tentative' discussions be started between the two bodies to explore church union or, failing that, closer cooperation between the two bodies.[116] In August 1929, a joint Baptist and Congregational committee recommended that future negotiations be conducted with the starting point that one denomination be established in which churches practised 'only one ordinance of baptism, viz: believers' baptism, (with liberty as to mode) but which also practised two dedication services for infants (neither called baptism) in one of which the symbol of water might be employed'.[117] It is likely that this proposal remains unique in the annals of ecumenical endeavour. For Congregationalists, the proposals meant the abandonment of infant baptism in favour of a type of 'wet' infant dedication service. If church union proceeded on the basis of the proposals, then 'Baptists' could witness this type of infant dedication service as well as believer's baptism without full immersion in 'their' churches.[118]

In response to the recommendations, the SABU appointed two church union committees in succession to investigate matters further.[119] The second committee did not make any recommendation to the SABU. It did, however, list several 'spiritual' and practical advantages that it believed would result from church union. They included widening 'the witness of believer's baptism', easing the financial strain on churches and ministers, and providing a strong appeal to those outside the Christian church for whom denominational divisions were a 'stumbling block'.[120] The committee listed only one disadvantage, 'the probability that the Federal tie [with the Baptist Union of Australia] might be broken'.[121]

---

[116] SABUGCM, 19 November 1928, SRG 465/51/7/7, SLSA.

[117] Minutes of the executive committee of the Congregational Union and Home Mission of South Australia, October 1929, SRG 95/3/4, SLSA; SABUGCM, 30 June 1930, SRG 465/51/7/7, SLSA. The joint committee recommended that ministers in local churches be permitted to 'set forth their views in a spirit of charity'. It further recommended that church membership and the holding of office be open to all irrespective of beliefs on baptism.

[118] Originating in Britain, the infant dedication service was introduced to South Australian Baptist churches in the 1890s. *SB* 28 September 1899, p. 206; 2 November 1899, p. 235.

[119] SABUGCM, 19 May 1930, SRG 465/51/7/7, SLSA.

[120] SABUGCM, 30 June 1930, SRG 465/51/7/7, SLSA.

[121] SABUGCM, 30 June 1930, SRG 465/51/7/7, SLSA.

While these deliberations were taking place among Baptists, church union discussions recommenced between Methodists, Congregationalists and Presbyterians following an initiative of the South Australian Methodist Conference. The Congregational Union of South Australia welcomed this initiative and informed the SABU in May 1930 that 'while we gladly proceed with the negotiations with the Baptist Churches we cannot accept any basis of union which would be detrimental to union with the other churches mentioned'.[122]

In response to the decision of the Congregationalists, the SABU general committee narrowly passed a resolution affirming its desire to continue negotiations with the Congregational Union 'first for the union with the Congregationalists and for a larger union with other Churches'.[123] The resolution also directed the reunion committee to prepare an educational campaign to inform Baptist churches concerning the issues involved in church union. The resolution was put to the annual meetings of the SABU in September 1930 and was passed with a thin majority. Although the sources do not indicate why the majority was so small, it is likely that some Baptists believed that church union talks were contributing to the continuing decline in membership numbers. It is also likely that some Baptists objected to any compromise on the question of baptism, while others were concerned about the possible expulsion of the SABU from the Baptist Union of Australia.[124]

New South Wales Baptists soon made known their response to the SABU resolution. The executive committee of the BUNSW issued a statement attacking the proposed South Australian action as 'involving the surrender of our distinctive witness concerning the ordinance of believers' baptism'.[125] The BUNSW executive further claimed to discern a distinct breach by the South Australians of the constitution of the Baptist Union of Australia for one of its chief objectives was 'to foster the spirit of fellowship and cooperation among the Baptist Unions of the Commonwealth of Australia, and to exhibit their substantial unity in Doctrine, Polity and Work'.[126] Bernard Tuck, South Australian vice-president of the Baptist Union of Australia, replied, rather lamely, that New South Wales Baptists need not fear that South Australian Baptists would be found disloyal to the principles of the Baptist Union of Australia. He provided no grounds for his confidence but pointed out that no decision had yet been taken regarding union with another denomination.[127]

---

[122] *South Australian Congregationalist* June 1930, p. 105.
[123] SABUGCM, 30 June 1930, SRG 465/51/7/7, SLSA.
[124] *BR* 15 October 1930, p. 7; 15 April 1931, p. 15; SABUGCM, 20 October 1930, SRG 465/51/7/7, SLSA.
[125] *BR* 15 April 1931, p. 12.
[126] *BR* 15 April 1931, p. 12.
[127] *BR* 15 April 1931, p. 12.

In October 1931, the Congregational Union wrote to the SABU asking for a response to the proposed basis for negotiations that had been recommended by the joint committee in August 1929.[128] The SABU general committee, aware that Baptists were divided on the issue, did not provide an official response, but indicated that the committee to educate Baptists about reunion had been reappointed.[129]

The SABU's reply to the Congregational Union was the last formal contact between the two denominations about organic union. The Congregational Union continued to work for union between Congregationalists, Methodists and Presbyterians on a national basis.[130] The SABU's church reunion committee continued to function, but it now focused on promoting good relations between Baptists and other denominations through means such as pulpit exchanges.[131] The drive by South Australian Baptists for organic union with other denominations, once so vigorous and full of hope, had petered out without formal resolution.

Conclusion

Wilson's thesis that secularisation was the main driver of ecumenism has some relevance to the actions of South Australian Baptists. Particularly following the First World War, South Australian Baptists were much concerned with a drift from their churches and the declining ability of churches to influence society effectively. They believed that these problems were partly caused by the war generation's disillusionment with denominational divisions and they hoped that church union would not only disarm complaints about disunity but would also help address falls in church attendance and membership and solve other problems such as ministerial supply.

Secularisation theory, however, can only give a partial explanation of ecumenical efforts in that theological and other factors were also important to interdenominational co-operation and the growth of church union sentiment. While the co-operative efforts and church union talks that South Australian

---

[128] This was in response to an enquiry from the SABU as to the Congregational position on the basis of church union discussions which had been agreed to by the joint committee in August 1929. SABUGCM, 18 May 1931, SRG 465/51/7/7, SLSA. Record of the annual meetings of Congregational Union and Home Mission of South Australia, 19 October–25 October 1931, in the minutes of the executive committee of the Congregational Union and Home Mission of South Australia, SRG 95/3/5, SLSA.

[129] Minutes of the executive committee of the Congregational Union and Home Mission of South Australia, 8 December 1931, SRG 95/3/5, SLSA.

[130] Record of the annual meetings of the Congregational Union and Home Mission of South Australia, 25 October 1932, SRG 95/3/5, SLSA.

[131] SABUGCM, 16 October 1933, SRG 465/51/7/7, SLSA.

Baptists undertook in the nineteenth century reflected modern concerns for organisational efficiency, they were mostly built on a shared Evangelical theology and identity with other Protestants. The Evangelical denominations in South Australia in the nineteenth century, far from being in decline, experienced strong growth and Evangelicals co-operated with each other so that the kingdom of God could be extended in South Australia and beyond. Indeed, the successful efforts of Angas and other South Australian Evangelicals in helping to shape the ethos and social structures of the 'paradise of Dissent' was one of the most outstanding examples of pan-Evangelical endeavour in the English-speaking world in the nineteenth century.

Other theological and internal factors were also important to the growth of favourable attitudes to church union. The theological fluidity associated with liberal theology, declining enthusiasm for believer's baptism, fear of Roman Catholicism, the practice of open membership and influential Idealistic currents in theology all played a part in shifting South Australian Baptists towards actively seeking church union after the First World War.

Why did the push for church union ultimately lose momentum among South Australian Baptists? First, factors outside their control had a marked impact. The decision of the Presbyterian, Congregational and Methodist denominations that negotiations with Baptists should take place only if the Baptist Unions across Australia agreed to take part, for instance, meant that South Australian hopes would inevitably be frustrated. Secondly, the formation of the Baptist Union of Australia in 1926 played a part in the loss of ecumenical momentum. As South Australian Baptists realised in their discussions in 1930 with the Congregationalists regarding church union, any union with them would probably fracture the federal Baptist link, especially given the attitude of the Baptist Union of New South Wales. This possibility weighed heavily on South Australian Baptists. Thirdly, there was a change of mood amongst South Australian Baptists. There was a widespread belief that church union initiatives, far from helping to solve denominational problems, had contributed to a decline in membership, falling interest in baptism and a decay of denominational consciousness.

By the end of 1931, supporters of church union came to the realisation that an era had passed and that church union was not likely in the foreseeable future.[132] While South Australian Baptists continued to co-operate heartily with other Protestant denominations in evangelistic, social and educational endeavours, most notably the introduction of religious instruction into state schools, never again were South Australian Baptists to pursue organic union with other denominations. While they could still lay claim to being Christians first and Baptists second, they chose to place renewed emphasis on being Baptist. In so choosing, they also affirmed their desire for continued

---

[132] SABUGCM, 30 June 1930, SRG 465/51/7/7, SLSA.

relationships with Baptists in other parts of Australia through the Baptist Union of Australia.

CHAPTER 13

From Baptist Leader to Presbyterian Leader: The Rev. Donovan Mitchell (1890-1954)

Ian Breward

Born in Erith, Kent, on 29 September 1890, Donovan Frederick Mitchell was nurtured in the Queen Street Baptist Church there and attended the local technical school, as well as completing a correspondence course in Greek.[1] He became a carpenter, as well as being very active in the family congregation. In 1911, he travelled to Australia to try to find his brother, Leslie, who had deserted ship there. He not only found his brother, but he also liked what he saw of Sydney. The family decided to migrate, but instead of staying went on to New Zealand to a farm at Wayby, between Warkworth and Wellsford, north of Auckland. It was an area already settled by English Dissenters.

Baptist Ministry

Mitchell's religious commitment was demonstrated by starting services in a disused local hall, but after two years he decided to return to Sydney, where he was powerfully influenced by the ministry of C.J. Tinsley, of the Stanmore Baptist Church, coming to feel a sense of call to ministry or missionary work. There was as yet no Baptist college in New South Wales, but he passed an entrance examination for the institution while it was still at the planning stage and began a two-year course of preliminary study while working as a home missionary at Mortdale from June 1914. The congregation grew from 31 to 58 under his leadership and effective evangelism.

In 1916, the Baptist college opened. Mitchell completed his course, as well as pastoring causes at Hornsby and Pymble, married Irene Ramage and was ordained at Hornsby on 28 November 1918. He had also enlisted in the Australian Imperial Forces in July 1918, but the war ended before he could serve overseas. His brief service made him eligible for university study, which he took up a little later. From 1919 to 1921 he served in Lismore, initially as a home missionary, where he began a church paper that earned him a rebuke

---

[1] The main sources for this article are the Donovan Mitchell File in the Baptist Union of Victoria Archives and information from his family.

from the editor of the *Australian Baptist* in New South Wales, who clearly did not welcome a rival. He was also attacked by William Lamb, of the Burton Street church, for allegedly dishonest use of scripture, in relation to Lamb's views on dispensationalism. Mitchell protested to the Union over this attack on his integrity and was upheld. Lamb did not apologise.[2]

It was becoming clear that the young minister had independent judgment and was prepared to take initiatives. In May 1920 he wrote to the Home Mission Committee requesting a transfer to Sydney, so that he could take up the matriculation he had been granted in virtue of his previous study and military service. Returning to Sydney, he ministered at Bankstown from 1921 to 1923 while simultaneously studying for an arts degree, majoring in 1924 with a first in philosophy under Professor Francis Anderson, after winning the prize in philosophy in 1922 and 1923. His ability was recognised by the Union, for he was invited to address the 1922 Australian Baptist Congress in Melbourne on 'Baptists and their Belief about the Spiritual Condition of the Young Child'.[3] He had also actively associated himself with the Student Christian Movement (SCM) at the University of Sydney, stimulated by its study groups, magazine and books. He argued in 1930 that that there should be a group of critically minded Baptists in every university.[4]

In 1923 Mitchell accepted a call to the struggling Hobart Tabernacle in Tasmania. It had been debilitated by a long vacancy, but Mitchell soon restored its influence. His leadership of young people was outstanding, both in the studies in which he led and the social activities in which he joined. He gained a reputation for substantial sermons, based on careful exegesis and wide general reading. Though not a showy preacher, his diction was clear and his material helpfully well organised. He was involved in the SCM and Toc H, became editor of the Tasmanian *Church Chronicle* and was active in the Hobart Council of Churches. His national reputation was growing and he was clearly concerned about a wide range of issues. Articles such as one in the *Australian Baptist* on 'The Lordship of Christ in the Arena of Industry' (1925) demonstrated that he was one of a minority of Baptists willing to venture into dealing with economic issues.[5]

His hopes for improving worship through the purchase of a pipe organ to celebrate the fortieth anniversary of the congregation were not achieved. Other debts were given priority by his office-bearers. His wearing of a gown for the conduct of worship was unusual among Baptists. The mayor of Hobart presided on 2 March 1927 at his farewell, at which the Anglican bishop was also

---

[2] M. Petras, 'The Life and Times of William Lamb', *Baptist Recorder* 101(May 2008), p. 9.
[3] *Australian Baptist* (*AB*) 5 September 1922, pp. 5-6; 10 October 1922, p. 9; 17 October 1922, p. 4.
[4] *AB* 5 August 1930, p. 3.
[5] *AB* 1 September 1925, pp. 1-2.

present, along with several aldermen and members of the Council of Churches, a tribute to his contributions to the city and to the partnership of Hobart churches.

In 1927 he accepted a call to Flinders Street, Adelaide, one of the denomination's most prestigious pulpits. He began on 3 April. His preaching soon made an impact, as did his teaching and pastoral gifts, but his attempt to found a men's Brotherhood in 1928 did not gather the momentum he had hoped. He was warden of the Baptist college in Adelaide, and began teaching at Parkin College, a Congregational institution with a strong Evangelical ethos. His long-standing interest in missions was increased by his appointment in 1931 as chairman of the South Australia Foreign Missions Board. The following year he wrote a short biography of Ellen Arnold, one of the first Baptist missionaries to India. An invitation to preach at the opening, in April 1929, of the Baptist church in Canberra indicated that he was seen as a minister of national standing.[6] He gave wise guidance in the pastorally demanding Depression years.

In 1933, he accepted a call to the Armadale congregation in Melbourne. In addition, he served on the board of Carey College, the Baptist boys' school, was secretary of the Board of Education of the Baptist Union of Australia and began teaching at Whitley College, the Baptist college in Melbourne, as an acting professor in systematic theology. Over four years, he stimulated many of the students by the freshness of his teaching and his ability to deal critically with recent theology and the controversies it brought because of the tensions between conservatives and liberals. In order to enhance his qualifications, the college authorities invited him in 1935 to commence a Bachelor of Divinity degree from the Melbourne College of Divinity, while at the same time being a member of the latter's governing body. This gave him close contact with the staff of the nearby Methodist and Presbyterian theological halls as well as updating his theological insights. He completed the degree in 1937, amidst all his other commitments.

The Crisis in Mitchell's Career

Principal F.J. Wilkin had retired from Whitley College in 1937 and was followed briefly by W.H. Holdsworth. Though Mitchell had not applied for the post of principal, he was persuaded by colleagues and was nominated by the college in July 1938 to the Baptist Union executive council. The council, however, asked the college to reconsider. Doubts were also raised intemperately by a newly founded and strident Evangelical magazine named the *Edifier*. Its editor, a Plymouth Brother who had formerly been a Baptist, alleged in the August 1938 issue that Mitchell was a modernist, which was quite

---

[6] *AB* 30 April 1929, pp. 1,10.

untrue.⁷ Nevertheless, anxiety about liberal theology was widespread among Evangelicals in Australia. The Presbyterian Church was deeply divided at the same time over the orthodoxy of Professor Samuel Angus of St Andrew's College in Sydney.

A sermon published by Mitchell in1935 re-interpreting the meaning of Armageddon would have offended believers in a very literal interpretation of the book of Revelation. He deplored the way that the sublime poetry of the Apocalypse had been turned into prose, a process he likened to turning sovereigns into base metal. Armageddon was a mystical name and the battle was for the hearts of men, not at a geographical place. 'Let us deliver ourselves and our churches from the notion that, in order to end militarism, God has predestinated a terrible war after the manner of men.'⁸

Student lecture notes were used to reinforce the allegation that Mitchell was 'unsound' and should not be appointed. He was a victim of malicious innuendo and misrepresentation and was given no opportunity to defend himself. When Whitley College reconsidered its nomination, it put Mitchell's name forward again. His nomination was defeated by 85 votes to 77 at the Baptist Union executive council on 8 September 1938. Mitchell was devastated. Some ministers, such as J. Allison of Elsternwick, had given notice of motion to the December meeting of the executive council, asking for publication of the relevant correspondence, if Mitchell would consent to letters marked 'Confidential' being included in this chronological list. Mitchell asked that this not be done in a letter of 27 February 1939. 'For the sake of the peace of the Church, the matter should be dropped forthwith.'⁹ He had no desire to reopen the issues and could see no value in doing so. He recognised that Baptists had become theologically more polarised because of Protestant divisions over interpretations of the faith, more so in Australia than in Britain.

Mitchell had been a loyal Baptist all his life, but after careful consideration felt that he had no option but to resign from the Baptist ministry, which he did in a letter to the general secretary of the Baptist Union on 29 March 1939. 'Since my Baptism I have been loyal to the teaching and the tradition of the Baptist Church as I learned it in England. But the fact is that recent events have been in the nature of a mental apocalypse to me; and I have become conscious of a fundamental incompatibility between my mind and the mind and heart of the Baptist movement as it has now disclosed itself to me.' In another letter, on 3 April 1939, he underlined that 'My decision was, as stated in my resignation, the result of a long intellectual process, stimulated by certain events and guided, as I firmly believe, by the Holy Spirit.'¹⁰

---

⁷ *Edifier*, 19 August 1938, p. 5.
⁸ *AB* 1 October 1935, p. 9.
⁹ BUV Executive Council Minutes, Baptist Union of Victoria Archives.
¹⁰ Donovan Mitchell File, Baptist Union of Victoria Archives.

The Baptist Union sent a deputation, pleading with him to withdraw his resignation, but he was adamant and finished his fruitful ministry at Armadale on 30 April. G.P. Rees, the general secretary, was deeply regretful at the course of events and provided Mitchell with a letter of good standing, which he needed in order to further his application to become a Presbyterian minister. He had already begun attending lectures at the Presbyterian Theological Hall on the Holy Spirit, church, ministry and sacraments given by Professor Norman MacLeish. In replying to Rees on 14 April, Mitchell wrote that he did not expect to be understood, 'but I have a secret conviction that my action will yet be to the praise of God's Word in ways that shall be understood'.[11]

Mitchell's application for admission to the Presbyterian ministry showed how his thinking had been changing for several years. The polity of the Presbyterians was more in harmony with the New Testament than churches with congregational order. The Presbyterian system was more effective in producing the apostles' fellowship than independency. The historic presbyterate and graded courts were better able to exercise oversight than congregational bodies. Presbyterian government was a more effective evangelistic instrument, since the gospel was able to be maintained with more honour within the church and with greater dignity and unity in the face of the world. Such considerations had gradually made him unable with good conscience to continue ministry within the Baptist churches, a process beginning with his address to the 1922 Baptist Congress, which some thought questioned the doctrine of total depravity.[12]

Mitchell also submitted that his doctrinal convictions would enable him to be a zealous and faithful minister of the Presbyterian Church. He had, for many years, not regarded immersion as obligatory. His views were, he believed, almost identical with the Westminster Confession of Faith. On the subjects of baptism he had also gradually come to the conclusion that baptism should not be confined only to believers. That had begun with his address in 1922 on Baptists and their belief about the spiritual condition of the child. The American theologian, Horace Bushnell, had profoundly influenced him.

Practical observation had also made aware of the evangelistic weakness consequent on refusal of Baptists to admit children into the family of the church. Deeper study had persuaded him that much Baptist exegesis was invalid. In particular, he mentioned the influence of Professor Gillies' lectures on Galatians and Principal MacLean's studies on the Hebrew background to New Testament sacramental teaching. A further factor was declaration of the British Baptist Union that it would never unite with Christians who practised infant baptism. This 1938 declaration had greatly distressed him and had 'the effect of making your petitioner feel that the Baptist conception of Christian baptism is schismatic in effect, and that it is a serious barrier to the full

---

[11] Donovan Mitchell File, Baptist Union of Victoria Archives.
[12] *AB* 10 October, 1922, p. 9; 17 October, 1922, 4.

manifestation of ecumenical love'. The cumulative effect of such considerations had created a yearning that he might be allowed to participate in God's gracious sacramental ministry to Christian families, for he could no longer be satisfied with an individualistic interpretation and practice of the sacrament of baptism.[13]

Presbyterian Ministry

In addition to this well-argued submission to the 1939 General Assembly of Australia, he had a stellar list of referees, including Presbyterian professors, Principals Kiek and Holdsworth, the general secretary of the Baptist Union of Victoria and Dr F.W. Boreham. After the end of his ministry at Armadale, he had done supply at St Kilda before, in 1939-40, becoming a home missionary at Daylesford, where he completed his MA. Then he was called to College Church, Parkville, where he ministered to staff and students of the Presbyterian Theological Hall and Ormond College and other university students. His preaching was always centred on the cross. His convictions about appropriate arrangements for worship were expressed in the rearrangement of the sanctuary, placing the table centrally and the pulpit to the side, as was favoured by Presbyterian ministers influenced by the Church Service Society in Scotland. Mitchell was always sharply focused in his use of time and not easy to know or relax with. That was one of the reasons for the extraordinary ability he showed to accomplish a wide range of tasks competently without ceasing to grow theologically. Those who remember him say that he had no equal in theological depth among parish ministers in Victoria.

From 1945 to 1950 he was minister at St Stephen's, Surrey Hills, where his ministry was greatly appreciated by ex-servicemen and their families. He was respected for his deep spirituality, which was expressed in prayer between 6 and 7 am every morning. Despite his ability, he was essentially a modest person who did not impose his convictions by force of personality, but rather by the quality of his persuasion. The Scottish *Book of Common Order* was regularly used in his services, imparting a new liturgical dignity, especially in celebrating the sacraments, which he performed with great dignity. The congregation was encouraged to say 'Amen' at the close of prayers. He was also active in educating his elders and other office-bearers by retreats and short courses.[14]

In 1950 the presbytery appointed him interim-moderator at Hartwell. He made such an impression that he was called and inducted by mid-year. The roll of some 330 members had increased to over 450 by the end of 1952. His personal and intellectual stature made him well able to hold strong elders together when relations became fractious. His session included G.U. Nathan, a barrister, who was session clerk, and the secretary of the Premier's Department,

---

[13] Proceedings of the General Assembly of Australia (1939), pp. 216-17.

[14] The Rev. W. Pugh supplied this information.

J.S. McGibbon. The former was theologically more conservative than Mitchell, but they valued and respected each other. There were some epic session disagreements and threatened resignations over sports clubs, dancing and Sunday tennis, as well as the eventual production of a statement on sabbath observance, sent on to the Victorian Assembly for consideration.[15]

Yet there was more than disagreement. Mitchell gave the lay leaders of the parish unity and fresh vision. Sunday School and youth work were put on a more satisfactory footing. The parish hummed with activity. Many talented young people came to active and intelligent faith as a result, including Max Griffiths, who became a notable minister. In 1951, the sudden death of Professor Duncan MacNicol left a serious gap on the Theological Hall staff. Mitchell was given leave by his session to help with lecturing in New Testament, in addition to his parish duties and other responsibilities in presbytery, the Victorian Assembly and the General Assembly of Australia.

These were considerable. He served as moderator of the Presbytery of Melbourne North in 1951, was a member of the Melbourne College of Divinity and its president in 1949-50, on the Ormond College council and a member of the General Administration Committee Executive. In addition, he served on the committees for Christian unity, life and work and theological education. His responsibilities to the General Assembly of Australia's committees were also considerable: aids to devotion, the church's attitude to its creed, the nature and function of ministry, marriage regulations. Then, in 1951, he was appointed convener of the college committee and charged with oversight of a restructuring of theological education nationally. Only a highly organised person, with experience in governance, could have accomplished such a range of responsibilities without getting lost in needless detail.

Reviewing the nature of theological education was a task involving a great deal of consultation, nationally, and then the drafting of new regulations. Mitchell and the committee rose to the challenge and he was greatly respected for winning consent to the new curricular patterns, which were trialled in 1953 and fully operational in 1955.[16] In brief, they involved a new introductory year involving introduction to theological study, English Bible, Hebrew and Greek for both those who were matriculated and those who were not, such as home missionaries. Those eligible were also expected to do a university subject, after which the Theological Hall Senatus decided which course should be followed. Thereafter, they did separate courses, before a shared exit exam in which they were tested for theological competence, knowledge of doctrine and polity and their ability to deal with pastoral matters in the light of their courses.[17] Unfortunately, Mitchell died suddenly on 31 May 1954, before the process was complete, but he made a lasting contribution to theological education, for which

---

[15] Hartwell Session Minutes, 1950-54, Uniting Church Archives.

[16] Proceedings of the General Assembly of Australia (1951), pp. 271-73.

[17] Proceedings of the General Assembly of Australia (1951), pp. 271-73, minute 112.

his wide experience had prepared him well. It was a tragic loss to the Presbyterian Church as well as to his family.

Nor should his contribution to theological scholarship be forgotten. He contributed occasionally to the *Messenger*, the Victorian Presbyterian paper, as well as writing a number of articles for the *Reformed Theological Review*, an Australian theological journal which began in 1941. He continued to read widely and came increasingly to value the Reformed heritage as a foundation to assess contemporary theological trends. He wrote on a variety of subjects, including 'The Reformed Doctrine of the Church', 'Calvin's Eucharistic Doctrines', 'The New Approach to Paradosis' and 'The Theologian and Divorce', but it was his article on 'Women and the Ministry: Whither Exegesis?' which is worth a brief discussion, for it was not only important in the long struggle over the ordination of women in the Presbyterian Church, but also had an influence on some leading Sydney Anglicans. Even more importantly, it directed attention to the need for a unified approach to exegesis, sorely lacking in many theological discussions and leading to what Mitchell regarded as needless confusion.

Mitchell argued that inadequate exegesis was one of the main sources of current disunity. Christians must be both sensitive to the mind of Christ and pay attention to apostolic tradition and the law of nature. Each of these had been used by the canonical writers, but they were too often ignored by those who placed too much weight on historical criticism as the master key to biblical interpretation, without seeing that this could lead to private interpretation, when people lacked adequate theological resources to assess their own work critically. Contemporary cries for change always needed to be critically tested.

Using Irenaeus as an exemplar of the methodology needed, Mitchell argued that apostolic tradition was clear that women do not have supremacy over men. 1 Corinthians 14:37 stated this as a divine command. He was clear that it was invalid to argue that the Holy Spirit was leading Christians to break with this tradition, because this tradition was established by divine guidance. Tradition ensured that there was continuity with what Christ deposited with his followers. Insisting that the law of nature was inseparable from understanding Christ as Logos and the foundations of the Christian ethic, Mitchell went on, following Brunner's Gifford Lectures, to suggest that absolute equality between men and women was impossible because of their functional differences. That did not contradict their equality in dignity and their share in a common destiny. 'What is wrong is not the exclusion of women from the Holy Ministry, but the assumption so commonly made that their exclusion is a sinful, masculine injustice.'

Freedom for the Word of God was essential, requiring the hard discipline of New Testament study, listening to the Fathers, heeding one another and constantly testing results in a spirit of deep humility. For Mitchell, there was a science of specifically theological exegesis in accord with the previously discussed assumptions. 'It would seem to me that any body of truth which flows from the mind of Christ, which was systematised and formulated under His influence and under that of His Apostles, which has been experimented with in the Church for nearly two millennia, and which is as soundly based on Nature as any of the so-called natural sciences – it would seem to me that such a tradition is entitled to be designated both scientific and just.'[18]

Some who move from one church to another become more ardent than those who grew up in a particular denomination, almost as though they needed to establish indubitably that they had made the correct decision. Mitchell did not have that insecurity. He built on his Baptist experience to grow into the related Reformed tradition present in the Presbyterian Church. Already equipped with a formidable philosophical education, very unusual for a Baptist, and a well-informed theology, he could find space in his personal experience of the risen Lord for fresh insights. His gifts for ministry, governance and education were speedily recognised by the Presbyterian Church of Victoria and some of its key parishes. Mitchell had already demonstrated his leadership gifts among the Baptist churches, both locally and nationally. While learning about the peculiarities of Presbyterian polity and governance took some time, Mitchell's ecumenical spirit and personal stature made the transition a rapid one. Baptist loss was a Presbyterian gain.

---

[18] *Reformed Theological Review*, 8.1 (1949), p. 10.

CHAPTER 14

Baptists and Indigenous Australians

Graham Paulson

Introduction

Most Australians are committed to reconciliation, in principle, but many seem to think that we should now be focusing almost exclusively on the future. A conference on Baptist history provides an important reminder about the significance of the past. We have to be clear about where we have come from, and what we need to repent of, before we can focus on the future with integrity.

Perhaps I should stress that we are here talking about living history. For example, my wife was in her early years compelled to live on a mission reserve in Queensland, she was not allowed to progress her education beyond year 8, and when she worked as a domestic servant in Queensland a portion of her wages was withheld. Those stolen wages have never been recovered, and they are the subject of ongoing legal action.

I was ordained as a Baptist minister in 1968, the first Aboriginal Baptist to be ordained, but under Queensland legislation at the time a police officer could compel me to live in an Aboriginal settlement, without requiring any legal process. Racism has been part of our family's everyday experience, whether sanctioned by Genesis, or by Darwin, or by policies that deprived Aboriginal and Torres Strait Islanders even of the right to vote.

While serving in the Northern Territory, one of the Aboriginal men within our congregation was a certain Vincent Lingiari, leader of the Wave Hill 'walk off' and land rights pioneer.[1] These were the experiences I brought with me into my roles as the inaugural president of the Baptist Union of the Northern Territory in 1971, as principal of Bimbadeen College in the late 1970s (a training college of the Aboriginal Evangelical Fellowship) and as the first Aboriginal president of the Queensland Baptist Union in 2004.

There are many stories that could be told, but this paper will attempt three things. First, it will seek to show the enormous barriers the social, scientific and

---

[1] For the history of the land rights movement, see especially Bain Attwood, *Rights for Aborigines* (Sydney: Allen & Unwin, 2003).

political contexts presented to successful cross-cultural mission to Australia's Indigenous people. Next, in spite of that context, the unique contribution of Australian Baptist individuals and ministries will be examined. And finally, given that history, it will seek to explore what special opportunities might exist to create and construct a ministry that will be effective and appropriate in the twenty-first century.

The Effects of Colonisation

An understanding of Baptist mission to Australia's Aborigines cannot be achieved without acknowledging the broader context of the history of colonisation and the global factors in that colonisation process. It is axiomatic that meaningful exchanges between the settlers and the Indigenous people could not exist without cross-cultural understanding. Cultural understanding, however, was not the primary ingredient of the colonising, 'might-is-right' philosophy. Not only was this philosophy so much a part of the reason why the settlers and convicts were in Australia in the first place, but it was also a philosophy that was affirmed in the global context. The 'might-is-right' philosophy was demonstrated by the international slave trade. It was demonstrated globally in 'social Darwinism', and it was confirmed for some in the church by the theology of the 'Hamitic Curse'.[2] Its impact on Aborigines is evident in the way the two societies interacted.

Notwithstanding the tragic history of misunderstandings, it is good to note that John Saunders set a prophetic tone in the early days of Baptist ministry in Australia. The first Baptist service of worship was held in Sydney on 24 April 1831, more than four decades after the British penal colony had begun in 1788. The first preacher was John McKaeg, who conducted baptisms in Woolloomooloo Bay in 1832. He gathered a motley group around him, a grant of land was received and plans for a chapel were made.[3] Later, a chapel was built in Bathurst Street, Sydney, and a church formed in 1836 under the leadership of John Saunders. Saunders exercised a prophetic ministry, and for example, he sounded a warning to the readers of the *Colonist* in 1838:

> Let the Hawkesbury and Emu Plains tell their history, let Bathurst give her account, and the Hunter render her tale, not to mention the South... The spot of blood is upon us, the blood of the poor and defenceless, the blood of the men we wronged before we slew, and too, too often, a hundred times too often, innocent blood... We have, therefore, reason to dread the approach of the Lord when he

---

[2] John Harris, *One Blood: 200 Years of Aboriginal Encounter with Christianity* (Sutherland: Albatross, 2nd edn, 1994), pp.49, 657-58; for a comprehensive historical discussion, see David M. Goldenberg, *The Curse of Ham: Race and Slavery in Early Judaism, Christianity, and Islam* (Princeton: Princeton University Press, 2003).

[3] Ken R. Manley, *From Wolloomooloo to 'Eternity': A History of Australian Baptists* (2 Vols; Milton Keynes: Paternoster, 2006), I, pp. 17-35.

cometh out of his place to punish the inhabitants of the earth for their iniquity: 'For the earth also shall disclose her blood, and shall no more cover her slain'.[4]

In this sermon, Saunders was actually echoing concerns expressed by the Colonial Office in London in the 1830s and 1840s. After the abolition of slavery in the early nineteenth century, and especially after the Emancipation Act of 1833, the Evangelical reformers focused their humanitarian attention on Aboriginal people in the colonies. In the understanding of these British parliamentarians, the Christian cause was being damaged by injustices done to Indigenous peoples in the name of the empire. Following in the footsteps of William Wilberforce in the campaign against slavery, the leaders were especially Thomas Buxton, James Stephen and Lord Glenelg.

In December 1835, for example, Lord Glenelg expressed a concern to the South Australian Colonial Commission, stating that:

> Before His Majesty can be advised to transfer to his subjects the Property in any part of the land of Australia, he must have at least some reasonable assurance that he is not about to sanction any act of injustice toward the Aboriginal natives of that part of the Globe. In drawing the line of demarcation for the New Province... the Commissioners therefore must not proceed any further than those limits within which they can show, by some sufficient evidence, that the land is unoccupied and that no earlier and preferable title exists.[5]

It was this kind of caution that lay behind the Treaty of Waitangi in 1840 in New Zealand, but the South Australia Act of 1834 had already declared that the colony was 'waste and unoccupied'. This particular clause was removed from the South Australia Act in 1836, but the underlying doctrine of *terra nullius* remained in place.

Aboriginal existence was recognised, but not ownership of land or resources. Property rights were linked to ideas of 'subduing the earth', interpreted largely in terms of farming, and Aboriginal people were legally invisible in that respect.[6] Moreover, the idea of *terra nullius* was linked to a feudal doctrine of land tenure that recognised only the sovereignty of the British crown, although in the 1830s the scope of that doctrine of sovereignty was still under construction. The Batman treaty with the Kulin nations in 1835 proved

---

[4] *Colonist* 17, 20 October 1838, pp. 91-92, cited in Henry Reynolds, *The Law of the Land* (Melbourne: Penguin, 2nd edn, 1992). Saunders is quoting from Isaiah 26:21.
[5] Quoted in Reynolds, *Law of the Land*, p. 106.
[6] For an account of the historical background, see Peter Harrison, '"Fill the Earth and Subdue it": Biblical Warrants for Colonization in Seventeenth Century England', *Journal of Religious History* 29/1 (2005), pp.3-24.

controversial, but eventually the Colonial Office in London decided that the treaty was not an act of the crown and so it was not valid.[7]

The historian, Bain Attwood, has recently investigated the inconsistency of British policy in Australia as compared with New Zealand, and his conclusion seems to be that in Australia it boiled down to a case of 'might makes right'. There is no doubt, however, that the Evangelical reformers in Britain were motivated by their faith. Following a select committee inquiry of 1835-36, Thomas Buxton expressed the view that all native peoples have 'an *inalienable* right to their own soil'.[8] Similarly, William Ellis, a representative from the London Missionary Society, said this:

> It has been our custom to go to a country, and because we were stronger than the inhabitants, to take and retain possession of the country, to which we had no claim, but to which they had the most *inalienable* right, upon no other principle than that we had the power to do so. This is a principle that can never be acted upon without insult and offense to the Almighty, the common parent of the human family, and without exposing ourselves, sooner or later, to the most disastrous calamities and indelible disgrace.[9]

It must be acknowledged that there were a number of voices of conscience in the colonies in the nineteenth century.[10] One Christian institution was the Baptist Merri Creek School, which began after the members of the Richmond Baptist Church had coaxed some Aboriginal children into attending Sunday School in 1845. The Baptists proposed a full-time school. In 1846 the government granted them the use of a house on the junction of Merri Creek and the Yarra River as a boarding school. The church raised enough money to employ Edward Peacock as teacher. He was regarded as a patient and successful teacher and by 1847 he was introducing what were then progressive ideas on schools for 'Coloured Races of the British Colonies' which had been proposed by James Kay-Shuttleworth, secretary of the Privy Council Committee on Education.[11]

---

[7] Bain Attwood, *Possession: Batman's Treaty and the Matter of History* (Melbourne: Miegunyah Press, 2009); Samantha Hepburn, 'Feudal Tenure and Native Title: Revising an Enduring Fiction', *Sydney Law Review* 27/1 (2005), pp.49-86.

[8] Buxton quoted in Reynolds, *Law of the Land*, p.85. See further Mark G. Brett, *Decolonizing God: The Bible in the Tides of Empire* (Sheffield: Sheffield Phoenix Press, 2008), pp.7-31.

[9] William Ellis in *British Parliamentary Papers* 1837, p.510, quoted in Reynolds, *Law of the Land*, p.95.

[10] See especially Henry Reynolds, *This Whispering in our Hearts* (St Leonards: Allen & Unwin, 1998), and Robert Kenny, *The Lamb enters the Dreaming: Nathanael Pepper and the Ruptured World* (Melbourne: Scribe, 2007).

[11] Harris, *One Blood*, p.128.

Twice in 1847 public meetings attended by Melbourne dignitaries were held to display the children's achievements. The Baptist experiment was described in glowing terms, the Peacocks praised and the intelligence and conduct of the pupils commended. When all but three of the students left later that year, Melbourne Baptists were quick to point out that it was not because the project in and of itself was a failure. On the contrary, the pupils displayed considerable academic aptitude. Baptists were pleased that the school was so well accepted by Aboriginal people, but because of cultural problems the school finally closed in 1850.

The demise of the Merri Creek school experiment, despite the best intentions of the pro-Aboriginal Baptists, was construed as a victory to the anti-Aboriginal lobby. The sad irony is that the pro-Aboriginal Baptists had given themselves an impossible dilemma. Desperately anxious to prove conclusively the intellectual capacity and equality of the Aborigines, they attempted to do so by showing that the Aborigines were capable of European civilisation. If we can think of a biblical contrast at this point, the Jews in Acts 15 did not think it necessary to 'Judaise' the gentiles, but it was impossible for Baptists in nineteenth-century Australia to know how to Christianise Aborigines without 'Westernising' them.

One more thing needs to be said about the nineteenth century. It has often been assumed that slavery was never a feature of the Australian experience, yet some forty years after the British Emancipation Act, French officials complained to England that one of its Australian colonies was stealing French citizens from New Caledonia and New Hebrides. Queensland was the focus of this concern, and the practice of stealing Kanaks was known as 'blackbirding'. In the mid-nineteenth century, before the practice of blackbirding was common, a ship sailed up the east coast of Tanna Island in the New Hebrides. My grandfather was picked up out of his fishing canoe in Waisisi Bay and brought to Queensland to cut cane at Bundaberg. He was just a young man at the time and when his canoe washed ashore, his family thought that he had drowned. Ironically, one of the first acts of the new Australian federation in 1901 was to exclude those very Kanaks, since they offended the White Australia policy.[12]

The White Australia policy grew out of an earlier Social Darwinism that put Aboriginal people so low in the evolutionary chain that even our humanity was questioned. Opinions such as the following were commonplace and newspaper editors, it would seem, happily published them:

Brutish, faithless, vicious, the animal being given fullest loose only approached by his next of kin the monkey…the Australian black may have a soul but, if he has,

---

[12] See especially Marilyn Lake and Henry Reynolds, *Drawing the Global Colour Line: White Men's Countries and the Question of Racial Equality* (Melbourne: Melbourne University Press, 2008).

then the horse and dog, infinitely superior in every way to the black human, cannot be denied possession of that vital spark of heavenly flame.[13]

European anthropologists, too, wondered if Australian Aborigines were the missing link between the monkeys and humans. Aboriginal people are still recovering the remains of their ancestors whose graves were desecrated and whose remains were sent to universities in Europe for study.

Missionaries, at least, believed that Aborigines possessed a soul.[14] They were human and therefore capable of salvation. It was on this point that popular opinion and missionary opinion divided. On many other points, however, Christian views on Aborigines were not clearly distinguishable from those of the rest of the community. To some missionaries, if Ham was the 'father' of all the black races, it followed that the Hamitic theory could be further applied to include Australian Aborigines. This was the theological counterpart to social Darwinism, combining to confirm a pattern of thinking and behaviour that persisted until the social challenge of the late sixties and early seventies. During my first assignment as an associate worker on the mission field in the early 1960s, my fellow Aboriginal colleagues and I were made rather acutely aware that one of the senior missionaries working with us was a firm believer in the Hamitic curse and, at that time, he thought it was appropriate to apply to it Australia's Aborigines.

International policies and practices had a flow-on effect on the attitudes and actions of the Australian colonisers, even into the twentieth century. The policies of protection from 1911 to1937 and assimilation from 1937 to1967 meant that under the guise of responsibility for the welfare of our Aboriginal people, the governments were free to do great damage to Indigenous culture and well-being. There were also failures on the part of officials to deal with even extreme violence. I heard white people boasting, even in 1971, of participating in the 'culling of Aborigines', and elders have told me stories of how they witnessed massacres first-hand. It was under the policy of protection that government agencies forcibly removed Aborigines from their homelands, transporting them several hundreds of kilometres to live on reserves and settlements and stealing any children who were of mixed racial parentage.

The government's White Australia policy further reinforced the perceptions and practices of racism. Aborigines only became full citizens of their own country after a constitutional referendum in 1967. Is it an historical accident that the Aboriginal Evangelical Fellowship was formed at the end of the same year as the referendum, when there was an encouraging sense that Indigenous people had finally found a public voice, in line with a number of international developments? But we also need to remember that it was still another eight years before the federal parliament would pass a Racial Discrimination Act

---

[13] Cited in Harris, *One Blood*, p. 28.
[14] Harris, *One Blood*, p. 30.

(1975), and although the Northern Territory had a Land Rights Act in 1976, land rights and native title would still be subject to fierce controversies in the subsequent decades. The legacies of nineteenth-century dispossession live on.

All this means that the gospel, being preached by people from the dominant racial group, was difficult to accept. By the year that the first Baptist Union was established in Australia, 1870, the denominations involved in Aboriginal mission reported a catalogue of failures, but there were to be some notable exceptions in the years leading up to federation.

Baptists in Mission

It was *individuals* from Baptist churches that helped lead Aboriginal mission forward in the era of federation. Two non-denominational missions grew out of the Christian Endeavour movement, and had their beginnings in New South Wales in the Woollahra Baptist Church and the Petersham Congregational Church. The first missionary was Miss J. Watson, who was soon to be followed by Miss Retta Dixon.[15]

A single woman, Miss Watson, feeling the call to live and work within a Sydney Aboriginal Community in 1895, sparked the beginning of a new era in Aboriginal cross-cultural mission. Two of the most influential missions in Australia sprang up out of the work begun by these two women. By agreement the Aborigines Inland Mission (AIM) worked the north and east of the country and the United Aborigines Mission (UAM) worked the west and south of the country. At the peak of missions in the early 1940s, they had over one hundred missionaries between them and more than half of all missionaries on the field. In addition, this number did not include the number of 'native workers' within each mission. The AIM called itself an interdenominational mission but in practice excluded those denominations with which it did not agree. And every missionary had to do a 'guide book' course that included the doctrine, principles and practices of that mission. An important point here is that those doctrines, principles and practices, including believer's baptism by immersion, would have been acceptable to any Baptist organisation of the day (and before the AIM was accepted as a denomination, I was told to register my denomination as Baptist at school or if I was in hospital). Baptist churches throughout the country gave the missions strong support. The impact of the Baptist contribution was far greater than expected given its size in proportion to the other denominations.

It was during the Second World War that Baptist bureaucracy became involved for the first time. After representation from a Baptist individual, Dr E. H. Watson, to the South Australian Baptist Union, that Union resolved in 1944 to survey the possibilities for mission in the Northern Territory. Eventually

---

[15] Manley, *From Woolloomooloo to 'Eternity'*, I, pp.634-40; Harris, *One Blood*, pp.553-55.

Baptist ministry was begun in 1947 at a settlement later to be called Yuendemu, in the southern region of Warlpiri country. Laurie Reece, a minister in charge of the survey, was still at Ali Curung, another mission station, when I first visited in 1961. The work of the Australian Baptist Home Mission in the Northern Territory was the single biggest Aboriginal mission task undertaken by an Australian Baptist institution. In particular, Tom Fleming was to serve the Warlpiri people for twenty-five years from 1950. Several other churches were established as a result of the post-World War II explosion of missionary activity in the north.

Our own contribution began in 1969, when we were based at Lajamanu but visiting other communities such as Kalkaringi, about one hundred and thirty kilometres to the north. On New Year's Day 1971, my family took up residence in Kalkaringi (otherwise known as the Wave Hill township) as pioneer resident missionaries in the new township built by the government.

Revival began among the children, and things moved quickly. A number of them signalled their desire to become Christians, and after they had been counselled they began bringing other children to the mission house. During one Sunday night service, I asked all the children to come out and line up across the front of the meeting. I then challenged the adults to consider their own position, and closed the meeting. Later that night, many came back to the mission house to advise us of their decision to follow the way of 'God the Father' (*Ngatchi*), and my wife and I were counselling people for many hours.

Within a matter of months, there was another movement in the nearby Gurindji camp called Daguragu, previously known as Wattie Creek. An elderly woman named Doris began bringing women to the mission house. It became clear to us that God was blessing her testimony in the camp, and many were turning to Christ. The day before a weekly camp meeting at Daguragu, Doris sat my wife down to tell her a story. She said that God had visited their area the night before. She described how a bright light had come down from the sky and briefly hovered over each home before moving on to the next one. When the light had visited each place it sped back into the sky. Doris was blind, but her vision proved powerful.

In the evening of the next day we gathered for our weekly fireside camp meeting. There seemed to be a different atmosphere about the place. People seemed to be more serious and quiet than before. Even the dogs were not fighting as usual. At the end of the meeting, I asked the people to think long and hard about the claims of Christ and what the Bible says. To my amazement, the whole meeting seemed to erupt at once with almost everyone trying to touch us to signify a desire to follow Christ. There was a loud and lively chorus of 'I want to follow *Ngatchi, maluka*'. This was not just a case of individual decisions for Christ; this was a people's movement. By the dying light of the central campfire, I prayed that God would keep the desire to follow Christ strong in their hearts until we could talk and pray together in the morning. On our way back to Daguragu in the morning, I was carefully negotiating our vehicle down a steep embankment and across a rocky creek bed when I discovered that another vehicle had deliberately blocked our way. The mixture of frustration and curiosity on my part soon dissipated, when the driver leapt out to inform me that he had not made a decision for Christ the night before, and asked if he could make it now. In the middle of the creek crossing, we led the man to Christ, and that began the events at Daguragu that day. Eventually we began an all-age Christian programme that included about 97% of the two communities, Wave Hill and Duguragu, which were about five kilometres apart.

One of the most important developments to come out of Baptist work in the Northern Territory in those days was in the area of contextualisation. This notion was first signalled by Tom Fleming back in 1968 when he involved the community in the 'handover' of land to God for a church building and represented the people's relationship to God in a stained glass window on which the cross at the centre was surrounded by symbols of various clan groups of the Warlpiri people. This had the effect of affirming the clan system within the body of Christ.[16] While Tom strongly acknowledged the connection between land and culture generally, it seems that he was not as keen to promote the use of local language in the church.

More formally, the subject of contextualisation was the topic of discussion by missionaries as early as 1971, when papers were written, but the concept did not catch the imagination of the people until the mid to late seventies. The process, actioned in concert by all the missionaries on the field at the time, was guided by Ivan Jordan and took root in Lajamanu. This was facilitated also through the leadership of one of the local 'lawmen' – a senior custodian of traditional law and custom – Maurice Jupurrula Luther, who was the first person to be baptised at Lajamanu in 1964, and, after him, Jerry Jangala Patrick. 'The development of the Christian '*purlapa*' [traditional dance] and Warlpiri iconography are two of the most significant phenomena in the history of missions in Australia', writes a reviewer of Ivan Jordan's book, *Their Way: Towards an Indigenous Warlpiri Christianity* (2003). 'The combined impact of the above is such that these Aboriginal people have given new understanding and gained new respect from the family of Baptist churches in Australia,' he continues.[17] Another significant cultural factor has been the discovery of the way the existing kinship system can inform styles of worship, leadership and ministry. These have resulted in greater involvement, participation and

---

[16] For an overview of Warlpiri culture and the relationships between 'skin', clan and country, see especially Steven Jampijinpa Patrick, Miles Holmes and Lance Box, *Ngurra-kurlu: A Way of Working with Warlpiri People* (Report 41; Alice Springs: Desert Knowledge CRC, 2008).

[17] See http://www.cdu.edu.au/cdupress/books/their-way.htm, summarising the book's contents when it was published by Charles Darwin University in 2003.

ownership of the church in the community. For example, it is 'skin' relatives who participate directly in baptism ceremonies, not just the pastor.

It may be an oddity within Baptist history that there has often seemed to be more excitement about the use of Christian Warlpiri iconography and *purlapa* (ceremony or 'liturgy') than about the use of the scriptures in Warlpiri translation.[18] Baptists have characteristically placed more emphasis on the Word than on ceremony.[19] In traditional Aboriginal ceremonies, however, there is a high value placed on the maintenance of the correct sacred words, and this cultural expectation raises a number of problems that will be discussed below.

The issues facing *urban* Indigenous people are slightly different from those in contexts where traditional law and custom are still strong, such as among the Warlpiri and Gurindji. In 1988, at the Baptist Unions' annual conventions along the eastern seaboard, delegates were asked to consider the establishment of a special ministry to urban Aboriginals. The Baptist Union of Australia soon considered the requests that were passed on from the state Unions and from the Australian Baptist Missionary Society, the mission agency responsible for Aboriginal work. In the ensuing discussion some felt that urban Aboriginal work was the responsibility of the urban and country churches, since this was not considered to be cross-cultural ministry. After further consultation with the Northern Territory field, the Baptist Union of Australia established the Aboriginal and Islander Baptist Council of Australia in 1991 (AIBCA). This ministry, through partnership with the respective state Unions, saw the establishment of Aboriginal churches in Brisbane and Perth and the emergence of new church leadership including the ordination of two Aboriginal pastors, Mark Kickert and Keith Truscott. The work closed down in 2001, although my understanding is that further ministries are still being considered.

Historic Challenges for Aboriginal Mission

Whether in remote areas or in urban areas, Baptists have been at the forefront of contextualisation of the gospel into Aboriginal communities. The work of contextualisation that has been done so far has largely been done in the area of

---

[18] It is the work of Steve Swartz, along with his leading co-translator Jerry Jangala Patrick, that lies behind the Bible Society translation *Yimi-nyayirni-wangu kaatu-kurlangu* (Canberra: Bible Society in Australia, 2001). Note that Steve Swartz's Warlpiri-English dictionary is available on the web at http://livinglanguages.wordpress.com/2006/07/16/warlpirienglish-dictionary/ .

[19] Analogies between the Christian eucharist and Indigenous ceremony were conceived more easily within the Lutheran missions. See esp. T.G.H. Strehlow, *Central Australian Religion: Personal Monototemism in a Polytotemic Community* (Bedford Park: Australian Association for the Study of Religions, 1978), pp. 27, 34, 60; Barry Hill, *Broken Song: T.G.H. Strehlow and Aboriginal Possession* (Milsons Point, NSW: Vintage, 2003), pp.49, 437; cf. Jürgen Moltmann, 'Ancestor Respect and the Hope of Resurrection', *Sino-Christian Studies* 1 (2006), pp.13-36.

the acculturation of processes of worship and styles of ministry. On these issues, I want to make three comments.

First, these initiatives have been valuable because Aboriginal people for centuries have relied on ceremonies and song to maintain the mythology of their animistic religion, using classical sacred vocabulary. For each story, the ceremonial process and their appropriate actions do remain critical to the maintenance of the myth. The use of ceremonies, and classical language, to embody the gospel stories corresponds to cultural expectations, but also raises certain difficulties.

Secondly, the message of the myths has been locked into the vocabulary of an ancient, classical expression, and publicly available translations into the common community expressions of today are not permitted. This has led to problems with acceptance and use of Bible translation work in some of our Aboriginal communities. The translator is sometimes very dependent on the perceptions of the native speakers, and they, depending on their Christian maturity and personal experience, might make use of both common and classical vocabulary to translate what they perceive to be a biblical concept. This leads to complications that need to be negotiated within the Aboriginal community.

Thirdly, in each tribe, there are clan or kinship groups that are allocated the responsibility for perpetuating selected stories and performing the appropriate rituals. These are classified as the owners and custodians of their respective traditions and as such retain authority over all ceremonial obligations. Consequently, in the first instance, when the missionaries brought the gospel to the Aboriginal community, they were considered to be the owners of the stories. The books from which they read contained the appropriate language of the story, and as the authoritative interpreters, they had control over all the related ceremonies. We might even suggest that Protestant missionaries against their intentions, have acquired the kind of honour that was accorded to mediaeval Catholic bishops, which is at least an irony – if not a departure from Baptist theology of the church. To the extent that Aboriginal people carry the new spiritual stories within the old cultural expectations, therefore, there may be a problem with pouring 'new wine into old wineskins'. The version of this parable in Luke 5:39 also throws up the troubling possibility that the goodness of the 'old wine' has not been appreciated as it might. In spite of the good work already undertaken in a number of denominations on the acculturation of Christian ceremony and ministry, we need to do more. We need to do more work on exploring redemptive analogies between the biblical texts and Indigenous cultures.[20]

---

[20] The idea of 'redemptive analogies' was promoted in the influential books by Don Richardson, *Peace Child* (Glendale, CA: Regal, 1974), and *Eternity in their Hearts* (Glendale, CA: Regal, rev. edn, 1984).

Beyond ceremony and ministry, there is an urgent need for the church to engage in Indigenous theologising. For example, the Bible devotes its first few chapters to creation. It begins with a cosmogony, and not enough work has been done on the relationship between Aboriginal cosmogony and the full breadth of biblical creation theology. There is an understandable reticence to do this when Aboriginal cosmogony and cosmology are part of ancient sacred traditions. Moreover, these sacred traditions are secret, known only to traditional elders, and the number of Christian Indigenous leaders who are also traditional elders is decreasing – although there are a number of Warlpiri people in this position.

There has been negligible encouragement from the mainstream Baptist churches to embark on this journey, but it must be undertaken. Cosmogony and cosmology are the prime movers of Aboriginal society. Most other aspects of Aboriginal culture derive their place and importance from the manner in which they preserve and protect Aboriginal cosmogony, cosmology and values. Thus, the cultural aspects of ceremony and ministry lose their relevance unless they are anchored in Indigenous beliefs, customs and values, yet these all need to be understood as reflecting the presence of God in Australia before the arrival of Christian missionaries.

The church in Australia is one of the great agents of change for Indigenous people, but change cannot be valued for its own sake.[21] What kind of theology will allow people's identity to be authentically Aboriginal and authentically Christian?[22] Unless this question can be answered with integrity, the church faces the danger of being seen as just another Western social institution that contributes, by default, to cultural genocide.

Baptists have made a significant contribution to the history of Indigenous mission. But outside of Warlpiri and Gurindji country, the question of what it means to be an Indigenous Baptist *church* in Australia has barely begun to find an answer. The body of Christ will always be multi-cultural, or culturally 'hybrid', but it also needs to be local and incarnational. Such a local identity, far from cloning North American or European models of the church, will be unique to Australia and the Asia-Pacific region. We need to turn redemptive analogies into redemptive practicalities.

---

[21] See the important collection of essays in Peggy Brock (ed.), *Indigenous Peoples and Religious Change* (Leiden: Brill, 2005).

[22] Graham Paulson, 'Towards an Aboriginal Theology', *Pacifica* 19 (2006), pp.310-22.

PART FIVE

Baptists in New Zealand

CHAPTER 15

THREE COUNTRIES, TWO CONVERSIONS, ONE MAN: J.J. DOKE - BAPTISTS, HUMANITY AND JUSTICE

Laurie Guy

Baptists in New Zealand have commonly not engaged to any great extent with major issues of social and public life beyond traditional concerns about sex, alcohol and gambling. Concern about even the latter two matters has largely subsided in the last generation. Is this frequent lack of larger concern linked with Baptist origins – perhaps an effect of having a 'gathered church' concept?

Baptist Silence on Public Issues

Baptists began in England in a time when it was assumed and expected that all members of society would also be members of the Church of England. This close linkage between church and state led to the church naturally having a major interest in the concerns of society. In stepping out of that arrangement in favour of a gathered church, Baptists conceptually were inclined to stand outside society. Their emphasis was much more on the individual and on the local church instead of society. This sort of perspective has commonly led Baptists to focus on saving and maintaining 'souls' and planting and growing churches, without much balancing concern for the larger issues of society. This is to be contrasted with the perspective of the great Evangelical, John Wesley, who remained in the Church of England, and whose vision was to 'spread holiness over the land', a holiness which, Wesley noted, was 'outward' as well as 'inward'.[1] Where public issues have been debated in society, Baptists have not uncommonly operated under 'trickle-up' theory: if we convert individuals this will trickle up to a solution of social problems.

Along with that has often stood a highly vertical view of Christianity: that it is all about one's relationship with God, as opposed to a perspective that Christianity is also very much a faith concerned with one's fellows. A 'trickle-

---

[1] Letter 'to a member of the Society', 16 September 1774, in John Emory (ed.), *The Works of John Wesley* (New York: Mason & Lane, 1839), Vol. VI, p. 779.

down' view has been common: when people get their relationship with God sorted out, right human relationships will surely follow. This sort of viewpoint has been reflected in the evangelistic approach of (Baptist) Billy Graham. At a press conference during his 2005 New York City crusade, Graham was asked to name the most critical societal problems of the time. He answered, 'Well the greatest problem that we have is poverty', before going on to say, 'And I believe that the Gospel of Christ is the answer. Not part of the answer, but the whole of the answer. We don't have any possibility of solving our problems today, except through Jesus.'[2]

Douglas Sturm has rightly identified this as a 'conversion approach' – a concentration primarily on the relationship between God and the individual self, a seeking of the transformation of the single soul. This is in contrast to a 'prophetic' model – a challenge to social sin based on principles of justice and solidarity, mutual respect and togetherness.[3]

This conversionist model requires scrutiny in the light of scripture and of Christ. What is needed is a deeper reflection on the nature of Christian conversion. Is it enough for an evangelist to urge hearers to come to Christ? Or is there also a second conversion – towards humanity? If people are converted to Christ but not also converted to humanity, are they only half converted? This is a vital question in contexts of racism, militarism, nationalism and injustice. How should the church respond in such contexts?

Joseph Doke as an Exception

Relatively few New Zealand Baptist voices have shown significant concern for larger social concerns. An outstanding example of this minority perspective, however, is Joseph J. Doke, who pastored in New Zealand for only seven years and whose ministry was cut short because of his opposition to the Anglo-South African (Boer) War.

Lacking a formal theological college education, Doke's development depended hugely on self-study. A friend and colleague in New Zealand, F.W. Boreham, later recalled Doke's passion for books:

> 'Read my dear man,' he exclaimed, one day, springing to his feet in his excitement and pacing the veranda in his characteristic way, 'read; and read systematically; and keep on reading; never give up!'[4]

---

[2] Douglas Sturm, 'You shall have No Poor among You', in Michael G. Long, *The Legacy of Billy Graham: Critical Reflections on America's Greatest Evangelist* (Louisville: Westminster John Knox Press, 2008), pp. 63-77, quoted at p. 63.

[3] Sturm, 'You Shall Have No Poor', pp. 65, 74.

[4] F.W. Boreham, *The Man who Saved Gandhi: A Short Biography of John Joseph Doke* (London: Epworth, 1948), p. 8.

Doke's searching and investigative mind frequently led him into social action. Social justice issues are often complex, requiring people to do their 'homework' before they can adopt an informed opinion. And Doke did his homework. His biographer, William Cursons, noted this in relation to Doke's becoming involved in the Indian cry for justice in South Africa:

> It would have been unlike Doke had he neglected to make himself acquainted with both sides of the dispute. . . . He had examined the whole position most carefully; and what grieved him was that, with few exceptions, the leaders of Christian thought and energy on the Rand were either apathetic or antagonistic. He could, to a certain extent, understand the feeling of opposition; but to him whose soul blazed out at any form of persecution, it did not seem right that the Churches should remain untouched and indifferent to the cry of a people where a question of conscience, even religion, was involved.[5]

Doke was a man of three worlds and two conversions. Born in England in 1861, and experiencing an Evangelical conversion and baptism in 1875, Doke had a brief pastorate at Dartmouth before becoming a Baptist pastor in South Africa (at Graaff Reinet) in 1882. Returning to England in 1886, he was successively pastor of two Baptist churches (at Chudleigh and then at City Road, Bristol). Called to the leading Baptist church in Christchurch, New Zealand (at Oxford Terrace), in 1894, he had a prominent ministry (serving as president of the Baptist Union of New Zealand in 1897), until his resignation from the pastorate in January 1902. Doke subsequently recommenced ministry in South Africa in 1903. There, he had two further pastorates (at Grahamstown and Johannesburg), also serving as president of the South Africa Baptist Union in 1906-07.

In 1913 Doke undertook a reconnaissance trip to what is now Zambia on behalf of the South African Baptist Missionary Society. On the homeward leg he caught enteric fever and died in Zimbabwe. Several services were held in his memory, one in Johannesburg being called by its mayor at the request of its citizens. People of all sorts of ethnicity and creed attended, with special seating being arranged for Indians, Chinese, Jews and others.[6] Mahatma Gandhi's weekly newspaper, *Indian Opinion*, mourned Doke's passing: 'To him every human being was truly a friend and brother. . . . Mr Doke was among the few who knew no distinction of race, colour or creed.'[7] This insight into Doke's character helps explain his efforts for racial justice in New Zealand and South Africa. It is to New Zealand that I now turn.

---

[5] William E. Cursons, *Joseph Doke, the Missionary-Hearted* (Johannesburg: Christian Literature Depot, 1929), p. 141.
[6] *New Zealand Baptist* (*NZB*) December 1913, p. 236.
[7] *Indian Opinion*, No. 33, v. 11, 23 August 1913, cited in the *Dictionary of African Christian Biography*: www.dacb.org/stories/southafrica/doke_jj.html, accessed 21 January 2009.

Anti-Asian Racism in New Zealand

On 18 August 1857 an Anti-Chinese Immigration Committee met in Nelson, New Zealand. Though no Chinese were then living in the region, 'all present expressed the greatest disgust and horror at the probability of Chinese immigrants arriving in this Province'.[8] The local newspaper, the *Nelson Examiner*, chimed in, voicing support for measures to block 'these bestial swarms' of 'Mongolian filth' coming into 'an English colony' (a colony which the English were then in the process of filching from the indigenous Maori).[9] Such racist sentiments were prevalent in New Zealand for the eighty or more years that followed.

The Anti-Immigration Committee failed in its aim of blocking Chinese immigration. Chinese did come in, especially during the time of the Otago gold rush of the 1860s. By 1874 there were 4,816 Chinese in New Zealand. However, under the Chinese Immigrants Restriction Act of 1881, Chinese immigrants were subject to a special poll tax of £10 (a tax later increased to £100 and persisting until 1944) and ships could convey only one Chinese per 100 tons of cargo. Subsequent legislation tightened the restrictions and also barred Chinese from citizenship (this applied until 1952).[10] Initially almost all Chinese immigrants were men. Chinese women were not allowed into New Zealand in any great numbers until the 1930s, and even in 1950 government memoranda indicated that 'Chinese are the only aliens who cannot freely obtain permits for the entry of their wives and children under our present immigration policy'.[11] Collectively the restrictions were largely successful. In 1951 the number of Chinese in New Zealand (4,832) was virtually the same as it had been in 1874.

Along with government restrictions went popular xenophobia. An anti-Asian 'White New Zealand League' formed in Pukekohe in 1925. The *Franklin Times* provided strong support for the League with highly racist articles, warning of the peril of allowing 'inferior races' to immigrate into New Zealand.[12] The newspaper urged a boycott of Asian businesses and published a correspondent's poem:

> And while we sing 'God save the King'
> And think we are the only thing,
> The alien builds his habitation

---

[8] *Nelson Examiner* 22 August 1857, p. 2.
[9] *Nelson Examiner* 19 August 1857, p. 2.
[10] Ng Bickleen Fong, *The Chinese in New Zealand: A Study in Assimilation* (Hong Kong: Hong Kong University Press, 1959), pp. 20, 24; Michael King, *The Penguin History of New Zealand* (Auckland: Penguin, 2003), p. 368.
[11] James Belich, *Paradise Reforged: A History of the New Zealanders from the 1880s to the Year 2000* (Auckland: Penguin, 2001), pp. 228-29.
[12] *Franklin Times* 18 January 1926, p. 4.

By means of 'peaceful penetration',
And notwithstanding scores of Diggers
The public buys its fruit from niggers.[13]

Xenophobia pervaded New Zealand for much of the hundred years that followed the 1857 *Nelson Examiner* articles. It affected leading citizens of the country as well as provincial bigots. A meeting of the Anti-Chinese League in Wellington in 1895, which passed resolutions supporting an increased poll tax on Chinese immigrants and calling for a boycott of their businesses, was attended by ex-premier Sir Robert Stout and at least seven other parliamentarians. The key speaker at the meeting was William Pember Reeves, then minister of labour. In his view, the alleged civilisation of the Chinese was 'no civilization'. Chinese 'lived in defiance of the rules of sanitation' and so were 'a danger to the health and morals of the people'. In warning of the threat posed by their industriousness to the employment of European labourers, Reeves compared the Chinese with baboons:

> Only that day he had read of an incident in South Africa where a baboon had been trained to work at a railway station and it worked very well. (Laughter). If they wanted labourers who were strong and cheap, let them import shiploads of baboons, because they would not cost anything, and if they were troublesome, at any rate they could kill them, which they could not do in the case of Asiatics.[14]

The speech was no political ploy, designed simply to garner popular support. Three years later, when Reeves was out of New Zealand as New Zealand agent general (later, High Commissioner) to the United Kingdom, he wrote of the Chinese as 'a true alien element' who 'work apart as gold-diggers, market gardeners and small shop-keepers and are the same inscrutable, industrious, insanitary race of gamblers and opium-smokers in New Zealand as elsewhere'.[15]

Doke as a Voice for Chinese

One Sunday evening in June 1899, the police arrested thirty-two Chinese and four Europeans at a Chinese gambling den, for being unlawfully on premises used for illegal gambling (some were playing fan-tan). Those arrested were handcuffed, marched along the street, crammed into cells that were barely large enough for half their number, left to sleep on a muddy floor with one blanket between four or five men, given a total of ten slices of bread to be rationed

---

[13] *Franklin Times* 8 February 1926, p. 4; 3 February 1926, p. 4. The term 'diggers' refers in New Zealand to soldiers, in this case to returnees from World War I.
[14] *NZ Times* 5 August 1895, p. 3.
[15] William Pember Reeves, *New Zealand* (London: Horace Marshall & Son, n.d. [1898]), p. 171.

among them all as a breakfast and then not fed again until 6 pm.[16] The police initially opposed bail for the Chinese on the basis that they all looked alike and if they absconded it would be impossible to identify them again.[17] Eventually, all those charged with being found without lawful excuse in a common gambling house were granted bail, the Chinese being required to provide a surety of £25, with the European bail amount being only £5.[18]

Into the fray stepped Doke.[19] He was already recognised in Christian circles as strongly sympathetic to Chinese mission.[20] Doke delivered an impassioned address at a Christian Endeavour rally in 1896 on the need to bring the gospel to New Zealand Chinese: 'These Chinese have souls to be saved, remember that; and remember that God loves them.' In making this appeal he denounced the shameful treatment by the West, in the earlier 'opium wars' in China and in New Zealand, of these 'uncut, unpolished diamonds', these 'natural gentlemen'.[21] Doke's church had started a Chinese Bible class in 1891.[22] Though the work was small for a time, it flourished a few years later to the extent that by mid-1897 its meeting room was too small.[23] This necessitated the building of a new meeting hall, costing £85, with most of the money coming from the Chinese themselves.[24] In 1898 the church baptised three members of the Chinese Bible class subsequent to their conversion.[25]

Six of those arrested in 1899 were attenders of the Chinese Bible class run by Doke's church, four of these also being lodgers at the gambling place. A number of those arrested frequently attended the gambling den, more to socialise in congenial society than to gamble (there was, according to Doke, no evidence that they ever did gamble).[26] When Doke heard about the arrests, he was returning from conducting an evangelistic mission at the nearby Spreydon Baptist Church.[27] He immediately went to the court and spoke up for the men and their potentially being refused bail.[28] He followed this up with public

---

[16] *Press* 16 June 1899, p. 3; 23 June 1899, p. 2; *Star* 17 June 1899, p. 6.
[17] *Press* 22 June 1899, p. 4.
[18] *Press* 13 June 1899, p. 3.
[19] *NZB* July 1899, pp. 105, 112.
[20] *Christian Outlook* 23 May 1896, p. 204.
[21] *NZB* May 1896, pp. 65-66; A.H. MacLeod, *Oxford Terrace Baptist Church: Centennial History 1863-1963*, (Christchurch: no pub., 1963), p. 49: NZ Baptist Archive: File 576/1.
[22] *NZB* August 1891, p. 115.
[23] *NZB* November 1891, p. 163; August 1897, p. 124.
[24] MacLeod, *Oxford Terrace*, p. 50; *NZB* August 1897, p. 124; June 1898, p. 94.
[25] Oxford Terrace Baptist Church records (Christchurch City Library archive: Z Arch 63, Box 2, series 1): Church minutes, 19 October 1898; also *NZB* October 1898, p. 157; December 1898, p. 190.
[26] *Press* 16 June 1899, p. 3; 19 June 1899, p. 3.
[27] Cursons, *Joseph Doke*, p. 96.
[28] *Press* 13 June 1899, p. 3; 22 June 1899, p. 4.

meetings and correspondence in the newspapers, eventually calling for a public inquiry into the matter.[29] Doke was troubled that the event could well be a setback for the gospel: 'They had been trying to teach these Chinese that "God is love" and that Christians were some faint echo of God.' What was needed was 'tender Christian sympathy'.[30] 'It might surprise the police to know that they [those arrested] actually were human beings with the rights – the birthrights of all God's human family, rights to justice, and humanity and love.'[31]

The outcome was a great deal of publicity and controversy in the national press, some of it quite sympathetic to the plight of Chinese in New Zealand. The affair was eventually debated in parliament. A departmental inquiry was held, leading to the disciplining of the officer who had failed to give the prisoners a mid-day meal, and to the sum of £350 being voted to improve the cell accommodation at Christchurch.[32] Doke was exuberant at the outcome: 'It was a time of great excitement through the colony and I got into all the papers, comic and others, in a friendly sort of way. But the gratitude of the Chinese knew no bounds.'[33]

The Breadth of Doke's Ministry

Doke was then in the midst of a flourishing ministry in his congregation. During his seven years at Oxford Terrace he welcomed 219 new members into his three-hundred-member church, while also engaging significantly in evangelistic preaching missions in other Baptist churches.[34] For example, the *New Zealand Baptist* noted in November 1897 that Doke had recently undertaken three series of evangelistic services at Spreydon, Oamaru and Greendale.[35] A large number publicly accepted Christ at Doke's Spreydon mission. He wrote at this time: 'To be used in the conversion of souls has been for a long time my highest ambition, but it seemed withheld from me. Now I feel, as the memory of those meetings comes back, "like singing all the time".'[36]

Despite his successful ministry, Doke fell foul of his church in 1900 in relation to the Boer War. A number of key English Baptist leaders opposed the

---

[29] *Press* 24 June 1899, p. 4.
[30] *NZB* July 1899, p. 112.
[31] *Press* 19 June 1899, p. 3.
[32] *New Zealand Parliamentary Debates* (*NZPD*) 109, 1899, pp. 426-27; *NZB* August 1899, p. 121.
[33] Letter to a friend, quoted in MacLeod, *Oxford Terrace*, p. 50.
[34] *NZB* October 1901, p. 154.
[35] *NZB* November 1897, p. 173; see also *NZB* July 1897, p. 109.
[36] Cursons, *Joseph Doke*, p. 94.

war with the Boers.[37] Given the strength of English influence in New Zealand, one might have expected New Zealand Baptists likewise to take a more neutral, if not an anti-war, stance. In this case, however, a more general New Zealand loyalty to imperial Britain overrode any New Zealand Baptist loyalty to their British Baptist mother church. Thus the *New Zealand Baptist* editor, in noting the anti-war stance of key English Baptist leaders in 1900, described it as 'extraordinary' and 'perplexing'.[38] The overall voice in the *New Zealand Baptist* magazine was markedly pro-war. As S.R. Ingold, long-standing secretary of the Oxford Terrace Baptist Church, said:

> [T]his war is 'our war'. It is not merely a conflict between the English and the Boers. . . . [T]he British nation is our nation; we are a living part of the Empire, and they and we – Britain and New Zealand – must rise *or fall* together.[39]

Ingold and Doke were leaders in the same congregation; so it behoved Doke to be cautious on this issue. However, his deep sense of the gospel and of justice, fuelled by his earlier experience in living in South Africa, led to his speaking out. A month after Ingold's article, Doke had a contrary article published in the same magazine. He saw the cause of the war as 'British aggression' fuelled by the machinations of imperialists such as Cecil Rhodes.[40]

Expressing such a viewpoint was risky. So nearly universal was New Zealand support for Britain in the Boer War that the Westland Harbour Board could threaten its employees with dismissal if they voiced 'disloyal and unpatriotic sentiments' in relation to the war. J. Grattan Grey, chief Hansard reporter at parliament, was dismissed from his position because he wrote a newspaper article and two pamphlets opposing New Zealand's involvement in the Boer War.[41] Stones were thrown through the Doke manse windows in response to his outspokenness.[42] And Doke's viewpoint almost certainly led to ongoing strain with his congregation. According to J.J. North, neighbouring pastor of Doke at Spreydon, Doke's sympathies with the Boers ended his New Zealand ministry.[43] This explanation seems likely because when Doke tendered his resignation to the church in September 1901 he indicated that he had 'no

---

[37] Ian M. Randall, *The English Baptists of the Twentieth Century* (Didcot: Baptist Historical Society, 2005), pp. 41-42. Randall indicates that at least half the English Baptist pastors were against the war.
[38] *NZB* March 1900, pp. 40-41.
[39] *NZB* April 1900, p. 61 (emphasis original).
[40] *NZB* May 1900, pp. 68-69.
[41] In J. Crawford and E. Ellis, *To Fight for the Empire: An Illustrated History of New Zealand and the South African War, 1899-1902* (Auckland: Reed Books, 1999), p. 29.
[42] *NZB* November 1962, p. 281.
[43] *NZB* December 1945, p. 303.

prospects and no plans'.[44] Pressure on Doke also seems implied in a *New Zealand Baptist* editorial linking Doke's resignation with 'disorder, I might almost say pettiness', in New Zealand church life.[45]

Doke's opposition to the Boer War was likely based not only on the wrongness of *this* war, but also on a broader opposition to militarism and war in general. Certainly, when later in South Africa, he opposed (without success) the South Africa Defence Bill in the interdenominational South Africa Church Council and in the South African Baptist Union, particularly the bill's requirements for compulsory military training. He wrote in the *South African Baptist* in March 1912:

> The Christian Church, with the sayings of the Master continually ringing in her ears, has acquiesced for so long in the growth of militarism, that she seems almost incapable of taking a stand against it.... I know of only one Spirit of Christ, and that is, the Spirit of Love; and, try as I may, I cannot reconcile Him with the military spirit of the age.... [O]ne of our greatest anti-Christian forces of the day is militarism; therefore the less Christian people have to do with it the better.[46]

Doke's larger concern about militarism helps explain the strong pacifist influence that surfaced among a small section of the Oxford Terrace church a few years after he left that pastorate, in particular in Charles Mackie, who was probably the key pacifist leader in New Zealand during World War I and who had joined the Oxford Terrace church a few months before Doke left that church.[47] It is perhaps significant that Mackie's pacifism surfaced in the public arena in New Zealand in 1911 over the issue of compulsory military training for young people – the same issue that provoked the expression of Doke's anti-militarism in South Africa soon thereafter.

Doke and Gandhi

When Doke went from New Zealand to South Africa, he came to embrace the struggle of Indians for justice, establishing contact with Indian leaders, including Mahatma Gandhi, who later wrote:

> When Mr. Doke came to the cause, he threw himself into it heart and soul and never relaxed his efforts in our behalf. It was usual with Mr. Doke to gain complete mastery over the subject he handled. He, therefore, became one of the

---

[44] Oxford Terrace Baptist Church records (Christchurch City Library archive: Z Arch 63, Box 2, series 1): Church minutes, 11 September 1901.
[45] *NZB* November 1901, p. 163.
[46] *South African Baptist*, March 1912, 25-26; Cursons, *Joseph Doke*, 132-33.
[47] For fuller exploration of this pacifism, see Laurie Guy, 'Baptist Pacifists in New Zealand: Creating Division in the Fight for Peace', *Baptist Quarterly*, 40.8 (October 2004), pp.488-99.

best informed men on the subject in South Africa. He loved passive resisters as they were his own congregation.[48]

Immediately after first meeting Gandhi at the end of 1908, Doke engaged in five powerful appeals for the justice of the Indian cause, sending letters to the *Transvaal Leader*, appearing in solidarity with Gandhi at his trial and sentencing to imprisonment, and preaching a sermon directly on the issue to his regular congregation.[49] Doke's friendship with Gandhi strengthened markedly in February 1908 when Gandhi was beaten up and left unconscious by Pathan Indians who felt that Gandhi was too compromising to the government in agreeing to be fingerprinted in relation to racially based registration. Doke brought Gandhi into his home for several weeks to recuperate. Apart from the sacrificial cost in caring for Gandhi, it was socially costly for the Doke family. Doke's son, Clement, later recalled that the family's neighbours, who had previously been friendly, 'cut us completely for so breaking caste as to entertain a black man'.[50]

Gandhi was touched by Doke's hospitality at the time of his recuperation. He later wrote:

> Every day marked an advance in our mutual affection and intimacy. Naturally, after I was injured, all classes of Indians flocked to the house, from the humblest street-hawker, with dirty clothes and dusty boots, to the highest Indian officials. Mr. Doke would receive them all in his drawing-room with uniform courtesy and consideration. The whole family gave their time, either to nursing me or else receiving the hundreds of Indian visitors who came to see me. Even at night Mr. Doke would twice or thrice tiptoe into my room to see if I wanted anything.[51]

Out of the recuperation sprang a continuing friendship. Doke edited the weekly newspaper, *Indian Opinion*, for Gandhi when Gandhi was in London, July to December 1909, pleading the South African Indian cause.[52] That same year, Doke also wrote the first biography written on the life of Gandhi, a copy of which Gandhi sent to Leo Tolstoy as a fuller introduction of himself and his aspirations. In its memoir to Doke at the time of his death, *Indian Opinion* noted that his commitment and zeal for the Indian cause put him at risk of

---

[48] In Anonymous, *The Late Mr. Joseph J. Doke: A Memoir* (reprinted from *Indian Opinion* 23 August 1913) (Phoenix, Natal: International Printing Press, n. d.), 11 (New Zealand Baptist Archive: MA 196, MS No. 1006478).
[49] James D. Hunt, *Gandhi and the Nonconformists: Encounters in South Africa* (New Delhi: Promilla, 1986), pp. 103-107.
[50] Hunt, *Gandhi and the Nonconformists*, p. 110.
[51] Boreham, *The Man Who Saved Gandhi*, p. 20.
[52] www.unisa.ac.za/Default.asp?Cmd=ViewContent&ContentID=11319, accessed 21 January 2009; Anonymous, *The Late Mr. Joseph J. Doke*, 4; Cursons, *Joseph Doke*, p. 145.

losing popularity among his congregation, '[b]ut that was no deterrent to him'. Biographer, William Cursons, came to a similar conclusion: 'nothing would keep him [Doke] quiet if an injustice reared its head'.[53]

Gandhi spoke of his experience in the Doke household at the Johannesburg memorial service for Doke in 1913: 'The whole family was at my disposal in order to nourish me, in order to serve me, in order to soothe me, although I was a stranger to them and had never done a single service to them…. With Mr. Doke it was a question of the conquest of hate by love, of the conquest of vice in others by the fullest exercise of virtue.'[54]

A Voice for the Underdog

For Doke, issues of truth and justice were of greater concern than issues of personal acceptance and popularity. For example, at one point in his Johannesburg ministry he drew attention in his sermon to the miserable pittance that many shop-girls were receiving and to the temptations to which this might well lay them open. This led to major outcry against Doke in the local newspapers. Unabashed, he told a friend, 'I am getting a tremendous frizzling in the papers.'[55]

Doke was outspoken but he was not angular. The writer and minister F.W. Boreham was a close colleague and friend in New Zealand. He later described Doke as having 'the most engaging and most lovable type of masculine saintliness of which I have ever had personal experience'.[56] Neither was Doke a liberal in twentieth-century terms, abandoning a traditional Evangelical focus for broader concerns. He was a passionate evangelist. This showed up in his dealings with Gandhi. When the two men first met, Gandhi was suspicious: had Doke come 'to convert me to Christianity'? Gandhi quickly changed his mind: 'we had not talked many minutes before I saw how sadly I had misjudged him'. While Doke did not talk of the gospel with Gandhi at that time, he did so later. Gandhi indicated this at the Johannesburg memorial service, saying of Doke that he 'missed no occasion to bring home to me the truth as he knew it and which brought him so much inward peace'.[57]

Doke's evangelistic passion spilled over also into a passion for foreign mission.[58] As an Evangelical of his times he was also passionately against

---

[53] Cursons, *Joseph Doke*, p. 129.
[54] Quoted in S. Hudson-Reed *et al.*, *The History of Baptists in Southern Africa, 1820-1977* (Roodepoort: Baptist Publishing House, 1983), pp. 108-109.
[55] Arthur C. Davies, 'Too Much Attention to the Pawns' (unpublished MS, n.d.): New Zealand Baptist Archive: MA 196, MS No. 1006478; Cursons, *Joseph Doke*, p. 130.
[56] Boreham, *The Man Who Saved Gandhi*, p.11.
[57] Hunt, *Gandhi and the Nonconformists*, pp.102-103; 123.
[58] *NZB* January 1902, pp.4, 9; February 1902, p. 27.

alcohol.[59] In addition, however, Doke was passionate for the underdog and for justice. Doke's Evangelicalism was a big Evangelicalism. He was a man of two conversions: to humanity as well as to Christ. That was the key to his remarkable life and ministry.

---

[59] *NZB* July 1899, p. 101; December 1899, p.187; August 1900, p.121.

CHAPTER 16

Prophets at the Gate?
New Zealand Baptists and Social Justice in the 1990s

John H. Tucker

Between 1984 and 1993 New Zealand underwent a revolution. Facing a severe economic crisis, and driven by a commitment to free market ideology, the country's Labour government (1984-90) introduced a series of radical economic and political reforms. One of the most regulated economies in the Western world suddenly became one of the most free. In an effort to create a more efficient economy the government stripped away the complex web of subsidies, tax breaks and protective tariffs supporting local businesses. Changes in the state sector were just as radical. The government sold off a raft of state-owned organisations and others were restructured along private-sector lines. In the process, thousands of people lost their jobs, tearing the heart out of many small communities. Another significant development was the introduction of 'user pays', a major extension of part-charges for government services. The effect was regressive. While the very poor were sometimes protected from this by special provisions, the fairly poor were not. To increase revenue further the government restructured the tax system, cutting substantially the top marginal tax rate for the rich and funding part of the shortfall by introducing a goods and service tax. Again, the outcome was regressive, impacting hardest on those least able to pay.

Labour's successor, a conservative National government (1990-99), spent its first term enthusiastically entrenching this New Right revolution. It extended Labour's policy of 'user pays' by increasing pharmaceutical charges, charging for hospital treatment and charging state housing tenants market rentals. It expanded the revolution from economics to industrial relations. The government's 1991 Employment Contracts Act left no institutional place for trade unions.[1] And in December 1990, facing a serious budget deficit, the government announced massive cuts in the level of social welfare benefits. The Prime Minister argued that the level of government spending was sapping the

---

[1] Union membership fell from 45% of the workforce in 1989 to 23% in 1994. Jane Kelsey, *The New Zealand Experiment: A World Model for Structural Adjustment?* (Auckland: Bridget Williams Books/Auckland University Press, 2nd edn, 1997), p. 184.

initiative and energy of New Zealand's wealth creators, and that these reforms would arrest New Zealand's 'drift from work to welfare' by removing the 'lure' of dependency.[2] These neo-liberal policies were by no means new. They had been sporadically applied elsewhere. What was new was their rapid and comprehensive application. It was a 'revolution'.[3]

Whether or not this revolution achieved its economic goals, the social cost appeared to be very high. During this period New Zealand had the fastest growing income gap between the rich and the poor in the industrialised world.[4] The proportion of the poor in the population as a whole rose sharply. Based on absolute measures, the proportion of children raised in a high poverty environment increased from 10.8% in 1984 to 24.7% in 1994, while the rate for solo parents went from 20% to 58%.[5] The government's policies seem to have been a major contributing factor.[6] The benefit cuts and the user-pays policy caused hardship for many and provoked bitter vigorous criticism. In the press a number of commentators argued that the government's policy was responsible for building a 'poverty prison'.[7] At the street level, unemployed workers and beneficiaries groups mounted turbulent protests. The finance and welfare ministers were burned in effigy and, for a period, allocated bodyguards. It was a bitter public debate that flared up several times during the 1990s.

The Christian churches, prompted by the growing pressure facing their social service agencies, and confronted with increasing evidence of poverty and social distress, became vocal and persistent opponents of the government's neo-liberal policies.[8] Indeed, one political commentator noted that for a while 'the

---

[2] Jim Bolger, 'Economic and Social Initiative', *New Zealand Parliamentary Debates*, 19 December 1990, cited in Andrew G. Gregg, 'Panic Attacks: The New Right, Media, and Welfare Reform in New Zealand, 1987-1998' (MA thesis, Victoria University of Wellington, 2004), p. 90.

[3] For use of this term to describe the restructuring of New Zealand's political economy in the 1980s and 1990s, see Keith Sinclair, *A History of New Zealand* (Auckland: Penguin, rev. edn, 2000), p. 337; James Belich, *Paradise Reforged: A History of the New Zealanders from the 1880s to the Year 2000* (Auckland: Penguin, 2001), p. 406; Michael King, *The Penguin History of New Zealand* (Auckland: Penguin, 2003), pp. 383-85.

[4] Sir Peter Barclay, *Joseph Rowntree Foundation Inquiry into Income and Wealth*, I (York: Joseph Rowntree Foundation, 1995), pp. 14-15.

[5] Robert Stephens, Paul Frater and Charles Waldegrave, *Below the Line: An Analysis of Income Poverty in New Zealand, 1984-1998* (Wellington: Victoria University of Wellington, 2000), pp. 29, 31.

[6] Brian Easton, 'Poverty in New Zealand: 1981-1993', *New Zealand Sociology* 10.2 (November 1995), pp. 202-203.

[7] G. Campbell, 'Building the Poverty Prison', *New Zealand Listener* 25 March 1991, pp. 14-18.

[8] Jonathan Boston and Alan Cameron, *Voices for Justice: Church, Law and State in New Zealand* (Palmerston North: Dunmore Press, 1994), p. 12; Peter Lineham, 'Social Policy

Churches were virtually the only effective opposition'.[9] Allan Davidson has argued that some churches in New Zealand, as they became marginalised, rediscovered their prophetic role in a newfound concern for social justice. No longer 'chaplain to the nation', they took on the role of 'prophet at the gate'.[10] Was this true of Baptists? Could it be said in relation to this debate that New Zealand Baptists stood like prophets at the gate of New Zealand society?

The 1992 Baptist Assembly

The government's decision to cut welfare benefits in December 1990 catalysed vigorous opposition from a number of churches, particularly the Anglicans and Methodists, who rebuked the government's veneration of 'individualism and economic efficiency' at the expense of the poor.[11] At an official level the Baptist Union made some early attempts to speak out on behalf of the poor and powerless.[12] But it was not until the national assembly in November 1992 that the Baptist Union's Public Questions Committee (PQC) took action. For some time it had been concerned that 'the gap between the haves and have-nots' was growing and that the 'trickle-down theory' was not working'.[13] At the 1992 assembly it tabled a remit challenging the government's neo-liberal policy settings because they 'emphasise a narrow, self-interested individualism ... ultimately destructive of human society'.[14] The remit was discussed, but only briefly. By the early 1990s public questions were usually assigned a place at the end of the assembly programme, when some delegates had usually left and

---

and the Churches in the 1990s and Beyond', in J. Stenhouse and B. Knowles (eds), *The Future of Christianity: Historical, Sociological, Political and Theological Perspectives from New Zealand* (Adelaide: ATF Press, 2004), p. 178; Campbell Roberts, 'Twenty Years of the Church as a New Zealand Public Citizen: A "punch drunk boxer," a "warrior" and "dancing with the wolves"', *Stimulus*, 13.3 (August 2005), p. 47.
[9] Barry Soper in *Counterpoint* 21 April 1993.
[10] Allan Davidson, 'Chaplain to the Nation or Prophet at the Gate? The Role of the Church in New Zealand Society', in J. Stenhouse and G. A. Wood (eds), *Christianity, Modernity & Culture: New Perspectives on New Zealand History* (Adelaide: ATF Press, 2005), p. 330.
[11] See, for example, the submissions of the Auckland Methodist Mission and the Anglican Diocese of Auckland on the Finance Bill 1991, SS/91/288, p. 6; SS/91/33, p. 1, Parliamentary Library, Wellington. Also Gregg, 'Panic Attacks', p. 102.
[12] E.g. the 1991 assembly endorsed an open letter to the Prime Minister brought by the Wellington Central Baptist Church. It noted the 'rising unemployment and dependency on charity' and argued that the burden of the government's reforms was 'not being equitably shared across society'. *New Zealand N. Z. Baptist* (*NZB*), December 1991, 9.
[13] Minutes of PQC meeting, June 1991, AN 1253, MS 1005966, New Zealand Baptist Research and Historical Society Archives (NZBRHSA).
[14] PQC remit, AN 1253, MS 1005966, NZBRHSA.

others were itching to go.[15] On this occasion time simply ran out.[16] The debate had to be cut short, and the issue referred back to the churches without a vote being taken or any decision made.

Early the next year the chairman of the PQC, Angus MacLeod, wrote to the general secretary of the Baptist Union to complain about the way public questions were dealt with at assembly and 'relegated to the very last moments … when reasonable discussion is impossible'.[17] In his opinion, 'this clearly reflected the view, increasingly obvious in recent years, that public questions are not a priority for Baptists compared with evangelism, mission, church growth'. He was also concerned that assembly was 'becoming more of an inspirational type of gathering than a deliberative one'. Indeed, by the 1990s the denomination's leadership had begun to see assembly more as a place to present their programmes and cast their vision,[18] and less as a place for 'corporate decision making' and 'discerning the Spirit's leading'[19] – in accordance with classic Baptist ecclesiology. Assemblies were being controlled to avoid any kind of debate.[20] In light of this, MacLeod asked if assembly council – the Baptist Union executive – would re-evaluate the way the denomination dealt with public questions.

The general secretary, Ian Brown, was frank in his reply: 'I know from my experience with the churches that to many there is neither time nor interest to discuss [controversial social or political] issues and that those who do present issues are often seen as detracting from the tenor of Assembly!'[21] 'Assembly delegations,' he admitted, 'don't seem to appreciate public questions being debated as perhaps they once did.' Therefore, while it envisaged a continuing role for the PQC, the assembly council did not want the PQC to stimulate debate on public questions at future assemblies.[22] In response, the PQC advised that it would no longer function. 'Our Baptist Assembly,' it lamented, 'is no longer a forum for debate or otherwise geared to go into social issues.'[23] The demise of the PQC was a significant development. For decades this committee – particularly at assemblies – played a crucial role in catalysing Baptist engagement in public debate. Never again in the 1990s did the issue of social justice come before a New Zealand Baptist assembly.

---

[15] Email from Gerard Marks to John Tucker, 22 April 2008.
[16] Ian Brown, interview by author, digital recording, Cambridge, 28 May 2008.
[17] Draft letter from Angus MacLeod to Ian Brown, 5 February 1993, AN 1254, MS 1005979, NZBRHSA.
[18] Stan Edgar, interview by author, digital recording, Auckland, 6 August 2007.
[19] Gordon Hambly, 'More Debate Needed', *NZB* February 1991, 2.
[20] David Wood, interview by author, telephone, 21 August 2007.
[21] Ian Brown to Angus MacLeod, 12 February 1993, AN 1254, MS 1005979, NZBRHSA.
[22] Ian Brown to Angus MacLeod, 21 April 1993, AN 1254, MS 1005979, NZBRHSA.
[23] Undated PQC statement, AN 1254, MS 1005979, NZBRHSA.

That is not to say that Baptists were not concerned about the poor. This period marked the proliferation in Baptist churches of social services like food banks and budgeting services.[24] This kind of response appealed to the inclination of most Evangelical Baptists towards the immediate and personal. It was less confusing than wrestling with difficult questions of social policy. And it was certainly less controversial and divisive. For most Baptists, therefore, social service effectively became a substitute for social action.[25] It was through their social services, however, that Baptist churches were challenged to take a stronger public stance over government policy.

The 1993 Social Justice Initiative

In 1993, at the request of the New Zealand Christian Council of Social Services,[26] the leaders of ten denominations – including the Baptist Union – embarked upon a co-operative project to promote the cause of social justice. The 'Social Justice Initiative', as it became known, involved a nation-wide study programme to help church members assess government policy in the light of biblical principles. The church leaders also published a 'Social Justice Statement', which was highly critical of the National government's New Right policies.[27]

According to one commentator, the Social Justice Initiative 'ranks as one of the most remarkable episodes in the history of the Christian church in New Zealand'. It 'marked,' he said, 'the first occasion when the nature of a just society had been seriously considered and then pronounced upon by the church leadership in a collective and ecumenical fashion. It was a bold and controversial move.'[28] It was certainly controversial. In an election year, the

---

[24] See *NZB* March 1991, pp. 7-9; May 1991, pp. 10-11; June 1991, pp. 5, 10-11.

[25] Comments by Royce Luck, Auckland Baptist City Missioner in the 1970s: personal conversation with author, Auckland, 7 July 2008. The director of Baptist Social Services in the early 1990s, Bruce Albiston, observes that, 'By and large, Baptists have been more activists than advocates'. Elaine Bolitho, *Meet the N. Z. Baptists: Post-war Personalities and Perspectives* (Wellington: Christian Research Association, 1993), p. 61.

[26] This council consisted of the social agencies of the Anglican, Baptist, Catholic, Methodist and Presbyterian churches, and the Salvation Army.

[27] The leaders asked the next government to review the adequacy of all benefits, adopt a more consultative style of decision-making, assess the equity of the present taxation structure, make full employment the basis of its economic policies and address the plight of the poor and vulnerable immediately. Ruth Smithies and Helen Wilson (eds), *Making Choices: Social Justice for Our Times: An Initiative of the Church Leaders in 1993* (Wellington: Church Leaders' Social Justice Initiative, 1993).

[28] Jonathon Boston, 'Christianity in the Public Square: The Churches and Social Justice', in J. Boston and A. Cameron (eds), *Voices for Justice: Church, Law and State in New Zealand* (Palmerston North: Dunmore, 1994), p. 33.

statement looked to many people like promotional material for the Labour Party. In spite of this, or perhaps because of it, the initiative generated a lively public debate and got the reality of poverty firmly on to the political agenda.[29] More importantly, perhaps, the Initiative achieved its primary goal of stimulating considerable discussion on social justice within the churches, particularly within the Catholic, Methodist and Presbyterian denominations. Thousands attended study groups. Many were prompted to write to the media. Others organised public meetings.[30]

Baptist churches, by contrast, were not widely involved. Robust discussion in the denominational magazine, the *N.Z. Baptist*, indicated a strong conviction among many Baptists that the church should not be 'bleating' to the government about social justice.[31] 'A lot of social ills,' wrote one correspondent, 'would disappear if moral values were upheld, if sex were confined to marriage', and people did not 'squander their income on alcohol, cigarettes, gambling'. If church leaders, he argued, would instead concentrate on their mission of preaching the gospel of Jesus Christ, 'social justice would follow without the need for appeals to government'.[32] In the minds of many Baptists, the solution to a problem like poverty was personal renewal. Indeed, the Baptist cabinet minister, Graeme Lee, articulated this very conviction in parliamentary debate on the Social Justice Statement. Fundamentally, he said, 'the Church has a role to look at matters that involve a change of heart and that will bring about a change of attitude. Through that, and only through that, does social reform actually take place.'[33] In all denominations there were those members who took this line and believed the church had no reason to be involved in this kind of political debate.[34] What this discussion revealed was the extent to which that perspective had gained a stranglehold on the Baptist movement. This was even more apparent when the debate about social justice re-ignited a few years later.

---

[29] Boston, 'Christianity in the Public Square', pp. 13-14; Ann Wansbrough, 'Making a Difference: What Can the Australian Churches Learn from the New Zealand Heads of Churches 1993 Program, Making Choices: Social Justice for Our Times?' (unpublished paper prepared for the Uniting Church in Australia, NSW Synod Board for Social Responsibility, 31 May 1994), p. 26.

[30] Wansbrough, 'Making a Difference', pp. 13, 18.

[31] E.g. *NZB* July 1993, p. 5; August 1993, p. 5; September 1993, p. 17. Not all Baptists held this view; e.g. *NZB* August 1993, pp. 3,5; October 1993, pp. 3,9.

[32] John Henwood, *NZB* September 1993, p. 3.

[33] *New Zealand Parliamentary Debates*, 21 July 1993, p. 16659.

[34] Allan Davidson, *Christianity in Aotearoa: A History of Church and Society in New Zealand* (Wellington: Education for Ministry, 1991), p. 173.

The 1998 Hikoi of Hope

In May 1998, concerned about the growing gap between rich and poor, and the prospect of further benefit cuts, the General Synod of the Anglican Church chose to launch a nationwide ecumenical march against poverty, the 'Hikoi of Hope'. This symbolic march or 'hikoi'[35] on parliament was designed not only to raise awareness of the 'intolerable levels of poverty and social breakdown',[36] but also to bring an end to policies which, the leaders said, 'have more to do with personal gain than the well being of all people'.[37] The Hikoi received considerable support from several denominations. About 40,000 people took part, with a crowd of 8,000 gathered for the final service on parliament's steps.[38] It certainly achieved its aims of drawing attention to poverty. The media gave the march considerable coverage.[39] And the government, consequently, came under real pressure.[40] One political commentator said of the marching clergy: 'The sight of those shiny, righteous faces, the woolly pullies and dog collars, was to National as the fingernails of God screeching down an eternal blackboard. It drove them nuts.'[41] In fact, some observers believed the Hikoi helped drive National to an election defeat the following year.[42] Whether that is true or not, the Hikoi represented one of the biggest single protests of the Christian church in New Zealand's history.[43]

Again, though, Baptists were not heavily involved. A number of Baptist leaders in Auckland joined sections of the march. The president and executive secretary joined other church leaders for the final Hikoi gathering in Wellington.[44] But there is little evidence of involvement beyond that. No Baptists were present when the Hikoi leaders met with the government in early December. The 1998 Baptist assembly, typical of most in the 1990s, passed no resolution on the issue. And the *N.Z. Baptist* magazine gave the matter very

---

[35] The New Zealand Maori word for 'march'.
[36] 'Briefing Sheet for General Synod', ANG 160/1/1, John Kinder Theological Library (JKTL), Auckland.
[37] Peter Beck, 'Church steps up pressure for relief from pain and despair', *New Zealand Herald* 17 August 1998, A13.
[38] Media release, 'The next step on the Hikoi', ANG 160/1/9, JKTL.
[39] Julia Stuart, 'The Hikoi of Hope: A Confrontation of Religious and Political Cultures mediated by the Media' (unpublished paper given at the Religion, Media and Culture Conference, July 1999), ANG 160/1/9, JKTL.
[40] Gregg, 'Panic Attacks', p. 165; Gordon Campbell, 'The Year that Was', *Listener* 26 December 1998, p. 24.
[41] Jane Clifton, 'Hearts and Vicars', *Listener* 17 October 1998, p. 19.
[42] Lineham, 'Social Policy and the Churches', p. 17; Roberts, 'Twenty Years of the Church', p. 47.
[43] Roberts, 'Twenty Years of the Church', p. 47.
[44] *NZB* October 1998, p. 5.

little editorial coverage.[45] Not a single letter on the topic appeared in its pages. Clearly, poverty and social justice were not live concerns for many Baptists.[46] It prompted one frustrated *N.Z. Baptist* correspondent, several years before, to call for a stronger public stance against the government's policies. 'If we can march for Jesus, we can march for the poor!'[47] But most did not.

Religious historians have observed that in New Zealand, from the 1960s, the focus of mainstream Protestantism moved increasingly away from a personal 'pietistic' moral focus to a more public, 'prophetic' morality, a morality concerned with broader questions of social justice.[48] By contrast, during that period, the New Zealand Baptist Union moved in the opposite direction. Like most Evangelicals, Baptists have tended, historically, to focus primarily on public issues 'that could be analysed in terms of personal responsibility'.[49] But in New Zealand there had always been a strong minority stream of influential Baptist leaders who saw the Christian gospel and the church's mission in broader terms, and who led or cajoled their fellow Baptists into public debate over issues of social justice.[50] By the mid-1990s, however, that stream had largely dried up.[51] The denomination's PQC had gone into recess.[52] Public questions – and debate generally – very rarely, if ever, figured at annual assemblies. And issues like poverty raised barely a flicker of interest in the *N.Z. Baptist* magazine. The range of public questions which still occupied Baptists had shrivelled down to questions of personal sexuality and the family unit.[53]

---

[45] Only one article appeared: *NZB* October 1998, pp. 1, 6. An editorial the following month discussed the merits of church 'kingdom banks', a social service initiative giving interest-free loans and free budget advice to the poor. *NZB* November 1998, p. 4.

[46] In the early 1990s only 8.5% of Baptist churches rated social justice as a priority: Bolitho, *Meet the N.Z. Baptists*, p. 61.

[47] Richard Manning to editor, *NZB* June 1993, p. 3.

[48] John Evans, 'Church State Relations in New Zealand 1940-1990 with Particular Reference to the Presbyterian and Methodist Churches' (PhD thesis, University of Otago, 1992), p. 128.

[49] See David Bebbington, 'Baptists and Politics since 1914', in K. W. Clements (ed.), *Baptists in the Twentieth Century: Papers presented at a Summer School July 1982* (London: Baptist Historical Society, 1983), pp. 86-87.

[50] See John Tucker, 'A Braided River: New Zealand Baptists and Public Issues, 1882-2000' (PhD thesis, University of Otago, 2010).

[51] Rob Bellingham, 'This World or the Next?', *NZB* March 1999, p. 8.

[52] A small PQC was resuscitated briefly between 2000 and 2004 on the initiative of a member of the Tawa Baptist Church. Since 2004 the Baptist Union has not had a Public Questions Committee.

[53] Laurie Guy (ed.), *N.Z. Baptists in Twentieth Century New Zealand: Documents Illustrating N.Z. Baptist Life and Development* (Auckland: NZ Baptist Historical Society, 2005), p. xiv.

And even these did not receive the attention they once did. By the end of the twentieth century, on most public issues, Baptists were virtually 'silent'.[54]

The Demise of the Baptist Social Conscience

The relative silence of Baptist churches during the 1990s can be explained partly by the changes that had occurred within society. In explaining its decision to wind down, the PQC observed that the issues of the 1990s were much more complex and confusing than issues like alcohol or gambling in earlier eras.[55] Staffing a PQC was, therefore, increasingly difficult. Volunteer committee members did not have the time and expertise to undertake the level of research that was now required to develop detailed policy proposals like those produced by some of the mainline churches.[56] While the committee believed that paid staff would have been desirable in principle, they recognised that for Baptists it was unlikely in practice. Moreover, the committee recognised that the public issues they now faced generated a much greater range of viewpoints than issues like alcohol or gambling. Consequently, assembly resolutions often reflected 'a cautious middle-of-the-road outlook, no doubt because only such resolutions could get through Assembly with any degree of unanimity'.[57] And when they got through, the committee chairman observed, these tepid statements were largely by-passed by the media and ignored by politicians.[58] Among Baptist leaders there was a growing sense by this time that these divisive assembly debates and bland resolutions achieved very little. What was the point of speaking out? No one was listening.[59]

---

[54] Guy, *N.Z. Baptists in Twentieth Century New Zealand*, p. 125.
[55] Undated PQC statement, AN 1254, MS 1005979, NZBRHSA.
[56] The Anglican Church's Social Responsibility Commission, for example, was able to make detailed submissions in early 1991 to the Social Services Select Committee on the Finance Bill and produced an extensive assessment from a social justice perspective on New Zealand's socio-economic direction: AN 1253, MS 1005966, NZBRHSA. The Joint Presbyterian-Methodist PQC also had paid staff, enabling it to operate relatively effectively in a complex policy environment.
[57] *NZB* August 1973, pp. 10-11.
[58] Draft letter from Angus MacLeod to Ian Brown, 5 February 1993, AN 1254, MS 1005979, NZBRHSA.
[59] Murray Robertson, interview by author, digital recording, Auckland, 29 July 2009. Not surprisingly, many of them decided that the best way to address social issues was through social service, not social action. Unfortunately, heavy reliance on state funding for their service ministries served to mute the ability of Baptist leaders to challenge government policy publicly. See Gerard Marks, 'Who Calls the Tune?', *NZB* February 1991, 2; Ian Brown, interview by author, digital recording, Cambridge, 28 May 2008.

Indeed, if once the churches had been expected to participate in public debate, it was not the case by the 1990s.[60] This was evidenced by the media's 'mostly harsh and disparaging' response to the Social Justice Initiative and the Hikoi of Hope.[61] A number of commentators argued that the church should not be engaging in this public debate at all: 'the church's business is not in business'.[62] Some reasoned that the church, with shrinking attendances, was not entitled to play such a public role.[63] 'Go and have your hikois within your church or hall walls,' screamed one. 'We don't need you, we don't want you among us. Go away, we tell you!'[64] Still others welcomed a public role for the churches, but insisted that the church's statements should be 'spiritual' or 'moral' in their focus. They argued that the churches should offer hope and inspiration to struggling individuals and support families in crisis, not wrestle with the broader issues like economic and social policy.[65] This debate revealed just how firmly New Zealand, like most Western societies by the end of the century, had come to embrace the assumption that religion belonged to the private sphere. That did not, however, prevent the mainline churches from speaking out and, at times, profoundly influencing the course of public debate. To understand the decay of the Baptist social conscience in New Zealand we need to look beyond changes occurring in society at large to changes occurring within the Baptist movement itself.

From the 1970s New Zealand Baptists were profoundly impacted by the charismatic renewal. The renewal movement tended to foster a highly individualised spirituality and distracted Baptists from broader considerations like social justice.[66] The focus for many became spiritual gifts, 'spiritual mapping',[67] or the Toronto Blessing and 'laughing revival'.[68] In July 1992 a

---

[60] Peter Lineham observes that by the 1990s there was a sense that governments had 'shut their doors to the churches'. 'The Voice of Inspiration? Religious Contributions to Social Policy' in B. Dalley and M. Tennant (eds), *Past Judgement: Social Policy in New Zealand History* (Dunedin: University of Otago Press, 2004), pp. 69-70.

[61] Roberts, 'Twenty Years of the Church,' p. 46.

[62] Marie-Agnes Brooke, 'Market doesn't need church advice', *Dominion* 25 November 1992, p. 10. See also Bernard Robertson, 'Law, religion and economics', *New Zealand Law Journal* (June 1995), p. 193.

[63] *Evening Post* 13 July 1993, p. 10.

[64] *Waikato Times* 29 September 1998, p.6.

[65] E.g. editorial, *New Zealand Herald* 14 July 1993, p. 8; Karl Du Fresne, 'Otherworldly posturing empties pews,' *Evening Post* 16 December 1998, p. 6.

[66] Tom Cadman, interview by author, digital recording, Auckland, 29 October 2007. For a similar assessment of the charismatic renewal in New Zealand and Australia, see Davidson, *Christianity in Aotearoa*, p. 173, and Stuart Piggin *Evangelical Christianity in Australia: Spirit, Word and World* (Melbourne: Oxford University Press, 1996), p. ix.

[67] *NZB* August 1994, p. 8; October 1994, p. 4. This was a spiritual warfare technique based on belief in 'territorial spirits'.

correspondent to the *N.Z. Baptist* complained about 'the advancing invasion of pentecostal and charismatic dogma into the Baptist churches'. He estimated that a third of Baptist churches in New Zealand were 'crusading under the charismatic banner', but suspected that he had only touched 'the tip of the iceberg'.[69] He was probably right. It has been claimed that the church stream in New Zealand most influenced by the charismatic renewal was the Baptist stream. By the late 1980s nearly 70% of Baptist churches identified with the charismatic movement.[70] And these churches carried significant influence within the denomination. They tended to be the growing churches. There was a sense that they represented the future. So it was common for ministers from these churches to be given positions of leadership on the executive councils of the Union.[71] It was, therefore, their narrower approach to public issues that came to dominate.

Baptists were evolving in other ways, too. After the 1992 assembly, the chairman of the PQC made a significant observation. 'Baptists', wrote Angus MacLeod, 'are much more varied in their theological and social views than in the past, and it is increasingly difficult to arrive at any real consensus.'[72] This was true. Throughout the 1970s and 1980s Baptist churches in New Zealand served as something of a refugee camp for Evangelicals from mainline churches from both sides of the increasingly polarised ecclesiastical spectrum. Not only did disenchanted Pentecostals and progressive Brethren find among charismatic Baptist churches a comfortable home. Conservative Evangelicals from the mainline churches also found among Baptists a safe refuge from neo-liberalism (with its 'dangerous' emphasis on social action). Importantly, both sets of exiles were predominantly conservative in outlook. Their priority tended to be personal holiness and the world to come – not the renewal of socio-economic structures in the here and now.[73] Moreover, many of these refugees came into Baptist churches with very little appreciation for Baptist congregationalism. They tended, instead, towards a strong emphasis on

---

[68] See, for example, letters to the *NZB* May 1995, p. 4; June 1995, p. 4; Ian Brown, 'To Laugh or Not to Laugh', *NZB* June 1995, p. 5; Editorial, 'A Mixed Blessing', *NZB* July 1995, p. 5; Gerard Marks, 'Include Me Out', *NZB* August 1995, p. 6. The 'Toronto Blessing' was a revival movement associated with a charismatic Evangelical church in Toronto, Canada.
[69] Joe Emmett to editor, *NZB* July 1992, p. 3.
[70] Bolitho, *Meet the N.Z. Baptists*, p. 37.
[71] Gerard Marks, interview by author, telephone, Auckland, 21 April 2008.
[72] Draft letter from Angus MacLeod to Ian Brown, 5 February 1993, AN 1254, MS 1005979, NZBRHSA.
[73] By the 1990s the Baptist Union was much more conservative theologically than it had been earlier in the century. This was reflected in – and compounded by – the Baptist Union's decision to withdraw from the ecumenical movement. *NZB* June 1986, p. 16; March 1987, p. 2.

eldership and apostolic approaches to leadership, which helps explain the general lack of interest in assembly debate.[74]

It would also be fair to say that many of these immigrants, who provided much of the numerical growth among Baptist churches in the 1970s and 80s, had very little sense of loyalty to the Baptist Union.[75] This was strikingly evident at the 1992 assembly, where the theme 'Absolutely Positively Baptist' provoked a strongly negative reaction from a number of delegates. Many of them, with histories in other denominations, simply did not identify with being 'Baptist'.[76] They could just as easily switch to another Evangelical denomination. The Baptist leadership was acutely aware of this. 'No one,' one leader observed wryly, 'was too eager to see them moving off to another church, so there was a considerable degree of accommodation of these people'[77] – and their views on social action.

Besides this theological evolution, New Zealand Baptists in the latter part of the twentieth century also underwent significant transformation in terms of their social and economic status. Research suggests that over the course of the twentieth century they became increasingly middle-class, increasingly affluent.[78] Management and professional people were much more highly represented among Baptists than in the general population. Conversely, Baptists had a much lower representation of working-class people. Many Baptists, it seems, had very little contact with the reality of poverty in New Zealand.[79] Nigel Wright has said of English Baptists, 'With increasing respectability and prosperity ... [w]e no longer feel ourselves to be in the vanguard of social change but are fearful of it ... We have a stake in the way things are.'[80] By the

---

[74] Laurie Guy and Martin Sutherland, 'Leadership: The New Zealand Experience Since the 1960s', in Graeme Chatfield (ed.), *Leadership and N.Z. Baptist Church Governance* (Eastwood NSW: Morling Press, 2005), p. 138. In the British context, Paul Fiddes argues that this blending of denominational streams explains the loss of confidence among Baptist churches in the church meeting or assembly: Paul S. Fiddes, *Tracks and Traces: Baptist Identity in Church and Theology* (Carlisle: Paternoster, 2003), p. 50.

[75] This was reflected in the failure of many to take up formal membership. Between 1993 and 1999 attendance in Baptist churches increased by nearly 10,000, while membership figures remained virtually static. This reflects a weakening commitment to membership generally, but the movement between denominations was a major contributor to this. See *NZB* February 1999, p. 4.

[76] Ian Brown, interview by author, digital recording, Cambridge, 28 May 2008.

[77] Gerard Marks, interview by author, telephone, 21 April 2008.

[78] Elaine Bolitho, 'In this World: Baptists and Methodist Churches in New Zealand, 1948 to 1988' (PhD thesis, Victoria University of Wellington, 1992), p. 59. Cf. John Stenhouse 'Christianity, Gender, and the Working Class in Southern Dunedin, 1880–1940,' *Journal of Religious History* 30.1 (February 2006), pp. 18-44.

[79] This was certainly the view of one *N.Z. Baptist* editor: *NZB* February 1991, p. 2.

[80] Wright, *Challenge to Change: A Radical Agenda for Baptists* (Eastbourne: Kingsway Publications, 1991), pp. 35, 207.

1990s much the same could be said of New Zealand Baptists. According to one study they were the most politically conservative of all the major denominations.[81] This explains their reluctance to enter this debate. They were largely comfortable with a neo-liberal, free-market world.[82]

Besides these theological and sociological factors, there were other pragmatic – and more significant – reasons for the reluctance of Baptists to engage in this kind of debate. David Bebbington has said that the numerical decline of British Baptists in the twentieth century produced a 'psychology of withdrawal, a sense that the Baptist house must be put in order before the nation's life could be swept clean'.[83] By the end of the twentieth century a similar dynamic was evident among New Zealand Baptists. After years of steady growth the Baptist movement hit a plateau in the early 1990s.[84] Relative to population growth it was in decline. At the local church level, ministers felt under enormous pressure. In a 1992 newsletter to pastors, the general secretary, Ian Brown, acknowledged this: 'I have concerns,' he wrote, 'for pastors (and spouses) who are struggling. It seems that as pastors we are in a time of considerable confusion. For some the ministry lacks a clear focus and purpose. For others there is … a sense of hopelessness or even overwhelming failure. (A number of churches seem to reflect these emotions as well!)'[85] For many of them, the focus became survival. The overriding consideration was numbers. The dominant question became: What do most people want to hear? What can we say that will draw people to our church?[86] The answer was not controversial public statements. Engagement in divisive political debates that could drive people away was the furthest thing from most pastors' minds. It was seen as a distraction. Baptists should 'stick to their knitting': winning souls.[87]

---

[81] A.C. Webster and P.E Perry, *The Religious Factor in New Zealand Society: A Report of the New Zealand Study of Values* (Palmerston North: Alpha Publications, 1989), pp. 19, 22, 73-81.
[82] See Richard Manning, *NZB* October 1993, p. 3.
[83] Bebbington, 'Baptists and Politics', p. 81.
[84] The census return of 70,155 in 1991 fell to only 51,426 in 2001. An attendance average of 31,299 in 1991 rose only slightly to 32,619 in 2001. Kevin Ward, 'Losing my Religion? An Examination of Church Decline, Growth and Change in New Zealand 1960 to 1999, with Particular Reference to Christchurch' (PhD thesis, University of Otago, 2003), p. 288. The total number of baptisms fell from a high of 1,874 in 1983 to 811 in 1996: figures supplied by Murray Robertson, personal communication to author, 31 July 2009.
[85] Ian Brown, newsletter to pastors, July 1992. Dunedin City Baptist Church, Elders and Officers Court minutes and papers, MS-2793/003, Hocken Library, Dunedin.
[86] For discussion of this kind of numbers-driven pragmatism in North America, see Mark A. Noll, *The Scandal of the Evangelical Mind* (Grand Rapids: Eerdmans, 1994), pp. 66-67.
[87] Gerard Marks, interview by author, telephone, Auckland, 21 April 2008.

Perhaps the most influential development within New Zealand Baptist churches over the dying decades of the twentieth century was the widespread adoption of American church growth principles.[88] The church growth movement, associated with Donald McGavran and Fuller Theological Seminary, promoted the use of quantitative research to develop sociological awareness of 'target populations' and factors affecting their receptivity to the gospel. The emphasis was on technique and method, deploying the right presentation or programme to achieve maximum evangelistic returns. In some respects this church growth reflected the kind of pragmatism that Jacques Ellul recognised had become such a feature of modern technological society, the incessant focus on quantifiable growth and measurable success – 'whatever works'.[89]

New Zealand Baptists embraced it enthusiastically. The Baptist Home Missions Department established a church growth school to train church-planting pastors.[90] Ministries and programmes were created to meet the felt needs of the 'target market'. Worship services were renovated so as to become 'seeker-sensitive'. The emphasis was on whatever would produce 'results' in numerical terms.[91] This church growth focus fostered a preoccupation with technique over theology, the internal structures of the church over the public implications of the gospel.[92] It shrank mission down to personal evangelism – 'getting bums on seats and people into heaven', as one leader put it.[93] Not surprisingly, the wider prophetic role of the church in society was neglected.[94] So the primary reason why Baptists in the 1990s held back from public debate

---

[88] For discussion of the growing influence of North American Evangelicalism on New Zealand Baptists, see Tucker, 'A Braided River', pp. 176, 290.

[89] See David Wells, *Above All Pow'rs: Christ in a Postmodern World* (Grand Rapids/Cambridge: Eerdmans, 2005), p. 36.

[90] Elaine Bolitho, 'In this World', p. 140. The goal during the 1990s – 'the decade of evangelism' – was 300 Baptist churches in New Zealand by the year 2000: *NZB* November 1988, pp. 8-9; April 1992, p. 5.

[91] Ward, 'Losing my Religion?', 327. This pragmatism was evident in a number of other developments. Rules for ordination were changed to include people who were not theologically trained but who, by virtue of their track record, had shown they could produce 'results'. Assemblies demanded that Baptist College staff be more than academics. They needed to be 'practitioners' who would produce not just theologians, but pastors 'who could lead growing churches': Gerard Marks, interview by author, telephone, Auckland, 21 April 2008.

[92] In the late 1980s the *NZB* acknowledged that churches had 'divorced religion and life'. The editor admitted, 'We [have] taught that life could be divided into compartments – sacred and secular. ... We [have] diminished God, putting him into a religious cubby hole, leaving the world of science and business to the devil'. Roy Bullen, 'Sharemarkets and Sinfulness', *NZB* March 1988, p. 2.

[93] Ian Brown, interview by author, digital recording, Cambridge, 28 May 2008.

[94] Ward, 'Losing my Religion?', 329.

over social justice was the simple fact that it did not produce conversions. As one pastor lamented to the 1988 Baptist assembly, the reason Baptist churches were not getting 'involved in issues of oppression' and social justice was that it 'does not always result in church growth!'[95]

In the 1980s Lesslie Newbigin declared that, 'Christianity in its Protestant form has largely accepted relegation to the private sector, where it can influence the choice of values by those who take this option. By doing so, it has secured for itself a continuing place, at the cost of surrendering the crucial field.'[96] With regard to New Zealand Baptists at the end of the twentieth century, it seems he was right. During this period, New Zealand's political and social economy underwent revolutionary changes. So, too, did New Zealand's Baptist churches. It certainly could not be said that they stood like 'prophets at the gate' of New Zealand society.

---

[95] *NZB* March 1989, p. 16. See also Neville Emslie, 'Silver and Gold Have I None', *NZB* August 1993, p. 5.
[96] Lesslie Newbigin, *Foolishness to the Greeks: The Gospel and Western Culture* (London: SPCK, 1986), p. 19.

CHAPTER 17

Baptist Worship and Contemporary Culture: A New Zealand Case Study

Steve Taylor

> Culture is *what we make of the world* – we start not with a blank slate but with all the richly encultured world that previous generations have handed to us.[1]

The story is true, but the names are changed in order to focus on the question at hand, that of the interface between Baptists and others. In the late 1990s members of First Baptist began to murmur. As a church in the city centre, it owned, through a trust, nearby property. A long-term tenant was of foreign descent and had, in recent times, placed some gods on display in the shop front window. Public prayer among church members began to focus on the need to remove the idols, and the shopkeeper. This is one response, that of *condemnation* and *critique*, to the interface – both ethnic and religious – between contemporary New Zealand Baptists and the other.

Down the street was 'Emerging' Baptist Church. Formerly a dying City Mission, a new minister had begun to experiment with liturgical and ecclesial innovation. The church adopted a new mission statement 'to provide a community of faith that is accepting and open to all who wish to be part of it, while maintaining a heart that is committed to serving Christ through engagement with contemporary society'.[2] With a new interface to explore, that of contemporary culture, a growing group of young adults had begun to gather.

---

[1] Andy Crouch, *Culture Making: Recovering our Creative Calling* (Grand Rapids, MI: Inter Varsity Press, 2008), p. 73.

[2] When interviewed about the values of 'Emerging' Baptist Church, its pastor described its interface with contemporary culture as follows: '[A]s a community we have a commitment to engaging with, reflecting on, participating in, not seeing as evil, questioning, reframing contemporary culture. So we would use without any apology contemporary movies, music, experiences.... [C]ontemporary culture.... It's the air [we] breathe.' Interview in Steve Taylor, 'A New Way of Being Church: A Case Study Approach to Cityside Baptist Church as Christian Faith "Making Do" in a Postmodern World' (PhD Thesis, University of Otago, New Zealand, 2004), pp. 397, 399.

Framing Baptists and the Other of Contemporary Culture

Both churches were Baptist in name and shared over a hundred years of history in the inner city. Yet the two churches embody contrasting approaches to the interface between Baptists and others. Andy Crouch summarises a range of contemporary stances toward culture:[3]

1. condemnation of culture
2. critique through intellectual analysis of culture[4]
3. copying, in which a subculture develops based on the imitation of the forms of a dominant culture
4. consuming, in which 'most evangelicals today ... simply go to the movies ... [and] ... walk out amused, titillated, distracted or thrilled, just like our fellow consumers who do not share our faith'.[5]

Crouch argues that these four stances are problematic and instead argues for *creating*, for the 'only way to change culture is to create more of it'.[6]

> I wonder what we Christians are known for in the world outside our churches. Are we known as critics, consumers, copiers, condemners of culture? I am afraid so. Why aren't we known as cultivators - people who tend and nourish what is best in human culture, who do the hard and painstaking work to preserve the best of what people before us have done? Why aren't we known as creators - people who dare to think and do something that has never been thought or done before, something that makes the world more welcoming and thrilling and beautiful?[7]

On the basis of Crouch's analysis, First Baptist sought to *condemn*, through prayer, an aspect of the culture of an/other. As prayer began, some suggested that if the shop was vacated, it could be turned into a Christian cafe. This, in effect, would be a *copying* of the surrounding cafe culture of the inner city.

It is the argument of this chapter that 'Emerging' Baptist Church offers another approach, that of *creating*. This argument is based on doctoral research carried out in exploration of how contemporary Baptists interface with the other and the implications for church, mission and discipleship.[8] It employed a

---

[3] Crouch, *Culture Making*, pp. 275-6.
[4] Crouch argues that critique, which tends to be the domain of academics, produces 'better art critics than artists.' *Culture Making*, p. 87.
[5] Crouch, *Culture Making*, p. 89.
[6] Crouch, *Culture Making*, p. 67.
[7] Crouch, *Culture Making*, pp. 97-98.
[8] The research involved ethnography, including participant observation of 'Emerging' Baptist Church over a five-month period, along with interviews, a participant survey and two focus groups. For results see Steve Taylor, 'A New Way of Being Church?' For a

research methodology that took seriously congregational liturgy as the basis for theological study.

Martin Sutherland argues for a distinct Baptist *way* of doing theology, based on the dynamics of church as becoming. He argues that for Baptists, 'the gathering *is* the sacrament, the moment of Christ's presence, the *telos* at once for the church and the world'.[9] Baptist theology thus becomes 'the dynamic interplay of two stories - the contemporary, local, "gathered" one, and the Christ story as revealed in scripture ... The story itself calls us forward and outwards rather than backwards ... Theology's task is to facilitate this harmonization, to bring us into consonance with Christ.'[10] For Sutherland, Baptist theology is to be found not in dialogue with philosophy, but embodied in local life, in things such as the church members' meeting or in the formation of church structures.

If Sutherland is right, then by extension, Baptist theology can also be found in Baptist worship, the how and what of prayer and preaching. This assertion would resonate with the work of Graham Ward and his argument that any practice (including an act of worship) is an 'embedded act of meaning and communication [that] operates within, and is invoked by, certain sets of social and cultural forces'.[11] Therefore, one way to address the question of the relationship between Baptists and the other is by analysing what Baptists pray and how Baptists worship, for in such practices will lie a Baptist theology of the interface. Initial analysis can then be followed by a second-order critical reflection probing the veracity of the practices of the gathered in light of the story of Christ and their harmonisation forward and outward, their 'becoming' (to use Sutherland) in interface with the world.

Hence this chapter will employ Sutherland's methodology. It will begin by exploring one particular act of 'becoming', specifically intercession undertaken at 'Emerging' Baptist Church, followed by a second-order reflection in relation to current discussions of the relationship between gospel and culture.

Let us Pray: Intercession with, for and through the Other

On Sunday 29 October 2000 at 'Emerging' Baptist Church, the worship leader introduced the theme of children's day. He then described the recent felling of a local landmark, a lone pine tree on One Tree Hill. This was linked to a

---

popular summary see Steve Taylor, *The Out of Bounds Church? Learning to Create a Community of Faith in a Culture of Change* (Grand Rapids, MI: Zondervan, 2005).

[9] Martin Sutherland, 'Gathering, Sacrament and Baptist Theological Method,' *Pacific Journal of Baptist Research* 3. 2 (October 2007), p. 53.

[10] Martin Sutherland, 'Gathering, Sacrament and Baptist Theological Method,' pp. 54-55.

[11] Graham Ward, *Cultural Transformation and Religious Practice* (Cambridge: Cambridge University Press, 2005), p. 8.

contemporary song entitled 'One Tree Hill', written by the rock band U2. Recent television news footage that had shown the death of a Palestinian boy in Israel was mentioned. The worship leader proceeded to play the U2 song along with a continuous loop of the video of the shooting of a Palestinian boy and invited the congregation to reflect and pray for children known to them. People did this for ten minutes. Without further explanation, the service resumed its normal structured pattern.

This act of intercession involved four elements: the story of protest; the U2 song; the video footage; and the invitation to pray. Each element can be analysed in order to understand the theology at work in this Baptist interface with the other.

A Local Voice: Axing a Tree on One Tree Hill

To begin to appreciate the 'social and cultural forces' at play in this liturgical act of 'becoming,' some background is instructive. A number of years ago a Maori protestor, Mike Smith, used a chainsaw in an attempt to cut down a lone tree that stood on a prominent hill overlooking Auckland City. His act provoked outrage from various quarters. Historically, in the eighteenth century, when European immigrants settled Auckland, a native tree was cut down and replanted with an imported Monterey Pine. This tree had become an identifiable local landmark, instrumental in the identity formation of Auckland, New Zealand's largest city. As a result of the chainsaw attack by Mike Smith, the tree was fatally wounded and, ultimately, a few years later, during the week preceding 29 October 2000, had to be cut down in the interest of public safety. Thus, the actions of Mike Smith, both in the initial attack and in the resultant slow death of the tree, served to focus attention on race relations and indigenous protest.

As this act of protest is named in worship, what can be gleaned regarding the Baptist interface with the other? Firstly, it is instructive to realise that this intercession began with the story of an/other, with the voice of protest from minority and indigenous groups. Second, it is noteworthy that the description was narrated in a way that neither *condemned, copied* nor *consumed.*

A Global Voice: A Lament from U2

The naming of the felling of the tree on One Tree Hill was followed by the playing of a song, 'One Tree Hill', from *The Joshua Tree* album. Again, some background is necessary. The song was originally written in honor of Greg Carroll, a Maori New Zealander, who died while working with the rock band U2.[12] It included a number of lyrical references to One Tree Hill. So is this

---

[12] U2, 'One Tree Hill', CD, *The Joshua Tree* (Dublin: Island Records, 1987). Lyrics transcribed by author. The album is dedicated to the memory of Greg Carroll and notes, 'Greg Carroll's funeral, Wanganui, New Zealand, 10th July 1986'.

simply an act of *copying* and *consumption*, in which a song references the same location and is used as a form of entertainment? Worse, is some Anglo-Saxon (Irish) music being imported in a manner that could once again colonise the voice of indigenous protest?

A more nuanced argument is that the song actually serves to endorse this church community and its posture toward the other. To follow the contours of this argument we need to understand the relationship between U2 and the Christian community in general. While contemporary Christian music is known primarily as a sub-cultural *copying* from mainstream rock music, the Christian band U2 adopted a different posture. Using Crouch's typology, U2 chose to *create*, rather than to *condemn, critique* or *copy,* contemporary rock music. By the late 1980s, U2's songs had begun to explore themes including doubt and darkness. 'Christians who had been overjoyed [that] a band powered by Christian conviction was competing in the higher echelons of rock were, naturally, dismayed. They felt hurt and let down.'[13] Given this background, to play a U2 song can be interpreted as an endorsement of U2's *creating* approach to culture. Further, it acts as an acknowledgement that *creating* with an/other (specifically contemporary culture) has a place in Christian worship, given it is now being creatively deployed as part of Christian intercession.

Further theological analysis is possible. With regard to lyrical content, the song can be argued to function as a contemporary lament. The subject in the first line of the chorus changes throughout the song: the initial 'You ran like a river' becomes, by song's end, 'We run like a river'.[14] This is an articulation of the inevitability of death, and has echoes of Ecclesiastes 1:7: 'All rivers flow to the sea, yet never does the sea become full. To the place where they flow, the rivers keep on going.' The first verse begins in lament, describing the need to face the chill of death. The second verse becomes a protest not just against one death, but against all death, followed by lyrics that reference the Cain and Abel narrative in Genesis 4:10 ('You know his blood still cries from the ground'). Yet lament is not the last word, for the song ends with the hope of reunion ('I'll see you again'). This is not a naive belief that all will be well ('I don't believe in painted roses or bleeding hearts'). Rather, it is an eschatology in which the world is changed at the end of time. The lines echo Revelation 6:13: 'Then I watched while he broke open the sixth seal, and there was a great earthquake; the sun turned as black as dark sackcloth and the whole moon became like blood. The stars in the sky fell to the earth like unripe figs shaken loose from the tree in a strong wind.' Hence, despite present darkness, the song offers the hope of a reunion with those we love and have loved, coupled with judgment on present evil.

---

[13] Steve Turner, *Hungry for Heaven: Rock 'N' Roll and the Search for Redemption* (Downers Grove, IL: IVP, 1995), pp.182- 83.
[14] Angela Pancella, 'Drawing Their Fish in the Sand,' *@U2* – http://www.atu2.com/lyrics/biblerefs.html, accessed 14 July 2009.

Such lyrical examination suggests that the an/other of contemporary culture is actually working as a vehicle for the expression of lament. The song's emotions, their articulation of doubt and darkness, could well be felt by those attending worship in 'Emerging' Baptist Church, resonating with their sense of loss over a famous local landmark and their uncertainty in the face of an act of protest. In other words, deploying Crouch's typology and the lens of interface, the use of the song by U2 is neither a stance of *condemnation, critique, copying* nor *consuming*. Rather, it affirms the art of *creating*, of culture-making, and allows the other of contemporary culture to be employed liturgically as a way to express communal lament.

A Local and Global Voice: Lament for Children Caught in Adult Cross-fire

The playing of the U2 song was also accompanied by the repeated playing of television news footage of the recent shooting of a Palestinian boy. Again, we find an/other artefact from contemporary culture being creatively used in this act of intercessory prayer. The visual images work to remind the community of how politicised rhetoric (whether in Palestine or Aotearoa New Zealand) can harm humanity and destroy the innocent. It might serve to encourage prayer for God's protection for any and all children caught in adult cross-fire.

Once again, using Crouch's typology, we are seeing neither a stance of *condemnation, critique, copying* nor *consuming*. Instead we are seeing an act of *creating*, in which the (visual) other of contemporary culture is woven into the worshipping life of the church in a powerful and provocative manner, inviting attenders to see the world with different eyes and to respond prayerfully in intercession for vulnerable children.[15]

A Local Earthing: Prayer for a Known Child

This mix of local news, contemporary music and video of news footage ends with the invitation to pray for children known to the participants. Often the realisation that one lives in a globalised world can evoke a sense of paralysis. In contrast, this act of intercession, the watching of television news, is framed as an opportunity for prayer to be expressed in the particular. A cultural engagement with the other of television news invites ethical consideration of how one might live locally. Christian faith is being presented as both globally aware and locally earthed.

In sum, one instance of contemporary Baptist theology has been analysed. The presence of the other of contemporary culture - a story of local protest, a contemporary song, visual news footage – has been discussed. This has been read as adopting a *creating* stance, as a way for this Baptist community to

---

[15] It is my understanding that visual images exist that widen the context to show that Palestinian gunmen are firing upon this Palestinian boy. This would add a further layer of meaning, a warning as to using the innocent for political ends.

express its relationship to culture. The other that is contemporary culture became a tool for prayer, employed to increase sensitivity to the other and to encourage protection of the vulnerable. What acts of culture-making might result in the coming days as a result of this intercession are unknown. Nevertheless an interface of creative culture-making is a different posture toward contemporary culture than one of *condemnation, critique, copying* or *consuming*.

One swallow does not a summer make. Nevertheless, this act of worship was consistent with my research of 'Emerging' Baptist Church. Of the ten services I participated in, twenty 'not explicitly Christian' music tracks (an average of two per service) and eleven videos (an average of one per service) were employed. When interviewed, participants described an important reason for coming to 'Emerging' Baptist Church was a desire to connect their faith with their cultural context.[16] In sum, a stance of *creating* in relation to the other of contemporary culture was essential to the theology and ecclesial identity of this Baptist church.

To date, we have analysed a moment of Baptist 'becoming'. We must now, using Sutherland's Baptist methodology, explore the interplay between this 'contemporary, local, 'gathered'' church and 'the Christ story as revealed in scripture'.[17]

'Sampling' as a Theology of Interface with the Other

A helpful metaphor for understanding 'Emerging' Baptist Church's interface with the other is that of 'sampling'. It is a metaphor drawn from the world of contemporary music and it involves taking a piece of music (a sample, for instance a drum beat or a base line) from one context and placing it with another sample, for instance a set of vocals, to create a new configuration in a new context. Using this metaphor, in the act of worship outlined above, four 'samples' have been mixed – children's day, an act of local protest, the music of U2 and the news footage of conflict – to become a contemporary intercessory prayer. In doing so, new meanings, new ways of being in relation to the world, have been suggested: a sensitivity to the other, a creating stance, a focus on children known to these Baptist participants.

This idea of sampling can be applied more generically to the interface between being Baptist, being Christian and the other of culture. Theologian Miroslav Volf, in considering the Christian interface with the other, observed:

> Christian difference is always a complex and flexible network of small and large refusals, divergences, subversions, and more or less radical alternative proposals,

---

[16] See Taylor, 'A New Way of Being Church', ch. 3.
[17] Martin Sutherland, 'Gathering, Sacrament and Baptist Theological Method,' pp. 54-55.

surrounded by the acceptance of many cultural givens. There is no single correct way to relate to a given culture as a whole, or even to its dominant thrust; there are only numerous ways of accepting, transforming, or replacing various aspects of a given culture from within.[18]

'Sampling' makes sense of Volf's proposal. The relationship between gospel and culture is being located in the context of everyday life – television news, contemporary music and children. Culture is being viewed not as monolithic, but as multi-faceted. 'Transforming the use of shared ideas from a non-Christian to a Christian one is a piecemeal process, in short; the items of another culture are not taken up all at once but one by one or block by block.'[19]

Sampling allows a simultaneous multiplicity of stances to be adopted – refusal, divergence, subversion – with regard to culture. Just as a DJ can sample in multiple ways – to reinforce or amplify a message, or ironically subvert or juxtapose, and in that contrast, suggest new meanings – so can Christian acts of worship and living move beyond binary notions of either a separation from (interface-as-wall), or an accommodation to (interface-as-permeable), contemporary culture.

Volf employs a similar taxonomy. He argues that Christians can amplify culture, they can 'adopt some elements of the cultures in which they live, possibly putting them to different use guided by the values that stem from their being "in God".'[20] Yet Christians can also subvert culture, taking images, festivals and practices from their culture and using them to reference their Christian faith: putting everyday 'things to different uses [in a manner that] will require changes in the things themselves ... taken up but transformed from inside'.[21] Further, Christians can juxtapose: they can take 'some elements of a given culture that Christians will have to discard and possibly replace [them] by other elements'.[22] Thus, sampling allows a plurality of responses to everyday practices.

Such an understanding is in contrast to readings of the other, including consumerism and globalisation, as a tsunami wave that will engulf the local. Such readings reduce local culture and people to passive, helpless victims in the face of culture. They marginalise resilience, creativity and adaptability and

---

[18] Miroslav Volf, 'When Gospel and Culture Intersect: Notes on the Nature of Christian Difference,' in *Pentecostalism in Context* (Sheffield: Sheffield Academic Press, 1997), p. 204. Italics have been removed.

[19] Kathryn Tanner, *Theories of Culture: A New Agenda for Theology* (Minneapolis, MN: Fortress Press, 1997), p. 117.

[20] Volf, 'When Gospel and Culture Intersect,' p. 203.

[21] Volf, 'When Gospel and Culture Intersect,' p. 203.

[22] Volf, 'When Gospel and Culture Intersect,' p. 204: Volf does not specifically employ the term 'juxtaposition.' However he does catalogue a comparison of the practice of slavery with scripture and the term 'juxtaposition' would seem to capture this comparison.

instead assume that imperialistic violation is the only outcome of cultural contact.[23] In contrast, Robert Schreiter argues that '[i]t is increasingly evident that local cultures receive the elements of the hyperculture and reinterpret them in some measure ... Some of the most salient features in religion and theology today can best be described from the vantage point of the *glocal.*'[24] Hence, the term 'glocalisation', which posits that rather than binary opposites, identity in a global culture involves the interaction between the global and the local.[25] The local and global can be enriching resources and sampling provides a mechanism by which this interface can proceed.

Having suggested that this metaphor of sampling is a way to understand 'Emerging' Baptist Church and its interface with the other, it is now important to tease out more generally the theological and ecclesial implications: in regard to place, to imagination, to community and to tradition.

Place: Embodied and Enculturated Within

> Christians do not come into their social world from outside seeking either to accommodate to their new home (like second generations immigrants would), shape it in the image of the one they left behind (like colonizers would), or establish a little haven in the strange new world reminiscent of the old (as resident aliens would) .... Christians are the insiders who have diverted from their culture by being born again.[26]

---

[23] For more on this from a missiological perspective, see for example Lamin Sanneh, *Encountering the West: Christianity and the Global Cultural Process: The African Dimension* (London: Marshall Pickering, 1993); Andrew F. Walls, *The Missionary Movement in Christian History: Studies in the Transmission of Faith* (Maryknoll, NY: Orbis Books, 1996).

[24] Robert J. Schreiter, *The New Catholicity: Theology between the Global and the Local* (Maryknoll, NY: Orbis Books, 1997), pp. 10, 12. Similarly, 'a global culture is a tradition that travels the world and takes on local colour. It has both a global, or metacultural, and a local, or situationally distinct, cultural dimension.' Irving Hexham and Karla O. Poewe, *New Religions as Global Cultures: Making the Human Sacred* (Boulder, CO: Westview Press, 1997), p. 41. A similar argument is advanced by David Lyon, 'Wheels within Wheels: Glocalization and Contemporary Religion,' in Mark Hutchinson and Ogbu Kalu (ed.), *A Global Faith: Essays on Evangelicalism & Globalization* (Sydney, NSW: Centre for the Study of Australian Christianity, Robert Menzies College Macquarie University, 1998).

[25] Term used by Roland Robertson, 'Glocalization: Time-Space and Homogeneity-Heterogeneity', in S. Lash and R. Robertson (eds), *Global Modernities* (London: Sage, 1995).

[26] Miroslav Volf, 'Soft Difference: Theological Reflections on the Relation between Church and Culture in 1 Peter,' *Ex Auditu* 10 (1994), p. 4 – http://www.yale.edu/faith/downloads/soft-difference-church-culture.pdf, accessed 14 July 2009. Similarly, 'Christian social existence is quite literally, then, without a homeland in some territorially localized society. Christians lead lives as resident aliens

Various writers describe liberal (interface-as-permeable) and separatist understandings (interface-as-wall) of gospel and culture as twins born out of the foundationalism of an Enlightenment context.[27] They argue that the cultural worldview of the Enlightenment demanded a foundation for knowledge to rest upon and that, consequently, this epistemology shaped the development of both liberal and fundamentalist theological approaches. Thus, separatist and accommodationist approaches exist as a contextualisation within modernity. As culture shifts, other forms of embodiment will become necessary.

A more recent response to gospel and culture is that of George Lindbeck, who argued for a cultural-linguistic approach, the presence of comprehensive interpretative structures through which the world is experienced and interpreted. His approach sought to describe the social world through the lens of the biblical story.[28] However, it raises some critical questions.[29] For instance, humans are invariably engaged in multiple cultural linguistic communities. Ward notes that 'members of the community of the Church are also members of other forms of fellowship, other bodies – industrial, commercial, agricultural, political, sporting, domestic'.[30] For Ward, this being part of multiple communities within a culture will not dilute the witness of the church. On the contrary, 'the Christian community's practices of transformative hope, executed in the name of Christ, are disseminated through the world because the living community of the Church is implicated in other "communities" and practices'.[31] Thus separatist, accommodationist and cultural-linguistic approaches to gospel and culture remain problematic. The first two exist as products of modernity, the latter fails to cater for the complex reality of everyday life.

Hence the possibilities of a 'sampling' approach, which assumes that the only place to innovate, to 'become', to make culture, is from within culture. Innovation is not possible when one is separated. Innovation is not necessary if

---

in the society of which they are a part, without, however, having migrated from any other society – they have no other homeland – and without setting up an alternative society of their own in a new land.' Tanner, *Theories of Culture*, p. 103.

[27] George A. Lindbeck, *The Nature of Doctrine: Religion and Theology in a Postliberal Age* (Philadelphia, PA: Westminster, 1984); Nancey C. Murphy, *Beyond Liberalism and Fundamentalism: How Modern and Postmodern Philosophy set the Theological Agenda* (Valley Forge, PA: Trinity Press International, 1996); Volf, 'When Gospel and Culture Intersect'.

[28] Lindbeck, *The Nature of Doctrine*.

[29] Miroslav Volf, 'Theology, Meaning, and Power. A Conversation with George Lindbeck on Theology and the Nature of Christian Difference,' in Timothy R. Phillips and Dennis L. Oknolm (eds), *The Nature of Confession: Evangelicals and Postliberals in Conversation* (Downers Grove, IL: IVP, 1996), pp. 46-66. Volf, 'When Gospel and Culture Intersect'. Tanner, *Theories of Culture*.

[30] Ward, *Cultural Transformation*, p. 55.

[31] Ward, *Cultural Transformation*, p. 55.

one chooses to assimilate. Innovation is problematic and, potentially, overwhelming when culture is considered as a unitary monolith. In contrast, sampling expects to occur from within a culture, by indwelling, without losing the possibility of culture-making and innovative creativity.

Consider the following contemporary discussion of the relationship between gospel and culture. Miroslav Volf likens the current task of Christianity in a Western context to that of rebuilding a city centre rather than erasing a suburb to create a brand new mall. For Volf, Western Christianity has no pure place from which to 'transform the whole culture ... to undertake that eminently modern project of restructuring the whole social and intellectual life'.[32] Rather, Christianity can only work from within, piecemeal, house-by-house, concrete practice by concrete practice.

Similarly Kathryn Tanner remarks that 'it is the *enculturated individual who may be innovative*'.[33] Sampling is thus a process, not of simple consumption, but of creative 'becoming', as the enculturated, indwelling Christian deliberately samples the artifacts both of the ecclesial tradition and contemporary culture.[34] Such sampling opens a process of transformation as in multiple ways everyday practices of the culture are metamorphosed.

Likewise, Graham Ward considers how Christianity might become 'a transformative public practice with respect to the cultures that contextualise it'.[35] Ward interweaves hermeneutics and imagination to argue that the only place one can be is embodied: 'a grammar of critical enquiry has to emerge - and emerge from *modifications* to *already existing* grammars'.[36] Further, 'Christian utterance, then, is constructed out of the cultural materials at hand. It is...always hybrid, improvised, syncretistic and implicated in networks of association that exceed various forms of institutional, individual or sectarian policing.'[37] Such an approach to culture – embodied and enculturated within –

---

[32] Christians 'have no place from which to transform the *whole culture they inhabit* – no place from which to undertake that eminently modern project of restructuring the whole social and intellectual life, no virgin soil on which to start building a new, radically different city. No revolutions are possible; all transformations are piece-meal transformations of some elements, at some points, for some time with some gain and possibly some loss. These transformations are reconstructions of the structures that must be inhabited as the reconstruction is going on.' Volf, 'When Gospel and Culture Intersect,' pp. 204-205. Italics are original.

[33] Tanner, *Theories of Culture,* p. 52. Italics are mine for emphasis.

[34] '[Christian social practices] create meaning through a process of consumption ... become a comprehensive way of life by working over the practices of others.' Tanner, *Theories of Culture*, p. 112.

[35] Ward, *Cultural Transformation*, p. 61.

[36] Ward, *Cultural Transformation*, p. 76. Emphasis added.

[37] Ward, *Cultural Transformation*, p. 47.

captures the practice of 'Emerging' Baptist Church.³⁸ From within their popular cultural world, through multiple mechanisms of amplification, subversion and juxtaposition, local happenings are described, contemporary music is played, TV footage is looped, as these cultural indwellers sample distinctly and embrace difference.

Imagination: Poetic and Ethical

Imagination is an essential component in this *creating* interface. Richard Kearney has provided a comprehensive survey of the place of imagination in human thought. He concludes by arguing for the need to cultivate in our contemporary context an imagination that is both poetical and second ethical.³⁹ For Kearney, central to imagination is the ability to be poetic, to play creatively. These acts of play open up new possibilities, new ways of being human. (Such an approach can be located in the Christian understandings of God as Creator and humans as culture-makers made in God's image.) Such theological affirmations provide a stance of creativity and inform a theology that undergirds practices of sampling. As humans, *creating*, 'becoming', offer a more life-giving way of being than *condemning*, *critiquing* or *copying* the other (of culture).

Secondly and equally, Kearney urges that imaginative play and relationships with an/other need to be grounded in an ethical imagination. For Kearney, we must neither culture-make for ourselves. Nor do we exist simply to copy or consume. Rather, imagination as ethical urges the moving beyond our rational, autonomous ethnocentrism. Any and all human interactions need to be shaped by the other, whether other humans, other organisms or other possibilities. Thus Kearney urges all available contemporary technologies - presumably including television news footage and contemporary music - be embraced and employed, because they can serve the ethical imagination.⁴⁰

Returning to the contemporary act of intercession, it is noteworthy that the intercession at 'Emerging' Baptist Church is both poetic, an act of creative play that opens up new possibilities, and ethical, as it offers sensitivity to the other of contemporary culture, indigenous voices and encourages prayer for children.

---

[38] Johnny Baker, writing from a UK context, makes a similar argument with regard to the centrality of the incarnation for 'alternative worship.' Baker, 'Alternative Worship and the Significance of Popular Culture' (April 2000) – http://www.jonnybaker.btinternet.co.uk/text/altw_popculture.pdf, accessed 14 July 2009.

[39] Richard Kearney, *The Wake of Imagination: Toward a Postmodern Culture* (London: Routledge, 1994).

[40] An example (from Ward) might be the seeing of a homeless person, in which the act of seeing becomes an invitation to a new imagination, which thus makes possible acts of resistance against the dominant social imaginary. Ward, *Cultural Transformation and Religious Practice*, p. 144.

Community and Tradition

In his book, *Culture in the Plural,* Michel de Certeau developed the idea that marginality, the places of interface, are the best sites for creativity. 'Every culture proliferates along its margins... it exists precisely along the interstice or the margin that it opens up.'[41] Further, this marginality produces a creative proliferation that is communal. 'In fact, what is creative, is the gesture that allows a group to invent itself. It mediates a collective operation.'[42] Thus, margins become the seedbeds of creative communities.

This appreciation of communities as marginal and creative is consistent with the history of the church. The people of Israel were birthed amid enslavement in Egypt. The exile was central in invigorating the Jewish scriptures and faith. Jesus was born in a cave, pursued as a refugee into Egypt and crucified outside the gate. The early church grew on the edges of Jewish culture and of Roman society. Borg suggests exile as one of the three macro-stories at the heart of scripture that shaped the imagination of ancient Israel and the early church.[43] He argues that the priestly story has dominated Christianity, and that the macro-story of exile needs to be recovered to shape anew our images of Jesus.[44] Miroslav Volf argues that

> the center is not the place where Christian faith should be anyway: it was born on the margins to serve the whole humanity ... social marginality is not to be bemoaned but celebrated ... as a place from which the church can, speaking its own proper language, address public issues and, holding fast to its own proper practices, initiate authentic transformations in its social environment.[45]

Certeau further developed this notion of marginal creative community when he described the relationship between the marginal creative community and their textual artefacts. 'Its trace will possibly outlive the group by assuming the form of an object fallen from life, taken, left aside once more, and redeployed for later practices: texts, tools, or statues.'[46] This is another way of understanding

---

[41] Michel de Certeau, *Culture in the Plural,* ed. Luce Giard (Minneapolis, MN: University of Minnesota Press, 1997), p. 139.

[42] Certeau, *Culture in the Plural,* p. 140.

[43] Marcus Borg, *Meeting Jesus Again for the First Time: The Historical Jesus and the Heart of Contemporary Faith* (San Francisco, CA: HarperSanFrancisco, 1995), pp. 119-40. The other two stories Borg discusses are those of the exodus and priest. In using Borg, I nevertheless remain uneasy about his methodology, which seems to read the ancient texts overly critically through the eyes of a deconstructive contemporary hermeneutic.

[44] We need to recapture a sense that we live 'estranged from the centre of our being and yearning'. Borg, *Meeting Jesus Again,* p. 132.

[45] Volf, 'Theology, Meaning and Power', p. 64.

[46] Certeau, *Culture in the Plural,* p. 140.

Crouch's call to be *creating*: marginal creative communities culture-make by producing marginalia, notes from the margins.

Viewed like this, sampling is never a pragmatic response to culture. Rather, in the production of new theological notes from the margins, including creative acts of intercession, it becomes a way of re-theologising. This has particular relevance for the Baptist interface with the other, especially given Sutherland's priority of the local gathered community as the primary site of Baptist ecclesiology. Terry Veling has argued that marginal Christian communities can learn much from the rabbinic *midrash* tradition, for they give to the Christian tradition a communal and dialogical mode of being.[47] These communities accepted their marginality. They located authority in their community of interpretation. Employing the concepts of Certeau, they produced marginalia: writing their interpretative scripts around the edges of their received text. This writing allowed them to re-read their tradition in light of their changing context, to re-theologise and, in doing so, to add vitality to their life of faith. Viewed this way 'Emerging' Baptist Church stands in continuity with these communities. It is a culture-maker, a producer of artefacts, of notes from the margins.

The notion of marginal creative communities producing marginalia has implications for the Christian understanding of tradition. Tradition need no longer be perceived as an oppressive external metanarrative. Rather it is 'product,' the theological notes from other communities who have applied the Bible, the history of the church and the way of Jesus to their unique context. In this understanding, tradition is not framed as monolithic but as the multiple perspectives of multiple communities. It acknowledges the context surrounding each of these communities and thus, the processes of selection, conflict and interpretation that surround the production of marginalia.[48] Acts of sampling will be sensitive to these other communities, seeking awareness of their story and the contexts surrounding these communities of tradition. In this understanding new perspectives can be expressed by exploring and ancient resources.

Such an approach offers a different approach to tradition within Baptist theology from that suggested by Sutherland.[49] He uses the notion of tradition as

---

[47] 'The rabbinic tradition provides a strong legitimation and rich resources for supporting the interpretive activity of intentional communities whose voices sound out from the margins of tradition.' Terry A. Veiling, *Living in the Margins: Intentional Communities and the Art of Interpretation* (New York, NY: Crossroad Herder, 1996), p. 152.

[48] Thus I disagree with Tanner, who sees the notion of tradition as being located in the texts of diverse Christian communities resulting in the masking of conflict. Tanner, *Theories of Culture*, pp.130-38.

[49] Martin Sutherland, 'Gathering, Sacrament and Baptist Theological Method,' pp. 55-56.

a train. The first carriage is the Jesus story. The last carriage is the church becoming. Sutherland notes how as the train goes around a bend, the last carriage can not only see the first carriage, but every other carriage. This for him is a picture of a Baptist approach to tradition. While applauding Sutherland's instinct, the use of sampling suggests his notion of tradition needs some further nuance. Sampling reminds us that in fact each carriage is not a monolith, but is piecemeal, a producer of multiple marginalia. To use the train analogy, each carriage is filled with boxes. Each box is able to be sampled by a culture-making community.

This suggests a two-fold dimension to the theological task of sampling. First, sampling as an act of creating will require a commitment to being not only a culture-maker but also a culture-keeper – engaging the historical disciplines of exegesis and contextual appreciation.[50] 'That is why the good screenwriter has first watched a thousand movies; why the surgeon who pioneers a new technique has first performed a thousand routine surgeries; and why the investor who provides funds to the next startup has first studied a thousand balance sheets.'[51] Second, humility as the marginalia of any and all communities is 'submitted, in the same way, for the consideration of others who are also concerned to establish the meaning of Christian discipleship' in their unique context.[52] Such an argument would thus reject the criticism that sampling engenders an emerging eclecticism that treats Christian tradition as 'a kind of bran tub into which we can dip for liturgical samples and other goodies'.[53]

In this section we have conducted a second-order critical reflection. This has involved the situating of sampling within the wider contemporary theological discussion regarding gospel and culture, concluding with an exploration of an explicitly Baptistic understanding of tradition and the gathered community.

Conclusion

This chapter has employed a distinctively Baptist method to focus on one act of intercession of a contemporary 'Emerging' Baptist and analysed what it might

---

[50] Crouch uses images of artist and gardener, noting their location in the Genesis story (creator and cultivator). Crouch, *Culture Making,* ch.6, pp. 101-17.
[51] Crouch, *Culture Making,* p. 77.
[52] Tanner, *Theories of Culture,* p. 137.
[53] Roberts, 'Thoroughly Modern Worship, Thoroughly 'Emerging' Culture,' Paper presented at the Gospel and Culture Conference, King's College, London, 1996, p.8. I am using the quotation from Roberts because of its expressiveness and not to suggest he makes this critique of sampling. Quite the reverse, he argues for sampling as essential to the vibrancy of localised liturgical praxis. However, he then advances respect for tradition and a revived doctrine of the community of saints as a way to avoid sampling. My argument advances a slightly different notion of tradition as the product of communities of faith.

say as a theological act about the relationship between gospel and culture. It has been argued that rather than historical postures of *condemning, critiquing, copying* or *consuming*, a posture of *creating* is possible. In one act of worship, the other that is contemporary culture was being employed to allow a vibrant and glocalised relationship with the other of indigenous voices, global conflict and children. This was accomplished through sampling, and as such allowed a Baptist church to make multiple responses – amplifying, subverting, juxtaposing – to gospel and culture and, further, to offer intercession that was an imaginative re-theologising in continuity with the Christian tradition.

This suggests that sampling is a sophisticated theological response to gospel and culture. It allows 'Emerging' Baptist Church to move beyond simplistic dichotomies of separation or accommodation and to embrace a simultaneous plurality of practice, drawing on an imagination that is both poetical and ethical, in an enculturated indwelling of culture. This has particular coherence with Baptistic understandings of church. It encourages the local gathering in a local theologising: 'the dynamic interplay of two stories – the contemporary, local, 'gathered' one, and the Christ story as revealed in scripture ... [that] calls us forward and outwards ... to bring us into consonance with Christ'.[54]

---

[54] Sutherland, 'Gathering, Sacrament and Baptist Theological Method,' pp. 54-55.

PART SIX

Baptists in Asia and Africa

CHAPTER 18

The First Australasian Baptist Missionary: Ellen Arnold and the Bengalis, 1882-1931

Rosalind M. Gooden

Onward Baptist brothers,
Marching through Bengal;
For our William Carey
Has trod there before,
Marshman, Ward, Fernandez
Were the first to share
The good news of Jesus
To those living there.

So begins a play of the 'History of Baptist Witness in Bengal'.[1] It summarised the story of the Baptist Missionary Society (BMS) work from 1792 until the formation of the Bengal Baptist Union in Calcutta in 1935, and was probably written for a Baptist celebration in 1984. The British Baptists have their story of relationships with India and particularly the Bengalis, but the aim in this paper is to give part of the Australasian story, involving Ellen Arnold, the first and longest serving missionary of the Australian Baptist Foreign Missionary Society.[2]

Samson Chowdury,[3] the leading Baptist layman in Bangladesh, has written:

> Ms Arnold was an icon because after her last furlough to Australia, she was not allowed by the Mission Board to come back to the then Bengal. Yet she took the trouble to come to Ataikola[4] on her own and started medical service. Before her

---

[1] Duplicated MS, probably produced for the Diamond Jubilee of the Bangladesh Baptist *Sangha*. 1984 marked the 62nd anniversary of the *Sangha*. BMS Archives, Angus Library, Regent's Park College, Oxford.
[2] The name has varied over the years, becoming the Australian Baptist Missionary Society (ABMS) and now Global InterAction.
[3] Samson H. Chowdury, Dhaka, to Rosalind Mary Gooden (R.M.G.), 5 April 2007.
[4] A village in Pubna District in rural Bengal.

death she handed over the property to the Australasian Baptist Union[5]. At last my father was asked to run the dispensary. I think that is reason she became the icon.[6]

But it was not just these events of 1931 that are the basis for Ellen Arnold's relationship with the Bengalis. On 9 July, the anniversary of her death, Ellen Arnold Day is celebrated by the Bangladesh Baptist Fellowship, particularly the Women's Department, even though very few of today's leaders remember her. It is seventy-eight years since her death at Ataikola. Written on her tombstone in the Pubna District of today's Bangladesh are the words: 'Jesus said, "I am the way, the truth and the life". Ellen Arnold walked this way, preached this truth, lived this life.' Why should this woman, out of the scores of Australian and New Zealand missionaries who have worked with the East Bengal Baptist Union and its derivatives, be so honoured or remembered? She was not the easiest to get on with, a loner who found submission to the authority of others virtually impossible, yet she is an icon to the Bengalis. Part of the explanation lies in the longevity of Ellen Arnold's service. Some of the reasons, however, are gender-based, including a woman's approach to working with Bengali male leaders and the significance of a matriarchal figure in Bengali society. Even more significant were the strengths and weaknesses of this particular woman. As John Bevan wrote at the conclusion of the play 'Ellen', composed for the centenary of the sending out of the first two Australasian women missionaries: 'You're a stubborn woman, Ellen Arnold, and proud. But you're what this place needs and you're what your mission needs if it's to accomplish what it's setting out to do'.[7]

South Australian Beginnings

Australian Baptist missionary activity began in South Australia in 1864 under the influence of Silas Mead, the founding minister of Flinders Street Baptist Church. It developed from British Baptist traditions. Yet South Australian Baptists formed their own missionary society, accepting responsibility for supporting work in the district of Furreedpore,[8] East Bengal, India. For Mead, 'small was beautiful'. For eighteen years the society employed national preachers supervised by BMS workers from Calcutta. In 1882 it sent out the first two women, Marie Gilbert and Ellen Arnold.

---

[5] Product of the work of the New Zealand Baptist Missionary Society and Australian Baptist Missions in East Bengal.

[6] See also D.D. Datta, *75 Year Jubilee Celebration* (Dhaka: Bangladesh Baptist Fellowship, 1994).

[7] J.C. Bevan, *Ellen* (Adelaide: J. Bevan, 1982).

[8] 'Furreedpore' and 'Faridpur' are both common in mission literature.

Arnold, the eldest daughter of Alfred and Ellen Arnold, was born in Aston, Warwickshire, England.[9] Her father was a successful jeweller in Birmingham. She worshipped in both Baptist[10] and Congregational[11] circles in that city, and she was knowledgeable about the work of the BMS[12] in the West Midland Baptist Association. The family migrated to Adelaide in 1879, and became associated with the Flinders Street Baptist Church. Here Ellen and her siblings were fired by the enthusiasm of Mead for missions. Ellen and Marie Gilbert were friends at the church and in the first intake of the Adelaide Teachers' College. They sailed for Bengal on 28 October 1882.

Furreedpore and Comilla

The two missionary women spent 1883 living with the Kerry family in Calcutta while their house was built. In 1884 they moved to Furreedpore, but Arnold was invalided to Australia by May of that year, and spent much of the time travelling around Australia and New Zealand, encouraging the other colonies to form their own societies and send out staff.[13] By the end of 1885 she returned, accompanied by four other women, affectionately known as 'The Five Barley Loaves'. These women lived together in the house in Furreedpore while they studied Bengali, and then scattered to open work in zenanas, the female quarters of the local homes, for the various colonial societies. Arnold was involved in the supervision of building an additional storey on the house in order to accommodate all these women, and when there was an over-run on the costs, she saw the hand of God in the suggestion of the New South Wales BMS that she should become its first worker at Comilla.

Arnold moved to commence zenana work in Comilla in 1890. While there she negotiated the purchase of land and brought Punchanon Biswas (who will be discusssed later) from Furreedpore for the building. By 1893 relations had become strained on the station and with the NSW home committee. Arnold's health was very poor, and she again went back to South Australia (SA) on furlough. It seemed unlikely that she would ever be able to return to India, but she recovered and rejoined the Furreedpore Mission.

---

[9] G.B. Ball, 'Ellen Arnold', in B. Dickey (ed.), *The Australian Dictionary of Evangelical Biography* (Sydney: Evangelical History Association, 1994), pp. 13-14.
[10] She became a member of Graham Street Baptist Church following baptism by its minister, Henry Platten.
[11] The family was commended to Flinders Street Baptist Church by Acocks Green Congregational Church but transferred from Graham Street.
[12] See her letters in *Our Bond* written from England in 1909. Also see R.M. Gooden, 'Birmingham - Crucible for Australian Baptist Missions' (unpublished paper given at the South Australian Baptist Historical Group, 2008).
[13] This is often referred to as the Arnold Crusade.

Pubna

The South Australian BMS then assigned her to its second station, Pubna, where she lived alongside the Summers family. They were joined by two independent Baptist doctors, Charles and Laura Hope, and William Goldsack, a rookie, in 1896.[14] Apart from a couple of years that she spent relieving for the Tasmanian Mission,[15] Arnold subsequently worked from Pubna town as her base. These were complex years with different philosophies and methods of ministry. There were issues of seniority, building programmes, institutional work and village itinerating. New missionaries (both Goldsack and Summers) struggled with the attitudes, opinions and even the theology of Arnold.[16] Finances were tight. Arnold spent more time travelling by bullock cart, boat or pony from village to village, proclaiming the good news. This was her passion.

Interest was shown in the village of Ataikola, and in 1902 a small hut was purchased there so that missionaries could stay and teach. Because of financial stringencies in SA in 1908, the Summers family transferred to the BMS. For 1909-11 Arnold was required to stay more in Pubna and look after the Haripur House for needy women while Miss Ings, its warden, was on leave. Ings raised money for buildings, and so there was a building programme requiring supervision, taking Goldsack from his primary role, and Arnold became involved. The Goldsacks transferred to the BMS in 1912 for specialised Muslim work. There were a number of preachers and colporteurs under the supervision of the men's department and one wonders if Arnold was envious of such resources for just one section of the work.

Arnold wrote a letter revealing deep tensions in the field situation and voiced criticisms of colleagues. In 1912 Arnold was instructed by the SA mission secretary to stop interfering in the Pubna men's department or come home.[17] A further, final decision was made in July 1913: 'hand over the accounts to Miss Ings and come home'.[18] Yet she remained in India and the next minute in the mission's records was that the secretary received a letter from Miss Arnold 'stating that she had taken up her residence at Ataikola and

---

[14] There is a wonderful source of unedited, uncensored information for this period in the correspondence books of the Fowler family. Jim Fowler, who was the principal of the firm D. & J. Fowlers in Adelaide, was the brother of Laura Hope, the independent doctor at Pubna and first woman medical graduate of the University of Adelaide. He was also a close friend and confidant of William Goldsack. They were both members of Glen Osmond Baptist Church. See Fowler Letters, PRG 34 Series 31, Vol. 4; and Series 29, Box 2, Vols 4-6, State Library of South Australia, Adelaide.
[15] 1903-1905.
[16] This could be well documented from the Goldsack-Fowler letters (see n. 14).
[17] Furreedpore Mission minute 629 (August 1912), 646 (October 1912), 680 (April 1913), Global InterAction Archives, Melbourne (hereafter GIA).
[18] Furreedpore Mission minute 685 (July 1913).

that she was well in health'.[19] In 1913 the Australian Baptist missionary societies federated,[20] and this was followed by a committee meeting held at Rajbari on 19 June 1913 to settle the question of the formation of a Field Council.[21] The responsibility for Arnold passed to the Field Council. Around this time she moved from Ataikola to Bera, gaining the grudging consent of the Federal Field Council.[22]

Exile

In a much later letter of 1930 Arnold wrote to the general secretary of the Australian Baptist Misssionary Society:

> For 17 years [i.e. from 1913] the mission has been experimenting by turning me out to the villages with an inclusive and fixed income, and got more economical work done. God kept me alive so long to let you weigh results.[23]

The development in 1913 marked a significant change in Arnold's life. She felt this was exile, even though her colleagues thought she was prone to interpret events irrationally and extravagantly.[24] She had believed that the only way for Europeans to remain healthy in the Indian climate was to live in substantial housing, and she had been responsible for attracting considerable resources to build several typical British Raj-style properties. However, she moved to a thatched, mud-floored village hut. She lived close to the people. She had described the Ataikola community as

> ignorant cultivators, dense headed and earthy minded to the last degree - torn by sickness, suffering and deformities, fever and cholera. At one time they hooted me out of the village; now they growl when I go away and rush for me when I come.[25]

Her appointed Bible women had lived in Ataikola early in its establishment as a centre, well before Arnold went to live there, and they remained faithfully dispensing medicines and teaching village women while Arnold travelled to outlying villages. The important development in the eyes of the people would seem to be that she chose to live among them, and she did this until her death in

---

[19] Furreedpore Mission minute 492 (August 1913).
[20] Tasmania was the exception, withdrawing from East Bengal. Field Council minutes, 23-25 June 1914, GIA.
[21] P.F. Lanyon, 'A Resume of Fifty Years Progress', in *Fifty Years of Mission Service in Eastern Bengal* (Glebe, NSW: Australian Baptist Publishing House, 1932), pp. 11-12.
[22] Field Council minutes, minute 24, 23-25 June 1914, GIA.
[23] Ellen Arnold to John C. Martin, 27 June 1930, GIA.
[24] This is often mentioned by Goldsack to Fowler (see n. 14).
[25] Missionary Echo, 2 May 1905.

1931. K.K. Das, one of the Pubna preachers, an eye-witness of this time in Pubna, wrote in his Bengali biography:

> Miss Arnold had wanted to work from the two [storeyed] home in Pubna – but God decided she should shew forth his glory from a tiny bamboo hut in the village of Ataikola: Ellen knew this at the end of her days and thanked God for this and was never disobedient to His call.[26]

Relationships

There were significant gender issues surrounding the work of women missionaries in the India of that period. Men directed the work of overseeing the preachers and colporteurs, controlling their movements and to some extent their finances and futures. Women, while essentially working among women, had an encouraging, caring role for these same preachers, particularly if they were older and more senior to the men. Relationships were important and the longer people served the more they knew and were known. The pattern can be illustrated for Ellen Arnold with three specific examples: Punchanon Biswas, the first 'South Australian' convert for the work in Furreedpore; Mouzi (later known as Mr Moses), a Muslim convert from Ramchandrapur, near Pubna; and Kailash Khrista Das, a second-generation student of Serampore College, a preacher in Pubna and Arnold's Bengali biographer.

In 1880-81 the South Australian BMS extended an invitation to its first convert in the Furreedpore work to visit SA. He was Punchanon Biswas, a Brahmin who had been baptised in May 1871, studied at Serampore and returned as one of the preachers. He spent six months visiting the SA churches and enthusing them. Income increased and his visit paved the way for the sending out of the first Australian Baptist missionaries. Both Gilbert and Arnold heard him speak. A disturbed Ellen commented:

> If I attended a missionary meeting it would upset me for days and yet if I heard of one being held I was bound to go.
>
> I heard [Punchanon Biswas] say that they wanted a school in Furreedpore so immediately the thought came 'There's hope for me yet', and perhaps I could be self-supporting and so no burden to the society. I told God about it and left it.[27]

So in a unique sense the Indian was the instrument of God for Arnold's specific call to work in India.

---

[26] K.K. Das, 'Australian Mission's First Missionary to Bengal' (Calcutta: Australian Bengal Baptist Union, n.d.), p. 14 (duplicated copy of translation).

[27] Ellen Arnold, 'How I have been led into Missionary Work', *Truth and Progress* (*T&P*), reprinted 1907.

Punchanon Biswas met the two women at Calcutta when they arrived at the end of 1882.[28] He was responsible for building the house at Furreedpore for the women, eventually reporting to the South Australians: 'I am glad to say that Misses Gilbert and Arnold are at last in our midst. Oh! How glad and happy we all have been to have them among us.'[29] His joy was reciprocated by Arnold and Gilbert in a letter written the same day.[30] The Biswas family became their friends, and was often mentioned affectionately in their letters. He was a strength to Arnold in her devastation at returning to Australia in 1884. In the midst of her appeal for more resources to extend the Furreedpore house for the newcomers, Arnold added a strong appeal for funds to build a new house for the Biswas family.[31] She enlisted Punchanon *Babu* to come to Comilla in July 1888 when she had obtained land for the building of the Zenana Mission House in order to supervise. The Comilla zenana log book records:

> Punchanon Babu, a very capable Bengali .... came to Comilla privately to assist Miss Arnold in the building of the new Zenana Mission House .... Punchanon Babu also feared to remain in his mat house [because the properties of Christians were being fired] and he also was given refuge in the Mission House with his wife and children.[32]

This was not an easy situation. Arnold confesses, 'It was hard for Punchanon Biswas to consult me, because I am only a woman and quite ignorant of building.... I found Punchanon Babu disinclined to confide in me and unwilling to return accounts until Mr Kerry[33] told him to do so.' He supervised the building until 3 October when the walls, roof and flooring were complete and Arnold released him to go back to Furreedpore.

The warmth of the relationship survived and Arnold continued to supply friends in SA with news of Punchanon Biswas's family and ministry. In 1902 he was released from responsibility in Furreedpore and Arnold rejoiced in his wider sphere of influence, entreating people to pray for him as they did for her. However, in 1905 he moved to live and work at Chinaurah, severing his ties with the mission. Arnold wrote to the home committee requesting a generous retirement pension, but the matter was referred back to the field.[34] Punchanon Biswas died in 1908 and Arnold conveyed the news in the following way:

---

[28] Arnold and Marie Gilbert to Sunday School scholars, 9 January 1883, *T&P* 1 March 1883, p. 29.
[29] Punchanon Biswas to editor, 3 February 1884, *T&P* 1 April 1884, supplement.
[30] *T&P* 1 April 1884, supplement.
[31] *T&P* 1 October 1885, p. 127.
[32] Comilla Zenana Log Book, introductory notes, p. 3, GIA.
[33] BMS missionary in Calcutta and the South Australian mission's agent.
[34] Furreedpore Mission minutes, December 1907, GIA.

> he was suffering from a very trying disease for years and one is fain to believe his late alienation from our mission was caused by this, and to remember his long years of devotion to Christ and kindness to fellow workers. Personally I have lost a dear and faithful friend, whose friendship dates back to 1881 when we met in Adelaide. After we came to Faridpur in January 1883 how he watched over us, practically did our housekeeping until we got hold of the language, sympathized in our sorrows - sympathy was perhaps his strongest characteristic. In my baffled hopes and sorrows at first leaving Faridpur in 1884 how tenderly he cared for us, making all arrangements for the journey! And I can never forget his gently wiping away the tears of the prostrate one when everyone else in the boat was resting and she thought she was unobserved. In bereavement he knew just what to say, for he suffered so much himself;[35] and our lots were so arranged that in Faridpur, Comilla and Pubna we lived together, his wife being my dearest friend after we got to know each other so well, and my heart must ever be grateful to them both for the will to share exile with me, though the proposal was not ultimately carried out. They knew my soul in adversity and I knew theirs.[36]

In a relational culture, such bonds were significant.

Mouzi was an early Muslim convert from the village of Ramchandrapur, near Pubna town. Arnold had visited his family home in 1895.[37] Mouzi was a Sunday School scholar in Pubna in 1897. During the visit of the home delegation, Dr Whitley and Silas Mead, he was baptised.[38] He was constantly described as a convert of Miss Arnold. He went to study at Serampore,[39] and took up ministry at Entally, Calcutta. He became known as Mr Moses. Occasionally he and his wife and children visited Arnold and the Christians in Pubna district. She records a trip of the couple to England in 1911, their visit to the Keswick Convention and them travelling on to America.[40] She had written to friends in England about receiving them. When she was sick in Kurseong she stayed with this family. On her return to India in 1930 the Moses family came to see her in Sealdah, Calcutta.[41] On her death the field secretary for the mission received a very warm letter, with testimony to their long-standing relationship and concern to be given a part of any memorial to her:

> Gradually I am realizing that my beloved mother in the Lord has passed away into the presence of our Lord....Miss Arnold's death leaves a blank in my life which I know will never be filled. For over 30 years we were one in spirit. There was

---

[35] The Biswas family lost seven out of the nine children. Arnold tragically lost two brothers and cousins.
[36] 'Pubna', *Our Bond* (*OB*) September 1908, p. 4.
[37] *OB* April 1895, p. 3.
[38] Included in remembrances of Laura Fowler in 1933. Pabna Zenana Work Log Book, p. 1, GIA.
[39] *OB* March 1898, p. 6.
[40] *OB* August 1911, p. 4.
[41] Arnold to Martin, 3 March 1931, GIA.

hardly a sorrow or joy in my life that she did not know, and the same was with her. Thus we together lived in the presence of God either to praise Him for blessings received or to implore His mercy. With us there was no race or colour prejudice....I left my father's home when I was quite young and thus I was deprived of my mother's affections and care. But Miss Arnold took her place. She not only cared for my body for some years but she faithfully cared also for my soul. What I am today, I am first by the grace of God and then by the love and prayers of Miss Arnold. She was an ideal missionary and one of the best soul winners I had known. Miss Arnold was one of the most unselfish European missionaries I had ever come across. Very early days of my acquaintance with her I was very much struck with her love and sympathy for the poor and suffering ones.

I, a fruit of her labour, have travelled throughout the length and breadth of India and up in the Himalayas preaching the everlasting Gospel of our God. Her sympathy, prayer and letters always followed me. I feel all the more keenly now to go and faithfully fulfill my calling.[42]

In 1965 a United Nations Conference in Auckland was attended by a Miss Dorothy Moses, who headed the Division of Social Affairs for the Economic Commission for Asia and the Far East (ECAFE) in Bangkok. Miss Gladys Collins, a previous missionary, read that she was the daughter of a Muslim convert living in Calcutta and contacted her. She proved to be the daughter of Moses *Babu*, and Collins wrote: 'Sure enough my conjectures were correct. Pubna had been her father's home and it was "a Miss Arnold who was responsible for the conversion of my father".'[43]

Finally there was the contribution of K.K. Das, one of the pastors of the Australasian Baptist Bengal Union. He had been a preacher at Pubna in 1913 when Arnold transferred to Ataikola and then Bera. He was asked by the Union to write her biography in 1931 (written in Bengali) and gives evidence of the regard she was held in by the Bengali church. There are some very telling personal recollections of Arnold's extreme exertions in distribution of famine relief: 'She did all the work herself, so that no one could be blamed and so that no one would be harmed.' Also, he records her personally nursing him and his son for typhoid in her own home to prevent others being infected. He witnessed her distress on leaving the Pubna house, and arranged for her transport by bullock cart to Ataikola. He details her work in famine relief, her care for children, her rescue of women, her evangelistic heart, her simple life-style. He sums her up:

She loved to honour people. Never did she despise any for being a Bengali, or for being uneducated. Rather did she seek to receive any who might be in the position

---

[42] M. Moses to A.J. Grace, from Calcutta, 23 July 1931, GIA.
[43] Copy of typed article by C.J. Collins and a newspaper cutting undated included with a letter to J.D. Williams from Aldgate, 24 January 1972, GIA.

to help others. Because of this in a place like Ataikola she never failed to have help from Government officers.[44]

Equally important was the relationship with the women who worked with her, particularly at Ataikola. Women whom she had appointed to work in the medical service before her exile were still there and nursed her at her death. Srimati Hironmayee Das[45] was the daughter of one of Arnold's early Bible women at Comilla and sometimes as a child accompanied them. She was sent to Calcutta for training and came back to Ataikola. She worked with Arnold for twenty-five years. She was one of the women there at Arnold's death and in her will Arnold wrote:

> It is my desire...that an old workers' home be provided for Heronmoy Das, her sister Shornomoy Baul, Mono-Mohinin Coondoo and such like mission workers when no longer able for active service. The Union must have the right to evict any who disgrace our Lord.[46]

Transition

As Arnold aged[47] and had to spend more and more weeks of the wet season in the Himalayas due to failing health, she made impassioned pleas to the field and home authorities for women to take over 'her' stations and itinerant work. The Australasian Baptist Union had been formed in 1919, drawing together the churches that were the fruit of New Zealand and Australian Baptist missionary work in East Bengal. Missionaries were included in the Union only when they were appointed by their churches as delegates. As early as 1925 the Union discussed the possibility of supporting the employed preachers. Arnold was present during those discussions.[48] At the meetings in 1928 and 1929 Arnold indicated that she wanted to hand over her work at Bera to the Union. She felt there was opposition initially, but, finally, there was a unanimous vote to accept responsibility for the work at Bera. The Union appointed a committee with power to act. Arnold was disappointed that the committee took so long to take up the work and that the appointment of a preacher was postponed. Arnold used this as an excuse for delaying her return to Australia despite her ill health and justifying her non-compliance with requests to return.[49] She believed she had

---

[44] Das, 'Australian Mission's First Missionary', p. 9.
[45] Within mission literature there are variations in the spelling of Bengali names.
[46] True Copy of Last Will and Testament of Late Miss Ellen Arnold, signed 5 March 1930, Arnod Box, GIA.
[47] She was 60 in 1918, the accepted retiral age for women, although at federation Field Council argued for case-by-case consideration.
[48] Datta, 75 Year, p. 8.
[49] Arnold to Martin, 2 March 1929, GIA. Arnold claims that the conditions of her previous letter had not been fulfilled. She needed to settle in the preacher, her health had

been appointed by the Union to stay as long as she was able. As she wrote to Martin:

> For 10 years a Bengal Union of New Zealand and Australian mission churches has been going. At the end of 9 years they decided on <u>independent</u> work...This decision in March 1929 called into existence an Executive committee of three under which I was working for my last year in India. At the 1930 meetings they elected another 2 men to this Committee...

She was most concerned that the home leadership should understand that the Field Council did not have authority over the Union. She also wished to convey that she was opposed to the tokenism whereby one or two of the Bengal preachers were included on Field Council. She reports that her women needed her:

> Really and truly I'm better cared for in East Bengal and fit the life better. I've no sheaves to show you, but have just been a plough boy all the time and the Master wants that work done well. The crops are His concern.[50]

In March 1930 Arnold finally agreed to return to Australia travelling on S.S. Cathay. She had to be carried off the ship at Fremantle. The mission assumed she would retire, and so did the Field Council, her colleagues and her family, yet the correspondence continued from this feisty woman:

> In their hearts the Indian Christians do not approve of our mission methods, though they are very afraid of offending the sahebs, and when they found this work more to their liking and within reasonable compass of their powers, they took it joyfully. My earnest plea to F.C. and Board is let them work it out themselves and don't muddle things up by trying to get them on to the F.C. They must rule in their own house....It seems to me the best thing the Board can do is to send a word of thanksgiving for their enterprise and ask the F.C. to release the man the churches have chosen.

> For 25 years I have been experimenting by putting more responsibility on Indians. Other missionaries warned me and disapproved, especially zenana missionaries who thought I was not guarding my women workers enough; but God has guarded them, and vindicated the policy.

> Many of the Indian men are senior and find it hard to be under youths. I am in a position to get more knowledge of this than others and have had it thrust upon me. Garos and Bengalis are so different....Missionaries may not agree to my

---

improved from early December, there was no one to take over from her and the Union had not yet finalised the decision.

[50] Arnold to Martin, 19 July 1929, GIA.

suggestions, unless the older ones do, and even since I have been here this time some of them have reprimanded me for believing what Bengalis have written.[51]

Retirement was virtually impossible for Arnold. Hers was an extreme case of reverse culture shock. Family relationships were strained and eventually she went to a retirement home. She started to enquire for a booking back to India. When she passed the test of the ship's doctor this was proof of God's will. She boarded ship and wrote to the field secretary from Colombo of her plans. She concluded that the fare back to Bengal cost no more than a funeral in Australia. Arnold went to live in Ataikola, adamant that she was not going to be any burden to missionary colleagues. Negotiations continued for the Union to take over the work at Ataikola and it agreed in March 1931. B.N. Eade, a New Zealand missionary, reported:

> The most important action taken by the Union was the acceptance of control and financial responsibility for one year of another small mission station. This is Ataikola, near Bera, and hitherto in the hands of Miss Arnold.[52]

He then went on to comment on the difference in atmosphere and attitude in the meetings from two years previously:

> I am fain to believe that the effort made to run Bera has been the greatest factor in bringing about this advance. Miss Arnold is to be congratulated on her enterprise. The Union is now on its feet. It is advancing. It has drunk the wine of success. "We can" is no longer a doubting hesitating whisper of hope. It is a triumphant shout of experience. Only those who have so long encouraged that trembling whisper and fought that terrible "We cannot" of Indian self-distrust can fully realise how grand it is not only to hear "We can" but also to see the "We can-ites" carry the day.

Ellen Arnold died four months later. Two of her friends gave money to build a dispensary at Ataikola. Her cry to the Australian mission was 'You have trusted me, now trust the Bengalis'. And the Bengalis believed she did.

---

[51] Arnold to Martin, 27 June 1930, GIA.
[52] *New Zealand Baptist* June 1931, p. 183.

CHAPTER 19

Baptists and the Reformed Church in Mission: Indonesian Papua in the Late Twentieth Century

David A. Groves

Global InterAction, then known as the Australian Baptist Missionary Society (ABMS), served in the western half of New Guinea and then Timor and Sulawesi in the closing years of the twentieth century. The work had its genesis in Australian-mandated New Guinea, spilled over the border and following the transfer from Dutch to Indonesian rule spread to other groups further west. This paper focuses on Baptist ministry among the Dani people in the North Baliem Valley from 1956 until 1963. It is now within the Indonesian province of Papua but was situated in the area known as 'Nederlands Nieuw Guinea' (NNG) during the period covered here.

The Reformed Church 'Utrechtse Zendings Vereniging' (Utrecht Mission Society) established its work in NNG a hundred years before ABMS arrived, the first Dutch missionaries landing in Dorei Bay in 1852. Pioneering was extremely difficult and 'after twenty five years of earnest striving the number of missionaries and family members who had died exceeded the number of natives baptised'.[1] Eventually the work began to grow and by the 1950s the national church 'Gereja Kristen Injili' (GKI) had planted congregations along the entire north coast and its immediate environs.

Penetrating the North Baliem

Following extensive media coverage given the previously unknown highland peoples in Dutch New Guinea by the Archbold Expedition of 1938[2] and the dramatic rescue of some downed American service personnel in what was called 'Shangri-La' in 1945, a number of Evangelical missions attempted to establish beachheads in Dutch territory to evangelise its unreached people as

---

[1] G. Souter, *New Guinea: The Last Unknown* (Sydney: Angus and Robertson, 1963), p. 23.
[2] R. Archbold, A.L. Rand and L.J. Bass, 'Results of the Archbold Expeditions No. 41: Summary of the 1938-39 New Guinea Expedition', *Bulletin of the American Museum of Natural History* 89, 3 (1942).

soon as practicable after World War II. At the invitation of Charles Mellis of Mission Aviation Fellowship (MAF), Norm Draper and senior missionary Victor White (ABMS) visited NNG in July 1955.[3] They had discussions with the government and other missions and made an aerial survey into the North Baliem Valley, 'buzzing' a fight in progress at Tiom. Their report to the ABMS in Melbourne[4] met with a favourable response, and Draper returned in the following year with his wife, Sheila, Gil and Pat McArthur, Ian Gruber, Hein Noordyk and John Betteridge.

Hollandia, the Dutch colonial capital built around Humboldt Bay, was the missions supply centre. Base camps were established adjacent to the airport at Sentani, forty kilometres inland, at a complex originally developed by the American Air Force during World War II. Missionaries from the Christian and Missionary Alliance (CAMA), the Evangelical Alliance Mission (TEAM), the Unevangelised Fields Mission (UFM), the Regions Beyond Missionary Union (RBMU) and the Australian Baptists, jostled good-naturedly for space on 'Mission Hill' at Sentani's Base 'Tujuh' (Seven). CAMA's American headquarters was 'laying claim to the entire area from the Wissel Lakes to the south end of the Baliem'[5] at the time, but the field missionaries agreed on suitable comity arrangements that allocated places for the groups inland. [6]

The Australians found that some members of the American 'faith' missions entertained reservations about them because of their denominational status. This mind-set appeared to be part of a cultural adjustment necessary to work in an 'inter-denominational' mission. It was in the mid-twentieth century that inter-denominational missions came into their own[7] and while the spiritual roots of individuals lay in a denominational home church, by joining an organisation that required raising personal support ('living by faith'), they developed a prejudice against those who seemed to be supported by their denomination. Most missionaries in denominational groups became aware that they were thought to be 'less spiritual' by those serving in the 'faith' missions. These suspicions increased when ABMS and the national church began to work together. It appeared to their detractors that the Baptists were providing a platform for GKI expansion into the highlands and as they were considered theologically liberal, Baptists were even more suspect.

---

[3] N. Draper and S. Draper, *Daring to Believe* (Melbourne: ABMS, 1990), p. 201.
[4] E.J. Steiger, *Wings Over Shangri La* (Anaheim, CA: self-published, 1995), p. 49.
[5] Steiger, Wings Over Shangri La, p. 58.
[6] A. Dube, 'At Your Own Risk', *Vision* (Melbourne) (April, 1956), p.6: 'The actual boundaries of the area....are to be determined by a Commission comprised of representatives of the various missions.' The comity agreements were generally adhered to even though they were initially quite informal.
[7] R.D. Winter, *The Twenty Five Unbelievable Years* (Pasadena: William Carey Library, 1970), p. 46.

Nevertheless ABMS co-operated with the inter-denominational groups to establish infrastructure (including a hangar for MAF) on the coast, and 'stepping stone' stations inland. In April 1956, MAF pilot Dave Steiger flew members of RBMU and ABMS into Lake Archbold to meet up with a UFM advance party. They then trekked to Bokondini to build an airstrip for UFM, thence to Pyramid Mountain in the Grand Valley, liaising with a CAMA party to construct a strip jointly for their work.[8] Draper, Gruber, Myron Bromley (CAMA's linguist) and Noordyk then walked along the North Baliem Valley to clear and level land for the first MAF landings at Tiom. As more staff arrived, other airstrips were opened at Makki, Danime, Pit River, Porga, Dimba and Kwiyawagi, effectively covering the area allocated to Baptist ministry. The missionaries began learning the language and commenced teaching among a people group who proved within a relatively short time to be wonderfully receptive.

Education Initiative

However, before commencing the push inland in 1956, Draper and McArthur had visited the Dutch mission headquarters at Joka on Lake Sentani to discover what strategies the Reformed Mission had developed to approach primitive stone-age people.[9] They had helpful discussions with schools' superintendent Nelis van der Stoep and his wife, Tine. The Dutch prioritised education and Nelis suggested that coastal Papuans, who already had seven years of schooling, could be trained for a further three years in the highlands to learn local language, qualify as teachers and become teacher evangelists living close to the people.[10]

The Baptists accepted the suggestion and agreed to recruit a Dutch-speaking Baptist teacher in Australia.[11] ABMS advertised the need for about twelve months without success. Consequently, when Draper returned to Joka to report that no suitable candidate had been found, he invited the van der Stoeps to take on the role themselves. Nelis had health problems that were aggravated by coastal living and after representation to his board was given permission to move inland. ABMS agreed and *Vision* (the ABMS paper) reported shortly

---

[8] N. Draper and S. Draper, *Contact* (Melbourne: ABMS, 2007), p. 15.
[9] E.J. Steiger, *Wings Over Shangri La*, p. 133.
[10] Personal conversation with Noel Melzer (March 1990). Melzer comments: 'the widespread outbreak of the Spirit of God among the Dani from as early as 1962 meant that, while the teachers' Christian influence among the children in the schools was positive and appreciated, they were not required to evangelise the adult population. Conversely, many coastal teacher trainees found Christ through the influence of Dani people.' N. Melzer, *In Pleasant Places* (Glenbrook: self-published, 2001), p. 77.
[11] A number of Australian teachers were involved teaching primary school children in Baptist missions in PNG at the time, using English and Pidgin.

afterwards that 'unexpected help has come in the availability of a Dutch educationalist. A long delay in the training of leaders will be obviated.'[12] They arrived at Tiom station in September 1957.

The Training Centrum Baliem (TCB), the Baliem Teachers' College, commenced in October 1957 in bush material buildings constructed by Ian Gruber and coastal carpenters.[13] Nelis was assisted from time to time by colleagues, Kees Sonke and Lammert Hukema, and in 1961 joined by a second teacher, Yaap Euwema, with his wife, Hanie, recruited and sent out jointly by Dutch Baptists and ABMS. The Australian missionaries at Tiom served as chaplains and their wives taught English.

The Campus

ABMS was committed to construct permanent buildings at Tiom. New missionary, Laurie Cawley, began saw milling and David Groves, in a gap year away from university, constructed a teacher's house, class rooms, dormitory and ablutions block with ancillary workshop and accommodation facilities. This significant commitment to an established programme was taking place within three years of first contact, with no government presence and no guarantee that local people might not suddenly require foreigners to leave.

Funds were sourced primarily from Semavi, a Dutch philanthropic organisation, through the good offices of the van der Stoeps, although not all agreed expectations were actually fulfilled. Craig remembers John Williams' and Max Hamer's visit in 1961, emphasising the 'mission was experiencing financial stress'[14] and hoping vegetable sales would reduce the deficit. Local farmers were growing good crops of vegetables from seed distributed by the mission and their produce was purchased with trade items such as beads, soap and salt, backloaded to the coast and sold to the Dutch for guilder.

The governor of NNG, Dr Plateel, visited the North Baliem in November 1960. He was impressed by the staff and students of the school and commented that the buildings reminded him of some he had seen when visiting the Snowy River scheme in Australia (meaning they were of very simple construction). Groves had combined Australian building techniques with some aspects of PNG's vertical board 'single thickness' Bulolo system to minimise costs.

The Students

The first intake was selected carefully from the Joka High School with the headmaster's recommendation and their parents' blessing. The families showed

---

[12] *Vision* (June, 1957), p. 6.
[13] *Vision* (February, 1958), p. 3.
[14] C. and P. Craig, *Sky People in a Stone Age Community* (Tauranga, New Zealand: self-published, 2006), p. 164.

interest when they saw the urgent need to introduce 'Education and the Gospel' in isolated areas. One of the fathers expressed his willingness, remembering the first missionary who came to his region. He was happy his family had listened to the gospel message and now his son would take part in mission work in the Baliem. It was also reassuring to him that a nurse would open a rural clinic for both the trainees and the Danis in Tiom.[15]

Fifteen students completed their three year training in the first class, gaining fluency in Dutch, English and Dani (besides 'Bahasa Malayu', the Malay tongue, and their own village language). There was some criticism that Dutch was used rather than 'Malay in the newly opened schools in the highlands in the early 1960s'.[16] In fact, Dutch was restricted to the TCB itself and village teaching was to be in the 'heart language' of the children, a particularly effective medium at that stage.

The students read European magazines, played good chess and football (no mean feat at an altitude of 2,000 metres), painted in the style of Albert Namatjira (an indigenous Australian landscape artist) and listened to BBC world news. In fact, their grasp of English enabled them not only to understand but also to be moved by the news content. Namatjira's gaoling for illegally supplying alcohol to fellow Aboriginals and his subsequent death on 8 August 1959 caused great sadness. During 1960 they followed the career of Patrice Lumumba, the Congolese nationalist leader, from grudging acceptance by the Belgian government to his ouster by Mobutu four months later. They entered into the racial ferment of the day and empathised with its winners and losers. This was the time of the Mau Mau rebellion in Kenya, the Sharpeville massacre in South Africa and forced desegregation of schools in Little Rock, Arkansas.

Groves appreciated their willingness to assist by lifting entire wall sections together as carpenters nailed braces and stays. He became aware of their national sensitivity as well. On one occasion, attempting to compliment a helper by saying, 'Lukas, you're a Briton', he was appropriately rebuked when Lukas replied tersely, 'I am not. I'm Papuan!'[17]

The students walked through the area on a number of occasions, familiarising themselves with locations considered suitable as future teaching posts and demonstrated a sensitive appreciation of local culture. When they were threatened by armed warriors or when possessions were stolen, they did not overreact. The Dani realised the coastal Papuans were as capable as the red men, but had brown skin and frizzy hair like themselves. The students were also spiritually sensitive, responding to the van der Stoeps' sincere faith and the chaplains' Evangelical teaching. The chaplains and their wives, the Drapers,

---

[15] Steiger, Wings over Shangri La, p. 134.
[16] R. Garnant, *Irian Jaya: The Transformation of a Melanesian Economy* (Canberra: Australian National University, 1974), p. 17.
[17] Personal conversation with Lukas, 1960.

Mountfords and Greens, taught the Bible and encouraged the young men to make their own personal commitment to follow Jesus.

The Staff

The van der Stoeps were an exceptional couple whose faith had preserved them through many amazing experiences prior to pioneering in the Baliem. They had been in the resistance in Holland during World War II. Nelis was once chased by a patrol after curfew. He ran into a house where a family was eating, dropping into a vacant chair as a plate was passed. When a German burst in there was no evidence of any thing untoward. The 'enlarged' family chatted about local issues until the coast cleared and Nelis could slip away. Tine's family provided shelter for a number of Jewish people with a bolt hole under the stairs. One of their guests died during the occupation and it was awkward to bury someone who was not even there! The only answer was to dispose of the body discreetly. Working as a district nurse, Tine dismembered the cadaver and carried packages containing its parts innocently on her bicycle on medical rounds to bury them clandestinely in the woods.[18]

Tine came to NNG as a nurse. She achieved local notoriety when the brakes failed on an ambulance she was driving, at the top of a steep hill leading down to Hollandia harbour. Activating the siren, she rode the vehicle down the hill, negotiating the many hairpin bends at ever increasing speed until eventually able to stop on the level ground in town. Nelis had been recruited from Holland to manage the schools on the north coast. They met and married at Joka, but, having no children of their own, found fulfilment in service.

The quintessential Dutch *domenie,* Nelis maintained an imposing magisterial presence that carried him through tense situations and while Tine was only slight she was also a force to be reckoned with. The local sorcerer, Pigarik Yoman, could see his power was threatened by Tine's medical clinic. He banned his people from attending and on one occasion climbed over the fence with a limb of wood to drive them out. Tine ordered him away and followed him as he went. He climbed the fence in a rage and threw the wood at her, bruising her shoulder.[19] But Tine's concern and compassion for her patients prevailed.

The Elephant in the Room

While relations between the Baptist missionaries and the Reformed teachers were generally excellent, there was one major contention. Many members of the 'Gereja Kristen Injili' (GKI), the Christian Evangelical Church that had been formed among the indigenous people on Reformed lines, held a form of

---

[18] Personal conversations with N. and T. van der Stoep, 1960.
[19] Steiger, Wings Over Shangri La, p. 136.

'folk-belief' surrounding infant baptism that was at odds with the Baptist practice of believer's baptism following spiritual rebirth. The mediaeval church had practised infant baptism and believed in baptismal regeneration. To correct this point of view the Reformers had taught that baptism was of no benefit without personal faith. Calvin saw regeneration as a life-long process.[20] The better educated GKI teachers and ministers grappled with Reformed theology concerning Christ's work in the soul, but the rank and file, only recently converted from animism, could be excused a tendency to believe the sacrament to be a new magic that of itself effected salvation.[21]

Groves lunched with the van der Stoeps each week day and the subject was often raised. Nelis struggled with Mountford's obvious desire to see the trainees make a personal commitment to Christ. While van der Stoep agreed that a decision to affirm faith could only be positive, he questioned whether that decision began one's Christian life and what it said about the hopes of the parents at their child's baptism? Mountford answered the concerns sensitively, affirming the parents' good intentions while comparing christening with presentation/dedication. He was then able to declare the need for personal affirmation. Each person could have the same experience as the first converts. The Baptists respected the van der Stoeps' opinions, but did not retreat from teaching a New Testament doctrine of salvation by grace through faith.

Yaap Euwema, having been recruited directly from Holland, understood the Reformed/Baptist issues. Several of Euwema's second-intake students made personal commitments through the combined influence of his gracious Christian attitude and the chaplain's Bible teaching. Another powerful influence, at that time, was the testimony and changed lives of Dani believers. A widespread movement of the Spirit of God that eventually touched the entire community in the North Baliem and beyond began at Tiom in 1961.

The Scheme Begins to Unravel

Political events are generally held to be responsible for the demise of the TCB and the unique partnership developing between Baptists and the Reformed Church and is partly true. The Dutch had encouraged Papuans to believe they would be granted self-government, and elections were held in 1961 for a house of representatives called the 'Nieuw-Guinea Raad' (New Guinea Council), with

---

[20] H. Burkhardt, 'Regeneration', in *New Dictionary of Theology*, ed. S.B. Ferguson and D.F. Wright (Leicester: IVP, 1988), p. 574.

[21] Ambivalence about baptism lies within one of the Reformed Church's earliest theological formulations, the 1561 Belgic Confession of Guide de Bres. Article 34 states: 'By baptism we are received into the church. As water washes the body...so the blood of Christ does the same to the soul. Ministers give us the (visible) sacrament...our Lord gives invisible grace. We believe children ought to be baptised and sealed with the the covenant.' *New Dictionary of Theology*, ed. Ferguson and Wright, p. 155.

twenty-two out of the twenty-eight members Papuan.[22] The proposition gained considerable support from Pacific Island states and African countries and won a majority at the UN General Assembly. Evangelical mission leaders had concerns about the intentions of this embryonic government, dominated as it would be by the GKI and Roman Catholics and awaited it taking office with some trepidation.

President Sukarno was even more concerned that his dream of a united Indonesia from Aceh (in the West) to Merauke (in the East) might slip away with the loss of the Dutch territory in New Guinea. At the time his new nation, throwing off the Dutch colonial yoke, was racked with secessionist turmoil and poor economic planning had produced rampant inflation of more than 600% per annum. To unite his people in a popular cause, Sukarno committed troops under General Soeharto to confront the old enemy in NNG. 'Volunteers' parachuted into the jungles and swamps of the south coast, most of whom were simply lost, never to be heard of again. According to Indonesian school text books, a legendary young woman from East Java met up with naked indigenous Irianese deep in the jungle, collaborating with them to defeat their Dutch oppressors.[23] In fact, starving survivors of paratroop sorties were regularly rescued by villagers and handed over to the Dutch military.

But Indonesia's financial commitment to defeating the Dutch was impressive. By August 1960 the Indonesians were thought to have secured $400,000,000 worth of Soviet arms.[24] The United States and Australia did not want either to be drawn into a war in which they would appear to be supporting colonialism or, on the other hand, fighting a North Atlantic Treaty Organisation member. After the United States reversed its stand of 'neutrality' and declared support for self-determination in March 1961 and Australia changed its policy position early in 1962 as well, they encouraged the Dutch to call it a day. This was a time of exacerbated international tension. The Cuban missile crisis was at its height, Dr Martin Luther King was facing his first arrest and it was an anxious time for the missions in West New Guinea. MAF had issued secret instructions providing details of last-resort evacuation plans if needed. But Melzer said: 'As we didn't use the plans I never discovered what they were.'[25]

By February 1962 the Kennedy administration had negotiated secretly with the UN and the Dutch to arrange a transfer of power to Indonesia. After that, an

---

[22] R. Chauvel and I. Bhakti, *The Papua Conflict: Jakarta's Perceptions and Policies* (Washington: East West Center, 2004), p. 9.

[23] Chauvel and Bhakti, *The Papua Conflict*, p. 12.

[24] N. Sharp, *The Rule of the Sword: The Story of West Irian* (Mitcham, Vic: Kibble Books, 1977), p. 42.

[25] Melzer, *In Pleasant Places*, p. 78.

'Act of Free Choice'[26] would allow the Papuans to make their own decision to join Indonesia or to become independent. The Netherlands' government was more than willing to quit the territory but needed this assurance as a face-saving gesture, even though it was widely understood to be 'political nonsense'. No one really believed that Papuans would ever be given an opportunity to choose their political future while under Indonesian control.

The handover to the United Nations Temporary Executive Authority (UNTEA) in 1962 prior to the Indonesian administration taking over government certainly produced significant anxiety and hardship for the teachers and trainees at the TCB. When it became obvious that the Dutch must return to Holland, an Ambonese, Godlief Pieter, was recruited with assistants Purba and Simatupang from Sumatra, to replace them. Unfortunately, the transition was tense and difficult. The Hollanders resented their imminent expulsion, taking out some of their bitterness on their Indonesian replacements, undermining their authority with the students and requiring Mountford and Green to fulfil an onerous disciplinary role with unsettled and rebellious young men.

Coup de Grâce

The major remaining difficulty plaguing the programme of co-operation between the Baptists and the GKI remained the denominational identity of the churches to be planted. While Draper and van der Stoep had trusted each other and had agreed that the churches to be planted would be Baptist, the rank and file maintained their own expectations. Draper had left the field in 1961and when the van der Stoeps quit for a new assignment in Africa in 1963, national church members encouraged TCB graduates to plant GKI congregations in conjunction with their schools. The missionaries believed that the problem could be resolved through discussion. In the Pit River area during 1963 a small number did commence (GKI) services in opposition to those of the Dani (Baptist) Bible School men but these problems were well on the way to being solved when the teachers left and the services were abandoned anyway.[27]

Ultimately, however, it was not the political upheaval or the theological issue that killed off the educational experiment, but the attitude of the 'faith' missions. Their prejudice against ABMS as a denominational entity allied with their criticism of any co-operation with the GKI was in the end responsible for scuttling the whole programme. In April 1963, an inter-missions conference was called to determine how the TCB and a wider village school programme would fit within the Indonesian government's education policy. ABMS was to be represented by Mountford as chaplain of the TCB at Tiom, ABMS general

---

[26] This referendum was initially ignored and then delayed, and when world opinion finally shamed Indonesia into complying with the UN requirement its blatant voter manipulation led to the occasion being widely described as an 'Act Free of Choice'.

[27] K. Green, diary entry, 25 April 1963 (transmitted by telephone).

secretary, John Williams, and Regional Committee secretary, Albert Dube. The Australian representatives had been advised by the Regional Committee in November 1962 to join the proposed educational foundation of the Missions Fellowship that was being set up in order to ensure that control of the TCB would remain in Evangelical hands,[28] although the delegation was empowered to discuss this on the field.[29] In discussions with the Reformed Church's head office staff in Java, Williams explained that 'Baptist Churches could not be integrated into a church based on the Reformed tradition but would be happy to co-operate as far as possible.'[30]

The attitude of the ABMS field staff was framed in a position paper drafted by Field Committee secretary, Charles Craig, in February 1963 to brief the members of the Australian delegation before they arrived. In it he raised the nature of the GKI, the original reasons for forming the TCB, risks of asset losses and control of the teachers.[31] Craig, from his base at Makki, felt some rivalry with the staff at Tiom.

A registered 'yayason' (foundation) was required as the entity to which the government could relate. Because the TCB had been established by Reformed Church personnel it was registered under the Education Foundation of the GKI. Dramatically 'in the Inter-Mission Conference ... UFM and RBMU opposed co-operation with the GKI declaring they were not a true church!'[32] With evident frustration Green asked of his diary, 'How long have UFM and RBMU been churches themselves? It is hoped that eventually a Dani church will commence but what will be its name? Its doctrinal basis? What will be its views on salvation and baptism, etc etc? Another denomination will be set up. Creating even more churches (denominations) demonstrates just how crazy is the thinking of those who are opposed to denominations.'[33] Because the faith missions would not join in work with the GKI, the Baptists had to choose their side.

The ABMS leaders vacillated for two weeks. The Missions Fellowship secretary, Harold Catto (CAMA), sent a letter to Mountford, dated 16 May 1963 stating that ABMS had not joined the new Inter Mission Foundation, but the authorities of the GKI claimed Williams and Dube had assured them that ABMS remained with them. Within a few weeks, however, ABMS officially switched loyalties and on 12 June, at the instigation of ABMS, Charles Craig

---

[28] ABMS New Guinea Regional Committee minutes, 23 November 1962, Global InterAction Archives, Melbourne (hereafter GIA).

[29] Personal conversation with J.D. Williams, 17 July 2009.

[30] J.D. Williams, 'Report on Visit to Djakarta', 13-16 March 1963.

[31] C. Craig, 'West New Guinea Field Council (letter to) General Secretary ABMS', 28 February 1963.

[32] Personal communication from Green, April 2009, GIA.

[33] Green, diary entry, 25April 1963, GIA.

refused permission for an appointee of the GKI to visit the TCB at Tiom. The GKI leadership was hurt by this slight and washed its hands of the problem.

The whole Baptist/Reformed Church programme was in total disarray. Most teachers returned to the coast, the TCB closed and the new Inter Mission Education Foundation insisted on re-interviewing all prospective teachers and applying strict new guidelines. The missions, instead of owning a functional educational system with trained, Evangelical, Dani-speaking teachers, were starting all over again and competing with established GKI, Catholic, Islamic and government systems.

With hindsight, greater transparency and co-operation with the inter-denominational missions covering issues other than mere comity agreements, might have produced better outcomes. Of special significance would have been earlier agreement on a secular education scheme involving the TCB and the Baptist village teacher programme of 1957. Under the heading 'Secular School Programs' at the inter-missions conference in April 1963 such a proposal came to be regarded *inter alia* as a combined Evangelical missions initiative that with superb irony the 'combined Evangelical missions' had just shut down.

The establishment and six-year operation of the TCB showed co-operation with the Reformed Church was possible. There were theological tensions, but the scheme achieved a great deal in exceptionally difficult political circumstances. In the end co-operation with the inter-denominational 'faith mission' societies at the same time as the Baptists were working with the Reformed Church produced a divisive and ultimately fatal triangulation.

CHAPTER 20

Baptists and Buddhists in Burma, 1813-2009

Samuel Ngun Ling

More than three centuries passed between the arrival of the first Roman Catholic mission in Burma in the sixteenth century[1] and the arrival of the first Protestant Christian mission, namely, the English Baptist mission in 1807. The first English Baptist missionaries, James Charter and Richard Mardon, were sent from India by the English Baptist Missionary Society[2] to see if a Baptist mission could be established in Burma, a country that had been ruled successively for centuries by Buddhist kings. They were then joined in 1808 by Felix Carey, son of William Carey, the famous English Baptist missionary in India, who later became known as the father of the modern missionary movement.[3] The English Baptist mission was faced, however, with failure because of the disintegration of the work carried out by Felix Carey and his fellows. The unfinished task of the English Baptist mission was taken up by the American Baptist mission led by Adoniram and Ann Judson who arrived in India at that time. It was during their voyage to India that the Judsons and their fellow missionary, Luther Rice, who were originally Congregationalists, changed their belief on infant baptism, adopted the doctrine of believer's baptism, and

---

[1] The first Roman Catholic mission under Pierre Bonfer, the French Franciscan mission pioneer, reached Burma in 1554, and returned in 1557. A group of Jesuit missionaries followed during the time of Fillipe de Brito, a Portuguese merchant, who arrived at Syriam with two Jesuit priests, Nicholas Pimento and Boves (1605-1688), and ruled Thanlyn city, which was located near Rangoon, as the viceroy. His descendants later became known as *bayinyis*, a name taken from the Persian language *feringhi*, meaning the Franks or Europeans. See Maung Kaung, 'The Beginnings of Christian Missionary Education in Burma, 1600-1824', *Journal of the Burma Research Society* XX, Part II, B (1930), pp. 62-63 (n.). See also G.E. Harvey, *History of Burma* (London: Longmans, Green and Co., 1925), pp. 348-349; D.G.E. Hall, *Burma* (London: Hutchinson's University Library, 1956), pp. 63-64.

[2] Brian Stanley, *The History of the Baptist Missionary Society* (Edinburgh: T. & T. Clark, 1992), p. 54

[3] B.R. Pearn, 'Felix Carey and the English Baptist Mission', *Journal of the Burma Research Society* XXVIII (1938), p.10.

became Baptists. They were all baptised by William Ward, a British Baptist missionary, on 6 September 1812 at the Lal Bazaar Chapel in Calcutta.[4] 'We are confirmed Baptists, not because we wanted to be, but because truth compelled us to be,' wrote Ann H. Judson.[5] As Baptists, their strong commitment to God's mission remained unwavering.

Less than a month after their arrival in India, on 17 June 1812, the Judsons were forced to leave as it was a time when the British East India Company banned the entry of missionaries, especially of Americans, to India.[6] When they prepared to leave India without knowing where to go, their first destination was actually Pulo Penang in the Straits of Malacca, rather than Burma. The only available ship in the harbour at that moment was the *Georgiana*, known as the 'crazy old vessel', which was bound for Rangoon, Burma. Undaunted, the young couple took the *Georgiana* on 22 June 1813, and made their voyage to Rangoon.[7] During their voyage, Ann Judson suffered from a severe attack of fever and almost died. Despite such experiences, the Judsons reached Burma after a month on the morning of 13 July 1813, to make this golden land their new home for the rest of their lives.[8] Soon after they arrived in Burma, they were appointed by the American Board of Commissioners for Foreign Missions as their first missionaries. The coming of the Judsons to Burma was not originally intentional but it was seen as providentially accidental.[9]

American Baptist Mission, British Colonisation and Buddhist Nationalism

It was during the reigns of six successive Burmese kings, namely, Bodawpaya (1782-1819), Bagyidaw (1819-1837),Tharrawaddy (1837-1846), Pagan (1846-1853), Mindon (1853-1878) and Thibaw (1878-1885), that the American Baptist missionaries launched their efforts in Burma. In his more than thirty years of service as an American Baptist missionary, Adoniram Judson spent most of his time in studying the Burmese language and in translating so that he hardly engaged personally in mission to the Buddhists in the Burmese kingdom. In his

---

[4] Courtney Anderson, *The Life of Adoniram Judson: To the Golden Shore* (Valley Forge: Judson Press, 1987), p. 146.

[5] Anderson, *Adoniram Judson*, p. 146.

[6] Edward Judson, *The Life of Adoniram Judson* (New York: Anson D.F. Randolph & Company, 1883), pp. 44-45.

[7] Judson, *Adoniram Judson*, pp. 47, 48.

[8] Maung Shwe Wa (Book I), Genevieve and Erville Sowards (Book II) (eds.), *Burma Baptist Chronicle* (Rangoon: Board of Publications, Burma Baptist Convention, 1963), pp. 1-4. This chronicle is a commemorative publication for the Sesquicentennial (1813-1963) Celebration in 1963. The Bi-Centenary (1813-2013) Celebration will be held in 2013, when the theme chosen by the Myanmar Baptist Convention is 'Your Will be Done in Myanmar'.

[9] *Missionary Cameralogs: Burma* (New York: American Baptist Foreign Mission Society, 1923), p. 16.

first conversation with a Burmese Buddhist king, Bagyidaw, Judson petitioned him for royal permission to propagate Christianity among Burman Buddhists, whose faith was strongly defended by the king against foreign interference. King Bagyidaw raised a number of questions with Judson regarding his missionary activity in the Burmese kingdom.

Most sympathetic with the work of the Christian missionaries among the Burmese kings was King Mindon. At the request of Anglican and Roman Catholic missionaries, King Mindon allowed them to build churches and schools including a high school and a college (St John College) for Burmese boys in the old capital, Mandalay, in Upper Burma. His patronage for the Anglicans was not designed to replace Buddhism with Christianity but to seek British favour following the loss of Lower Burma to the colonial power in 1852-53. A Burmese Buddhist historian praised the open-mindedness of King Mindon:

> Although the Christian missions were openly hostile to Buddhism, King Mindon had no prejudice against them and granted plots of land to the Reverend Dr. Mark, head of the English Society for the Propagation of the Gospel, and to Bishop Bigandet, head of the French Roman Catholic Mission, to enable them to build their churches and schools. He even sent his sons to study English under Dr. Mark.[10]

King Mindon was succeeded by King Thibaw, the last king of the Burmese dynasty, who was dethroned on 28 November 1885 by the British following the Third Anglo-Burmese War and exiled at Ratnagiri on the coast of India near Bombay, where he died in 1916. During his reign, the American Baptist mission operated in Lower Burma under British protection. Upper Burma was then annexed to British India by proclamation on 1 January 1886.[11]

During this period Judson set the pattern for missionary activities. His mission to the Buddhists can be divided into three categories. The first was his work in Buddhist literature and the Burmese language. Judson was quite aware of the fact that a foreign missionary needed to communicate the gospel of Christ to local peoples in their own terms and languages. In fact, literature and language formed Judson's first concern. In a letter of 1813 to his brother-in-law, Joseph Emerson,[12] Judson wrote: 'My only object at present is to prosecute, in a still, quiet manner, the study of the language, trusting that for all

---

[10] Maung Htin Aung, *A History of Burma* (New York: Columbia University Press, 1967), p. 241.

[11] John LeRoy Christian, 'Thibaw, Last King of Burma', *Far Eastern Quarterly* III. 4 (August, 1944), pp. 309-311.

[12] Joseph Emerson was the husband of Rebecca Hasseltine, the sister of Ann Judson, and was pastor of the Dane Street Church in Beverly, CA, USA, in Judson's time. Anderson, *Adoniram Judson*, pp. 80, 84, 113.

the future God will provide.'[13] Judson studied the Burmese language, Pali vocabularies and translation methods with two lay Buddhist teachers, U Aung Min and Maung Shwe Gnong.[14] Judson's translation of the Bible into Burmese could not have been accomplished without their assistance.[15] After a year and half of studying Burmese and Pali, Judson wrote, 'I have been here a year and a half and so extremely difficult is the language – perhaps the most difficult to a foreigner of any on the face of the earth, next to the Chinese that I find myself very inadequate to communicate divine truth intelligently.'[16] After two years, he again wrote, 'I just now begin to see my way forward in this language, and hope that two or three years more will make it somewhat familiar;…For a European or American to acquire a living oriental language, root and branch, and make it his own, is quite a different thing from his acquiring a cognate language of the West….I once had occasion to devote about two months to the study of French. I have now been about two years engaged on the Burman; but if I were to choose between a Burman and French book to be examined in, without previous study, I should, without the least hesitation, choose the French.'[17]

After four years of hard study in Burmese language and in Buddhist Pali, Judson started writing and printing gospel tracts in Burmese. He then translated the Bible, beginning with the Gospel of Matthew, and completed the first draft of the entire Bible in January 1834. The final revision went to press in 1840. The American Baptist Foreign Mission Society gave special recognition to Judson's translation work, stating, 'Judson's Bible is to the Burmans what Luther's is to the Germans and the translation of 1611 to readers of the English language.'[18] Judson's translation of the Bible was and is still considered by both Buddhist and Christian Burmese scholars to be one of the finest existing examples of the classical Burmese language at its best. In the remaining years of his life, especially from 1845 when he came back from a visit to America, Judson came to be fully occupied with work on English-Burmese and Burmese-English dictionaries. He completed the former before he died, and the latter was published after his death (12 April 1850) by E.A. Stevens at Moulmein in 1852.[19] By 1913, the centenary of the Judsons' arrival, the Bible was already

---

[13] Judson to Joseph Emerson, 7 January 1814, quoted in Judson, *Adoniram Judson*, p. 78.
[14] Maung Shwe Wa, *Burma Baptist Chronicle*, p. 12.
[15] Randolph L. Howard, *Baptists in Burma* (Philadelphia: Judson Press, 1931), p. 9.
[16] Howard, *Baptists in Burma*, p. 30.
[17] Judson to Lucius Bolles, 16 January, 1816, in Judson, *Adoniram Judson*, 89. See also James D. Knowles, *Memoirs of Mrs. Ann H. Judson: Late Missionary to Burmah* (Boston: Lincoln & Edmanns, 1831), pp. 148-49.
[18] *Missionary Cameralogs: Burma*, p. 22.
[19] F.G. Dickason, ' Preface', in *Judson's Burmese-English Dictionary* ed. Robert C. Stevenson and F.H. Eveleth (Rangoon: Baptist Board of Publications, 1953).

translated and printed in six different local dialects in Burma.[20] One of the most impressive of Judson's literary works, both in his translated Bible and in his composition of the tracts, was his expression of the gospel message in terms comprehensible to native readers and in a form suitable to the Buddhist socio-cultural context. He was able to employ a number of Buddhist Pali terms in the Burmese Bible whose meaning reflected the local Buddhist language, literature and culture.[21]

Judson's public mission began only after he had become acquainted with the Burmese language. His mission methods to the Buddhists then included both the circulation of Christian tracts and personal dialogue with the Buddhists at a *zayat* (dialogue house),[22] which Judson erected in 1819 after the Burmese Buddhist fashion on a hill adjoining his mission house, facing the main road that leads to the great Shwetagon Pagoda.[23] Ann Judson reported to her parents:

> The *zayat* is situated 30 or 40 rods from the Mission House, and in dimensions, is 27 by 18 feet. It is raised 4 feet from the ground, and divided into three parts. The first part is laid entirely open to the road, without doors, windows, or a partition in the front side, and takes up the third part of the whole building. It is made of bamboo and thatch, and is a place where Mr. Judson sits all the day long...The next and middle part, is a large airy room with four doors and four windows opening in opposite directions, made entirely of boards, and is white-washed to distinguish it from the other *zayat* around us. In this room, we have public

---

[20] Robert G. Torbet, *Venture of Faith* (Philadelphia: Judson Press, 1955), p. 227. The six versions of local dialects were Burmese (by Adoniram Judson), Pwo Karen (by Durlin Brayton), Sgaw Karen (by Francis Mason), Shan (by Josiah Cushing), Kachin (by Ola Hanson) and Mon or Talaing (by James Haswell and Robert Halliday).

[21] The Pali terms used in Judson's Burmese translation of the Bible include contextualised terms such as *Dhamma saya*, which originally means 'teacher of the teachings of Gautama the Buddha' and is used for 'servant of God' in 2 Cor. 6:10; *U-poh neih,* which originally means 'Buddhist devotion day' and is used for 'sabbath' in Mk 2:23, 27-28; and *Anan-dah-tha-kho*, which originally means 'the divine power of one of the Buddhist deities' known as *Anan-dah* and is used for 'Almighty' in Rev. 11:17, 15:3. 16:7. Judson also used the Buddhist honorific form *dow* in his Burmese Bible. To mention a few instances, he uses *dow* with the Trinitarian God (*kha-me-dow; taa-dow; than-shin-thaw-wih-ngin-dow*) in Mt. 28:19; *dow* with 'logos', the word of God (*hnok-kap-pat-dow*) in John 1:14; *daw* with the glory of God (*bun-dow*) in 2 Cor. 6: 17; and *dow* with the disciples of Christ (*tha-peik-dow*) in Mk 14:17-18.

[22] *Zayat* is a Burmese Buddhist term for a small building, often with a platform, erected beside a road or a street for a shelter or a rest house or for public accommodation. The word seems to have originated from the Burmese word *sa-yat*, a combination of *sa* (eat) and *yat* (rest or stop), which implies 'a rest place for a meal' or 'a stop to eat'. See *Judson's Burmese-English Dictionary*, ed. Stevenson and Eveleth, p. 425.

[23] Today this road is called Shwedagon Paya road.

worship in Burman on the Sabbath; the third and last room is only an entry way which opens into the garden which leads to the Mission House.[24]

On 4 April 1819 Judson held the first public service in the form of a dialogue with a congregation of fifteen persons. This *zayat*, the first dialogue house erected by the American Baptists in Burma for the worship of God, had a platform designed contextually in Burmese Buddhist architectural style, where Judson would have an open conversation with the Buddhists.[25] It was at this dialogue house that Judson engaged in dialogue with the Buddhist pilgrims and passers-by on religious issues. Judson used to set aside a time to spend with visitors at this *zayat*:

> My time, for the last few months, has been divided between reading Burman, writing some portions of Scripture, and other things preparatory to public worship, holding *zayat* (as the Burman call it), or place of public resort, where we intend to spend much of our time, and where we hope to have an attempt under this Government...And should this *zayat* prove to be a Christian meeting-house, the first erected in this land of atheists, for the worship of God – a house where Burmans, who now deny the very existence of Deity, shall assemble to adore the majesty of heaven, and to sing with hearts of devotion the praises of the incarnate Savior – But.....Can this darkness be removed? Can these dry bones live? [26]

A few months after the opening of the *zayat*, a number of curious visitors came to hear, to enquire and to learn from Judson about the Christian religion. The gospel thus spread out to more and more people, and a number of enquiries were received daily from people of different backgrounds.

Among the enquirers was Maung Nau, the first Burmese Buddhist convert, who had a serious dialogue with Judson at the *zayat*. A missionary colleague of Judson, named Colman, explained his first experience with Maung Nau:

> Maung Nau came to the *zayat*, sat behind the company...after visiting brother Judson several times, he became considerably affected, and at last, discovered some true penitence on account of sin...when it was attempted to convey instruction to his mind on the subject of God, he would reply, 'I never heard of the true God before. Had I been acquainted with his character, I would not have sinned against him,'...the religion of Gautama provides no atonement...There is no way of avoiding punishment. But here is a religion that discovers a way by which

---

[24] Ann Judson to her parents, 4 August-8 December 1819, in *American Baptist Magazine and Missionary Intelligencer* 1:10 (July, 1820), p. 380.

[25] Jonathan Wade's Journal, 20 June 1828, in *American Baptist Magazine and Missionary Intelligencer* IX:2 (November, 1829), p. 415.

[26] Ann Judson to the Corresponding Secretary, 20 February 1819, in Judson, *Adoniram Judson*, p. 123.

we can be delivered from the consequences of sin, Jesus the Son of the eternal God has suffered in our stead, and redeemed us by his own blood.[27]

Maung Nau was thus won eventually to Christ after six years of Judson's labour. On 6 June 1819 he wrote to Judson asking for the ordinance of baptism. This letter, the first confession of faith by a Burman Buddhist convert, naturally used Buddhist forms of expression. The letter read:

> I, Maung Nau, approach your feet...I believe, that the divine Son, Jesus Christ, suffered death, in the place of men, to atone for their sins....I feel my sins are very many....Since it is so, do you, sirs, consider, that I, taking refuge in the merits of the Lord Jesus Christ, and receiving baptism, in order to become his disciple, shall dwell one with yourselves... in the happiness of heaven, and (therefore) grant me the ordinance of baptism...[28]

The method of dialogue was proving effective.

Judson also undertook dialogue with the Burmese king. Although no official record was made of any audience with other Burmese kings, Judson had a religious conversation with King Bagyidaw three times during his mission in the Burmese kingdom. King Bagyidaw (1819-1838), grandson of King Bodawpaya, succeeded to the throne in 1819. Judson's first dialogue with the ruler occurred in on 27 January 1820 when he petitioned the king for religious tolerance towards the American Baptist mission and Christian converts. He approached the king with a present of an English Bible in six volumes, covered with gold leaf in Burmese style and with each volume enclosed in a rich wrapper. Several pieces of fine cloth and other articles were also taken as presents for members of the government. Judson and his fellows were received at the palace gate, where they first introduced themselves as propagators of religion and asked that they be allowed to appear before the king to present the sacred book, which was accompanied with a petition. But Judson's effort to secure religious toleration from the king at this time was not successful. He reported:

> The important interview with the emperor is past. The result is the most unfavorable. His majesty refused our petition, and sent us away from his capital. 'No toleration to any foreign religion,' is the standing policy of the Burman government. Every Burman subject who renounces the established religion of the empire is liable to imprisonment, torture and death.[29]

---

[27] Mr Colman to E. Lincoln, 14 June 1819, in *American Baptist Magazine and Missionary Intelligencer*, I:8 (March, 1820), pp. 287-88.

[28] Judson to one of the editors, 28 June 1819, in *American Baptist Magazine and Missionary Intelligencer*, I:8 (March, 1820), p. 290.

[29] Judson to Thomas Baldwin, 16 March 1820, in *American Baptist Magazine and Missionary Intelligencer* I:12 (November, 1820), p. 435.

Judson's second dialogue with the king took place on 1 October 1822, when the ruler invited Jonathan Price, a medical doctor,[30] to the capital with Adoniram Judson as his interpreter. As they arrived at royal palace, the visitors were met by the king and after a moment the king asked Judson, 'And you in black, what are you? A medical man, too?' to which Judson replied, 'Not a medical man, but a teacher of religion, your majesty.' As the king continued by asking him whether any had embraced the Christian religion, Judson immediately replied, 'Not here.' The king persisted, 'Are there any in Rangoon?' and Judson replied, 'There are a few.' 'Are they foreigners?' the king kept asking. Judson trembled at this point since he feared that his answer to this question might bring some trouble to the church he had established. But Judson decided that 'the truth must be sacrificed, or the consequences hazarded'. So he replied, 'There are some foreigners, and some Burmans.' The king remained silent for a few seconds, but soon showed that he was not discontented by asking other questions on religion, geography and astrology.[31] In this way, Judson boldly witnessed to the gospel before the Burmese king and his officers, though his witness proved unnoticed by them.

Judson's third dialogue with the king took place on Christmas Day 1822. This time Judson initiated a visit to the king's court. On this occasion the king asked him four crucial questions: 'Are Judson's Christians real Burmans?' 'Do they dress like other Burmans?' 'How does Judson preach?' and 'What does Judson have to say of Gautama Buddha?' The first question was concerned with social and political issues. The king's primary concern was to clarify whether the Burmans still remained Burmans when they became Christians. Judson assured the king by explaining that there was no change of status, race or nationality on becoming a Christian. The second question was cultural. The king wanted to know whether Burman Christians still looked like other Burmans. To this question, Judson replied: 'Yes, they dressed like other Burmans; they wore *longyis* (long skirts for men), and *eingyis* (shirts) just like their fellow countrymen.'[32] The third question was quite ecclesiastical. The king wanted to know how Judson worshipped. To this question, Judson explained, 'I began with a form of worship, which first ascribes glory to God, and then describes the commands of the law of the Gospel, after which I stopped.' The last question asked by the king was most potentially dangerous for Judson. The question was religious and the king wanted to know Judson's views on the religion of Gautama, which the Burmese kings had protected and

---

[30] Jonathan Price was born a Presbyterian and educated at Princeton. As part of his preparation for a missionary life, he studied medicine in Philadelphia, where he became a Baptist. It was Price's medical knowledge that was responsible for securing the missionaries an audience with the king.

[31] 'Dr. Judson's Journal', 21 August 1822, in *American Baptist Magazine and Missionary Interlligencer* IV:6 (November, 1823), p. 211.

[32] Maung Shwe Wa, *Burma Baptist Chronicle*, p. 42.

propagated for many centuries. No matter how dangerous it was, Judson did not hesitate in responding, 'we all knew he was the son of King *Thog-dau-dah-nah*; that we regarded him as a wise man and a great teacher, but did not call him God'.[33] Listening to Judson's reply, the king remained silent, and after a while, he abruptly arose and left. What the king really thought about Judson's answer was not known.

Identifying the Christian Missionaries as Colonial Agents

A fundamental problem that confronted the American Baptist mission in Judson's time and over subsequent years was the perception of the missionaries as colonial agents. As the first American Baptist missionaries in Burma, the Judsons were suspiciously eyed by nationalist Buddhists as companions of the British intruders who had invaded Burma and had enslaved the Burmese under their iron-heel colonial rule. The Burmese Buddhist nationalists considered Judson, his fellow missionaries and their Christian converts as an expression of the power of the British Indian Empire. In fact, in the eyes of Burmese Buddhist nationalists, the British colonial administrators, the American Baptist missionaries and their Christian converts were the same. Such a political suspicion was intensified when the Judsons happened to receive their monthly allowance through the East India Company, suggesting a connection with the British administration in Burma.[34] There was further intensification when Judson served the British as interpreter in the peace negotiation known as 'Treaty of Yandabo' which was held on 24 February 1826 between the British and the defeated Burmese King Bagyidaw. What Judson as a missionary expected from this treaty was, first of all, to make peace between the two countries, Britain and Burma, and second, to open up doors for the Baptist mission to evangelise Buddhists in Burma. At this point, Judson seemed not to be aware of the problems he would face in his future mission if he worked closely with the British rulers. 'This gentleman (Dr. Judson),' wrote a British administrator, 'avows himself predisposed for war, as the best if not the only means of eventually introducing the humanizing influence of the Christian religion.'[35] His determination to work as an interpreter for the Treaty of Yandabo was,

---

[33] *American Baptist Magazine and Missionary Intelligencer*, IV:6 (November, 1823), p. 216.

[34] *The Religious Tract Society, The White Foreigners From Over the Water: The Story of the American Mission to the Burmese and the Karens* (London: The Religious Tract Society, n. d.), pp. 68, 71.

[35] Helen G. Trager, *Burma through Alien Eyes: Missionary Views of the Burmese in the Nineteenth Century* (London: Asia Publishing House, 1966), p. ix. The foreword was written by a Burmese scholar and anthropologist by the name of Maung Htin Aung who had served as the vice-chancellor of the University of Rangoon and chairman of the Burma Historical Commission.

however, not necessarily because he supported the British colonisation of Burma, but because he was the only foreigner who could speak Burmese well at this time. Judson's political involvement in this peace treaty was opposed neither by the American Baptist Foreign Mission Society nor by his Baptist missionary fellows who joined him later. Nevertheless the result was that the Baptist mission came to be labelled as a pro-British colonial movement. U Pe Maung Tin, a prominent Burmese Christian scholar, explained it:

> The Buddhists of Burma blame the Christian missionaries for causing as they say in Burmese, the division of blood among Burmese. A Burman is synonymous with a Buddhist, and so when a Burman turns Christian he is looked upon with suspicion; he is pro-British, pro-American, a traitor to Burma...[36]

A further reason for identifying American Baptist missionaries as agents of British colonisation was that they often took political protection from the British. They saw the British conquest as God's providential chance for the expansion of Christianity, interpreted the British conquest as their own conquest[37] and did not repudiate the British colonisation. 'The American Baptist mission,' wrote D.M. Smeaton, a British official, about imperial authority, 'proved to be its loyal ally in Burma, for the missionaries identified themselves with the all-conquering Englishmen.'[38] Not only the missionaries but also the first Christian converts, particularly the Karen Christians (mainly Baptists), took sides with the British soldiers in fighting against the Burmese independence movement. As the Karen Christians openly declared that they fought for the British, they were singled out by the Burmese Buddhist nationalists as non-patriotic or stooges of Western imperialism. Among the British officials who first used the term 'Loyal Karen' was Smeaton. He clearly stated,

> The Karen people are at heart loyal to us, and have proved their loyalty by freely shedding their blood in defence of our rule and in the cause of order...The story of the deeds and sufferings of the Karens in defence of the Queen-Empress's government in Burma...deserves an honored place in the records of the Empire.[39]

In fact, for Buddhist nationalists, the American Baptist missionaries, their new converts (mainly Karen Baptists) and the British intruders were simply different groups who worked together for the same colonial scheme known as

---

[36] A.C. Bouquet, *The Christian Faith and Non-Christian Religions* (London: James Nisbet and Co., 1958), p. 291.
[37] S.B. Gitterington, *History of our Baptist Missions in Burma* (Washington: American Baptist Publication Society, 1892), p. 49.
[38] Maung Htin Aung, *A History of Burma* (New York: Columbia University Press, 1967), p. 224.
[39] D.M. Smeaton, *The Loyal Karens of Burma* (London: Kegan Paul, Trench, Trubner & Co., 1920), pp. 9-10, 11.

the white men's 3-M scheme, which means 'Merchant, Military and Missionary'.[40] In the histories of other nations, it was not unusual for colonial rulers to precede missionaries of the cross and for the flag of the nation to go in advance of the banner of Christianity.[41] In Burma, however, British colonial rule came first and then was followed by the Baptist mission. The British colonial administrators and the American Baptist missionaries worked together for the same purpose of subjecting the people to their different interests, in the former case political and in the latter spiritual.

Why was the Christian mission seen as part of the colonial scheme? The first reason was because of the alliance of Christian missionaries with the British rulers. The authorities tried to incorporate the work of Christian missionaries into their administrative framework in the hope that the missionaries' efforts might improve several sectors of Burma's national life. The British government fully supported, for instance, nationwide educational work by the American Baptist mission, employing some missionaries in their respective mission fields as inspectors of schools. Thus Herbert J. Cope, an American Baptist missionary at Tedim, Chin state, was appointed the inspector of schools for the whole Chin Hills in the 1920s. Cope formalised the Chin scripts in three dialects of the Northern Chin Hills, Hakha, Laizo and Tedim, and his innovation has been taught in the vernacular schools in the locality since 1925.[42] The second reason for suspicion of the Baptist mission arose from the Buddhist ideology of Burmese nationalism that rejected all foreign intrusions including the Christian mission. It was an undeniable fact that the American Baptist mission and the British colonisation came together to Burma in the same period. Because of such a coincidence, the Burmese Buddhists could not understand how to separate the Christian mission from colonisation. In their eyes, both American Baptist missionaries and British colonial administrators were defenders of the Christian faith who were strongly opposed to Buddhist nationalism. In fact, whenever the Burmese read the Christian mission with the eyes of a Buddhist nationalist, they definitely found it a destructive foreign element that could threaten the values of Burmese Buddhist society.

Only a few missionaries and administrators in the colonial period could foresee the need for the contextualisation of the church in an independent Burma. The urgency of this need was pointed out by U Hla Bu, a great native Burmese leader. Professor Hla Bu was the first national principal of the Judson Baptist College and later the chairman of the department of philosophy at the

---

[40] Samuel Ngun Ling, *Communicating Christ in Myanmar: Issues, Interactions and Perspectives* (Yangon: ATEM, 2005), p. 35.

[41] H.P. Cocharane, *Among the Burmans: A Record of Fifty Years of work and Fruitage* (New York: Orbis Book, 1904), p. 152.

[42] C. Thang Za Tuan, 'Some Reflections on Christianity and Formal Education in the Chin Hills', in Cung Lian Hup (ed.), *Thinking About Christianity and the Chins in Myanmar* (Yangon: Editor, 1999), p. 52.

University of Rangoon. During a period of service as Henry W. Luce Professor of World Christianity (1959-1960) at the Union Theological Seminary in New York he pointed out

> that the church in Asia is suspected of denationalization and tends to be regarded as an alien community. It has therefore become imperative for the Asian Church to be itself, to domesticate its work and worship, to witness in indigenous ways and endeavor to be really the 'salt of the earth' and 'the light of the world.'[43]

As Buddhists cannot understand nationality apart from their religion, it is natural that they tend to see Christians as disloyal citizens of their Buddhist society. Donald E. Smith was right when he stated, 'The Burmese people cannot think of nationality apart from the religion that they hold, for it is Buddhism which welded the Burmese together and the idea of a nation-hood owes its inception to Buddhism.'[44] Many Buddhists identify Christians as anti-Buddhists, pro-Americans and even traitors to the nation. In a typical Burmese Buddhist context, to become a Christian means to become a foreigner and to abandon Buddhist identity. The following remark of Pe Maung Tin, a prominent Burmese Christian scholar, may be helpful for a better understanding of the alienation of Christianity from the bulk of the population in Burma:

> The Buddhists of Burma blame the Christian missionaries for causing as they say in Burmese, the division of blood among Burmese. A Burman is synonymous with a Buddhist, and so when a Burman turns Christian he (or she) is looked upon with suspicion; he or she is pro-British, pro-American, a traitor to Burma...[45]

In fact, the strong spirit of nationalism led Buddhist nationalists to think that the Christians were betrayers of the nation simply because they denounced Buddhism, which they thought to be the core of nationalism. These people also thought of the Christian religion as a remnant of British colonisation that could rise again to exploit the nation culturally and politically. Again, the movements of Christian Karen and Kachin insurgencies were believed to be stimulated by their missionaries. 'Because the leaders of the rebellious Karen National Union were for the most part Baptist Christians and the outbreak started in three mission centers, the Burmese government tend to blame the American missionaries and dub the uprising the Baptist rebellion.'[46] The ethnic Christians, including the Karen and Kachin, had interpreted the British

---

[43] U Hla Bu, 'The Luncheon Address', *Union Theological Seminary Quarterly Review* XV.2 (11 January 1960), pp. 120-21.
[44] Donald Eugene Smith, *Religion and Politics in Burma* (Princeton: Princeton University Press, 1960), p. 82.
[45] Trager, *Burma Through Alien Eyes*, p. ix.
[46] John F. Cady, *A History of Modern Burma* (Ithaca, NY: Cornell University Press, 1958), p. 596.

conquest as God's sign that Buddhism was to be destroyed forever.[47] Because of the escalating misconceptions and misunderstanding between the Christians and Buddhists, the Christians came to be treated as second-class citizens on their own soil.

Post-Judson Period (1850-1948): Baptists and Buddhist Nationalism

Once the British colonisation of Burma began in 1886, the British authorities made a clean sweep of the older Buddhist system, abolishing not only the Buddhist court but also the ecclesiastical commissions.[48] The Buddhists feared that their centuries-old faith and tradition would swiftly disappear under alien rule, and these fears increased when the British rulers disestablished the Buddhist church and replaced it with their imperial institutions.[49] The Buddhist monastic schools that served as the keystone of the Buddhist educational system were disestablished and even replaced by Christian missionary and Anglo-Burmese schools where the Buddhists and Buddhism were reported to be belittled and even ridiculed.[50] Because the colonial government abolished the organisation of the *Sangha* (the Council of the Buddhist Monks) and denied the legitimate status of Buddhism as an official religion, the traditional monarchical pattern of church and state collapsed. The reactions of Buddhists and Christians in regard to the disestablishment were totally different. While the Buddhists felt endangered in their socio-cultural existence because of the loss of their Buddhist institutions and monastery education,[51] the ethnic Christians tended to look to the Baptist mission as what gave them a place in the sun.[52] The Baptists were alienated from the mainstream of national life.

The rise of Buddhist nationalism (1900-1947) combined with a resurgence of Buddhist tradition, culture and literature. The Buddhist nationalists including the monks took leadership in mass struggles for independence against the British intruders, strongly opposing all foreign and non-Buddhist elements.

Christianity, particularly the American Baptist mission, in this nationalistic period was strongly opposed as a religion of the imperialists and the Christians were politically suspect as supporters of the British Indian Empire. National identity in the period was re-defined as patriotism against external (foreign

---

[47] Letter of J.B. Vinton, 28 February, 1886, quoted in Smeaton, *Loyal Karens*, pp. 14-15.
[48] John F. Cady, 'Religion and Politics in Modern Burma', *Far Eastern Quarterly* XII (February 1953), p. 153.
[49] C.P. FitzGerald, *A Concise History of East Asia* (New York: Frederick A. Praeger, 1966), pp. 253-54.
[50] FitzGerald, *Concise History of East Asia*, p. 240.
[51] *Report of the Administration of Burma, 1929-30* (Rangoon: Gov. Printing Office, 1930), pp. vi-ix.
[52] San C. Po, *Burma and the Karens* (London: Elliot Stock, 1928), pp. 38-39.

intruders) and internal (ethnic insurgents) destructive elements.[53] There were new Buddhist movements such as the Young Men's Buddhist Association, which was organised in 1906 on the Christian model of the Young Men's Christian Association with the objective of re-shaping valuable elements of the Buddhist tradition in the context of Western learning and standards.[54] It later developed into a larger organisation called the General Council of Burmese Associations, a body which was strongly influenced by the religious-political movement of a prominent Burmese Buddhist monk, U Ottama.[55] Burmese Buddhism in this period appeared to be politically aggressive and therefore instrumental in a series of political uprisings led by the Buddhist nationalists and political monks against the British rulers.

Democracy and Religious Conflict

Burma regained independence from the British in 1948. The country, for the first time, enjoyed democratic elections and self-rule under U Nu, the first elected Prime Minister of Burma, from 1948 to 1962. During this short democratic period, freedom of worship, freedom of speech and freedom of the press were fully in operation. U Nu made it clear that all religions were given equal rights to profess their faith. In an address given to a conference of the Burma Baptist Convention in October 1954, U Nu strongly urged the Baptist leaders of the Christian community and the leaders of the Burmese Union that he would entrust them with an assignment to practise the forbearance taught by Lord Buddha and by Jesus Christ, and to work for religious harmony and for the increasing stability of the Union.[56] He made an apology to the Baptists for mistaken rumours critical of the American mission and urged all religious peoples in Burma to stand for unity. His address went as follows:

> If there is any instance whereby the government suppresses the profession of any religion in the Union, please bring it to my notice....I want to mention a very sad instance of...a piece of news...that the Union Government was bullying the adherents of the American Baptist Mission...there is not a vestige of truth in this rumor... Among the insurgents...there are Baptists [i.e. the Karen] as well as Buddhists and adherents of other religions...they are suppressed not on account of the religion they profess but for the obvious fact that they are taking up arms against the government...As a Buddhist, I am prepared to give my life, if necessary, for the defense of Buddhism...in the same spirit, I, as Prime Minister,

---

[53] Smith, *Religion and Politics in Burma*, p. 85.
[54] John F. Cady, *Southeast Asia: Its Historical Development* (New York: McGraw-Hill Book Company, 1964), p. 403.
[55] Fred R. von der Mehden, *Religion and Nationalism in Southeast Asia* (Madison: University of Wisconsin Press, 1968), pp. 134-35. See also U Ba Yin, *U Ottama* (in Burmese) (Rangoon: Thamaeittha Press, n.d).
[56] *Burma Weekly Bulletin* (20 October 1954).

am prepared to defend any religion professed by any section of the people in the Union of Burma.[57]

U Nu's short leadership ended with the issue of making Buddhism the state religion, which was promulgated as law on 26 August 1961.[58] This constitutional amendment included two bills: one declaring Buddhism to be the state religion and making the government responsible for the protection and promotion of the religion; the other, a State Religion Promotion Bill, empowering the government to provide compulsory teaching of Buddhism to all Buddhist students, to close government offices on the Buddhist sabbath and to provide images of the Buddha in every court building. Article 13, Section 21, of this 1961 constitutional amendment reads as follows: 'Buddhism being the religion professed by the great majority of the citizens of the Union shall be the State Religion, and...'.[59] To protect this constitutional amendment on state Buddhism, U Nu tried to restore the traditional Buddhist pattern which had been de-institutionalised by the British colonialists. Between 1954 and 1956, he had convened the two-year-long World Sixth Buddhist Synod at Rangoon, commemorating the 2500th anniversary of the *Maha-parinibbana* (Entering *Nibbana*) of the Buddha. For this event, U Nu built a great *Kaba-Aye pagoda*, meaning 'World Peace Pagoda', in a location seven miles from Rangoon, and many Burmese Buddhists viewed it as a great event of the 'Golden Age'.[60]

U Nu's scheme of making Buddhism the state religion caused a disintegration of religious harmony and a rise of internal conflict within the national leadership.[61] This conflict exacerbated problems caused by ethnic insurrections, of the Karen in 1949 and the Kachin in 1962. The Burmese army, fearful that the non-Burman tribes such as the Karen, Kachin, Chin, Shan, Mon and Rakhine would break away from the Union, took power in a military *coup d'état* on 2 March 1962, installing a military revolutionary government under General Ne Win.[62] This revolutionary council introduced a new programme of 'The Burmese Way to Socialism', and formed the single political party called the 'Burma Socialist Programme Party' (BSPP) in the same year.[63]

---

[57] U Nu's speech delivered at the YMCA annual meeting on 11 February 1950, in *From Peace to Stability* trans. Thakin Nu (Rangoon: Ministry of Information, 1951), p. 73.
[58] Smith, *Religion and Politics in Burma*, pp. 230-31.
[59] Von der Mehden, *Religion and Nationalism*, p. 105.
[60] Emmanuel Sarkisyanz, *Buddhist Backgrounds of the Burmese Revolution* (The Hague: Martinus Nijhoff, 1965), pp. 206-209.
[61] Von der Mehden, *Religion and Nationalism*, p. 102.
[62] Hnin-ketaya, *Burmese Administrations: From the Nineteenth Century to the Twentieth Century A.D.* (in Burmese) (Yangon: Mya-watti Press, 1993), p. 205.
[63] Maung Maung, *Burma and General Ne Win* (Bombay: Asia Publishing Company, 1964), p. 5.

Baptists and Socialism (1962-1987)

The U Nu period was succeeded by Ne Win's socialist period (1962-1987). Ne Win's 'Burmese Way to Socialism' could otherwise be interpreted as the 'Burmese Way to Burmanisation'. Burmanising all religious and ethnic language minority groups culturally, socially and politically became a priority. In 1964 all foreign Christian missionaries including teachers, medical doctors and humanitarian social workers were ordered without any reason to leave the country, and all mission schools, Christian hospitals, foreign banks, private schools, national mass media and commercial enterprises were nationalised in the following year. From the time of nationalisation, Baptist missionary education was replaced by a new socialist educational system whose ideologies and philosophies were based solely on the teachings of Theravada Buddhism and its *Abhidhamma* philosophy. In the pre-socialist period, the languages of minority groups were allowed to be taught for five years in primary schools. But during the socialist period, the minority languages were allowed to be taught only for three years. The Burman ethnic language (Burmese) became not only the official common language of all ethnic groups of the Union but also the only medium of instruction for all education in Burma. The study of Burman language (*Mianma-sa* in Burmese), in which Buddhist Pali, myths, legends and stories are included, came to be taught as compulsory at all levels of schools from primary to high school. Ne Win abandoned U Nu's idea of making Buddhism the state religion and made a new constitution in 1974, which guaranteed the 'right of everyone to profess and practice his or her religion freely'. Yet Buddhism continued to enjoy a special position under the patronage of the socialist government.[64] In the past, the *Sangha*, the council of monks, was endowed with a special power to play mediation roles between the state and the public. It was through this *Sangha* that the king and the Buddhist monks could work together for various state affairs. The *Sangha* and the state were interdependent in that the *Sangha* took the responsibility of keeping the state steadfast to Buddhist teaching and the state took the responsibility of protecting, preserving and purifying the *Sangha*.[65] In the socialist period the structure of the *Sangha* changed from its old monastic model to a new type of ecclesiastical pattern, which came to be known in Burmese as *Tha-tha-na-baing*.[66] Special favouritism continued to be given to Buddhism by the socialist government and this favouritism eventually came to be recognised as a special

---

[64] Maung Htin Aung, *History of Burma*, p. 327.
[65] Donald K. Swearer, *The Buddhist World of Southeast Asia* (New York: State University of New York Press, 1995), p. 64.
[66] The Burmese term *Tha-tha-na-baing*, used with reference to the Pali word *Sasana*, which means 'the lord or owner of the Buddhist religion', was not very much appreciated by the native Burmese Buddhists, for they assumed that the Buddhist faith could not be owned by any body. The term they preferred is *Buddha Tha-tha-na Saungh* which means 'Guard of Buddhist Faith.'

power reserved for Buddhism which would, in turn, limit the freedom and rights of other religious and minority ethnic groups. The resulting high degree of participation by Buddhist leaders in national politics had not gone unchallenged in the past. A number of Buddhist monks and laymen, alike, used to oppose the *Sangha's* active involvement in national politics as they believed that such an involvement was contrary in theory to the original teachings of the founder.[67] More orthodox and conservative Theravada Buddhist monks in this line used to view the *Sangha* and state not only as mutually exclusive but also as opposing domains based on the Buddhist distinction between *lawki* (secular and worldly) and *lawkottara* (sacred and otherworldly).[68]

The separation of church and state and the secularisation of the government, which were the original intention of General Aung San, who had negotiated Burmese independence in 1947, were ignored in socialist period. The unconstitutional and unofficial recognition of Buddhism as the state religion continues to persist in the minds of a majority of Buddhists even up to the present day. Since Buddhism under Ne Win enjoyed special favour, freedom of other religions like Christianity, Islam and Hinduism was subject to the control of the government limited by certain restrictions. Baptist pastors were free to preach, for instance, but their preaching had to be restricted to the non-political and had to avoid any anti-Buddhist tone. The churches were free to worship, but only within the compound of the church. Christian literature could be published, but only with a limited circulation. Bibles in different ethnic languages were not allowed to be printed in the country, and so they had to be printed outside the country in India, China, Hong Kong and Malaysia. Only a limited number of church leaders were allowed to obtain travel documents either for attending overseas Christian conferences or for further studies.

Until the end of Ne Win period, the Baptist churches were growing in number, especially among ethnic minority groups. These people with an animistic background tended to be more adaptable to Christianity than the majority people with a Buddhist background. It was in this socialist period that the Baptist and other churches had to struggle very hard for the preservation of their own existence. The need for theological responses to Burmese socialism and Buddhist nationalism forced the Christian churches to re-examine their expression of the Christian message in all aspects of life and action. In other words, the young Baptist churches in this period were challenged to look at the fundamental questions that were concerned not only with their existence but also with their roles in relation to the larger Buddhist community. The church was being established under national leadership, practising the three Baptist principles of self-government, self-propagation and self-support. The Baptist

---

[67] Than Tun, 'Mahakassapa and his Tradition', *Journal of the Burma Research Society*. 42, Part II (1959), p. 114.

[68] Melford E. Spiro, *Buddhism and Society: A Great Tradition and Its Burmese Vicissitudes* (Berkeley: University of California Press, 1982), pp. 392-93.

churches continued to grow among the major ethnic groups, the Karen, Chin and Kachin, and the number in church membership increased every year.

Baptists and Post-Socialist Militarism (1987-2009)

Ne Win's three-decades-long socialist rule ended in 1987 and was followed from August 1988 by a new military regime, the 'State Law and Order Restoration Council' (SLORC), with General Saw Maung as its first president. Leaders of this regime held the same aims as Ne Win, their predecessor. Their original scheme was to restore the traditional monarchy with a democratic system, and to legitimise their government with the support of the people, rather as in countries like Thailand, Japan and England.[69] In this period Aung San Suu Kyi, the leader of National League for Democracy Party, which won a landside victory in the 1990 general elections, was denied power and detained under house arrest for about two decades.[70] The recipient of the 1991 Nobel Peace Prize for her non-violent democracy movements in Burma, she was described by the *Economist* magazine as Asia's Mandela.[71]

Buddhism continues to play a significant role at both government and community levels. The Buddhist philosophy of 'to be an authentic Burmese is to be a Buddhist'[72] continued to dominate the psyche of majority Burmans, whose Buddhist world-views, thought forms, ways of life and belief-systems remained unchanged. As a faithful successor of the previous socialist government, the post-socialist military government repeatedly makes a claim that there is freedom of worship and no discrimination on religious grounds. But Buddhism, which before was a religion simply favoured by the socialist government, is now not only reaffirmed by the succeeding military government, but it also enjoys a *special distinctiveness or status* over other religions, and has the state's backing as before in all its activities.

The ideology of this *special status* or favoured religion tends to minimise the freedom of other *unfavoured* religions, those which do not have *special status*, although the government claims to expect all religions to flourish together peacefully and harmoniously.[73] Upholding this *special status* claim, the

---

[69] *Asian Week* (November, 1990), p. 27.

[70] Aung San Suu Kyi, *Freedom from Fear and Other Writings* (New York: Penguin Books, 1991). See also Bruce Matthews, 'Buddhism Under a Military Regime', *Asian Survey* 33:.4 (1993), pp. 408-23. .

[71] *Economist* (15-21 July, 1995), p. 11.

[72] Gerald H. Anderson, *Christ and Crisis in Southeast Asia* (New York: Friendship Press, 1968), pp. 22-23.

[73] Samuel Ngun Ling, 'Our Hope and Their Hope: Reading Amos' Justice Message in Myanmar Context', *CTC Bulletin*, Bulletin of the Program Area on Faith, Mission and Unity (Theological Concerns), Christian Conference of Asia, XXIII:2 (August, 2007), p. 68.

government launched a new movement to propagate Buddhism, taking any possible step to make Buddhist belief and Buddhist philosophy known to all ethnic groups, most of whom were already Christians. This movement, called *Buddhist Taungtan Tatana* in Burmese, which means 'Buddhist Mission to the Hill Regions', was a counter-mission being carried out aggressively among ethnic Christians with a strong back-up by the government in all its activities.[74] The only aim of this movement was to convert all ethnic Christians, especially the Baptists, back to Buddhism to make the whole of Burma a Buddhist land. To help fulfil this master plan, the military government tried to use every possible means. Many Christian children and parents from poor family backgrounds were openly persuaded, for instance, to become Buddhists by promising them needed food, education, jobs and so on. Such is the situation in which the Baptists and Buddhists in Burma have so often encountered each other, ending sometimes in tension and confrontation. In a number of mission fields in the lower part of Burma, especially in Rakhine state, it has been reported that some local Baptist missionaries were often confronted with oppression, arrest and even imprisonment just because they were Christian missionaries and were trying to convert the Buddhists, while the Buddhist monks and missionaries who were sent to the ethnic Christian areas were neither oppressed nor arrested.

This post-socialist military government reaffirmed the use of the Burmese language as the official common language of all ethnic groups of the Union and as the medium of instruction for all education in Burma. The languages of minority groups which were taught for three years in primary schools during the socialist period were now not allowed to be taught at all. A crucial problem for minority ethnic Christians was not necessarily the use of Burmese as a common language but the government's attempts to eliminate the long existing languages of minority ethnic Christians,[75] which are considered an essential part of their social existence and cultural identity.

Mission and Theology: Post-Missionary Period

By the time when the American Baptist missionaries arrived in Burma (1813), Theravada Buddhism and folk religions such as *Nat* worship (*Nat* means 'spirit' in Burmese) were already flourishing. Hence there was no religious gap on Burmese soil for the Christian religion to fill. It was in this context that

---

[74] Samuel Ngun Ling, *Communicating Christ in Myanmar: Issues, Interactions and Perspectives* (Yangon, Myanmar: Asociation for Theological Education in Myanmar, 2005), p.70.

[75] Samuel N. Lynn (Samuel Ngun Ling), 'Voices of Minority Ethnic Christians in Myanmar', in *CTC Bulletin,* Bulletin, Bulletin of the Program Area on Faith, Mission and Unity (Theological Concerns), Christian Conference of Asia, XVIII:2 –XIX:2 (December, 2002 – August, 2003), p. 17.

Adoniram Judson claimed, 'It is more difficult for a Burman to become a Christian than it is to extract a tooth from a tiger's mouth.'[76] Nevertheless, Judson was able to bring a single Buddhist soul to Christ in the person of Maung Nau in 1819, that is after six years of his missionary service in Burma. Judson's lack of success among the Burman Buddhists was due not to the weaknesses of his mission strategies but most significantly to the rooting of Theravada Buddhism in the soul of the Burman people since the eleventh century. Helen G. Trager described that situation as follows:

> Dr. Judson and his missionaries also felt frustrated because they found among the Burmese no religious vacuum which their religion could fill. Since the beginning of their history, the Burmese had professed Buddhism, one of the noblest faiths mankind has ever known, and the Burmese way of life itself had always been under the all pervading influence of Buddhism... As years passed and their endeavors among the Burmese continued to meet with failure, the missionaries were forced to seek converts in the remote areas where Buddhism had not penetrated and where the pre-Buddhist religion of animism still prevailed.[77]

Although the Buddhists, to whom the Judsons were primarily sent, denied God's salvation message, their reaction opened a way of salvation for the non-Buddhist ethnic groups. It was reported that there were over seven thousand Baptist converts during the lifetime of Adoniram Judson.

From the end of Judson's period into the twentieth century, the American Baptist missionaries continued their work with renewed mission zeal for Burma and extended their mission to the tribal/ethnic peoples with animistic backgrounds who reside in the mountainous regions and in the remote border areas. Statistically speaking, there are altogether more than a million Baptists in number, 4,522 local churches, 120 local associations, and 18 language and regional conventions under the Myanmar Baptist Convention.[78] The growth of Baptist churches continues to be viewed with suspicion by the government not only as part of the Western cultural and political dominance in the country but also as part of the foreign support for an inrenal development which the government banned after nationalisation in 1965.

Contextualisation of the Church and Mission

In response to the challenges made by the unexpected expulsion of their missionaries, by the negative impacts of British colonial rule upon the churches, and further by the anti-Christian movements of Burmese socialism, the Baptist churches in Burma tried to maintain their denominational identity

---

[76] Paul D. Clasper, *Christianity and Buddhism* (Rangoon: Thudhama Press, 1960), p. 10.
[77] Trager, *Burma through Alien Eyes*, p. xi.
[78] Simon Pau Khan En, 'The Ecumenical Perspective of Christianity by the Churches in Myanmar', in *RAYS MIT Journal of Theology*, 10 (January, 2009), p. 22.

based on the practice of three Baptist self-dependent principles: self-support, self-propagation and self-governance. These Baptist principles are predominantly Western-oriented. That is also true of the Baptist translation of doctrine into practice, in the understanding of dimensions of the church such as the form of worship and the structure of church organisation (ecclesiology), in the ideas of God and his salvation (theology) and in the concepts of mission and strategies of mission outreach (missiology). This Western orientation came to the Baptist churches not only through their missionaries' teaching but also through the influence of their colonial rulers, administrators and civil educators. That is why Professor Erick Sharpe, a former missionary to India, described Burma's situation as being 'tarred with a colonialist brush'.[79] As the churches took shape alongside the cultures and religions of other faith communities, the Baptist churches began to feel the need to practise not only *self-propagation* but also *self-theologising*, that is, *contextualisation* of Baptist belief and tradition, theology and mission, and faith and practice in relevance and response to the challenges and needs of the context. In this process of contextualisation, the Baptist churches took steps to re-consider the whole patterns of their inherited tradition, faith and practice. Contextualisation requires of the Baptist and other Christian churches to deconstruct all Western thought forms, Western forms of worship and Western structures of the churches, and at the same time to reconstruct them in a Burmese way and thought forms with the use of Burmese religious/ cultural resources. This work of theological reconstruction, namely, the deconstruction and reconstruction of missionary Christianity, was the main theological task that the Baptist and other churches had been undertaking since the beginning of post-missionary period. The Baptist churches had determined to stand on their own feet for survival on the basis of three Baptist *principles* that we have indicated above. It was from this post-missionary period that the Baptist churches began to have Bibles, hymn books and liturgical readings translated into various local terms and ethnic languages, and worship styles, pastoral leadership manners, sermons, music, song composition and many other activities restructured in indigenous forms, contextual styles and local tones. *Self-theologising* had thus become a theological task required of post-colonial churches. In this process of self-theologising, the Baptist churches are forced to rethink their theological stand on the relationship between church and society, and to begin to take new steps to engage in community building. The churches would need to remove the so-called 'missionary-compound mentality' that always looks to the West alone for a model of life and value. This kind of mentality does not take sufficient notice of the Buddhists but views them rather as objects of missionary love,

---

[79] Samuel Ngun Ling, 'The Encounter of Missionary Christianity with Resurgent Buddhism in Post-Colonial Myanmar', *Quest: An Interdisciplinary Journal for Asian Christian Scholars, Religion and Globalization*, 2:2 (November, 2003), pp. 66-67.

concern and preaching.[80] The Baptists are to abandon such an exclusive and arrogant mentality or *holier-than-thou* attitude that makes them feel superior to their neighbours of other faith communities.[81] It is this exclusive Christian mentality that has led to very little attention being paid to the questions and challenges posed by people of other faiths in present-day Burma.

It is, therefore, important for the Baptist churches in Burma, first of all, to liberate themselves from the exclusive theological framework of the West and, secondly, to pursue a new theological reconstruction that is more relevant to the Burmese Buddhist context. A majority of Baptists in Burma today are not deeply convinced about the need to relate Christian faith and practice to current socio-politico-economic issues, though these issues are closely linked with religious community life as a whole. Contextualisation at this point represents the reality of 'here and now' that deals with all issues and challenges that are facing the Baptist churches today. It will redirect the Christian mission to shift its paradigm from a proselytising form of mission to a dialogical form of mission which cares for all peoples and respects all religions. We need a mission that does not look down on non-Christian neighbours and their religions; that is, one that is not bent on condemning good non-Christians to hell. The Baptist churches in Burma do not need a proselytising evangelism that calls arrogantly for statistics of conversions but a servant-modelled mission that is carried out with genuine Christian love and humility.[82]

Interfaith Dialogue and Baptist Mission

When the American Baptist missionaries came to Burma, they came with the existing ideologies and theologies of their own time. Their exclusive understanding of mission in relation to culture, their dualistic understanding of the church and the world, their otherworldly interpretation of salvation and spirituality, and their holier-than-thou attitudes towards peoples of other faiths proved the fact that they belonged to the old school of nineteenth-century theology. They are not to be blamed today for what they believed and practised as they were the product of their own time. While there were valuable things that they did for peoples of the Third World countries, there were also regrettable estimates that they made of cultures, religions and traditions of peoples in those countries. To speak from the experience of Burma, the American Baptist missionary theology did not seem to provide much room for intercultural studies of tribal peoples and issues of interfaith relations, especially Christian-Buddhist dialogue, while they carried out holistic mission among tribal peoples in Burma.

---

[80] *Southeast Asia Journal of Theology* 3:2 (October, 1961), p. 28.
[81] *Southeast Asia Journal of Theology* 3:2, p. 68.
[82] Ling, *Communicating Christ*, pp. 70-71.

The encounter of the American Baptist mission with the challenges and issues of the various periods made its missionaries significantly defensive in their approach, exclusive in their theological thinking and alienated in their relationship with other faiths. It was Adoniram Judson, however, who tried to adopt a dialogue model of mission in reaching the Buddhists in Burma. His initiative was the beginning of the story of Baptist-Buddhist dialogue in Burma. Judson's idea of mission to the Buddhists through dialogue was, however, neglected by later Baptist missionaries and young national Christian leaders in post-missionary Burma. Among reasons for this discontinuation was the confinement of the Baptist mission to culturally and politically distinct tribal and religious groups. When culturally diverse ethnic groups with different local languages in Burma responded to the Baptist mission in different ways, multicultural versions of Christianity have come up, creating internal divisions on racial and religious lines. The American Baptist mission in this respect divided peoples into groups on racial and cultural lines, and hence as the churches grew, they became separated not only from each other but they also became isolated more and more from the larger Buddhist society. That is a reason why the Baptists and Buddhists need to come together for dialogue to remove isolationism and alienation, to build a healthy relationship and to strive for common growth.

From Selfhood to Ecumenical Relationship

When the Baptist churches came to suffer from nationalisation in 1965, with the unexpected expulsion of their missionaries, they were faced with the great difficulty of preserving their own identity. The period from 1965 to the end of the socialist period, about two decades long, constituted the silent years of the churches in independent Burma. The Baptist churches during this period tried to maintain their own selfhood based on three Baptist self-principles. There were fears that all the churches would be swept out by nationalisation and that the Christians would suffer from severe persecution. These fears flew away when the socialist government made a new constitution in 1974, which guaranteed the 'right of everyone to profess and practise his or her religion freely'. It was only after 1974 that the Christian churches in Burma began to revive themselves anew with enthusiastic missionary zeal, refreshed ideas of ecumenism (unity in diversity) and church development. All the churches' activities and mission movements during this early socialist period were carried out only on a racial and regional basis.

The Kachin Baptist Convention celebrated the hundredth anniversary of the arrival of the American Kachin Baptist missionaries on 21-25 December 1977 at Naung Nan, Myitkyina in Kachin State.[83] The theme of the celebration was,

---

[83] The first missionary couple assigned from America for work among the Kachins were Albert J. Lyon and his wife, who arrived at Bhamo on 13 February 1878. Tragically,

'Remember the days of the old, consider the days of many generations...' (Deut. 32:7). It was during this specific centennial celebration that a hundred ordained pastors baptised 6,214 persons within an hour in the Irrawaddy River.[84] As an outcome of this centennial celebration, there came the birth of a regional mission, commonly known as three years three hundred mission (3/300 mission), on 24 December 1977. The founding father of this 3/300 mission was M. Janaw who served as president of the Kachin Baptist Convention at that time. 3/300 mission meant the selection of three hundred volunteers for three years of mission, without pay. Divided into eight groups for seven mission fields, 3/300 missionaries were thereby sent to work from 1978 to 1981. The three successive themes of this mission were: 1978 Jesus serves; 1979 Jesus frees; 1980 Jesus unites. The total number of converts from animistic and Buddhist backgrounds to the Baptists was estimated to be altogether about 7,638 persons.[85]

In a similar vein but with different visions, the Chin Christians began to launch their national mission programme known as 'Chin for Christ in One Century' (CCOC) with effect from 1983 and completed it with a great success in 1999, with the result of making about 98% of the Chin people Christian in a century. The aims and objects of this historic mission were: (1) to preach the salvation message to all Chin people before the end of the century, (2) To have the existing Baptist churches renewed and even empowered for the furtherance of God's mission among the Southern Chins, (3) To celebrate the centenary of the arrival of the first American Baptist missionary couple[86] and (4) To continue, after the celebration of the centenary, doing mission among the non-Chins after the year 2000. To accomplish the above aims and objects, the Zomi Baptist Convention laid out five programmes to be carried out as follows: (1) To preach the gospel among southern Chins, 1983-86; (2) To establish new churches, 1986-89; (3) To enable the new churches to become self-supporting, 1989-92; (4) To form regional associations, 1992-95; (5) To strengthen regional associations and to prepare them for 1999 centenary celebration.[87] Myanmar Golden Mission to the Buddhists, which was launched by the Myanmar Baptist Convention in 2000, has made steady progress, although it has been faced with

---

because of his serious illness, Lyon passed away within one month of his arrival at Bhamo. Lyon was replaced, after a year, by William Henry Roberts who, with his wife, arrived in Bhamo on 12 January 1879. See Wa and Sowards (eds), *Burma Baptist Chronicle*, pp. 368-69. See also Herman G. Tegenfeldt, *A Century of Growth: The Kachin Baptist Church of Burma* (Pasadena, California: William Carey Library, 1974), pp. 97-100.

[84] Mading Hkaw Sau, '3/300 Mission of Kachin Baptist Convention' (Myanmar Institute of Theology B.D thesis, 1990), p. 15.

[85] Trager, *Burma through Alien Eyes*, pp. 22-45, 114.

[86] The first American missionary couple to the Chins, Arthur and Laura Carson, arrived at Hakha, Chin State, on 15 March 1899. See *Burma Baptist Chronicle*, pp. 383-87.

[87] Zomi Theological College, *Chin Church History* (Falam: ZTC, 2007), p. 220.

unprecedented challenges from the Buddhist communities and also certain reactions from the local authorities.

When the churches grow on racial and cultural lines, racial-based divisions of the churches followed. This unpopular tradition of 'divided missions' began with the missionaries, following the 'divide and rule' colonial policy of the British Indian Empire. The Baptist missionaries concentrated, for instance, on reducing the local languages of their missionaries' centres to a written form, but lacked a vision for the future of those they evangelised as people with dignity, identity and unity. Their visionless missions resulted in shameful and divisive competition and schism among the regional churches of different Christian mission fields. Again, fearing that the ethnic people would have no influence in society if Christianity were represented overwhelmingly by the poorest and the most ignorant elements (though this has actually happened today), the missionaries and mission administrators were not much concerned about the growth of Christianity among them.[88] This idea was completely opposed to the original idea of mission as servanthood. Hence, divisions introduced by Western missions later became major disruptive factors, especially for self-supporting Baptist churches in post-socialist Myanmar. An ecumenical call for unity and solidarity of the churches, therefore, becomes a great demand and also a challenge for all the Baptist and non-Baptist denominations in Burma.[89]

Beginning in the socialist period, the idea of the ecumenical movement emerged in Burma under the leadership of the Burma Christian Council, which today is the Myanmar Council of Churches.[90] The young church leaders, Bible school teachers, and seminary professors during this socialist period developed theology by identifying the Christian concept of 'God's kingdom' with socialist ideals.[91] Indigenous theology, Asian theology and ecumenical theology began to be taught at theological schools and seminaries. The native Christian theologians like U Hla Bu, U Pe Twin, U Kyaw Than, U Khin Maung Din, U Tha Din and other church leaders sought a wider scope for Christian theology by employing Buddhist concepts or categories of faith within the framework of Christian theology to make it more at home to Buddhist thinkers to whom the Christian message was preached. Khin Maung Din's essay 'Some Problems and

---

[88] Charles W. Norman (ed.), *Christianity in the Non-Western World* (Englewood Cliffs, NJ: Prentice Hall, Inc., 1967), pp. 52-53.

[89] Samuel Ngun Ling, 'Communicating Christ Cross-Culturally: A Dialogical Approach to Mission and Theology in 21st Century Myanmar', in *Our Theological Journey: Writings in Honor of Dr. Anna May Say Pa* (Yangon: Festschrift Committee, MIT, 2006), pp. 36-37.

[90] U Kyaw Than, 'Theologizing for Selfhood and Service', in *Asian Voices in Christian Theology*, ed. Gerald H. Anderson (New York: Orbis Books, 1976), p. 54.

[91] Alan Saw U, 'Justing Love', in *Living Theology in Asia*, ed. John England (Maryknoll, NY: Orbis Books, 1982), p. 136.

Possibilities for Burmese Christian Theology Today' (1975)[92] and Kyaw Than's 'Theologizing for Selfhood and Service' (1976)[93] reflected the development of inclusive Christian theology in socialist Burma. Along with the shift in Christian theology and mission at the educated level, Christian mission grew among the illiterate tribal peoples in the frontier areas of Burma. There was no record of Christian persecution in Burma in the socialist period, though the successive governments never lost sight of their suspicions of any Christian movement.

Concluding Remarks: The Future of the Christian-Buddhist Relationship

Burma (Myanmar), known as a hermit nation, is a country where the two wheels of Dhamma (Buddha) and Logos (Christ) have rolled together peacefully, but at a certain distance. Owing to this situation of peaceful co-existence and the lack of any real encounter, the churches, organisations and theological institutions in Burma have been too silent theologically for almost two centuries. In fact, it is time for Myanmar Christians to liberate themselves from the ideological captivity of their Western missionaries' theological thinking and to lift their theological voices in their own context. To do a contextual theology in the Burmese Buddhist setting would mean to take into very serious consideration Buddhist philosophy, culture, belief and practice. To put it in other words, any doing theology in Burma cannot ignore the theological significance of Christian-Buddhist relations, their mutual impacts and interactions. This implies that any theology practised in Burma today ought to be a dialogical theology, a theology that is informed and shaped by inter-religious experiences or a theology which is self-consciously dialogical in content and orientation. It is imperative, therefore, that Burmese Christians develop a theology in dialogue with theologies of other faiths in order to help articulate a genuine contextual theology out of the interfaith encounter. The common socio-political experiences of the Buddhists and the Christians during the war and postwar periods have forced them to take common action against the fundamental issues that have confronted them (for example, environmental crisis, health care, religious freedom) in Burmese society, so that the two religious communities have been compelled to develop mutual understanding and inter-religious co-operation.[94]

The practice of theology in Burma cannot be meaningful unless it takes seriously into account the importance of interfaith relations and their impact on community building and interpersonal relationships. In Burmese Buddhist

---

[92] Khin Maung Din, 'Some Problems and Possibilities for Burmese Christian Theology Today', in *Christianity and the Religions of the East: Models for a Dynamic Relationship*, ed. Richard W. Rousseau (Scranton, PA: Ridge Row Press, 1982), Vol. I., pp. 77-89.
[93] U Kyaw Than, 'Theologizing for Selfhood and Service', p. 54.
[94] U Kyaw Than, 'Theologizing for Selfhood and Service', pp. 59-60.

culture, the person-to-person relationship is more important than the religion-to-religion relationship. In fact, in its first stage, building a good interpersonal relationship is more important than undertaking interreligious co-operation and dialogue. If there is no healthy relationship between religious persons, there will be no peace between their religions.[95] In this respect, dialogue between persons plays a significant role in building a peaceful interreligious community. Dialogue at this point means partners of different religions thinking and acting together for building a healthy human environment and relationship. Dialogue is not a conceptual meeting of religions but is a creative relationship of persons who adhere to the different teachings of those religions. Its very nature stems from the profound recognition of the mutuality of common life.[96] Wilfred Cantwell Smith insists that inter-religious dialogue is fundamentally the concern of religious persons, that is, a person-centred approach.[97] In fact, as long as the Baptists and Buddhists take defensive and hostile approaches toward each other, it is evident that an unhealthy relationship between the two religions will persist in the future and, finally, no peaceful relationship between the Baptists and the Buddhists will be ever possible. Building a peaceful and democratic future in Burma would depend very much on how healthy and free a relationship the Burmese government would be able to build between the majority Buddhists and the minority religious peoples like the Christians and Muslims. If there is no healthy and free relationship between religious peoples, there will be no inter-religious cooperation, and if there is no inter-religious co-operation, there will be no peace in the community. In fact, any practice of contextual theology in Burma must be inter-religiously redemptive rather than offensive. The central focus of a contextual theology of liberation in Burma should be to set at liberty the poor, the oppressed and the marginalised in order to demonstrate solidarity with the powerless masses in their struggles for justice, peace and freedom. Any kind of Burmese theology must enable the grassroots peoples to rediscover their lost human dignity, rights and identity.

---

[95] Samuel Ngun Ling, 'Interfaith Dialogue: Theological Explorations from Myanmar Context', in *Ecumenical Resources for Dialogue between Christians and Neighbors of other Faiths in Myanmar*, ed. Samuel Ngun Ling (Yangon: Judson Research Center, MIT, 2004), p. 31.
[96] Samuel Ngun Ling, 'Encounter of Missionary Christianity', pp. 71-72.
[97] Wilfred Cantwell Smith, *Religious Diversity* (New York: Crossroad, 1982), pp. xviii, xix.

CHAPTER 21

Baptists and New Christian Movements in West Africa

Matthews A. Ojo

After over 180 years of the Baptist faith in West Africa, there are indications that Baptists are facing a number of challenges regarding the Baptist heritage. While some Baptist churches insist on maintaining Baptist heritage, some are ready to adapt to contemporary Christianity. The irony is that in many cases Baptist churches want to remain Baptist but are, to a great extent, accepting doctrinal emphases and practices of other Christian traditions. They normally keep the Baptist distinctive of the baptism of believers by immersion. Others who have joined Baptist churches as adults have noticed the consistency of Evangelical messages preached in Baptist churches, or the demonstrable equality of members in meetings in Baptist churches as part of Baptist distinctiveness. Although it is rather difficult to determine the level of awareness among West African Baptists, in general, of their own distinctiveness, one recurring denominator of Baptist heritage is the emphasis among West African Baptists on the autonomy of the local church and the congregational polity that gives equality to every member to participate in the decision-making of his or her local church.

It is this interest about Baptist distinctiveness and the challenge this heritage has faced since the 1970s that has informed this paper about Baptists and New Christian Movements in West Africa. The paper examines the growth of the Baptist faith in selected West African countries, and further examines the relationships that exist between Baptists and other Christian bodies in the region. Particular attention is paid to the contemporary Pentecostal and charismatic movements and their impact on the Baptist faith. I wish to argue that contemporary Baptists in West Africa hold on to two different values or religious cultures simultaneously. However, these values have not yet been welded together; hence from time to time conflicting situations arise as each value seeks relevance and tries to supplant the other. The first religious culture is the Baptist heritage formulated over four hundred years of Christian experience and theological reflection which in its manifestations includes equality of all believers within a congregational polity, autonomy of the local church as self-governing, the centrality of the scriptures as a determinant of doctrines and Christian conduct, believer's baptism upon a public affirmation of faith in the vicarious death of Christ, separation between church and state and a certain pietistic ethos. While not abandoning their Baptist heritage, West African Baptists have, since the mid-1970s, appropriated some doctrinal emphases and practices of Pentecostals. This new religious culture is characterised by emotionalism in worship with singing and dancing to modern musical instruments, and the culture of pomp, grandeur and beauty, particularly among pastors, which is characteristic of modern Pentecostalism in Africa. Furthermore, there is a quest for deeper experience connected with the baptism of the Holy Spirit, the affirmation of miracles and the miraculous and the demonstration of power – whether construed as healing or 'breakthrough' or 'deliverance' – and the quest to utilise spirituality to address existential needs about life and living, whether in its traditional moorings or in its modern perspectives. This utilitarian view of spirituality finds some congruence with the general aspirations of the traditional African quest for long life, wealth, power, success and fame in a competitive, but dislocated, society. However, it contrasts sharply with the substantive conservative Evangelical spirituality of deep theological thinking. The dilemma of either maintaining a rational theological tradition or exalting religious experience above other things has caused the dissipation of much energy among West African Baptists in the last three decades.

'New Christian Movements' is so general a term that it is hard to apply it with any certainty to our present enquiry, and the sociological term 'New Religious Movements' is also an umbrella term for an overwhelming diversity of religious phenomena. However, what is 'new' to many observers of African Christianity is the independent Pentecostal and charismatic churches and organisations. Hence, I will largely restrict the term to this religious phenomenon. Independent Pentecostal and charismatic churches in West Africa are of different varieties. Some are this-worldly and publicity-seeking while others are world-rejecting and sectarian. However, what is common is that they first emerged in the 1970s and centred their spirituality on a new interpretation of the events in Acts 2. They claimed a new religious experience often attributed to the baptism of the Holy Spirit, as a second experience after conversion, which is evidenced by speaking in tongues, and the exercise of the gifts of the Holy Spirit, principally the gift of healing. The methods they utilise to broadcast their message and enlist members are equally new – using marketing strategies and investing greatly in media publicity and in large open-air evangelistic services. They are, therefore, new and different from the existing Christian traditions – the Roman Catholic Church, the mainline Protestant churches and the African Indigenous Churches.

There are, generally, four types of Baptist bodies or traditions in West Africa. The largest are the Baptists forming the mainstream and are, largely, represented by the national conventions in each country. Almost all were the results of the missionary enterprise of the Southern Baptist Convention and other Baptist bodies from Europe and North America in the nineteenth century or early twentieth century. From the late 1980s, other similar Baptist bodies have surfaced in Ghana and Sierra Leone. The second are the Fundamentalist Baptist congregations whose beginnings were in the 1960s, in Ghana, and 1980s, in Nigeria. In Ghana, they have formed the Association of Fundamentalist Baptist Churches which has a seminary for training its own crop of ministers. The Fundamentalist Baptists have also been growing, though slowly, since the early 1990s with newer congregations. Both in Ghana and Nigeria, Fundamentalist Baptist churches are small, usually with an average of 100 members. The Free Will Baptists started in Nigeria in 2006 when a Nigerian who had been resident in the United States and had been worshipping with the Free Will Baptists returned to Nigeria and established the first Free Will Baptist church. By early 2009, there were six churches in some villages in southwestern Nigeria. The Indigenous Baptist groups which were formed as a result of schisms from other Baptist bodies over doctrinal issues or cultural nuances constitute the fourth group. In the 1930s and 1940s certain churches, calling themselves the 'African Baptist Church', were formed after seceding from the national convention in Nigeria when polygamists were excluded from holding leadership positions in the Nigerian Baptist Convention. The Gospel Baptist Conference was established in 1974 over the failed leadership quest of one of the Nigerian Baptist Convention leaders, while the Upper Room Baptist Church and the Evangelical Baptist Church were formed over disagreements over Pentecostal doctrines and practices. Attention in this paper will focus on the national Baptist conventions because they are more visible and there are ample records about their activities.

Baptist Beginnings and Growth in West Africa

While accurate statistics of religious affiliation in Africa are difficult to come by, a conservative estimate, provided in 1995, put the population of Baptists in fourteen West African countries at 775,673 members and 6,171 churches, of which 80% were found in Nigeria.[1] A recent and much more reliable estimate from the Nigerian Baptist Convention indicated about 6,000 churches in Nigeria alone.[2] With a membership numbering about four million, Nigerian Baptists are perhaps the second largest Baptist group in the world, next only to the Southern Baptist Convention.[3] Of the estimated 52 million Christians in

---

[1] Albert W. Wardin (ed.), *Baptists Around the World* (Nashville, TN: Broadman & Holman, 1995), pp. 11, 67.

[2] *National Church Census: Pilot Project Report* (Ibadan: Nigerian Baptist Convention, 2007), p. 1.

[3] A base count carried out by the Nigerian Baptist Convention and the International Missions Board of the Southern Baptist Convention in the late 1990s indicated Nigerian Baptist churches to be 5,814. See *National Church Census: Pilot Project Report*, p.1. It

Nigeria, the Baptists are second only to the Anglicans with about 6 million adherents, though the Nigerian Baptists are more dynamic in missionary commitment than any other Protestant denomination in the country.

Although Nigeria has the largest Baptist population, Sierra Leone and Liberia had Baptist congregations as far back as 1792 and 1822, respectively. The abolitionist movement from the late eighteenth century promoted the colonisation project which was funded by the British crown in order to repatriate freed slaves to their homelands. Consequently, Freetown was founded in 1786 by the British government. Among the emigrants to Freetown, there was a Baptist preacher from Canada who gathered a small congregation among the emigrants in 1792. For a few years, there was support from the Baptist Missionary Society in England but the church was abandoned about 1797 due to lack of supervision.[4] However, in Liberia, there has been a continuous history of Baptists since 1822, when two ex-slaves, Lott Cary and Collin Teague, went to Liberia under the sponsorship of the African Baptist Missionary Society of Richmond, Virginia. This initial effort of freed slaves led to the establishment of Providence Baptist Church in Providence Island (later Monrovia) among the emigrants who had come from North America.[5] A number of American missionary organisations, including the Southern Baptist Convention, sent missionaries and supported the mission work in Liberia from 1826 till the twentieth century.

A new era opened for the Liberian Baptists when Dr William R. Tolbert served as the president of the Baptist World Alliance (BWA) from 1965 to 1970.[6] During his tenure in the BWA, he also served as the vice-president of the Republic of Liberia, and from 1972 was the president of the country. While in this leadership position in the BWA, an invitation was extended to Southern Baptist Convention to commence additional missionary work in Liberia. The Southern Baptists responded and sent missionaries from the early 1970s, which eventually helped Liberian Baptists to expand in educational ministries, evangelism, church development, mass media ministries and theological education.[7] However, this progress was stopped by the Liberian civil war which began in 1989.

---

is best to accept this as an estimate rather than an actual figure because a national census of Baptist churches is still progressing.

[4] Baker J. Cauthen and Frank K. Means, *Advance to Bold Mission Thrust: A History of Southern Baptist Foreign Missions, 1845-1980* (Richmond: Foreign Mission Board, Southern Baptist Convention, 1981), pp. 140-41. See also Christopher Fyfe, *A History of Sierra Leone* (London: Oxford University Press, 1962), pp. 70-71, 73.

[5] Cauthen and Means, *Advance*, pp. 136-37.

[6] Richard V. Pierard (ed.), *Baptists Together in Christ, 1905-2005: A Hundred-Year History of the Baptist World Alliance* (Falls Church, VA: BWA, 2005), p. 143.

[7] Cauthen and Means, *Advance*, pp. 381-82, 385-86.

Jamaican Baptists under the sponsorship of the Baptist Missionary Society in England introduced Christianity into Cameroon when it sent two missionaries to the island of Fernando Po in 1843, and within a short time the missionaries moved to the mainland of Cameroon. However, the German occupation of Cameroon forced the English Baptists out and the work was taken over by the Presbyterian Basel Mission. Although some German Baptists began mission work there in the 1890s, this was short-lived. Disruption was also caused by the First World War, and in the 1920s France occupied Cameroon and forced out all German missionaries. However, some Baptist churches continue to exist, and later formed l'Union des Eglises Baptistes du Cameroun (UEBC). The American Baptist missionaries who had worked with the German Baptists returned to Cameroon in 1935. Again, in 1941, when all the German missionaries had to leave because of World War II, the North American Baptist General Conference took over part of the German mission work and, later, created the present Cameroon Baptist Convention with a concentration in the English-speaking western Cameroon.

The mercantile and migratory lifestyle of the Yoruba from southwestern Nigeria, among whom the Southern Baptists have had a fruitful missionary work, and who were seeking economic opportunities outside their homeland, contributed in spreading the Baptist faith to other West African countries such as Togo, Ghana, Cote d' Ivoire, the Niger Republic and Burkina Faso within the first three decades of the twentieth century. These Yoruba migrants with little Western education, a factor which had excluded them from the cash crop economy in their homeland, were engaged in the distributive and retail trade in these West African countries. Wherever they settled, homogeneous Yoruba-speaking Baptist churches emerged, which also served as the nucleus of the Yoruba communities in these towns. By the 1950s, about eighty Baptist churches had been established in Ghana, two in Togo, eight in the Benin Republic, one each in the Niger Republic and Burkina Faso, and four in Côte d'Ivoire.[8] It was an indigenous initiative with far-reaching socio-political implications. Although inward-looking and closely attached to the Baptist churches in their Nigerian homeland, some of these churches embarked on evangelistic and missionary activities to the indigenous peoples. It was reports of these efforts sent back to Nigeria and shared by the missionaries of the Southern Baptist Convention in the country that partly stimulated the Foreign Mission Board to initiate mission work as a way of strengthening these churches and also of expanding Baptist work to nationals of these countries. The first missionary couple was sent from Nigeria to Ghana in February 1947. Thereafter, missionaries were appointed from USA and sent to Togo in 1964,

---

[8] Paul O. Kolawole, 'The Dynamics of Trade and Religion Among Diaspora Yoruba Baptists in West Africa, 1919-2004' (PhD thesis, Nigerian Baptist Theological Seminary, Ogbomoso, Nigeria, 2007).

Côte d'Ivoire in 1966, the Benin Republic in 1970, Burkina Faso in 1971 and other West African countries in the 1970s.[9]

The expulsion of aliens from Ghana in December 1969 initially disrupted and retarded Baptist work when most of the Yoruba traders returned to Nigeria. Of the over a hundred Yoruba Baptist churches, only three survived the disruption, though much later others were reopened with nationals. The renewal of work by the Southern Baptist Convention missionaries from 1970 and the conversion and enlistment of Ghanaians into Baptist churches aided the indigenisation of Baptist work in Ghana.[10] By the 1980s, Baptist work across West Africa had grown substantially through an increase in evangelistic and missionary efforts. This could be judged by statistics from the Foreign Mission Board of the Southern Baptist Convention. In 1948, the Foreign Mission Board had a total of 112 missionaries in Africa, all of whom with two exceptions were in Nigeria.[11] By 1970, the Foreign Mission Board had begun work in fourteen additional countries and at the end of 1969 there were 614 missionaries serving in Africa, of whom 247 were located in Nigeria.[12] Ghana received special attention from 1948 and had 41 missionaries at the end of 1968.[13] By the beginning of 1980, 339 Southern Baptist Convention missionaries were working in nine West African countries,[14] though Nigeria continued to have the largest Baptist work with the highest number of Foreign Mission Board missionaries. The Nigerian Baptist Convention was the largest result of Southern Baptist Convention mission work in Africa. A little attention will be devoted to the Baptist faith in Nigeria.

There are four major epochs in the history of Nigerian Baptists. The first is the missionary era that began when the Foreign Mission Board of the Southern Baptist Convention sent its first missionary, Thomas Jefferson Bowen, a native of Georgia, to Nigeria in August 1850. The period was characterised by pioneer work, mostly in southern Nigeria. Bowen had been preceded in Yorubaland in southwestern Nigeria eight years earlier by the Anglicans and the Methodists working under the Church Missionary Society and the Wesleyan Methodist Missionary Society, respectively, and four years earlier by the Church of Scotland (Presbyterian) mission that concentrated its work around Calabar in southeastern Nigeria. Against a background of a country that was still then steeped in inter-ethnic wars, a major means of supplying captives to the Portuguese slave merchants, and against a background of the English trying to enforce the abolition of the slave trade and open up the country to legitimate

---

[9] Kolawole, 'Dynamics of Trade and Religion', p. 382.
[10] J.A. Boadi, *A Brief History of the Ghana Baptist Convention* (Kumasi: no pub., 2007), pp. 92-98.
[11] Cauthen and Means, *Advance*, p. 153.
[12] Cauthen and Means, *Advance*, pp. 153-54, 180.
[13] Cauthen and Means, *Advance*, p. 156.
[14] Cauthen and Means, *Advance*, p. 391.

commerce, the missionaries were the vanguard of a new civilisation and a new culture. Generally, they had an enthusiastic welcome in many towns partly because their superior material culture announced their presence ahead of them. The message they preached was rather strange but their schooling system and medical skills created inroads into the traditional society. The missionaries learnt the local languages, preached and taught, and eventually won converts and built churches. The first indigenous ministers emerged from 1875, most of whom were previously interpreters to the missionaries or trained by the missionaries. Bowen's monumental book on the Yoruba people and culture,[15] and, later, his grammar and dictionary of the Yoruba language,[16] gained him recognition and provided more impetus for the mission work. Additional missionaries joined Bowen, and despite a short break in 1869-1875, caused by the aftermath of the American Civil War, the work progressed rapidly, partly fuelled by competition with the Anglicans who also concentrated their efforts in this same geographical area. By hard work, heroism and persistence, converts were won and Baptist churches were planted in many major towns in southwestern Nigeria by the close of the century.

In the second period, beginning from 1888, indigenous leadership became more assertive. A schism from the Lagos Baptist Church in February 1888 when the resident missionary relieved the indigenous pastor of his services and failed to give adequate explanation to the members of the church, showed how mature Nigerian Baptists had become in their own understanding of Baptist congregational polity. This incident precipitated similar schisms in the Anglican and Methodist churches, resulting in the African Church Movement – a movement that promoted Christianity under African leadership and was more accommodating to African culture.[17] Under African leadership, the Baptist faith spread to the Niger Delta area in 1893, from a partnership in mission between William Hughes of the Colwyn Bay Institute, Wales, and the First Baptist Church, Lagos, under the indigenous pastor, Dr Mojola Agbebi, an energetic, visionary leader who initiated other missionary activities that expanded Baptist faith to midwestern and southeastern Nigeria.[18]

---

[15] T.J. Bowen, *Adventures and Missionary Labours in Several Countries in the Interior of Africa from 1849 to 1856 [1857]* (London: Frank Cass, 1968).

[16] T.J. Bowen, *Grammar and Dictionary of the Yoruba Language* (Washington, DC: Smithsonian Institute, 1858).

[17] For more on this issue see J.B. Webster, *The African Churches among the Yoruba, 1888-1922* (Oxford: Clarendon Press, 1964). See also Matthews A. Ojo, 'The 1888 Schism in the Lagos Baptist Church and its Aftermath', *Ife Journal of History* 2:2 (September, 1998), pp. 114–43.

[18] J.A. Atanda (ed.), *Baptist Churches in Nigeria, 1850-1950* (Ibadan: Ibadan University Press, 1988), p. 258. See also Hazel King, 'Cooperation in Contextualization: Two Visionaries of the African Church: Mojola Agbebi and William Hughes of African Institute, Colwyn Bay', *Journal of Religion in Africa*, 16:1(1986), pp. 2-21.

The third period was from the 1950s, when political independence in many African nations speeded up the indigenisation of the leadership and structures of many organisations in Africa, including the church. With courage and commitment, an indigenous missionary board, the Foreign and Home Mission Board, was established in 1953 to direct the missionary efforts of the Nigerian Baptist Convention. Hence, there was expansion into other regions of the country. By 1960, it had embarked on foreign missions to Sierra Leone, while the Yoruba traders in other West African countries continued to sustain a Baptist missionary presence. Attention was also given to educational work in elementary and secondary schools and in teachers' training colleges, and leadership training for the Convention also accelerated.

In the fourth period, beginning from 1970s, Nigerian Baptists initiated new projects within the Convention including the establishment of more theological institutions, taking over student and youth work from the Southern Baptist missionaries and increasing their funding, which soon made them self-independent and self-sustaining. Foreign missions also received a boost with the opening of a second international mission field in Côte d'Ivoire in 1996, and, thereafter, more missionaries were appointed and sent to the Niger Republic, Sierra Leone, Burkina Faso, Chad, the Benin Republic, Guinea and Mali. In 2006 partnership began with the Mozambique Baptist Convention as part of its bold foreign mission thrust. Quite important for this paper, it was during this period that Nigerian Baptists witnessed the influence of the charismatic renewal in various ways. Attention will be given to this issue later.

Overall, the Baptist faith in West Africa is largely characterised by its conservative tone. It is very Evangelical, and a pietistic culture is strongly represented in Nigeria and Ghana. The leadership of the various conventions is dominated by highly educated middle-class individuals, many of whom were trained in Southern Baptist Convention institutions in the USA or have gained postgraduate qualifications in secular institutions. The pastors are also well trained and since the 1990s, most of those entering the seminaries have had some secular education at the tertiary level. In the rural areas, however, the membership consists largely of poor people. West African Baptists are very evangelistic and missionary; hence the number of churches and the membership are increasing yearly. However, unlike the Southern Baptists, women are in full-time pastoral ministry and some of them have been ordained.

Nigerian Baptists in Ecumenical Relations

The ecumenical movement was a major movement towards Christian unity in the twentieth century. In Nigeria, this movement first developed in 1926 with the aim of streamlining missionary penetration into the interior and avoiding competition among the mission agencies. The movement began in southeastern Nigeria among the Primitive Methodists, Anglicans, Presbyterians and the Sudan United Mission and Qua Iboe Mission, two inter-denominational faith missions from the United Kingdom. Although the two faith missions soon withdrew from the proposed union, consultations continued into the 1960s with the goal of forming a united Church of Nigeria.[19] The signing of an agreement and the take-off of the new body were fixed for 11 December 1965. However, at the eleventh hour suspicion and fear took over, and the project was abandoned to the surprise of everyone. Nigerian Baptists were not involved in this enterprise, neither did they participate in any of the consultations.

The first co-operation on a formal level in which Nigerian Baptists were involved was the meetings and consultations that resulted in the formation of the Christian Council of Nigeria in March 1930. An education edict of the colonial government that was going to affect the co-operation of government and mission in the provision of Western education by requiring some stringent demands on mission societies before their elementary and secondary institutions could be given government aid sparked off the anger of the leadership of the mission societies. Two initial meetings in November 1929 led to a more formal one on 16 December 1929, and in March 1930 there was a decision at a meeting attended by representatives of ten mission agencies to consider the educational law and put up a common response. The Nigerian Baptist Convention was represented in these meetings and eventually became a founding member of the Christian Council of Nigeria (CCN) when its establishment was approved.[20] Participation in the Christian Council of Nigeria, which in the 1960s became a member of the World Council of Churches, is limited to the leadership of the Nigerian Baptist Convention who attend CCN's meetings. Selected leaders in various regions also attend CCN's meetings in their own regions. According to the decision of 1930, 'questions of doctrine and ecclesiastical polity lie outside the province of the Council'. The 1930 constitution determined the functions of the body as 'to foster and express the fellowship and unity of the Christian Church in Nigeria and the realization of its oneness with the Church throughout the world'; 'to be the medium through which the church may speak on such matters social, moral, religious, educational and the like, as affect the entire Christian Movement in Nigeria and where necessary to take joint action'; and 'generally, to discuss all matters tending to affect the stability and expansion of Christianity in Nigeria'.[21] The first issue the Council took up was the proposal of the director of education in the colonial government. In subsequent meetings, there were discussions and resolutions on such things as Sunday observance, the issue of bribery and corruption, 'Christians and chieftainships'[22] and 'reception of African Soldiers

---

[19] Ogbu U. Kalu, *Divided People of God: Church Union Movement in Nigeria, 1875-1966* (New York: Nok Publishers, 1978), pp. 17-25, 66-78.
[20] Christian Council of Nigeria minutes, 14-19 March 1930, Nigerian Baptist Theological Seminary Library, Ogbomoso, Nigeria.
[21] Christian Council of Nigeria minutes, 14-19 March 1930.
[22] Christian Council of Nigeria, minutes, 23-26 February 1938, pp. 6-9.

When Demobilized' after the Second World War.[23] Issues taken up by CCN were mostly administrative and governmental issues involving the mission agencies and their denominations, and, secondly, outreach programmes of the WCC such as educational scholarships, relief and development programmes and health education issues. As agreed in 1930, questions of doctrinal beliefs or the independence of member denominations have never been discussed. Officers of Christian Council of Nigeria are elected usually on a rotational basis among members.

On the local level, however, the Bible Society of Nigeria, formed in 1965 to promote the translation and distribution of the Bible in English and Nigerian languages, has fostered much more inter-denominational co-operation than the Christian Council of Nigeria. Each town or each designated area often has a Bible Society auxiliary unit that meets regularly to deliberate on ways of distributing Bibles, usually through sales to member churches, and also ways of gathering support for Bible work in Nigeria. Both lay people and the clergy participate actively. More important, once a year on a designated Sunday, pastors are rotated among member denominations for the observance of 'Bible Sunday', a service devoted to the promotion of the work of Bible translation and distribution. Almost all the major segments of the Nigerian churches, mainline Protestants, Pentecostals and African Independent Churches, are represented in the Bible Society of Nigeria, though the mainline Protestant denominations are the most active.

Lastly, the Christian Association of Nigeria, formed in 1979, has a larger constituency than the Christian Council of Nigeria. Its aim is to provide a united Christian response to the political events and decisions that could negatively affect Nigerian Christian churches in the religious pluralistic context of the country.[24] Nigerian Baptists have participated in the activities of this body.

Generally, the affinities of location and pressing administrative matters have determined the nature of the relationship of Nigerian Baptists to other Protestant bodies. On a local level, Baptist churches have co-operated and still co-operate with other Christian bodies as the need arises either to present a united Christian voice on any issue or to promote evangelism.

Charismatic Renewal in Africa

Previous studies of the Independent Pentecostal and charismatic movements have largely been historical and situated within specific countries. Ojo examined the growth of charismatic movements in western Nigeria, while Ruth

---

[23] Christian Council of Nigeria, minutes, 8-12 July 1944.
[24] Iheanyi M. Enwerem, *A Dangerous Awakening: The Politicisation of Religion in Nigeria* (Ibadan: IFRA, 1995).

Marshall focused on the socio-political involvement of the movements.[25] Larbi traced the historical development of the movements in Ghana from indigenous roots in the early twentieth century to their contemporary manifestations.[26] Gifford's *New Dimensions in African Christianity* presented the growth of charismatic movements in many countries within one edited volume.[27] Gifford further described the major charismatic organisations in Ghana.[28] Recently, Gifford has examined the growth of charismatic movements in Ghana and Africa within their socio-economic and political contexts.[29] Recent works have often been anthropological in content. For example, Birgit Meyer examined the construction of a cosmology of power in modern Ghana.[30] Meyer's recent works have focused on the connection between Pentecostalism and popular media culture.[31] Hackett examined the linkage in the appropriation of media technology by Pentecostal and charismatic movements in Nigeria and Ghana.[32] Kalu provided some re-interpretation of Pentecostal movements in Africa from an African perspective of culture and worldview.[33] Omenyo situated his study of charismatic movements within the mainline churches in Ghana, while Asamoah-Gyadu provided a theological examination of the doctrinal emphases and practices

---

[25] Matthews A. Ojo, 'Deeper Christian Life Ministry: A Case Study of the Charismatic Movements in Western Nigeria', *Journal of Religion in Africa* 17:2 (1988), pp. 141-62; Matthews A. Ojo, 'The Contextual Significance of the Charismatic Movements in Independent Nigeria', *Africa: Journal of the International African Institute* 2, 58:2 (1988), pp. 175-92. Ruth Marshall, 'Pentecostalism in Southern Nigeria: An Overview', in Paul Gifford (ed.), *New Dimensions in African Christianity* (Nairobi: All African Conference of Churches, 1992), pp. 8-39.

[26] E. Kingsley Larbi, *Pentecostalism: The Eddies of Ghanaian Christianity* (Accra: Center for Pentecostal and Charismatic Studies, 2001).

[27] Paul Gifford (ed.), *New Dimensions in African Christianity* (Nairobi: All African Conference of Churches, 1992).

[28] Paul Gifford. 'Ghana's Charismatic Churches', *Journal of Religion in Africa* 24:3 (1994), pp. 241-65.

[29] Paul Gifford, *Ghana's New Christianity: Pentecostalism in a Globalising African Economy* (London: Hurst and Company, 2004).

[30] Birgit Meyer, '"If you are a Devil you are a Witch and if you are a Witch you are a Devil": The Integration of "Pagan" Ideas into the Conceptual Universe of Ewe Christians in South-eastern Ghana', *Journal of Religion in Africa* 22:2 (1992), pp. 98-132.

[31] Birgit Meyer, 'Pentecostalism, Prosperity and Popular Cinema in Ghana'. *Culture and Religion* 3, 1 (2002), pp. 67-87; and Birgit Meyer, 'Pentecostalism, Prosperity, and Popular Cinema in Ghana', in S. Brent Plate (ed.), *Representing Religion in World Cinema: Filmmaking, Mythmaking, Culture Making* (New York: Palgrave Macmillan, 2003), pp. 121- 44.

[32] Rosalind J. Hackett, 'Charismatic/Pentecostal Appropriation of Media Technologies in Nigeria and Ghana', *Journal of Religion in Africa* 28:3 (1998), pp. 258-77.

[33] Ogbu U. Kalu, *African Pentecostalism: An Introduction* (Oxford: Oxford University Press, 2008).

of the movements.[34] Ojo has noted cross-cultural missionary activities of the Pentecostal and charismatic movements as an important part of the African initiative in Christian missions in the twentieth century.[35] Corten and Marshall-Fratani largely examined Pentecostal movements in Africa within the context of trans-nationalism and globalisation.[36] This paper, on the relations between West African Baptists and the charismatic movements, is another contribution to the study of inter-religious activities and Pentecostalism.

Although Pentecostal churches of both foreign and indigenous types have existed in Nigeria and other West African countries since the 1930s, it was the rise of charismatic renewal from 1970s that greatly enlarged the Pentecostal constituency and afterward engaged Baptist churches and their membership. The response of Nigerian Baptists was varied, but at the end the essentials of Baptist heritage and identity stood the test.

The rapid spread of the Pentecostal and charismatic movements in Africa since the 1970s have been noted to be an important feature of the changing African religious landscape. The Pentecostal and charismatic movements have also been recognised since the 1980s as the fastest growing segment of Christianity as Pentecostal groups proliferated under founders and general overseers and self-styled bishops. In fact, an essay in the African Concord in 1985 noted that charismatic movements were the fastest growing endeavour in West Africa.[37] From about ten independent Pentecostal and charismatic organisations in the mid-1970s, largely restricted to Nigeria, the number has grown to over ten thousand groups across the continent. By 2000, the membership had become substantial, with about eight million of the 48.42 million Christians in Nigeria,[38] about two million of the Christian population in Ghana, and not less than 200,000 in Cameroon and Côte d'Ivoire, about 300,000 in each of Benin and Burkina Faso, about 100,000 in Togo and about 2,000 in the Niger Republic. The differences in regional growth are partly due to different social and political experiences. The decentralisation of the political

---

[34] Cephas N. Omenyo, *Pentecost outside Pentecostalism: A Study of the Development of Charismatic Renewal in the Mainline Churches in Ghana* (Uitgeverij, Netherlands: Boekencentrum, 2002). J. Kwabena Asamoah-Gyadu, *African Charismatics: Current Developments within Independent Indigenous Pentecostalism in Ghana* (Leiden: Brill, 2005).

[35] Matthews A. Ojo, 'Transnational Religious Networks and Indigenous Pentecostal Missionary Enterprises in the West African Coastal Region', in *Christianity in African and the African Diaspora: The Appropriation of a Scattered Heritage.* ed. Afe Adogame, Roswith Gerloff and Klaus Hock (London: Continuum, 2008), pp. 167-79.

[36] André Corten and Ruth Marshall-Fratani (eds), *Between Babel and Pentecost: Transnational Pentecostalism in Africa and Latin America (*Bloomington: Indiana University Press, 2001).

[37] *African Concord* (London & Lagos), 18 February 1985, pp. 7-8.

[38] Figures worked out from annual percentage growth statistics and other reports released by the National Population Commission between 2002 and 2007.

arena in the English-speaking countries – Nigeria and Ghana – has fostered religious creativity as a cultural phenomenon, whereas the centralised unitary systems in Francophone countries have retarded similar developments. Secondly, the liberalisation of electronic and print media in the Anglophone countries has favoured a healthy contest for public space by religious organisations. On the other hand, the media in the Francophone countries still operated under government restrictions into the early twenty-first century.

The rapid growth of charismatic renewal since the 1970s has produced a substantial religious and social change with a differing impact on various denominations in the country. By the late 1980s, the proliferation of independent charismatic and Pentecostal churches and groups erecting bill boards on street corners, holding services in rented or temporary spaces and publicising themselves using the electronic and print media was visible everywhere and could not be ignored. Generally, their sermons, healing and miracle services, breakthrough programmes, Holy Ghost Night services, and advertisements of conventions and special programmes – all providing utopian escape from the deteriorating socio-economic and political conditions – still dominate the airwaves, providing huge and easy revenue to many cash-strapped radio and television stations. Charismatic movements were important because they created a new religious visibility to the middle class, already decimated by harsh economic realities in the region. By the late 1970s, most of the mainline Protestant churches – Anglican, Baptist, Methodist and Presbyterian – have had cause to react to the growing influence of charismatic renewal that was seeping into these denominations and causing apprehension among the leadership of these denominations.

Although charismatic renewal[39] had become worldwide by the late 1960s, the movement in Nigeria took its roots from the Evangelical witness already laid in Nigeria's educational institutions from the 1950s by such inter-denominational student organisations as Scripture Union, the Evangelical Christian Union and the Student Christian Movement.[40] From some previous contacts with Pentecostal literature, a revival which centred on the Pentecostal experience of baptism of the Holy Spirit and speaking in tongues arose among these students in January 1970. Eventually the revival precipitated a substantial religious awakening in Nigeria's higher educational institutions. Its progress from 1970 was very rapid, and by the mid-1970s the revival had saturated the Evangelical circles in most of the universities in southern Nigeria, and in the late 1970s it spilled over into the larger society, where it was initially sustained within the Scripture Union Pilgrims Groups. By the mid-1980s, charismatic

---

[39] It was a new religious phenomenon which began in the US in the 1960s that emphasised that apostolic Christianity is grounded in the experience of 'being baptised in the Holy Spirit' as a second blessing.

[40] For more details see Matthews A. Ojo, *End Time Army: Charismatic Movements in Modern Nigeria* (Trenton, NJ: Africa World Press, 2006).

renewal had become a major social movement as Pentecostal spirituality affected millions of citizens in various ways.

In the 1970s, charismatic organisations operated like Bible study or evangelistic groups, holding their meetings only on weekdays and offering Bible studies or prayer meetings to their members in addition to the regular activities in their churches. Hence they described themselves as inter-denominational or non-denominational organisations. However, by 1983 some of the groups had initiated Sunday worship services, thus adopting a denominational status. They also began to erect permanent places of worship instead of holding meetings in rented spaces. By the mid-1980s, paid clergy, mostly trained in Bible schools or associated with the founders, had emerged, and the structure of administration became formalised with a discernible hierarchy and line of authority. This denominationalisation indirectly aided the proliferation of the charismatic organisations. From one group in May 1970, the movement grew to about ten organisations in 1974, and by the early 1980s, there were already over a thousand such groups. The number grew steadily to over five thousand independent groups by 2000.

The charismatic movements, despite being so recent, have exerted a wide influence because they were sustained by the educated elite, which, though a small class, enjoyed an enviable status and great potentialities in African society. Moreover, charismatic organisations have an interesting variety.[41] Some are large, while others are small. They also differ in their doctrinal emphases. Some are other-worldly, maintaining a strict holiness ethos, while others are this-worldly, preaching prosperity and encouraging members to upward social mobility – an emphasis that has some congruence with contemporary secular values.

The movements are almost entirely urban, which is the best environment to sustain a religious phenomenon that relies heavily on the electronic and print media to gain membership. Manifestations of urban life such as a cosmopolitan and youth membership, preaching against ethnic divisions (they use choruses of multi-lingual appeal and call themselves brothers and sisters in Christ), conducting services with electronic keyboards, drum sets and public address systems, all feature prominently in the movements. The use of literature – their own printed magazines, tracts and booklets – has aided the wider dissemination of charismatic spirituality in the country. The modernising orientation of Pentecostalism and its global outlook appealed greatly to youth. Pentecostal ritual steeped in the English language – a global communication language – became the defining principle of the new religious phenomenon in the country. Besides, the utilisation of the print media and modern media technology has

---

[41] I have earlier constructed a typology of the charismatic movements. See Matthews A. Ojo, 'African Charismatics', in *Encyclopedia of African and African-American Religion*, ed. Stephen Glazier (New York: Routledge, 2001), pp. 2-6.

greatly helped Pentecostal and charismatic churches to widen their horizon and to conceive their mission in global terms.

Doctrinal Emphases and Practices of the Charismatic Movements

It is the doctrinal emphases and practices of the charismatics and Pentecostals that have had most impact on the mainline Protestant denominations, and the disagreements have centred on these issues. First, charismatic movements are intensely biblical and so most of their doctrinal emphases are rooted in a literal interpretation of Bible verses. Moreover, the teachings are often backed up with personal testimonies that make them relevant to most situations. Charismatics understood their own teachings to be a restoration of apostolic Christianity. Were it not for this conviction, nothing substantial might ever have been written about them.

The greatest emphasis has been on healing, which has often been demonstrated with a very wide application. They insist that once Christians pray and have faith, healing must take place, and even the dead can be brought back to life and blood genotype can be changed. Generally, charismatics focus primarily on physical healing and, secondly, on 'casting out of demons', which is termed 'deliverance'. In recent years, another dimension which has developed is healing over difficulties of life, which is termed 'success and prosperity'. Lastly, there is healing of the political and socio-economic conditions of a nation, which is termed 'prayer for the nations'. These definitions of healing have taken positive account of traditional causative factors of diseases as well as coming to terms with the dislocation of contemporary life. Moreover, charismatics have deployed their literal interpretation of the scriptures with potentially far-reaching implications. They have looked at illness as evil and have utilised the symbol of Satan to pinpoint social and religious tensions. These definitions, thus, have an explanatory function as well as an ethical dimension.

Charismatics have also emphasised prosperity, through which they have engineered personal empowerment and have also provided motivation for rapid upward social mobility. From the quest for personal material comfort, charismatics have moved to strengthen personal ambition from a very strict biblical perspective. What sustains their apparent quest for material resources is, partly, the traditional African quest for wellbeing and wealth in all their ramifications. Wealth is a means to recognition in society and a means towards political power. People have used various means to acquire wealth. For charismatics, it is their access to spiritual knowledge through which they believe power will accrue to them. Therefore, they teach that it is sinful for Christians to be poor; rather everyone can and must enjoy abundance. It is against this broad background that we can evaluate the charismatics' worldview.

Thirdly, Charismatics insist that miracles, signs and wonders are part of the common experiences of Christians. Hence, as noted by Ademola Ishola and Travis Collins, they 'claim that evangelistic efforts, unless accompanied by signs and wonders, are incomplete and inadequate'.[42] This obsession with miracles has now come to dominate most camp meetings, Holy Ghost services and evangelistic activities. Indeed, the quest for miracles has made Christianity become utilitarian, always serving the interests and needs of Nigerians.

Furthermore, charismatics insist that all Christians must undergo the baptism of the Holy Spirit at a certain point in their lives, and they must speak in tongues to confirm the inward experience. The gifts of tongues are accepted to be part of corporate worship, and can also be used in private devotional worship. It is assumed that the person who speaks in tongues is a better Christian than the others who do not speak in tongues. In fact, charismatics teach that 'baptism in the Spirit offers a quick and easy spirituality'.[43] Many pamphlets and sermons from Pentecostal pulpits have emphasised this doctrinal position.

Lastly, evangelism or soul winning is a central belief and practice among charismatics. They teach that a Christian must engage in evangelistic activities all the time. This could be by distributing tracts, preaching in buses and on street corners, or going from one house to another, from person to person and so on. This emphasis on evangelism soon developed into a consciousness of missions with much political significance because charismatics insist that Nigeria, as the acclaimed 'giant of Africa', should be a bastion for the evangelisation of the continent. Unlike the existing Protestant churches, charismatic movements have made significant strides in indigenous African missions, and their missionary activities have spread to many parts of Africa and beyond.

Largely through the formation of indigenous and mostly non-denominational mission agencies for the recruitment, training, sending, supporting and supervising of missionaries,[44] and through the territorial extension of branches of charismatic organisations to new areas, charismatic missions are advancing rapidly all over Africa. Since the early 1980s, charismatics have been training Nigerians and other Africans in cross-cultural missions in the indigenous School of Missions and sending them out as missionaries within and outside

---

[42] Travis Collins and Ademola Ishola, *Baptists and the Charismatic Movement* (Ibadan: Nigerian Baptist Convention, 1995), p. 47.

[43] Collins and Ishola, *Baptists and the Charismatic Movement*, p. 30.

[44] In 1975, Calvary Ministries (CAPRO) was formed as the first indigenous missionary organisation promoting cross-cultural missions.

Nigeria.[45] Indeed, charismatics' missions have been successful in spreading the charismatic renewal and in contributing to church growth in Africa.

Nigerian Baptists and Charismatic Renewal

The Baptist response in Nigeria to charismatic renewal passed through three phases, and each epoch revealed certain peculiarities of that age. First, throughout the 1970s and 1980s, the response was antagonism and opposition to Pentecostal spirituality and religion by most Baptist leaders (deacons, pastors and leaders of associations and the Convention) and Baptist churches. In the 1990s, secondly, there was tolerance of Pentecostal spirituality arising from the fact that Pentecostalism had grown and become popular, and some Baptist pastors had been influenced by it. Thirdly, by the new millennium, there was a realisation that certain aspects of Pentecostal spirituality could be utilised as a tool for church growth. To this end, there was an expansion of space for Pentecostal spirituality with the aim of retaining the youth, women and others who had already adjusted to Pentecostalism through earlier participation in Pentecostal activities, particularly on the campuses of universities and colleges. The position then shifted to acceptance of Pentecostal spirituality as many Baptist churches adopted the contemporary free liturgy characteristic of Pentecostal churches. Some also adopted Pentecostal practices such as display of emotionalism in worship services, noisy prayers, greater emphasis on healing and deliverance, and, in some cases, extending invitations to Pentecostal pastors and freelance evangelists to lead revival or special services.

Baptists have been involved in various ways and levels with charismatic renewal from the early 1970s, and some of these men and women have participated actively in the programmes of their churches and even occupied leadership positions. Groups such as the Scripture Union Pilgrims Groups in various towns, the Christian Unions on various campuses of tertiary institutions and evangelistic groups that had backgrounds in charismatic renewal were some of the avenues through which Pentecostal spirituality seeped into the Nigerian Baptist churches. Also Pentecostal literature and broadcasts were freely in circulation in the 1970s. Besides, there were many others who also had participated in programmes of Pentecostal and charismatic organisations before they became Baptist pastors. In comparison with the generality of Baptists, these 'Pentecostal' Baptists claimed to possess a deeper understanding of spiritual truth, and hence sought to rekindle revival in the Nigerian Baptist Convention.

Another Pentecostal organisation that was attractive to many of the educated elite in the 1980s was the Full Gospel Businessmen's Fellowship International

---

[45] For more on this see Matthews A. Ojo, 'The Dynamics of Indigenous Charismatic Missionary Enterprises in West Africa', *Missionalia*, 25: 4 (December, 1997), pp. 537-61. Internet edition in http://www.geocities.com/missionalia/ojo1.htm.

(FGBMFI). It was established in the USA in the early 1950s by Demos Shakarian and his wife, both Armenian Christians whose grandparents had emigrated to California in the nineteenth century. With the growth of charismatic renewal in the USA in the 1960s, FGBMFI also gained popularity as an interdenominational Pentecostal organisation patronised chiefly by upper- and middle-class white Americans.

First introduced to Nigeria in 1983,[46] it later experienced growth and planted branches in major towns such that by the early 1990s membership in the FGBMFI became a social index of success among middle-class Nigerians – lecturers, managers, professionals and so on. The monthly breakfast or lunch meetings, always held in hotels, attracted large numbers of nominal Christians who normally would have nothing to do with charismatic organisations. A constant theme by the speakers at the breakfast and lunch meetings was that the mainline Protestant churches were unable to offer any assistance when people were in spiritual crises, until they came into contact with Pentecostal groups. The selective testimonies were sometimes bold, but they tended to de-emphasise affiliation to any of the existing churches, and to uplift the Pentecostal experience. In some of these meetings, Baptists who had experienced renewed faith gave testimonies or participated enthusiastically in the FGBMFI.

Without any doubt, the major institutional channel for the penetration of Pentecostalism into the Nigerian Baptist Convention was through the Baptist Student Fellowship (BSF), one of the oldest and the most developed of all denominational Christian student organisations in the post-secondary institutions of the country.[47] Baptist Student Fellowship was established in 1958 from the missionary efforts of Southern Baptist Convention missionaries among students in colleges, polytechnics and universities. By the mid-1960s, the BSF became co-ordinated as more missionaries were evangelising among students in post-secondary institutions.[48]

It was in the mid-1970s that charismatic renewal reached its peak in the universities, where it influenced a number of Baptists. In the universities of Ibadan, Lagos and Ife, some Baptist students came into contact with Pentecostal spirituality on their campuses and began to disseminate their Pentecostal experience. Experiences such as crying while praying, open confession of sinful habits and speaking in tongues were reported among some Baptist students. Some of these 'excesses' were attributed to Miss Mary Frank Kirkpatrick, the Southern Baptist student minister, who was stationed in

---

[46] *Full Gospel Business Men's Advance* 1:4 (September, 1991), pp. 1-8.

[47] Records show that the first worker, Miss Mary Kirkpatrick, also worked among secondary schools students in western Nigeria in the 1960s and 1970s. However, the BSF has had a permanent and continuous life in post-secondary institutions, mostly in the universities.

[48] Baptist Mission of Nigeria 1964 Minutes, p. 84, Nigerian Baptist Theological Seminary Library, Ogbomoso, Nigeria.

southwestern Nigeria. Her expulsion from Nigeria by the federal government on 15 December 1977 in a general clampdown on Christian youth activities in the country[49] was unconnected with her pervading influence among Baptists and Christian young people. Some parents felt that Miss Kirkpatrick supported the fanaticism that accompanied the charismatic revival and encouraged Baptist students to participate fully in the renewal.[50]

Pentecostal Manifestations in Nigerian Baptist Churches[51]

The charismatic upsurge continued in various Baptist Student Fellowship groups, particularly in southwestern Nigeria, throughout the 1980s. The problem increased from 1985, when BSF groups were established in local Baptist churches as part of an institutional change. Although this development guaranteed a steady membership as many of those who were gaining admission to colleges and universities and joining the BSF groups had been members of church groups, it nevertheless brought the Pentecostal influence closer to the churches. By the late 1980s, some churches were taking steps to ban BSF from operating, or disallowing the hosting of BSF programmes in their churches on the ground that they were spreading 'unBaptistic' practices. It was at this time that leaders of BSF began to curtail excesses among students and also to open discussion with churches. Besides, Deaconess Bettye McQueen, a Southern Convention missionary and the national director of student ministries, in 1989 issued the pamphlet *Does the Church Need BSF?* to explain the official position of the department to churches and their pastors. In addition, Emiola Nihinlola, then the western zone co-ordinator of the student ministries, and Dr Matthews A. Ojo, a leader of the BSF Alumni Association, made several visits to pastors and churches to plead for tolerance and acceptance, despite what were considered as excesses on the part of the students.

By the 1990s, several churches that had had contacts with students or other Baptists already influenced by charismatic renewal, were presenting Pentecostal spirituality as the only means for renewal in Baptist churches. In response, opposition to BSF by some pastors and churches increased. In fact, from the late 1980s, all-night prayer meetings, deliverance services, the casting

---

[49] Baptist Mission of Nigeria 1978/79 Minutes, p. 48. Folu Soyanwo, a Nigerian and the general secretary of Scripture Union, was also detained for some days by Nigerian security services in December 1977 for undisclosed offences.

[50] *Minutes of the Sixty-Fifth Annual Session of the Nigerian Baptist Convention* (Ibadan: Nigerian Baptist Convention, 1978), p. 19.

[51] This section is closely related to my earlier article, Matthews A. Ojo, 'The Nigerian Baptist Convention and the Pentecostal Resurgence, 1970-2000: Critical Issues for Ecclesiastical Dynamics', in Ademola Ishola and Deji Ayegboyin, *Ecclesiastes: The Preacher, the Church and the Contemporary Society* (Ibadan: Sceptre Prints, 2006), pp. 327-64.

out of demons and slaying in the Spirit were being reported to convention leaders as unBaptistic activities. True as these allegations were, many pastors failed to realise that some of these Baptist students actually did not belong to BSF groups and neither were these activities promoted on BSF platforms. Rather, some of these students had been greatly influenced by their peers in the colleges.

It was at this time that the leadership of the student ministries wrote out some basic Baptist beliefs and practices as a small pamphlet for students.[52] This write-up accepted new experiences of baptism of the Holy Spirit and tried to explain them from the Evangelical tradition. This was the first systematic attempt to approach the Pentecostal upsurge with understanding. Furthermore, Dr Matthews A. Ojo, as a member of the Student Ministries Advisory Committee, was requested by the leadership of the student ministries to produce a new book expounding Baptists' doctrinal beliefs for the BSF. This work, which incorporated beliefs on baptism of the Holy Spirit and healing, was completed and submitted in late 1992, but it was never published.

On the Convention level, in February 1990, Dr S.T. Ola Akande, the general secretary, invited Mrs A. Aderoju, a school principal and the chairman of the Student Ministries Advisory Committee, to present a paper at the General Workers' Conference. The paper, which was well written and well received, provided a better understanding of the Pentecostal upsurge, particularly through the avenue of the BSF. However, no concrete policy was formulated from the discussion, and so controversy about Pentecostal spirituality continued.

In the presidential address to the 77th annual session of the Nigerian Baptist Convention held in Kaduna in April 1990, D.H. Karo called on his hearers to accept BSF, both in schools and churches.[53] However, despite this official support, some associations and conferences continued to act in a panic and responded with general condemnation of the Pentecostal spirituality in any form – whether it was noticed within BSF or found among some other Baptists.

About 1992, the executive committee of Oyo West Baptist Conference issued guidelines regarding what were considered unBaptistic practices in a booklet titled *Baptist Beliefs and Practices* and published in English and Yoruba for wider dissemination. That the publication was informed by Pentecostal experiences and practices was reflected in its introduction, which says in part:

> The reason why the Executive Committee embarked on this exercise is due to various occasional allegations and accusations by some Baptist youth and adults that worship services in Baptist churches are very lukewarm. They have alleged

---

[52] *Doctrinal Statement and Guide* (Ibadan: Student Ministries Department Nigerian Baptist Convention, 1990).
[53] Nigerian Baptist Convention, *Minutes of the 77th Annual Session of the Nigerian Baptist Convention* (Ibadan: Nigerian Baptist Convention, 1990), p. 26.

that our prayers are weak and not 'hot enough'. They said we do not heal the sick or raise the dead. They have also alleged that in Baptist churches, miracles do not happen and people are not baptised by the Holy Spirit neither are they able to speak in tongues.... But surprisingly enough, many of these people still stay in the Baptist Churches and insist on forcing these Pentecostal beliefs on members.[54]

Although, the executive committee gave very moderate Evangelical positions on certain Pentecostal beliefs and practices, it went to an extreme on its comments on 'Night Vigils' and in a very caustic manner asked all churches and individual to cease holding night vigils immediately.[55] Likewise, some associational moderators and pastors took it upon themselves even to pontificate on what they knew little about.

The only informed opinion, perhaps coming late, was the publication by Drs Ademola Ishola and Travis Collins, both at that time lecturers in the Nigerian Baptist Theological Seminary, Ogbomoso. Published in mid-1995, the book provided a theological appraisal of charismatic renewal from the Baptist point of view, and offered ways of responding positively and systematically to the phenomenon.[56] It should have been adopted by the Convention as the basis of its response, but that opportunity was allowed to slip away. Consequently, the success of the book was limited because initially only 2,000 copies were published for a Baptist constituency of over three million. At the same time, Emiola Nihinlola, the western zone BSF co-ordinator, in his book, titled *Nigerian Baptist Convention and Pentecostal-Charismatic Worship Practices* (1995) gave an objective analysis of the concerted opinion and reactions of the Nigerian Baptist Convention family to the Pentecostal and charismatic awakening. The book covers many aspects that deal with corporate worship like prayers, fasting, speaking in tongues, emotional shouting of 'Praise the Lord', testimonies, night vigils, singing choruses, laying on of hands and deliverance. Nihinlola concluded that since Nigerian Baptist young people had a strong sympathy and appreciation for the Pentecostal worship practices and were active members of Baptist churches, it would be inappropriate to continue to describe such practices as 'unBaptistic' since it appeared that the impact of the charismatic renewal on the denomination had been positive.

By the mid-1980s, lacking any precise definition, a new offence of 'unBaptistic practices' had been created at association, conference and Convention levels. Under this rubric, some Baptists and certain individuals were charged. Perhaps the most interesting case was in connection with Orita Mefa Baptist Church, Ibadan, one of the largest and most evangelistic churches

---

[54] *Baptist Beliefs and Practices* (Ibadan: Executive Committee, Oyo West Baptist Conference, c. 1992), p.1.
[55] *Baptist Beliefs and Practices*, p. 11.
[56] Travis Collins and Ademola Ishola, *Baptists and the Charismatic Movement* (Ibadan: Nigerian Baptist Convention,1995).

in Nigeria. It was reported in 1986 that some unBaptistic practices were going on in the church with the active support of the pastor, S.M. Leigh. Despite the success of the church in terms of its evangelism and church planting, and as it was one of the major financial contributors to the Nigerian Baptist Convention's co-operative programme, some Baptist leaders felt that the church should be brought to book. Unfortunately, a report of a committee set up to look into the matter was judged by the Board to be inconclusive. Even among the leaders of the convention, there was disagreement on the matter until 1987, when the matter was amicably resolved.[57]

It was not a success story everywhere. In some churches, the Pentecostal spirituality caused division and schism. For example, it was reported in 1986 that two churches, Ebenezer Baptist Church, Ijokodo, Ibadan, and Oworonsoki Baptist Church, Lagos, were de-fellowshipped from their various associations due to unBaptistic practices. Such unBaptistic practices included 'wailing, crying during worship, and dancing during thanksgiving'.[58] In addition, in Lagos there were splits in two Baptist churches, and one of the schismatic groups, The Upper Room Baptist Church, has remained as an independent Baptist denomination. In early 2006, it celebrated its tenth anniversary with much media publicity. In other cases, some of the seceding groups retained their membership in the Nigerian Baptist Convention. Therefore, by the mid-1990s, Pentecostal influences had gone beyond the BSF constituency and, to the dismay of some conservative pastors, were becoming a wider phenomenon.

Official response to the Pentecostal upsurge was never co-ordinated; hence, panicky measures were adopted to curtail the spread of the revival. With hindsight now, it seems that the various leaders in the associations, conferences and the Convention did not appreciate charismatic renewal as a revivalist ethos, while some did not consider change as necessary for religious progress. One of such panicky measures was the set of instructions issued by the Oyo West Baptist Conference, about 1992, stating what beliefs and practices were accepted or not. Moreover, a report from Oyo East Conference, about 1992, banned starting any prayer with 'In Jesus' Name' or shouting 'Praise the Lord' and 'Hallelujah' too often!

It is necessary to ask what actually were those beliefs and practices described as 'unBaptistic' and upon which the controversies centred. Certainly, it is difficult to say because opinions varied depending of the person's background and Christian maturity. However, the Oyo West Baptist Conference listed the following:

---

[57] See various reports of the Ministerial Board on this matter in Nigerian Baptist Convention, *Book of Reports 1986*, p. 29; *Book of Reports 1987*, pp. 81-83, 89-91.

[58] Nigerian Baptist Convention, *Book of Reports, 1986* (Ibadan, 1986), p. 29.

a. Shouting during prayers as if God were deaf.
b. Foot stamping and fingers snapping at prayer sessions followed by sentimental responses like 'Yes, it shall be done', 'you must do it', 'Jesus', etc.
c. Weeping and rolling on the ground during prayers.
d. Holding separate prayer meetings while the church is holding one in the sanctuary.
e. Night vigil.
f. Praying for the gifts of the Holy Spirit so that one would be able to speak in tongues as it happened on the day of Pentecost to the Apostles.[59]

To the above, the following could be added:
1. Any affirmation of baptism of the Holy Spirit as a post-conversion experience.
2. Speaking in tongues and any demonstration of that belief.
3. Moving about or jerking or throwing hands about while praying.
4. Shouting 'Hallelujah' and or 'Praise the Lord' during worship services or prayer meetings.
5. Claims of seeing visions or having prophecies.
6. Belief in and the practice of deliverance from what are perceived as satanic agents and demons.
7. Believing all the time that calling on the name of Jesus can effect physical healing.
8. Any emphasis placed on the 'End Time' or the events that will herald the 'End Time'.
9. Any semblance of deep devotion beyond the ordinary.
10. Spasmodic interjections of phrases such as 'Praise the Lord', 'God bless you', 'Amen', 'the blood of Jesus', 'God is good', etc., while worship is going on.
11. Excessive use of choruses to the neglect of hymns.
12. Attending and participating in programmes organised by Pentecostal churches and ministries.
13. Not wearing of earrings, necklaces, bangles or costly dressing from religious conviction or piety.
14. Dressing in a particular mode, depicting certain religious inclinations.
15. Laying on of hands as means of blessing or effecting 'anointing'.
16. Belief in 'slaying under the anointing of the Spirit'.
17. Anointing people with oil or using anointed handkerchiefs or anointed water as a ritual formula.
18. Any deep devotion to miracles, signs and wonders or any expectation of such.

---

[59] *Baptist Beliefs and Practices*, p. 7.

The above listings clearly indicate that any objective approach would have been difficult, as some of the practices could not be considered as undesirable or unbiblical. Eventually, by the late 1990s, worship in some Baptist churches had changed so much that some of the things earlier condemned as unBaptistic practices became acceptable. With hindsight, Emiola Nihinlola was probably right when, in reference to the sweeping charismatic renewal, he recommended as follows: 'Don't Ignore It, Don't Reject it, Don't Adopt It, Study It, Moderate It, and Experience It.'[60] He added that while the BSF was not a Pentecostal organisation, the organisation was responding positively to what he called 'the move of the Spirit biblically and practically', and that pastors and churches tying to stop Pentecostalism were wasting their time.[61]

An institutional change came in 1993 when the Nigerian Baptist Theological Seminary, Ogbomoso, introduced the three-year Master of Divinity programme, and was strengthened in 1996 when it introduced the same course as a sandwich programme. These programmes provided opportunities for many graduates with a first degree to be trained as Baptist pastors. Before then, the seminary offered only the three-year Diploma in Theology and four-year Bachelor in Theology programmes which were not attractive to graduates from the universities. Most of those admitted into the Master of Divinity programme were former members of the BSF, and some had been influenced by charismatic renewal on the campuses. This class of students whom the churches had complained about as peddling unBaptistic practices soon became the vanguard for the rejuvenation of the Nigerian Baptist Convention. By the late 1990s, these M.Div. graduates were exercising successful ministries in their churches. Membership of their churches rose considerably, there was demonstrable spiritual alertness and commitment and the financial contributions of their churches were enormous and challenging to the generality of Baptists. Though never documented, it is clear that Pentecostal spirituality and awareness of renewal have, largely, sustained this spiritual awakening in Baptist churches pastored by M.Div. graduates or by others who have had equivalent contacts with charismatic renewal.

The key person who took advantage of this new development for Baptist growth was Ademola Ishola, who earned a doctoral degree in missiology from Southwestern Baptist Theological Seminary, Forth Worth, Texas, USA, in 1992, and who had spent his youth in the Yoruba Diaspora communities in Ghana. Upon his election as the general secretary in 2001, Dr Ishola adopted the motto 'Empowering Churches for Kingdom Growth' to mobilise the churches for growth in all dimensions. In addition, he carried out a restructuring of the programme of the annual general session of the Convention. The traditional emphasis on debates, taking reports and the

---

[60] Emiola Nihinlola, *A Biblical Evaluation of Pentecostalism* (Ibadan: Sceptre Prints, 1998), p. 22.
[61] Emiola Nihinlola, 'The BSF Vision (Part III)' *Nigerian Baptist*, March 1997, p. 11.

business meetings was retained from 8.00 a.m. till 4.00 p.m. each day. However, Dr Ishola introduced evening worship programmes, usually held from 5.00 p.m. to 8.00 p.m. each day, consisting of large open services with singing and dancing, sermons and ministry for healing that are characteristic of Pentecostal churches. The charismatic fervour in these services was glaring, and within two years the success of the innovation was widely reported, and, thus, attracted more Baptists and others to the evening programme. However, Ishola's delicate attempt to replace congregational polity with an episcopal polity in 2006 soon awakened some Baptists to the imperative of defending the Baptist heritage.

In 2005 there were discussions about restructuring the Nigerian Baptist Convention and making it more relevant in the contemporary world. A committee was set up which submitted its report to the 93rd annual convention session held in April 2006 in Owerri.[62] Certain points in the proposal were very alarming as it sought to modify congregational polity by giving executive powers to elected officials. In fact, considerable executive powers were proposed for the general secretary, secretary of conferences and moderators of associations. To crown it all, the nomenclature of 'general overseer', 'regional overseer' and so on, already popularised by Pentecostals for their authoritarian leadership, was put forward. The general secretary as 'general overseer' was to 'have spiritual oversight responsibilities for all the churches of the denomination' and the funds of each local church 'will be managed by the General Overseer and Regional Overseers according to the vision that they have for the denomination. They will allocate the funds to churches as they deem fit instead of the co-operative plan.'[63] In Nigerian Pentecostal churches, a general overseer is really the pastor of the denomination and every local pastor or area or regional pastor is subordinate to the general overseer who can transfer, promote, demote or discipline any pastor at any time as he deems necessary without reference to any body or to any constitution, and most often appeal is not possible.

There was immediate opposition to this proposal, and some Baptists alleged that the Nigerian Baptist Convention was about to be turned into a denomination with a Pentecostal structure and an episcopal polity. They, therefore, urged going back to the Baptist heritage of the autonomy of the local church and the Baptist co-operative programme which had worked in Nigeria for over 150 years.[64] The total rejection of this restructuring package partly indicated that though Nigerian Baptists were seeking spiritual renewal and

---

[62] Nigerian Baptist Convention Restructuring Committee Report (Ibadan: Baptist Press, 2006). Addendum to the Book of Report, Nigerian Baptist Convention, *Book of Reports, 2006* (Ibadan, 2006).
[63] A.O. Ilupeju, *Reactions to the Proposed Plan for the Restructuring of the Nigerian Baptist Convention* (Lagos: no pub., 2006), pp. 1-2. See also A.O. Tella, *The Nigerian Baptist Congregational Restructuring Update: Matters Arising* (Ibadan: no pub., 2006)
[64] Ilupeju, *Reactions to the Proposed Plan*, p. 1.

social relevance in the contemporary world, they still wanted to keep their distinctive Baptist heritage and identity and not be like any Pentecostal denomination.

Ghana Baptist Convention and Charismatic Renewal

Although the Baptist faith was a latecomer to Ghana in comparison to the Presbyterians and Methodists, whose beginnings go back to 1828 and 1835, respectively, and who were widespread in the country,[65] yet charismatic renewal also exerted an influence upon the Baptists in Ghana. However, it did not have any long-lasting disrupting impact. At the time charismatic renewal was spreading in the 1970s and 1980s, the Ghana Baptist churches were just regrouping after the expulsion of the Yoruba Baptists who had dominated the Baptist faith in Ghana. Secondly, the Baptist faith in Ghana was not anywhere large and neither did it have many branches in the 1970s and 1980s, so contacts with charismatic renewal were limited. More important, most converts in Baptist churches came from other denominations, including Pentecostal churches, and so Pentecostal spirituality was one of the varied backgrounds for Ghanaian Baptists during that period. In fact, almost all the Ghanaian leaders in the 1980s and 1990s were converts from other Christian churches. Lastly, some of the churches did not have pastors; hence leadership opposition to charismatic renewal was very limited.

After the exit of the Yorubas, Southern Baptist missionaries embarked on a more concerted missionary effort through intensive evangelism using the media, tracts, outreach to university students and lastly church planting. This yielded fruit and brought into the church a largely middle-class membership in the big cities.

Although Ghana's population of 22 million is small compared to Nigeria's 140 million population, 69.1% of Ghana's population claimed to be Christians, which was the highest percentage in West Africa. Christianity in Ghana is widespread and has had much pervasive impact on every institution in Ghana. One clear indication of this is the fact that Christian prayers are said at every public function and gospel music has become part of popular culture.

Although from one locality to the other Baptist churches have co-operated with other Christian churches in many evangelistic and ecumenical activities, it was the New Life for All evangelistic programme of the late 1960s which brought all Christian churches together for a concerted effort at evangelisation that drew Baptist churches into the mainstream of ecumenical relations. Later the Ghana Baptist Convention became a member of the Christian Council of Ghana.

---

[65] Alfred Koduah, *Christianity in Ghana Today* (Accra: Advocate Publishing, 2004), pp. 22-29.

After the exit of the Yoruba Baptists, the largest and the most vibrant Baptist church was the Calvary Baptist Church situated in the centre of the city of Accra, and it was in that church that Pentecostal spirituality was first manifested. Established by the missionaries of the Southern Baptist Convention in 1968, its membership was mostly young people who had been recruited from other Christian churches.[66] They were enthusiastically evangelistic and also Evangelical. Some had participated in the Scripture Union, an Evangelical organisation for children and young people, and in the Ghana Fellowship of Evangelical Students (GHAFES), an Evangelical student association whose history is closely tied to the Evangelical Christian Unions in UK. Despite their conservative backgrounds, Pentecostal manifestations were noticed in these groups in the 1970s as some of their members also participated in the evangelistic activities of Pentecostal televangelists that visited the country.

About 1976, Stevenson Alfred Williams, an African American with a music ministry, began to participate in worship services in Calvary Baptist Church. His enthusiastic religious lifestyle, coming from the background of the black churches in the United States, and his generosity made him an endearing figure in the church. In the absence of any theologically-trained minister, he was appointed the pastor of the church in October 1977.[67] Under his pastorate, Pentecostal spirituality and charismatic manifestations of the baptism of the Holy Spirit, speaking in tongues, healing and miracles and what Pentecostals call the 'nine gifts of the Spirit' became prominent in worship services.[68] As noted by Cephas N. Omenyo, 'the charismatic renewal in the Calvary Baptist Church brought a lot of vibrancy' as it grew tremendously in numbers. Worship became livelier and eventually transformed the financial base of the church such that by the mid-1980s, it was financially independent and was self-propagating. Evangelistic, Bible study and prayer ministries sprang up in the church.[69] This background provided the impetus for inviting Pentecostal evangelists from Nigeria and USA to conduct revivals in the church between 1987 and 1993.[70]

Likewise, in another big church, Grace Baptist Church, Kumasi, the leadership promoted charismatic renewal and invited freelance evangelists to conduct revival services in the church. As a result, the church witnessed tremendous growth and its church planting activities spread charismatic renewal within the Baptist tradition in Kumasi and its surrounding towns and

---

[66] *A History of Calvary Baptist Church* (Accra: Calvary Baptist Church, 2003), pp. 11-20.
[67] *Calvary Baptist Church*, p. 25.
[68] *Calvary Baptist Church*, pp. 25-26.
[69] *Calvary Baptist Church*, p. 26. See also Omenyo, *Pentecost outside Pentecostalism*, pp. 193.
[70] *Calvary Baptist Church*, p. 44.

villages.⁷¹ Alfred Nyamekye, one of the pastors of Grace Baptist Church, who had spearheaded charismatic renewal, eventually left the church and established an independent Pentecostal congregation in the same city.⁷² In all these developments, the Southern Baptist missionaries did not intervene, though there were indications that they were apprehensive about charismatic renewal and were worried about how Baptist heritage was gradually being eroded.

In 1985, Williams became the president of the Ghana Baptist Convention, and the conflict regarding Pentecostal spirituality was played out at the 1986 annual session of the Convention. In his presidential address, Williams severely criticised the Southern Baptist missionaries and affirmed his support for charismatic renewal. The Southern Baptist missionaries walked out of the Convention session and gave notice that they were severing their relationship with the Ghana Baptist Convention until things were sorted out and Baptist principles put into operation once again. The conflict resulted in two fractions of the Ghana Baptist Convention.⁷³ The churches that supported Williams were those which had become charismatic, while those that opposed Pentecostalism sided with the Southern Baptist Convention missionaries.⁷⁴ Initially, many Ghanaian Baptists sided with Williams but within a year, it became clear that he was autocratic and had no regard for Baptist principles. Williams's supporters believed that the cause of the conflict was the Pentecostal spirituality which had been accepted by Williams and Calvary Baptist Church and not the caustic remarks about the American missionaries in the presidential speech.

In May 1992, reconciliation was effected and co-operation once again resumed with the Southern Baptist Convention. Interestingly, in the discussions leading to reunion, not much was discussed about charismatic renewal. At the first convention session in August 1992, it was reported that 'every delegate present…on that occasion burst into 'tongues' and acknowledged that the reunion was a divine gift from the Holy Spirit'.⁷⁵ Indeed, this was a happy ending to a bitter struggle.

Ghanaian Baptists, like their Nigerian counterparts, have accommodated certain Pentecostal practices. In fact, through the influence of Pentecostals and charismatics, Ghana Baptist ministers are now required to wear clerical collars as part of their costume at any public function. In the recent code of ethics approved by the Convention, the wearing of clerical collars was mandated, though no punishment was prescribed for defaulters.⁷⁶

---

⁷¹ *Grace Baptist Church: 40ᵗʰ Anniversary Celebration, 1968-2008* (Kumasi: Grace Baptist Church, 2008), pp. 7-8.
⁷² Omenyo, *Pentecost outside Pentecostalism*, p. 194.
⁷³ For more details of the crisis, see Boadi, *Ghana Baptist Convention*, pp. 99-116.
⁷⁴ Calvary Baptist records admitted this fact. See *Calvary Baptist Church*, pp. 53-54.
⁷⁵ *Calvary Baptist Church*, p. 54.
⁷⁶ 'Code of Ethics and Discipline for Ministers', Ghana Baptist Convention, 45ᵗʰ Annual Session Report Book (Accra: Ghana Baptist Convention, 2008), pp. 27-47.

Conclusion

Charismatic renewal has made a great impact on many denominations, including Baptists, in Ghana and Nigeria. As a renewal movement, it is a religion that calls for intense religious experience, and also calls attention to the text of the scriptures. It is still spreading across many denominations, partly, because its doctrinal emphases are contextually relevant to the contemporary situation facing millions of West Africans. While it has become the vehicle for renewal in some churches, it has also been the cause for conflict and misunderstanding in many others.

While in certain cases, Baptist heritage has been eroded, charismatic renewal has eventually contributed to growth in some Baptist churches. The proliferation of these new churches and their activities offer many challenges to the existing churches, including Baptist churches. First, religious experience plays a crucial role in the life and thought of the charismatic movement. Charismatics are attempting to integrate experience into a doctrinal system that has developed with minimal reference to the experiential side of Christianity. The experience that is greatly emphasised is the work of the Holy Spirit, something which was strongly reflected in the lives of the early Christians. Moreover, the simplicity of the means used by the new churches enabled them to reach the masses at the grass roots. The movements are laying a new emphasis on spontaneous oral expression, and thus they are answering the contemporary need for experience and authenticity. The emphasis on experience in Pentecostal theology makes the theology, itself, quite difficult to assess from a non-Pentecostal viewpoint.[77] Hence, theologians of non-Pentecostal churches may not be capable of examining the teachings of the movement perceptively.

Baptist heritage has survived four hundred years of upheaval and changes, and it is still surviving in the face of the onslaught of Pentecostalism. In this contest between Baptist distinctiveness and giving primacy to religious experience, 'much is at stake – the content of the Baptist vision, the integrity of the Baptist witness, and the quality of the Baptist future'.[78] Unless there is internal weakness, West African Baptists will continue to maintain their distinctiveness within global Christianity.

The implications of the interaction of West African Baptists with Pentecostalism are that a living faith must exercise a growing understanding of its environment and the needs of the people. This is what has happened in the past three decades in West Africa. Secondly, it is really obvious that charismatic beliefs and practices can be accommodated as other forms of Baptist expression as long as no aspect of traditional Baptist heritage is

---

[77] Matthew S. Clark and Henry I. Lederle et al., *What is Distinctive About Pentecostal Theology?* (Pretoria: University of South Africa, 1989), p. 38.

[78] Charles W. Deweese (ed.), *Defining Baptist Convictions: Guidelines for the Twenty-First Century* (Franklin, TN: Providence House Publishers, 1996), p. 17.

jettisoned. West African Baptists have shown that they want to remain as Baptists but require a dynamic faith for achieving that amidst the competitive religious landscape. Indeed, for Africans, theology is increasingly shaped by religious experience and not by rational thinking. Hence it was necessary to enlarge the charismatic space to accommodate young people and larger numbers, and thus bring renewal to the faith. Consequently, in the twenty-first century, a new African tradition of Baptist faith is already emerging. Therefore, the Baptist faith will no longer be defined solely by the Anglo-American or European traditions, but also by the new African religious expression.

Index

A Practical View of the Prevailing Religious System of Professed Christians in the Higher and Middle Classes (1797), 60
A Sigh for Peace: or The Cause of Division Discovered (1671), 24
A Tribute to the Memory of the Apostles (Henry Grew), 51
Abercrombie, Charles, 53
Abolition Bill, 85
Aboriginal cosmogony and cosmology, 262
Aboriginal Evangelical Fellowship, 251
Aborigines Inland Mission (AIM), 257
Abraham-Williams, Gethin, 133
Aderoju, Mrs A., 380
African Baptist Church, 363
African Baptist Missionary Society, 364
African Church Movement, 367
Agbebi, Dr Mojola, 367
Akande, Dr S. T. Ola, 380
Aked, C.F., 169
Alberta Baptist Association, 149
Alfred Place Baptist Church, Aberystwyth, 133
American Baptist Foreign Mission Society, 157, 160, 335, 337, 343
American Bible Society, 105
American Board of Commissioners for Foreign Missions, 335
American or Know Nothing Party, 104, 112
American Protestant Society, 111
American Republican Party, 104, 111, 112
Amsterdam, 3, 15, 16, 22, 27, 128, 172, 174
An Address to the People of Great Britain, on the Propriety of Abstaining from West India Sugar and Rum. See Fox, William

Anabaptism, Anabaptists, xv, 3, 4, 5, 6, 7, 8, 9, 10, 11, 12, 13, 14, 15, 16, 17, 18, 19, 21, 24, 26, 27, 28, 189
Anderson, Christopher, 72
Angas, George Fife, 220
Anglicanism, Anglicans, 29, 33-36, 40-46, 56, 59, 61, 62, 65, 75, 76, 79, 83, 119, 121, 125, 127, 134, 139, 141-145, 157, 158, 170, 171, 181, 189, 196, 203, 218, 219, 225, 229, 235, 243, 249, 279, 281, 283, 285, 336, 364-368, 373,*See* Church of England
Anglo-South African (Boer) War, 266, 271-273
Angus, Joseph, 204
AntiBurgher Secession Church, 50
Anti-Catholicism, xvi, 113, 114
Anti-Chinese Immigration Committee, 268
antisacramentalism, 4
anti-Semitism, 188
Armadale Baptist Church, Melbourne, 244, 246, 247
Arminianism, xv, 53, 90, 91
Arnold, Ellen, 244, 311, 312, 313, 314, 315, 316, 318, 320, 322
Ashworth, John, 58
Associating Evangelical Churches of Wales, 133
Ataikola, Bengal, 311, 312, 314, 315, 316, 319, 320, 322
Aubrey, M.E., 170, 175, 192
Auchtermuchty, Fife, 52
Aung San Suu Kyi, 351
Australasia, 158, 166, 167, 174
Australia, xvi, xvii, 53, 54, 81, 124, 126, 158, 161, 166, 167, 174, 197, 201-216 *passim*, 216-241 *passim*, 242-250 *passim,*, 251-262 *passim*, 282, 286, 300, 311-327 *passim*, 330, 332
Australian Aborigines, 251-262 *passim*
Australian Baptist, 174, 216, 219, 229, 232, 243, 313

Australian Baptist Foreign Missionary Society, 311
Australian Baptist Home Mission, 258
Australian Baptist Missionary Society (ABMS), 311, 315, 323, 324, 325, 326, 331, 332
Australian Baptist Research Forum, xvii
Australian Baptists, xvii, 167, 174, 201, 203, 215, 216, 219, 220, 222, 223, 224, 228, 229, 230, 231, 232, 233, 234, 238, 239, 240, 312
Auvache, F.W., 139
Axling, Dr William, 165
Ayr Baptist Church, 125
Badger, David, 223
Baker, Moses, 63
Baker, Robert A., 4, 5, 63, 64, 68, 156, 178, 217, 303, 364
baptism, xvi, 3-28 *passim*, 50, 53, 55, 107, 121, 122, 127, 128, 131, 140, 146, 147, 153, 154, 170, 181, 182, 205, 216, 220-223, 226, 227, 230-238, 240, 246, 257, 260, 267, 313, 328, 329, 332, 334, 340, 361, 362, 373, 376, 380, 383, 387
baptismal regeneration, 107, 153, 329
Baptist Catechism, The, 20
Baptist Convention of Manitoba and the Northwest, 142, 152
Baptist Convention of Ontario, 145
Baptist Convention of Quebec, 143, 145, 150, 153, 154, 163, 164
Baptist Convention of Western Canada, 137
Baptist Federation of Canada, 145, 164
Baptist historians, 18, 26, 99, 100, 102
Baptist Home Mission Society, 114, 115, 116
Baptist Home Missions Department (New Zealand), 290
Baptist Magazine, 67, 68, 71, 73, 157, 204, 219, 339, 340, 341, 342
Baptist ministry, 235, 245, 252, 258, 323, 325
Baptist Missionary Society (British), 50, 56-85 *passim*, 134, 157, 159, 165, 203, 260, 311-314, 317, 334, 364, 365
Baptist Protestant Society, 111
Baptist Record, 235, 236

Baptist Student Fellowship (BSF) (Nigeria), 378-382, 384
Baptist theology, 3, 16, 27, 30, 45, 261, 294, 297, 305
Baptist Times, 129, 157
Baptist Times and Freeman, 157
Baptist Union of Australia, 167, 238, 240, 241, 260
Baptist Union of Canada, 136, 153
Baptist Union of Great Britain [and Ireland], xv, 29, 119-122, 126-135, 157, 169-171, 228
Baptist Union of New South Wales, 233, 234, 238, 240
Baptist Union of New Zealand, 267, 284
Baptist Union of Scotland, 53, 125, 157, 171
Baptist Union of the Northern Territory, 251
Baptist Union of Victoria, 208, 209
Baptist Union of Wales, 120, 124, 130-135, 169, 171, 175
Baptist Union of Wales and Monmouthshire, 120
Baptist Union of Western Canada, 136-155 *passim*, 164
Baptist Watchman, 104
Baptist Women's Missionary Society of Manitoba, 151
Baptist World Alliance (BWA), 94, 121, 131, 168, 177-198 *passim*, 364
Baptist World Congresses, 180-197 *passim*, 246
Barreira, Paul, 235
Bartlett, E.B., 113
Barton, John, 58
Bathurst Street Baptist Church, 205, 252
Bathurst, Lord, 71
Bayley family, 51
Bebbington, David, xv, 178, 284, 289
Bengal Baptist Union, 311, 312, 316
Bengal, Bengalis, xvii, 311, 312, 321, 322
Benin Republic, 365, 368, 372
Bible, 10, 72, 87, 105, 106, 107, 111, 121, 133, 177, 180, 195, 205, 213, 230, 248, 254, 258, 260-262, 270, 305, 315, 320, 328, 329, 331, 337,

Index 393

338, 340, 358, 374, 375, 387, *See* scripture, scriptures
Bible Society of Nigeria, 370
Billington, Ray Allen, 103, 104, 105, 109
Bimbadeen College, 251
Bingham, H.H., 139
Birks, Rosetta, 224
Birmingham, Alabama, 191
Bishop of Rochester, 61, 62
bishops. *See* episcopacy
Biswas, Punchanon, 313, 316, 317, 318
Black, James, 146, 147
Blunt, Richard, 19
Bonaparte, Napoleon, 70
Booth, Abraham, 27, 58
Boreham, F.W., 247, 266, 275
Bowbrick, A.J., 150, 151
Bowen, Thomas Jefferson, 366, 367
Bradshaw, Nick, 135
Breconshire Association, 120
Bretherton, Luke, 215
Brethren, 54, 165, 180, 287
Briggs, John, 201, 215
Bristol, 56-85 passim, 124, 169, 170, 267
Bristol Baptist Academy, 57
Bristol Baptist College, 57
British and Foreign Bible Society, 72, 134
British colonial rule, 344, 353
British Columbia Baptist Convention, 139
British Council of Churches, 129, 170, 171
British Empire, 56, 63, 149, 178, 203, 219
Broadmead, Bristol, 57, 68, 77, 80
Brougham, Henry, 79
Brown, Charles, 127, 185
Brown, Ian, 280, 285, 287, 288, 289, 290
Bruce, Archibald, 50
Buck, William, 112
Buddhism, xvii, 336, 345-354
Bulyea, Mrs G. H. V., 143
Bunting, Jabez, 80, 84
Bunyan, John, 34, 195
Burkina Faso, 365, 368, 372
Burls, William, 66

Burma, xvii, 159, 165, 174, 334-361 *passim*
Burmese nationalism, 344
Burton Street Baptist Church, Sydney, 243
Bushnell, Horace, 246
Butterworth, Joseph, 80, 84
Buxton, Thomas, 253, 254
Calcutta, 66, 72, 81, 126, 311-320, 335
Caldicott, Thomas Ford, 108
Calvin, Calvinists, Calvinism, 19, 20, 49, 50, 53, 55, 89, 98, 99, 125, 164, 220, 249, 329
Cambridge, 32, 33, 57, 58, 62, 65, 69, 72, 156, 175, 180, 182, 280, 285, 288, 290, 294
Cameroon, 365, 372
Cameroon Baptist Convention, 365
Campbell, Alexander, 49, 50, 87, 88
Campbell, Thomas, 50, 51
Campbellism, Campbellites, 50, 51, 52, 53, 54, 55
Canada, 53-55, 115, 136-155 *passim*, 158, 161, 163-165, 173, 193, 287, 364
Canadianisation, 142, 143, 154
Canberra Baptist Church, 211
Cardiff Baptist College, 127, 133
Carey Baptist Grammar School, 81, 211
Carey, Felix, 334
Carey, William, 60, 61, 65, 67, 70, 81, 83, 84, 114, 195, 311, 324, 334, 357
Carlile, J.C., 169, 187
Carmichael, Robert, 50
Cary, Lott, 364
Castlereagh, Lord, 68
Catholicism. *See* Roman Catholicism, Roman Catholics
Cawley, Laurie, 326
Central Baptist Church, Regina, 149
Certeau, Michel de, 304, 305
Ceylon, 159
Chambers, Paul, 134
Chance, T.W., 124
chaplains, 124, 125, 170, 212, 228, 326, 327
charismatic movements, 361, 370-376
charismatic renewal, xvi, 286, 368, 372- 389

Charlestown, Massachusetts, 104
Charter, James, 334
Charteris, W.C., 125
China, 111, 157, 159, 165, 174, 224, 270, 350
China Inland Mission, 160, 224
Chowdury, Samson, 311
Christchurch, New Zealand, 267
Christian and Missionary Alliance, 160, 324, 325, 332
Christian Association of Nigeria, 370
Christian Council of Nigeria, 369, 370
Christian-Buddhist relations, 359
Christianisation, 142, 188, 193, 194, 197
Christianismus Primitivus (1678), 25, 31, 38, 39, 40-43
church and state, 3, 18, 36, 45, 79, 190, 201, 202, 203, 205, 210, 211, 215, 218, 265, 346, 350, 362
church growth movement, 290
Church Missionary Society, 60, 65, 366
Church of England, xv, 31-33, 43, 59, 65, 66, 75, 85, 126, 139, 142, 203, 218, 219, 225, 228, 229, 234, 265, *See* Anglicanism, Anglicans
Church of Nigeria., 369
church union, xvi, 137, 142, 163, 216, 217, 226-240
Churches at the Crossroads A Study in Church Unity, The (1918, J.H. Shakespeare), 126, 228
Churches of Christ, xvi, 25, 49-55, 106, 162, 165, 166, 173, 196, 220, 226, 227, 236
Churches Together, 129
Churches Together in England (CTE), 129, 133
Clapham, 56, 60, 62, 64
Clarke, John, 63
Clifford, John, 177, 181-183, 189, 194, 195
Clifford, N. Keith, 146
close communion, 92, 93, 123, 126, *See* open communion
Collins Street Baptist Church, 204-209
Collins, William, 20
Colwyn Bay Institute, 367
Comilla, Bengal, 313, 317, 318, 320

Commission of Covenanting Churches, The, 129
Committee of Protestant Dissenting Ministers for the West Riding of Yorkshire, 58
Communism, 178, 191, 192
Conference of Missionary Societies of Great Britain and Ireland, 161
Congregational Union of Canada, 147
Congregational Union of England and Wales, 122, 170
Congregationalism, Congregationalists, 71, 114, 121-128, 131, 136-139, 142, 144-147, 150, 154, 157, 163, 165, 167, 168, 170, 182, 204, 207, 216, 221-244 *passim*, 257, 313, 334, 385
Connecticut Baptist Convention, 110, 115
conscience, 3, 9, 12, 14, 25, 34, 45, 46, 66, 70, 108, 113, 187, 201, 210, 223, 246, 254, 267, 286
Conservative Baptist Association, 173
contextualisation, 259, 260, 301, 344, 354
conversion approach, 266
Cope, Herbert J., 344
Correspondence of William Wilberforce, The, 56, 57
Côte d'Ivoire, 365, 368
Council of Churches for Britain and Ireland, 129
Council of Churches for Wales, 129, 133
Council of Churches in South Australia, 225
Cox, F.A., 80
Craig, Charles, 332
Criccieth, 52
Crieff, Perthshire, 52
Crosby, C.C.P., 108
Cross, Anthony, 133
Crouch, Andy, 292, 293, 296, 297
Crowell, William, 95, 96
Cumberland Presbyterians, xv, 88, 90, 91, 92, 94, 99, 100
Curry, J.L.M., 113
Cursons, William, 267, 275
Cyprian, 34
Cytûn: Churches Together in Wales, 129-134

Index 395

Daguragu, 258
Danbury, Connecticut, 50
Dani people, 323, 325
Das, Kailash Krista, 316, 320
Das, Srimati Hironmayee, 320
Davidson, Allan, 279, 282
de Ries, John, 15
Declaration and Address (Thomas Campbell,1809), 51
deconstruction, 101, 354
deism, 59
democracy, 180, 184, 187, 189, 193, 351
Denbigh, Flint and Merioneth Association, 123
Denck, Hans, 4
denominationalism, 147, 148
Depression, 177, 184, 186, 187, 194, 244
Derrida, Jacques, 101
Disciples of Christ, 49, 52, 54, 55, 145, 148, 152, 153, 154, 162, 226
discipleship, 46, 150, 191, 293, 306
Dissent, Dissenters, 34, 56, 59-67, 70, 72, 73, 79, 82, 242, *See* Nonconformity, Nonconformists
divine presence, 43
Dixon, A.C., 193
Dixon, Miss Retta, 257
Doke, Clement, 113, 274
Doke, J.J., xvi, 265-276 *passim*
Dore, James, 58
Doris (of Wattle Creek), 258
Dowling, Henry, 204
Dowling, John, 106
Downey, Alexander, 91, 92
Dr Pritchard Memorial Church, Llangollen, 126
Dr Williams's Library, 73
Draper, Norman, 324, 325, 331
Dunbar, 53
Dundee, 49
Dutch Collegiant Mennonites, 3
Dutch Reformed, xvi
East Asia, 165, 166, 346
East Asian Christian Conference, 174
East Glamorgan Association, 120
East India Company, 60, 65, 69, 335
East Melbourne Baptist Church, 209
Ebenezer Baptist Church, Ijokodo, Ibadan, 382

ecclesiology, 3, 280, 305, 307, 354
ecumenism, xvi, 18, 83, 121-137, 144, 153, 156-176, 190, 217, 221, 239, 353, 356, 360, 368
Eddy, Daniel Clarke, 112
Edinburgh, 50, 52, 53, 65, 72, 84, 156-161, 171, 173, 175, 181, 182, 196, 227, 334
Edmunds, Thomas, 123
Education Bill (1820), 79
Edwards, William, 124
Ellis, Tom, 119
Ellis, William, 254
Ellul, Jacques, 290
England, 3, 16, 17, 30-35, 41, 49-51, 63, 65, 69, 77, 79, 100, 107, 119-132, 169, 189, 206, 218, 225, 228, 229, 232, 235, 245, 253, 255, 265, 267, 313, 318, 351, 358, 364, 365
England, Bishop John, 107
English Baptist Church at Commercial Street, Newport, Monmouthshire, 126
English Baptist Union, 204
English Separatists, 3, 17
Enlightenment, 218, 220, 221, 232, 301
episcopacy, 29-38, 43, 46, 228, 229
Errett, Isaac, 50
Estep, William, 16, 17, 171-173
European Baptist Federation, 131, 175
Evangelical, 72, 105, 121, 130, 132, 140, 157, 163, 178, 194, 205, 221, 224, 228, 286, 287, 289, 313
Evangelical Baptist Church, 363
Evangelical Christian Union, 373
Evangelicals, Evangelicalism, xvi, 50, 56-62, 72, 81, 85, 94, 109, 121, 122, 126, 130-134, 157, 158, 160, 163, 166-169, 176-180, 193, 194, 203, 206, 216, 219-225, 230, 232, 233, 240, 244, 245, 251-256, 265, 267, 275, 281, 284, 287, 288, 301, 323, 324, 327, 328, 330, 332, 333, 361, 362, 368, 373, 380, 381, 387
evangelism, 37, 38, 45, 61, 62, 71, 82, 116, 138, 139, 178, 188, 193, 242, 280, 290, 355, 364, 370, 376, 382, 386
Evans, Beriah Gwynfe, 119
Evans, Caleb, 58

Evans, Percy, 175
Evansville, 88, 90
Evening Post, 78, 286
Ewing, Greville, 50
ex opere operato, 4, 6, 10, 25, 28
Fairey, Samuel, 209
Fawcett, John, 57, 58
Federal Council of the Evangelical Free Churches, 169
Fellowship of Independent Evangelical Churches, 130
Fiddes, Paul, 18, 27, 202, 215, 288
Fifth Baptist World Congress (1934), 187
First Baptist Church, Pearl Street, Brooklyn, 109
First Baptist, Vancouver, 139
First Baptist, Winnipeg, 140
Fleming, Tom, 258, 259
Flinders Street Baptist Church, 227, 244, 312, 313
footwashing, 12
Foster, John, 67
Fountain, John, 70
Fowler, Stanley, 16, 20, 22
Fox, William, 58
Free Church(es), 3, 5-7, 11, 15, 18-20, 24, 25-27, 122, 126, 167-170, 181, 228, 229
Free Will Baptists, 89, 162, 164, 363
Freeman, Curtis, 3, 27
Freeman, J.D., 180, 181, 194
Fridén, George, 197
Full Gospel Businessmen's Fellowship International (FGBMFI), 378
Fuller Theological Seminary, 290
Fuller, Andrew, 27, 57-62, 65-72, 78, 80-85, 107
Fuller, Richard, 107
fundamentalists, 186, 193
Furreedpore, Bengal, 216, 312-317,
Gambrell, James B, 162
Gandhi, Mahatma, 266, 267, 273, 274, 275
Garner, Robert, 20-22
Garrett, James, Leo, 105-107, 158, 163, 165-168, 170, 173
gathered church, 7, 9, 265
gathering as sacrament, 294
General Association of Regular Baptists, 173

General Baptist Herald, 93
General Baptists, xvi, 16,-20, 24, 25, 36, 37, 41-43, 86-102 *passim*
Georgia, 29, 110, 111, 366
Georgia Baptist Convention, 110
Gerrits, Lubbert, 15
Ghana, xvi, 158, 362-389 *passim*
Ghana Baptist Convention, 366, 386, 388
Gibbs, Edward, 206, 209
Gilbert, Marie, 312, 313, 317
Gillette, A.D., 109
Glamorgan English Strict Baptist Association, 124
Glas, John, 49, 50, 55
Glasgow, 50, 53, 125, 161
Glasites, 49, 50
Glenelg, Lord, 253
glocalisation, 300
Glover, T.R., 127, 169
Goertz, Hans-Jürge, 8, 14
Going, J., 114
Golding, Elfed, 134
Goldsack, William, 314, 315
Gonsalves, M.J., 109
gospel and culture, 294, 299, 301, 302, 306, 307
Gospel Baptist Conference, 363
Gotsiridze, Rusadan, 29
Grace Baptist Church, Kumasi, 387
Graham, Billy, 266
Graham, Elaine, 214
Grant, John Webster, 136, 154
Grantham, Thomas, 20, 24, 25, 26, 31, 38-43
Graves, J.R., 86, 87, 112
Great Commission, 114, 185
great reversal, 178, 179, 193
Grebel, Conrad, 4
Green, A.E., 225
Gregory, Olinthus, 57, 62
Grew, Henry, 51
Grey, J. Grattan, 272
Griffith, Gwilym Oswald, 119
Grigg, Jacob, 70
Groves, David, xvi, 30, 323, 326, 327, 329
Guinea, 323, 329-332, 368
Gurindji people, 258, 260, 262
Gurney, Martha, 58
Gurney, W.B., 57, 58, 62

Index 397

Gutteridge, Joseph, 58, 67, 83
Gwaltney, L.L., 191, 192
Haiti, 75, 76, 77, 85
Haldane tradition, 54
Haldane, Robert, 50, 69, 75
Haldanes, James and Robert, 50
Hall, Robert, 57, 58, 62, 69, 77
Ham, John, 204
Hamitic Curse, 252
Hancock, Gordon, 189
Hardy, Colonel James G., 113
Harford, John, 59
Harkness, D.B., 141, 146, 149
Hauerwas, Stanley, 215
Hay, William, 147
Hayford, Mark, 158
Heath Street, Hampstead, 126
Helwys, Thomas, 3, 15, 17, 30
Henderson, J. Raymond, 188
Higlett, William, 210
Hikoi of Hope (1998, New Zealand), 283, 286
Hinton, James, 72
History of Romanism (1848), 106
Hobbs, Herschel H., 4
Hofmann, Melchior, 4
Hogan, Michael, 212
Holden, H. J. (Harry), 225
Hole, Charles, 60
Holland, 3, 16, 19, 174, 328, 329, 331
home mission, 115, 141, 185, 210
Hooker, Richard, 33, 34, 35
    The Laws of Ecclesiastical Polity, 33
Hope, Charles and Laura, 314
Horsey, Joseph, 58
House of Commons, 60, 67, 119
Hubmaier, Balthasar, 5, 6, 7, 8, 10, 12, 14, 15, 18, 19, 26
Hudson, William, 58
Hughes, H.E., 220
Hughes, Hugh Price, 122
Hughes, William, 367
Hull, 59
Hungary, 168, 175
Hunter, Hiram, 91
Hyper-Calvinism, 51
Ide, George B., 109
Idealism, 119, 231, 232
imagination, 259, 300-304, 307

India, xvii, 56-86 passim, 159, 172, 188, 244, 311-322 *passim*, 334-336, 342, 350, 354
Indian Decennial Missionary Conference, 159
Indiana, USA xvi, 86-102 passim, 110, 372
Indiana Baptist Convention, 110
Indigenous Australians, xvii
indigenous peoples, 188, 365
Indonesian Papua, xvi, 323
Indonesian province of Papua, 323
infant baptism, 107, 146, 237, 329, *See* paedobaptism
Ingold, S.R., 272
Ings, Miss, 314
Inter-Church Forward Movement, 149
International Conference on Baptist Studies, xvii, 102
International Missionary Council, 156, 159, 160, 161, 172, 182
International Review of Missions, 159
intolerance, 113, 236
Ireland, 54, 116, 119, 120, 129, 230
Ishola, Ademola, 376, 379, 381, 384
Ishola, Dr Ademola, 381
Jackson Avenue Baptist Mission,, 139, 143
Jamaica, 56-85 *passim*
James, Henry, 126
Japan, 159, 165, 166, 351
Japan Baptist Convention, 165
Japanese Baptist Churches, 165
Java, 71, 78, 330, 332
Jefferies, James, 222
Jefferson, Thomas, 202
Jeffery, Will, 38, 41
John, E.T., 119
Johnston, Kerr, 204
Jones, A.E.O., 125
Jones, Dr Martin Lloyd, 132
Jones, J. Ithel, 128
Jones, Philip, 183
Jones, R. Tudur, 121, 122, 127, 128, 129
Jones, Sir David, 128
Jones, Thomas, 125
Jones, W.E., 125
Jones, William, 50, 51
Jordan, Ivan, 259

Judson, Adoniram, 15, 26, 39, 60, 88, 136, 153, 158, 160, 195, 334-360 *passim*
Judson, Ann H., 57, 335, 338
justice, 186, 191, 266-275 passim, 276, 279-290 *passim*, , 360
Kachin Baptist Convention, 356, 357
Kalkaringi, 258
Karen people, 338-351 *passim*
Karo, D. H., 380
Kautz, Jacob, 4
Keach, Benjamin, 20, 27
Kearney, Richard, 303
Keeney, William E., 11, 13
Kentucky, 88, 91, 104, 110, 113, 114, 179
Kettering, 67, 72, 84
Kickert, Mark, 260
Kierstead, G.F.C., 149, 150
Kirkpatrick, Mary Frank, 379
Klaassen, Walter, 4, 8
Knapdale, 54
Korea, 159
Kulin nations, 253
l'Union des Eglises Baptistes du Cameroun (UEBC), 365
Lagos Baptist Church, 367
Lajamanu, 258, 259
Lamb, William, 233, 243
Landmark Baptists, 112
Langdon. Thomas, 57, 58
Latin America, 158
latitudinarianism, 59
Latvia, 29
Lawrence, Henry, 20, 22, 24
Laymen's Missionary Movement, 137, 146, 148
League for the Preservation of Religion, 219
League of Nations, 190, 192
Leeds, 57, 58
Leigh, S. M., 382
liberalism, 230, 231
Liberia, 364
Liberty Association of General Baptists, 89
Lindbeck, George, 301
Lingiari, Vincent, 251
Litch, J. Willard, 139
Little Prescot Street, London, 58
Liverpool, 50, 51, 67, 73, 119, 169

Llangollen Academy, 127
Lloyd George, David, 52, 189
Lloyd, Robert, 124
Lobo Township, Middlesex County, 54
Lochgilphead, 54
Lockhart, Ninian, 52
London Confession, 19, 20, 40, 42
London Confession (1644), 37
London Missionary Society, 254
London Society for Effecting the Abolition of the Slave Trade, 58
London Society for Promoting Christianity among the Jews, 72
Lonsdale Street Baptist Church, Melbourne, 206, 209
Lord's Supper, 3-28 *passim*, 146, 169, 226, See open communion
Louisville, Kentucky, 110
Luther (Martin), Lutherans, 4, 6, 19, 21, 136, 160, 165, 167-169, 175, 218, 221, 260, 337
Luther, M.J., 259
Mabry, Eddie, 5, 6
MacBeath, John, 161, 182
Macdonald, D.G., 147
Macintosh, Professor D.C., 141, 145, 146
Mackie, Charles, 273
Maclean, J.N., 144-148
MacLeish, Norman, 246
MacLeod, Angus, 280, 285, 287
MacNicol, Duncan, 248
Maddox, Marion, 213
Magarey, Thomas, 54
Magill Baptist Church, 232
Malcom, T.S., 110
Mali, 368
Manchester, Duke of, 68
Mander, Henry, 126
Mardon, Richard, 334
Maritimes, Canada, 54
Marpeck, Pilgrim, 7-15, 18, 26
Marshall, A.N., 226
Marshall, Ruth, 371, 372
Marshman, Joshua, 57, 65, 81
Martin, James, 207, 208
Mathews, Shailer, 141, 196
Maung Nau, 339, 340, 353
Maze Pond, Southwark, 57, 58
McClendon, James W., 44
McCormick, W.J., 144, 147

Index 399

McCullough, Robert, 235
McDermid, James, 153
McDonald, A.M., 148
McDonald, Alexander 'Pioneer', 150
McFarlane, Thomas, 206
McGavran, Donald, 290
McGuire, U. M., 187
McKaeg, John, 203, 252
McLaren, David, 53
McLaren, E.D., 141, 142
McLaurin, C.C., 137, 145
McLean, Archibald, 50, 52, 55
McNaughton, Norman, 151
McNicol, Donald, 228, 230, 233
Mead, Silas, 223, 227, 312, 318
Meek, Donald, 54, 55
Melbourne, Australia, xvii, 166, 201-215 *passim*, 218, 225, 229, 233, 243, 244, 248, 253-255, 286, 314, 324, 325, 332
Mennonites, 4, 9, 11, 14-17, 19, 27
Merri Creek School, 254
messengers, 37-45, 109
Methodism, Methodists, 56, 59, 62-65, 76, 79, 80, 94, 110, 121, 122, 125, 128, 129, 131, 132, 136, 138, 140, 142-146, 149, 150, 151, 154, 157, 160, 163, 166, 168, 203, 216, 223, 226, 229, 234, 238-240, 244, 279-288, 366-368, 373, 386
Methodists, 63, 145
Meyer, F.B., 193
midrash, 305
Miles, F.J., 126
military chaplains, 228
Millennial Harbinger and Voluntary Church Advocate, The, 50, 51, 54
Milner, Thomas, 53
Missionary Aviation Fellowship (MAF), 324, 325, 330
missions, 56, 59-61, 64, 69, 71, 75, 77, 82, 85, 89, 98, 105, 114-116, 140, 145, 148, 152, 158, 159, 161, 184, 211, 244, 257, 259, 260, 271, 313, 323-325, 330-333, 336, 358, 368, 369, 372, 376
Missouri Synod (Lutheran), 172
Mitchell, D.F., 242-250
modernity, 301
Mol, Hans, 150
Moldova, 29

Moriah Baptist Church, Risca, 130
Mormons, 54
Morse, Samuel, 103
Mott, John R., 156, 159, 161
Mount Pleasant Baptist Church, Swansea, 126
Mouzi, (Mr Moses), 316, 318
Muir, John, 53
Mullins, E.Y., 181, 194, 196
Münster, 7, 8
Myanmar. *See* Burma
Myanmar Baptist Convention, 335, 353, 357
N.Z. Baptist, 272, 273, 279, 282-284, 287, 288
Namatjira, Albert, 327
Nassau Street Baptist Church, Winnipeg, 147
National Association of Evangelicals, 94
National Baptist Convention of America, 163, 173
National Baptist Convention, U.S.A., Inc., 163
National Churches of Christ in the USA, 173
National Council of Evangelical Free Churches, 122
National Council of the Churches of Christ in the USA, 163
National Council of the Evangelical Free Churches, 169
National Free Church Council, 126
nativism (U.S.A.), 111, 112
Nazism, 192
Ne Win, 348, 349, 350, 351
Nederlands Nieuw Guinea (NNG), 323, 324, 326, 328, 330
Nelson, New Zealand, 268
neo-liberalism, 287
Netherlands, 11, 30, 161, 167, 331, 372
New Christian Movements, 361, 362
New England, 49
New Hebrides, 255
New Jersey Baptist Convention, 114
New South Wales, 166, 174, 203-205, 212, 213, 217, 218, 233, 234, 238, 242, 243, 257, 313

New Testament, 51, 52, 100, 106, 134, 143, 147-154, 177, 188, 201, 204, 209, 234, 246, 248, 249, 329
New Westminster Baptist Church, 139
New York Baptist Register, 108, 110, 111
New Zealand, xvii, 54, 161, 167, 174, 242, 253, 254, 265-276 *passim*, 277-291 *passim*, 292, 295, 297, 312, 313, 320-322, 326
New Zealand Baptist Public Questions Committee, 279, 280, 284-287
New Zealand Christian Council of Social Services, 281
New Zealand Council of Churches, 167
Newbigin, Lesslie, 291
Newman, William, 80
Nicholson, J.F.V., 36-41
Niger Delta, 367
Niger Republic, 365, 368, 373
Nigeria, xvi, 362-389 *passim*
Nigerian Baptist Convention, 363, 366, 368, 369, 376-385
Nigerian Baptist Theological Seminary, Ogbomoso, 365, 381, 384
Noel, Baptist Wriothesley, 205
Nonconformity, Nonconformists, 81, 122, 129, 134, 218, 232, 234, *See* Dissent, Dissenters
Norbury, Dave, 134
North Adelaide Baptist Church, 219
North Baliem Valley, 323-325
North Melbourne Baptist Church, 207
North Wales Baptist College, 125
North Wales English Baptist Union, 121, 134
North, J. J., 272
Northern Baptist College, 132, 135
Northern Baptist Convention, 157, 162, 173
Northern Baptist Learning Community, 135
Northern Territory, Australia, 251, 257, 258, 259, 260
Nottingham, 50, 51, 58, 129, 130
Nova Scotia, 54, 124, 164
Nyamekye, Alfred, 388
Obbe, Philips, 11

Ojo, Dr Matthews A., 379, 380
Okotoks Baptist Church, Alberta, 147
Old Paths Churches of Christ, 49
Oldham, J.H., 159
Old-School Baptists of Ontario, 54
Oliver, Frank, 141
Olivet Baptist Church, New Westminster, 151
Olney, 61
One Tree Hill, 294, 295
Ontario, 54, 137, 142, 145, 150, 163, 164, 173
open communion, 90-95, 123, 124, 153, *See* Lord's Supper
open membership, 126, 223, 232, 236, 240
Orchard, M.L., 143, 147, 151
ordination, 12, 32, 33, 38, 41-43, 91, 95-99, 170, 228, 249, 260, 290
Orita Mefa Baptist Church, Ibadan, 382
Orkney, 125
Orthodox Churches, 18, 19, 24, 39, 168, 172, 181, 191
Orthodox Creed (General Baptist), 18, 19, 24, 39
Ottawa, 140, 142
Owen, Marc, 134
Owen, Owen, 122
Oworonsoki Baptist Church, Lagos, 382
Oxford Movement, 137
Oyo West Baptist Conference, 380, 381, 382
Packer, J.I., 5
paedobaptism, 16, 50, 93, 107, 146, 152, 162, 163, *See* infant baptism
Paisley, 54
Palestine, 188, 297
Pan-Evangelicalism, 221
Particular Baptists, 19 24, 27, 36, 37, 43, 44, 54, 204, 206, 209
Patterson, F.W., 146
Payne, Ernest, 175, 191, 201
Paynter, John, 227
Peacock, Edward, 254
Pennsylvania, 51, 110
Pennsylvania Baptist Convention, 110
Pentecostalism, Pentecostals, 168, 287, 299, 362, 370-378, 384, 385, 387-389

Index

Peterloo Massacre, 76
Peto, Samuel Morton, 57
Philadelphia, 6, 15, 50, 88, 104, 106, 107, 109, 110, 114, 133, 160, 172, 177, 178, 180, 301, 337, 338, 341
Philips, Dirk, 10-17, 26
Phillips, Obbe, 11
Phillips, Thomas, 127, 185
Pitt, William (the Younger), 81
Playford, Thomas, 220
Plumer, William, 106
political activism, 73, 111
Poole, William, 208
Pope John XXII, 107
Portsmouth, 58
Potter, William, 207, 208
premillennialism, 193, 220
Presbyterian Church of Wales, 125
Presbyterianism, Presbyterians, xv, xvi, 35, 36, 86-102 *passim*, 104, 110, 121, 122, 125, 126-155 passim 157, 160-166, 182, 203, 216, 224-226, 229, 230, 234, 235, 238, 239, 240, 242-250 *passim*, 281-285, 341, 365, 366, 368, 373, 386
Price, Charles, 139
Price, J. Arthur, 119
Price, William, 58
Primitive Christianity, 49, 55
Prince Edward Island, 54
prophetic model, 266
Protestant Magazine, 78
Protestant Reformation, 3, 6, 11, 31, 32, 35, 86, 87, 100, 104, 108, 109, 201
Protestant Reformation Society, 104
Protestantism, Protestants, 4, 6, 7, 25, 27, 28, 58, 60, 73-80, 103-116 *passim*, 129, 136, 137, 156-176 *passim*, 182-185, 193, 196, 211, 216, 218-221, 225, 227-230, 234, 235, 240, 245, 261, 284, 291, 334, 362, 364, 370, 373, 375, 376, 378
public issues, xvii, 197, 265, 284, 285, 287, 304
Pugh, F. W. Walker, 147
Qua Iboe Mission, 368
Quakers, 59, 63
Quebec, 137, 142, 145, 163, 173
Queensland Baptist Union, 251

Queensland, Australia, 174, 210, 213, 251, 255
racism, 251, 268
Radnorshire, 122
Radnorshire and Montgomeryshire Baptist Association, 123
Randall, Ian, 88, 127
Rauschenbusch, Walter, 140, 196
Rawlyk, George A., 141
Raws, John, 217, 227, 229, 230, 233
Ray, Stephen, 107
Reardon, Timothy, 9
Reavis, William, 89, 92
Reece, Laurie, 258
Rees, A.M., 125
Reeves, William Pember, 84, 269
Regent's Park College, 57, 60, 84, 125, 311
religious liberty, 105, 113, 116, 164, 169, 180, 181, 189, 195, 212, 218
restoration, 49, 51, 207, 375
Re-thinking Christian Missions, 185
revival, 51, 71, 89, 92, 94, 96, 99, 125, 137, 138, 191, 286, 287, 373, 377, 379, 382, 387
Rhys, Thomas Tudor, 125
Rice, Luther, 334
Riley, W.B., 193
Rippon, John, 66
Roberts, Evan, 120, 125
Robinson, H. Wheeler, 27, 182
Robinson, Robert, 58
Rodway, John, 70
Roman Catholicism, Roman Catholics, xvi, 6, 11, 13, 63, 73, 75, 78, 80, 103-116 *passim*, , 129, 134, 137, 158, 162, 164, 166, 168, 169, 172, 181, 203, 206, 210, 211, 218, 219, 225, 230, 232, 240, 330, 334, 336, 362
Romania, 168
Romanticism, 231
Rose Street, Edinburgh, 52
Ross, Britton, 139
Rothmann, Bernhard, 7, 8
Rowe, John, 64, 68, 85
Roxburgh Terrrace, Edinburgh, 53
Rushbrooke, J.H., 169, 171, 194
Russia, 191, 194
Ryland, John, xvi

Ryland, John E., 56-85 *passim*, 163, 173
sacraments, sacramentalism, xv, 3-28 *passim*, 32, 33, 107, 121, 181, 232, 246, 247, 329
Saffery, John, 60, 61, 84
salvation, 4, 11, 12, 20, 23, 24, 93, 132, 138, 140, 179-181, 185, 186, 256, 329, 332, 353, 354, 355, 357
Salvation Army, 145, 214, 281
Sampey, John R., 173
sampling, 298-307
Sandeman, Robert, 49, 50, 55
Sandemanians, 49, 50
Saskatoon Baptist Church, 139, 148
Saunders, John, 203, 252, 253
Schmidt, Paul, 183, 192
schools, 59, 79, 81, 111, 112, 189, 205, 210- 215, 219, 240, 254, 325, 327, 328, 331, 336, 344, 346, 349, 352, 358, 368, 374, 378, 380
Schreiter, Robert, 300
Schwenckfeld, Caspar, 10
Scotch Baptists, xvi, 49-55 *passim*, 125, 220
Scotch Itinerant Society, 54
Scotland, 32, 35, 49-55, 63, 69, 87, 94, 125, 127, 157, 159, 161, 171, 175, 247, 366
Scott, Thomas, 81
Scott, Walter, 49, 50
Scottish Council of Churches (SCC), 171
Scripture Union, 373
scripture, scriptures, 10, 13, 20, 43, 51, 68, 79, 105-107, 109, 115, 148, 177, 233, 243, 260, 266, 294, 298, 299, 304, 307, 361, 375, 389, *See* Bible
Second London Confession (1677), 19
Secularisation, 239
Separatists, 3, 15, 19, 222
Serampore, 65, 67, 68, 81, 83, 316, 318
Seventh Day Adventists, 210
Seventh Day Baptists, 158, 163
Shakarian, Demos, 378
Shakespeare, Dr J.H., 125, 126, 127, 169, 170, 179, 180, 183, 190, 194, 228, 229
Shanghai Baptist College, 159

Shanghai Missionary Conference, 159
Sharp, Granville, 58
Sharpe, Dores R., 140
Shaw, Avery A., 140
Shaw, Benjamin, 80, 84
Sherman, Dr Hazel, 133
Shields, T.T., 151, 193
Shropshire Baptist Association, 123
Sidmouth Bill (1811), 62
Sierra Leone, 70, 78, 363, 364, 368
Sifton, Clifford, 141
signs and wonders, 376, 383
Silcox, J.B., 138
Simons, Menno, 11, 13, 14, 15, 26
Sims, John, 34
Sinclair Baptists, 54
Sinclair, Dugald, 54, 55
slave trade, 56-60, 64, 77, 78, 252, 366
slavery, 56, 67, 73, 74, 76, 105, 221, 253, 255, 299
Smith, Donald E., 345
Smith, J. Viner, 225
Smyth, John, 3, 15-18, 27, 88
social Darwinism, 252, 256
social evangelism, 188
social gospel, 137, 140, 141, 154, 196
Social Justice Initiative (1993, New Zealand), 281, 286
South Africa, xvi, 158, 267, 269, 272, 273, 274, 327, 389
South Africa Church Council, 273
South African Baptist, 267, 273
South African Baptist Missionary Society, 267
South African Baptist Union, 273
South America, 165
South Australia, xvi, 53, 166, 174, 203, 204, 209, 210, 216-241 *passim*, 244, 253, 312, 313, 314
South Australian Baptist Association, 220, 223, 225, 232
South Australian Baptist Association (SABA), 220, 224
South Australian Baptist Union (SABU), 216, 225, 226, 227, 229, 231-239
South Melbourne Baptist Church, 206, 208
South Wales Baptist Association, 134, 135

Index 403

South Wales Baptist College, 124, 127, 128
Southern Baptist Convention, 162, 163, 166, 172, 173, 362-368, 378, 387, 388
Southern Baptists, 111, 116, 158, 159, 162, 163, 165, 173, 197, 364, 365, 368
Soviet Union, 191
Spreydon Baptist Church, Christchurch, 270-272
Spurgeon, C.H., 195
Spurgeon's College, London, 175
Spurr, F. C., 170, 188, 189
Stackhouse, W.T., 152
state aid, xvii, 201, 204-206, 209, 210, 212, 213, 219
Stephen, James, 63, 66, 253
Stepney College, 80
Stettler Baptist Church, Alberta, 150
Stinson, Benoni, 88-100 passim
Stockford, O.B., 147, 148, 152
Stone, Barton, 49
Stonehouse, George, 219, 221, 222
Stout, Sir Robert, 269
Strong, Augustus, 185, 189
Student Christian Movement (SCM), 160, 243, 373
Sturm, Douglas, 266
successionism, 43, 86-88, 100
Sudan United Mission, 368
Sukarno, President (Indonesia), 330
Sutcliff, John, 61, 72, 83, 84
Sutherland, Martin, xv, 167, 252, 288, 294, 298, 305, 306, 307
Sweden, 161, 165, 167
Swedish Missionary Society, 165
Switzerland, 3, 127, 161, 167
Sydney, Australia, 203, 204, 208, 224, 236, 242, 243, 245, 249, 251, 252, 254, 257, 300, 313, 323
Tabernacle Baptist Church, Winnipeg, 146, 147
Tanner, Kathryn, 299, 302
Tasmania, 174, 203, 204, 243, 315
Tatersall, T.N., 125
Taylor, James, 86, 98, 132, 185, 205, 206, 207, 292-294, 298
Taylor, Michael, 132, 133
Teague, Collin, 364
Tealing, 49

Teignmouth, Lord, 66
Temple, William, 171
Tennessee Baptist, 112
Teraudkalns, Valdis, 29
Test and Corporation Acts, 57-59, 70, 78
Thomas, H. Geoffrey, 133
Thomas, John, 60
Thornton, Henry, 61
Tinsley, C.J., 242
Togo, 365, 372
Tolbert, Dr William R., 364
Towler, Robert, 217
Townley, Athol, 210
Training Centrum Baliem (TCB), 326-333
Treaty of Waitangi, 253
Trowt, Thomas, 71
Truett, George W., 173, 181, 184, 186, 190, 194, 195
Truscott, Keith, 260
Truth and Progress, 209, 219, 222, 232, 316
Tuag at Uno (Towards Union), 128
Turner, John, 206, 209
U Hla Bu, 344, 345, 358
U Nu, 347-349
U Pe Maung Tin, 343, 345
U2, 294-298
Ulster, 50
union churches, 127, 151, 222
Union of Welsh Nonconformists, 122
Unitarianism, Unitarians, 58, 206
United Aborigines Mission (UAM), 257
United Baptist Convention of the Maritime Provinces (UBCMP), 145, 164, 165
United Church of Australia, 216
United Church of Canada, 145, 147, 150, 163, 164
United Church of Wales: The Way Forward, The, 131
United Free Church of England, 169
United Missionary Council of Australia, 161
United Reformed Church, 49, 129, 131
Upper Room Baptist Church, 363, 382
van der Stoep, Nelis, 325, 326, 328, 329
van der Stoep, Tine, 328

Van Diemen's Land. *See* Tasmania
Vancouver, 136, 139, 140, 143, 145, 146, 147
Victoria Baptist Foreign Mission, 158
Victoria, Australia, 81, 124, 126, 158, 166, 174, 204-212, 216, 218, 242, 245-247, 250, 278, 288
Victorian Baptist Witness, 211, 212
Victorian College (Whitley College), 209
Victorian Education League, 208
Volf, Miroslav, 298-304
Voller, James, 205
voluntaryism, 204, 218, 219
Wales, xvi, 49, 51, 62, 119-136 *passim*, 169, 175, 367
Waleswide (Cymrugyfan), 134
Wallis, James, 51
Ward, Graham, 294, 302
Ward, William, 83, 335
Warlpiri people, 258-262
Waterlanders, 3, 15-19
Watson, Dr E.H., 257
Watson, E.L., 124
Watson, Miss J., 257
Wave Hill, 251, 258, 259
Webster, Marilyn, 214
Welsh Home Rule, 119
Wenger, J.C., 13
Wesley, John, 265
West Africa, 361-89
West Indies, 60, 63, 64, 68, 69, 74, 76, 85
West Melbourne Baptist Church, 206
West, Stephen, 71
Western Australia, 174
Western Baptist Convention, 115
Western Canada, xvi, 136-155 *passim*, 164, 173
Western Outlook, 140, 141, 144, 146-148, 152-154
Westminster Confession, 49, 246
Westminster Theological Seminary, 133
White Australia policy, 255, 256
White New Zealand League, 268
White, G. J. Coulter, 144
Whitley College, xvii, 212, 244, 245
Whitley, W.T., 41, 158, 209
Whole Faith of Man, The, 39, 41
Wilberforce, Robert, 57

Wilberforce, William, xvi, 56-85 *passim*, 178, 253
Wilkin, F.J., 209, 210, 244
Willard, F.A., 110
Williams, J.S., 133
Williams, M.J., 128
Williams, Stevenson Alfred, 387, 388
Williamson, H.R., 159, 165
Wilson, Bryan, 217
Wilson, C.E., 157
Windmill Street, Finsbury Square, London, 51
Windsor Baptist Church, 126
Winnipeg, 143, 149, 150
women, 97, 101, 157, 185, 194, 197, 224, 249, 257, 258, 268, 312-316, 319, 320, 321, 368, 377
Wood, William, 58, 59
Woolloomooloo, 126, 166, 174, 197, 203, 205, 211, 219, 222, 233, 252, 257
Works of Andrew Fuller, 78
World Alliance of Reformed and Presbyterian Churches, 121
World Congregational Conference, 121
World Council of Churches, 128, 156, 171-176, 182, 369, 370
World Missionary Conference (1910), 156-161, 175, 182, 227
World War I, 124, 125, 141, 143, 170, 171, 179, 183, 186, 189, 190, 216, 227, 228, 230, 237, 239, 240, 269, 273, 365
World War II, 164, 166, 168, 170, 172, 186, 210, 257, 258, 324, 328, 365, 370
Wright, A.F., 211
Wright, Nigel, 288
Wyeth, Peyton C., 51
Yorkshire, 58
Yoruba people, 365-368, 380, 384, 386, 387
Young Men's Buddhist Association, 347
Young Men's Christian Association (YMCA), 162, 163, 228, 348
Young Women's Christian Association (YWCA), 224
Zenana missions, 157, 313, 317
Zwinglianism, 4

www.ingramcontent.com/pod-product-compliance
Lightning Source LLC
Chambersburg PA
CBHW071436300426
44114CB00013B/1458